D1548847

DISCARD

PUBLISHED UNDER THE AUSPICES OF

THE CENTER FOR JAPANESE AND KOREAN STUDIES

UNIVERSITY OF CALIFORNIA, BERKELEY

SOCIALIZATION FOR ACHIEVEMENT

SOCIALIZATION FOR ACHIEVEMENT

Essays on the
Cultural Psychology of the Japanese

by GEORGE A. DE VOS *with contributions by*
HIROSHI WAGATSUMA, WILLIAM CAUDILL, *and*
KEIICHI MIZUSHIMA

UNIVERSITY OF CALIFORNIA PRESS
Berkeley, Los Angeles, London

University of California Press
Berkeley and Los Angeles, California

University of California Press, Ltd.
London, England

ISBN: 0-520-01827-3

Library of Congress Catalog Card Number: 78-132420

Printed in the United States of America

To WINNIE,

whose understanding saw me through from the beginning.

In the preparation of this manuscript, I received the tireless supportive assistance of MRS. JUNE KAZUKO ONODERA *and the able editing of* MRS. ANN BROWER *and* MR. DAVID CAMP.

Contents

vii

Preface

In this series of essays on the cultural psychology of the Japanese, I have attempted to bring together what, to me, are the unnecessarily divergent approaches of psychology, anthropology, and sociology into a framework that will increase our understanding of human behavior in the conceptual context of "culture and personality."

The researches described are the result of individual work and of collaboration extending over twenty-five years. Some of the conclusions represent my personal interpretation of themes in Japanese culture and personality, but most are distillations of lively discussions with colleagues and of solitary arguments with the written works of social scientists who have preceded me.

Social scientists are more the product of their society than they are shapers of it. Each of us wishes to communicate his experiences and by so doing to change the perceptions of others toward some social end. Writers who use the humanities as a vehicle of communication convey their personal avowal of common humanity in expressive subjective terms. In contrast, the social scientist attempts to step outside himself, to objectify his observations, hoping to arrive at conceptual generalizations that will deepen the understanding of the psychological and the social structural laws underlying man's social behavior. But the social scientist, in what he chooses to study, does not escape himself. His approach is determined by the tensions and the incongruities of his own social experience deeply embedded within him.

My approach has been syncretic; I have attempted to resolve inconsistencies and differences in human relationships and in social theory. For reasons still not clear to me, I came at an early age to an acute awareness of ethnic differences in those about me and thence to observation of those differences. As a son of a Catholic Belgian immigrant, I grew up in the so-called "melting pot" of urban Chicago. Actually, it was much more of a *bouillabaisse* with large flavorful pieces (as Nathan Glazer has aptly observed) than a hash in which the ingredients have lost their individual consistency, flavor, and texture. I have never felt myself to be melted down; as far as I was concerned, Pieter Brueghel was, in my youth, still alive and well in Chicago.

But Flemish Belgians in the United States are too small a segment to be accorded the questionable advantage of a stereotype such as that bestowed upon the Irish, Czech, and Polish Catholics with whom I went to parochial school, or upon the others in ethnic "Logan Square" Chicago: the Protestant Swedes; a sprinkling of "real" Americans who attended the Episcopalian church, a remnant in a neighborhood that had changed; and the Jews who went to public school. Each group was set apart as "different" by members of other groups; to each group was assigned a set of real or fancied traits and characteristics.

Adolescence, with its inner trials left me stripped of my religious faith (a process somewhat like that described by Will Durant in his autobiography, *Transition*). Thus I arrived by some chance of self-will or "intellectual arrogance" (as previous mentors in my Catholic school days would have it) at the University of Chicago. My discovery there of social science helped me to resist the temptation of "passing" as what is now termed a "wasp" and thereby losing my sense of myself as a European.

The social science survey courses at the University of Chicago were staffed by intellectual liberators. I discovered that what I had learned through observation and by reading novels could be applied in a world of conceptual discourse, to enhance comprehension of how our society shaped us. In more personal terms, I could comprehend the social circumstances that caused pain to my parents and to others who in one way or another were defeated by their environment.

At this time the world of self-revelation in literature took on new meaning with my deepening interest in Freudian psychology. I found Freud a provocative man to read. My retrospective distortion of my early impressions would have it that he was saying in asides to his reader, in a somewhat hurt but resigned tone, that his ideas would be rejected by society at large.

World War II interrupted my career as an undergraduate in sociology. Through a set of circumstances possible only in the American army in 1943–1945 I found myself studying the Japanese language at Yale and after that at the University of Michigan and Fort Snelling, Minnesota. This period of study not only established my future professional interest in Japan, but was also in itself the most intense intellectual experience of my life. Among those in the Japanese language programs was a group of young American intellectuals who were thrown into a situation of constant communication with each other. As one of the younger students, I was exposed to every form of political or social philosophy in the course of attending, all night long, vigorous discussions and arguments.

When I returned to Chicago to resume my studies, after the war, I thought I had escaped Japan and the dreadful necessity to continue learning a language so remorseless in its demands. I received my bachelor's degree in sociology, but decided in graduate school that anthropology was more congenial to my new perspective. The personal attention and kindness of Lloyd Warner, then professor in both the sociology and the anthropology departments, helped convince me that graduate work in anthropology and, subsequently, in an interdisciplinary program in human development, would be a way to resolve intellectually my dual interest in culture and in human psychology.

At about this time I undertook to remedy what I considered to be certain deficiencies in my training. During my "leisure time" in the army I had devoted a considerable amount of my reading to psychiatric literature. The companionship of a perceptive wife had sent me deeper into myself with probing questions not to be answered by sociological theory. I was dissatisfied with my almost too ready capacity to theorize, and I began to worry about the necessity for empirical checks upon facile conceptualization. Personal psychoanalysis, which I entered at the time, made me critical of social science generalizations that left out the intense reality of personal experience; such generalizations did not adequately consider the wellsprings of human motivation.

At this time, the study of "culture and personality" was cresting in a wave of popularity among anthropologists. But I wanted more than promises and avowals of what research would bring. I felt it necessary to develop methods for demonstrating conclusions. I was impressed by the works of Kardiner, Mead, Bateson, and Hallowell, and I began taking courses related to psychological testing. I was encouraged by a number of specialists in the Rorschach and Thematic Apperception Tests (TAT) methods who were then giving a variety of courses in the University and in various clinics and hospitals in Chicago. Psychologists Al Hunsicker, Hedda Bolgar, Allen Rosenwald, Samuel Beck, and William E. Henry were encouraging. David Shakow, then chief psychologist at Illinois Neuropsychiatric Institute, understood what I was groping for and provided a year's intensive internship at the Institute.

In short, after receiving my master's degree in anthropology and completing a number of post-master's courses in human development, I ended up in 1949 immersed in the world of psychodiagnostic testing and therapy. I strongly hoped that it was possible to objectify and communicate what is so deeply subjective and hidden from view in the functioning of human beings.

In the meantime, in 1947, I had joined a research team interested in studying the effects of the wartime relocation of Japanese-Americans from the West Coast. This team was made up of Charlotte Babcock, a psychoanalyst; William Caudill in anthropology; Setsuko Nishi in sociology; later Estelle Gabrielle, a psychiatric social worker; Lee Rainwater and Allen Jacobson in human development; and Adrian Concoran in sociology.

This wartime relocation was an unconscionable act arising out of the still unexpunged racism plaguing American society. It forced most West Coast Japanese-Americans into concentration camps. Fortunately, the conduct of perceptive camp administrators and the capacity of the Japanese themselves to endure through adversity made the best of what could have been a shattering experience for all concerned. When the European war ended, the American-born Nisei, first, and later the immigrant Issei were released from the camps and helped to relocate in the more "neutral" territories of the eastern and midwestern United States. When the war with Japan ended, all Japanese were allowed to return to their prewar homes.

Our research group was concerned with the problems of psychological adjustment and with the forms of community adaptation that accompanied the relocation.

We were somewhat surprised by what we found. The Japanese community as a whole was able to surmount the difficulties encountered without manifesting much evidence of social disorganization or personal maladjustment. A number of community groups had quickly been organized among the Japanese themselves. They sought little outside help. Use of existing social agencies in the Chicago area was minimal. The anticipated need to assist a group of disturbed and distraught people did not materialize. Japanese-Americans found work quite readily in Chicago in occupations previously familiar to them in California. Employers quickly formed a favorable stereotype and, after some initial reluctance, began to seek out the Issei and Nisei for employment. Our survey showed that, despite severe discrimination, the Nisei generation of Japanese-Americans was quietly entering the American middle class. Why? For me this was a challenging question and I have been concerned with it ever since.

My contribution to the research project was to use the Rorschach test as a means of systematically comparing the perceptual patterns and the intrapsychic adjustment patterns of the American-born Nisei with those of their immigrant parents. I was also able to study a sample of "Kibei," American-born Nisei who had been sent to Japan for several years of schooling. In my work on my doctoral dissertation at Chicago, I compared the three groups of Japanese with samples of normal, neurotic, and schizophrenic Americans under study as part of a project being conducted under the direction of Samuel Beck at

Michael Reese Hospital. William Thetford and Herman Molish had just completed gathering a systematic comparison sample of these Rorschach protocols for a research project on schizophrenia.

Although sharing the skepticism of some about projective tests, I was deeply impressed with the results I obtained. The two generations of Japanese differed remarkably in their perceptual patterns. The Nisei norms approximated in most respects the statistical norms of the American group; the Issei showed characteristic patterns of perception significantly different in many respects. The small Kibei sample varied widely, but, when averaged out, the Kibei norms were generally between those for the Issei and those for the Nisei.

As we found subsequently, the Rorschach test results obtained from Japanese immigrants, most of whom had entered the United States after they were eighteen years old, were highly similar in normative scores to the results later obtained for a larger sample living in rural and urban environments in Japan.

The records of Thematic Apperception Test protocols obtained from the same Chicago subjects by William Caudill showed signs of intellectual effort that suggested strongly internalized achievement motivation. Chapter 9 of this volume represents the collaborative conclusions drawn by William Caudill and me about the meaning of the results of our projective tests with the Chicago Japanese. (As this book goes to press I have learned of Bill's untimely death. Peace to a fellow traveler on the path.)

Although I did not know it at the time, I had not completed my work on the subject of Japanese achievement motivation. In 1951, Dr. Tsuneo Muramatsu, professor of psychiatry at Nagoya University, visited the Chicago Institute of Psychoanalysis. Our research team discussed with him the results we had obtained. He was interested and took back with him a set of Murray TAT cards. Shortly thereafter, Caudill and I received invitations to do research in Japan, taking advantage of the newly instituted Fulbright program. Neither of us then felt capable of responding. I had just taken on the job of Chief Psychologist and Director of the Graduate Internship Training Program in psychology at Elgin State Hospital. At this time I was interested in exploring, with whatever means possible, the nature of what are termed schizophrenic reactions. However, Dr. Muramatsu's persistence eventually paid off, and finally, in 1953, I took my wife and young daughter to Japan for what I thought would be a one-year program; instead it extended over a period of twenty-five months.

The enthusiasm of Dr. Muramatsu and his collaborators at Nagoya University for doing some large-scale work on Japanese culture and personality was such that we quickly sought the help of American foundations. We received grants from the Rockefeller Foundation and the Foundation Fund for Research in Psychiatry, and later were given some additional funds from the Center for Japanese Studies at the University of Michigan. This funding enabled us to assemble a large team of psychiatrists, social workers, psychologists, and sociologists.

I learned a great deal about Japanese culture during my work with the research team. The group included, as my principal colleagues, Eiji Murakami, Akira Hoshino, Fumio Marui, Tsuneo Yamane, Haruo Kawaii, Hiroshi Yoshikawa, and Yasao Hori. We first developed questionaires to augment our projective test methods. We eventually studied a sample which totalled 2,400 Japanese: residents of the cities of Okayama and Nagoya, and of a farming village, a fishing village, and a mountain village in Central and Southwest Honshu.

I returned to the United States in 1955 to join the department of psychology at the University of Michigan and the Center for Japanese Studies there, benefiting from association with Fred Wyatt, Richard Beardsley, John Hall, Robert Ward, R. B. Hall, and Joseph Yamagiwa.

While at the University of Michigan, I met Hiroshi Wagatsuma, who was to become a close friend and colleague, sharing my subsequent work on Japanese culture and personality. Wagatsuma had come to Michigan as a graduate student and he worked with me there in the preparation and analysis of the psychological materials on Niiike village, done under sponsorship of a grant from the Behavioral Science Division of the Ford Foundation. Some results of this work are included in Chapters 2, 3, 4, and 5 of the present volume.

Wagatsuma and I continued our collaborative work after my transfer to the School of Social Welfare at the University of California at Berkeley, where I remained from 1957 to 1965, and after I joined the Department of Anthropology in 1965.

During this period my interest was shifting to the study of social deviancy in the United States and Japan. In 1958–1959 I collaborated as a consultant in some research on Mexican Americans and Negroes in correctional institutions in California, and I determined to do a study of my own on various forms of social deviancy in Japan. In 1960, I received a grant from the National Institute of Mental Health to launch a large-scale comparative research project on delinquency. Harold Jones suggested that I locate my work within the Institute of Human Development, which housed and encouraged the project in every way possible.

Part III of the present volume covers some of the work done on delinquency, work which is continuing. Among my collaborators was Keiichi Mizushima, who is a co-author of a number of the chapters on Japanese delinquency. Mizushima, Eiji Murakami, and Takao Murase all assisted in the processing and analysis of data. The Social Science Research Institute of the University of Hawaii under William Lebra was helpful in providing funds for the final stage of the data preparation.

The work during this period was not limited to the specific questions of delinquency formation. With Hiroshi Wagatsuma, we took advantage of an unusual opportunity to investigate the social problems related to the formerly outcaste Burakumin minority still living in ghettos in the cities of southwest Japan. The results of this research are published in *Japan's Invisible Race* of which excerpts appear in Chapters 15 and 16.

Wagatsuma and I have had a continuing interest in problems of alienation. I have directed my attention mainly to questions concerned with suicide, whereas Wagatsuma has focused on more general questions of alienation among Japanese intellectuals. Some results of our collaborative thinking on these topics are given in Chapters 17 and 18.

Finally, as represented in the central portion of this volume, I have repeatedly returned to a concern with the initial absorbing problem posed by my first observation of Japanese-Americans, that of achievement motivation. In the course of our delinquency research, Wagatsuma and I gathered a great deal of ethnographic data on the lower-class ward in Tokyo that was the focus of our study. We worked intensively with fifty Japanese families and again noted the pervading concern with achievement apparent in our interview data. Although the families studied were in some ways relative occupational failures, they demonstrated clearly the strong psychological dynamic in Japanese culture. The complete results of our ethnographic and of our research findings on delinquency are being published in another volume, *The Heritage of Endurance.* I have borrowed from that work a chapter on the "entrepreneurial mentality" of lower-class Japanese, As Chapter 8, it rounds out the section on achievement motivation in Japanese culture.

Introduction

Essays on the Cultural Psychology of the Japanese as a Contribution to a General Study of Human Socialization

The principal theme bringing some unity to this volume of essays and research reports written over a period of twenty years is the cultural psychology of the Japanese. In their inception, the various chapters were prompted by a number of theoretical issues relevant to the role to be taken by a psychological approach to human motivation in the construction of a general social science theory. In my mind the volume as a whole elaborates a general contention that some form of personality theory based on principles of human psychosexual and cognitive maturation is essential, and has to be integrated into a general theoretical approach to man as a culture-bearing animal. All I have written has been as a partisan of this point of view.

The approach of what is now frequently termed "psychological anthropology" is not accepted by a good number of colleagues who are working in the disciplines of sociology, anthropology, political science, and economics. Be this as it may, psychological anthropologists see human psychology in all its complexity at work everywhere and cannot conceive of applying theory to behavior without attending to the psychological determinants of human motivation. No theoretical conclusions concerning any form of behavior, be it seen as structured by political, economic, or other social institutions, can ignore the influence of personality variables that are the transmitted heritage of different cultural traditions.

This need to consider psychological structure as part of culture is even more apparent when directly approaching the subject of "socialization." That is, the study of those processes of social learning whereby the biological potential of humans is given cultural content and form.

1

A human being can only become human, that is to say, become "socialized," by experiencing some form of culturally transmitted social life from early infancy on. Although most influential in childhood, the social processes acting on the individual to "socialize" him are at work throughout the life cycle.

One can note throughout the various chapters of this volume a continual implicit partisan reference to a general theory of socialization based on psychoanalytic precepts concerning human psychosocial maturation. Hopefully, it will be recognized that these precepts are neither unnecessarily intrusive nor uncritically applied. Equally apparent should be the fact that my concern with socialization has been as profoundly influenced by the major currents of sociological and anthropological theory derivative of the writings of Emil Durkheim and Max Weber.

In tracing Japanese history back into the premodern period, I try to demonstrate how a "Japanese" culture has persisted in spite of self-conscious modernization. What makes a Japanese "Japanese," that is to say, what comprises Japanese cultural psychology, has persisted in spite of changes in legal institutions, in technology, and in spite of an absorption of a great deal of scientific and esthetic tradition from the industrialized West. Sociological theory based only on an examination of present social structure by itself cannot explain this persistence. It is obvious that Japanese cultural traditions can persist well in spite of change in basic social institutions. One therefore has to examine the methods and nuances of cultural transmission as they occur in the young in each generation.

Whereas human social behavior is inescapably modified by political, economic, and educational institutions that together comprise what sociologists call the "social structure" of a culture, at the same time there are to be found as part of every society *culture patterns* that remain relatively "functionally autonomous." Some of these autonomous culture patterns have to do with the structuring of interpersonal relationships within the family. Child-rearing patterns in particular are relatively autonomous and can persist in influencing modes of cognition and social perception despite very great changes in economic and political institutions. The structuring of the emotional life of primary families within a culture persists despite radical changes in technology and in legal institutions. Hence, primary socialization patterns are much less amenable to legal and economic changes than the social planners would like to have us believe. Conscious social attitudes and ideologies learned in later periods of life can be changed more rapidly than the more deepset emotional responses learned in the very earliest years within the primary family. Hence many cultures, while experiencing rapid social change, manifest what I term a "psychological lag."

Such a psychological lag is manifest, for example, in a persisting Japanese discrepancy between positive attitudes toward making a free marriage on the basis of personal choice and the fact that the majority of marriages made in Japan even today are arranged by the family. To help explain why one finds such discrepancy between socially avowed attitudes and actual behavior, it is necessary to go beneath the surface of conscious attitudes and to explore the emotional life of Japanese as can be done with psychological techniques and tools.

I have titled this volume *Socialization for Achievement* to stress the recurring theme that socialization within the Japanese culture causes its members to internalize and perpetuate a culture pattern that demands much from succeeding generations in standards of performance. To become ethnically Japanese by growing up in a Japanese family, whether in Japan, the United States, or Brazil, is to become motivated in such a way that energy is mobilized and directed toward the actualization of long-range goals. A strong need for accomplishment in some form, be it traditional or modern, artistic or economic, motivates Japanese generally. Why this is so and how it operates is the central theme unifying this volume.

A psychological approach to culture emphasizes conflict as potentially occurring both within and between individuals. No society functions without some forms of tension. The fact that much of human behavior is "internalized" in childhood and rigidified into fairly fixed cognitive and emotional patterns is a source of continuity in both a positive and a negative sense. These patterns persist automatically, influencing the perception of the social world in such a way that they are not easily modified by adult experiences. These earlier socialization patterns are therefore actually a part of a persisting cultural tradition that is passed on from one generation to the next in culturally characteristic child-rearing practices. These practices capacitate the individual so that he can, with *more* or *less* success, fulfill the expected adult social roles. There is never a complete congruence between the normative role patterns and role expectations of a society and the personality patterns of the individual, although in most stable cultures there is sufficient congruence to maintain positively evaluated cultural continuity. Whatever the unique features of the individual and his unique experiences, it is the cultural tradition that gives social behavior its meaning. Whatever the internal conflicts between the ideal normative role and the idiosyncracies of the individual, he is constrained by his society to manifest socially acceptable behavior. Each society provides for the individual adult normative role patterns which the individual more or less successfully attempts to actualize.

The first two parts of this volume are concerned with how an internalized need to achieve is socialized as part of Japanese personality structure. Japanese learn to direct their efforts with persistence toward the realization of long-range social goals. Immediate pleasures are sacrificed to future-oriented purposes. The resulting culture pattern is characterized by the maintenance of high standards of attainment ranging from art to economic development. I attempt in the first few chapters to demonstrate achievement motivation at work in rural villages as well as in the charged atmosphere of the modern Japanese city.

The last part of this volume turns from an exploration of the very visible social effects of a generally internalized need for achievement to the less visible social problems and deviant patterns of failure and antisocial behavior which are also equally characteristic of Japanese culture. Seen in a comparative anthropological perspective, each well-studied culture reveals not only patterned definitions of social accomplishments, but also characteristic ways to fail and to become deviant from the expected norms. Patterns of socially approved achievement are always in dynamic contrast to patterns of personal alienation and what is perceived to be criminal or antisocial behavior.

To understand a culture thoroughly one must therefore examine both what is positively expected in social roles and what is considered deviant and unacceptable. The social definitions of failure and deviancy are as persistent a part of any given culture as are its definitions of success and achievement. Particular patterns of deviant behavior continue from one generation to the next; they are the ever present dark sides of what is expected, condoned, or praised. The latter part of the present volume therefore deals with what can be learned about Japanese culture by examining its historical continuities in crime, social ostracism, and personal alienation. My research on deviancy in Japanese culture has been an attempt on a theoretical level to combine the sociological approach of Emil Durkheim and Robert Merton with what is to be learned about human deviancy from psychoanalytic psychology.

In sum, it is not sufficient for a social scientist studying Japan to arrive at the surface conclusion that psychologically and socially the Japanese are a nation of energetic, self-motivated, hard-working people. Nor is it sufficient to say simply that achievement is a cultural tradition in Japan. The major purpose of my research in Japan has been to explore the peculiarly Japanese psychological patterns operative beneath their manifest success in modern economic development as well as in meeting other challenges of rapid social change. As part of the totality of the culture I have also explored persistent patterns of failure, deviancy, and alienation that run concurrently in submerged channels from the premodern past into the frenetic present. The reader is to judge whether I have helped explain how and at what price the Japanese accomplish their "socialization for achievement."

Part One:

Normative Role Behavior

Part One Introduction

Social Role Behavior:
Basic Motivational Concerns in
Primary Interpersonal Relationships

I have been concerned throughout my work as a social scientist studying Japanese culture and personality with combining an understanding of individual psychological motivation with a knowledge of how social structure determines cultural behavior. While I have consistently used a basically psychoanalytic approach in examining various features of Japanese culture I have found it most helpful to combine my concern with psychodynamics to an equal interest in the social determinants of behavior by using social role behavior as a bridge concept between what can be termed the psychological and the sociological dimension of human behavior. Use of a role concept is essential to what I term a psychocultural approach since it permits the independent examination of the patterning effect of both personality variables and social role expectations witnessed in actual behavior. My purpose throughout has been to forward understanding motivations resulting in witnessed behavior rather than to create a formal conceptual scheme of Japanese social organization.

The first five chapters of this volume are basically written around a study of actually perceived normative role behavior. Among the various psychocultural forces influencing normative behavior discussed in Chapter 1 it is immediately apparent that I have concerned myself most in this volume with *achievement motivation*. It is, in effect, the central thread running throughout the entire volume. I recognize, however, that a well-rounded discussion of the cultural psychology of the Japanese requires attention also to a number of the other motivational dimensions involved in a role behavior as discussed in Chapters 1 and 2 in regard to positively sanctioned role behavior and, in Part

Three, especially Chapter 17 on suicide, in regard to socially deviant responses. Indeed, it is in the interweaving of a multitude of socially conditioned interpersonal concerns, both conformist and deviant, that one finds the peculiar flavor of any given culture.

My first chapter attempts a broad overall discussion of what I perceive theoretically to be the essential dimensions of normative role behavior as they are manifest in Japanese culture. This chapter, written in 1968, is more recent than the four chapters that follow, and benefits somewhat in its organization from the more recent developments of my thinking about the motivational structure in work with material from other cultures as well as that obtained from Japan.

The remaining chapters of this first section are earlier reports on data collected from 1953 to 1955 in both rural and urban settings as part of an interdisciplinary research effort with Japanese colleagues working out of Nagoya University. Most of the data analysis was finished at the University of Michigan, working collaboratively with Hiroshi Wagatsuma from 1955 through 1957.

Chapter 2 reports an empirical examination, by means of projective tests, of various social values and personal attitudes to be found in the primary human relations of one of the Japanese rural villages, Niiike in 1953. A number of the conclusions concerning role relations discussed in this chapter are derived directly from psychological test results. The illustrations used were taken from answers to a Problem Situation Test (PST) and stories given in response to Thematic Apperception Test (TAT) cards, modified slightly from the Standard Set used in psychological testing within the United States. This report includes a brief summary of Rorschach findings which are compatible with normative Rorschach results obtained elsewhere in Japan.

Chapter 3 compares some of the attitudes about the expected role behavior of women found in this farming village with the contrasting attitudes found in a fishing village. The discrepancies between the results obtained in these two settings are discussed in relation to the disparate traditions of farmers and of fisher-folk. Especially to be noted are the differences in social status that exist between well-to-do farming villages and chronically impoverished fishing villages.

The fourth chapter is concerned with the tendency of the Japanese, as part of expected role behavior, not to externalize blame. Instead, they turn guilt in on themselves. This is evident in the way they perceive death and illness, in contrast to how these afflictions are perceived in some other cultures. The themes of role dedication and internalized guilt, which recur repeatedly throughout the volume in subsequent chapters, are introduced here in terms of particular research findings.

In Chapter 5, I marshal more specific evidence, derived from the

Thematic Apperception Test, to shed light on the question of how and in what form guilt is internalized within the Japanese. I contend that the internalization of guilt is culturally quite manifestly related to patterns of occupational achievement and arranged marriage. I conclude, therefore, in spite of many published statements to the contrary, that Japanese behavior is strongly motivated by guilt rather than by more superficial concerns with shame and "face." I have found considerable evidence to support my contention that individual Japanese are driven by a need to repay parents for the sufferings incurred in their behalf and must in a puritanical sense find self-justification through hard work. They are in this sense Oriental Calvinists, who are concerned with problems of evil related not so much to their sexual drives as to the symbolic meaning of failure as a destructive act. The need to repay the sacrifices of hard-working parents is not unknown in the West, but nowhere has it found such direct institutionalization and enforcement as in the Japanese traditional concepts of expected role behavior within the family. In the psychological motivation underlying *on,* or parental repayment, so sensitively described by Ruth Benedict in *The Chrysanthemum and the Sword,* one finds the key to the Japanese need to adhere to life-long patterns of dedication to socially prescribed roles and their attendant goals.

The social consequences of the internalized motives considered in Chapter 1 through 5 are related in greater detail in Part Two to an overall discussion of economic development and achievement motivation.

Chapter I

Status and Role Behavior in Changing Japan: Psychocultural Continuities

with HIROSHI WAGATSUMA

One basic question the Japanese ask themselves today is how is rapid industrialization influencing family life and the fundamental conceptions of the widely different roles of men and women.[1] Changes there are, but despite these changes Japan continues to function as an amazingly stable society. No major breakdowns of family living patterns are evident. The Japanese divorce rate is much lower than that of the United States, and comparable to that of most European states, although present Japanese divorce laws are perhaps the most liberal of those in any major country. Dramatic episodes of suicide or socially deviant behavior as well as student unrest have attracted public attention to malaise in youth since World War II. Nevertheless, the behavior of Japanese youth generally is not as disorderly as the newspaper accounts might indicate. Although the political attitudes of youth are more revolutionary than in the past, the relationship of children to parents generally remains close.

Among intellectuals there is much discussion of alienation and of confusion about the direction to be taken by Japanese society; but among many ordinary Japanese one still finds a fair degree of acceptance of, if not genuine contentment with, the patterning of their private lives. Japanese parents are most concerned with making a

---

[1] This chapter was originally published in *Sex Roles in Changing Society*, Seward and Williamson (eds.) (1970), pp. 334–370. Additional material added to present chapter appeared as part of Wagatsuma and DeVos, "Attitudes Toward Arranged Marriage in Rural Japan" in *Human Organization* (1962), pp. 187–200.

better world for their children through hard work, saving for the future, and providing the best possible educational opportunities. Family life in Japan continues to reflect a fairly optimistic view of the future. The overall stability of the Japanese society, in spite of rapid change, is due in no small part, in our opinion, to the manner in which role behavior within the family has remained relatively cohesive and relatively satisfying for individual Japanese. The emphasis on the formal role one is expected to play in the immediate family and in external relationships has seemed, to some Western observers at least, in general more extreme than that found in Western societies. What is, in our opinion, extreme is not the playing of roles (which one finds everywhere), but the degree to which the sense of a personal self has been deemphasized in Japanese culture.

ROLE DEDICATION: A CONTINUING TRADITION IN MODERN JAPAN

Even for a modern Japanese, role behavior becomes a means of self-realization. He learns to dedicate himself to the role prescribed for him by his culture and finds it difficult to think of himself apart from it. The modern Japanese dedication to role is a carryover from a very successful indoctrination in Confucian philosophy which dominated the thought of the samurai elite in the nineteenth century. This Confucian influence still underlies differences between the Japanese view of role and the Western view.

Essentially, the difference between the concept of "social role" and a more independent sense of self aside from expected role behavior was less developed in Japanese moral teaching and ethical training. The Confucian influence is still observable in Japanese life whether at home, in industry, or among athletes representing Japan. Such dedication to occupational role is at present the envy of developing nations wondering at the rapidity of Japanese economic growth.

In Western cultures the concept of the individual and the goal of personal development have been basic in religious and social thought since the Renaissance. It has been generally assumed to be "good" in Western philosophy that man should develop his potentials out of a need for self-realization, whether this self-realization is viewed within the context of a religious ideology or that of a more materialistic moral philosophy. At the same time, man's sense of social responsibility in Western social ethics has been *universalized* to include at least the welfare of all the members of his own country if not of all humanity. In this Western system, tensions can occur between individual religious commitment and commitment to the state, as well as between individual ends and the common good.

The social philosophy of Confucianism tended to deemphasize the individual as an end in himself and to emphasize instead the network of *particularistic* obligations and responsibilities that the individual assumed as a member of his family and of his community.[2] Living in accordance with one's prescribed role within the family and within a political and social hierarchy was the ultimate basis of moral values, subjectively sanctioned by one's own conscience and objectively reinforced by the informal sanctions of the community and the legal codes of the state. In Japan no conflict arose between religious ideologies and loyalty to superiors, but conflict could occur between individual passion and role responsibility.

In traditional Japan, the self-awareness of a Japanese was fused with some conception of expected role behavior, often idealized in his mind as a set of internalized standards or directives. Accordingly, in psychological terms, his "ego ideal" was conceptualized as some *particular* form of idealized role behavior. A Japanese would have felt uncomfortable in thinking of his "self" as something separable from his role. When he "actualized" himself he became what in his status and role position he was expected to be, a member of a particular family and of a particular community, or a man with a given occupational position in a particular economic enterprise. A woman most often conceived of herself as a wife or mother dedicated to the exacting requirements of these roles. To allow oneself to be devoid of any role commitment was to produce in oneself a sense of moral disarray or guilt. In the traditional Japanese mind, to be individualistic in Western moral sense is almost equal to being "selfish" (thinking only of one's self). According to any ethical traditional Japanese, a person could not actualize himself, that is to say, accomplish his destiny as a human being without playing his proper social role.

Various forms of role dedication can still be observed in the way Japanese carry out prescribed tasks. There is in many Japanese such an intensity of commitment to the occupational role on the part of men and to the marital role on the part of women that their total energies seem to be directed to the end of actualizing their roles. Long-range lifetime goal objectives are pursued from childhood through periods of training in youth and by hard work and endurance until old age. Sacrificing oneself for a cause seems for some to become the meaning of life itself.

Such dedication when pursued very rigidly can lead to behavior

---

[2] Particularism in moral philosophy is not unique to Japanese culture. Members of numerous cultures feel no need to generalize the sense of moral obligation beyond family and immediate kin. However, the degree of generalized dedication to expected role behavior found in Japan is difficult to find elsewhere so widespread through a population.

that becomes difficult for the Western observer to understand. Role dedication can result in what we describe in Chapter 17 as "role narcissism." For some Japanese the occupational role completely takes the place of any meaningful spontaneous social interaction. Traditions of role dedication still can lead to what appears to be an extraordinary capacity for self-sacrifice, such as, in the very recent past, that of soldiers going to certain death.

Role dedication can be viewed as the core of the two chief Japanese traditional virtues of loyalty and endurance. Traditionally, a Japanese expressed loyalty to master or lord by assuming repayment of the obligations incurred within the network of social life. This network as part of the samurai tradition was well described by Ruth Benedict.[3] *On-gaeshi* is the child's never-ending repayment to the parents for their love and care; *gimu* is the obligation inherent in one's vocational position; a sense of *giri* is involved in maintaining the interdependent reciprocal obligations that bind extended family, community, or professional networks together. The maintenance of obligations is still an essential part of Japanese life. Although the fulfillment of obligations does not play the primary role it played in the past, any careful examination of a professional community or a business organization will reveal that networks of obligation remain an extremely important part of professional and economic intercommunication and negotiation.

PSYCHOLOGICAL LAG: MARRIAGE AND FREE CHOICE

Of particular issue in modern Japan are changes in attitudes toward arranged marriages. These attitudes are in obvious transition. Social change influences given attitudes differentially, causing internal incongruities and inconsistencies. Japanese manifest what I have termed "psychological lag." Conscious avowals to the contrary, they still are profoundly influenced by some premodern attitudes and expectations concerning the nature of marital life.

In the Confucian-feudal pattern (as is often the case with a patriarchal and patrilineal society) the object of marriage was to forward the interest of the family concerned, and not to secure the happiness of those who married. Continuity of "house" and prosperity of the lineage were dominant preoccupations. Hence transmission of family name and property were essential considerations in marriage choice. The name of the family (*ka-mei*) was carried by male members. Usually the eldest son would inherit the family property and assume the duty of maintaining respect for the ancestors. The younger sons remained

---

[3] Benedict, *The Chrysanthemum and the Sword* (1946).

in their elder brother's household after marriage, or established branch households.

In families without a suitable male heir, adoption of an adult "son" (*yōshi*) who takes the name of his wife's parents is still a common practice, especially in business and professional families. In families where an actual son is not extant or does not prove adequate, the adoption of a *yōshi* insures the continuation of a business or profession in the hands of an individual of demonstrated competence.

Marriage, under the prewar Japanese civil code, was officially the simple act of changing the registry of a woman from that of her own family to that of her husband, an act requiring the agreement of the head of the family if the man was under thirty, after which age he could act independently. A man under thirty and a woman under twenty-five could not legally marry without parental consent. Marriage registration without the consent of the family head was sometimes accepted by the county office, but if a family member married without consent, the family head was still legally authorized to punish the offender by expelling him from the family or by refusing him reentry into the family after divorce.

After marriage, a bride's name usually was changed to that of her husband, but this was not simply a result of the marriage. Legally, the bride first entered her groom's family and, becoming a member of the family, took the name of this family. Thus, her family name became the same as that of her husband.

In keeping with these legal provisions, the general value attitudes held a love marriage (*ren-ai kekkon*) to be improper, indecent, "egoistic," or similar to an extramarital affair in Western Christian moral codes. To be "proper," a marriage had to be "arranged" by parents and other elder members of the families concerned.

However, it appears that there have always been deviations from this general value attitude. In the country and among urban lower social strata, many marriages were initiated by the individual's personal choice, although "arrangements" for the sake of formality were increasingly prevalent after Meiji. Also, even in the marriages arranged by parents, some young people were given a right to veto the proposed marriage, thus having opportunities to express, even though negatively, at least some element of choice. Further, there has always been a relatively small group of parents who, in arranging marriages for their children, were—or thought they were—concerned more with the happiness of their children than with the interests of their family. Such parents often considered an arranged marriage not as primarily for the sake of the families concerned but rather as necessary, since young people were not experienced or mature enough to choose their own spouse properly and reasonably. Hence, the parents had to take the responsibility of finding a suitable partner for their child. In many communities in remote country areas, and especially in many fishing villages, where the indoctrination with Confucian values was less operative than in cities and farming villages, people's attitudes toward marriage remained freer, and marriage based upon individual choice and love was more frequent. Such attitudes are illustrated in Chapter 3 comparing the farming village of Niiike with the fishing village of Sakunoshima.

The recent social and political changes in Japan have increased the tempo of change toward the individualistic idea that marriage is a mutual concern of the marriage partners, not of their families. In the post–World War II revision of the Japanese civil code, which was the natural consequence of the revision of the Japanese Constitution, legal support for the traditional family system was all but abolished. Men and women over the age of twenty can now marry legally without the consent of parents. The new constitution explicitly states that a marriage should be based upon the mutual consent of both parties and be maintained through mutual cooperation, with equal rights for husband and wife. New laws were enacted with regard to individual dignity and equality of the sexes in choice of spouse, property rights, domicile, and in other matters pertaining to marriage and the family. Along with the general endeavor to "democratize" family relationships and people's thoughts generally, there appeared numerous writings, speeches, and lectures by more liberal Japanese encouraging young people to think of their marriage as a matter of their own responsibility.[4]

Some changes in expressed attitudes toward marriage have become apparent, especially in cities, as evidenced by some interesting figures quoted by Steiner from Statistics of the Population Research Office of the Welfare Ministry (1948). According to these statistics, the number of so-called "love" marriages in the prewar period was approximately 10 percent of the total number of marriages in the Tokyo "uptown" area (Yamanote, a middle- and upper-class residential area) and 15.3 percent in the "downtown" area (Shitamachi, an area of industrial and commercial activities with mainly lower-class residences). In the postwar period, the numbers of "love" marriages reported increased to 37.8 percent in the Yamanote area and to 40 percent in the Shitamachi area.[5] Similar but less radical increases were observed also in farming

---

[4] As for the postwar change in Japanese civil codes, see Steiner, "Postwar Changes in the Japanese Civil Codes" (1950), and Wagatsuma, "Democratization of the Family Relations in Japan" (1950).

[5] These statistics do not necessarily represent the number of love marriages there were in actuality before or after the war. They reveal only what proportion of people report the fashionable or approved form. One may doubt whether anything like 40 percent of Tokyo marriages in the period reported here were in fact love matches.

and mountain villages in Saitama Prefecture near Tokyo. These figures are from the area of Japan most subject to Western influence.

Supporting evidence of this postwar change is found, for instance, in the results of a more widely dispersed opinion survey by the Japanese National Public Research Institute in connection with UNESCO research on the postwar Japanese youth.[6] A total of 2,671 people from various urban and rural areas were asked, along with a series of other questions, "Do you think that the choice of a husband or a wife is a matter of the chooser's concern or for his (or her) family?"

In the urban areas most people marry between the ages of twenty-five and twenty-nine, and in the rural areas between twenty and twenty-four. Of the 153 men and women questioned in the former age group, 53 percent answered that marriage is a matter of individual concern, 31 percent gave intermediate opinions, and 12 percent expressed the opinion that marriage should be exclusively a matter of family concern. Of the 255 men and women in the rural group, 47 percent considered marriage to be exclusively an individual matter, 39 percent had intermediate opinions, and 13 percent expressed the opinion that marriage should be a family matter exclusively. If this survey reflects attitudes generally, it would seem that marriage arranged only on the basis of family concern is no longer in favor with any but a small minority in either the urban or the rural areas. Other results in the same survey show that individuals over thirty years of age are more likely than younger people to suggest some sort of compromise solution. (See Table I-1.)

More recently, in his survey on Japanese youth's attitudes toward marriage and family, Baber collected responses from more than 4,000 university and high school students of city, town, and village upbringing.[7] Among the numerous questions he asked, eleven are pertinent to the problem of marriage and mate-selection. On the whole, the responses indicate more "progressive" attitudes than do the results cited above from the Japanese National Public Research Institute. For instance, on the question of whose interest should come first in the choice of a husband or wife, 98.3 percent of boys and 98.8 percent of girls considered that the young couple's interest should come first. No significant differences are found among university and high school students, or those of city, town, and village upbringing. When asked if they considered the "love match" (ren-ai kekkon) to be the ideal method in the choice of a husband or wife, four-fifths of the boys and nearly three-fourths of the girls responded affirmatively. (See Table I-2.) When the parents disapprove of the girl their son wants to marry,

---

[6] Stoetzel, *Without the Chrysanthemum and the Sword* (1955).

[7] Baber, *Youth Looks at Marriage and the Family: A Study of Changing Japanese Attitudes* (1958).

TABLE I-1

ATTITUDES TOWARD MARRIAGE AS PREDOMINANTLY FOR
THE INDIVIDUAL OR FOR THE FAMILY

Age group	Number of subjects	For "family" exclusively (percent)	Intermediate opinions (percent)	For "individual" exclusively (percent)	No opinion (percent)
Urban					
16–19	139	17	24	51	8
20–24	145	10	36	49	5
25–29	153	12	31	53	5
30–over	604	14	39	45	2
Rural					
16–19	200	15	30	49	8
20–24	255	13	39	47	1
25–29	224	15	36	47	2
30–over	954	14	47	38	3
Totals	2,674	14	39	44	3

SOURCE: See Table 50, p. 183, Jean Stoetzel, *Without the Chrysanthemum and the Sword* (1955).

TABLE I-2

ATTITUDES OF YOUTH TOWARD "LOVE MATCH"
QUESTION: *Do You Consider the Love Match in the Choice of a Husband or Wife to Be the Ideal Method?*

Boys				Girls			
University		High school		University		High school	
Yes	No	Yes	No	Yes	No	Yes	No
76.6	23.4	83.6	16.4	75.2	24.8	67.3	32.7

SOURCE: Modified from Table 21, p. 65, Ray Baber, *Youth Looks at Marriage and the Family* (Tokyo, 1958).
NOTE: N = 4,946

the boys and the girls from university and high school are over-whelmingly agreed (approximately 85 percent) that the son's will should prevail, with a relatively small difference in the viewpoints of urban and of rural youth. Should the parents disapprove of the young man their daughter wants to marry, more than 70 percent of both boys

TABLE I-3

ATTITUDES OF YOUTH TOWARD PARENTAL DISAPPROVAL
QUESTION: *When the Parents Disapprove of the Girl Their Son Wants to Marry,
Whose Will Should Prevail—the Parents' or the Son's?*
(in percent)

Boys				Girls			
University		High school		University		High school	
Parents'	Son's	Parents'	Son's	Parents'	Son's	Parents'	Son's
13.5	86.5	14.6	85.4	11.6	88.4	16.8	83.2

SOURCE: Modified from Table 19, p. 62, Baber, *Youth Looks at Marriage and the Family.*

TABLE I-4

ATTITUDES OF YOUTH TOWARD PARENTAL DISAPPROVAL
QUESTION: *When the Parents Disapprove of the Young Man Their Daughter Wants
to Marry, Whose Will Should Prevail—the Parents' or the Daughter's?*
(in percent)

Boys				Girls			
University		High school		University		High school	
Parents'	Daughter's	Parents'	Daughter's	Parents'	Daughter's	Parents'	Daughter's
26.0	74.0	26.5	73.5	17.2	82.8	29.0	71.0

SOURCE: Modified from Table 20, p. 63, Baber, *Youth Looks at Marriage and the Family.*

and girls believed the daughter's will should prevail, although some respondents became less sure of themselves when a daughter was involved. (See Tables I-3 and I-4.)

These results seem to indicate that the majority of young Japanese students consider that marriage should be primarily for the sake of the young couple and that their will should not be thwarted by their parents' opinion or by their families' interest. However, these surveys are somewhat misleading; there is an obvious lag between survey responses and actual marriage practices. Baber's students, who are seemingly very "pro–love match" on the general problem, as we saw, become much less so when the question is put on a more "realistic" basis: on being asked which method of choosing a marriage partner they think will be used *in their own case,* about 40 percent of the boys and less than 20 percent of the girls answered that they will make the choice themselves. Although a minority expects parents to make the choice, more than half of the boys and two-thirds of the girls think that their parents and they will make the choice together. It is difficult to tell exactly what is meant by this answer. It may mean that the young people want to find their future mate themselves and yet need their parents' support for their marriage, or that they will not blindly accept their parents' choice, but will accept it only when they find the candidate agreeable. It probably means both. In any case, it is noteworthy that although these young students subscribe to a "love match" *in principle* and are of a "progressive" opinion in regard to the general problem of marriage, when it becomes their own problem many reveal dependency on their parents and would not defiantly veto parental choice.

Actually, then, marriages are still arranged, even for individuals who express preference for a marriage of personal choice. Why this discrepancy? One obvious answer is the effect of social pressure exerted by family and community on the individual, an effect that is beyond dispute. In the following chapter I document a less obvious consideration from indirect evidence taken from projective test materials obtained in the farming village of Niiike, namely, that there is a "psychological lag" in internalized sanctions. An arranged marriage is psychologically easier for many individuals. Free choice in marriage very often involves rebellious attitudes toward parents, and guilt feelings may be aroused in making such a marriage.

In the research material presented in the chapters immediately following, it will be possible to demonstrate specifically the presence of such guilt as well as some general incongruities in attitudes toward marriage.

CULTURALLY PREDOMINANT SOCIAL AND PERSONAL CONCERNS IN JAPANESE INTRA-FAMILY BEHAVIOR

In our research on Japanese cultural psychology we have made extensive use of the Thematic Apperception Test, a series of pictures with one or several individuals in a variety of settings and moods used to elicit stories from the subjects interviewed. Some of the pictures used and results obtained are described in detail in several of the following chapters. In working out a conceptual scheme for categorizing the emotional and social content of the themes elicited I have developed a system of scoring self and social attitudes according to ten basic motivational concerns, which I believe encompass the major modalities of interpersonal behavior in every culture (Table I-2). What I have been

TABLE I-5

Basic Thematic Concerns in Human Relations

Thematic Concerns	Positive (Socially Sanctioned)		Negative (Socially Unsanctioned)	
	Active, initiated and/or resolved	Passive or unresolved	Active, initiated and/or resolved	Passive, withdrawal and/or resolution

INSTRUMENTAL BEHAVIOR

Achievement (will do) internalized goals (S)	Goal-oriented activity	Internal conflict, overcommitment, role diffusion, daydreaming	Goal-oriented criminal activity	Anomic withdrawal, alienation from social goals
Competence (can do) internalized standards of excellence (S)	Avowal of capacity	Doubt about capacity, worry, diffuse anxiety, chagrin	Failure due to personal inadequacy	Sense of incapacity and inadequacy
Responsibility (ought to do) internalized moral standards and controls (S)	Sense of duty, assumption of obligation *Some forms of "altruistic" suicide**	Remorse, guilt, regrets over acts of commission or omission	Profligacy, irresponsibility	Avoidance, escape *Some forms of "anomic" suicide**
Control-Power (must do) external power *superordinate:* (V)	Legitimate authority, power—mastery, persuasion	Defensive insecurity	Authoritarian dominance, security, control through destruction of feared object	Failure to assert proper authority (spineless, gutless)
subordinate: (V)	Liberation, autonomy or compliance	Ambivalence about authority or power	Rebellion, trickery	Submission
Mutuality (with or against) interpersonal ethics *competitive:* (H)	Regulated competition, games, contests	Envy	Unethical competitive behavior	Capitulation withdrawal from competitive situation
cooperative: (H)	Concerted behavior (mutual trust)	Distrust, disagreement	Plotting, deception of a cohort	Sense of betrayal

TABLE I-5 (*Continued*)

Thematic Concerns	Positive (Socially Sanctioned)		Negative (Socially Unsanctioned)	
	Active, initiated and/or resolved	Passive or unresolved	Active, initiated and/or resolved	Passive, withdrawal and/or resolution

EXPRESSIVE BEHAVIOR

Harmony (with, emotionally) (H-V)	Harmony, peaceful relationships	Jealousy, fear of threat, emotional discord	Violence, injury, revenge *Some "egocentric" suicides**	Withdrawal into hostility and resentment
Affiliation (toward someone) (H)	Affiliation, intimacy, union, responsiveness, contact	Isolation, loneliness, alienation	Rejection of another	Sense of loss due to rejection or separation *Some "egoistic" suicides**
Nurturance (for someone) (V)	Nurturance, care, help, comfort, succor	Dependency	Withholding	Sense of personal, social, or economic deprivation *Some "egocentric" suicides**
Appreciation (from someone) *others:* (H-V)	Recognition of achieved or ascribed status	Feeling ignored, neglected, unappreciated	Disdain, disparagement	Sense of degradation *Some "anomic" suicides**
self: (S)	Self-respect	Doubt about worth, sense of shame	Self-abasement, self-depreciation	Sense of worthlessness *Some "egoistic" suicides**
Pleasure (within oneself) self-expression (S)	Satisfaction, sense of curiosity or creativity, enjoyment	Indifference, boredom	Masochistic behavior, asceticism	Suffering

FATE

Fortune Health, social, economic conditions	Good luck, fortunate circumstances	Anxiety over environmental or health conditions	Bad fortune, accident, injury, bad economic circumstances	Handicap, illness, death

NOTE: In each category the relationship between actor and others changes relative to the observer's perspective in the thematic concerns. Some categories are actor initiated and some are actor responsive. There are internalized concerns (self-oriented) coded (S) and other-oriented themes concerned either with horizontal interactions coded (H) or vertical interactions coded (V).

* *See explanation of types of suicide in Chapter 17.*

trying to do in order to understand Japanese culture relative to others is to define the relative priority of these major concerns, the intensity of interest in each, and the manner in which these concerns are expressed through culturally prescribed social role behavior. It is also culturally significant to define how these themes are combined into complex interpersonal relationships differing from culture to culture. The following discussion of interpersonal relationships within the Japanese family is organized around these ten dimensions.

Five of these interpersonal dimensions are primarily "instrumental" in nature. The other five are "expressive" in motivation.[8] In instrumental role behavior, action is perceived by self and others as motivated as *a means* of achieving a goal or to meet a standard by which behavior is judged. Action is a means to an end rather than for the immediate satisfaction inherent in the action itself. The five basic instrumental dimensions we considered are (1) *achievement*—behavior motivated by the desire to attain a goal, positively within a given set of standards or social codes, or negatively through what is socially defined as "criminal behavior"; (2) *competence* or adequacy—behavior related positively to actualizing personal adequacy or capacity, or to a need to acquire competence negatively with a sense of failure and inadequacy; (3) *responsibility*—behavior motivated by a sense of responsibility or obligation to internalized social directives, or the opposite: avoidance of or flight from responsibility, or neglect of responsibility due to profligacy, or irresponsible self indulgence; (4) *control*—behavior directed toward the actualization of power, authority, or control in social relationships negatively perceived, problems of dominance and submission; (5) *mutuality*—the phrasing of instrumental behavior in cooperative or competitive terms positively within socially prescribed norms or negatively outside of them.

Expressive behavior can be primarily defined in terms of a feeling rather than of its consequences. There may be an inherent sense of gratification gained in an act itself or in the situation or relationship

---

[8] In their now classic sociological discussion of instrumental and expressive role behavior within the primary family, Parsons and Bales included only a simplistic two-generational picture of roles within the family (*Family Socialization and Interaction Process* [1955], p. 9). The "father" role is an instrumental dominant one, the "mother" an expressive dominant, the "son" an instrumental subordinate, and the "daughter" an expressive subordinate role. This model of role behavior is far too simple and needs amplification and modification to approximate actual role-behavior patterns found within most family configurations in any culture. Their dichotomy of "instrumental" and "expressive," however, has universal application. Although emphases differ with role position, all family configurations involve instrumental and expressive behavior by all members in at least a three-generation frame of reference. There is considerable interpenetration of instrumental and expressive motives in the actual behavior occurring within any given cultural pattern.

in which the behavior is expressed. The five expressive concerns are (1) *harmony-discord*—positively behavior involving maintenance of peacefulness or harmony, or negatively concern with disharmony, discord, even violence and destructiveness in human relationships; (2) *affiliation-separation*—behavior related to feelings of interpersonal closeness and intimacy or their opposites, isolation, rejection, or interpersonal avoidance; (3) *nurturance-deprivation*—behavior involving care, succor, nurture, or, looked at from the standpoint of the recipient, behavior based on fulfillment of a dependent need or on its frustration; (4) *appreciation*—a need for recognition or response from others—or its opposite, a concern with feeling ignored, unimportant, or disdained or depreciated by others; (5) *pleasure-pain*—behavior generally governed by a direct experience of satisfaction or pleasure or their opposites, of dissatisfaction or suffering within the self.

When one goes beneath the surface appearance of the family in Japan to understand the motivations underlying the observable interaction patterns, one finds a complex network of attitudes and expectations in which various instrumental and expressive motives are inextricably intertwined. Nevertheless, there are culturally consistent variations in the strength of and the direction taken by the particular role interaction variable characteristic for the various possible role positions. These consistencies can be defined in formulating an ideal normative picture of Japanese life. The remainder of this chapter is an examination of these normative patterns in motivational variables in some progressive order as they shed light on the nature of traditional Japanese role patterns now being influenced by social change.

INSTRUMENTAL COMPONENTS OF ROLE RELATIONSHIPS WITHIN THE FAMILY

Achievement Motivation

In subsequent chapters we describe the socialization of achievement motivation within the Japanese as related to a sense of obligation incurred by parental sacrifice. In our research we have documented the strong sense of need achievement in Japanese society, expressed as a need to sense personal accomplishment and thereby to "justify" oneself to society. The Japanese are guided by a work ethic as compelling as that demonstrated by Northern European Protestants.[9]

Today, as in the past, the Japanese mother canalizes a culturally structured need to achieve and a desire for competence on the part of

---

[9] Bellah, *Tokugawa Religion* (1957), and Tawney, *Religion and the Rise of Capitalism* (1926).

her children by fostering in her sons a direct identification with the male familial role as the major goal of life.

The male role still emphasizes internalized responsibilities in a hierarchically structured control system. It also emphasizes self-control and restraint. It deemphasizes overt competition within the family lineage conceived of as a cooperative corporate enterprise.

It must be noted that the identification fostered by the mother (emphasized especially in the case of the first son) is with the *status* and *role* of the father than with the father as a particular individual. Traditionally, the father's authority position was never challenged nor did the successfully dedicated mother change her attitude toward this role, no matter what the behavior of the actual father might be. Male adult status was never brought into question by any deprecation of the specific individual holding this office. Such deprecation would be considered as unseemly as for an experienced army sergeant to allow his men to know his private attitudes toward a young inexperienced lieutenant who has just been put in charge of his company. For the Japanese mother, as for the sergeant, duty demands role performance toward the office rather than toward the person.

Similarly, the small girl in Japan learns to identify with the mother's role as a part of her sense of personal achievement. She has ample opportunity to identify with her mother in learning the nurturant, appreciative, "maternal" behavior to be exercised toward males and the maintenance of a harmonious atmosphere within the home. If she is an older sister (*nesan*) she will assume early the role of secondary mother toward her younger sibs. The male role, externally directed toward society, seen superficially emphasizes instrumental qualities, but men derive their strength from the expressive support provided by the women. Examined psychodynamically, however, both male and female roles are compounded of instrumental and expressive components.

In much of social science and literature the concept of "achievement" as related to social role is too narrowly focused on economic definitions of the male vocational role. It is not recognized that, for women in many cultures, achievement motivation is toward the realization of the maternal expressive role and that for a woman this represents a need achievement as much as the realization of more instrumental occupational success does for a man. There is in our own culture an implicit derogation of the adult maternal role in favor of the more culturally appreciated economic vocational achievement. There has been less emphasis in modern Western societies, especially in the United States, on the female marital role as a specialized counterpart to the adult male vocational role. The woman's role, implicitly at least, is seen as less worthy, since women as housewives are not given the same status as are men in an economically oriented society. Arnold Green[10] states ironically that American middle-class housewives spend half of their time doing the unappreciated tasks they dislike and the rest of their time thinking of how to get even with their husbands. Such an attitude, even without the exaggeration, is curious when viewed from the perspective of the traditional Japanese woman. She countenanced no confusion in her mind about becoming a dedicated mother, or, alternatively, about selecting one of a number of possible career choices that are clearly seen as excluding the maternal role. Marriage meant the production of children to insure the continuity of a family. This role entailed exacting training and preparation through the observation of her own mother's behavior and through training before marriage, very often as a maid or servant in another household. Special schools prepared the young woman in the graces attendant on her role, and in the more mundane daily skills of running a household. The conduct of a Japanese household was not considered a simple matter but one requiring a great deal of planning and a sense of organization. Moreover, when a woman entered a household as a bride she had to be trained in the particular traditions and values of her husband's lineage, whatever its social function—economic, military, or artistic.

Japanese women could choose an alternative role to that of marriage. There were professional roles for women in Japanese culture, but most of these were in the field of entertainment, ranging from the relatively high status afforded a gifted geisha to the pathetic status accorded an ordinary prostitute. There was ample opportunity in the world of entertainment for personally aggressive, dominant, or specially gifted women to exercise both dominance and control, as well as to actualize a sense of competence and achievement as a business woman.[11] Success in these various roles outside the marital sphere again demanded special training and a dedication of purpose from a relatively early age. But most women felt they gave up more by forgoing the maternal role than they would by assuming it. Becoming a mother was of higher value than becoming a professional outside the home.

In Japan as elsewhere, today as in the past, there are attempts to actualize achievement needs, not only through socially condoned channels, but also through illegal or antisocial means. In the latter portion of this volume I return to a detailed examination of criminality and deviance in Japanese culture as the obverse of normative or idealized achievement.

[10] Green, "The Middle Class Male Child and Neurosis" (1946).
[11] Yamata, *Three Geishas* (1956).

The Actualization of Competence:
The Apprentice Role, Becoming an Adult

In traditional Japan there was no adolescent period ritually separating childhood from adulthood; each class had its own traditional form of preparation for full adult status, which varied considerably from epoch to epoch in Japanese history. Samurai used marriage to enhance the status of a lineage, and, as parents tended to seek earlier and earlier liaisons, the age of marriage was gradually pushed back from that obtaining at the beginning of the Tokugawa period, around 1600, until by the end of that same period (circa 1850) the age of adulthood for samurai warriors was about fifteen.[12] During this period the women of the warrior class were considered to have become adults before age fifteen. In the merchant and artisan classes, in contrast, the period of apprenticeship became increasingly protracted, and some individuals remained in an apprentice relationship with a master even into their middle thirties.

Today, throughout Japanese society there is a recognition of "adolescence" very similar to that found in the West, with increases in all the attendant problems of psychosexual maladjustment that are prevalent in Western adolescent youth. (See Chapter 12.) Although in Japan the patterns of transition into adulthood remain somewhat different for middle-class, as compared with lower-class, youth, the differences in this respect are actually less noticeable in respect to the appearance of delinquent behavior, since in Japan a continuing apprenticeship pattern allows for less alienation. The "acting out" behavior of lower-class Japanese youth is less apparent. Nevertheless, in Japan, as well as in the United States, school dropouts and so-called delinquent behavior are more prevalent among lower-class youth. (See Chapter 13.)

The apprenticeship of youth during premarital years in traditional Japanese culture was an essential part of socialization and deserves particular attention. Such patterns persist in Japanese industry in modified form today. To understand adult Japanese it is necessary to understand the work mentality as it is developed for many around an apprenticeship experience. The intensity of the adult role dedication in both men and women receives strong reinforcement during a formative period prior to formal entrance into adulthood.

Before the modern period, the Japanese, whether samurai, merchant, or artisan, were expected from about age twelve to undergo rigorous training under an adept master in order to develop the technical competence necessary for adult performance. There was no easy acceptance

---

[12] Ema, *Complete History of Japanese Customs* (1925, in Japanese).

of incompetence or of lack of application to the task of learning. Standards were exacting in every field of endeavor. The apprentice was expected to work hard for long hours with little pay. He had no time for "selfish pleasures" and interests, but had to put such thoughts out of his mind, or limit himself to fantasies about the future day when he would enjoy the pleasures allowed a person of recognized status.

The apprenticeship period was not limited to the male vocational role. There were many apprentice-like equivalents for women during their premarital period. Just as many boys were sent out of their own homes to work under someone other than their fathers, girls were frequently sent out of the home to work as maids in the homes of wealthier folk of higher status to learn proper marital-housewife behavior. If they remained at home, they were required to perform some service for their parents to train themselves for future performance.

In marrying an eldest son, the young bride coming into a new household was in a sense entering her second period of apprenticeship, under the severe and sometimes jealous tutelage of her new husband's mother. If she failed in any way to meet the exacting requirements, or showed herself to be inept, she could be sent back to her family as a failure.

Boys were very often sent out even when they were to inherit their father's craft or business, because it was considered more rigorous, hence better training, to be apprenticed to someone other than the father. The second sons from farm families were encouraged to seek apprenticeships in an urban setting, most often with an artisan but sometimes with a merchant. The girl from a wealthy family was required to attend a special school, which was to train her in the polite arts so necessary for a bride marrying into a respectable lineage. A lineage kept its pride by requiring refined behavior of its in-marrying women.

One of the real changes in socialization noticeably occurring in today's Japan is in respect to the vocational "imprinting" preceding marriage. The traditional forms of apprenticeship described above are being replaced by formal education, on the one hand, and by mass communication media, on the other. This change is especially evident as it influences the woman's role. Mass media have almost entirely supplanted the direct, first-hand experience of the preparatory "maid" period for women as a means of acquiring knowledge concerning the expected role of the housewife. Until recently, most "proper" young women were learning domestic skills by emulating the "refined" behavior observed in upper-status households during a period of domestic apprenticeship outside the home. With the lapse of this custom, the traditional Japanese definition of a maid has now shifted toward the Western concept of a lifelong occupational role.[13] As a consequence, class-limited role diffusion of domestic patterns from higher-status households into lower-status households no longer occurs through direct experience. Young girls instead turn to popular magazines and television for inspiration and instruction in homemaking. The "Westernization" of Japanese women is going on at a rapid pace in the inculcation of a mass-media concept of what a home should be.

Apartment-house dwelling is increasingly prevalent in congested urban areas. The young bride learns to make the most of a small living space in which many of the domestic refinements of the old culture no longer have any pertinence. There has been widespread use of the recently developed ready-made foods, such as "instant noodles" and soups. The small Japanese home kitchen has become mechanized with such devices as toasters and electric rice cookers. The complicated and time-consuming skills once needed for food preparation are rapidly disappearing. For most housewives there remains the necessary daily shopping in neighborhood shops, since the buying of large quantities is difficult for those traveling on foot. Increasingly, however, those who can afford cars do stock up refrigerators that are continually growing in size and capacity. More housewives are buying at large food centers and department store basements. Western cooking is demonstrated on daytime television and is very popular as a home diversion for the housewife who finds herself with increasingly greater periods of leisure.[14]

In many households in Japan, the diet is shifting so that rice is no longer a three-meal staple but may be consumed once a day. Government-controlled rice stocks are accumulating owing to a shift from rice to bread and milk in the morning diet. The modern housewife has been made very nutrition conscious; the Japanese are well aware that the shift toward more calcium, protein, and vitamins in the diet has resulted in an increase in stature of from three to four inches in present-day youth as compared with those of the prewar period.

Today some women, with proper business skills, can work in a

---

[13] In 1954 I noted that American families in Japan had many difficulties with Japanese "maids." They wanted to pay them more than they expected, as they considered the Japanese salary "exploitative" (about $15 a month in 1954). But many maids, although highly paid by Japanese standards, would leave when they discovered that the American housewives for whom they worked assumed no responsibility for "training" them in English or European cooking, which had been the major reason many young girls sought maid service in American households.

[14] The detailed description of personality and social change in Japanese apartment houses has been made by Christie Kiefer, "Social Change and Personality in a White Collar Danchi," University of California, Berkeley, Department of Anthropology, doctoral dissertation (1968).

company prior to marriage, usually to a fellow employee. The prewar "discrimination" in patterns of formal education given men and women is still somewhat in evidence, although all the major universities, including the University of Tokyo, admit qualified women on an informal quota basis. Any determined woman, if she so chooses, can seriously consider taking on a professional career. Most educated women in Japan, very much as in the United States, forgo their careers when they marry. Some women may choose to follow a professional career after the death of a husband.

For men, the apprenticeship pattern still has considerable vitality as a means of vocational socialization, in spite of the rapid inroads on this pattern by large-scale factories. Nevertheless, many young men are no longer tolerant of the psychological dependence, the hard work, and the occasional harshness experienced in a formal apprenticeship. After being graduated from nine years of compulsory school, many prefer to find as quickly as possible some position in a large factory that will afford them security and wages that increase steadily with seniority. The focus of vocational concern is shifting from acquiring special skills mastered with difficulty to finding positions with shorter hours and higher pay—attitudes that have already been primary for years among Western blue-collar workers. (See Chapter 8.)

Japanese youths wish to have time free for after-hours recreation. A variety of such recreation is afforded by the many places of amusement now accessible through the transportation ganglia of modern Japanese urban areas. For urban workers the virtue of loyalty, and the interdependent responsibilities incumbent in a network of associations, related to the apprentice-master structure of the past are beginning to disappear. In professional, clerical, and managerial positions, however, the network of expectations is more apt to endure for some time, since there is still considerable emphasis on loyalty of service in the middle-class segment of the population.

The process of change does not terminate the many continuities in Japanese personality configurations and role performance related to the concern with competence and adequacy. The culture continues to be a demanding one in its definition of the adequate performance of adult social roles. Even today it is no mean task for most Japanese to actualize adult role expectations, to have a sense of achievement or success. In various studies over the past fifteen years with the Thematic Apperception Test (TAT) in Japan we have continued to find evidence of very strong achievement motivation or, as some psychologists term it, a "need-achievement" related to family responsibility and interdependent nurturant concerns. These achievement concerns are almost invariably expressed in the context of worry over potential

incapacity to realize one's own internalized standards.[15] High standards
pervaded the full range of traditional culture, from the specialized
world of art represented by exacting traditions such as the Noh drama,
the Kabuki stage, or the various forms of graphic arts, to the everyday
world of the lowliest artisan or cook. Everything in Japan is still judged
and ranked—the relative position of the major universities, the "belts"
worn by judo experts, the ratings of *go* players.

No field of endeavor in Japan has escaped concern with refinement
and finesse. During the traditional apprenticeship period, an individual, whether he was treated leniently or harshly, was required to
continue until he showed himself to be sufficiently aware of what was
expected of him in the way of proper standards. Only then would he
be considered worthy of independence.

The concern with shame, and with community approval discussed
at length by Ruth Benedict in *The Chrysanthemum and the Sword* [16]
is related to patterned socialization that sanctions the child by drawing
to his attention that all behavior is constantly observed by the outside
community and can reflect shamefully on other family members,
causing them "social injury." The sensitivity to "face," so often remarked upon by visitors to Japan, is the external manifestation of
the continual awareness that one is being judged against a demanding
set of social standards.

Seen in its expressive aspects, Japanese socialization not only causes
an internalized self-appraisal of adequacy and inadequacy; it also
stimulates a continuing need for the recognition and response of
others. Compared with Western culture, there is indeed an acute
sensitivity to lack of appreciation and potential disdain. In their external relationships with Westerners, Japanese have sometimes seemed
to go to extremes to avoid social disapproval. In my opinion however,
the obvious need for appreciation and fear of disdain has been too
simplistically generalized to characterize Japanese as a "shame" culture—I cannot agree with Ruth Benedict in this regard. As the subsequent chapters will document, I am most impressed by the deeper
cause of internalized standards found as a consequence of Japanese
socialization. Hence I would regard instrumental concerns with inadequacy and expressive concerns with appreciation less prepotent
when they are viewed within a total context of interpersonal concerns,
including instrumental concerns with achievement and responsibility,
and expressive concerns with interdependency and nurturance. If so

---

[15] DeVos and Wagatsuma, *Heritage of Endurance* (to be published). It is interesting to note that concern with adequacy has not diminished as revealed in TAT protocols taken in 1965 from Arakawa Ward from both adults and fifteen-year-olds.
[16] Benedict, *The Chrysanthemum and the Sword* (1946).

perceived, Japan can hardly be called a "shame" culture. In fact, problems related to "guilt" are culturally much more in evidence.

In the premodern past the pressures experienced in Japanese vocational socialization made ever becoming really "adequate" a difficult and problematical process. It demanded of the individual a strong endurance and a capacity to maintain himself in submissive and subordinate positions until his mentors deemed him capable of independent action. For the man, ideally achieved social status was that of master merchant, or artisan, or of successful bureaucrat in the premodern samurai hierarchy. Similarly, farmers prided themselves on their proficiency and diligence in producing the maximum crop from poor soil. For a wife and mother, endurance continued until her children showed to the world their capacities attesting to the mother's years of careful nurture and training and preparation. Much of what Freud [17] and Reik[18] have described as "moral masochism" applies directly to the apprentice mentality in its attitude toward the endurance of suffering maintained by Japanese throughout their preparatory years of training. One must not overlook the fact that submissiveness was and still is related to a sense of the future long-term goal of acquiring competence in order eventually to become independent or dominant in relation to others. This ability to endure tutelage helps explain past and even present Japanese relations with the West.

It is often said in present-day Japan that concern with standards among artisans is disappearing in direct proportion to the increase in mechanically standardized products that are displacing the various handicrafts in the marketplace. However, the mentality of seniority starting with an apprenticeship is still strong. Despite increased mechanization, the Japanese vocational career in industry is still characterized by very low salaries for beginning workers and the gradual increase in those salaries within a rigidly adhered-to system of seniority. Fringe benefits begin from the first. A reciprocal relationship between worker and employer in which the employer has a paternalistic responsibility is carried over from the Japanese concept of preparatory apprenticeship training. (We shall discuss this continuity more fully in Chapter 8.)

The mechanization of Japanese technology has not yet altered fundamental attitudes; the evidence from projective psychological tests of young and middle-aged Japanese shows a continuity of concerns by each subject with his capacity to meet standards and expectations. Japanese concerns with success or failure remain focused, on

<hr>

[17] Freud, "The Economic Problem of Masochism," in *Collected Papers* (1955).
[18] Reik, *Masochism in Modern Man* (1941).

a conscious level at least, on problems of personal adequacy rather than on issues of self-interest or self-will. Japanese still see themselves as meeting social expectations rather than as concerned with their own individualized motivation, or lack of motivation, in contrast to comparable American subjects. Even though choice of vocation may have been made by one's family rather than by oneself, most Japanese do not have leeway for conscious awareness of any motivational ambivalence on their own part. There are many Japanese for whom it is still psychologically impossible to consider directly their own unwillingness to perform an expected vocational role. One can be excused to some degree for lack of performance only if one is physically or mentally incapable of performing in an expected role. This enduring cultural characteristic is related to the fact that in traditional Japan the assertion of an individual's will was considered destructive to the harmony of a cooperative community and—even more basic from a psychodynamic standpoint—destructive to one's own parents. (See Chapter 5.) Feelings of unwillingness can give rise to a very strong sense of guilt, and such guilt is still to be found deeply motivating the behavior of modern Japanese.

Responsibility and Obligation

The profound sense of responsibility of the Japanese is the residue of the familialism of the past, in which the individual ego was not differentiated from an intense sense of social belonging; each person shared this sense, whatever his particular position within the family or organization. In the Japanese family it has been and still is the mother who is responsible for bringing up the children. Traditionally, this has meant that when children acted badly the mother apologized to others for the behavior of her child. Often when a criminal is apprehended, the mother (much less frequently the father) of the culprit is quoted in the newspaper as saying that she feels inexpressibly sorry, hence responsible (*mōshiwake ga nai*), for her son's behavior. A mother may feel impelled to make a public apology, taking full responsibility for her son's act. In Japan, if one's dog bites someone, one apologizes, very often not for one's carelessness in allowing it to happen, but on behalf of the dog, who in a sense "belongs" familially, the dog's behavior thus reflecting upon his "family." Again we can see how Japanese would be socialized to be sensitive to what might be considered socially "shameful" behavior.

Children know intuitively that they can cause their parents pain through their sharp sense of responsibility. Such knowledge often leads in consciously explicit terms to the inhibition of improper behavior outside the family that could cause pain by shaming its members.

Similarly, in employment relationships, workers in Arakawa[19] today

---

[19] DeVos and Wagatsuma, *Heritage of Endurance* (to be published).

still tend to identify in a familial sense with the boss, assuming the operation of a reciprocal relationship that goes far beyond the so-called paternalistic practices in the West. Japanese paternalism still derives much of its strength from the traditional expectation that a person playing the role of a boss (literally, in Japanese, *oyabun*, "parent role") will assume almost total responsibility for the health and welfare of his workers. The belief that one's boss has a strong feeling of responsibility allows subordinates the complementary expressive feelings of dependency and loyalty toward authority. Such feelings of responsibility are continuities of an internalized code of leadership of the past, whether the leaders were bureaucrats, businessmen, artisans, or petty merchants.

This code of leadership is illustrated in "I Want to Be a Sea Shell," a rebroadcast on American educational television of an earlier Japanese TV production of the story of the war-crime trial of a simple Japanese soldier during the American occupation. The film depicted a scene that must have seemed strange, although touching, to its Western audiences. The private, who has been condemned to die, was forced by his immediate superior to carry out the ambiguous order of a general "to take care of" two American flyers who had been shot down over Japan in a B-29 raid. A lieutenant interpreted this order to mean the execution of the Americans and ordered the private to carry out the death sentence, for which he in turn has been sentenced by an American tribunal. The general who had given the initial ambiguous order, himself still a prisoner, visits the death-row cell of the private and humbly apologizes to him, asking forgiveness for his responsibility for the private's fate.

There have been numerous recorded instances of *sekinin jisatsu* ("responsibility suicide"), in which a superior, although totally ignorant of the action of his subordinates, nevertheless assumes responsibility and commits ritual suicide.

In Japan the definition of "responsibility" outside the family usually involves explicit allegiance to some organization such as a business firm, an intellectual clique, or a political faction. For *both* psychological and social reasons few Japanese work independently. So-called independent entrepreneurs usually function as members of some informal interdependent economic organization. Role definition within each such group has some sense of implicit hierarchy. The leader role depends on the support of the collective efforts of the other members of the groups. Yet, in one sense, subordinate roles are not so carefully defined as they are in the United States. For example, if a person officially assigned to a job in a business cannot carry out the job effectively, others in the organization will informally supplement his efforts so that the task gets accomplished. In American business, an individual usually functions only within his assigned role and tends not to cover for the failure of others. The Japanese *kaisha,* or company, is more like a football team. Except for that of the quarterback, positions are not always clearly maintained; once the ball is in play, everyone does what he can in competition with an opponent to get the ball across the goal line. It is this continuous teamwork rather than individualistic action that has contributed much to Japanese economic success. All are responsible together.

SELF-CONTROL AS AN ASPECT OF RESPONSIBILITY.—Sex roles in traditional Japan differed in the degree to which "self-control" was necessary. As a whole, the role requirements put strong emphasis on maintaining self-control in order not to bring any injury on one's family. As we shall discuss further, in respect to concepts of self-expression of pleasure related to bodily functions, the traditional Japanese concept of self-control differs somewhat from that of the West in that a man can indulge in sexuality, for example, if it in no way interferes with the well-being of his *ie,* or house. Unfortunate sexual commitments or possessive feelings toward an inappropriate person, however, can lead to a deep sense of guilt.

Japanese men could act impulsively, even violently, toward members of their own family, but such action was not usually defined as violence. Such expressions, prevalent in the traditional culture, were not matched with freedom to behave impulsively in outside relationships since such behavior would in such contexts be considered a violent rupture of the expected. Women, particularly, still are expected to practice restraint over their impulses to anger or discord vis-à-vis both husband and children.[20] For a woman violence is usually irrevocable and marks an end to a maintenance of social role.

In Japan, the practice of self-control in role behavior differs somewhat from that in the West in that Japanese depend very heavily on mechanisms of *suppression,* whereas Western Europeans or Americans tend to practice *repression.* That is to say, Japanese very often are totally aware of their underlying emotional states when those emotions are not appropriate to expected role behavior, but they choose to suppress them. Westerners often control emotions by modes of repression, which they buttress by placing a strong value on the maintenance of "rational" logical behavior. Although Japanese in similar circumstances are often painfully aware of their own inner feelings and the feelings of others, because of the "self-control" re-

---

[20] In my more recent research we found that the most striking differences between delinquent families and nondelinquent normal controls were the relatively unrestrained impulsive behavior and other marks of inadequate maternal supervision, as well as the overt expressions of dissatisfaction with the marriage, on the part of the women in families with a delinquent child.

quired by the expected role, they maintain a blandness of surface behavior that Westerners often consider "inscrutable." In a sense Westerners expect behavior to be in accord with underlying spontaneous feelings, and when it is not, it is considered insincere. The Japanese concept of sincerity, in contrast, is the maintenance of behavior that is fully in accord with what is required by the individual's role. Needless to say, the Japanese understand and are aware of one another's covert attitudes in spite of the surface control, whether the hidden feelings are intense anger or profound sorrow.

Cooperation and Competition

Today, as in the past, an individual cannot function in any Japanese society without explicit interdependency and therefore responsibility to some group in his professional and vocational life. Those who fail to meet obligations soon isolate themselves, and a person who seeks to circumvent seniority or who becomes too independent finds himself almost totally alienated. An old proverb, *Deru kugi wa utareru* ("The nail that sticks out gets hit"), still seems to express Japanese thought on this matter. This interdependent network makes it difficult for Japanese to behave individualistically unless they are exceptional artists or individuals who for other reasons do not have to give any form of symbolic allegiance and avowal of cooperation to a particular group or competitive segment of the society. Competition in Japanese society, as Nakane[21] describes in detail, is among groups of hierarchically organized, yet cooperative and mutually nurturant individuals. For further discussion of the mutuality dimension of cooperative and competitive behavior in the world outside the family, we commend Nakane's excellent discussion.

The deemphasis of overt disharmony within Japanese culture generally should not lead us to assume a lack of intense competition among families or groups. The obverse of the loyalty to one's own group is an underlying competitiveness toward others.

One is always continually maneuvering with one's allies against other competitors, who are similarly allied in cliques and factions. Partisanship is intense. Loyalties within conglomerates shift, resulting in the success or failure of certain ventures. Hence, one must insist on the maintenance of harmony within one's own group in order to succeed against others. Competition among factions within the major political parties on the basis of intensely loyal leaders and followers gives a special flavor to Japanese political life.

The Japanese business world in some respects is a modern version of the shifting allegiances of the daimyo (lords) of the feudal period.

[21] Nakane, *Japanese Society* (1970).

An interesting aspect of Japanese competition is that its purpose is not to destroy the enemy completely, but to take over the lion's share of a particular area of enterprise. In the competition among publishing companies, for example, it was recently within the power of one major company to put a longtime competitor completely out of business. It did not, however, and the defeated rival continues operation on a much reduced level.

KYŌIKU-MAMA. The education of children is perhaps the most intense arena for competition observable within Japanese culture today. A phrase one frequently hears in summarizing the behavior of particular women with respect to the education of their children is *kyōiku-mama* ("education-mama"). This usage refers to the intense nurturant control a particular mother will exercise over her children in direct competition with other mothers in her neighborhood or special circle to see to it that her own children do better in their educational progress. A good majority of middle-class children, for example, are required or encouraged to take extra schooling given after regular school hours. Many children are given private tutoring, a service that provides extra income for grade-school or high-school educators, who are highly sought after for this purpose.[22]

Japanese middle-class as well as lower-class mothers will make countless sacrifices, including taking on extra work, to provide the money necessary for tutors and other additional educational expenses so that their children will be in a better competitive position. The reason for the widespread increase in the use of tutors is that, with recent changes in the curriculum, mothers are no longer able to help their children or to do their homework for them. Attempts to see that the teacher pays special attention to one's own child lead to a great deal of what Americans would consider the tacit bribery of teachers.

To illustrate, the city of Ashiya between Osaka and Kobe has a large number of upper-middle-class and upper-class residents. School teachers there receive lavish "gifts" including tailored suits. It has been considered quite a plum to become a teacher in this area. It has been traditional for teachers to receive gifts from the parents of their students and it was not considered unethical to do so. Nevertheless, the gift-giving competition in Ashiya reached such a point that the teachers themselves held a meeting in order to find some means of holding this practice within acceptable bounds. The parental competition had become so fierce that the teachers became concerned about maintaining their integrity in the face of the implicit obligations incurred.

---

[22] DeVos and Wagatsuma, *Heritage of Endurance* (to be published).

One of the worst features of this intense preoccupation with the education of one's own child is the tensions that arise between neighbors. As indicated, a woman can judge herself a failure unless her children do well at school, and mothers are made to feel inadequate to the point of suffering a clinical depression or severe neurotic debilitation—in attempting to keep up with the Tanakas. Moreover, the pressure causes a considerable strain on many of the children throughout their childhood and preadulthood.[23]

Status competition among Japanese families in the middle class is not limited to the education of the child, but extends to material possessions. Competition is especially critical today in acquiring household appliances. In the small urban apartments that are increasingly used as dwellings for middle-class so-called salary men, electric appliances have become more important for status than furniture. When television sets first appeared in large numbers, they immediately became a status symbol. It was reported that families living in apartments would put up television aerials before they were able to purchase a set so that they would not be seen by their neighbors as deficient. Very recently, the most prized competitive possession necessary to the maintenance of proper middle-class status has shifted to color television and to the automobile.

For housewives, status is sometimes defined by such nuances as the quality of the bedding aired over the tiny balcony attached to each apartment.[24] Kiefer, in a study of apartment-house living, reports that one housewife would hang out rich-looking undergarments to add status to her laundry, although she considered them far too expensive ever to wear. Salesmen visiting apartment-house areas take full advantage of these competitive attitudes.

Authority and Control

DISTRIBUTION OF POWER AND DECISION-MAKING IN THE JAPANESE FAMILY. Many who read about the Japanese authoritarianism assume simply that Japan was traditionally a hierarchical society in which the individual on top made the decisions and took initiative. But this is rarely the case either in the external political sphere or within the family. Decisions are often collective efforts "on behalf of" the family or company head. If a person in such a leadership position too often counters the collective efforts of his subordinates (who in many circumstances take initiatives that would not be acceptable in the West) he may lose his power base entirely by withdrawal of the active support of his subordinates or by some sort of silent resistance that makes it difficult

[23] Vogel, "Entrance Examinations and Emotional Disturbance" (1962).
[24] Kiefer, "Social Change and Personality in a White Collar Danchi" (1968).

to continue functioning. In actuality, therefore, the distribution of power in the Japanese society is a very complex matter. It is well known that in Japanese political history the nominal leader was very often controlled by his "advisers" or by individuals who continued to manipulate events after their so-called "retirement." Much as in the performance of a drama, real direction came from behind the scenes while the audience observed only the role performances taking place on stage.[25]

It is often assumed that Japanese women have no power. They generally have been delegated to subordinate roles in which their behavior continually symbolized their inferior social position vis-à-vis men. What is overlooked when only overt behavior is observed, however, is the frequent operation of actual control of the family by women within the family household. No matter who actually exercised power in premodern Japan, women always carefully deferred to men in accordance with role requirements, just as a powerful regent in public defers to a royal figurehead on the throne.

Recent trends toward a more overt expression of latent dominance by women are more apt to appear in urban lower-class families where women are less restricted than those in middle-class families by status considerations and therefore are more likely to give freer vent to emotional expression, whether of a sexual or an aggressive nature. The appearance of strong-willed wives and dependent husbands, however, is not totally a product of any postwar "emancipation" of Japanese women or of any sociological factor such as the effects of industrialization on the whole society.

In the traditional culture many comic stories and anecdotes (called *rakugo*) about the common people's life in the Tokugawa period describe an impulsive and somewhat careless husband as a foil to his more realistic, practical, and dependable wife. It is clear in all these anecdotes that the boss is actually the so-called "dependent" marital partner.

Dominant or submissive role behavior and dominant or submissive personality structure are independent of one another. A sample of 800 records of the Rorschach Tests administered by DeVos and others[26] in rural and urban Japanese communities revealed no basic, significant,

---

[25] For a careful description of political functions of the Privy Council (the most powerful semiadvisory and semiadministrative organ) and Genro (the extra-Constitutional advisory organ) in prewar Japanese government, see Linebarger, Chu, and Burks, *Far Eastern Government and Politics: China and Japan* (1954), chap. 17, "Government under the Meiji Constitution."

[26] Muramatsu, *The Japanese: An Empirical Study in Culture and Personality* (1962, in Japanese).

consistent structural differences in personality between Japanese men and women. The general results would indicate that the distribution of personality traits does not produce obvious personality differences corresponding to the obvious Japanese dichotomy in observed social sex-role behavior. Hence we would assume that in the past, as in the present, there was no significant difference between men and women in Japan in the incidence or distribution of structural traits of personality, in basic active or passive attitudes, dominant and submissive needs, and the like. Thus, while a dominant man could assert himself directly within the behavioral prerogatives of the male role, a potentially dominant woman had to find some indirect means of expressing dominance within the narrow strictures confining female role behavior. The means taken come readily to view when one looks beneath the surface and examines the actual distribution of dominant and submissive traits within specific Japanese families. A potentially dominant woman learns to manipulate susceptible men in such a way that they are very often totally unaware they are "deciding" in accordance with the woman's wishes. A dependent male child naturally is most susceptible to the exercise of his mother's nurturant control.

The role of the paternal grandmother is one of the key points of tension in Japanese family life. Tensions arise out of the harsh dominance with which a mother-in-law (*shutome*) very often exercises control over a politically powerless in-marrying daughter-in-law (*yome*) and out of the way she manipulates the dependent-nurturant ties between herself and her favorite adult son. There is, in essence, a competition for the husband that is only infrequently won by the wife, even today in situations where the mother no longer lives with the nuclear family. The defeated wife, in turn, when she has such propensities in herself, learns quickly to play the game and shifts her affective needs and emotional requirements from her husband to her growing children. Many major decisions within the family, and sometimes even outside the family, are subject to the mother-in-law's control. It was interesting to us to note in the study of Niiike village[27] that the strongest sense of household tradition and lineage in this tradition-oriented farm village was found among the older women who, as young brides, had come in as strangers from the outside, but who, through the process of severe hazing and rigorous training over a period of time, themselves became "keepers of the flame" for their adopted households. These in-marrying women are eventually given chief responsibility for the care of the *butsudan* in which are kept the ancestral tablets memorializing persons they themselves probably never knew.

---

[27] Beardsley, Hall, and Ward, *Village Japan* (1959).

The paternal grandfather, conversely, plays a minor, somewhat withdrawn role in many families, and in some he may express an almost maternal kind of nurturance toward the young. If the grandfather is a sufficiently dominant personality, however, he will continue in business matters to exercise control even after his so-called retirement.

Power within the Japanese family was in the past always exercised in the name of preserving lineage and enhancing family status. Therefore, the family head was never considered to hold true personal power but to inherit a role through which power was exercised for family benefit. A family head who was a dominant person, of course, would exercise personal direction of the other members of his family, whereas a more passive person, if not totally inadequate, would heed "suggestions" made directly to him.

EXPRESSIVE COMPONENTS OF ROLE RELATIONSHIPS WITHIN THE FAMILY

So far this discussion has focused mainly on the instrumental motivations to be found in Japanese role behavior. The same behavior may also be viewed in terms of its expressive motivational components. Only in the abstract can we look at behavior as solely goal-oriented. Sustained goal-directed behavior cannot be maintained for most individuals, whatever their culture, without some continuing sense of expressive gratification. The socialization process within any culture can be viewed as changing primary needs and gratifications into culturally specific secondary ones.

As was already indicated, expressive role behavior has positive and negative dimensions of (1) harmony and discord, (2) affiliation and isolation, (3) nurturance and deprivation, (4) appreciation and depreciation, and (5) pleasure, gratification, self-expression, and suffering. Expressive concerns are themselves inextricably intertwined. Therefore, in examining any type of expressive behavioral motivation, we will have to relate what we say to other forms of instrumental as well as expressive motivation.

In examining Japanese sexual behavior generally, for example, one finds that sexual congress can be not only a means of satisfying physiological needs, but also, as it can be in any culture, a means of satisfying affiliative needs, evoking response and appreciation or supplying feelings of nurturance and dependency. Sex can even be sublimated when direct expression comes in conflict with other instrumental or expressive needs which are not fulfilled. In short, there is no form of expressive behavior that can be viewed in total isolation.

Harmony and Discord: The Suppression and Repression
of In-group Discord and Violence

In most of their social relations Japanese are expert at maintaining a Confucianist harmony and peacefulness on the surface, at least, and suppressing any obvious forms of discord, let alone violence.

If we limited our examination of Japanese culture to normative patterns and overt social role behavior, we would fail to understand how disruptive or destructive impulses are displaced and interests expressed through culturally patterned forms. In Chapters 4 and 5 we take a look beneath the surface and we make a specific examination of the unconscious psychological mechanisms operative in the channeling of aggression into relatively nondestructive social channels. Chapter 4 discusses how circumscribed outlets for aggressive behavior in Japanese are transmuted into what has been termed "moral masochism." We draw some cross-cultural contrast between the projection of aggression, which in some cultures is indirectly manifest in concern over witchcraft and sorcery, and Japanese ways of introjecting hostility.

In Chapter 5 I continue the discussion of the introjection of hostility in respect to the internalization of guilt in Japanese children. The manner in which this occurs I perceive to be an essential motivational push to the achievement motivation that characterizes Japanese culture. Finally, in Chapter 17 I discuss the relationship of aggression to the special conditions, forms, and cultural content to be found in Japanese suicide related to what I term "role narcissism."

In examining social sex roles as expressively motivated, we must again start with a general consideration of the traditional Japanese family. Both modern and traditional family in Japan provided and is providing a sense of well-being and security through a sense of "belonging." This sense of belonging today, however, had changed from one that is realized through a quasi-religious reverence for the family as an enduring corporate entity to a more secularized ideal of the establishment of relationships through which one can realize, as the Japanese term it, *shiawase*—comfort, contentment, and happiness defined in very material terms. In the past, the sense of expressive contentment within the household was to be attained by following Confucian ideas of harmony and order. (See Chapters 2 and 3.)

It would be helpful perhaps to point out again that the traditional Japanese word *ie* is not a direct translation of the English word "household," "family," or "house," at least in their usual connotations. Usage of the English word "house" in special phrases such as "house of Rothschild" is the closest connotative approximation. The phrase connotes a corporate entity existing beyond the span of individual lives, a group closely bound together by intimately, harmoniously conceived ties of blood and kinship. The leadership is passed on. An *ie* may develop subsidiary branches, as did the Rothschild "cadet" line. In some regions of Japan, mainly in the Northeast, a similar extended family structure called the *dōzoku* became prominent.[28]

For Japanese, the *ie* was a framework for clearly divided roles; members derived personal satisfaction from working cooperatively. Nurturant and dependent needs could be realized within this framework. This realization did not necessarily occur primarily in the husband and wife relationship. The sharing of one's intimate self in companionship and communion was not considered a goal of marriage; it was not an institutionalized expectation of the marriage bond, and indeed at times such sharing was considered detrimental to proper role behavior in marriage.

The Japanese sense of belonging does not derive from any achievement of mutual understanding, but is related to a diffuseness of oneself in which any painful awareness of an existential separateness can be avoided by holding a sense of one's self as a family member. Such a loss of self is found satisfying to many members of religious bodies, as Durkheim discussed in the *Elementary Forms of the Religious Life*.[29]

Conversely, in Chapter 17 I discuss in some detail how loss of a sense of belonging is related to patterns of suicide to be found in Japan as well as elsewhere. A sense of group identity gives one strength to go beyond one's personal defects or limitations in the interdependence that occurs in religious collectivities. For some of its adherents, Christianity today satisfies such a basic social need instead of merely offering a dogma. In this context, it is significant that the Christian concept of "church" bears some psychodynamic similarities to the Japanese quasi-religious concept of "house"; *kyriakon,* the Greek word from which "church" is derived, represents this directly. The Church is the "House of the Lord" to which all Christians belong, as brethren under God the Father, and it offers a sense of transcendental affiliation that answers the deepest need for dependent security in the Christian sense of self. It is sometimes overlooked that although many so-called psychologically independent Christians are independent in their human relationship, underlying this independence is some psychodynamic primitive sense of a special dependent relationship with God.

Many modern Japanese women who seem to be maritally well

---

[28] Brown, " 'Dōzoku' and the Ideology of Descent in Rural Japan" (1966), pp. 1129–1151; Cornell, "Dōzoku: An Example of Evolution and Transition in Japanese Village Society" (1964), pp. 449–480; Kitano, " 'Dōzoku' and 'Ie' in Japan" (1962), pp. 42–46; Nagai, "Dōzoku, A Preliminary Study of the Japanese 'Extended Family' Group and Its Social Economic Functions" (1953).

[29] Durkheim, *The Elementary Forms of the Religious Life* (1947).

adjusted and satisfied still give evidence of the well-developed capacity manifested in the traditional culture to relate to the *role* of the husband rather than to the *person*.

This emphasis on role behavior rather than on personal communication is well illustrated by differences we found among the families in Arakawa Ward.[30] Our normal controls and sample families with delinquent children differ significantly in the manner in which harmony is maintained and discord avoided. In respect to achievement and competence, there is no difference in the role behavior of the fathers of these families; many in both groups are obvious economic, vocational, and personal failures. But the mothers of nondelinquents express far less direct criticism or disdain of their husbands' shortcomings. In six interviews with each mother, more than three-fourths of the mothers of problem children expressed a direct and unequivocal dissatisfaction with or sometimes even contempt for their husbands; many of them described in graphic terms the types of discord and disharmony that characterized their marital life. Although the mothers of nondelinquent children also criticized their husbands, they did so less frequently and less intensely.

In both groups we found many women whose basic personality propensities were not at all in accord with the demands of their social sex role. Many of these women felt themselves to be more dominant and aggressive, and even more impulsive, than acceptable role behavior warranted. We felt that the psychologically available techniques for role maintenance, especially dedication to self-controlled behavior within the role, made the critical difference. On a psychodynamic level, the integrative mechanisms available to mothers of the normal controls were somewhat better than those of the mothers of delinquents; thus the mothers of nondelinquents, whatever their propensities, had better psychological means at their disposal to maintain self-control.

In the Confucianist concept, the Japanese father was never to be treated in any way that was disrespectful to his role position. Whatever the woman's unrealized need for mutual affection or dependency, she was required to treat the husband as the symbol of authority and succession in the family. As we report in Chapter 3, in comparing farming and fishing villages we found in the fantasies elicited by the Thematic Apperception Test that, depending on class and role background, the implicit expectations of women could vary considerably from the self-sacrificing samurai ideal. As we shall describe more fully in Chapters 3 and 4, in the farming village of Niiike women's fantasy was more clearly in line with written works describing traditional

---

[30] DeVos and Wagatsuma, *Heritage of Endurance* (to be published).

normative expectations. Marriage for love was never described as succeeding, nor were there any references to a woman's aggressive behavior toward a husband in a situation of discord or dissatisfaction. In a fishing village, however, we elicited a number of stories of women who were physically abusive to a drunken or profligate husband. In the farming village, when a woman was depicted in any violent scene, the violence was attributed to her deep sense of responsibility for the careful upbringing of her children. Such behavior could end in suicide as a symbol of her total failure in her role as a mother.

In the traditional Japanese culture, the terms of address used within a family further suggest that the relationships are primarily in terms of roles. As a general rule, only those with higher status can call those of lower status by their given names with or without affix (such as *san, kun,* or *chan*). Parents call their children by their given names, and so do the older children in addressing their younger sibs. Those of lower status, however, when addressing those of higher status, must use the words designating the role of the addressee (with affixes such as *sama* or *san* or *chama chan,* in an exceptionally intimate and informal relationship or in the case of a child). Accordingly, children must address their parents as *"o-to-sama"* ("honorable father") or *"o-ka-san"* ("honorable mother"). Younger children do not call their elder brothers and sisters by their given names unless there is little age difference and great intimacy. As a rule a younger child will address the elder brother as *"o-ni-san"* ("honorable elder brother) and the elder sister as *"o-nei-sama"* ("honorable elder sister"), or will use a combination of name and role, such as *"Takako-Nei-san"* (comparable to "Sister Emily"). Particularly different from American practice is the way husband and wife address each other. The husband, as a person of higher status, can and does call his wife by her given name, but this is not reciprocated by his wife except in extreme privacy. In an old tradition, the wife would call her husband by a deferential word such as *"danna-sama"* ("honorable master"), or more recently by a vague term such as *"anata"* (meaning "you"). Today, both husband and wife, and the wife in particular, generally use names designating parental roles, the husband calling his wife "mother" (*o-kā-san*) and the wife calling her husband "father" (*o-tō-san*) as soon as they become parents of children. A more recent trend, especially in urban middle-class families, is to use foreign words for father and mother; thus a husband calls his wife "mama" and a wife calls her husband "papa."

Individuals from cultures accustomed to more direct spontaneous family relationships, particularly between sibs and husband and wife, may find it difficult to understand the emotional implications of these forms of address. Such usage in Japan puts continual symbolic emphasis on the fact that direct personal relationships interfere with the performance of duties related to roles.

A similar emphasis is clearly found, for example, in authoritarian structures such as an army, which depends for its organization on the fact that orders given by a superior must be obeyed without question. The army discourages officers and noncommissioned officers from "fraternizing," and forbids their using the same recreational facilities or addressing one another by first names.

This emphasis on role maintenance, whatever the personal feeling of the man and wife toward each other, has certain expressive advantages as well as the disadvantages of hindering intimacy of communication. There is a sense of security attached to the role in that the individual knows he can maintain himself within the protective armor of his role position. Such use of role maintenance is especially important for individuals with an underlying sense of inadequacy. A person, whatever his sense of personal inadequacy (which, given Japanese standards, is a widespread inner experience), can maintain himself within his formal family pattern without a sense of threat. Most vulnerable, of course, is the individual holding the position of family head, since this position carries the expectations of family success and the responsibility for failure. Ideally the individual is placed *in* the role rather than measured *against* the ideal requirements of the role. For the children being socialized within a family, emphasis on role behavior fosters the continuity in vocational identification useful in a lineage system. Observation of the respect accorded the adult male is a continual psychological inducement to the growing male child to take over the privileges of the same vocational-marital position. Identification with the father is fostered, at least in respect to the father's role position, whatever the father's deficiencies as an individual.

Some Western contrasts bring out clearly the implication of this emphasis on the expressive aspects of roles. One can cite numerous instances, especially in lower-class segments of Western society, where the mother's ideas of what a "man" is do not at all coincide with her perception of her husband. In fact, in certain segments of American Negro society and of Irish society there are almost institutionalized discongruities between what a wife expects of her mate in contrast to the implicit idealized male image. In the Irish family, for example, the role of "father" was often given over in ideal form to the desexualized priest, whereas the actual husband was often depreciated as an inadequate drunkard. James Joyce gives poignant testimony to the identity conflict occurring in a young boy in such a disharmonious situation. Again to cite a literary example, this time Welsh rather than Irish, D. H. Lawrence in *Sons and Lovers* depicts the internal conflict in a young man whose mother has middle-class pretensions and directs expectations toward him, hoping he will achieve some type of middle-class vocation and will avoid any identification with a drinking father, who makes a living for his family as a coal miner. Such lower-class working men are not given even perfunctory respect by their wives, but are continually measured against the role ideals taken from another class. The black American boy growing up must cope with the fact that, whether it is consciously acknowledged or not, his mother's picture of an adequate male is very often a white middle-class man. When he is being disciplined, his mother will often brutalize him not only physically but psychologically by making it apparent to him that she has no hope for him that he can possibly fulfill.[31]

The traditional Japanese emphasis on role behavior, while de-emphasizing intimacy and companionship between man and wife, can also serve as a protective buffer against the appearance of discord and disharmony in family life in situations where the expressive and emotional gratification is minimal for both spouses. Impressionistically, therefore, one of the reasons for the relative lack of discord in Japanese family life compared with that in other countries is the degree to which women derive personal satisfaction from being competent in their roles rather than from having a mate who meets their personal needs.

Some of the negative consequences of Japanese emphasis on role are discussed further in Chapter 17 on "Role Narcissism and the Etiology of Japanese Suicide." The subjective experiences of affiliative loss and alienation are centrally involved in some forms of Japanese suicide.

Nurturance and Appreciation in the Socialization of Dependency

To understand the emotional patterning underlying Japanese role behavior, it is essential to examine peculiarities of socialization that lead modern Japanese, like those in preceding generations, to emphasize emotional interdependency, whether in the family or in other organizations. Caudill, in comparing maternal care and infant behavior with that in the United States, finds that, in the socialization of children, intensive and continual body contact between the mother and her young children facilitates certain attitudes.[32] The Japanese are much more conscious than Westerners are of the satisfaction to be found in skin contact and oral sensuality. This consciousness of the pleasures of the body is further encouraged by customs of bathing and

---

[31] Kardiner and Ovesey, *The Mark of Oppression* (1962); Grier and Cobbs, *Black Rage* (1968).

[32] Caudill and Weinstein, "Maternal Care and Infant Behavior in Japanese and American Urban Middle-Class Families" (1966).

massaging, by the attention to textural details of food, and by art and language.

Hovering nurturance, which persists in a child's life to a far later age in Japanese than in American culture, tends to impede aggressive independence. The child is disciplined by threats of isolation rather than by the inhibition of free movement.[33] He learns to rely upon ready access to gratifications afforded by his mother. He is not encouraged to physically separate himself from the mother or to seek independent means of coping with his environment as he is in Western socialization. He is encouraged to be *sunao*, or obedient. In this context of dependency the Japanese also develop a capacity, by passive means, to induce nurturant behavior toward themselves by others. The inductive manipulation of others to secure care of oneself is expressed in the Japanese word *amae*.[34]

Sunao behavior receives positive evaluative reinforcement. The nearest English equivalent translation, "upright," [35] does not convey what is meant by the word. *Sunao* connotes compliance and obedience to the wishes of others.

For example, *sunao ni kiku* means to listen without objection or to follow directions. The opposite of *sunao* is *hinekureta* ("twisted or warped"). When a person's need for nurturance dependency is not satisfied and he feels an acute frustration, he resorts to sulking in a characteristic way described by the verb *suneru*, which means to pretend indifference to dependent needs or, even worse from the Japanese standpoint, to display envy of others apparently favored over oneself. This latter attitude is expressed in the Japanese verb *higamu* (to be "soured"). When *higamu* becomes a chronic attitude, seen as an integral part of a child's or an adult's personality, the individual is described as a *hinekureta* person—distrustful, embittered, and cynical.

These words indicate that the Japanese mothers are conscious that, in order to maintain compliance and obedience, they must satisfy the feelings of dependency developed within an intense mother-child relationship. Goodwill must be maintained so that the child will willingly undertake the increasingly heavy requirements and obligations placed upon him in the school and the home. There is a direct cul-

---

[33] Takeo Doi has told me that when a child is put in a separate room in Japan he feels he is being isolated from contact with others. An American child in similar circumstances would probably feel that his liberty had been curtailed.

[34] The Japanese language is extremely rich in terms for tactile sensations and other descriptions of texture. Many of the terms used in Japanese depict relative degrees of smoothness, softness, etc., and have no directly comparable words in English. See Doi, "'Amae': A Key Concept for Understanding Japanese Personality Structure" (1962).

[35] Derivatively the word comes from *nao*—"straight," as in the verb *naosu*, to straighten, correct, or cure. The *su* is an emphatic prefix.

tural linkage between contentment and compliance. A *sunao* person maintains basic trust in authority and finds it easy and natural to follow the directives of others with the implicit assumption that he will be taken care of should special needs arise. Only those who are warped in character would suspect, object to, or protest against any legitimate authority. It is this implicit "psychological" equation stretched through time that makes it possible to endure the periods of rigorous training or apprenticeship discussed above. The equation is implicit in *oyabun-kobun* paternalistic relationships within the Japanese economy.[36] It is this equation that underlies vocational role relationships and makes it difficult for the Marxist-oriented labor unions in Japan to develop the cleavages in loyalty necessary to separate workers from management. Unions have been relatively unsuccessful in redirecting patterns of loyalty from those expressed toward the boss to those expressed in terms of class identity. The owners of even progressive factories have realized the necessity to maintain worker goodwill by continual emphasis upon what are termed "fringe" benefits in the United States. For the Japanese worker these are not fringe benefits, but essentials expected from one's boss in an occupational setting.

This "psycho-logical" equation can be applied to the special affectional preference given the eldest son in the traditional culture. Since he is to receive the heaviest burden of responsibility, it is only natural that he be given the most intense care and nurturance so that he will be *sunao*.

On a deeper psychodynamic level, being *sunao* sometimes means continuing as an extension of the mother's own ego. Many women have strong achievement needs or desire to express potentials for dominance and other instrumental potentials within their personality; by binding the son permanently to herself through the maintenance of nurturant control the mother in effect uses the son as a masculine extension of her own ego. This helps explain why many mothers become so fiercely competitive with the daughter-in-law, who may seek to intrude and break up the hold the mother maintains over the son.

Such emotional undercurrents may be too much for some individuals to bear, and various forms of psychological neurotic debilitation or even psychosis can result. The burdens imposed by the traditional cultures are still evident in the revelation of William Caudill's research that there is significant overrepresentation of eldest sons in Japanese mental institutions.[37] What is apparent in past patterns of socialization, and what seems to be continuing today in intense mother-

---

[36] Bennett and Ishino, *Paternalism in the Japanese Economy* (1963).

[37] Caudill, "Sibling Rank and Style of Life Among Japanese Psychiatric Patients" (1963).

child relationships, is the exercise of seemingly unconscious mechanisms of control by women through the manipulation of the dependent needs of a child.

Sensitivity to appreciation and vulnerability to feeling depreciated, slighted, degraded, or ignored is strongly developed in Japanese socialization, especially in males. Japanese social control relies heavily on sensitivity to shaming. Japanese children are sanctioned to sense they are being observed by outsiders. Few Japanese achieve a sense of self, that is, independent of the attitudes of others. There is a vulnerability to depreciatory attitudes which makes some Japanese dependent on nurtural reinforcement of signals of social approbation. They are socialized to provide such signs of approbation to one another. Women or subordinates in our occupational hierarchy learn to provide the expected compliments to their social or occupational status superiors. Japanese readily respect such signs of pleasure to be accorded minor accomplishments. For example, Japanese sometimes suck in their breath to indicate the "importance" of what someone is saying. Foreigners are particularly captivated when they become subject to the minor social flatteries that make them feel "appreciated" in a way seldom experienced in their own culture.

Japanese who have achieved social status readily feel ignored and unappreciated when alone in a strange environment. They are highly dependent in this sense on their own social atmosphere, which shields them from crudely objective industrial evaluations that lack some expressive coating of appreciation. While Japanese learn as part of status sensitivity both to expect and to give appreciation to others, they are not taught how to remain independent or invulnerable to what they perceive in the attitudes of a continually evaluative social world.

The converse of the manipulation of nurturance or appreciation in dyadic relationships is the manipulation, again either consciously or unconsciously, of a potential giver by one who is dependent. This type of manipulation is explicitly recognized by the culture in the well-used words *amae* (noun) or *amaeru* (verb) whereas in Western European languages one finds no direct counterpart for the idea. *Amaeru*, as Doi[38] points out, is an active verb in Japanese, designating a passive induction of nurturance toward one's self from others. Such passive induction cannot be directly expressed in an active intransitive verb in Western languages. To *amaeru* is to produce passively the state of being loved and indulged or appreciated by another, a form of emotional judo.

Doi relates *amaeru* to a peculiar lack of individuation frequently found in Japanese. He points out that the attitude of *amae* is related

---

[38] Doi, " 'Amae': A Key Concept for Understanding Japanese Personality Structure" (1962).

to a lack of realization, or even the desire for realization, of an autonomous ego on the part of many Japanese. This is consonant with the emphasis on interdependency noted in Japanese role relationships.

The passivity and dependency of *amae* can be much more ego-syntonic or acceptable as part of the self for a Japanese than for a Westerner and is without the sense of shame or personal discomfort that a Westerner would feel if, as an adult, he gave himself over to a passive, dependent, yet manipulative role in his social relationships. Such a posture, if conscious, goes counter to the Western ideal of personal autonomy.

For the Japanese male who maintains a lifelong dependent attachment to his mother, there is no feeling of internal conflict, no matter how disappointed his wife may be when he fails to assert himself in the frequent conflicts between mother and wife. Characteristically, the disappointed wife learns, in turn, to manipulate her husband's passive dependence to her own purposes. She also affectively turns to her own children, ensuring the continuation of the pattern into the next generation.

Although Japanese women may be more psychodynamically independent than men in some respects, many of them, through their manipulations, are eliciting *amae* from a grown son. The role requirements for Japanese women wean them from whatever expectations they may have had of remaining dependent on their own mothers. Sometimes dependent expectations are transferred to the exacting mother-in-law by a young bride, with resultant tensions and unhappiness. In the past, in some sections of Japan, some young brides suffered from "fox possession." Clinically viewed, this behavior was essentially an hysterical psychological disturbance, which, while indicative of expressed needs, would also have the unconscious instrumental purpose of bringing forth on one's self the nurturant attendance of others.

The disproportionate numbers of youngest daughters in Japanese mental hospitals, reported by Caudill,[39] gives evidence that the peculiarities of this role position, which are related to the practice of *amaeru,* can cause serious internal disturbances in psychological integration.

Alcoholism in Japan (which, according to our impression, is prevalent in Arakawa Ward)[40] receives less attention from the public and the psychiatric profession than the same problem does in the United States. Perhaps one reason for this lack of concern is that tensions over dependency, which often underlie alcoholic problems, are considered more "natural" by Japanese than unresolved dependency problems are by Westerners. Only when alcoholism is combined with some form

---

[39] Caudill, "Sibling Rank and Style of Life Among Japanese Psychiatric Patients" (1963).

[40] DeVos and Wagatsuma, *Heritage of Endurance* (to be published).

of violent expression does it receive much attention. Individuals who drink over a quart of cheap sake every day are rarely considered "sick" in any way. We have found such drinking habits fairly common in lower-class Japanese. In our sample of fifty families the descriptions of a considerable number of fathers and of paternal or maternal grand-fathers gave us the impression that they would be classified as alcoholic were they to be diagnosed in an American clinical setting.

This lack of concern is related to the lack of negative sanctions applied to any form of oral indulgence not leading to the complete disruption of one's required role activities. It is not considered outside the boundaries of the acceptable male social role to become drunk so long as there is no interference with one's work pattern. In fact, drunkenness is frequently an excuse for mistakes or unseemly behavior. In many Japanese professional and business organizations a *bonenkai* ("a forget-the-old-year party") is held at the end of the year. A *bonenkai* is an occasion when, under the influence of alcohol, individuals can breach the formal boundaries of communication between hierarchical levels and inform superiors of problems that it would be unseemly or unacceptable to discuss when sober. Much information that a man imparts while drunk is supposed to be forgotten by the recipient, so that the informer is in no way punished.[41]

Evidence from our lower-class sample confirms the rather frequent appearance of stomach complaints among Japanese. Some of these complaints, affecting overwhelmingly more men than women, are apparently of a psychosomatic nature. Cases of so-called hyperacidity strongly suggest underlying problems concerning dependency very often related to tensions in a job situation. In our sample, the complaints seem to disappear when the person quits his job or finds some other form of employment. Some individuals are so severely affected that they remain home "ill" and their wives must seek employment in their place.

The widespread use of insurance policies has contributed heavily in recent times to the deemphasizing of the dependent role of the aged. The attitude that financial provision can be made in advance for one's parents has tended to further the development of nuclear family thinking in many younger Japanese. Nevertheless, the tendency to avoid responsibility for the care of the aged is much less than that in the United States, where beds in mental hospitals are filled with aging parents who can no longer take care of themselves owing to some form of mental deterioration. Although there is some increase in the number

---

[41] Recently in the Diet there occurred unseemly conduct on the part of one mischievous congressman, who kissed a very stout congresswoman in the presence of many others. Although his behavior was considered quite reprehensible, he was partly forgiven on the grounds that he was drunk and so did not know better.

of old people's homes, this form of care for the aged is not yet in any way characteristic of the Japanese social scene. The aged generally can still depend on their middle-aged children for care and assistance.

In spite of this cultural emphasis on nurturance, it is quite apparent that in Japan as well as elsewhere there are deprived children who become delinquents during adolescence.

Affiliation in Changing Japan: From Role Commitment to Companionship in Modern Japan—An Incomplete Transition

As was indicated, affiliative needs such as intimacy and companionship were not institutionalized as desiderata of an ideal Japanese marriage. Marriage in traditional Japan was a family connection, not an attempt to fulfill individual needs. A woman became a wife by becoming a member of her husband's family. The objective of the marriage was to produce children to continue the *ie*. The role emphases were parental and familial not conjugal.

Sex as an expression of mutual affection was not only deemphasized, but sometimes even suppressed; undue emphasis on affective sexual needs was considered a form of selfish assertion of individuality that could disrupt the harmonious functioning of the total household. The important role for a woman was to serve her children, husband, and parents-in-law. Sexual reciprocity and feelings of companionship between spouses might appear but were not to be expected. To make a rather exaggerated comparison, one might almost equate the Japanese housewife in the traditional family to an efficient secretary in an American business organization, where undue emphasis on the sexual aspects of the secretary as an attractive young woman could disrupt the smooth functioning of role relationships within the office. The wife was also expected to continually "appreciate" her husband and avoid giving signs of depreciation or devaluation. Japanese men continually expect such ego support.

For the man, sexuality was regarded as a secondary source of pleasure to be satisfied periodically away from home in the special world of entertainment where again women were explicitly trained not only to please the sexual needs of men but also to enhance men's vulnerable sense of self by appreciative behavior. Sex and bodily feelings were never considered "bad" as defined by Shinto or Confucian ethics. Acceptable sex was, rather, a matter of time and circumstance. A man could easily indulge in outside sexual activities without feelings of guilt, as long as he did nothing to disturb the good order and functioning of the *ie*. It was even considered permissible to maintain a mistress on a long-term basis if this did not decrease the financial support of the family. However, should the outside affair become a serious financial drain, everything would be done to apply sanctions to the offending individual. Such flagrant maintenance of a mistress is not tolerated by modern wives; mistresses have gone underground, as has prostitution.

Because of their strong emotional attachment to their own mothers and their basic dependence on women for both nurturance and appreciation, many Japanese men in the traditional culture, as well as today, suffer in varying degrees from fears of sexual inadequacy or anxiety about their physical prowess as males. Since the man's role vis-à-vis the woman's role in the traditional Japanese culture was clearly defined and prescribed, underlying anxiety about one's sexual prowess could be covered up. As long as a man played the role of a man and husband, supported by his wife playing her role, he was to some degree protected from facing possible internal sexual problems. Today, however, when the marriage of companionship has become a recognized ideal and women's magazines emphasize women's right to sexual expressiveness and satisfaction, a new type of confrontation often occurs. More explicit resolutions become necessary.

The amazing number of bars and places of amusement having bar girls and hostesses in today's Japan indicate that female companionship outside the home remains highly desirable for many men. But, even in the world of bar hostesses, one must note that the sexuality of the man is often pregenital, not necessarily leading to completion of the sexual act. The role of the bar girl often takes the form of a type of ego boosting, making the man feel important and appreciated while supplying him minor oral gratifications. Aggressive phallic male behavior is a positive ideal realized by relatively few Japanese men although found frequently in fantasy. Vicarious gratification in this direction is partially supplied by pornographic publications and movies that frequently dwell on rape or the flagellation of bound women. Violence is satisfied voyeuristically. The Turkish bath has become a site for present-day prostitution, and very often the sexual behavior consummated there is a form of passive masturbation, rather than active genital congress in which aggressive as well as sexual needs are satisfied.

One of the major changes within Japanese culture is in the role of the prostitute. In the past, the attitude toward the prostitute was romanticized. She was often viewed as a basically innocent person who, through the impoverishment of her family, was sold into a house of prostitution, where she dutifully submitted to her role on behalf of her family. The modern prostitute or "pan pan" girl is a more active, aggressive, and "tough" type of person, whose activities are controlled by gangsters. In the past, houses of prostitution were run by traditional families, who passed on their business from one generation to the next. The owners of houses of prostitution lived within the brothel with their entire family, and often the wife assisted in its management.

SLEEPING PATTERNS AND SEXUAL INTIMACY. Japanese sleeping patterns tend to limit the opportunity for sexuality between parents. There is a persistence of patterns in which children sleep in the same room as their parents.[42] In the usual progression in family sleeping patterns, the youngest child continues to sleep next to the mother, the second youngest by the father, and older children sometimes by a grandmother or other adult. A Japanese house offers little privacy, so that the parents must use opportunities when children are absent or asleep for sexual congress. A frequent sexual position, therefore, is that in which the husband approaches his wife from the rear while the couple are lying on their sides. A minimum amount of noise is created in this position. The amount of sexual play allowed for under these circumstances is minimal.

The material from our lower-class working samples substantiates the conclusions drawn by Plath and Caudill that even where separate space is available, child and adult members of the family tend to sleep together, thus preventing sexual privacy. In our sample there were some cases where mothers slept with the children while the father slept alone. Young children, especially, are never put to sleep by themselves in a room. There is no provision for protective confinement, such as a crib. Therefore, it seems necessary for a mother or some other person always to sleep by an infant or small child.

POSTWAR CHANGES IN PREMARITAL SEXUAL COMMUNICATION. During the past five or six years, there has been a notable increase in the practice of "dating." Before World War II, the sexes were segregated beyond the primary schools, but with reforms all public schools became co-educational. Until quite recently, however, one could observe patterns of informal segregation. High school boys and girls could not be unduly familiar with one another in any form, and dating by couples in the American sense was considered extremely improper. Informal sanctions were maintained by the students themselves. But in the last five years, in the very large cities at least, one can observe much more companionship between youths of opposite sexes. Not only is dating taking place, but couples may also be observed walking hand in hand; generally speaking, much more direct physical contact occurs among youth in public than formerly.

The amount of change in this area is documented by Shinozaki, who

---

[42] Caudill and Plath, "Who Sleeps by Whom? Parent-Child Involvement in Urban Japanese Families" (1969).

has compared recent and earlier behavior, in a study of colleges, and who reports that most students in his sample, taken more than ten years ago, had never dated.[43] If dating occurred, it usually started after graduation from college. Asayama, comparing Americans and Japanese and referring explicitly to the material in the Kinsey report, found that only 10 percent of eighteen-year-olds in his Japanese sample reported any experiences of kissing, compared with more than 90 percent of American youth.[44] If a similar survey were taken today, the dissimilarities between Japanese and American students would be notably less striking.

Nevertheless, arranged marriages persist throughout Japan even today, as was discussed above. Marriage for modern Japanese still involves responsibility and obligation to parents, but even more important on a psychodynamic level is the general unwillingness of many Japanese to assume individual responsibility for decision-making either in marriage or, often, in choosing a career. Many Japanese remain emotionally dependent. Making one's own marriage decision is a frightening prospect; it implies the necessity to affirm symbolically one's independence from parents and relatives, an independence that means one can no longer turn to them for assistance or succor in times of need. Although most Japanese consider personal autonomy to be highly desirable, it is too frightening a responsibility to assume in making the major decisions of life related to vocation and marriage. Vogel cites a number of forms of marriage arrangement still current in contemporary Japan.[45]

Today, therefore, dating must be considered a form of "playing around" prior to firm commitment to the serious business of life. Similarly, on an intellectual level, youths will espouse political and social causes that they immediately renounce once they commit themselves to some particular business or professional organization. In our interviews with lower-class subjects we noted that there may be some informal sexual liaisons before marriage, but if a child is born, there is usually serious job commitment and the assumption of family responsibility. Such drifting into marriage is not frequent, even in the Japanese lower class. More characteristic is the pattern in which either a boss or a relative decides for a young man that it is time for him to settle down and helps him find a suitable mate.

Even when the young couple decide to marry on their own initiative, in order to maintain interdependent ties with their parents and relatives some form of arrangement will usually be established by an ac-

---

[43] Shinozaki, *Nihonjin no Sei Seikatsu* (1953).

[44] Asayama, *Sex in the Twentieth Century* (1958, in Japanese).

[45] Vogel, *Japan's New Middle Class* (1963).

commodating go-between to give the marriage the proper aura of respectability. An example of the continuity of marriage tradition under new guise is a recent occurrence in an upper-middle-class family known to one of the authors. The son of an American-educated university professor, before leaving for the United States for his graduate work, brought his intended wife home and introduced her to his mother, his purpose being to have her "trained properly" by his mother for the role of a competent Japanese bride. The "responsible" behavior on the part of their son pleased the parents very much. However, psychodynamically what was involved was the son's continuing sense of dependency on his mother; he was actually seeking some assurance that he could maintain the maternal tie unbroken.

PROBLEMS OF COMPANIONSHIP IN "BED TOWN." One of the chief complaints voiced by modern apartment-house dwellers is the lack of time for companionship between married couples because so many men commute to offices which are sometimes up to an hour and a half distant from home. In fact, however, many husbands do not hurry home in the evening, but stop at bars for an hour or two, or even longer, arriving home just in time to go to bed. Hence the nickname "Bed Town" for some of the apartment areas. Men also earn the nickname *Gozensama* ("Mr. Early Morning") by returning home after midnight most of the week. The prevalence of this practice means that, whatever their ideals of companionship and home life, in many middle-class families the actual time spent together by husband and wife is limited to Sundays, which by new norms are supposedly devoted to wife and children. However, there are cartoons—such as one depicting an exhausted husband trailing behind a more energetic wife and children visiting a zoo or some other place of recreation on a weekend—which give the impression that the husband would truly like to lie down and sleep through the weekend break. Apartment-house wives interviewed in 1959 by Masuda gave as the three most important traits for an ideal husband, good health, a stable high income, and an understanding, appreciative attitude toward wife and children.[46] They did not select other possible choices, such as that the husband return home early at a regular time. Implicit in this survey and others like it is that women's expectations of their husbands' role do not include, even today, much sustained companionship or affiliative interest in the wife, beyond showing periodic consideration. The chief concern of the wife is that the husband maintain his health and not strain himself unduly, so that their income will be assured. In a number of these new "Bed Town" communities women have taken on most of

---

[46] Masuda, *Exploration of Life in Concrete Apartment Houses* (1960, in Japanese).

the concern with the community functions through women's organization; people often joke about the PTA as actually being an MTA
(Mama-Teacher Association).

Robert Blood reports a study done among middle-class apartment
dwellers in Tokyo approximately ten years ago.[47] His sample was
drawn from among the so-called salary men (that is, men employed by
large corporations), the majority of whom were college graduates. By
and large, the apartment-house dwellers tended to be younger couples
with preadolescent children,[48] and a fairly large proportion of the
women did some sort of part-time work. In Blood's sample of fairly
progressive people, he compared the affectional ties of those who had
made a self-initiated love marriage and those who were married
through the more traditional forms of arrangement. The differences
are not so great as some might expect. Nevertheless, certain slight
trends reach significance on some variables. Comparing marital satisfaction, the affectional attitudes within love marriages are significantly
better than those in arranged marriages. But, interestingly enough,
women in arranged marriages tend to be slightly more appreciative
of role adequacy, being satisfied with the husband's vocational ability,
decision-making capacity, and actual helpfulness in the home. Blood
also compared his Tokyo sample with a sample of household residents
in the Detroit area. There was striking similarity in the answers to a
number of questions asked of couples in Detroit and Tokyo, although
there was a different ranking of what produces marital satisfaction.
Whereas love and affection are cited by both samples as the highest
source of satisfaction, the Tokyo sample ranks role appreciation
of "wife as mother" or "husband as father" as a close second in
the hierarchy of factors leading to satisfaction. Sex ranks sixth for
husbands and wives, and companionship ranks tenth for husbands
and ninth for wives in Tokyo. Companionship, in contrast, ranks
second to love and affection as the principal source of marital satisfaction for the Detroit sample.

In the Tokyo sample, frequency of sexual intercourse has a direct
correlation with marital satisfaction; in only 27 percent of those having intercourse less than once a week did both partners see themselves as basically satisfied with their marriage. It should be noted
that the emphasis on sexuality and the frequency of sexual intercourse
is greater in couples making a love marriage than in those whose
marriage was arranged.

Adultery on the part of wives is quite rare in Japan. It is part of

---

[47] Blood, *Love Marriage and Arranged Marriage* (1967).

[48] Christie Kiefer had similar findings about the composition of apartment dwellers
in the city of Kobe in his doctoral dissertation, "Social Change and Personality in a
White Collar Danchi" (1968).

the Japanese conception of the woman's role to remain faithful to her husband, ideally even after his death. Although faithfulness is also part of a Western's woman's role expectations, the Japanese woman adheres to her role requirements much more strongly than does her Western counterpart. To commit adultery is to give up and to consider oneself a failure as a wife or mother. When adultery occurs in Japan, the wife's motive is most frequently retaliation. Even in the past, when it was the wife's role to submit to a double standard of marital fidelity, many women deeply resented their husbands' mistresses. Although, among successful businessmen of the more conservative type, it is still considered a mark of status and male prowess to be able to maintain a mistress, there is a besetting fear of the potential wrath of the wife. The attitude is something like that of a small boy stealing cookies from his mother's kitchen. In episodes in comic strips or movies of male adultery, much humor is extracted from the man's fear of discovery by his wife. The wife is most often depicted as a fearsome person, more like a mother catching a boy at some indecent activity. The male is seldom depicted as a browbeating tyrant as he is in the Western stereotype of a Japanese husband.

One of the favorite Japanese comic strips is "Kappa Tengoku" (*kappa*—heaven) in which the latent dominance that men fear in women within their own society is satirized in the mythological world of Japanese water sprites (*kappa*). The male *kappa* has a difficult time contending with his formidable spouse.

One of the benefits of belonging to a new religious sect, such as Rissho Koseikai or Seicho-No-Ie, is the individual counseling received by middle-aged wives, who are helped to resign themselves to the fact that, after all, husbands are really grown-up boys who sometimes consort with women much as children become intrigued by new toys. Women are taught not to take this flighty behavior of their husbands too seriously, but to rely on the fact that the maternal behavior binds the man to his wife by dependent ties. The women are reassured in these sessions, in which they can share in an institutionalized way in understanding that the maternal nurturant role of marriage puts the wife in the controlling position within her own household. This emphasis on the maternal aspect of the traditional woman's role rather than on the sexual role reconciles many middle-aged women to the necessity of deemphasizing their own sexual needs or to their incapacity to experience the pleasures of the female orgasm. Increasingly, however, the younger women are taught through the women's magazines to seek some sense of personal adequacy in "a capacity for orgasm." More recently the tone of some of these articles has taken on a more extrapunitive note, and husbands are blamed for their lack of finesse and "stamina" (now a Japanese word) in helping women

achieve sexual satisfaction. Japanese academicians writing about marriage roles tend to ignore the apparently considerable impact of these
women's magazines on the expectations of the younger generation of
Japanese couples.

With the postwar legal emancipation of women from their previous
inferior position, there has been overt recognition of their potential
for self-assertion and dominance, always latent in the woman's role in
the past. A favorite expression among Japanese men on the subject
of modern women is: "In postwar Japan, both the soles of stockings
and the character of women have taken on an increased toughness"
(*kutsushita no soko to onna ga tsuyoku natta*).[49] One can state that
the younger Japanese today is no longer content in marriage with the
necessity to give up expressive needs for communication and to lapse
into a type of proximate living in which one's thoughts remain private
and uncommunicated within the family unit. They are seeking,
whether they find it or not, some form of companionship in marriage
as the ideal for themselves. Characterologically, however, there is an
impaired capacity in many Japanese to realize this ideal owing to the
continuity of emphasis on dependency and its manipulation as basic
in interpersonal situations.

In writing of the role behavior of Japanese women toward the end
of the last century, Lafcadio Hearn declared that "the most wonderful 'aesthetic' products of Japan are not its ivories . . . nor any of
its marvels in metal or lacquer—but its women," and that "the Japanese woman is an ethically different being from the Japanese man." [50]
While living examples of these role polarities can still be found, they
by no means represent the reality of Japanese social sex roles as they
are played in the present day, or as they were played in the past.
Japanese marital relationships and patterns of family life in the past,
as in the present, allowed for considerable mutual satisfaction in some
spheres of expressive behavior, in fact considerably more satisfaction
than appeared to Western eyes. Basic traits of character never divided
as clearly along sex lines as the more rigid and ritualistic quality of
the formalities of premodern Japan would suggest. Although the
range of permitted role behavior has vastly broadened in the present
day, men and women in actualizing their behavior still to a great degree show continuities with the past in motivational structure. The
degree to which one is gratified or not gratified in interpersonal relationships within the family still relates to underlying implicit role

---

[49] There is a play on words here in which the word *tsuyoi* implies both durability
and strength when applied to material things, and power when applied to individuals.

[50] Hearn, *Japan: An Attempt at Interpretation* (1904).

expectations that do not differ much from those of the past in spite of the freer manners of today.

Nor are instrumental patterns related to achievement, competence, responsibility, control, competition, or cooperation greatly dissimilar to those found in the past culture. Changes are occurring in modern Japanese, especially in those under thirty, but it is not yet possible to determine whether the ultimate direction taken by Japanese culture in defining role relationships will be completely congruent with that of Western modernization. To some degree, at least, patterns of instrumental behavior, as well as patterns of self-expression, harmony and discord, affiliation, appreciation and nurturance, will be maintained in terms of the interpersonal needs of individuals whose personality characteristics have been conditioned or socialized by Japanese culture.

Chapter II

Social Values and Personal Attitudes
in Primary Human Relations in Rural Japan

INTRODUCTION

This chapter[1] and the three following discuss results obtained from psychological tests given in 1954 to inhabitants of Niiike Village in Okayama Prefecture, Japan. No special attempt is made here to sketch the material culture and social background of the people whose social values and personal attitudes we are considering. For a detailed study of this community the reader is referred to *Village Japan*.[2]

Niiike is a *buraku* (hamlet) located on the lower slopes of a hill, an ancient burial mound, some twenty miles west of Okayama City in Okayama Prefecture. It is situated about 400 meters north of the highway running between the cities of Okayama and Kurashiki, separated from other buraku by fields, but not isolated. In 1954 there were twenty-four households in Niiike and one hundred thirty people, of whom forty-nine were farmers, twelve were office workers, and sixty-nine were women and children. Life depends primarily upon the paddy fields, most of which yield a winter crop of barley and wheat in addition to the summer rice. Niiike also has some upland dry fields for vegetable and fruit production. The villagers also grow a kind of rush (*i-gusa*) as a subsidiary money crop, and each family weaves these grasses into *tatami-omote* between the periods of heaviest labor demands. The people of Niiike are relatively well off as farmers go in

---

[1] This chapter is modified from that originally published as "Social Values and Personal Attitudes in Primary Human Relationships in Niiike," in *Occasional Papers* of the University of Michigan Center for Japanese Studies (1965). Additional material added to the present chapter appeared as part of Wagatsuma and DeVos, "Attitudes Toward Arranged Marriage in Rural Japan," in *Human Organization* (1962).

[2] Beardsley, Hall, and Ward, *Village Japan* (1959).

61

Japan, especially if compared with those in the northeastern section of the country.

In this chapter we examine social values related to specific social role relationships as they are subjectively experienced in Niiike. We present results of those tests properly called "projective," tests which elicit spontaneous, unselfconscious responses; such tests are in contrast to opinion questionnaires or attitude schedules which require from the subject direct expressions of agreement or disagreement with specific statements.

I shall describe briefly the derivation of social values from a traditional premodern social code at a time when undercurrents of change in the village had not yet reached overt expression. Any empirical approach challenges notions that values are static or that they are arranged in a completely harmonious system. Various values, even though fairly general throughout a group, may be basically incompatible. Such disharmony underlies potential conflict, not only among individuals but within the psychic structures of individuals. At any point in time, moreover, values are in flux and are held on varying levels of consciousness in varying degrees of intensity. Values are not necessarily held in common by all the individuals in a group. In times of rapid change special inconsistencies appear. Today Japan is experiencing radical shifts in behavior and attitudes; these are not only pronounced in urban life but are also evident in more tradition-bound rural areas. Niiike is one example of what was to be found in rural Japan in 1954.

In their general overt behavior, the people of Niiike adhere rather firmly to the social values of the traditional Japanese family system. This system views the family as the legal unit of responsibility and loyalty. During the Tokugawa era (1608–1868) hierarchical loyalty was stressed; family members owed their loyalty to the head of the household. Social mobility and change of occupational status were considered disruptive influences. Growth, by developing new lands or raising the agricultural yield in other ways, was encouraged, as long as it did not disrupt the framework of traditional loyalties. The Tokugawa concept of family life for the farmer stressed the virtue of hard work, and so functioned positively to maintain both social and personal stability in agricultural communities. The code had functional utility to Japanese farming methods and to psychological stability, as such a code must have to survive without severe legal enforcement.

Industrialization on the Western model has contributed to higher regard for individual initiative and responsibility in Japan. Recent revisions in Japanese social legislation have emphasized these individual values over collective ones. Social values, however, run deeper than legal codes and their revisions. Modes of living and attitudes about human relationships are influenced by deeply set emotional patterns learned from early childhood and they often persist in the face of conscious efforts to bring about change through formal institutions. Therefore, even though the present government operates on a basic philosophy drastically changed from that of Tokugawa times, many farm families still find economic utility as well as moral virtue in the old ideas and tend to maintain them even without legal support.

Japanese farmers in general have been less overwhelmingly exposed to economic and social change than have the urban segments of the population. The evidence gathered in 1954 pointed to a tendency to cling with some tenacity to traditional attitudes toward lineage and household, parent-child relationships, marital-family relationships, and to the traditional measures of success and achievement in adult occupational roles. Values in these areas of life are unlikely to change much unless the overall way of life described in *Village Japan* also changes radically, as indeed it has in the last few years with the introduction of factories in rural areas.

RESEARCH IN NIIIKE: METHOD OF APPROACH

To understand the motives behind expressed values on the instrumental and expressive concerns discussed in Chapter 1, one must deal with the universal emotions of love, fear, and hate, and their most complex derivatives, as they are shaped by family and other social relationships. A culture, from one psychological viewpoint, is a mode of expressing, in all their complexity, these primary emotions, which are aroused by inner biological urges or occur as reactions to specific outer stimuli. The agency through which these feelings are integrated and expressed is the individual's personality structure. Much that might be said about the feelings of the people of Niiike toward family relationships or about their ideals of life adjustment would be true of people anywhere. For the sake of brevity this discussion is limited to peculiarities in the integration of attitudes and emotions that may be considered "rural Japanese"; we do not deal with features that are more broadly human.

The degree of unanimity and the firmness of various social values held by Niiike residents in 1954 were investigated through a large-scale survey employing psychological tests and opinion scales. These methods were applied in 1954 to most of Niiike's adults as well as to some of the children over twelve years of age. The tests and interviews of 80 of the 124 persons over twelve at Niiike were conducted as a joint enterprise by the members of the Human Relations Interdisciplinary Research Group at Nagoya University: T. Muramatsu, director, with my cooperation as a Fulbright research scholar. The Center for Japanese Studies of the University of Michigan helped sponsor the project with participation by faculty and students of Okayama University.[3] Analysis of the projective story material was conducted at the University of Michigan by Hiroshi Wagatsuma and myself aided by a grant from the Behavioral Science Division of the Ford Foundation.

To compare Niiike with other rural communities and urban communities, similar surveys were conducted in two other villages. The following scales and tests were used: (1) intensive interviews; (2) opinion scales: (a) the "F scale" used in *The Authoritarian Personality* (Adorno, et al. 1950), (b) excerpts from the "Tough, Tender, Liberal, Conservative Scale" used by Eysenck, (c) a direct opinion scale on the family system, and (d) an indirect "liberal-conservative scale of Japanese psychological attitudes"; (3) the Rorschach Test; (4) the Thematic Apperception Test used by Murray (with drawings revised to provide Japanese features of face, dress, and background details); (5) Spontaneous Figure Drawings; (6) the Problem Situation Test (adapted from Sargent's "Insight Test" method).[4]

By getting people to tell stories or to imagine what one would do when confronted with a particular situation, it is possible to elicit a spontaneous expression of social attitudes as well as of personality variables. In psychological terms, subjective experience of values occurs at various levels of consciousness. For purposes of simplicity we consider three such levels: (1) values self-consciously expressed; (2) values indirectly expressed in the context of real or hypothetical behavior; (3) values expressed unconsciously in real or hypothetical behavior and interpreted by the analyst's inference from the data.

In the analysis of the stories and other materials obtained from inhabitants of Niiike, there is a sufficiently detailed exposition to make clear the mode of approach. (See Appendix A for detailed description of methods.) Interpretation is based not only on manifest content, that is, the type and manner of behavior depicted in story material produced or what is manifestly expressed as the feelings of a particular individual in a particular situation; it is based also on other less overt or conscious aspects of the material elicited. The emotional tone of a story may be as significant as the description of the behavior of a par-

---

[3] A report of many of these results by Muramatsu and associates has been published in Japanese under the English title *The Japanese: An Empirical Study in Culture and Personality* (1962).

[4] See Appendix A for a technical description of the tests used as the basis of the conclusions of this chapter: The Problem Situation Test, TAT, and the Rorschach Test.

ticular character. To illustrate: in constructing a story to the card depicting a sleeping figure, two individuals may describe the figure as sleeping, but whereas one condemns the sleeper as "lazy," the other may see him as a person exhausted from hard work, as in the following:

(M, age 27, picture M3M)[5] This person is sleeping. He is supposed to study. But he is lazy. Or he prefers playing.
(M, age 38, picture M3M) This—girl. She is resting, is taking a nap between labors at a hospital. She is exhausted from her work.

In the course of the following exposition, the reader should become further acquainted with the way in which a psychologist uses expressive data of individuals to gain a picture of personal values held in the context of individual personality. In addition, in analyzing a group quantification of all materials one must obtain the relative incidence of a particular emotional tone revealed in a specified social context in order to come to conclusions concerning what social values and personal attitudes are most characteristic for a particular social group, such as Niiike village.

RESULTS

The Expression of Primary Emotions in Niiike:
Certain Psychological Correlates

In Niiike, even more than elsewhere generally in village Japan, few opportunities exist for the expression of feelings with any vehemence or abandon. Ceremonial activities consist mainly of quiet visits to shrines or temples. Niiike does not encourage even those forms of dancing and drinking that occur in other Japanese communities. The only dancing that is general in Japan is the joyous and rhythmic, but controlled, Bon dance; Niiike does not celebrate the Bon festival with dancing. Drinking is a minor form of release throughout Japan, but Niiike seems relatively puritanical in this respect as well, and drunkenness, except on the occasion of certain feasts, is not at all characteristic of Niiike men. Moreover, although Niiike has not been completely without incidents of criminal violence and open conflict among individuals, relationships within the village characteristically avoid any direct conflict or overt expression of hostility or aggression.

Psychological evidence concerning personality structure also shows very little pressure of any directly aggressive attitudes. Even beneath the surface, the people of Niiike do not seem to have any undue hos-

---

[5] The TAT pictures used are described in Appendix A. M3M refers to picture by number.

tility or anxiety. The Rorschach test results,[6] for example, do not reveal seething emotions, but suggest that, by American standards, the
people of Niiike as a group are quite rigid and constricted. On the
same tests they are significantly more rigid than the inhabitants of
nearby Okayama City. Such rigidity, however, is not unique to Niiike;
research with other rural groups in Japan and elsewhere indicates that
it may be widespread in rural communities. Rigidity in Niiike is expressed in a rather overcautious and inflexible approach to problems
and a constriction in free access to feelings and impulses. The people
of Niiike restrain positive as well as negative expressions to the extent
that both happy and disturbed feelings generally remain muted and
suppressed. The Niiike Rorschach records are notably free from signs
of freely expressed anxiety. It is possible that anxious feelings are
quickly resolved by adherence to the fixed rhythm of daily work activities.

In respect to measures of overall maladjustment, the Niiike group as a
whole scored higher than a normative sample of Americans in respect
to constrictive defenses and pervasive blocking of thought processes,
but they also scored significantly higher, when compared with American
neurotics and schizophrenics, in ability to maintain ego control. People
in Niiike have a strong sense of reality. They see the world as it is, without distortion.

The Rorschach results suggest the prevalence of two basic patterns
for what is termed "outer control" or control over affective reactivity
to outer stimuli: first, a cautiousness in affective responsiveness while
maintaining a capacity for some spontaneity; second, for a considerable
number, a complete constriction of spontaneity.

In regard to measures of what is termed "inner control" (the relationship of thought processes to kinesthetic experiences, awareness of
motivational pressures from within, the socialization of imagination
and fantasy, etc.) the evidence suggests that, as a group, the people
of Niiike are potentially strongly introversive in orientation. There is,
however, considerable blocking of this introversion by strong repres-
sions, together with a lack of maturation in whatever imagination or
fantasy is consciously available. One must note, however, that there
are a number of individuals in Niiike who escape this generalization
and who do show superior potentials in respect to creativity and imagination. Considering the village as a unit, it cannot be assumed,
therefore, that it completely lacks imaginative capacities. For a well-

---

[6] Detailed results with the Rorschach, as well as comparative material from two
other villages and two cities, have been published by Murakami, "Special Characteristics of Japanese Personality Based on Rorschach Test Results" in Muramatsu
(1962). Also Murakami, "A Normative Study of Japanese Rorschach Responses"
(1959).

functioning small community, it is probably sufficient that such traits find representation in a few of its leading personalities.

The thematic test material supports the conclusions drawn from the Rorschach records, showing that Niiike men are highly cautious and restrained in their descriptions of appropriate behavior. Women, however, in suggesting solutions to problem situations, often give answers with strong emotional content. This may seem to be a discrepancy within the test results, since no such difference between the sexes appears in the Rorschach test material, but it may be explained by the differences between the consciously acceptable social roles of men and women; Japanese women are characteristically denied overt action in dealing with situations of conflict, whereas men are continually oriented toward goal-directed behavior. Therefore, women tend to think about what they feel, whereas men think about what they do. Neither men nor women are necessarily given to overt labile affective displays except where they are socially sanctioned. Actual affective behavior in situations where it could be socially disruptive is notably well controlled.

Attitudes Concerning Achievement and Success

On the surface, rural Japanese society presents a picture of stability and continuity, and embedded in rural (as well as in urban) culture is a strong emphasis on values of hard work, achievement, and educational advancement which rivals the force of these values in socially and professionally mobile middle-class Americans. Even in a rural hamlet such as Niiike one hears stories, told by teenagers and by older people, of growing up to be a great man (or, as in one story given by a girl, of marrying a prime minister). It is as if some Oriental Horatio Alger were one of the patron deities of the local shrine.

As discussed more fully in Part II of this volume, the rapidity of Japan's development into the modern industrial giant of Asia was due in part to the remarkable energy of its people, who can apply diligence and hard work with equal intensity to industrial expansion and to agriculture. Part of this energy and application is related to basic social values and can be explained in psychological terms.

In many respects, achievement values in Niiike resemble those found in American culture, but there are emphases that have a distinctively Japanese tone. The Niiike villager usually molds his achievement needs within a framework that does not force him to leave his family.[7] One notes here a major difference from the stories told by many middle-class Americans, who, in their fantasies, leave their parents' homes to

---

[7] Since we have not tested or interviewed villagers who have left Niiike, we cannot compare these results with those of individuals who were motivated strongly enough to leave the village for the city or other areas.

strike out for themselves. The Japanese tested in our survey do not
desire to leave home; the strong need to remain close to the family
takes precedence over the need to achieve.[8] On a deeper psychological
level, the data suggest that the Niiike man does not want to give up
the primacy of his relationship to his mother by leaving the household.
In TAT stories, however, the Niiike people envisioned achievements
that were not limited to the field of agriculture; they were very much
aware of broader horizons. Nevertheless, stories in which achievement
took a person away from his family often ended with his subsequent
return. In stories about leaving home there were often indirect expressions of guilt over the evasion of filial responsibilities. In such
stories the departure was frequently due to domestic conflict and was
not merely a matter of the pursuit of individualistic ambitions.[9]

Despite the emphasis placed on achievement as a means of gratifying
one's immediate family, there were few stories in which a person sought
success in order to bring honor to his *ie*. It seems that a person's emotional relationship to the real members of his household—to those
who are close around him—plays a more important role in achievement and success than any abstract notion of the *ie* as an institution.
Since the TAT stimuli are focused on primary family situations, it is
to be assumed that the appearance of this characteristic is partially due
to the nature of the test; nevertheless, the results emphasize the strongly
affective ties which underly the formal social structure of values concerning the household.

Achievement stories showed certain values that are characteristically
Japanese. To elucidate these values, the 83 stories (out of a total of
807 stories elicited) that contain an achievement theme have been
categorized into four basic groups: (1) self-motivated achievement (48
stories); (2) encouraged or inspired achievement (13 stories); (3) achievement as repayment (10 stories); (4) achievement as expiation (12 stories).
These stories were elicited by nearly all the TAT cards presented, not
merely by cards such as cards J1 and J2, which most commonly evoke
such themes.

SELF-MOTIVATED ACHIEVEMENT. A major characteristic permeating the
first group of achievement stories is an emphasis on the pursuit of suc-

---

[8] Chapter 6 amplifies my criticism of ethnocentrism in American psychological
theories of achievement motivation generalized principally on the basis of American
results.

[9] In the stories told by Japanese emigrants to America, one finds a much stronger
expression of feelings of guilt than in those given by Niiike villagers, for the Issei
have actually left their families behind to emigrate. Such feelings of guilt are most
often expressed toward a mother, who often rejects her son in Issei stories. The son
in such a story sometimes asks for forgiveness from his mother.

cess at all cost. The virtues of persistence and tenacity will help to overcome all difficulties, and so, even if one is at a loss or feels inadequate, he must not give up. This value was illustrated by the following story:

(M, age 16, card JM1) I like music and I used to go to a teacher to receive violin lessons. One day he told me that I'd better give up the violin because I was not doing well. However, I swore in my mind that I would become a good player. I practiced day and night, as hard as possible, and finally my teacher had to admit I was playing well.

The fact that such stories occur with fair frequency in Niiike well illustrates that such social values are especially strong in this village. Reading of stories given to the same card in other cultural settings reinforces this impression. In my judgment, stories with themes of persistence toward success must be considered more characteristic of Japanese when compared with other cultures on which similar data has been obtained.

There were age and sex differentials among those who told stories of self-motivated achievement. Proportionately fewer such stories were told by women at all age levels, with the exception of those from eighteen to twenty-four years of age. The men of this age group tended to be more concerned with stories of family conflict and heterosexual problems than were any of the other groups considered. On other measurements, also, such as a maladjustment score on the Rorschach test, they showed signs of interpersonal disturbance. The meaning of these findings for this young age group in Niiike is difficult to ascertain, but one has the impression that there may be an undercurrent of social and intrapsychic tension in a good number of the young men of this village who are under twenty-five. For the women in the village generally there was more emphasis on a self-effacing social role; they were more apt to give themes of death and illness of a member of the family, sometimes involving stories of self-sacrifice.

ENCOURAGED OR INSPIRED ACHIEVEMENT. Many stories expressed the feeling that a father should serve as a respected and admired example for his son. The son should strive toward success with the encouragement and advice of his father:

(W, age 40, card J7M) This is a father and this is a son. The father is encouraging his son, who is very studious; the son tries very hard and becomes successful.

However, the father may not always be a great and successful man. A son may actually exceed his father's accomplishments, thus putting the son into a situation similar to that in which many American sons find themselves. In such a case, an attitude of respect or idealization is maintained by treating the father as one richly experienced in life, a man of noble character or superior wisdom.

The TAT stories sometimes displayed an idealization of the image of a dead father. Some achievement stories (mostly those told by people under thirty-five) show a son inspired by a portrait or an image of his father rather than by his father in person. The father as an idealized image inspires the child; when the father is dead, realistic limitations cannot inhibit his inspirational function:

(M, age 17, card J7M) I think that this man has not been very successful in business so far (pointing at the young man). But since his father was a great man, I think he will remember his father and will make strong efforts to be as successful as his father.

(M, age 15, card J7M) This young man's father died forty-nine days ago. Today he gazes at his father's picture and thinks about whether he should become a farmer cultivating a big field—a rice field—according to his father's will, or whether he should become an engineer as he himself would like to do. He cannot decide, and he consults his former high-school teacher. His teacher receives him pleasantly, listens to his opinions about his problem, and thinks it over seriously. His teacher finally says that he should become a farmer and try to become a leader of his country [district] just as his father was. Afterward, he talked over various other matters with his teacher, and decided that he should remain in his country and take care of his ancestral land. Since then he has worked very hard at farming and has become a popular young man in his country.

(M, age 23, card J7M) He is thinking of his dead father. This is the image of his father—this—he is recalling his father and is making up his mind to strive toward success. I don't know what his profession is; anyway, he has an ambition now.

Although this image of an encouraging and inspiring father is prevalent in Niiike, it is somewhat weaker here than in our other Japanese village samples. Niiike women, especially, tend to think of a son as more independent of his father. In certain stories, a son is described as going counter to parental advice:

(M, age 17, card J7M) A conventional and obstinate father is in conflict with his son. They live separately.

(W, age 16, card J7M) A father who is conventional and feudalistic, told his son to marry a girl. The son does not obey but walks out. He lives on his own, establishes himself and marries a girl he likes. The father will forgive him and they will live in contentment.

Such negative stories, however, were in a minority.

ACHIEVEMENT AS REPAYMENT. The third category of stories concerning achievement stresses the reciprocity of what have been termed *on* relationships: parents should willingly undergo hardships to raise and educate their children; the children, out of gratitude to their parents, should try to be successful so that they will be able to care for their parents when they are old. Thus achievement can satisfy the sense of obligation to one's parents:

(M, age 29, card J2) They are farmers, pretty well off. The parents work very hard and send their daughter to high school. The girl is studying hard and is deeply grateful to her parents. She will study hard, and even though she is a woman, she will accomplish good research work in the field of agriculture. (W, age 45, card J2) It is the country. The father and mother are farmers and this is the daughter. The father and mother think it will be good if they have a nice crop. The girl is studying very hard. She wants to improve herself and be able to take care of her parents and make their life easy.

The same virtue of repayment of *on* (*on-gaeshi*) seen from the viewpoint of the parent may become a realistic expectation that if you raise your children well and if they observe filial piety, you will be cared for by them when you are old and cannot support yourself. This rather prosaic and realistic aspect of *on* was depicted in some of the stories:

(M, age 17, card J2) They are farmers. They are doing painful work. They raise their children and send them to school by doing hard work so that in the future, when they are old, they will be taken care of by their children.

ACHIEVEMENT OF SUCCESS AS EXPIATION. Hard work and success are not undertaken only in repayment of good done by parents; they may also represent a measure of unconscious guilt for having hurt one's parents in some way by one's behavior, often by an act of self-will about marriage, or a lack of seriousness toward education:

(M, age 40, card J5) In a middle-class family their single child does not like to study. The mother gets worried and comes to see whether the child is working. The child gets addicted to philopon [a stimulant drug used widely in Japan from 1950 to 1956] and becomes an outlaw. The mother becomes very worried, gets sick and dies. The child reforms himself and becomes successful in the future.
(W, age 17, card J7M) A father scolded his son for being stupid. The son walks out. The father dies. This inspires the son to work hard and he becomes successful.

These stories have pictured vocational achievement in the man. For women in Niiike, there are relatively few stories suggesting that a woman's accomplishment lies in any direction other than conforming as closely as possible to the ideal of wife and mother. It is apparent throughout the psychological material that this role revolves around a deep sense of responsibility for the care and well-being of the hus-

band and the support of his purposes and, even more, for the development of her children into successful adults.

Attitudes Concerning Work and Leisure

ACHIEVEMENT VS. PLEASURE. Work itself is positively valued in Niiike
regardless of goals and achievement. The necessity to work hard, whatever the personal cost, is stressed in certain TAT materials. In some
stories excessive work results in ruined health:

(W, age 17, card M3M) What's this appearing on the side [talking to herself]?
[Interviewer: "Just say what you think it is."] It is hard to say—. This girl
lives on dress-making. It does not bring in enough income, but she has to
keep on living just the same. No matter how hard she works, the situation
doesn't improve. Her body gets weaker from the hard work, and she can't
stay up late at night because of fatigue. If this goes on, what will become of
her? She won't be able to recover. The reason I mentioned dress-making is
that this thing [pointing] looks like a pair of scissors.

An item in the Problem Situation Test was constructed to measure
the relative importance of health and work: "A person who is ill is
told by a doctor to rest for some time, but if he takes a rest it will
seriously interfere with his life's work." In only 60 percent of the replies
did the person follow the doctor's orders. Four women directly stated
that work is more important than health. Several who said they would
leave their jobs, as well as some who said they would continue to work,
stressed concern with possible economic distress if they were to stop
working. A young man stated, "Life is but fifty short years." Two older
men resignedly, and in indirect religious terms, left their problem in
the hands of fate or providence.

One characteristic of certain TAT stories was the separation of the
farmer's life from lives of greater leisure or ease. In this regard, farming was seen as distinct from other occupations. This is illustrated by
the fact that the girl with books in picture J2 is seen as unrelated to
the working figures in two-fifths of the stories told in Niiike. In the
following story, a defensive identification with farm life and a rejection
of the easy life were made very explicit:

(M, age 39, card J2) What idea does this picture contain? This is a problem.
They would be the same when they are small, and they look like individuals
of rather mature years, but from different circumstances. One of them works
in the field and the other is a spoiled daughter of a certain family and . . .
when they have happened to meet on the road, one of them is thinking of
her hard field work and the other is thinking that one can live easily without doing such laborious work. The one working in the field intends to live
close to the soil and by so doing to be free of insecurity. The other is thinking that here the farmers are engaged in hard work while her own life is

enjoyable. In the future, the person at work will lead a happy life, but this spoiled daughter's family will become unstable. Nothing else especially.

Leisure was depicted positively by some respondents but negatively by others. The attitude toward leisure was directly related to the age of the story teller. The pattern of distribution recalls the description of Japanese life as a U-shaped curve, with the middle years full of responsibility, and the early and late years happier and freer from pressure. The combined total of "leisure" stories told by men and women from ages eighteen to fifty is sixty-two; only eleven of these, or approximately 18 percent, are positively toned, but if the stories of teenagers from twelve to eighteen are combined with those of men and women over fifty, there is a total of forty leisure stories, approximately two-thirds of which are positively toned. There is only one positive story of leisure told by any woman between eighteen and thirty, and only two positive stories by men between twenty-four and fifty. Conversely, there were many more stories told by people in these age groups that described leisure activities in negatively colored terms. (See Table II-1.)

TABLE II-1

DISTRIBUTION OF TAT STORIES IN WHICH LEISURE OR RECREATIONAL ACTIVITIES ARE DEPICTED ACCORDING TO AFFECTIVE TONE OF THE STORIES
(in percent)

	Age of subjects						Number of stories by	
	12–17	18–24	25–34	35–49	50–64	65+	men	women
Positive or neutral tone	72	26	7	17	60	89	17	21
Negative tone	28	74	93	83	40	11	29	35

The high incidence of negative stories about leisure told by individuals in their middle years is related to the large number of stories of drinking or drunkenness told by the same people. Men often associated drinking with violence and conflict, and sometimes linked it to extramarital affairs with bar hostesses. Some stories very self-consciously pointed out the evil effect of drunkenness on family life:

(M, age 37, card J5) The husband came back home drunk, and his wife quarreled with him. He got angry and went out again. She is anxiously seeing him off.

Drinking is a fairly common leisure-time activity throughout Japan, but it did not appear in a positive light in any story. Niiike residents seem restrained in this matter; no one in the community is noted as

a drunkard. Niiike may be somewhat more puritanical in attitudes
toward drinking than rural Japanese villages in general.

The most positive among leisure situations depicted were those
which told of families together at home or traveling together for a
visit:

(M, age 68, card J7M) [Man in picture is visually distorted into old woman.]
An old couple are going to worship at the grave [*hakamairi*]. They pay deep
respect to their ancestors, and they will end their life in peace and contentment.

These traveling stories usually involved an older retired couple or a
grandparent and a grandchild. Most such stories were told by people
over fifty. They reflect the attitude that one's old age should be a time
of peace and enjoyment of one's family. In these years, free from the
responsibilities and conflicts that filled one's earlier years, one may
find companionship with one's spouse. These stories also indirectly
emphasized the relaxed attitude of older people toward their grandchildren.

Autonomy and Affiliation vs. Obligation: Attitudes Concerning Marriage Relationships

CHOICE OF MARRIAGE PARTNERS IN NIIIKE. The psychological investiga-
tions in Niiike generally reflect marriage as a stable and fixed institution. Parents and other authorities are thought, in general if not in
specific instances, to have more wisdom concerning the suitability of
marriage partners than younger people who lack life experience.

In Niiike, as indirectly revealed by TAT materials, there was marked
distrust of free choice in marriage. There was not only some change
and lack of unanimity noted among Niiike inhabitants in this regard,
but intrapsychic ambivalence was also in evidence. On the one hand,
no spontaneous TAT stories attributed marked unhappiness in a
consummated marriage to the fact that the marriage partners had
been chosen by outsiders. On the other hand, to a far greater degree
than was found later in a fishing village, failure was often assumed
to result from free-choice marriages. To some individuals a love marriage seemed dangerous, unstable, and unconsciously guilt-producing,
although there was no unanimity in the village on this matter.

Some positive value was attached to individual choice of a marriage
partner, and love was not completely overlooked as a valid and force-
ful consideration. On a conscious level, in contrast to the unconscious
fear of free choice revealed in the TAT, the positive value of free
choice in marriage was expressed in Niiike by a relatively large minority in answer to Problem Situation Test items. A love marriage,
even in opposition to the wishes of parents, found some acceptance
by a number of men and women. (See Table II-2.) The number who

TABLE II-2

DISTRIBUTION OF RESPONSES TO PROBLEM SITUATION TEST ITEM 14

A man is loved by a girl who is "below" him in wealth and social position. Reciprocating the love, he wants to marry her. He talks to his parents about it, but they are against the idea. What would he (or she) do? (The same question for men and women, with change of subject and object.)

Age codes:	18+(a)	25+(y)	35+(m)	50+(o)	65+(s)	Men (total)	Women (total)
Men	3	3	4	3	1	14	
Women	1	3	6	4	1		15
I—Marry							
A. Marry						9	6
1. for one's self							1(m)
2. because social position is not important							4(a-m-m-o)
3. because he loves her						6(a-y-m-m-m-s)	1(o)
4. because a marriage should be made freely						2(y-o)	
B. Leave home and marry unless he is permitted to by persuading the parents							
1. because he does not regard social position as important						1(a)	
II—Make efforts to marry						3	3
A. Ask the parents for permission							
1. in order to marry						1(m)	2(y-y)
2. because he hopes for happiness						1(o)	
3. for future						1(a)	
B. Ask a mediator for help							
1. in order to marry							1(o)
III—Not marry						2	6
1. because marriage results in undutifulness to the parents						1(o)	3(y-m-o)
2. because trouble may happen in the future						1(y)	1(m)
3. because the parents are right							1(m)
4. because love does not last long even though they are tied by the impulse of the moment							1(s)
5. for the parents and *ie*							

would oppose parental wishes varied with the hypothetical circumstances under which free choice and obligation were opposed in the
problem situation items used. In a hypothetical problem in which the
parents raised strong objections to a marriage even after having been
introduced to the potential spouse, there were fewer advocates of the
love marriage. (See Table II-3.) Three-fourths of the women and two-
thirds of the men would not have persisted in making the disapproved
match. Some of the men would hope that with patience they might
persuade their parents to change their opinions. Only a few individuals
explicitly stated an autonomous position; they would go counter to
parental wishes, since marriage was for them a lifelong relationship
between two people and should be based on mutual love. The primacy
of the marriage bond over the ties of lineage was thus explicitly con-
firmed by a minority in Niiike.

When faced with a problem situation in which an intended spouse
is opposed by parents because of a somewhat "lower" social status, only
one-seventh of the men and two-fifths of the women queried would
consider giving up the idea of marriage. (See Table II-2.) Overcoming
a concern about status in the name of love is a noble concept for most
Niiike villagers.

Nevertheless, in response to other items, some of the women made
occasional references to status. They were concerned, for example, that
nothing should injure the good name of their families, lest their possibilities for a "good" marriage be impaired thereby. Even in these cases,
the primary concern was for marriage and not for status as such.

When faced with the question of marrying to satisfy a parental
obligation to an outsider, men and women revealed different attitudes.
(See Table II-4.) Three of the fourteen men queried, including one
adolescent, directly accepted marriage on such terms. Five men definitely rejected the idea of the marriage, however, and there was a
great deal of hedging in the replies of the other men. For example,
two said that they would marry if the other person were suitable, but
not merely for family obligations. While four men directly supported
the principle of marrying *only* according to one's own will, one of
these added that "he would marry in this case because he had the will
to marry." No age differences appeared among the men with regard to
these attitudes.

Among the women, eleven of the sixteen queried on this item (including all nine women over thirty-five) accepted the idea of a marriage of obligation. Most of their replies explained directly that if
one's family owed much to another family, one must aid in returning
the favor because one owed so much to one's parents and because it
would "set the parents at ease." In women under thirty-five more conflict appeared: one woman refused to answer; one hoped for further

"investigation," since one cannot be married more than once; and two girls under eighteen directly refused to get married because of "shame" or "dislike" for the person selected as a potential mate.

These responses bring out rather clearly an interesting value differential operative in Niiike; all but the youngest women showed little conflict between filial piety and obligation, on the one hand, and individual choice on the other. They clearly accepted the older collective virtues. Adolescent girls were troubled, but they had little tendency to phrase their concern in terms of principles. They probably had had no experience in defending their feelings by an appeal to such ideals as "women's rights." Men of all ages, however, showed a hesitancy and a qualification in their answers and were more visibly caught in a dilemma between a sense of obligation and gratitude toward the parents and a respect for individualism. As a group they appreciated the value of self-will as opposed to passive submission to obligation. In the hedging that appeared, however, it is evident that there was only a veneer of active, masculine self-will over a deeper attitude signifying submission to possible family pressure.

Another problem posed (see Appendix A, item 17) was that of inability to support both a mother and a potential mate whom one loves. In general, men were apt to seek a solution, whereas a greater number of women gave up the idea of marriage out of consideration for the potential mother-in-law. The most common solution, suggested by one-third of the men and women, was that the couple marry and the wife find work. Such a solution is probably more readily available to farmers, who have a tradition of women working, than to individuals of a higher status, who would consider it shameful for a wife to work. Two individuals considered establishing a residence separate from the mother, and a few men suggested postponement of the marriage. However, no women considered delay a satisfactory solution to this problem, perhaps because women are more conscious of age as a factor in marriageability than are men.

One-third of the men and more than half of the women gave up the idea of marriage. Most in this group were individuals between thirty-five and fifty, some of whom stated resignedly that the marriage would "make life too difficult." The greater number of the women who resigned themselves to the impossibility of marriage under these circumstances did so because they felt strongly the emotional side of a man's attachment to his mother; the men phrased the problem more consciously in terms of their duty to take care of their mothers. One woman gave as a reason for forgoing the idea of marriage "the look in his mother's eyes," possibly suggesting the feeling of jealousy implied in this kind of relationship. In general, the men seemed more concerned with the love relationship, the women with economic pressure and

TABLE II-3

DISTRIBUTION OF RESPONSES TO PROBLEM SITUATION TEST ITEM 19a

A man is engaged to be married to a girl whom he loves; however, when he introduced the girl to his parents, one of them raised strong objections. What should he or she do? (The same question for men and women.)

Age codes:	18+(a)	25+(y)	35+(m)	50+(o)	65+(s)	Men (total)	Women (total)
Men	3	3	3	3	3	15	
Women	5	2	5	2	2		16
I—Marry							
A. Marry						6	4
1. because they have been close for a long time						1(o)	1(m)
2. in order to keep a promise to marry						1(m)	1(m)
3. because it is O.K. if they love each other							1(a)
4. because his mother agrees							1(a)
5. because this marriage is their own business						2(a-o)	
6. because the fiancée is beautiful						1(a)	
B. Marry *if* the fiancée is good for him							
1. no reason						1(y)	
II—Talk with the parents						4	2
1. in order to have the parents cooperate							
2. because it is better to be in agreement							
3. because if he does so he can marry						1(m)	1(a)
4. because he thinks the parents will allow the marriage						1(a)	1(y)

5. wait until the marriage is allowed — 1(s)
6. have the parents investigate the fiancée, because he has confidence in her — 1(m)

III—Not marry

	3	8
1. for the sake of the parents	1(s)	1(m)
2. because it is bad to be scolded by the father		1(s)
3. because she loves her father much more than the fiancé		1(o)
4. for the peace of the home		
5. because it is not necessary to marry against reason	1(y)	
6. because it is not allowed in Japan. The national character of Japan is different from America's	1(s)	1(m)
7. because he thinks of his relatives		2(a-o)
8. because he was opposed by the parents		1(y)
9. because there are many men in the world		1(a)
10. and marry another man because the first was opposed severely by the father		

IV—React emotionally

	2	2
1. can't give up		
2. be disappointed because parents' opinion is different	1(y)	1(s)
3. be distressed	1(o)	1(m)
4. be sad because parent is opposed to the marriage		

TABLE II-4

DISTRIBUTION OF RESPONSES TO PROBLEM SITUATION TEST ITEM 12

A man's parents are indebted to an individual for help. (Men) One day he asks the parents to accept his daughter as a bride for their son. The man's parents are very happy about the request. (Women) One day he asks for their daughter as a wife for his son. The woman's parents are very happy about the request. What would he (or she) do?

Age codes:	18+(a)	25+(y)	35+(m)	50+(o)	65+(s)	Men (total)	Women (total)
Men	3	3	4	3	1	14	
Women	5	2	5	2	2		16

	Men (total)	Women (total)
I—Not marry	5	2
1. because he dislikes the other person	1(a)	1(a)
2. because he already has a lover and dislikes the other person	3(a-y-s)	
3. because one should get married by one's own choice	1(o)	
4. because it is better to give things as thanks for receiving help		
5. because he is ashamed		1(a)
II—Marry if the other person is suitable	3	
1. because people should get married for themselves, not for parent and family or obligation	3(y-m-o)	
III—Investigate		1
1. because one can't get married more than once in a whole lifetime		1(y)
IV—Marry	6	12
1. for obligation	3(a-m-o)	5(m-m-m-o-s)
2. for setting the parents at ease		6(a-y-m-o-s)
3. because he has had the will to be married	1(m)	1(a)
4. because he finds the other a suitable person	2(y-m)	1(a)
V—No response		1(a)

indirectly with the primacy of a man's obligation to his mother. Nevertheless, resolving the situation through hard work on the part of both marriage partners was also a notable factor in the responses of both sexes.

The people of Niiike clearly demonstrated their conservative attitude toward free choice in the matter of the remarriage of a widow. (See Appendix A, item 20). Almost all of the women refused to consider remarriage; only two suggested the possibility of remarriage "for a happy home life." The most common reason given for refusal to remarry was the "future" of one's children. Other answers involved concern for both the children and the "house," since remarriage would deprive children of their right to inherit their dead father's household.

To understand why women do not consider it possible to remarry and still secure their children's future, one must know that a second husband has no responsibility toward the children of another man, nor would his family be interested in them. Children belong to the house of their own father, and a man can totally ignore the children of a widow whom he marries. He need provide no financial support for them; hence a widow remains dependent on the house of her former husband for their support, and if she were to oppose the wishes of members of this house, they might not give her any money for her children. A woman is expected to sacrifice herself for her children, and she should not be selfishly concerned with her own happiness. The question of remarriage theoretically involves the matter of infidelity, since a woman is supposed to remain faithful to her husband after his death. Moreover, her obligation to her mother-in-law, at least in theory, does not cease with her husband's death. These concerns, however, were not reflected in the test results. The responses of the women of Niiike make it clear that the obligation of a mother to her children is the primary consideration in such a question.

It is obvious from the above items that the more concretely and directly an item put free choice into conflict with other values, the weaker the attitude in favor of free choice became. In romantic fantasy, many may contemplate opposition to parental wishes and marriage to a person of their own choosing. Reality, however, gives young people little opportunity for such individualism in the face of the social sanctions of their own and neighboring communities. Moreover, a strong sense of the "rightness" of obedience to parents and of potential guilt for rebellion insures eventual submission to parental and community pressure. In short, whatever the attitudes held, few people in Niiike possess the degree of personal autonomy required to attempt a love marriage. When it actually occurs, such a marriage is usually an act of rebellion against the parents and generally produces a disharmonious situation. Although structured in terms of positive feelings of mutual love, the bond between the young people is more often one of shared antagonism toward parents. As such, love marriages do not often have a sufficiently stable base to ensure permanency, and the internal sanctions of guilt eventually take their toll.

In Niiike up to 1954 only one "love" marriage was reported to have occurred in recent years. It did not succeed, according to the villagers. In effect, Niiike evidences "psychological lag" in its attitude toward love marriage.

PROBLEMS IN MARRIAGE RELATIONSHIPS. Two main problems were spontaneously depicted in TAT stories pertaining to marriage: the wife's adjustment to her mother-in-law, and infidelity and profligacy on the part of the husband. Both men and women tended to see these problems as central issues in marriage, although there was some difference in their views.

The mother-in-law problem is a conscious and important issue in Niiike, as it is elsewhere in Japan. Countless articles in Japanese magazines deal with this perennial sore spot. Evidence from both TAT and problem situation tests indicate that very little is required to stimulate strong feelings on the subject in women. No matter what TAT card was presented, some women (usually a younger one) managed to depict a conflict situation involving an unreasonable mother-in-law. Men, on the other hand, preferred to avoid conscious concern with the problem.

Although they were quick to recognize that a problem did exist, women taking the role of wives would concede only that they must have patience and endure. Not one woman expressed any possibility of direct opposition to the excessive demands of a mother-in-law. (See Appendix A, item 26.) Such results reflect the degree to which the women of Niiike accept the fact that a bride has no personal rights in her new house until she has established her status, usually by bearing children. As an outsider, she is not readily accepted as a true member of the family. Fulfillment of her responsibilities to her husband is not sufficient; she must also develop and display a deep feeling of respect for his ancestral lineage. When her mother-in-law is present, the new wife is never considered the manager of the home; and the mother-in-law, herself once an outsider, is considered the proper disciplinarian. She should see to it that the proper attitudes are established in the young wife, a process of indoctrination that may include a great deal of cruelty and jealousy.

Two of the women who suggested submission to the mother-in-law also stressed a need to "avoid" falling ill. The juxtaposition of these two topics suggests an unconscious mechanism at work. It would be impossible to malinger, but becoming ill can be used unconsciously as one way of escaping excessive demands.[10] One of these women suggested the possibility of returning home to avoid illness, and the other suggested ignoring what the mother-in-law said so far as possible, but doing one's work. It can be inferred here that, by ignoring, one can avoid internalizing excessive requirements, and hence avoid illness.

Two other women gave culturally noteworthy reasons for "enduring." One said that there was no alternative because she would have no other opportunity for marriage. Another stated that even if she were to marry again the chances were that her new mother-in-law would be no better. To maintain autonomy is often to remain unmarried, and a person who remains unmarried is considered strange in Japan; national statistics demonstrate that it is comparatively rare. Most unmarried women are entertainers or prostitutes and these alternatives are avoided by most women, especially those in the rural areas. For the village woman, then, there is no real escape from the mother-in-law problem, unless one is fortunate enough to marry a second son whose residence is different from that of his mother.

Men were more likely than women to see divorce as a solution to the friction between a husband's mother and his wife. (See Table II-5.) In responses to a problem situation in which one's spouse suggests divorce because the wife's relationship with the mother-in-law is impossible, the men were divided about evenly between those who would accept the wife's desire for divorce and those who would seek reconciliation. The reasons most frequently given by the men for accepting divorce were that parents must be given paramount consideration and that one must take account of social considerations, such as the scandal involved in continued friction between a woman and her mother-in-law. Those men who would reconcile the differences expressed a variety of reasons: love for the wife, concern for the children, and a man's responsibility to resolve differences between his wife and his mother. It is noteworthy that only one man mentioned the possibility of setting up a residence separate from that of the parents. Sixty percent of the women subjects, in solving a situation wherein a husband recommends divorce, suggested apology to the mother-in-law or self-reform, or both. Only 20 percent would accept the husband's suggestion of divorce; two women expressed disappointment with the weakness the husband displayed in failing to give moral support to his wife. Two other women suggested that the couple establish a separate residence.

---

[10] As is discussed further in Chapter 4, numerous cases have been reported among farm women of *hisuteri*, an hysterical illness which is recognized by some professional Japanese to be related to interference by the mother-in-law in the sexual life of a young married pair, or else a reaction to excessive work demands made by the mother-in-law.

TABLE II-5

DISTRIBUTION OF RESPONSES TO PROBLEM SITUATION TEST ITEM 6

A man's wife does not get along well with her mother-in-law. They have conflicts over all sorts of matters. (Men) As a result, his wife one day tells him she would like a divorce. (Women) As a result, her husband one day finally suggests divorce. What would he (or she) do?

Age codes:	18+(a)	25+(y)	35+(m)	50+(o)	65+(s)	Men (total)	Women (total)
Men	3	3	3	3	3	15	
Women	3	3	6	4	1		15

I—Divorce						7	3
A. Because parents are paramount, and							
1. it is necessary that he support his parents						2(y-s)	
2. she is one who does not know how to obey						1(s)	
B. For social considerations							
1. it is socially scandalous						1(o)	
2. it is foolish from the standpoint of the state of the world						1(y)	
C. For egocentric concerns							
1. because he is unhappy						1(a)	
D. Because of loss of feeling for husband							
1. because she heard it from her husband, who should take care of her							2(m-m)
E. For other reasons (avoidance of issue)							
1. because she is not beautiful							1(a)
2. use a mediator for divorce							1(y)

	7	9
II—Not divorce		
A. Become reconciled to each other		
1. because the husband loves his wife	2(y-o)	
2. for the parent	1(s)	
3. because this is his responsibility	1(m)	
4. because there are many examples like this in the world and he thinks of his child in the future	1(m)	
5. no reason	1(o)	
B. Investigate		
1. in order to know what the cause is	1(a)	
C. Apologize to her husband and have him think it over again		
1. because she thinks that her husband and mother-in-law have responsibility too		1(y)
2. because she is ashamed to divorce		1(m)
3. because it is difficult to marry again		1(m)
4. because appearance is bad		1(o)
D. Reflect and reform herself		
1. because it is the duty of a bride to submit to her husband and mother-in-law		1(o)
E. Be patient out of filial duty		3(a-o-s)
III—Husband and wife set up separate living	1	2
1. for their own future happiness	1(m)	2(y-m)
2. no reason		
IV—Answer unclear		1(o)

Some women gave reasons for a fear of divorce which were more realistic than those offered by the men. One woman stated that it would be difficult to marry again. Others talked about the personal shame. Generally, the women showed, on the surface at least, an attitude of self-reproach and submission that clearly delineates both traditional values and the actual social reality of the Japanese wife who lives with a mother-in-law. From the woman's standpoint, the vertical relationship of a man to his mother and family seems much stronger than his horizontal relationship to his wife.

The second major marital problem, that of infidelity, clearly involves a double standard. Japanese wives do not usually elicit much jealousy from their husbands; in cities, women can and do go about by themselves, and husbands only rarely become suspicious or possessive. The possibility of adultery on the part of a wife does not enter into the spontaneous thinking of men or women in Niiike. On the TAT, the only suggestion of a woman once married having extramarital contacts was in reference to a widow. In a problem situation item worded to suggest straying affections or possible unfaithfulness in a wife (see Appendix A, item 25) the men were content to "investigate," implying a general caution against jumping to conclusions and a maintenance of emotional distance. They seemed unwilling to consider the possibility seriously unless it was stated in more direct terms.

In solving a problem in which it is actually stated that a wife loves another man (Appendix A, item 8), more than half the men suggested divorce, but usually only after the husband had definitely established that the reports were true. Moreover, several individuals suggested discussion with the wife to reestablish harmony. Those who did recommend divorce justified it in diverse ways: concern about the children's future, the need to ensure the peace of the entire family, concern over one's own loss of happiness, and incompatibility. One old man blamed the parents in such a case for having made a poor marriage arrangement.

Women's responses to the same items showed none of the caution expressed by the men. They quickly assumed unfaithfulness on the part of a husband in doubtful situations, but they were characteristically resigned to the difficulty of doing anything about it. The usual answers involved advice or admonition. Some women expressed only anger, with no course of action indicated. Only two women would consider divorce, and for reasons quite different from each other's and from those given by men; one suggested divorce as a matter of principle, whereas the other suggested divorce so that the man might be happy with the other woman.

Three women thought that increased care for the husband might solve the problem of his infidelity, and two women saw the wife as somehow directly responsible for having allowed her husband's interest to wander. The tendency to blame the wife for the husband's infidelity or for his general dissatisfaction was exhibited by both men and women. This theme was often evoked by picture J13 of the TAT series, which depicts a seminude woman lying in bed in a posture usually interpreted as that of sleep, illness, or death. The man, shown with his arm across his eyes, seemed to some male respondents to be angry or disappointed over a lack of wifely care. To other men the carelessness in the sleeping posture of the woman suggested a lack of wifely devotion.[11] In their stories they complained that "such a wife" would not care for a husband properly and would even go to sleep before his return at night rather than wait up for him. Women also saw a lack of attention to the husband as a potential source of discord between a man and his wife. The converse, discord due to a husband's inattention to his wife, was never elicited.

TAT pictures evoked many stories of a husband or father who stayed out late to drink, and, in a certain number of these, extramarital affairs on the part of a husband were also suggested. Many of the stories about a husband's dissipation told by both men and women had a moralistic tone. Drinking and impulsive behavior under the influence of alcohol were not condoned but seemed to be acknowledged as part of the nature of certain men. Aggressive quarreling was generally associated with drinking.

The profligacy of men was not seen by either sex as a common cause of permanent rupture of the marriage bond. The wife was never pictured as "fearful" of losing her husband to another woman, as wives frequently are in stories told by American women. The Japanese wife may suffer from neglect in such situations, but she does not characteristically fear permanent loss. One may infer that she is secure in providing the basic maternal care for her husband, which ultimately builds a stronger bond than does satisfying sexual impulses. American wives, on the other hand, are more conscious of having to maintain the interest of their husbands or lovers by remaining sexually attractive, and therefore display more anxiety.

Nurturance: Parent-Child Relationships

ATTITUDES CONCERNING CHILD SOCIALIZATION: CARE AND TRAINING OF CHILDREN. Many stories given in response to TAT pictures dealt with the means by which mothers advise, admonish, and care for their children to assure their successful futures. Long-range goals were expressed so often that one cannot escape the impression that Japanese mothers

---

[11] Decorum in Japanese women extends to the sleeping as well as the waking state. A young girl is taught to control her body even while asleep.

are constantly self-conscious about the possible influence of their behavior on the future development of their children. The nature of his
mother's care is considered crucial in a child's chances of becoming a
success in life.

While the mother's role is usually expressed in terms of direct, active
influence, the father's is more that of a model image to be emulated.
His role is to encourage or inspire, and his inspiration may be effected
not only through daily contact, but also through a child's memory of
his image. Some stories depicted a dead father who inspired a child
to achieve in order to care for his mother, as his father had done. In
a small minority of stories, the absence of a father made it impossible
for a mother to cope with the discipline of their son and hence led to
a negative outcome. In other stories a widowed mother, through selfish
interest in other men, allowed herself to be distracted from proper
devotion to her child's upbringing. The strong feeling that it is wrong
for a mother to remarry is linked directly to her need to devote herself
to her children, whom she would ordinarily have to leave with her
first husband's family were she to remarry.

Methods of control or discipline in Niiike differed with the age of
the child and the problems presented. The mother was usually the
admonishing figure, although she would sometimes involve a child's
elder brother by having him intercede actively as disciplinarian in her
support. In stories involving younger children, indirect refusal of a
child's demands by ignoring them or by distracting the child with other
activities was more prevalent than direct verbal refusal or physical
punishment. Excessive scolding was linked to unsuccessful results. Children are thought to develop negative attitudes if punished with any
severity, and it was said that children so treated become "soured" or
"distorted in their attitudes" toward life. The principal source of
trouble in these stories of conflict between parents and younger children was "laziness," or lack of application to study on the part of the
child.

Violent chastisement did occur in some stories. The figure of the
cruel stepmother was often evoked in negatively toned stories to depict
the lifelong evil effects of cruel or severe punishment of children:

(M, age 56, card J18) This is—ah—a stepmother and a daughter, I suppose.
And the stepmother is—to her stepdaughter furious—at present—I suppose
the stepmother is chastising her stepdaughter.

As the stepmother is always hard on her daughter, the daughter has a
"jaundiced" mind and does not obey her stepmother. It seems to me that
the daughter has contradicted her mother on something, and the mother is
chastising her by gripping her neck. If such a relationship between the stepmother and her daughter continues indefinitely, their minds will grow more
opposed to each other and a coolness will grow up between them, and . . .

but they have pure thoughts in the bottom of their hearts, I think. Finally, even if they cannot keep a good intimate relation with each other, they will surely come to know that they have been wrong, if they meet on an occasion when one of them dies of illness.

Conversely, in some stories, selfish children failed to recognize the self-sacrifice of a good stepmother until much later in their lives.

There were no stories of cruel stepfathers, of fathers who were severe disciplinarians, or of violent behavior in a man toward his son or daughter. In the nine stories told by men about physical violence within a family, all nine violent acts were committed by women; in seven of these stories the violence was actually extreme discipline directed toward an adult son. Among seven stories of this kind told by women, four involved acts of violence by a woman toward her son, and three described violence inflicted by a man on his wife.

Violent chastisement occurred in a more positive light in some stories, which suggested a deep sense of the continuing responsibility of the mother toward society for the proper behavior of her child, even after he has reached adulthood. Such stories are related to those which unconsciously depicted a mother who masochistically punished herself or her son by becoming ill and dying, after which the son usually reformed himself and worked hard. Parents in such stories never turned to legal sanctions, such as the police, to punish delinquency. The responsibility for delinquent behavior was clearly the mother's:

(M, age 20, card J18) Mother severely chastises her disobedient child who committed a crime.
(M, age 20, card J18) A parent is choking a son who committed burglary. The son is arrested by a policeman, reforms himself, and lives with parents happily.
(M, age 17, card J18) A mother strangles to death her prodigal son. She will be imprisoned.

In a few stories, a woman killed herself after killing a delinquent young son, and one older person constructed a traditional story of a mother who kills her son in order to fulfill an unspecified *giri* obligation.

The figures on the same TAT card (J18), when interpreted as a mother-daughter situation, evoked only three stories of conflict. Violence toward a daughter was rarely inferred, and the picture was usually seen as a depiction of a mother's tender concern for her daughter during illness or malaise. It is to be noted as well that a mother-in-law was never described as physically abusive toward a bride no matter how negatively she was seen in other contexts.

One sees reflected in these data the fact that fathers in Japan are not usually considered active disciplinarians. The responsibility for child-rearing rests upon the mother, and mothers, in assuming this responsibility, are not passive in their relationship to children even after they are grown. On the contrary, women are considered capable of violent chastisement of their wayward children. Such an active attitude appears in other contexts as well; stories of marriage arrangements, for example, ordinarily showed a mother taking the initiative and handling matters with a firm will. Much as a man conceives of his adulthood in terms of occupational achievement, a woman sees the successful maturation of an adult son as a prerequisite to a sense of fulfillment. This is her principal goal in life.

CARE AND SOLICITUDE TOWARD PARENTS—ON-GAESHI AND RESPONSIBILITY. The relations of parents and children in Niiike are characteristically intense and positive. Even though direct comparison with other social relations is difficult because of limitations in the stimuli values of the tests, the sentiment between children and parents is undoubtedly very strong. The people of Niiike expressed this sentiment in ways resembling those of Americans, but they appeared to feel an attachment that was more intense and less subject to ambivalence. Any strongly negative feelings were buried so deeply that they were expressed only unconsciously.

The strength and spontaneity of parental attachment varied, of course, with the individual. This variation was evident in the reactions to problem situations and TAT pictures that involved a choice between the value of obedience to parents and that of self-motivated achievement. Care and solicitude for a mother were of paramount concern. In one such problem test men and women were asked what a son who was studying or working away from home should do if his father died and he was asked to return. Another hypothetical situation posed the question of whether one should carry on with one's own plans or come home in response to a parental request for help, to care for one's mother, for example, or to succeed to the house leadership. Taking responses to all such situations together, we find that most men (70 percent) and women (75 percent) judged it best for the hypothetical person to return home. Most of the respondents stated specifically, or seemed to assume, that a person living away from home would be a younger son, who would be less implicitly obliged by custom to continue in the parental household. Some men (27 percent) and fewer women (16 percent) felt it proper for such a person to refuse to return home permanently. The following stories are examples of the majority and minority points of view:

(M, age 36, problem situation 1a) He returns home to stay because it is his duty to become the head of his family.

(W, age 25, problem situation 1a) He returns home only temporarily to take care of funeral ceremony, and so forth, but afterwards continues to work toward his own goal away from home.

Men who recommended the traditional role of returning home, to succeed as family head or to take care of a mother, nonetheless spoke of the regret that would accompany giving up one's chosen studies or occupation. Women who submitted to the need for their husbands to accept the duty of head of the household were apt to treat this situation as a required service to their mother-in-law. The women who rejected this tradition were younger, all but one of them under thirty-five. Three women explicitly rebelled against life with a mother-in-law, and one went so far as to say that divorce would be preferable to such a life. It appears that these women accept marriage to a younger son, which has its own disadvantages, because of the freedom it offers from the mother-in-law problem; to have to contend with a mother-in-law after making such a choice would be too much of a burden.

In opposing the community pressure to observe tradition, the younger women's attitudes led to a certain amount of inner conflict. In late adolescence girls are apt to reach for a freedom that they later resign themselves to doing without. Therefore, we are probably on safer ground if we view the clash of attitudes shown here as part of the maturation process in the individual, rather than as a sign of changing times and the transfer of values. Quite possibly if an identical problem were posed to the same young women and girls ten years later, it would bring answers comparable to those of today's older women.

In the responses discussed above, care and solicitude for the parents gave strong emotional shading to the practical problem of succession to the leadership of a household. Only a few men, and they were the elders of the village, mentioned the formal concepts of obligatory succession and family duty. These few elders also stressed the responsibility of leaders to serve as examples for others and created self-consciously moralistic stories in which vice was always punished and virtue triumphant. The majority of the men framed their responses to these parent-child problem situations as if the emotional sense of responsibility for care of the aging mother were uppermost in their minds. If they rebelled against the idea of returning (always specifying that their role was that of a second son), we may judge that their attitude reflected the parents' tendency to lavish greater affection on the oldest son, whose sense of gratitude for their sacrifice should thus surpass that of a younger son. Surely the majority of men who urged return also recognized this invidious distinction. It is thus noteworthy that they resigned themselves to the abandonment of self-set goals to repay the sacrifice and hard work of their parents and not to fulfill the overt, formal duty of succession. They followed custom willingly through an emotional motivation, and not merely to meet a formal requirement.

OBEDIENCE TO PARENTS AS OPPOSED TO OTHER VALUES. In a problem situation (see Appendix A, item 10), in which the values of personal achievement were opposed to those of obedience to parental wishes, men showed a surprising amount of concern for personal achievement. The duty of a son to follow in his father's occupation was apparently not strongly felt in Niiike.

Men and women both tended to consider positive interest and talent more important than parental wishes in the choice of a career; not a single man spontaneously suggested obedience to the wishes of parents. Nevertheless, disregard of parents' desires was phrased with concern for their feelings. One man stated, for example, that, even though to ignore parental wishes was impious, one could eventually repay his parents by achievement. Another expressed the idea that failure itself is impious, so that it is better to follow one's own interests and talents:

(M, age 36, problem situation 5) He gets the job he is interested in rather than succeeding his father because his parents are successful in their own profession, and it is filial piety for him to be successful in his own.

Others regretted that they must disappoint their parents, but felt that the parents would eventually see the wisdom of the son's choice.

Another problem situation item (Appendix A, item 10) posed the question of whether a child should continue his education over parental objections or despite the pressure of poverty on his parents. More than half the men answered that they would continue their schooling. The answers often included some indication that, since mental labor promises more economic advantage than does physical labor, education is a guarantee of a profitable future. On the other hand, all but two women said they would give up their education if their parents requested them to do so. Their concern was with their duty to help their parents. Few women in Niiike envisioned any career other than that of housewife. The woman's role as they saw it did not include higher education, so their responses to this problem did not reveal many signs of conflict. Although education did not seem to mean a great deal personally to women, they did appreciate the benefits it held for them.

On items that assessed the relative strength of parental pressure and individual choice in the selection of marriage partners, a surprising number of men answered that they would persist in a choice their parents opposed, but would attempt to gain parental approval. A number of men said that they would not consent to a marriage that had been arranged in repayment of an obligation incurred by their parents.

With the exception of a few younger girls, women were usually sub-missive in their expressed attitudes concerning obedience to parents in this situation, whereas men much more often asserted self-choice and disregard of parental wishes. (See "Choice of Marriage Partners" above.)

In a situation where a child and his parents clash on religious or political issues, only one man of the twenty-nine tested said he would change his opinions to conform with those of his parents, but five of the thirty-one women tested would do so. About one-third of the women felt free to urge their views on their parents. The women tended, at least in their imagined behavior, to become directly assertive or else completely submissive, and they showed less submissiveness in response to the item concerning religious and political opinions than to any other. A number of women showed a rather assertive but friendly attitude toward their parents, saying that they would defend their own beliefs because they were right or because there were differ-ences between one generation and the next.

Men, on the other hand, suggested that one would best attempt to assume a neutral attitude in order to keep peace in the family. Their attitude toward their parents was conciliatory; they wished "to keep friendly relations with parents." Half of the men and one-third of the women showed such constrained attitudes. The men especially tended to avoid the problem by claiming that an individual in this situation would leave home, keep silent, or listen to parents' views for his own information. Such an attitude may exemplify the Japanese saying "Keep clear of the devil"; in other words, do not pursue matters too far and avoid emotional involvement.

These results—especially the open assertiveness in the answers of some of the women—contrast to some degree with results obtained on other items. There may be several reasons for this difference. One possible factor is the degree to which religion and politics are removed from the requirements of the family and from community sanctions in Japan. Hence, expression of political or religious opinions contrary to those of parents would not constitute such an affect-laden situation as it does in the West, where such differences can cause extreme tension within families. Religion has never played such a central role in Japan; morality is related to systems of obligation to family and social hier-archy, and not to God and a system of abstract principles. People seem to consider theology a personal proclivity rather than a burning issue. Politics is also a minor matter for most of the people of Niiike. Radical younger people in the city might see more potential conflict in this problem than do the younger people of Niiike.

Another factor to be considered is that, although the family demands conformity in behavior and to a certain extent seeks to orient feelings, individuals feel free to keep their own opinions on matters not directly

related to daily behavior. Since the opinions in question do not immediately involve important social sanctions or social and family obligations, individuals feel freer, in general, to champion the right to their
own opinions.

When asked about the reactions of a son or daughter who got into
trouble outside the family (Appendix A, items 7 and 21), women were
most concerned about parental feelings. In sharp contrast, only a small
minority of men were so oriented; most men seemed to be primarily
concerned with resolving the difficulty in which they found themselves
and less emotionally involved in a dependent way with their parents.
Women, whatever their age, continue to feel very dependent upon their
parents or parental surrogates and to show little development of any
ideas of self-reliance. (Such attitudes contribute to the conservative,
authoritarian modes of thought exhibited by women in their responses
to opinion scales as well as in the projective psychological data.)

Attitude Toward Authority—The Control Dimension
in Role Behavior

FAMILY SANCTIONS: FAMILY RESPONSIBILITY AND FAMILY SOLIDARITY.
When a problem situation was presented in which a family member
had done something disgraceful (Appendix A, item 4), Niiike respondents did not usually feel sympathetic toward the offending member,
nor were they particularly concerned with his reform (cf. Table II-6).
Their concern was principally with the disgrace to the whole family
and with the social rectification of the misconduct. The family itself
turned upon an errant member instead of protecting him against the
outside world or leaving him to his own resources and fate. These reactions reveal the extent to which the Niiike family feels responsible
for the behavior of its members, in spite of postwar reforms stressing
the legal responsibility of the individual.

Men and women reacted differently to situations involving this sense
of family responsibility. Men were most concerned with the social rectification of the misconduct of a family member. A number of them,
particularly men who held active and responsible roles in the village,
spoke of a public apology by the family head. One suggested type of
public apology was *kinshin:*

(M, age 24, problem situation 4) He does *kinshin* and makes an effort himself to restore the previous state of affairs, because to do so is the duty of a
person who is in the position of a leader.

Traditionally *kinshin* was the social behavior required of a samurai
when he had committed some act that was disgraceful but not serious
enough to require *seppuku,* or formal suicide, when one was compromised by subordinates for whom he was responsible. The samurai

would confine himself to his house and give up ordinary affairs for a fitting period of time. A superior could ask a samurai to do kinshin, just as he could order *seppuku* for more serious offenses. Kinshin seems to be rather similar to medieval European public penance, but it was undertaken in expiation of "disgraceful" behavior, and not to atone for "sin." One individual felt, however, that kinshin was not enough. Since a member of his family had disgraced his household, he could no longer be a fitting leader; he had lost his moral force over others:

(M, age 39, problem situation 4) I think he was a rather high-placed person. Probably he stood above others in public position. If such a thing occurs within a family, an attitude of kinship is probably expressed. If one's house produces such an individual, one loses any qualifications for leading others by his own example.

The women's reactions were generally more passive. They worried about the shame they would feel, and suggested the necessity to avoid people, or even to leave home. One said that a woman might fall ill as a result of being disgraced by a family member. (As was indicated elsewhere, illness is sometimes unconsciously used as a punishment of others, or as an excuse to avoid a hopeless situation or one in which a person fears future failure.)

Some respondents were more concerned with admonishing the offending family member. But even among this group, three men also showed concern with public appearances, while only one man was worried about the internal harmony of the family. One of the two women who would directly admonish the offender was anxious to reform him; the other concentrated on the personal harm the offender's behavior had caused her.

Since the Niiike family tends to accept responsibility for the behavior of its members and to show little sympathy toward the errant member, the offending individual faces not only community sanctions, but also the possibility of severe rejection by his own family. The existence of these two complementary sanctions probably helps to explain the general lawfulness of the Japanese, not only in Japan, but even among those who have emigrated to America (where their delinquency rates are very low).

The difference between the Japanese attitude and that of an Italian family, for instance, where family ties are often held above the law, is striking.

EXTERNAL SANCTIONS OF AUTHORITY. By their nature, the TAT cards used brought out little data on attitude toward possible external authority. There is some indirect evidence in the material to indicate that the teacher is a figure of authority in village life, but priests,

TABLE II-6

DISTRIBUTION OF RESPONSES TO PROBLEM SITUATION TEST ITEM 4

A man who came from an honorable family has been respected by his neighbors. But one of his family did a dishonorable thing so that he is not able to show his face in public. (The same question for men and women). What would he (or she) do?

Age codes:	18+(a)	25+(y)	35+(m)	50+(o)	65+(s)	Men (total)	Women (total)
Men	3	3	4	3	1	14	
Women	5	2	5	2	2		16

I—Not change behavior

1. continue usual activity because people will gradually change their opinions as a result of his efforts

2. not leave home and not do anything, because his actual neighbors are not the ones who speak ill of the offender — 1(s) | 1(a)

II—Admonish or apologize (emphasis on correction of difficulty)

A. Publicly apologize — 8 | 2

  1. kinshin and make efforts to recover the previous state of affairs, because it is duty for him who is in the position of leader to do so — 1(a)

  2. kinshin and retire from public affairs. He can't any longer be respected in a position of leadership — 1(m)

B. Publicly apologize and admonish the family member

  1. because it is publicly inexcusable — 2(m-o)

  2. because it is reasonable — 1(m)

C. Admonish (constructively or aggressively) the offending member and console the family

  1. in order to restore peace to the family — 1(y)

  2. because the other member harmed him — 1(y)

D. Caution the offending person not to do it again		
1. because he must not repeat it		1(y)
E. Give up shameful behavior because he did something shameful in appearance [mistakes behavior as his own]	1(o)	
F. Work as hard as possible	1(y)	
III—Escape and avoid (emphasis on dire results)	3	6
A. Avoid meeting people and give up some usual activities		
1. because he is afraid of punishment from the neighbors	1(a)	2(y-m)
2. because he is ashamed to meet people	2(m-o)	2(m-o)
B. Leave home		
1. because he is ashamed to show his face		1(m)
C. Get ill		
1. because he is ashamed to meet people		1(s)
D. Marry a person who is lower in status		
1. because she abandons a hope of marriage with a person who is of good birth		
IV—React emotionally		6
1. hate the family member, because when she marries she must marry a person who is lower in status		1(m)
2. be ashamed and sad, because she is ashamed to show her face		3(a-m-o)
3. be distressed		1(s)
4. be ashamed to show her face to the family because she was severely scolded [mistakes behavior as her own]		1(a)
V—Investigate		
1. for his brother		1(a)
VI—No response	1(y)	1(a)

doctors, and other figures never appear in such a role. The teacher sometimes appears (especially in the stories by younger women) as a counselor in times of stress. As a teacher, he is a secondary father figure, whose advice is respected by the community. The teacher was also seen, in general, as an unquestioned authority on problems of child-rearing.

Both men and women seemed to accept without question or disapproval the advice or admonition of teachers on the subject of child behavior. In response to one problem situation (Appendix A, item 27), men showed an attitude of passive noninterference in a situation where a child's behavior met with disapproval from the teacher; they expressed the feeling that it was the mother's duty to correct the child. Women felt more need to respond personally to rectify the child's behavior.

Stories of antisocial actions by older children outside the home were most commonly told by younger men and, to a lesser extent, by women under twenty-four. Six of these TAT stories were about stealing, two about murder, and others about mixed or unspecified crimes. Punishment or reform was mentioned in all but three of the stories. Such results are in striking contrast to the data from records of similar TAT pictures with American lower-class and certain American Indian samples. These latter groups showed a much higher incidence of concern with crime and with avoidance of punishment through some sort of escape. Crime enters the fantasies of young people in Niiike more often than it does those of older individuals, but even the fantasies of the young don't allow crime to go unpunished.

There was some tendency in the young people to see rebellious or antisocial behavior in story characters of the opposite sex; young girls tended to depict bad behavior in boys, and vice versa. Women told more stories of rebellion by sons than did men. Some men gave stories of a girl who leaves home and falls into prostitution in the city:

(W, age 14, card M3M) This boy quarreled with his parents. He runs away from home, but commits suicide after all.

(M, age 27, card J3F) This girl was scolded by her parents. She ran away from home—sexual promiscuity—she cannot go back home. She finally kills herself to apologize to her parents.

When the sex of the parent against whom the child rebelled was specified (in forty-three of fifty-two stories) it was the mother who was defied. In many stories of rebellion no outcome was indicated. In other stories, especially those told by women, there was an eventual submission to the wishes of parents. In only about one-fifth of the stories was a child successful in his opposition to parental wishes, and most of these stories of successful rebellion dealt with the reconciliation of parents to a marriage choice.

Stories of misfortune following an act of rebellion were told by one-fifth of the men and by a few women. In such stories punishment for rebellion often seemed to come as a stroke of fate (such as the death of parents or the beloved), and was less often caused by a human agent. Except in some moralistic stories, the ill fate following rebellion was not consciously defined as a punishment; this sequence of association was unconscious:

(W, age 13, card J7M) A father died and the son walked out of home because his mother repeatedly told him to become like his father. The mother lived a lonely existence. When she finds her son again, she dies. The son becomes a hard-working man.

(M, age 39, card J6F) A daughter whose mother is dead, is listening to her father urging her to be married to a certain person. She refuses, having her own choice—her father agrees finally. After her marriage she takes good care of her father, but her father dies.

In stories that depict no outcome, or a successful outcome, of rebellion, there was often an emphasis on severe scolding or admonition by the parent. Such a story was used unconsciously to depict the ineffective or negative results of oversevere scolding or punishment.

THE NEGATIVE SANCTIONS OF CONSCIENCE (OBLIGATION AND RESPONSIBILITIES). Errant behavior called forth conscience more often than external authority as a sanction. In the stories concerning bad behavior (twenty-five by men and eleven by women), many modes were employed to resolve the internal pressures of conscience. In eleven of the men's stories and in two of the women's, these feelings were finally resolved by reform of one's behavior and by expiatory hard work. In five stories by men and one by a woman, suicide was taken as a way out. Three stories by men and three by women suggested a public apology or a confession to police. The situation was left unresolved, and the individual continued to feel regret or sadness in six other stories. These stories reemphasized the pragmatic orientation of Niiike men; they tended to solve the problem positively by reform rather than to dwell passively on guilt. In American stories there tends to be more concern with conscious guilt or with other feelings, such as regret, and less emphasis on eventual reform.

Some stories presented suicide as the only solution. This was true in two stories of failure in studies due to neglect, in two stories of sexual promiscuity of women, in a story of marriage failure followed by crime, and in a story of murder. In response to items in different categories, other suicide stories were told with a variety of reasons given for the suicide.

The results suggest that women may experience guilt for sexual behavior not because it is sinful per se, but because parents are hurt by it. In a few stories told by men about girls who went to the city and fell into a life of prostitution, the outcome was regret, even suicide; such a girl could not return home, and there was no way out of her predicament.

Certain stories of marriage failure were categorized as "bad behavior" stories because in each of five such stories the teller specifically stated that the marriage was a love match (implying its unsanctioned nature). In addition to one story of suicide as a result of the failure of a love marriage, there were stories of regret (one story) and divorce (three stories), and one melodramatic story of a man who so regretted having opposed parental wishes that he murdered his wife and gave himself over to the police. After serving time in jail, he started a new life:

(W, age 22, card J13) He got married with a woman for love in spite of opposition by his parents. When they were first married, they lived happily. But recently he reflects on his marriage and the manner in which he pushed his way through his parents' opposition—and the present wife—he wishes his present wife would not exist—he attempts to push away the feeling of blame within his breast. One night on the way home he buys some insect poison and gives it to his wife to drink and she dies. What he has done weighs on his mind. He gives himself up to the police. He reflects on how wicked he has been in the past. He completes his prison term and faces the future with serious intent.

This story brings out a feeling of guilt for having attempted a love marriage. Such a marriage is psychologically forbidden fruit to many Japanese, and tasting it brings punishment upon the transgressor like that following extramarital sexual experiences in the fantasies of some more puritanical Westerners.

There were no stories by Niiike respondents revealing guilt in men for extramarital sexual activities; this is in sharp contrast to the relative prevalence of such stories told by American groups in response to similar TAT pictures. In the stories of some Japanese men there was guilt, not for sexuality itself, but for the fact that a lack of self-control could lead to a love marriage:

(M, age 35, card J13) Well, this man and woman married for love. The woman was a café waitress and married the man for love. But they have not lived happily, so the man repents the marriage very much. Well, this man used to be a very good man, but he was seduced by the waitress and lost his self-control and at last he had a sexual relationship with her. Afterward [after they marry] he becomes afraid, and he has to think over their [impulsive] marriage. If their married life has any future at all—I hope they will maintain some better stability. But if this woman doesn't want to do so, he needs to think over their marriage, I suppose.

In certain of the stories of love marriage, regret seemed to stem not only from a sense of guilt for having acted contrary to filial obligations under the influence of sexual attraction and because of other considerations, but also from a sense of chagrin over having married an unsuitable woman. There was perhaps a projection of some of the man's guilt onto the woman; she must be somehow worthless, since she was sufficiently active to enter a love marriage, thus disregarding the rules of proper conduct and submissiveness to parental wishes required of the model Japanese woman. The projective material related to guilt is examined in greater detail in Chapters 4 and 5.

Turning Blame on Oneself Masochistically—Suffering

In many responses to TAT pictures a woman handled a stressful situation by turning the blame on herself. This self-blame was of a sort that can only be understood psychologically as masochistic; there are many examples in Japanese culture of relief from a stressful situation by the assumption of blame, even where the blame is not apparent. In TAT stories one finds themes of this nature related to a strong sense of ultimate responsibility that women assume for the behavior of men. In two of these stories a woman apologized for having quarreled with her husband. In two more a wife blamed herself for her husband's unfaithful behavior:

(W, age 23, card J4) Her husband comes back very late at night. She thinks it is because of the lack of her affection. She tries hard, and he reforms himself finally.

In another story, when a man who committed a crime was arrested and finally reformed, his sister (with no explanation given in the story) felt that she was somehow culpable:

(W, age 15, card J9) The elder brother did something wrong and is examined by the policeman. He will be taken to the police station, but he will return home, reforming himself. The younger sister is also thinking that she was wrong herself.

A few women construed certain problem situations to include a young woman who gets the blame.

In certain stories wifely devotion was expressed in extreme forms of self-immolation:

(W, age 17, card J13 [Gazes at the picture a long time.] Although this couple was married and have lived happily, the wife is not healthy. She was put to bed with a cold. Her husband took care of her and did not attend to his work at the company. On this day he thought she was somewhat better, and he went to work. When he came home that night, he found his wife dead.

From her diary lying there, he learned that she had felt sorry for her husband (having to take care of her) and had committed suicide by taking poison. He is now crying with grief. Having lost his wife he continued to work very hard and . . . he led a lonely life by himself without ever forgetting his dead wife.

As in the stories in which a parent dies, subsequent devotion to duty was emphasized here. This story recalls many sentimental novels written around the theme of noble self-sacrifice on the part of the sick wife who commits suicide to relieve her husband of the burden of her care. It is further implied that her motive was to inspire him to devote himself completely to his work; how could a man, without experiencing the most severe guilt, ever be able to treat his work lightly, after his wife had so sacrificed herself? (The feeling of this story recalls stories of a mother's sacrificial behavior, even unto death, as a source of guilt in her children.) From a Western standpoint such fantasies may seem to be excessively masochistic, but to a Japanese they are very moving, since they are supposed to reflect the degree of devotion of a wife to her husband and his purposes. Tears are brought forth in the older members of a Kabuki audience when such a story is presented in a dramatic form. The young Niiike girl who told this story perhaps romantically envisioned her future married role in such self-sacrificing terms.

General Sources of Worry

Niiike men and women told an approximately equal number of stories about a figure who was depicted as worried over some matter; but the nature of the anxieties differed according to the sex of the subject. Women saw possible illness as a chief source of worry, but they also inferred anxiety about the safe return of a loved one (usually a husband or a son), or they worried about some form of personal inadequacy. Men showed no strongly dominant pattern in their stories; worry over personal inadequacy or illness was only slightly more common than other anxieties they depicted.

ILLNESS AND DEATH. A dominant concern of the women of Niiike is the possible ill health or death of a family member. About one-fifth of all the stories told by women in response to TAT pictures included a character who was grieving or worrying about the illness or death of someone close to him, or who was ill or dead himself. Men gave only about half as many such stories, and the endings of their stories involving illness were far more optimistic. Women tended to give no outcome in such stories or else to see eventual death, exhibiting in many instances the masochistic quality already mentioned. Some of the stories told by men about illness or surgical operations revealed a less pronounced masochistic quality.

The distribution of TAT stories indicates that whereas women see the mother-son relationship in the emotional context of problems of accomplishment or rebellion, they put the mother-daughter relationship much more into the context of problems of physical care and death. The family member most often described as ill by women was a mother or a daughter, and less often a father or a husband. Men most often thought that a dying figure must be a wife. Men over fifty seemed especially concerned with the possible loss of the care and attention of a beloved wife.

No specific illness was singled out as a major source of anxiety. There were, however, in the stories of younger women, a number of references to vomiting or stomach upset, suggesting the possibility of unconscious concern over sexuality and pregnancy. There were also four references to tooth trouble, a most unusual specification never encountered in American TAT stories. The interpretation of these stories of death and illness is expanded upon in Chapter 4.

ACCIDENT. Stories of accidental death or injury were told more often by men than by women, and in such stories the most common victim was the husband or the eldest son. These responses are probably related to the fact that men are naturally more prone to hazards than are women, but they may also involve anxiety over the threat to family security that such a mishap would entail. Almost totally absent from the preoccupations of the villagers was any evident concern over the dislocations or sorrows caused by World War II. In all the material, there was but one story of a war death, one story of a family impoverished by war, and two indirect mentions of war casualties. In the stories of younger people, contemporary catastrophes such as the sinking of a ferry and the radiation sickness of the fishermen on "The Lucky Dragon" were used for dramatic effect in stories of accidents.

MENTAL ABNORMALITY. A small number of stories manifested concern over the kind of mental abnormalities that lead to strong affective display. Insanity or neurotic behavior in women was mentioned in eight stories. When specified, these abnormalities were attributed to the loss of a loved one or to the unfaithfulness of a husband. (Similarly, one encounters in traditional Nō plays the figure of a woman driven insane by jealousy or sorrow.) In one other story pertaining to mental abnormality, a "weak-minded boy" dreamed about his mother being pierced by a dagger; in another, a sister killed her "idiot" brother to spare him the torment of his cruel stepmother; and in a third, a mother devoted herself to trying to improve her "unintelligent" daughter.

FINANCIAL CONCERNS WITHIN THE FAMILY. The TAT pictures produced only a small number of stories concerning financial difficulty, in contrast to numerous instances of such stories reported for other cultures. These stories were most commonly told by people from eighteen to thirty-five and most frequently by men. A number of them dealt with the difficulty of a family in the event of the father's death. In constructing such stories, young men showed their concern with possible financial responsibility resulting from such an eventuality.

The projective test material indirectly affirms the fact that patterns of inheritance are relatively fixed in Japan. Inheritance is not seen as a source of difficulty among family members. Except in two stories, one in which a mother disinherited a profligate son and another in which two brothers quarreled over succession to property, the subject did not appear.

Another type of story dealing with economic matters pertained to the payment of taxes and the use of family connections to mediate tax reductions. A few stories suggest that financial success may be seen as an aggressive act of revenge for insult or injury in a family or love relationship.

In a large proportion of such stories, financial difficulties were connected with obligations to more or less distant relatives. Certain individuals in Japan readily take advantage of such feelings of obligation and impose upon a more responsible relative who feels unable to refuse. A lender cannot ask for proof of a transaction, such as a written I.O.U., from a family member because to do so would insult the relative by casting doubt on his integrity and would make it a business relationship rather than a purely family matter. This allows an unscrupulous person to borrow freely from relatives without concern about repayment. Such a person can also claim to have lent money to a dead person, and the new family head or the widow may be compelled to preserve the dead man's honor by paying, even without actual proof of the existence of the debt. In one story, after a father's death, the widowed mother was plagued by an uncle whose claims against the dead man proved to be untrue:

(W, age 17, card J11) When a boy has come back home from high-school . . . his mother and a guest are talking, so he is eavesdropping. And . . . the guest is his uncle. While his father was alive, the uncle pretended to be kind, but since his father died he changed his attitude suddenly and begins to harass the boy's mother, saying that she has owed some money to his uncle since before his father died. He understands this by hearing it through the wall. Having heard this story he told it to his class teacher to make sure whether the debt [in his uncle's story] is true or not. The teacher determined the story was not true, and the uncle was put on trial and punished, and the boy could then live peacefully without any interference.

Many stories of money were told in a manner suggesting that financial matters are something secret or private in Japan. The extent to which borrowing actually occurs in Niiike cannot be readily determined; it is a part of the secret life of the community. Sometimes in stories about money there was a suggestion that the widowed mother was sexually involved, indicating that economic matters, like sexual relations, are to be kept from the curiosity of innocent children. In one story an element of jealousy about one's mother was directly expressed:

(M, age 25, card J11) A nephew comes to his aunt to ask for money to get out of his business failure. Her child listens to them, wishing that the nephew would go away. His mother must be going out with the nephew as she is in pretty clothes. She will come home and console her child with presents.

Money is a "touchy" matter between parents and sons in Japan; usually it is not given very readily to children, and when it is freely given, it is a mark of an exceptionally close relationship. In responses to TAT cards, when a mother rejected an older son's request it involved either money or the selection of a marriage partner.

SUMMARY

Japan is changing. Rural Japan is aware of the new attitudes and modes of living already established in the cities. Some individuals leave the farms to take up urban life, but those who remain in the villages are able to ward off the potentially disruptive influences of new values by maintaining their firm identity with traditional values. These values, when realized in behavior, become sources of deep personal satisfaction and lend meaning to the lives of the villagers.

In Niiike, and probably in other rural communities, certain accommodations and shifts in emphasis from traditional ways of thinking can be perceived. There are some expressions of uneasiness about the new generation: Will the younger men maintain their attitude of respect for parental figures in the face of individualistic propensities? Will the younger generation lose interest in a life of virtuous hard work and forget its obligations?

In general, at the time of this research, however, the "cup of custom" remained unbroken. The village had assimilated changes in laws of succession and in the legal position of women without a disruption of community life. Older women maintained traditional value patterns with great intensity. Some of the young unmarried girls gave evidence of internal conflict about submission to their prescribed roles as adult women in a farming community, but they could not voice their conflict in any articulate fashion. They were willing to depend on their elders for guidance.

The men of Niiike showed a great respect for individual initiative
and self-will. This is in part incompatible with traditional values of
individual subordination to family goals, and the men did express
certain attitudes that conflict with what is supposed to be the traditional system. Occupational succession, for instance, was not considered
a necessity; the value of doing what one can do best was recognized,
and the young people sought education, even at the expense of opposition to parents.

To a certain extent, the results presented here suggest that the continuity of tradition and values in Niiike is maintained not merely by
inculcated formal attitudes concerning lineage, but also by the force
of underlying patterns of affection for parents. When a Japanese speaks
of *on*, he refers to a deep-seated feeling within himself for his parents,
which is the basis of his moral feelings toward all others. These feelings are related to the Japanese sense of social purpose and success.
The emphasis on effort and perseverance, and the manner in which
this is reflected in hard work, suggest a puritanlike ethic for Niiike as
a whole. As an aspect of the rapid industrialization of Japan, this Japanese ethic recalls the role of the Protestant ethic in the industrialization
of Europe. In Niiike one must toil diligently, but not for God's salvation; success in hard work proves that one is dutiful toward parents
and loves them. There is no transmutation of feelings toward one's
parents into a personal relationship with a transcendental deity. In
fact, there is little concern with such a deity, but there is instead a
respectful idealization of a father image, and a feeling of loving devotion to a mother who deserves eternal gratitude. Part II of this
volume examines these attitudes in broader perspective.

Although it is often stated that the Japanese are without a sense
of "sin" or "guilt," our evidence suggests that this is not so. What
might be called Japanese "puritanism" does not view bodily functions
as evil; one's impulses are good if they are directed properly and with
control. But although there is not a single expression of guilt over
sexual transgressions per se, some projective test stories displayed guilt
over the loss of control that leads to an unsanctioned love marriage,
countering one's life purposes as prescribed by one's parents. Generally,
a person in Niiike feels guilt for rebellion against his parents and not
for transgressions against a code of behavior sanctioned by a supernatural deity or by a religious code. One works hard, not in order to
stay in a state of grace or to do penance, but to repay one's parents in
gratitude or to expiate their sacrifice in honest toil. Chapter 5 develops
these interpretations further as reflecting central features of the cultural psychology of the Japanese.

Within the traditional Japanese value system, the worst possible
eventuality is "excommunication" from one's house and community.

There seem to be psychological analogies between *ie* and Church, with resulting similarities between certain of the social values and personal attitudes of the inhabitants of Niiike and those of Americans. Japanese interest in self-motivated achievement, at least, strikes a familiar chord, even if the motivational source in Japanese rural family and community life would at first glance seem an unlikely origin for what we have come to define as values prevailing in the American middle class.

A cultural-historical analysis of rural groups would be concerned with changes in attitudes and practices in specific rural areas consequent upon changes in centers of social and political dominance. In many rural communities in Japan in recent times one noted, for example, the permeation of Confucianist ethics concerning the nature of the family, which influenced marriage practices and helped define what is "proper" in marriage among rural villagers. These values are now being modified by changes in modern postwar Japan. Processes of urbanization and industrialization along lines found in Western societies are very much in evidence on the modern urban Japanese scene. Evidence of these influences, backed by recent postwar changes in legal sanctions, is not lacking in rural villages as well.

Approached psychologically, the acculturative processes involved show that the rate of change in attitudes differs from the change in overt behavior. Some previously deeply internalized values about marriage and family obligation may be consciously disavowed, but they remain as inner constraints, preventing behavioral implementation of newer values by many young people who would like to adopt a different way of life. To demonstrate the working of these inner psychological processes is not, however, to dispute the determinant influences of overall cultural and economic forces on acculturation generally.

Opinion survey methods based on direct questioning and tabulation of the proportion of individuals affirming one idea or another are insufficient by themselves for gaining insight on the inner integration of values within the individual. Specifically, this chapter has attempted to demonstrate on a small scale the efficacy of using psychological test data either independently or as part of a survey. By utilizing psychological tests that reveal attitudes indirectly as well as directly, we have shown an apparent difference between consciously stimulated attitudes and attitudes appearing indirectly in the context of spontaneous stories depicting interaction in primary relationships. The PST data are more in line with the results of direct opinion survey results reported in Chapter 1 than are the less self-conscious expressions of attitudes in the context of TAT stories.

In Niiike, internalized sanctions that function in relation to marriage choice are inferentially more closely related to earlier dominant cultural attitudes than to newer consciously accepted values. This phenomenon can be considered a manifestation of psychological lag. A concept of psychological lag in the persistence of internalized sanctions is essential to understanding the effects of culture and personality on attitude change in any acculturation process. The concept may help explain the nature of inner discord of an individual in whom the older and newer attitudes are both present without as yet being resolved. Santayana, in *The Last Puritan,* brought out that the American culture of his time, although it seemingly had left the Puritan tradition behind, still manifested that tradition in a lurking residue of emotional constraint among many individuals. The premise that life's purpose is the pursuit of happiness seems sometimes to run into inner restraints that help to explain America's proneness toward a work ethic. Many Americans are not so free to pursue happiness as they would like to believe. The same sort of lag is found in Japanese attitudes toward family life. In many Japanese there is an avowed value in being able to be "free" in a love relationship, but there is also a curious inability to implement this value in a successful way behaviorally. In one sense, this dilemma concerning the potential tragedy of loving is not new in Japanese culture. Love romances, usually ending unhappily, have for generations been enormously popular in Japan. Ruth Benedict made this point when she wrote that the Japanese had made things extraordinarily difficult for themselves by idealizing love matches in fiction but forbidding them in reality. What is different now, however, is that the government, and to a certain extent the society generally, is avowedly committed to a "new Japan"—a Japan relating herself to Western traditions of equality and individual self-determination.

The psychological test data presented in this chapter only hint at some of the complexities of the relationship between the internalization of older standards and the avowal of new ones. I believe, however, that I have shown in a rural Japanese village some disparity between conscious and less conscious attitudes toward changing marriage patterns.

This chapter does not exhaust the possible topics related to social values or interpersonal relationships, but I believe I have been able to present, by means of the instruments used, a quantitative as well as qualitative picture of how the people of Niiike thought and felt in 1954. For me the challenge was to develop anthropological methods superior to the simple gathering of impressions from selected informants. By using projective methods, in addition to necessary field work, it is possible to let the subjects speak for themselves and express their views without undue structuring. Quantitatively, one can assess the relative prevalence of specific social attitudes and determine how they are interrelated by the people holding them. Methods such as those used in the study also permit one to test the relative strength of social attitudes when they become opposed to one another in conflict situations.

In retrospect now in 1972, the report adequately represents the social relationships of Niiike twenty years ago. Modern technology has changed the basic farming patterns in use in Niiike at the time of the study. Other factors are increasingly at work to bring about change. It would be interesting, therefore, to know how much the attitudes revealed in this report have further shifted with time. In Niiike, as elsewhere, the majority of villagers are now working in factories. How this industrialization of the countryside finds reflection in a changing view of social life can only be ascertained by an intensive restudy employing the same means of inquiry demonstrated in the present chapter.

Chapter III

Value Attitudes Toward
Role Behavior of Women
in Two Japanese Villages

with HIROSHI WAGATSUMA

Chapter 2 has presented our general results with material from Niiike village. In this chapter[1] we more specifically compare the attitudes in Niiike about women's social role with comparable data obtained from a fishing village, Sakunoshima, where the social status of the entire village has been traditionally lower than that accorded fairly well-to-do farmers such as those of Niiike. The overall results on the psychological tests were in general strikingly similar, yet we could find consistent differences in attitudes concerning the role behavior and social attitudes expected of women within the primary family. Our original effort was to determine whether we could demonstrate the sensitivity of our projective tests to the status differences of women obtaining in these two rural communities located in what is described generally by Japanese social scientists as "Southwestern" Japan.

HISTORICAL DIVERSITY IN FAMILY RELATIONSHIPS
IN RURAL JAPAN

The accumulation of intensive data on Japanese rural culture has revealed many regional differences in Japanese values and attitudes. Scholars concerned with Japanese culture are now more aware than

---

[1] Chapter 3 is slightly modified from the article of the same title by DeVos and Wagatsuma appearing originally in *The American Anthropologist* (1961).

they once were that they must distinguish between what is broadly characteristic of the society as a whole and what is specific to smaller segments. The full range of variation, however, is still far from clear.

Japanese scholars[2] characterize premodern rural social organization as having two principal forms: a Northeastern pattern emphasizing kinship and pseudo-kinship relations,[3] and a Southwestern pattern giving a greater role to communal organizations not based on kinship. Although attitudes and values concerning the social position of women varied greatly within the Northeastern pattern, they emphasized a relatively low position for females within a hierarchically organized patriarchal family structure.[4] In the Southwestern area, the status of women was considered to be somewhat higher; there was a greater tendency toward bilateral kinship, and familial and other relationships were less strongly hierarchical. Within the range of these broad regional variations, anthropologists have further described many local differences in status and social values related to specific occupational groups.[5]

Throughout Japan, as in the southwest areas we investigated, it is recognized that the relative status of women tended to be higher in

[2] See Ariga, *A Study of Social Organization in Japanese Farming Villages* (1940, in Japanese), *Study of History of Marriage in Japan* (1948, in Japanese), and "Contemporary Japanese Family in Transition" (1955); Ariga, Nakano, and Morioka, "The Japanese Family," *Transactions of the Second World Congress of Sociology* (1954); Fukutake, *Social Character of Japanese Farming Villages* (1949, in Japanese), and *Analysis of Social Structure of Japanese Farming Villages* (1954, in Japanese); Izumi and Gamo, "Regional Differences in Japanese Society" (1952, in Japanese); Kawashima, *Familial Structure of Japanese Society* (1948, in Japanese); Ogyu, "Local Distribution of Selected Culture Elements in Japan and the Structural Relationships of Their Lineage" (1957, in Japanese); Omachi, "History of Japanese Marriage Customs" (1937, in Japanese); Okada, "Kinship Organization in Japan," *Journal of Educational Sociology* (1952, in Japanese).

[3] Befu and Norbeck, "Japanese Usage of Terms of Relationships" (1958).

[4] Large sections of northeastern Japan were populated in recorded history by forcing out the Ainu. Warriors were the dominant group; a basic agricultural tradition did not predate the ascendancy of the feudal warrior tradition with its kinship structure. In contrast, the southwest region had been agricultural from before the dawn of recorded history. Interaction among farmers using large irrigation systems encouraged modes of cooperation not limited solely to considerations of kinship. The pattern of suppressing competition discussed in Chapter 1 is much in evidence in agricultural villages in the Inland Sea area.

[5] Beardsley, "The Household in the Status System of Japanese Villages" (1951); Cornell, "Matsunagi—a Japanese Mountain Community" (1956); Donoghue, "An Eta Community in Japan: The Social Persistence of Outcaste Groups" (1957); Hulse, "Status and Functions as Factors in the Structure of Organizations Among the Japanese" (1947); Ishino, "The Oyabun-Kobun: A Japanese Ritual Kinship Institution" (1952); Nagai and Bennett, "A Summary and Analysis of the Familial Structure of Japanese Society by Takeyoshi Kawashima" (1953); R. Smith, "Kurusu—A Japanese Agricultural Community" (1956).

fishing villages than in farming villages. It is obvious that socioeconomic factors operated to differentiate fishing communities from
others. The occupations of men and women in fishing communities
were such that the wife tended to assume day-by-day authority in the
household. Her relationship to her own parents was better maintained,
and unilateral patrilinial ties did not tend to develop as strongly as
they did in farming communities. The relative poverty and isolation of
fisherfolk did not allow them to give much heed to possibilities of
bettering their social status by emulating the samurai-Confucian patterns governing the relationship of the sexes. Communities therefore
historically differed in the degree to which they were influenced by
the Confucian values of the socially superior samurai class. In some
communities, for example, arranged marriages did not appear until
the turn of the century. Sexual behavior was freer, and the test of the
desirability of a woman for marriage was her fertility not her virginity.
In some villages today the grandparents and grandchildren have attitudes toward sexual behavior more similar to those of one another
than to those held by their thirty-five- to fifty-year-old parents. The
"modern" changes occurring in some lower-status villages are in actuality a reversion to older, looser patterns. Women in fishing villages,
like women we have studied subsequently in a working-class area of
Tokyo,[6] show very little evidence of the deferential behavior expected
of women emulating the samurai tradition, such as the women of
Niiike in 1954.

The "democratization" of Japan with modernization in the Meiji
period after 1868 in effect lowered the relative status of women in much
of the rural areas including the Southwestern area where we did our
fieldwork. For the first time the ordinary farmers and fisherfolk were
to be included in the army, go to school, and so forth. They were also
to be taught proper social behavior which emphasized the relative
status of the head of the family and all males vis-à-vis women. This
teaching seemingly had less effect on the lower-status fisherfolk than
on the better placed farmers, who in a sense could more readily aspire
to higher status mobility.

After being temporarily infatuated by Western thought, the leaders
of the new state redirected Japanese governmental ideology back toward the traditional samurai values as standards of conduct for the
nation as a whole. These values, including the assignment of women
to a social position much inferior to that of males, became an integral
part of the moral education imparted to all rural and urban commoners through the newly established compulsory education system.
The samurai values also served as a foundation for the new Japanese

---

[6] DeVos and Wagatsuma, see especially Chapter 11, "The Arakawa Families Social
Status Considerations," in *Heritage of Endurance* (to be published).

civil code. Rural Japan had previously had little direct contact with government except through the local feudal lords. With increased communication, the rural areas were permeated with new ideas. Rural modes of marriage selection were altered by samurai ideas as to what was proper and fitting. The arranged marriages characteristic of the samurai, not previously practiced in many villages, were widely adopted.[7] As the tempo of communication increased, long-established local marriage practices tended to disappear.

Despite government pressure at the turn of the century, the industrialized urban areas began to show the effect of increasing contact with Western ideas of individualism. One can safely say, however, that for most individuals, attitudes toward family relationships did not change radically or abruptly. It was not until after World War II that any number of Japanese showed clearly observable evidence of radical changes in their concept of the family.

Some changes in the relation between the sexes can now (1969) be observed in both urban and rural areas. But the rural life we observed in 1954 tended to remain more conservative than urban life because the individuals most seeking change were migrating to the urban centers. At this time the more conservative elements remained in their rural homes, and the rural communities were thus able to maintain more traditional forms of economic and social stability. What we find in our research results obtained in 1954 is essentially village attitudes that are still traditional. The differences in Niiike and Sakunoshima are in their traditions and do not reflect differences in postwar change of attitudes.

The Communities Compared

Niiike as a representative farming community has already been briefly described. There are noticeable differences from Sakunoshima. The villagers of Sakunoshima were living on an island at the entrance of Mikawa Bay in Aichi Prefecture when we visited in 1954. The island consists of two hamlets; the eastern one, which we studied, has a population of 618 individuals in 138 households. From some time in the thirteenth century until the end of the Tokugawa period (1868), the island of Sakunoshima was on a central route of water transportation connecting Edo (Tokyo) in the east and Kyoto and Osaka in the west. The subsequent development of land transportation and the use of larger steamships diminished the usefulness of this small island as a stopping-off place. In 1954, the inhabitants of Sakunoshima were making a poor living by fishing or small-scale farming. Some of the younger individuals spent a number of years working on the mainland nearby

---

[7] Ariga, *A Study of Social Organization in Japanese Farming Villages* (1940, in Japanese).

or traveling as far as the Keihan district of Osaka, or to Kyoto and
Kobe, seeking menial work. The fields were small and inadequate for
raising rice. Only wheat, potatoes, and some vegetables were grown.
Self-sufficiency in food was impossible, and therefore fishing was in-
dispensable as a supplementary industry. About 68 percent of the total
households were engaged in 1954 in some form of fishing in addition
to farming. Earning a living usually required the combined efforts of
the whole family; the men worked on fishing boats or in the cities,
some of the younger women worked in nearby industries on the mainland, and the married women worked in the field and at home.

As observed in 1954, the two communities of Niiike and Sakunoshima differed considerably in how they viewed themselves in contact
with the world outside their immediate communities. The farming
community self-consciously traces its founding to samurai, and this
historical view of origin probably contributes heavily to coloring the
attitudes of the villagers. The fishing people have no such tradition
of alignment with a higher class nor social pretensions vis-à-vis others.
They maintain relationships with certain family members who at various times migrated to port cities such as Yokohama or Osaka, and these
ties are maintained bilaterally, with occasional visiting.

The attitudes expressed in the farming community of Niiike exemplify what has been said by Beardsley[8] and many others concerning
the centrality of the concept of the family or "household" (ie) as the
cornerstone of rural social life and the concept of clearly defined social
role found in the Japanese family.

In contrast, the fishing community studies on Sakunoshima showed
much less evidence of samurai-Confucian attitudes in family relationships. The social status of fishermen has always been low. Women do
not assume a significantly deferential role.[9] Relationships within the
village seemed more relaxed than in Niiike. There was evidence of
considerable drinking by some of the men, in contrast to the relative
absence of drinking in Niiike.

Analysis of TAT Materials: The Nature of the Sample

Differences in attitudes about social roles of women between the
inhabitants of Niiike and Sakunoshima appear throughout the projec-

---

[8] Beardsley, Hall, and Ward, *Village Japan* (1959).

[9] This picture presented by Sakunoshima in regard to the relationship of the sexes
is not dissimilar from that presented in detail by Edward Norbeck in his study of
a fishing village, *Takashima: A Japanese Fishing Community* (1954). It is to be noted
that Norbeck found arranged marriage to be a very recent custom, gaining ascendancy
in the last two decades with universal education in the schools. It became increasingly "improper" to have marriage initiated without the formalities of the go-
between working with the two "families" concerned. Older practices are still in the
memory of the elders in the village, however.

tive test material. We have selected for illustration four areas from the TAT that point up certain noteworthy differences: (1) attitudes toward an arranged marriage and a love marriage; (2) attitudes toward sexual relationships; (3) fantasies of self-assertion and the expression of violence in conflicts involving women; and (4) concern over conflict between the wife and her husband's mother.

The records we are considering in this report include 807 TAT stories from 80 individuals in Niiike and 385 stories to the same cards from 35 matched individuals from among those tested in Sakunoshima. In Niiike approximately two-thirds of the inhabitants were sampled. In Sakunoshima less than one-fifth of the population was sampled. We were successful, however, in seeing that age and sex distribution of the total village was proportionately represented.

ATTITUDES TOWARD A LOVE MARRIAGE VS. A FAMILY-INITIATED MARRIAGE

In attitude surveys, such as that conducted by Stoetzel,[10] a surprising number of young Japanese—close to 50 percent—state in answer to a direct question that marriage is an individual affair. This is true in both urban and rural areas. One would presume from such results that individually initiated marriages are on the increase. Steiner[11] quotes statistics from areas near Tokyo that support this supposition. However, as the previous chapter indicated, according to material from Niiike, there was a tendency to accept the *idea* of marriage for love in response to direct presentation of problem situation items requiring a direct answer, but the TAT test stories, given more spontaneously by the same villagers, did not tend to support such a positive acceptance of a love marriage. Rather, when subjects constructed stories of love marriage, they tended to view such marriages as ending in some form of failure. In the problem situation test responses, the emphasis was not on how the marriage subsequently turned out but on the "right" to enter into such a marriage on the part of individuals. This emphasis on individual rights has become part of the conscious value system—whether it can be emotionally implemented or not.

These rather negative attitudes in Niiike toward love marriage contrast with a more relaxed and freer attitude in Sakunoshima toward love and marriage as indicated by the ethnographic data as well as the projective instruments. Our TAT evidence substantiates the impressions gained informally by observations and interviews in both villages.

---

[10] Stoetzel, *Without the Chrysanthemum and the Sword* (1955).
[11] Steiner, "Postwar Changes in the Japanese Civil Code" (1950).

In our 807 TAT stories obtained from eighty individuals in Niiike, there were 42 explicit spontaneous references to the circumstances of marriage (see Table III-1). (None of the cards used necessarily suggests the theme of marriage per se.) Thirteen references were to some form of arranged or family-type marriage, and 24 references were to love marriage or to an individual-type marriage. Only 3 of the stories mentioning arranged marriage showed tensions existing between individuals, whereas in only 2 of the 24 stories mentioning a love marriage was there absence of tension. Most frequently (10 stories) a love marriage was depicted as ending in some form of failure.

TABLE III-1

EXPRESSION OF TENSION IN TAT STORIES IN WHICH THE CIRCUMSTANCES
OF MARRIAGE ARE EXPLICITLY MENTIONED

	Niiike			Sakunoshima		
	M	F	Totals	M	F	Totals
Total respondents	36	44	80	17	18	35
Total stories			807			385
Stories giving circumstances						
of marriage	22	20	42*	7	12	19*
Arranged marriage—totals	3	10	13	2	7	9
No tension	3	6	9†	1	4	5
Tension	0	3	3†	1	3	4
Indefinite	0	1	1	0	0	0
Love marriage—totals	15	9	24	4	5	9
No tension	1	1	2†	0	4	4
Tension—totals	14	8	22†	4	1	5
Eventual conformity to						
family pressure	2	0	2	1	0	1
Conflict without outcome	4	3	7	2	0	2
Successful persistence	3	0	3	1	1	2
Eventual failure of marriage	5	5	10	0	0	0
Other	4	1	5	1	0	1

* It should be noted that the percentages of stories giving the circumstances of marriage are similar in both communities (5.2 percent for Niiike; 4.9 percent for Sakunoshima).

† Chi-square, Yates Cor. P > .001.

In Sakunoshima the evidence is of a different nature. Of 385 stories to the same cards obtained from thirty-five individuals, 18 made some mention of marriage, and there is no difference in distribution of tension stories and stories without tension with respect to love marriage or to arranged marriage. A qualitative examination of differences in the stories strongly suggests the nature of the differences in attitudes in the two villages.

For example, in Sakunoshima we find the following stories:

(W, age 19, card J4) They are dancing together. They will live together. They will marry, in the future they will get along all right.

(W, age 55, card J4) Two of them; they are looking at something. This is a well-drawn picture. They are looking at something passing by outside from the window. Looking at their lives (what are they thinking?). They are thinking of marrying and living happily, as the people they are looking at. Both of them are working laborers. They came to love each other. They will marry, live happily, work together, I suppose.

There is marked contrast between these stories and those given in Niiike. The following two stories were given to card J13 in Niiike:

(M, age 35–49, card J13) A young man regrets his love marriage with a maid of a bar who cajoled him. He regrets his marriage when he sees her slovenly attitude.

(M, age 35–49, card J13) A husband is addicted to drinking and comes back home to his slovenly wife, who is sleeping. He had married her as a result of a love relationship. They are divorced, they each go on to terrible ways—the woman becoming a procuress, the man contracting an infectious disease. He goes to prison and eventually kills himself on the railroad tracks.

These stories are extreme, indicating by their moralistic tone and graphic depiction the terrible end that can result from going contrary to an arranged marriage. No such stories appear in Sakunoshima; instead, positive stories of love marriage appear proportionately more frequently. It must be noted, however, that arranged marriages also are represented in the Sakunoshima stories. It cannot be said, therefore, that one village subscribes to arranged marriages as proper and the other to love marriages; but the residents of the fishing village place less emphasis on arranged marriage and are more optimistic as to the outcome of love marriages. Both villages show the presence of traditional Japanese core values about arranged marriage.

COMPARISON OF GENERAL ATTITUDES TOWARD SEXUAL RELATIONSHIPS IN NIIIKE AND SAKUNOSHIMA

There are numerous stories from both villages in which the principal concern is some form of heterosexual relationship. These stories again demonstrate consistent differences between the two villages in viewing problems in heterosexual love relationships. There are thirty-one stories in Niiike depicting nonmarital love relationships between young individuals. Fourteen of these stories involve conflict between a child and a parent, most of them with no resolution (see Table III-2).

(M, age 25–34, card J6M) A mother scolds her son on account of his indulgence in female company. The son is antagonistic toward his mother.
(W, age 12–17, card J18) A parent and son quarrel over son's love affair and the parent strangles the son to death.
(W, age 34–50, card J9) A son was scolded by his father about his love affair. Finally he will leave home.

There are no comparable stories in the Sakunoshima sample. There are seventeen stories in Niiike of various other tensions in a love relationship, in twelve of which a woman is rejected by her lover in one way or another. Only one story of this kind appears in Sakunoshima. The remaining stories in Niiike depict either violence of a man toward a woman or a separation.

There is no notable difference between the two villages in the manner of depicting nonmarital triangular relationships, in which, characteristically, two men quarrel over a woman. The principal concerns in the stories from Sakunoshima are extramarital triangular affairs involving a husband (father), or transient sexual relationships of various kinds.

(Saku M, age 50–64, card J11) The mother looks sad over something. This is her son—I see the hat and the briefcase of her husband but she looks very sad—I guess she is sad because her husband's conduct is not good. The child is sorry for the mother and is worried too. They were happy in the past. They were well off and had a child, but now the husband's conduct is not good, and the wife is sad and the son is worried. If the husband reforms himself, the son and the wife will be happy.

In the Niiike sample, seduction is depicted as leading to an unhappy marriage and regret. In Sakunoshima, seduction or casual sexual contact is seen as leading to regret or to some personal demoralization of the individual concerned but not to marriage (Table III-3).

(Niiike M, age 25–34, card J13) This does not look like too good a place. This young man was seduced by a prostitute, a woman taking the initiative. They did bad play in such a place, I suppose. This young man had never done such a thing before, I think. From now on . . . he will be interested in such things and will become a delinquent . . . well, I think that's all that it is. The woman is urging him to sleep with her and he is at a loss, not knowing what to do, I guess. He becomes a delinquent and then reforms himself again. He will become a serious person again.

In all but two of the extramarital relationships depicted, one in each village, it is a man who goes to a mistress or has an affair, causing unhappiness at home. Characteristic throughout these stories in both

TABLE III-2

Heterosexual Relationships in Stories Given to Ten TAT Pictures in Sakunoshima and Niiike

	Niiike			Sakunoshima			Signifi-cance
	M	F	Totals	M	F	Totals	
Total stories given on 10 cards*	257	273	530	170	180	350	
Total stories on heterosexual relationships†	31	24	55	18	11	29	Not sig.
Percentage of such stories to total stories†			(10.4‡)			(7)	
Nonmarital love relationships (marriage not an outcome)							
Essentially involving parent-child-conflict	7	7	14	0	0	0	P < .001
Aggression-violence	2	1	3	0	1	1	
Separation	1	1	2	1	0	1	
Rejection of women	5	7	12	0	2	2	P < .01
Totals	15	16	31	1	3	4	P < .01
Nonmarital triangular							
Man—two women	1	0	1	1	1	2	
Two men—woman	8	5	13	3	2	5	
Totals	9	5	14	4	3	7	Not sig.
Extramarital triangular							
Husband's affair	4	2	6	7	3	10	
Wife's affair	1	0	1	0	1	1	
Totals	5	2	7	7	4	11	P < .05
Transient sex relationships leading to							
Regret or reform	1	1	2	4	0	4	
Demoralization or suicide	1	0	1	2	1	3	
Totals	2	1	3	6	1	7	P < .05

* The 10 cards are J2, M3M (J3F), J4, J6M, JM7M, J9, J11, J13, J18, J22.
† Excluding circumstances of marriage stories shown in Table III-1.
‡ Significant differences in proportion of stories on heterosexual relationships between Niiike and Sakunoshima.

TABLE III-3

COMPARISON OF PRINCIPAL THEMES IN NIIIKE AND SAKUNOSHIMA ON CARD J13

A. Distribution of Major Thematic Categories

	Niiike			Sakunoshima		
	M	F	Totals	M	F	Totals
Total responses	20	22	42	17	18	35
Main emphasis in the stories:						
Concern over death and illness						
Of wife	4	9	13	2	5	7
Of mother	1	5	6	2	3	5
Totals	5	14	19	4	8	12
Emphasis on aggression or violence						
Husband to wife	0	2	2	0	0	0
Man to woman	2	1	3	0	0	0
Totals	2	3	5	0	0	0
Sexual aggressiveness						
Man to woman	1	0	1	1	0	1
Woman to man	2	0	2	2	1	3
Totals	3	0	3	3	1	4
Marital quarrel and discord						
Wife dominant—total	0	1	1*	5	3	8*
Wife scolds	0	1	1	(2)	0	2
Wife ignores	0	1	1	(2)	0	2
Husband apologizes or reforms behavior					1	1
Husband defeated or helpless				1	2	3
Husband dominant—total	7	2	9*	1	1	2*
Husband scolds	1	0	1	0	0	0
Husband regrets marriage, considers divorce	2	0	2	0	0	0
Husband divorces	4	0	4	0	0	0
Wife apologizes or reforms	0	0	0	1	0	1
Mutual reconciliation	0	2	2	0	0	0
Totals	7	3	10	6	4	10
Other	3	2	5	4	5	9

B. Total Stories of Aggression, Discord, and Illness, Depicting Relative Activity or Passivity in the Relationship, by Protagonist

Man active	8	3	11	1	0	1
Woman passive or sick**	5	14	19**	5	8	13**
Man passive	2	0	2	3	4	7
Woman active**	2	1	3**	4	1	5**
Mutual	0	2	2	0	0	0
Other	3	2	5	4	5	9

* Fischer's Exact Test, P < .01.
** Chi-square, P < .05.

villages is a moralizing attitude of the teller about the consequences
of this sexual behavior on the future of the individual.

In summary, in spite of certain overall similarities, the differences
in the stories are sufficient to indicate marked differences in what is the
concern of the two villages toward sexual behavior. In Niiike the focus
is on the effects of going against the moral code requiring arranged
marriage and obedience to parental figures. Tension between parents
and children over sexual behavior is not a theme in Sakunoshima.
The villagers are more concerned with the potential evil outcome of
the infidelity of the father and of transiency and irresponsibility in
sex. These results are clearly in line with the other attitudinal differences in the two villages toward aspects of the Confucianistic ethical
code concerning marriage.

PERCEPTION OF WOMEN AS CAPABLE OF VIOLENCE OR AGGRESSION

The traditional Japanese ethical ideal is that women were,
under no condition, to express a violent or aggressive attitude toward
their husbands. However, under the stress of extreme circumstances,
violence could be turned toward the self in the form of suicide to
preserve one's honor, or toward one's children if the greater honor of
the family or some overriding obligation made it necessary. By examining in some detail two of the TAT cards calling forth stories of violence or aggression between individuals, one can readily document
differences between the two villages in the underlying attitudes toward a woman's capacity for aggression or violence. The two cards
most suited for this analysis are card J18, which depicts a female
figure readily interpreted as choking either another woman or a man,
and card J13, often interpreted, by the Japanese at least, as a situation
of quarreling or discord between husband and wife.

Situations of Violence on Card J18

Stories to card J18 involve either themes of violence, on the one
hand, or some form of affiliative concern, such as illness or the reunion with a beloved, on the other. The stories from Niiike emphasize
the mother's intensity of feeling about raising her son to become a
responsible adult in the traditional culture. Such feelings, although not
absent in Sakunoshima, are proportionately less frequently expressed
(Table III-4).

There is little difference between the total percentage of stories of
violence given to this card in the two villages (48 percent in Niiike to
46 percent in Sakunoshima), but in Niiike there are markedly more

TABLE III-4

STORIES ON TAT PICTURE J18 IN NIIIKE AND SAKUNOSHIMA

	Niiike			Sakunoshima			Signifi- cance*
	M	F	Totals	M	F	Totals	
Total	22	26	48	17	18	35	
Total stories of violence	14	9	23	6	10	16	Not sig.
Severe or violent chastisement of a child							
Mother or stepmother to son	4	5	9†	2	1	3	
Mother or stepmother to daughter	3	2	5†	2	3	5	
Mother or stepmother to child	2	1	3	0	1	1	
Totals	9	8	17	4	5	9	
Mercy killing	2	0	2	0	1	1	
Quarrel and aggression between adults							
Woman to woman	2	0	2	1	0	1	
Woman to man	0	1	1	0	0	0	
Wife to husband	0	0	0	1	2	3	
Man to man	1	0	1	0	0	0	
Man to woman	0	0	0	0	1	1	
Husband to wife	0	0	0	0	1	1	
Totals	3	1	4	2	4	6	Not sig.
Total stories of positive concerns	5	16	21	9	5	14	
Expression of affection							
Mother to son	2	0	2†	0	1	1	
Mother to daughter	0	2	2†	2	1	3	
Mother to child	2	3	5	2	1	3	
Totals	4	5	9	4	3	7	Not sig.
Concern over illness							
Mother to son	1	1	2†	0	1	1	
Mother to daughter	0	9	9†	2	1	3	
Mother to child	0	1	1	3	0	3	
Totals	1	11	12	5	2	7	Not sig.
Other	3	1	4	2	3	5	

* Significant difference of proportion of stories on J18 between Niiike and Sakunoshima.

† Differences in stories concerning chastisement of sons or positive concern in relation to daughters in Niiike. P < .05 (Fischer's Exact Test).

stories involving the chastisement of an errant son. Four stories given in response to J18 follow; the first two are from Niiike and the second two from Sakunoshima.

(M, age 12–17, card J18) A mother strangles to death her prodigal son and she will be imprisoned.

(M, age 18–24, card J18) A mother chastises severely her son who played a trick on a child next door.

(M, age 35–49, card J18) A mother scolded her son—the son always asked for money and played all the time. He did not want to work. She could not stand to see the attitude of her son any longer and chastised her son very severely. Though she did, the son did not change his mind. But, I think, he will reform himself later, perhaps when the mother gets sick or he loses his mother. He has no father. The father died when he was small.

(M, age 12–17, card J18) There was a parent and her child. The child became a delinquent and was doing bad things every day. The mother was told about her child by somebody and chastised her son very severely. The mother looked at her son's face and shed tears. She said, "Why do you like to make trouble around here?" The mother began chastising her son frequently.

From these examples it is clear that men see a woman capable of violence in disciplining her child. The chastisement is not depicted as the expression of an uncontrollable anger or of fury, but as arising from the deep sense of responsibility to society for the behavior of one's child. The bad behavior of a child, especially when it is directed against societal norms, may threaten the reputation of his parents or violate their sense of responsibility to society. In the traditional Confucian pattern, the parents and their children are emotionally tied together and are not altogether differentiated out of the psychological unity of the family. Therefore, what children do may have a direct emotional effect upon their parents. Parents may experience what their children do almost as if a part of their own ego were responsible. Accordingly, when their children's behavior is negative and threatens their own ego-ideal, they may react by chastisement, which may primarily express their resentment against the uncontrollable part of themselves. Parents may even want to kill their children, which actually means punishing themselves, in order to be faithful to their ego-ideal and to maintain their psychological security. (The stories of chastisement in Niiike have a more severe tone than those in Sakunoshima.) Parents expect their children's behavior to support the parental aspirations for their children's success and to brighten the reputation or honor of their parents and the lineage. Thus, all that is required of children may be phrased in terms of fulfillment of the parents' sense of duty and responsibility to their family and society. Parents may not know how to cope with a situation in which a child goes so against the expectations of the parents as to make them fail in their responsibility. One reaction would be to disown the child; the response in the extreme situation, in fantasy at least, would be to kill the child who has failed in his duty.

In the traditional pattern, parental pressure, expectation, or control, is exerted more strongly on a son than on a daughter because important social status and roles were usually limited to men and much more social responsibility was required of men. One may also point out that when children act against parental expectation, it is more often their mother who is exposed to a strong sense of failure. The mother, coming as an outsider into the family, has to demonstrate her capacity by being responsible for the correct upbringing of her children.

In Niiike an interesting contrast between the attitudes of mother toward daughter compared with those of mother toward son is to be noted throughout the TAT material. In responses to card J18, in stories of affection or concern over illness where the sex of the figure is explicitly noted, the mother is most often seen as concerned over the health or well-being of her daughter. This is true throughout the remainder of the Niiike TAT material. There are fewer stories of such affectionate concern over the health of a son.

Throughout the remainder of the Niiike TAT material, the mother-daughter relationship is almost invariably idealized as one in which the mother is lovingly concerned with the health and well-being of her daughter. When a negative mother-daughter relationship appears, it is most often attributed to a stepmother or a mother-in-law. On the other hand, the mother is more often seen in a disciplinary role toward her son. Responses in Niiike to card J18 show that a mother's desire to see her son grow up properly can lead to violence on her part. In Sakunoshima stories such a difference between the mother's behavior toward the son and that toward her daughter is not evident.

Chastisement of a son by a mother is not exhibited in the stories from Sakunoshima; there is as much aggression expressed by a woman toward a daughter or another adult as toward a son. Whereas card J18 evokes several stories of aggression between adult married individuals in Sakunoshima, in Niiike no such stories were elicited. In three of the Sakunoshima stories a wife is described as choking her errant husband.

If we examine more specifically the stories of violence between adults, we note that, even in these stories, certain differences between Niiike and Sakunoshima are apparent. In Niiike when a woman is seen as violent or aggressive toward other adults, she is depicted as being either insane or a widow (unusual social statuses in which role expectations are more relaxed). The following stories are from Niiike:

(M, age 18–24, card J18) A mother strangles to death a woman who tempted her innocent son. Mother becomes insane and dies. The son begs his mother's forgiveness.

(W, age 12–17, card J18) A woman and a man fight. The woman is insane and does not know what she is doing.

(M, age 65 or over, card J18) A mother strangles to death her small child because she is bound to some *giri* (obligation) and has no other solution. She will commit suicide.

(M, age 18–24, card J18) A widow strangles another widow in their quarrel over money.

In contrast, in the following stories told to card J18 by Sakunoshima villagers, a woman kills both herself and her child because her husband is poor, which can be considered as violence directed toward her husband; a woman fights with another woman; and in two stories a wife is directly aggressive toward her husband.

(W, age 50–64, card J18) Because of the poverty or the idleness of her husband this woman is going to kill her child and commit double suicide. Both will die.

(M, age 18–24, card J18) It's terrible. The hands are not normally shaped—a parent?—well, I don't know. In their past, this woman bore that woman an ill will and now she is trying to vent her spite. A love affair—a rivalry, I mean. She cannot live happily because of her ill will toward this woman.

(W, age 25–34, card J18) They are married. The husband was playing the prodigal—drinking all the time and gambling, playing with his mistress. So, the wife tries to grip his throat. He will change his mind and become a good husband.

(M, age 18–24, card J18) Well, trying to kill somebody? Oh—they are a married couple. The husband deceived his wife. This is the husband who deceived his wife and he is going to be killed by his wife.

No comparable stories of a wife's aggression toward her husband appear in the entire Niiike TAT sample.

> *Themes of Discord on Card J13: Perception of Active*
> *and Passive Attitudes in Heterosexual*
> *Relationships*

The stories given in response to card J13 (which depicts a woman in the background lying on bedding with her breasts exposed and a man standing in the foreground with his arm thrown before his eyes), when considered solely from the standpoint of the aggressive or passive behavior of the principal figures, show a striking difference between the two villages.

In the stories from Niiike, in a domestic quarrel or in other situations as well, a man is much more likely to be depicted as active, even violent or aggressive, toward a woman. In Sakunoshima, there is a greater tendency to depict a woman as sexually aggressive and, in a story of a quarrel between husband and wife, the man may be pictured as helpless or passive in relation to the woman. In only one story from Niiike is the woman depicted as scolding or dominant in any respect, whereas the husband is pictured by a number of men as regretting his marriage and initiating divorce as a consequence. In Sakunoshima, in eight out of ten stories, the wife asserts herself, or the husband is depicted as weak or helpless in the quarrel. The following example is from Niiike:

(M, age 35–49, card J13) I don't know—how shall I think. I want to do this later. [Rejects card; card is given to him again after he finishes the sequence.] A young salaried man lives with his young wife. His wife is an extravagant woman, so he cannot support them with his salary. One day the young man came back home late at night. His wife became sulky and did not speak to him, showed contempt in her attitude. Her husband was really angered and began to feel miserable. He thought in his anger that his marriage was a failure, and he cried with mortification. He is at a loss whether he should start a new life or continue to live with her. He is afraid that if he divorces her, he will miss her, but he will divorce her just the same.

In contrast we find the following three examples in Sakunoshima:

(W, age 25–35, card J13) In this family a husband came home later than usual. The wife had gone to bed alone. The husband had been drinking, that's all. He will apologize to his wife for having come home drunk. Yes, he will apologize.

(M, age 34–50, card J13) A husband and a wife quarreled. They are still young. The husband is working in an office. Sometimes he drinks a little *sake* on the way back, and his wife complained about it. It is not a serious quarrel at all, and they will be on good terms again. They will live as ordinary people. He is now excited and wishes he could go out somewhere again, but he cannot do it. He is thinking, "Why cannot she act a little more gently toward me."

(M, age 50–64, card J13) This must be a husband and wife. Looks like a petticoat-government situation (*kaka-denka*). Therefore, they always quarrel. They cannot have a good child that way. The woman is sleeping, you see. They have often quarreled like this. This is not a good family. Anyway, this wife is egocentric (*wagamama*). They will come to no good in the future. The husband has come back from the office and is crying.

It is noteworthy, in regard to the question of initiative between men and women, that whereas five individuals in Niiike saw a man or husband in picture J13 acting violently toward a woman, there is no single person in Sakunoshima who saw a man in this picture as violent in the same manner. Following are three examples from Niiike of stories of the man as violent or aggressive.

(W, age 12–17, card J13) A husband killed his wife because the wife complained too much about his low salary. He regrets it very much.

(M, age 25–34, card J13) A man kills a woman who is a dancer and entertainer because she rejects him when he makes advances toward her. He runs away.

(M, age 12–17, card J13) A man who is rather licentious carries a woman to his room and perspires because it is hot. He forced her to come, bewitched by her sexual charm.

The results of card J13 strongly indicate that in a heterosexual relationship in Niiike the man is expected to take the initiative. In contrast, in Sakunoshima there are numerous stories indicating a dominant attitude on the part of a woman. Both groups give stories to this card depicting the wife as ill or dead, but such stories are much more evident in Niiike and most Niiike women give such a response. This evidence is in line with that previously cited and emphasizes the different perceptions of role relationships in the two villages.

CONCERN OVER THE MOTHER-IN-LAW
RELATIONSHIP

In viewing their family system self-consciously, the Japanese are well aware that the point of greatest difficulty between family members is in the relationship of a young bride to her mother-in-law. There are many accounts of conflict between a mother-in-law and her daughter-in-law or bride. A mother-in-law is seen as prone to torment or maltreat her daughter-in-law, who comes from another family and who must therefore be indoctrinated into the different ways of living in her new home. Numerous instances of tension in this relationship are found in Japanese novels, family court cases, and everyday life.

The phenomenon of a mother whose emotional attachment to her son tends to make her jealous of her son's bride, whom she sees as possibly taking her son away from her, is not peculiar to the Japanese. However, this tendency seems to be accentuated by many factors peculiar to the traditional hierarchical pattern of the Japanese family. A woman is bound to be dutiful to her new parents-in-law. The mother-in-law in her turn has come to realize status in the family through her son, whom she has reared to take over the family responsibilities. Once an outsider herself, she becomes the most vigilant of all in protecting the family's interests. The son has always been for her a means of self-realization, and it is only with difficulty that she allows him to be detached from her as a primary object of love. In a traditional family a young bride is in no position to alienate her husband from his mother, because the marital bond is not conceived as a primary relationship between a husband and his wife, but as a family contract. The mother, however, is well aware of the potential intimacy between the new couple, which may act as a wedge between her and her son. In effect, the wife's role is defined very much as is that of the mother, in terms of maternal solicitude and emphasis on the nurturant relationship to the husband. These factors combine to make an old woman feel that her role, her position, her self-assertion through her son, are all threatened and endangered by the young bride.

The Nichiren priest who was the head of the parish in which Niiike was located clearly saw this particular conflict as the main problem of his parishioners. He told us that more than 90 percent of the individuals who came to see him were either mothers-in-law concerned with the new brides of their sons, or new brides coming to complain bitterly against unnecessary harassment by the mother-in-law.

In Niiike, we originally included a TAT card depicting an older and younger woman figure. The responses to this card were so consistently stories of a mother-in-law harassing a young bride that we deleted the card from the series given in the fishing village. It is therefore impossible to compare the two villages in regard to the stories on this card; however, stories of a mother-in-law tended to be stimulated by other cards in our series in Niiike to a much greater extent than in Sakunoshima.

In Niiike there were eleven stories in which there was explicit mention of a mother-in-law, whereas in Sakunoshima there were only two such mentions. In Niiike a number of responses were given in which the mother-in-law was introduced into the story although no such figure actually appeared on the card; although absent, she was deeply involved in the story of what was happening between the two principal characters. In Sakunoshima the two stories that explicitly mention a mother-in-law were in response to card J9, picturing a family scene in which one of the individuals depicted might be identified as a mother-in-law. In only one of these two stories in Sakunoshima is there acutal conflict between a man's mother and his wife; in the other story, on the contrary, the mother is seen in a conciliatory role in a conflict between man and wife. The two stories from Sakunoshima follow.

(M, age 25–34, card J9) They are the members of a family and the elder brother made some mistake and his mother and sisters are worried. I guess he made some mistake concerning his wife. Well—after all, the relationship between his wife and his mother is not good. If I look at the face of the mother I feel that this family is not harmonious and the young sisters are sorry for their elder brother and they are worried, too. Future? Thanks to the sisters, the mother's anger will be calmed down, the elder brother's anger will be calmed down, and they will not be worried any longer. The

elder brother is sad, not knowing which side he should take, his mother's or his wife's.
(M, age 25–34, card J9) A husband and a wife quarreled and, well—his mother came out and is calming them down. This is their young daughter, crying, embraced by the wife. The quarrel will be solved happily—the man is a prodigal and his wife was about to leave the house, taking their child, and the quarrel started.

In Niiike the mother-in-law is described directly as an aggressive, scolding person in most of the stories. In four stories from Niiike the mother-in-law scolds her daughter or is aggressive to her. For example:

(W, age 18–24, card 3BM) She was scolded by her mother-in-law; she cannot talk to her husband, leaves him, and cries but eventually comes back.
(W, age 25–34, card J3F) A mother-in-law is not satisfied with her daughter-in-law. The daughter-in-law will leave home and tell the story to her own family.

When a conflict takes place with a mother-in-law in the traditional setting, there is no guarantee that the husband will attempt to protect his wife. He is most likely to remain inactive, although he may take his mother's side against his wife when his emotional attachment to his mother and his loyalty to the family is greater than any feeling of affection he may have toward his wife. Many Japanese women know of this possibility in the event of a conflict. In a story told by a woman under thirty-four in Niiike, there is an implicit expression of the wish that a husband would be assertive against his mother and take the part of his wife.

(W, age 12–17, card J4) A husband is feeling violent against his mother who is jealous of the couple, and his wife tries to stop him; she talks to his mother. The couple decide to live separately from his mother.

Actually, it would be highly unlikely in a rural village that a man would move away from his mother and live separately with his wife. Finally, two fanciful stories were told in Niiike demonstrating rather extreme attitudes toward the *yome-shutome* conflict.

(W, age 18–24, card J3F) Ghost of a dead bride come back to haunt a severe mother-in-law.
(M, age 64 plus, card J6M) A mother and a son are going to visit the grave of her dead daughter-in-law (his dead wife). The family relations will become better than they were before.

In the first of these stories the dead bride can get back at her mother-in-law only by haunting her after her death. In the second story the interpretation that because a son and mother visit the grave of a dead daughter-in-law the family relationships become better suggests that the daughter-in-law was a cause of alienation between mother and son. The evidence from the TAT stories would strongly support what was suggested by observation, namely that in the fishing village the role of the mother-in-law was not one of a guardian of family custom as it was in Niiike. In Sakunoshima, with the relationship between husband and wife considered primary, the mother-in-law had no unusual authority over the wife, who tended to be autonomous in her own home to a degree not realized in the farming village.

SUMMARY AND CONCLUSION

Starting with the hypothesis that differences in social status and role of women would be reflected in projective psychological materials, we compared TAT stories told by people of two Japanese rural villages: one, a farming village in which it was obvious from other behavioral evidence that traditional samurai-influenced values were still held with considerable firmness; the other, a fishing village that appeared ethnographically to be relatively free from emphasis on these values. The major findings of the TAT material support the hypothesis well.

In each instance the evidence is consistent with the picture of greater emphasis on lineage and hierarchical relationships in defining role relationships between the sexes in the farming village as compared with the fishing village. The fishing village shows much more emphasis on more freely conceived and less structured relationships in family role relationships. In the fishing village there is more willingness to perceive love and aggression expressed between individuals, regardless of specified traditional sex or family roles.

It is suggested that these differences between the two villages represent different value emphases related to functional differences in social organization found in various occupations as well as in various regions in Japan. In certain areas and in certain segments of the population, the position of women has been higher, and less emphasis has been put on formal social roles, status, and lineage. The pattern most often considered traditionally Japanese was by no means as universally dominant as certain authors would lead us to infer.

Chapter IV

The Psychocultural Significance
of Concern over Death and Illness

with HIROSHI WAGATSUMA

INTRODUCTION

Cultures differ widely in their explanations of the causes of death and illness and in the degree and nature of their preoccupation with them.[1] In societies where naturalistic appraisements are lacking, malevolent sorcery or witchcraft is often used as a ready explanation. Whatever the explicit explanation accepted within the culture, social scientists have been interested as well in understanding the implicit psychological meanings of concern over death and illness.

Interpretations such as those of Hallowell[2] and Kluckhohn[3] point out that the attribution of illness to sorcery or witchcraft is not due solely to a lack of naturalistic explanations. Such beliefs may also have a specific function in relation to the handling of aggressive feelings. Thus, continual concern over potential illness or death, especially when related to ideas concerning the possible evil intentions of one's avowed or secret enemies, may function as a "projection" of aggressive impulses.

Another type of relationship between concern over death and illness

---

[1] This chapter previously appeared in "Psycho-Cultural Significance of Concern over Death and Illness Among Rural Japanese," by DeVos and Wagatsuma in *International Journal of Social Psychiatry* (1959).

[2] Hallowell, "Aggression in Saulteaux Society" (1953); and Hallowell, "The Social Function of Anxiety in a Primitive Society" (1941).

[3] C. Kluckhohn, *Navaho Witchcraft* (1944). The terms *sorcery* and *witchcraft* are used interchangeably by many anthropological writers.

and a culturally determined mode of structuring aggression has become apparent in the course of work with the Thematic Apperception Test materials. Concern with death and illness for the Japanese often seems related to the introjection of guilt, as compared to the projection of aggression reported for the American Indian groups.

The fact that concern over illness is associated with belief in sorcery in some culture groups but not in others is most probably related to differences in the nature of the social systems, of the structuring of responsibility in adult social roles, and of child-rearing practices. Beatrice Whiting[4] suggests in her study of Paiute sorcery that belief in sorcery is related to the distribution of power or control in certain features of social organization. She indicates that a survey of the Human Organization area files demonstrates a statistically significant presence of sorcery in nonhierarchical societies, in comparison with its relative absence in societies with class or status difference in the distribution of power, as evidenced by superordinate justice or punishment for crimes. The Japanese have been noted for the hierarchical nature of their society and would seem to fit this generalization. However, this explanation is somewhat unsatisfactory unless examined further in specific cases. Careful examination of the factors contributing to the developmental patterning of adult social roles would help demonstrate the way in which sorcery is functional or not functional psychologically.

The Berens River Saulteaux, as described by Hallowell, for example, live in a fairly simple nonhierarchical society. They are characterized by a lack of overt aggression in face-to-face situations. These Indians appear to have placid character, patience, and self-restraint. Murder and theft are rare, and there is no open expression of anger or quarrels involving physical assault. In spite of the notable lack of violence in the social behavior of this Indian culture, the Saulteaux feel themselves constantly threatened by the hostile intentions of others. If a Saulteaux becomes ill and if ordinary medical treatment fails to produce improvement, he is bound to suspect that he has aroused another person's hostility by some action or attitudes and that, therefore, the offended person has retaliated. In fact, sick persons almost always believe that their illness is due to revenge. Hallowell concludes that their belief in sorcery provides a major outlet for aggression— that aggressive feelings are, in a sense, projected and resolved through external means.

Such belief in sorcery as an instrument of covert aggression in causing illness or death is two-edged. Whether or not the individual him-

---

4 Whiting, "Paiute Sorcery" (1950). What Whiting calls *sorcery* is termed *witchcraft* by Kluckhohn.

self uses this means of aggression, the threat that another may be using such techniques against him constantly lurks in the background of his daily life; thus, in spite of overtly minimizing the personal friction and hostility that periodically arise in their human relationships, the Saulteaux are dogged by anxieties and fears over possible illness or death arising from the belief that others may be prompted to covertly do them positive harm. It is not the practice of witchcraft but the prevalent belief in it that is of prime importance, because, from the standpoint of the individual who interprets his illness and misfortune as being due to sorcery, it makes little difference whether someone has gone through certain magical procedures or not.

Another major source of illness in Saulteaux belief is punishment from a supernatural being for what they call "bad conduct." In this society certain classes of sexual behavior (incest, homosexuality, auto-eroticism, bestiality, etc.) proscribed by the guardian spirits, may be punished by disease. It must be noted that such a fear is not generically different from the belief in sorcery. Both envision an external agent as reacting to an enraging act with destructive intent. Projection rather than introjection is operative in the Saulteaux in their fear of supernatural punishment and in their belief in sorcery. In both cases any tendency toward what is conceived of as a transgression or an impulse toward an aggressive act is held in check by a firm belief in and fear of consequent attack by an external force, be it visited on the victim in the form of illness or of some other misfortune.

In most communities in modern Japan, rural and urban, social sanctions emphasizing harmony and discouraging open antagonism are as pronounced as they are among Saulteaux studied by Hallowell or the Navaho discussed by Kluckhohn. However, in strong contrast to these American Indian groups, belief in sorcery is of little or no importance in the concerns of the ordinary villager. This is not to say that such a belief is entirely absent in Japanese communities. Magical practices such as sticking pins in an image can be documented, but fear of such practices is not part of the ordinary concern of the Japanese. Illness is not generally regarded by Japanese as a punishment from an external source, yet it seems likely from the intensity of concern over possible illness noted in many Japanese that some form of displacement of affect is generally operative in these preoccupations.

Considerable concern with illness can be noted in the modern literary productions of the Japanese; such concern often appears when there is some sort of emotional crisis. In many stories there is a masochistically tinged theme of heroic suffering to attain a goal despite such difficulties as the long-term illness or death of a beloved. Only in the most ancient tales does one find much concern with the super-

natural in relation to disease. One can roughly generalize that death
or illness is most often seen in Japanese literary works in relation to
the self-sacrificing nurturant role of women; or, when seen as related
to men, illness is presented as a hindrance to one's undistracted dedication to achievement in life.

The content of fantasy productions of Japanese given the Thematic
Apperception Test, when considered in the light of certain psychoanalytic formulations, suggests that excessive concern over either death
or illness, may be related to hostility, as in the Saulteaux, but that the
mechanism most operative, especially in tradition-oriented women, is an
introjection of aggression. Concern over illness in many Japanese, then,
seems ultimately related to unconscious internalized guilt feelings
rather than to fear of projected hostility. In the Saulteaux, while possible guilt reactions may also be operative, the psychological processes
involved in the use of an external agent of punishment to cope with
guilt are different from those involved in the more "internalized" form
of guilt in which the punitive agent is introjected and the individual
in a sense punishes himself.

TAT STORIES OF DEATH AND ILLNESS
AS RELATED TO INTERNALIZED CONSTRAINTS

The internalization of social expectations and its relation to
guilt phenomena depend largely on how these expectations are inculcated in children in the context of primary family relationships. In
Chapter 5 we discuss the projective test evidence suggesting the
presence of a great deal of unconscious guilt in Japanese and explain
the pertinence of this to an understanding of their need for achievement and success as a people. The Japanese virtues of self-sacrifice,
persistence, and endurance toward long-range goals are learned by
children from the mother, through her living example. The proper
status and role behavior of the Japanese adult demands much self-
discipline. The manner in which this self-discipline is inculcated in
childhood makes it impossible for the Japanese to find ready outlets
for external projection of hostility or to attribute to outside causes
any failure in expected performance. The effect of what may be termed
the mother's moral masochism on her children makes escape from
expected behavior most difficult.

Differences in the degree of internalization of the woman's role
between Niiike and Sakunoshima, discussed in the previous chapter,
are apparent in a comparison of stories about death and illness.

The responses to the TAT pictures, analyzed quantitatively, showed
in the Niiike farm women an unusually high degree of concern over
problems of illness in family relationships. A comparison of the re-

sponses of farm and fishing groups to eleven TAT cards showed that approximately 20 percent of the stories given by women in the farming village were characterized by a theme involving some form of death or illness (see Table IV-1). The farm men used such themes in about 10 percent of their stories. This is still a high number in comparison with American norms, but not unusually so. The difference between men and women in Niiike was significant even at the 0.1 percent level.

TABLE IV-1

TAT STORIES OF DEATH, ILLNESS, AND INJURY—NIIIKE AND SAKUNOSHIMA

Classification	Niiike			Sakunoshima		
	Men	Women	Total	Men	Women	Total
Total stories	291	313	604	187	198	385
Death	11	22	33	12	9	21
Illness	13	38	51	10	12	22
Injury	0	3	3	4	1	5
Accidental death	6	1	7	1	1	2
Totals	30	64	94	27	23	50
Percent of all stories	10.3	20.4*	15.5	14.4	11.6	12.9

NOTE: The eleven pictures used are J1, J2, J3 (F & M), J4, J6M, J7M, J9, J11, J13, J18, and J22 in the Marui-DeVos set. Other cards used only in Niiike were excluded from this comparison.

* Niiike women significantly differ from men: D/6D-4.2 sig. > .001.

As demonstrated in Table IV-1, a specific comparison of the stories of death and illness from the two villages shows a high number of these stories from Niiike women, supporting our supposition that such stories are related to the degree of emphasis on a traditional self-sacrificing type of women's role in Niiike. The Sakunoshima women do not show a similar concern. In Sakunoshima there is no significant difference in incidence of such stories between men and women. The discrepancy between the women's groups accounts for most of the difference between the two villages in respect to the incidence of death and illness stories.

Analysis of the stories (Table IV-2) shows that the main difference between the two villages is the tendency for people, and especially women, in Niiike to see women as ill. The person most often specified as ill is the wife; the next is the mother. Women particularly tend to see a wife as dead, dying, or, if ill, as not recovering. This concern with a woman's illness or death is an indirect reflection of a masochistic conception of her social status.

TABLE IV-2

STORIES OF DEATH, ILLNESS, INJURY, AND ACCIDENTAL DEATH
TOLD BY NIIIKE AND SAKUNOSHIMA VILLAGERS, CLASSIFIED
ACCORDING TO THE AFFECTED SUBJECT

Affected subject	Death				Illness				Accidental death and (injury)			
	Niiike		Sakuno-shima		Niiike		Sakuno-shima		Niiike		Sakuno-shima	
	M	W	M	W	M	W	M	W	M	W	M	W
Father	1	5	3	2	1	4	2	3	3	0	1	1
Mother	2	5	3	2	1	6	1	3	0	0	0	0
Son	0	0	0	1	1	1	0	1	2	0	(1)	0
Daughter	0	1	0	0	1	8	1	1	0	(1)	(1)	0
Child	1	1	1	0	0	2	2	0	0	(1)	0	0
Husband	0	0	0	0	0	2	0	0	0	0	0	0
Wife	4	8	1	3	3	3	1	2	0	0	0	0
Other man	0	1	2	0	1	2	1	0	1	1	(1)	(1)
Other woman	1	0	0	1	4	6	1	2	0	0	0	0
Other person	0	1	0	0	1	2	1	0	0	(1)	(1)	0
Parent(s)	2	0	2	0	0	2	0	0	0	0	0	0
Totals	11	22	12	9	13	38	10	12	6	1 (3)	1 (4)	1 (1)

NOTE: Niiike: Total TAT (604). Total men's stories 30; total women's stories 64. Sakunoshima: Total TAT (385). Total men's stories 27; total women's stories 23. Parentheses indicate injury stories.

Another dimension of analysis of the TAT stories is the theme around which the death or illness is perceived. Grief, worry, and anxieties over the death or illness of a beloved are the most prevalent themes in the Niiike women's stories. Women's themes in general tend to be more pessimistic than those of men. Women seem to enjoy depicting in detail the grief of a man losing his beloved wife. Themes of anxiety usually concern the health of some individual in the family. A second theme noted in the stories given by many Niiike women and in none of the other groups considered is that of caring for a daughter who is ill. In a few stories sons are described as caring for a mother who is ill.

There is a scattering of stories from Niiike and Sakunoshima suggesting certain other Japanese ethical themes (see Table IV-3). One theme appearing in a few stories is the diligence and hard work of a son whose mother or father has died. In some of these stories in the Niiike sample there is a suggestion that the death has changed the son's attitude to one of greater diligence and application. A few stories depict illness as a result of overwork. And in another vein there is a story of suicide as an act of self-sacrifice on the part of a wife, removing herself as an obstacle to the husband's devotion to his work. In other stories, suicide is an act of dedication by a mother to a son who has died, or by a son who joins a dead father. These latter stories occur in the Niiike sample; no counterpart is found in Sakuno-shima.

TABLE IV-3

STORIES OF DEATH, ILLNESS, INJURY, ACCIDENTAL DEATH
TOLD BY NIIIKE AND SAKUNOSHIMA VILLAGERS,
CLASSIFIED ACCORDING TO MAJOR THEMES

Major themes	Niiike		Sakunoshima	
	Men	Women	Men	Women
Situational description of death and illness, injury	6	15	4	2
Care and nurturance related to death and illness, injury	8	17	6	4
Grief, worry, and anxieties concerning death and illness	7	23	9	13
Achievement and hard work related to death and illness	1	2	1	1
Reform and expiatory achievement related to death and illness	2	4	3	1
Masochistic themes of self-sacrifice, overwork, suicide	5	2	3	1
Poverty and financial concern related to death and illness	1	1	1	1
Totals	30	64	27	23

The number of such stories emphasizing death or illness is in marked contrast to the few stories about being attacked or attacking with resultant injury or death.

The few stories recorded can be interpreted along psychoanalytic lines as indicating the presence of some pressing, even though unconscious, hostility. These results were in marked contrast to those obtained in another TAT study done in collaboration with MacNeish and Carterette[5] on a Canadian Slavey Indian group. Among the Slavey Indians, stories of aggressive violence leading to death or injury

[5] MacNeish, DeVos, and Carterette, "Variations in Personality and Ego-Identification Within a Slavey Indian Kin-Community" (1960).

were very much in evidence; there were fewer stories of illness. Behaviorally, the Slavey community showed no more overt personal aggression than did the Japanese village. Nevertheless, one could see that there was more fear of personal attack, and preoccupation with violent hostile feelings; themes of self-sacrifice were entirely lacking.

This difference in emphasis on illness in TAT themes does not seem related to realistic concern with illness in the communities considered. It is to be noted that the Slavey Indians, for example, worry a great deal about illness; they have considerable fear of diseases, such as tuberculosis, against which their resistance is poor.

In Niiike, the Japanese farming village, the figure seen in five of the six stories of accidental death told by men is the father or son. No such trend is evident in the Sakunoshima material. Some difference between the Sakunoshima and the Niiike men in regard to the possible unconscious hostility toward a father seen in a dominant role (as he is in the farming village) is apparent also when we look at another class of stories which are related to consequences of the absence of a parent long-since dead, usually a father. These consequences are depicted in positive and negative terms. In Sakunoshima, the men emphasize a theme of the dead father as an inspiration to the achievement and success of the son. Memory of the father is sometimes evoked as an image inspiring the son.

In contrast, in a scattering of stories, the absence of a parent is seen as leading to evil conduct, specified as being caused by lack of guidance or example. There are three stories in which a mother's conduct after the death of her husband is described as licentious, encouraging the son to learn evil ways. In Niiike there are fewer such stories, and, in contrast, certain stories emphasize expiatory themes in which a son, by reflecting upon the image of his dead father, changes his attitude toward life and reforms.

The fantasy material from Niiike includes instances in which the illness of the parent seems related to the improper behavior of a child. If such a parent becomes ill or dies, the child reforms. Introjection of guilt is strongly suggested by these stories. One's evil conduct has injured the sorrowing parent; hence, one must pay by assuming the responsibilities for hard work and diligence previously avoided. Such stories of parental illness as related to introjective guilt are particularly stimulated by the ideal cultural requirements of status and role in relation to achievement, and they also indicate a relative unavailability of aggressive outlets in traditional Japanese social relationships.

A few stories depicting mental aberration deserve special attention. Such stories given by men depict women as "hysterical" or "insane." For instance, in one story by a man, a woman is seen as "hysterical" because she "hates her husband who fools around with other women."

TABLE IV-4

STORIES OF CONSEQUENCES RESULTING FROM PARENTAL
DEATH IN NIIKE AND SAKUNOSHIMA VILLAGES

	Niiike		Sakunoshima	
	Men	Women	Men	Women
A. Classified according to the major theme				
Evil conduct	3	2	1	3
(Wife's)	(2)	(0)	(0)	(1)
(Son's)	(1)	(1)	(1)	(2)
(Brother's)	(0)	(1)	(0)	(0)
Achievement, son's	3	1	8	2
Expiatory achievement, son's	2	0	0	0
Poverty	1	1	2	0
Loneliness	0	0	1	2
Other	0	0	0	1
Totals	9	4	12	8
B. Classified according to the role of the dead person				
Grandfather	0	0	1	0
Parents	0	1	2	2
Father	9	3	9	5
Mother	0	0	0	1
Totals	9	4	12	8

Conversely in one story given by a woman, a young son is depicted as having gone insane. Mental deficiency or idiocy is depicted for sons in two other stories and for a daughter in yet another. Men give more stories of mental problems than do women. Men tend to see the women as mentally disturbed when they act in an overly emotional manner, and, conversely, the three stories of mental deficiency or insanity in boys or men are given by women. These stories of concern with mental functioning are unique to Niiike, and no counterparts are found in Sakunoshima. This difference in sensitivity to mental malfunctioning is not readily explicable directly from the ethnographic data. It may be another reflection of differential stresses in status and role performance in the two villages. A woman seen as "violent" is sometimes explained by men in the farm village as losing the ordinary ego controls that would prevent her from expressing her aggressive feelings directly to her husband. In Niiike, a boy with a weak intellect would not be considered fit to carry out ascribed adult role functions.

CONCLUSIONS AND DISCUSSION

In contrast to the American Indians' "projection" of aggressive feelings suggested in the concern over sorcery, the Japanese rural villagers tend to show introjection of hostility. Through the operation of moral masochistic mechanisms involving internalized guilt, the Japanese are prone to concern themselves with self-denial in terms of long-range goals. Concern with death and illness as displayed in the TAT responses is often related to the self-sacrifice and suffering necessary for the attainment of such goals. The generally greater concern over death and illness by women from the farming village can be interpreted as related to the greater degree to which sexual and aggressive impulses are prohibited in women in this particular village. The prohibition against outer expression of these impulses is more severe in Niiike than in Sakunoshima; hence their appearance is less tolerated in the fantasies of the farming women than in those of the women of the fishing village.

As is discussed more fully in the following chapter, Japanese behavior raises speculation as to how introjective defense mechanisms can be related to the use of illness in various situations involving achievement drive. For some Japanese, illness may take the unconscious form of self-inflicted punishment for failure, or, if understood more deeply, for unacceptable hostility to a parent or authority figure and his expectations. It may also be used as an excuse to the self or to others for lack of accomplishment or failure to complete expected goals. Other Japanese seem to use physical illness as an unconscious mode of escape from an intolerable situation that allows no way out. Studies into the mechanisms of reaction involved in physiological and psychological stress suggested why certain Japanese were in the 1950s particularly prone to suffer a reactivation of tuberculosis, for example, when under some form of social pressure to succeed in a difficult situation, such as studying abroad.

For women the emphasis is on the role of nurturance within the home rather than on some form of the external achievement required of men. The sacrifice of women in caring for a son after the death of a husband and her obligation to instill in him a desire for accomplishment is a favorite theme in Japanese literature generally, and such stories appeared in our TAT sample. Reik[6] points out that if we are to understand moral masochism, we must recognize that inherent in it is the expectation of eventual triumph after perseverance.

In the TAT stories, as in Japanese literature generally, the virtue

---

[6] Reik, *Masochism in Modern Man* (1941).

most lovingly emphasized in both men and women is endurance toward the accomplishment of a goal taking lifelong dedication.

The traditional ability of the Japanese man to demonstrate endurance and self-sacrifice in his role of warrior is well documented for the samurai period and more recently for World War II. However, it is especially in the day-by-day conduct required in the ideal role for women that one finds the apotheosis of Japanese ethics concerning traditional virtues.

Speculating on the basis of psychoanalytic theory derived from American clinical cases, one can conceive of several possible psychological processes that could underlie such a strong concern with death and illness as that found in the TAT stories. One possibility is that with the denial of external expression there may be a turning in of affect on the body in the form of hypochondriac concerns. This sort of mechanism could be a basic character defense in the ego controls of aggression, depending on a narcissistic withdrawal of affect from outside objects generally into an inner preoccupation. Such a process is sometimes revealed through increased concern with possible illness.

Another somewhat different possibility is that unacceptable destructive or sexual impulses are converted into excessive anxiety over the possible illness of others. Related to this sort of transmutation of feelings is what we have suggested as the moral masochistic tendencies appreciably present in Japanese. Concern over death or illness could be related to some sort of masochistic dedication to the persons of one's immediate family. Illness and death involve forms of sacrifice and suffering to be endured. The manner in which many of the illness stories are structured favors this latter type of analysis, rather than analysis in terms of hypochondriacal leanings per se.

Data from representative samples of the Rorschach test do not suggest the presence of much hypochondriacal concern of either men or women. Anatomical material is not present to any notable degree in the test results. The pattern of high anatomical content found in Japanese-American groups undergoing an acculturation process in the United States is not found in the representative sample of rural and urban Japanese, obtained in our interdisciplinary study.[7] More evident, but not to the degree that it could be termed characteristic, are certain indications of hysteroid ego defenses.

---

[7] The reports on Japanese-Americans are found in DeVos, "A Comparison of the Personality Differences in Two Generations of Japanese-Americans by Means of the Rorschach Test" (1954); and DeVos, "A Quantitative Rorschach Assessment of Maladjustment and Rigidity in Acculturating Japanese-Americans" (1955). Reports on the representative samples of Japanese Rorschachs are presented by Eiji Murakami in Japanese in "Special Characteristics of Japanese Personality Based on Rorschach Test Results" (1962).

One notes sometimes a tendency to confuse what Japanese villagers themselves aptly call *"hisuterii"* with hypochondriasis. *Hisuterii* is related structurally *not* to affective withdrawal but to hysterical conversion phenomena. Even so, such phenomena as fox-possession which are reported elsewhere in rural Japan, are not present in Niiike. At the time of the study there were no obvious cases of hysterical flights into illness or false pregnancies or any other notable symptomatology of a hysterical nature such as those reported in certain brides in instances where there is trouble with a severe mother-in-law. Phenomena of this sort tend to be interpreted as clinically hysterical in nature by Japanese psychiatrists who have first-hand contact with such cases.

Hysterical phenomena are to be distinguished from the more severe types of affective withdrawal found in hypochondriacal cases. According to general psychoanalytic theory, hypochondriasis will result from difficulties in very early parent-child relationships. Hysterical phenomena, on the other hand, are related to an arrest of maturation at a later stage, usually related to an Oedipal conflict. Evidence from the Rorschach test and from TAT drawings obtained in Niiike does indeed suggest some tendency in several of the women toward a "little girl" type of feminine identification of a type often related to hysterical character defenses, but there is very little evidence in the projective material from our sample of either urban settings or the rural villages that suggests the more severe ego disturbances found in hypochondriasis.

We contend that high incidence of concern over death and illness in the TAT stories should not be related to personality defenses derived from difficulties at early developmental levels, and subsequent withdrawal of affect to an overconcern with illness in one's own body. It is more meaningful to discuss these results in the context of the effects of severely circumscribed adult social roles especially on women. Such tendencies toward aggression as do exist are, according to our inference, well transmuted by the Niiike women into a masochistic identification with a traditional role in which they feel they are expected to sacrifice themselves to the care of the family. The stories often suggest themes in line with these ethical expectations. They depict women who are dutifully concerned over the illness of others or women who suffer illness or death in the course of maternal or wifely devotion.

Although traditional patterns are changing, Japanese fiction still contains many stories involving a father's death that illustrate this psychological equation: mother keeps son, but mother and son both pay by maintaining diligent submission to a far-off life goal demanding endurance and self-sacrifice. In these stories the father's death is followed by the mother's aiding her son, through her sacrifice, to make a success of his life, and the implication is that for her sacrifice the son owes the mother a continued dedication to success. In these stories, the father is removed quickly so that the relationship of mother to son is an exclusive one throughout most of the telling. The mother becomes a completely desexualized figure, often ill or suffering as a consequence of her dedication to her child. Any interest in sexuality on her part would be perceived as bringing about the ruination of her son. Stories in which the theme of success is spelled out in terms of a mother's love rather than in terms of the establishment of a family are not uncommon in American literature or for that matter in American TAT stories. However, American stories point up the goal of leaving the mother and going off to marry, albeit sometimes with great reluctance. The latter stories are quite infrequent in the Japanese material. According to American standards, a son leaves the generation of the mother and takes up his own tasks in life, and his failure to do so is often attributed to some unhealthy tie to the mother.

As contended throughout this volume, sacrifice and masochism are, unconsciously, forms of control. A woman's ego in the traditional Confucian ethics is encouraged to broaden itself to include her male child. She, in a sense, does not want to lose this male "principal" that is attached to her. Men, however, are often covertly perceived as weak and prone to a dependent attachment to a woman. A woman gives up the goal of direct physical fulfillment and replaces it with the subtler goal of maintaining a long-range unbroken control over the husband or the son as a masculine part of herself. The image of the terrible mother-in-law in the Japanese family, therefore, is not explicable solely as that of an older woman who is permitted displaced aggression toward a young bride as part of her status; the mother who feels a son is attached to her becomes uncontrollably aggressive when someone threatens this deep attachment.

The basic differences hypothesized in the psychocultural meaning of concern over death and illness between the Japanese in our study and the American Indian groups reported on by Hallowell and others, in conclusion, are a differential cultural emphasis on mechanisms of introjection and related masochistic defenses, on the one hand, and fear of retaliation and projection of hostile impulses, on the other. In the one, guilt is internalized as a part of the ego and ego ideal; in the other, punishment or hostility is perceived as coming from the outside. Cultural conditioning is responsible for differential emphasis on the use of these mechanisms insofar as a culture, including its socialization process, makes certain controls necessary in handling prohibited aggressive impulses, and at the same time selectively provides learning experiences in which these mechanisms are observed being used by others who are objects of future identification.

Chapter V

Some Observations of Guilt in Relation to Achievement and Arranged Marriage

IS JAPAN A "SHAME" CULTURE?

A central problem in understanding Japanese cultural psychology is whether the Japanese emphasis on achievement drive may be motivated by a sense of shame or guilt inculcated in childhood.[1] Despite the assertions of other observers and writers, including Ruth Benedict,[2] about the sense of "face" as a strong motive in behavior, I contend that a sense of guilt developed in the basic interpersonal relationships with parents is a much stronger motive.

The characteristic beliefs, values, and obligatory practices that provide emotional security and that are usually associated in the West with religious systems and other generalized ideologies—and on a conscious level at least are related only indirectly to family life[3]—are in tradition-oriented Japanese related much more explicitly to their family system. The structuring of guilt in the Japanese personality is hidden from Western observation, since there is a lack of empathic understanding of what it means to be part of such a family system. Western observers tend to look for guilt, as it is symbolically expressed, in reference to a possible transgression of limits imposed by a generalized ideology or religious system circumscribing sexual and aggressive impulses. There is little sensitivity to the possibility that a sense of guilt can be centrally related to a possible failure to meet expectations in a moral system built around family duties and obligations.

---

[1] This chapter is modified slightly from DeVos, "The Relation of Guilt Toward Parents to Achievement and Arranged Marriage Among the Japanese" (1960).

[2] Benedict, *The Chrysanthemum and the Sword* (1946), pp. 221–227.

[3] Kardiner, *The Individual and His Society, The Psychodynamics of Primitive Social Organization* (1939), pp. 89–91.

Piers and Singer, in distinguishing between shame and guilt cultures,[4] emphasize that guilt inhibits and condemns transgression, whereas shame demands achievement of a positive goal. This contrast is related to Freud's two earlier distinctions in the functioning of the conscience. Freud used *shame* to delineate a reaction to the ego ideal oriented toward a goal of positive achievement. He related *guilt* to superego formation in regard to transgressions of taboos. A great deal of Japanese cultural material, when appraised with these motivational distinctions in mind, would at first glance seem to indicate that Japan provides an excellent example of a society concerned most with shame as its chief internalized social sanction.

Historically, the Japanese have been pictured as having developed extreme susceptibility to group pressures toward conformity as a result of several hundred years of tightly knit feudal organization. This strong group conformity is often viewed as associated with a lack of the personal qualities that foster individualistic endeavor.[5] In spite of, or, according to some observers, because of these conformity patterns, which are embedded in governmental organization as well as in personal habits, the Japanese—alone among all the Asian peoples coming in contact with Western civilization in the nineteenth century—were quickly able to translate an essentially feudal social structure into a modern industrial society and to achieve eminence as a world power in fewer than fifty years. This remarkable achievement may be viewed as a group manifestation of what on the individual level is presumed to be a striving and achievement drive.

Achievement drive in Americans has been discussed by Riesman,[6] among others, as shifting in recent years from puritan, inner-directed motivation to other-directed concern with conformity and outer group situations. Perceived in this framework, the Japanese traditionally have had an "other-directed" culture. Sensitivity to "face" and attention to protocol suggest that the susceptibility to social pressure, traced psychoanalytically, may possibly derive from underlying infantile fears of abandonment. Personality patterns integrated around such motivation, if culturally prevalent, could lead to a society dominated by a fear of failure and a need for recognition and success.

Intimately related to a shift from Puritan patterns in America were certain changes in the patterns of child-rearing. Similarly, it has been observed in Japan that prevailing child-rearing practices emphasize social evaluation as a sanction, rather than the more internalized, self-

---

[4] Piers and Singer, *Shame and Guilt: A Psychoanalytic and Cultural Study* (1953).
[5] See, for example, Lafcadio Hearn's statement that Japanese authoritarianism is that of the "many over the one—not the one over the many," *Japan: An Attempt at Interpretation* (1904), pp. 435 ff.
[6] Riesman, *The Lonely Crowd* (1950).

contained ethical codes instilled and enforced early by parental punishment. The child-rearing patterns most evident in Japan manifest early permissiveness in regard to weaning and bowel training and a relative lack of physical punishment.[7] There is, moreover, considerable emphasis on ridicule and lack of acceptance of imperfect or slipshod performance. There is most probably a strong relationship between early permissiveness and susceptibility to external social sanctions. In line with the distinctions between shame and guilt, the Japanese, again, could easily be classified as shame-oriented, and their concern over success and failure could be explicable in these terms. This formula, however, does not hold up well when reapplied to an understanding of individual Japanese, either in Japan or in the United States. For example, the five clinical studies of Japanese-Americans in *Clinical Studies in Culture Conflict*[8] consistently give evidence of depressive reactions and an inability to express hostile or resentful feelings toward the parents. Feelings of guilt are strongly related to an inability to express aggression outwardly, leading to intrapunitive reactions. Feelings of worthlessness also result from the repression of aggressive feelings.

    Emphasis on shame sanctions in a society does not preclude severe

---

[7] See, for example, the empirical reports by Lanham, "Aspects of Child Care in Japan: Preliminary Report" (1956), and by Edward and Margaret Norbeck, "Child Training in a Japanese Fishing Community" (1956). See also Norbeck and DeVos, "Japan" (1961), which presents a more comprehensive bibliography, including the works of native Japanese on child-rearing practices in various areas in Japan.

[8] Seward (ed.), *Clinical Studies in Culture Conflict* (1958). The Nisei woman described by Norman L. Farberow and Edward S. Schneidman in chapter 15 (pp. 335 ff.), "A Nisei Woman Attacks by Suicide," demonstrates the transference to the American cultural situation of certain basic intrapunitive attitudes common in Japan related to woman's ideal role behavior. The Kibei case demonstrates a young man's perception of the manifest "suffering" of Japanese women. The case described by Charlotte G. Babcock and William Caudill in chapter 17 (pp. 409 ff.), "Personal and Cultural Factors in Treating a Nisei Man," as well as other, unpublished, psychoanalytic material of Babcock's, amply demonstrates the presence of deep underlying guilt toward parents. Such guilt is still operative in Nisei in influencing occupational selection and marriage choice. Seward, in a general summary of the Japanese cases (p. 449), carefully points out the pervasive depression found as a cohesive theme in each of the cases. She avoids conceptualizing the problems in terms of guilt, perhaps out of deference to the stereotype that Japanese feel "ashamed" rather than "guilty." She states: "Running through all five Japanese-American cases is a pervasive depression, in three reaching the point of suicidal threat or actual attempt." Yet she ends with the statement: "Looking back over the cases of Japanese origin, we may note a certain cohesiveness binding them together. Distance from parent figures is conspicuous in all as well as inability openly to express resentment against them. In line with the externalization of authority and the shame-avoidance demands of Japanese tradition, hostility is consistently turned in on the self in the *face-saving devices* of depression and somatic illness." (Italics mine.)

guilt. Although strong feelings of anxiety related to conformity are evident in Japanese society, severe guilt becomes more apparent when the underlying motivation contributing to manifest behavior is more intensively analyzed. Shame is a more conscious phenomenon among the Japanese, hence more readily perceived as influencing behavior, but guilt often seems to be a stronger basic determinant.

Although the ego ideal is involved in Japanese strivings toward success, day-by-day hard work and purposeful activities leading to long-range goals are directly related to guilt feelings toward parents. Transgression in the form of laziness or other nonproductive behavior is felt to injure the parents and thus leads to feelings of guilt. There are psychological analogues between this Japanese sense of responsibility to parents for social conformity and achievement and the traditional association sometimes found in the Protestant West between work activity and a personal relationship with a deity.[9]

Any attempt to answer questions about guilt in the Japanese raises many theoretical problems concerning the nature of the internalization processes involved in human motivation. It is beyond the scope of this chapter to discuss theoretically the complex interrelationships between feelings of shame and guilt in personality development. But I believe that some anthropological writings, oversimplifying psychoanalytic theory, have placed too much emphasis on a direct one-to-one relationship between culturally prevalent child-rearing disciplines and resultant inner psychological states. These inner states are a function not only of observable disciplinary behavior but also of more subtle, less reportable, atmospheric conditions in the home, as well as of other factors as yet only surmised.

Moreover, in accordance with psychoanalytic theory concerning the mechanisms of internalizing parental identification one would presume on an *a priori* basis that some form of internalized guilt is almost universal, although its form and emphasis differ considerably from one society to another. Nevertheless, this chapter, while guided by theory, is based primarily on empirical evidence and *a posteriori* reasoning in attempting to point out a specifically Japanese pattern of guilt. Developmental vicissitudes involved in the resolution of Oedipal relationships are not documented. Concisely stated, the position is as follows:

Guilt in many of the Japanese not only operates in respect to what are termed superego functions, but is also concerned with what has

---

[9] Bellah, in *Tokugawa Religion* (1957), perceives, and illustrates in detail, a definite relationship between prevalent pre-Meiji, Tokugawa-period ethical ideals and the rapid industrialization of Japan that occurred subsequent to the restoration of the emperor. A cogent application of a sociological approach similar to that of Max Weber allows him to point out the obvious parallels in Tokugawa Japan to the precapitalist ethical orientation of Protestant Europe.

been internalized by the individual as an ego ideal. Generally speaking, the processes involved in resolving early identifications as well as in assuming later adult social roles are never possible without some internalized guilt. The more difficult it is for a child to live up to the ideal behavior expected of him, the more likely he is to develop ambivalence toward the source of the ideal. This ideal need not directly emphasize prohibited behavior, as is the case when punishment is the mode of training.

When shame and guilt have undergone a process of internalization during the course of an individual's development, both become operative regardless of the relative absence of external threats of punishment or overt concern with the opinions of others concerning his behavior. Behavior is automatically self-evaluated without the presence of others. A simple dichotomy relating internalized shame only to ego ideal and internalized guilt only to an automatically operative superego is one to be seriously questioned.

Whereas the formation of an internalized ego ideal in its earlier form is more or less related to the social expectations and values of parents, the motivations that move a developing young adult toward a realization of these expectations can involve considerable guilt. Japanese perceptions of social expectations concerning achievement behavior and marriage choice, as shown in experimental materials, give ample evidence of the presence of guilt; shame as a motive is much less evident.

Nullification of parental expectations is one way to hurt a parent. As here defined, guilt in the Japanese is essentially related either to an impulse to hurt, which may be implied in a contemplated act, or to the realization of having injured a love object toward whom one feels some degree of unconscious hostility.

Guilt feelings related to various internalization processes differ, varying with what is prohibited or expected; nevertheless, some disavowal of an unconscious impulse to hurt seems to be generic to guilt. In some instances there is also emphasis on a fear of retribution stemming from this desire to injure. Such seems to be the case in many of the Japanese. If a parent has instilled in a child an understanding of his capacity to hurt by failing to carry out an obligation expected of him as a member of a family, any such failure can make him feel extremely guilty.

With the following TAT materials taken from Niiike, I will attempt to demonstrate how Japanese view guilt related to possible rebellion against parental expectations. Two possible ways for the male to rebel are: (1) by dissipating energies in some sort of profligate or otherwise unacceptable behavior; or by failing to apply the diligence and hard work necessary to obtain some achievement goal; (2) by rejecting arranged marriage and making a marriage of passion, a so-called love marriage.

In women guilt seems related to becoming selfish or unsubmissive in the pursuit of duties involved in adult role possibilities as wife and mother. Such behavior could consist, as in the case of men, in refusal to accept the parents' marriage arrangement, or, after marriage, in failure to devote oneself with wholehearted intensity, without reservations, to the husband and his purposes and to the rearing of the children. Failure to show a completely masochistic, self-sacrificing devotion to her new family is a negative reflection on the woman's parents. Deficiencies in her children or even in her husband are sometimes perceived as her fault, and she must intrapunitively rectify her own failings if such behavior occurs. TAT stories taken from the Niiike sample bring out, directly and indirectly, evidence to support these contentions.

The Japanese mother has perfected the technique of inducing guilt in her children by quiet suffering. A type of American mother often encountered in clinical practice repeatedly tells her children how she suffers from their bad behavior, but in her own behavior reveals her selfish motives; in contrast, the Japanese mother does not verbalize her suffering for her children to the same extent but lives it out before their eyes. She takes on the burden of responsibility for her children's behavior—and her husband's—and will often manifest self-reproach if they conduct themselves badly. Such an example cannot fail to impress. The child becomes aware that his mother's self-sacrifice demands some recompense. The system of *on* obligation felt toward the parents, aptly described by Ruth Benedict,[10] receives a strong affective push from the Japanese mother's devotion to her children's successful social development, which includes the standards of success set for the community. As will be discussed in Chapter 9, the educational and occupational achievements of Japanese-Americans also show this pattern, modified in accordance with American influences.

The negative side of accomplishment is the hurt inflicted on the parent if the child fails or if he becomes self-willed in marriage or loses himself in indulgence. Profligacy and neglect of a vocational role in Japan—and often in the West as well—are an attack on the parents, frequently unconsciously structured.

The recurrence of certain themes in the TAT data, such as the occurrence of parental death as a result of disobedience (as was discussed in the previous chapter) suggests the prevalence of expiation as a motive for achievement. Themes of illness and death not only seem to be used to show the degree of parental, especially maternal, self-

---

[10] Benedict, *The Chrysanthemum and the Sword* (1946), pp. 99–117.

sacrifice, but also seem to be used as self-punishment in stories of strivings toward an ideal or goal with a single-minded devotion so strong that its effects may bring about the ruin of one's health.

These attitudes toward occupational striving can also be seen in the numerous examples in recent Japanese history of men's self-sacrifice for national causes. The sometimes inexplicable logic—to Western eyes at least—of the self-immolation practiced in wartime by the Japanese soldier can be better understood when it is seen not merely as an act of sacrifice resulting from pressures of group morale and propaganda stressing the honor of such a death; the emotions that make such behavior seem logical are first experienced when the child observes the mother's attitude toward her own body, as she exhausts it in the service of the family.

GUILT RELATED TO PARENTAL SUFFERING

The relation of guilt to parental suffering is apparent in certain TAT stories in which the death of the parent follows the bad conduct of a child, and the two events seem to bear an implicit relationship, as expressed in the following summaries.

(M, age 41, card J6GF) A daughter marries for love against her father's will; she takes care of her father, but the father dies.
(W, age 22, card J6GF) A daughter marries against her father's opposition, but her husband dies and she becomes unhappy.
(M, age 23, card J18) A mother strangles to death the woman who tempted her innocent son; the mother becomes insane and dies. The son begs forgiveness.

In such stories one may assume that a respondent first puts into words an unconscious wish of some kind but then punishes himself by bringing the death of a beloved person quickly into the scene.

One could also interpret such behavior in terms of cultural traditions. Many Japanese have punished others by killing or injuring themselves. Such self-injury or suicide became an accepted pattern of behavior under the rigid feudal regime where open protest was an impossibility. Numerous works on Japanese history contain accounts of the severe limitations on behavior and spontaneous self-expression.

The emotional logic of this behavior, however, requires psychological explanations as well as such valid sociological explanations. This moral masochistic tendency is inculcated through the attitudes of parents, especially of the mother. Suffering whatever the child does, being hurt constantly, subtly assuming an attitude of "look what you have done to me," the Japanese mother often gains by such devices a strong control over her child, and by increasing her overt suffering she can punish him for disobedience or lack of seriousness of purpose. Three of the stories given above suggest that a mother or father is "punishing" a child by dying. Parents' dying is not only the punishment of a child, but also, more often, the final control over that child, breaking his resistance to obeying the parental demands.

This use of death as a final admonition lends credence to a story concerning the Japanese Manchurian forces at the close of World War II. The young officers in Manchuria had determined to fight on indefinitely, even though the home islands had surrendered. A staff general was sent by plane as an envoy of the emperor to order the troops to surrender. He could get nowhere with the officers, who were determined to fight on. Returning to his plane, he took off and circled the field, sending a radio message that this was the final directive to surrender. The plane suddenly dived straight for the landing field, crashing and killing all on board. The troops then promptly surrendered. (See Chapter 17 on admonition suicide.)

It is not unknown for a mother to threaten to die as a means of admonishing a child. In a therapy case with a delinquent boy,[11] the mother had threatened her son, with very serious intent, telling him that he must stop his stealing or she would take him with her to the ocean and commit double suicide.

The mother reasoned that she was responsible and that such a suicide would pay for her failure as a mother, as well as relieve the world of a potentially worthless citizen. The threat worked. For the man, this threat of possible suffering becomes related to the necessity to work hard in the adult occupational role; for the woman, it becomes related to working hard at being a submissive and enduring wife.

In other of the TAT stories the death of a parent is followed by reform, hard work, and success. For example, these are summaries of some of the stories given to various cards:

(W, age 16, card J7M) A son, scolded by his father, walks out; the father dies; the son works hard and becomes successful.

(M, age 39, card J5) A mother worries about her delinquent son, becomes sick, and dies; the son reforms himself and becomes successful.

(M, age 54, card J13) A mother dies; the son changes his attitude and works hard.

(W, age 17, card J7M) A father dies; his son walks out as his mother repeatedly tells him to be like the father; when he meets her again, she dies; he becomes hard-working.

(W, age 38, card J9) Elder brother is going to Tokyo, leaving his sick mother; his sister is opposed to his idea; his mother dies; he will become successful.

(M, age 15, card J6M) A son becomes more thoughtful of his mother after his father's death; he will be successful.

---

[11] Personal communication from a Japanese psychiatrist, Taeko Sumi.

Emphasis on hard work and success after the death of parents clearly suggests some expiatory meaning related to the moral masochistic attitude of the mother. The mother's moral responsibility is also suggested by other stories, such as a mother being scolded by a father when the child does something wrong, or a mother—not the father—being hurt when the child does not behave well. The feeling experienced by the child when he realizes, consciously or unconsciously, that he has hurt his mother is guilt—because guilt is generated when one hurts the object of one's love. The natural ambivalence arising from living under close parental control supplies sufficient unconscious intent to hurt to make the guilt mechanism operative.

The expiatory emphasis on hard work and achievement is also evident as a sequel in TAT stories directly expressing hurt of one's mother or father:

(M, age 17, card J11) A child dropped his father's precious vase. The father gets angry and scolds the mother for her having allowed the child to hold it. The child will become a fine man.

(M, age 53, card J18) A child quarreled outside; his mother is sorry that his father is dead. The child makes a great effort and gets good school records.

(M, age 24, card J11) A mother is worrying about her child who has gone out to play baseball and has not yet come back. When he comes home he overhears his mother complaining about his playing baseball all the time without doing his schoolwork. He then makes up his mind not to play baseball any more and to concentrate on his studies.

Although the realization of having hurt one's parents by bad conduct is not explicit in the following story, it is another example of the use of hard work or study—obviously as the means to achievement —to expiate possible guilt:

(W, age 17, card J3F) A girl worries about the loss of her virginity, consults with someone and feels at ease. She studies hard in the future.

In the same context, if one fails to achieve, he has no way to atone. He is lost. The only thing left is to hurt himself, to extinguish himself —the one whose existence has been hurting his parents and who now can do nothing for them. Suicide as an answer is shown in the following summaries:

(M, age 57, card 3BM, original Murray card) A girl fails an examination, kills herself.

(W, age 32, card J3F) Cannot write a research paper, commits suicide.

On the level of cultural conditioning, the traditional teaching of *on* obligations enhances the feeling of guilt in the child, who is repeatedly taught by parents, teachers, and books that his parents have undergone hardship and trouble and made many sacrifices in order to bring him up. For example, parents may have suffered financial strain and ill health because of overwork for the sake of this child. Of course, the child did not ask for all this sacrifice, nor does he consciously feel that he has intentionally hurt the parents, but there seems no way out; all this suffering takes place somewhere beyond his control, and he cannot avoid the burden it imposes. Certainly the child cannot say to himself, "I did not ask my parents to get hurt; their hurt is not my business," because he knows his parents love him and are also the objects of his love. What can be done about it then? The only way open to the child is to attain the highest goal expected of him; by working hard, being virtuous, becoming successful, gaining a good reputation and the praise of society, he brings honor to himself, to his parents, and to his *ie* (household lineage), of which he and his parents are, after all, parts. If he is virtuous in this way, the parents also receive self-satisfaction and praise from society for having fulfilled their duty to *ie* and and society by raising their children well. The pattern repeats itself; the child sacrifices himself masochistically for his own children, and on and on.

My assumption is that among many Japanese people such a feeling of guilt very often underlies the strong achievement drive and aspiration toward success. If this hypothesis is accepted, then it can easily be understood that the death of a parent—that is, the symbolic culmination of the parent's being hurt following some bad conduct of a child—evokes in the child a feeling of guilt strong enough to bring him back from delinquent behavior and to drive him toward hard work and success. This is what underlies the TAT stories of parental death and the child's reform.

GUILT IN JAPANESE MARRIAGE RELATIONSHIPS

The feeling of *on* obligations generated in the family situation during childhood is also a central focus in Japanese arranged marriages and in this context is very pronounced in women. In a sense, a woman expresses her need for accomplishment and achievement by aiming toward the fulfillment of her roles as wife and mother within the new family she enters at marriage. A man does not face giving up his family ties in the same way. Interview data suggest that, for a Japanese woman, failure to be a dutiful bride reflects on her upbringing, and therefore any discord with her new family, even with an unreasonable mother-in-law, injures the reputation of her parents.

Marriages that, counter to family considerations, are based on individual passion or love are particularly prone to disrupt the family structure. Such marriages are often an expression of rebellion, and any subsequent stresses of adjustment to the partner or the respective families tend to remind the participants of the rebellious tone of the marriage and to elicit guilt feelings.

The TAT stories give evidence of guilt in regard to both types of "unacceptable" behavior in marriage; they show the wife's readiness to blame herself for difficulties with her husband, and they show both men and women expressing self-blame or blame of others for having undertaken love marriages.

The Wife's Self-Blame in Difficulties with Her Husband

In several of the stories involving discord between a man and his wife, the woman feels herself to be wrong in a situation that in the United States would be interpreted as resulting from the poor behavior of the husband. There are no stories showing the reverse—a man being blamed in an even slightly equivocal situation.

Of five such stories, four are given by women. The one story given by a man involves a need for reform by both partners, who are united in a love marriage and therefore conform to the guilt pattern of such marriages. In summary, the four women's stories are:

(W, age 26, card J3F) A wife quarreled with her husband when he returned from drinking. She leaves her house to cry, feels guilty for the quarrel.
(W, age 54, card J4) A husband and wife quarrel because the former criticized her cooking. The wife apologizes to him.
(W, age 37, card J4) A husband and wife quarrel, and after it the wife apologizes to her angry husband.
(W, age 22, card J5) A husband comes home very late at night; the wife thinks it is due to her lack of affection and tries hard; he finally reforms.

Such attitudes seem to be reflected also in other test data, such as the "problem situations" material described in Chapter 2. It is especially interesting to note that women may attribute a husband's profligacy to the wife's failure. The husband's willfulness—like that of a male child—appears in some instances to be accepted as natural; somehow it is not his business to control himself if he feels annoyed with his wife, but nevertheless the wife must take responsibility for her husband's conduct. In one case of a psychotic reaction in a young wife,[12] the mother-in-law blamed the bride directly for her husband's extramarital activities, saying, "If you were a good and satisfying wife, he would have no need to go elsewhere."

In connection with this point it may be worth mentioning that probably on the deepest level many Japanese wives do not "give" themselves completely to their husbands, because the marriage has been forced on them as an arrangement between the parents in each family. Wives often may not be able to adjust their innermost feelings

---

[12] Described in personal communication by the Japanese psychiatrist Kei Hirano.

in the marital relationship so as to be able to love their husbands genuinely. They may sense their own emotional resistance, and believe that an evil willfulness keeps them from complete devotion as dictated by ethical ideals of womanhood. Aware in the deepest level of their minds of their lack of real affection, they become sensitive to the slightest indication of unfaithful behavior by the husbands. Feeling that their husbands are reacting to their own secret unfaithfulness in withholding, they cannot blame their husbands, but throw the blame back upon themselves. When, for example, their husbands happen to be late in getting home, they may become very anxious, reflecting upon their own inadequacies and attempting to remedy them. Another possible interpretation is that Japanese women, lacking freedom to express their own impulses, identify with male misbehavior and assume guilt as if the misbehavior were their own.

This propensity for self-blame in women is not necessarily limited to the wife's role. In the following story, already cited in a previous chapter, a younger sister somehow feels that she is culpable when an older brother misbehaves.

(W, age 17, card J9) An elder brother did something wrong and is examined by the policeman; he will be taken to the police station but will return home and reform. The younger sister also thinks that she was wrong herself.

One might say, in generalization, that the ethical ideal of woman's self-sacrifice and devotion to the family line—whether to father or elder brother before marriage, or to husband and children after marriage—carries with it internalized propensities to take blame upon oneself and to express a moral sensitivity in these family relationships that no religious or other cultural sanctions compel men to share.

Love Marriages and Other Heterosexual Relationships

The TAT stories from Niiike concerning marriage circumstances show, as we demonstrated in Chapter 2, that many of the men and women in Niiike who bring up the subject of love marriage still do not see it in a positive light but rather as a source of disruption. In certain stories, such as the following, a love marriage made in open rebellion against the parents is punished by the death of a beloved person.

(M, age 41, card J6F) They are father and his daughter. The mother has died. The daughter is sitting on a chair in her room. The father is looking in, and she is turning around to face him. He is very thoughtful of his daughter, and as she is just about of age for marriage he wants to suggest that she marry a certain man he has selected. But she has a lover and does not want to marry the man her father suggests. The father is trying to read her face, though he does know about the existence of the lover. He brought up the subject a few times before, but the daughter showed no interest in it. Today also—a smile is absent in her face. The father talks about the subject again, but he fails to persuade her. So finally he gives in and agrees to her marrying her lover. Being grateful to the father for his consent, the daughter acts very kindly to him after her marriage. The husband and the wife get along very affectionately also. But her father dies suddenly of apoplexy. The father was not her real father. He did not have children, so he adopted her, and accepted her husband as his son-in-law. But he died. He died just at the time when a baby was born to the couple.

(W, age 22, card J6) The parents of this girl were brought up in families strongly marked with feudal attitudes—the kind of family scarcely found in the present time—so they are very feudal and strict. The daughter cannot stand her parents. She had to meet her lover in secret. She was seeing her lover today as usual, without her parents knowing it. But by accident her father found out, and she was caught by her father on the spot. When she returned home her father rebuked her severely for it. But she could not give up her lover. In spite of her parents' strong objection, she married him. [Examiner: Future?] The couple wanted to establish a happy home when they married, but probably she will lose her husband. He will die—and she will have a miserable life.

There are a number of stories about unhappy events in the lives of couples married for love. Many of these are told in response to card J13 of the TAT. Since responses to this card bring out in clear focus some basic differences between guilt over sexuality in Americans and in the Japanese, it will be well to consider them here in some detail although some have already been cited previously.

Card J13 in the Japanese series is a slight modification of the original Murray TAT card 13, with furniture and facial features altered.

Comparing Japanese and American responses to card J13 makes it clear that while Americans never express remorse over "committing" a marriage the Japanese, at least those of Niiike, express remorse in a heterosexual situation in the context of a love marriage. For Americans, card 13 is apt to evoke stories of guilt related to intercourse between partners not married to each other; the woman is sometimes identified as a prostitute or sometimes as a young girl. When the figures are identified by Americans as married, the themes are usually around the subject of illness. In contrast, in the sample of forty-two stories given in response to this card in Niiike village, not one story depicts a theme of guilt over sexuality between unmarried partners. Remorse is depicted only when it is related to regret for having entered into a love marriage.

Most themes of Japanese stories given in response to this card fall into one of three categories: sex or violence or both (ten stories); marital discord (ten stories); and sickness or death (twenty stories). Some striking differences in themes are related to the age and sex of the subjects.

CARD J13: RESPONSES INVOLVING SEX AND/OR VIOLENCE. Six stories involve themes of extramarital sexual liaison. In three, the woman is killed by the man. Five of the six stories are given by men who, with one exception, are under thirty-five, and one is given by a woman under twenty-five. In the young woman's story, a man kills a woman because she was too jealous of him. One young man sees a man killing an entertainer who rejects him. Another sees a man killing a woman who was pursuing him "too actively." Another young man tells a story of a student and a prostitute, in which the man is disturbed by the prostitute's nakedness, not by his feelings of guilt over his activity.

The man over thirty-five sees the picture as depicting disillusionment in a man who unexpectedly calls on a woman with whom he is in love, only to find her asleep in a "vulgar" fashion. As is true in the stories about marital discord told by other men over thirty-five, the man is highly censorious of the woman's position on the bed. A relaxed appearance reflects a wanton or sluttish nature.

Japanese men are apt to split their relationships with women into two groups: those with the wife and those with entertainers. Other evidence supports the conclusion that, for many men, genuine affection is directed only toward maternal figures, and that little deep affection is freely available toward women perceived in a sexual role. Moreover, the Japanese male must defend himself against any passivity in his sexual relationship, lest he fall into a dependent relationship and become tied. By maintaining a rude aloofness and by asserting male prerogatives, he protects himself from involvement.

Men can resort to a violent defense if threatened too severely. Younger women especially tend to see men as potentially violent. In the stories discussed above, three women under thirty-five see a man killing a woman, in two cases his wife. In addition to the jealousy mentioned before, the motives are the wife's complaint about low salary (a man must be seen as particularly sensitive about his economic prowess if such a complaint results in murder), and regret for entering a love marriage. The story which follows is particularly pertinent to understanding how guilt is related not to sexuality per se but to becoming involved.

(W, age 22, card J13) He got married for love with a woman in spite of opposition by his parents. While they were first married they lived happily, but recently he has reflected on his marriage and the manner in which he overrode his parents' opposition—and the present wife—he wishes his present wife did not exist—he attempts to push away the feeling of blame within his breast. One night on the way home he buys some insect poison and gives it to his wife to drink and she dies. What he has done weighs on his mind. He gives himself up to the police. He tells his story frankly to them. He reflects on how wicked he has been in the past. He completes his prison term and faces the future seriously.

This story indirectly brings out a feeling of guilt for attempting to carry out a love marriage.

CARD J13: RESPONSES INVOLVING MARITAL DISCORD. The flavor given stories concerning marital discord is unique to the Japanese. Seven of the twenty-one Niiike men giving stories about card J13 mention marital discord. Five of these men and all three women giving such stories, are between thirty-five and fifty years of age. The men tend to see the marriage as ending badly, whereas the women are more optimistic about seeing the discord resolved. Both sexes usually place the blame for the discord on the women.

As in one of the stories mentioned previously, the men take a cue for their stories from the position of the woman in the bed. They do not see the woman as ill, as do many of the women, but use the woman's posture as a basis for criticizing her. One of the chief complaints is that such a woman obviously does not take "proper care" of her man. The following stories bring out the nature of some of the feelings leading to the castigation of the wife for "looseness" and lack of wifely concern for her husband. The man, too, is castigated in some of the stories, but not with the strength of feeling that is turned toward the woman.

(M, age 39, card J13) This is also very difficult for me. What shall I say— I can't tell my impressions—what shall I say—it seems to me that they do not lead a happy life. The man often comes back home late at night, I suppose. But his wife does not wait for her husband. She has decided to act independently of her own accord, I suppose—he is back home late again, and his wife is already asleep. He thinks that it might be well to speak to her. I suppose there is always a gloomy feeling in this family. Well, if they led a peaceful life, such a scene as this would never occur. It is customary that a wife takes care of her husband, as she should when he comes home—and afterward she goes to bed. But, judging from this picture, I suppose this wife wouldn't care a bit about her husband. Such a family as this will be ruined, I think. They should change their attitude toward each other and should make a happy home. [Examiner: What about the future?] They will be divorced. It will be their end. [Examiner: Do you have anything to add?] Well, I expect a woman to be as a woman should be. A man also should think more of his family.

(M, age 41, card J13) This is also—this man is a drunkard, and his wife also a sluttish woman. And the man was drunk, and when he came back his wife was already asleep—and, well—finally, they will be ruined. They have no child. They will become separated from each other. This wife will become something like *nakai* or a procuress. The husband will be held in prison—and the husband will kill himself on the railroad tracks. And—the wife will work as a *nakai,* and after contracting an infectious disease will die. The infectious disease that attacks her is dysentery. They worked together in a company and were married for love. That is their past. [Examiner: What does it mean that they will be ruined?] He became desperate. He became separated from his wife, so he became desperate. If a man commits a bad thing, nobody cares for him. He could not hope for any help, so he killed himself.

(M, age 35, card J13) Well, this man and woman married for love. The woman was a café waitress and married the man for love. But they have not lived happily, so the man repents the marriage very much. Well, this man used to be a very good man, but he was seduced by the waitress and lost his self-control, and at last he had a sexual relationship with her. Afterwards [after they marry], he becomes afraid and he has to think over their [impulsive] marriage. If their married life has any future at all I hope they will maintain some better stability. But if this woman doesn't want to do so, he needs to think over their marriage, I suppose.

The last story, especially, brings out strong feelings of guilt related to an attempt to maintain a love marriage. The story directly depicts the guilt as related to losing self-control and becoming involved with an unsuitable woman, not with sexual activity per se.

Implied, too, is the idea that any woman who would make a love marriage is not really capable of being a very worthy wife. Therefore, in addition to depicting guilt for going counter to the parents in a love marriage, card J13 is seen as indicating the potential avenue for projecting guilt onto the woman who is active enough to enter a love marriage. Such a woman's conduct obviously does not include the proper submissiveness to parental wishes and therefore she would probably fail in giving attention to the needs of her spouse.

This castigation of the woman is therefore directly related to an expectation that the wife, instead of being a sexual object, should be a figure fulfilling dependency needs. The man sees his wife in a maternal role and is probably quick to complain if she renders him less care and attention than he received from his mother. Since the wife-mother image tends to be fused in Japanese men, they have little conception of companionship or of the mutual sharing of experience; moreover, the too-free sexual behavior of the wife excites in the husband aspects of sexuality that were repressed toward the mother in childhood. The wife-mother image cannot be conceived in gross sexual terms. It is speculated by some that some Japanese need a mistress because their sexual potency toward their wives is muted by the fused wife-mother image. Free sexual attitudes on the part of the wife would tend to change her image from mother to prostitute.

One may say that this fusion of images has a great deal to do with the conflict often arising between the young bride and her mother-in-law. The mother-in-law's jealousy is due in part to her fear of being directly replaced in her son's affection by the bride, since their roles are essentially similar. The wife becomes more intimate with the husband after she becomes a mother, and comes to treat him essentially as the favorite child.

These attitudes were evident in the case mentioned previously in which a woman's psychotic episode was precipitated by her mother-in-law's attacks, including her interpretation that the alliance of her son with other women was proof of the wife's incompetence. It is interesting to note in connection with this case that during the wife's stay in the hospital the husband was able to express considerable feeling of concern for her. There was no doubt that he loved her. In effect, however, this feeling was more for her as a maternal surrogate than as a sexual partner. His mother knew she had more to fear from the wife in this respect than from her son's liaisons with other women, with whom he never became too greatly involved. He, on the other hand, had no manifest guilt for his sexual activities—in effect, they were approved of by his mother in her battle with the wife.

In six responses, of which five are from women, three of them teenagers, card J13 is interpreted as a mother-son situation with the mother either sick or dead. The son is pictured specifically as working hard or studying; in one story the son steals because they are so poor. The younger girls especially seem to need to defend themselves from the sexual implications of the card by inventing a completely desexualized relationship. Unable to make the card into a marital situation, much less a more directly sexual one, some fall back on the favored theme of a sick mother and a distraught but diligent son. Emphasis on studying hard suggests the defensive use of work and study to shut out intrapersonal problems. Diligent work to care for the mother is again unconsciously used to avoid any feelings related to possible guilt. The way out is the one most easily suggested by the culture. Seeing card 13 as a mother-son situation is rare in American records, even in aberrant cases.

Seeing card J13 as depicting illness or death of a wife is the most characteristic response of women; fourteen women, most of them over thirty-five, gave such stories. Six men, including four of the five in the sample over age fifty, selected this theme. The middle-aged women were strongly involved in their stories about the death of a wife. Such stories were the longest of any given to the card. In sharp contrast to the derogatory stories directed toward the women by the men, the women use respectful concepts, such as *otoko-naki* ("manly tears"), in referring to the men. On certain occasions it is expected that manly tears are shed. Although a man is usually expected not to cry freely

when sober, the death of a wife is an occasion on which he is expected
to cry. Much emphasis is placed on the imagined love felt toward the
wife by a husband, on his loneliness, and on his feeling of loss because
of the absence of wifely care. Concern with potential loneliness and
possible loss of such care is certainly reflected in the fact that most of
the older men select similar themes. All but one of the women see the
wife as dead or dying; the man is frequently seen as remarrying.
Conversely, the men are more optimistic about recovery of a wife
from illness and more pessimistic about remarriage if she does not
recover.

One woman constructs a story of a sick wife who commits suicide
so as not to be a burden to her husband. This type of story, which
recalls many sentimental Japanese novels is very moving to the Japanese, since it is supposed to reflect the degree of devotion of a wife
for her husband and his goals and purposes. To the Westerner, the
stories seem to be excessively masochistic and exaggerated. The Japanese ethical ideal of the self-sacrificing role of woman is here emphati-
cally displayed.

CONCLUSION

The foregoing material from Niiike which other evidence suggests
is deeply imbued with traditional attitudes, is consistent with the
interpretation that the potentiality for strong guilt feelings is prevalent in the Japanese. Such feelings are aroused when there is failure
in the performance of expected role behavior. Among the Japanese
there is little pronounced guilt or otherwise negatively toned attitude
directed toward physical expression of sexuality per se. Rather, sexuality is related to guilt indirectly in the concern with possible loss
of control through the individual's becoming involved in a love relationship that interferes with his prescribed life goals.

From a sociological standpoint, Japanese culture can be considered
to manifest a particularistic or situational ethic as opposed to the
more universalistic ethic built around moral absolutes found in Western Christian thought.[13] This evaluation can be well documented,
but it does not mean that the Japanese people evidence a relative
absence of guilt. Whereas in many situations the more universalistic
Western ethic may tend to transcend the family, the Japanese traditional ethic is actually an expression of rules of conduct for members
of a family, and filial piety has in itself certain moral absolutes that
are not completely determined situationally, though they tend to be

[13] See Parsons, *The Social System* (1951), p. 175, for a description of the particularistic achievement pattern. This category suits traditional Japanese culture very
well.

conceptualized in particularistic terms. This difference between family-oriented morality and a more universalistic moral system is, nevertheless, a source of difficulty in the understanding of guilt in the Japanese.

Another reason for the failure of Western observers to perceive guilt in the Japanese stems from the West's customary relation of guilt to sexuality. Missionaries in particular, in assessing the Japanese from the standpoint of Protestant moral standards, were often quoted as being perplexed not only by what they considered a lack of moral feelings in regard to nonfamilial relationships, but also—and this was even worse in their eyes—by a seeming absence of any strong sense of "sin" in Japanese sexual relationships. It seems evident that the underlying emotional content of certain aspects of Christianity requiring repression and displacement of sexual and aggressive impulses has never appealed to the Japanese, in spite of their intellectual regard for the ethics of Christianity. Many modern educated Japanese recognize Christianity as advocating an advanced ethical system more in concert with modern universalized democratic ideals of man's brotherhood than are traditional Japanese ethics. As such, Christianity is favored by them over their more hierarchically oriented traditional system with its rigidly defined particularistic emphasis on prescribed social roles. For the educated Japanese, however, the concept of sin has little place in attitudes toward Christianity. This lack of interest in sin is most probably related to the absence of childhood disciplines that would make the concept important to the Japanese.

Traditional Western disciplinary methods, guided by concern with the inherent evil in man, have been based on the idea that the child must be trained as early as possible to conquer evil tendencies within himself. Later, he learns to resist outside pressures and maintain himself as an individual subject to his own conscience and to the universalist laws of God. The traditional Western Protestant is accustomed in certain circumstances to repress inappropriate feelings. "Right" thoughts are valued highly, and one generally tries to repress unworthy motives. Justice must be impartial, and one must not be swayed by the feelings of the moment or be too flexible in regard to equity.

In Japanese Buddhist thought one finds a dual concept of man as good and evil, but in Shinto thought, and in Japanese thinking about children generally,[14] the more prevailing notion is that man's im-

---

[14] It is significant that in Japan the ceremonials for marriage and fertility and to celebrate various periods in childhood are Shinto, whereas Buddhist ceremonials are used mainly in paying respect to parents—that is, in funerals and in memorial services at specified times after death. It must be noted that the material in this chapter does not include any references to fear of punishment in an afterlife; al-

pulses are innately good. The purpose of child training is merely the channeling of these impulses into appropriate role behavior.

The definitions of proper role behavior become more and more exacting as the child grows and comes into increasing contact with others as a representative of his family. As such, he learns to be more and more diplomatic and to contain and suppress impulses and feelings that would be disruptive in social relations and that would put him at a disadvantage. He does not bring a system of moral absolutes into his relations with others any more than does a diplomat who negotiates for the advantage of his country. The Japanese learns to be sensitive to "face" and protocol and to be equally sensitive to the feelings of others. He learns to keep his personal feelings to himself as a family representative. It would be fallacious to assume, therefore, that the Japanese is without much sense of guilt, just as it would be to assume that a career diplomat has no personal sense of guilt. The fact that so much of their conscious life is concerned with a system of social sanctions helps to disguise the underlying guilt system operative in the Japanese. This system is well disguised not only from the Western observer but also from the Japanese themselves. The Westerner, under the tutelage of Christianity, has learned to "universalize" his aggressive and other impulses and feel guilt in regard to them in general terms. The modern Japanese is moving toward such an attitude, but he is affected by the traditional moral structure based on the family system, or, in expanded form, on the nation conceived of in familial terms.

Lastly, some difficulty in perceiving Japanese guilt theoretically, if not clinically, arises because psychoanalysis—the psychological system most often consulted for help in understanding the mechanisms involved in guilt—tends to be strongly influenced by Western ethical values. Psychoanalytic writers, in describing psychosexual development, tend to emphasize the superego on the one hand and concepts of personal individuation and autonomy on the other. For the Westerner a major goal of maturation is freedom of the ego from irrational social controls as well as from excessive internalized superego demands. For an understanding of the Japanese this emphasis is somewhat out of focus. Maturational ideals valued by the traditional Japanese society put far more emphasis on concepts of "belonging" and on adult role identity.

---

though such references have been present in traditional Buddhism in the past, they are not much in evidence in modern Japan. Relatively few modern Japanese believe in or are concerned with life beyond death. (See Chapter 4.) It is my contention that fear of punishment either by the parents, society, or God is not truly internalized guilt. Insofar as the punishment is perceived as external in source, the feeling is often fear or anxiety, as distinct from guilt.

In studying the Japanese, it is helpful, therefore, to try to understand the nature of internalization of an ego ideal defined in terms of social role behavior. Concern with social role has in the past been more congenial to the sociologist or sociologically oriented anthropologist,[15] who in examining human behavior is less specifically concerned with individuation and more concerned with the patterning of behavior within a network of social relations.

However, the sociological approach in itself does not provide a sufficient explanation of the presence or absence of a strong achievement motive in the Japanese. It is necessary to use a psychoanalytic framework to examine the psychological processes whereby social roles are internalized and influence the formation of an internalized ego ideal. The ideas of Erikson,[16] in his exploration of the role of "self-identity" in the latter stages of the psychosexual maturation process, form a bridge between the psychoanalytic systems of thought and the sociological analyses that cogently describe the place of role as a vital determining factor of social behavior. Erikson's approach offers promise for an understanding of the Japanese social tradition and its effect on individual development.

---

[15] This approach is also evident in the theorist in religion. Also, the recent interest in existentialist psychiatry is one attempt to bring in relevant concepts of "belonging" to the study of the human experience. See the further discussion in Chapter 17 on Japanese suicide as related to a failure of belonging.

[16] Erikson, "The Problem of Ego Identity" (1956).

Part Two:

Achievement Motivation

Part Two Introduction

Achievement Motivation
and Social Change

In the following four chapters I evaluate critically various theories of economic development and social change as they relate to achievement motivation. I bring to center stage the larger socioeconomic issues raised by my previous discussion of internalized guilt and achievement motivation in the Japanese.

Chapter 6 returns to a consideration of the instrumental-expressive dichotomy in human social role behavior discussed in Chapter 1. The discussion here elaborates my position in much broader terms; I maintain that there is an ethnocentric bias in much of social theory, especially economic theory. Both classic and Marxian economists implicitly assume that the human behavior governing the segmentation of human groups is instrumentally motivated; such behavior, therefore, largely determines the directions taken in the history of change in societies or culture. I question this assumption.

Western psychological theory, too, has its biases. The gist of Chapter 6 is an attack on ethnocentrism in a well-respected psychological theory of achievement motivation. Principally, I attack the theoretical approach of David McClelland and his associates for the way it generalizes a relationship between need achievement and individualism that is recurrently apparent in West European culture. I cite my interpretation of Japanese need achievement as an argument against the universality of McClelland's theory.

Chapter 7 continues my critique of theories of economic development viewed from the perspective of a psychocultural approach to social change in Japan. From the standpoint of my own emphasis on the peculiarities of internalized Japanese values related to achievement, I also criticize briefly Everett Hagen's theory of social change. I do not differ with Hagen's generally cogent attempt to apply a psychocultural approach. However, he adopts a prevalent cliche about "shame" as a basic behavioral motive in Japanese culture, whereas I contend that the Japanese achievement motives cannot be seen apart from underlying processes in socialization that induce *guilt* internally, and *trust* externally, in the Japanese social structure.

Chapter 8, written in collaboration with Hiroshi Wagatsuma, relates Japanese social role motivational patterns more specifically to features of Japanese traditional social structure still operative in the life styles of the petty merchants and artisans of a lower-class urban ward in Tokyo. This chapter spells out in some detail the interaction of psychological motivations with the economic determinants in social structure. In Japan one still finds, partially operative at least, paternalistic *oyabun-kobun* ("patron-client") structures derived from Japan's premodern past. Psychological as well as economic dependencies, based on long-term apprenticeship experiences in youth, develop into continuing patterns of social and economic reciprocity in later life. Also peculiarly Japanese are the pervasive entrepreneurial attitudes developed among even the lowest social strata of urbanized Japanese. No Western society to my knowledge exhibits a comparably prevalent pattern.

Data for this chapter were generated by the standard method of face-to-face anthropological interviewing. Firsthand material was analyzed against a background of economic data and the well-researched analyses of culturally sophisticated economists such as William Lockwood and of economic historians such as Thomas Smith, whose writings are largely responsible for structuring my view of Japanese economic development.[1]

In the final chapter in this section I come, in effect, full circle in the expression of my theoretical interests. It was in collaboration with William Caudill in 1947[2] that I first addressed myself to the issue of achievement motivation in Japanese culture; this work dealt with Japanese as immigrants to the United States. We wanted to understand and explain the relatively successful social and economic adaptation of Japanese-Americans. During World War II, Japanese immigrants and their families suffered severe forms of social and economic discrimination—including being sent en masse to American concentration camps—yet they have managed to sustain themselves against discrimination without showing any of the usual social indices of personal disorganization. They have the lowest crime and delinquency rates of any of the definable ethnic groups in California. The Amer-

---

[1] Lockwood, *The Economic Development of Japan: Growth and Structural Change* (1954); T. Smith, *The Agrarian Origins of Modern Japan* (1966), and "Landlords' Sons in the Business Elite" (1960).

[2] Cf. n. 7 in Chapter 9 for other collaborators on research in Chicago.

ican-born Japanese-Americans continue to average approximately four years more schooling than does the nation as a whole. They have gone into white-collar and professional employment in very high proportions. In our joint paper, first published in 1956,[3] Caudill and I presented the argument that the cultural tradition of Japan, mediated by socialization within intact Japanese family units, was responsible for passing on a strong need for achievement (called need-achievement in psychological literature) from one generation to the next.

The Japanese-American evidence confounds the often too facile sociological generalities about the invariably negative effects of social discrimination. The Japanese acculturation to the United States amply demonstrates that the acculturation patterns of immigrants to a new society depend heavily not only on their acceptability to the host society but also on the nature of the cultural response by the immigrant group itself to external social stimulations and challenges. Any ethnic-group response to the possible stresses of acculturation is governed by psychocultural reaction patterns that are characteristic for the specific group. This was the point that Caudill and I made in our original study. The values and role expectations sanctioned within the family by immigrants are of major importance in understanding the direction taken and the relative facility of acculturation of any group. This earliest study, conducted shortly after the dislocation of Japanese-Americans by the enforced relocation from the West Coast during World War II, has proved to be prophetic of trends that have continued to the present. We have been pleased to find that time has supported our conclusions and that I can again publish this article without need to modify it in any way.

---

[3] Caudill and DeVos, "Achievement, Culture and Personality: The Case of the Japanese Americans" (1956).

Chapter VI

The Cultural Context of Achievement Motivation: Comparative Research

INSTRUMENTAL AND EXPRESSIVE BEHAVIOR IN SOCIAL CHANGE

Rapid social change is taken for granted today. Forces of change are manifestly at work in every culture.[1] Many previously isolated cultural groups are now gradually being absorbed in an interrelated world-society with a pervasively secularized set of implicit values. Even the seemingly disparate and opposed ideologies of socialism and capitalism, when examined closely, are found to be based on similar premises and to have similar goals. They differ only in the economic and political means advocated for the realization of these goals.

The major forces at work in this gradual worldwide homogenization of values are economic and political in nature; however, the peculiarly different responses of individual cultures to the economic and political forces pressing them toward accelerated social change cannot be explained solely by economic or political theory. The conception of the challenge and the adequacy of the response differ widely, depending on the culture. To the objective observer it becomes quickly apparent that the cultural history and the psychological peculiarities of a people must be considered significant as forces impeding or facilitating change. What is sometimes less apparent is that these peculiarities have to do more with the expressive than with the instrumental aspects of culturally determined behavior.

It has been relatively easy for anthropologists or sociologists to classify, categorize, and conceptualize the instrumental aspects of cul-

---

[1] Part of this chapter has appeared in "Achievement and Innovation in Culture and Personality," Norbeck, Price-Williams, and McCord (eds.) *The Study of Personality: An Interdisciplinary Appraisal* (1968), pp. 348–370.

ture. Man has used considerable ingenuity and rationality to cope with the essential difficulties of any of the highly diverse geographic or social environments within which he has found himself. Whatever the culture, much of man's behavior becomes understandable when one views it as directed toward realizing some understandable economic or social-political end. It has been much harder to comprehend man's behavior cross-culturally when various forms of expressive behavior are considered.

Although man has adapted himself rationally to the demands of his natural and social environment, he must be considered a peculiarly irrational animal. He creates for himself curious problems and complexities uncalled for by a direct simple need for either survival or social dominance. Expressively, man is a religious, artistic, and playful animal as much as he is a political or economic animal. Man developed not only into a Promethean rebel, a violator of nature and a killer of his own kind, but also into a dreamer and an idealist.

These aspects of man's nature are difficult to fathom and are not often satisfactorily accounted for in social science theory. Each observer, as he examines the behavioral motives in cultures other than his own, finds it difficult to shed his own implicit values, which subjectively color his perception of man's expressive nature. Although he may well comprehend the rational elements of another culture, his own unexamined, irrationally based values make a truly relativistic approach virtually impossible when it comes to studying expressively determined beliefs and behavior. Man's behavior is never limited to establishing a means for survival. Aspects of a culture that start out as utilitarian, such as particular techniques used in the development of material artifacts, eventually become ends in themselves and in this sense expressive. The shape of material artifacts, grammatical structures in language, or modes of artistic representation come to be cherished in themselves not merely as utilitarian forms but as social values, and they may end up by becoming something quite nonutilitarian. Changes gradually occurring in previously functional aspects of culture may come to be governed more by a sense of style than by a continuing need for utilitarian adaptation.

We can observe psychologically that all men are motivated. The social scientist, whatever his specialized discipline—economics, political science, or sociology—works with some more or less well-differentiated, implicit theory of human motivation. Few would hold that man's behavior is totally guided by the immediate external sanctions of his society. Most recognize the presence of internal motivations or "needs" that govern and direct human action. One such generally recognized need is the need to achieve or accomplish. This is usually considered as a need which leads to an emphasis on the instrumental rather than the expressive elements in behavior; achievement behavior is directed toward the realization of a future goal and is not simply an end in itself, or a source of pleasure for the individual so behaving.

For any culture to survive, the younger generation must become motivated to take on expected roles. In this sense, all individuals are achievement-oriented when they conform to the cultural pattern in which they grow up. To grow up, one must want to move from the status of a child to that of an adult and must direct one's behavior toward some form of future accomplishment.

However, achievement motivation, as ordinarily defined in modern societies in contrast to tradition-oriented societies, is not static but a dynamic force for social change in society; it is seen as taking place within some system of social stratification in which individuals do not attempt solely to repeat the past role of a parent but tend to work to win higher status through a capacity to take risks, to excel, or to innovate. Nevertheless, in most social systems, simple or complex, higher status can usually be obtained by acquiring material wealth or through a developed capacity to dominate by the manipulation of personal or group power. Behavior carefully guided toward the realization of a goal of higher status is by definition highly instrumental in nature.

In every culture, higher status can also be realized, in more subtle ways than by direct economic or political means, by individuals who exemplify or express the "sacred" or the basic unquestioned values of the society. Such an individual finds himself accorded some form of relative social status reflecting his position in a hierarchy of the sacred that exists in even the most instrumentally oriented societies. No society is without its exemplars of the ideal, as personified today in the social roles of the scientist, the artist, the teacher, or the religious leader. These roles have their precursors; established values are not static, even in simple societies.

Innovation and invention in social behavior are not limited to politics and economics; either may take the form of religious innovation or social reform, often brought about by a charismatically directed reordering of general social values. Llewellyn and Hoebel [2] and Barnett[3] give examples from American Indians and New Guinea natives, respectively, of how social change can occur essentially in the area of values rather than of politics or economics. Llewellyn and Hoebel discuss the emergence of certain law patterns among the Cheyenne and Barnett discusses cultural, economic, and political changes brought about through religious innovation in New Guinea. These two anthropological studies present case examples of changes

---

[2] Llewelyn and Hoebel, *The Cheyenne Way* (1941).

[3] Barnett, "Peace and Progress in New Guinea" (1959).

that result from the rise of particular charismatic leaders operating within the context of the expressive aspects of the culture, who through these means obtain eventual political dominance. The sociologist Weber[4] was well aware of the expressive aspects of leadership, as evidenced in his discussion of the charismatic leader and his influence in bringing about social innovation.

Static societies discourage innovation, however. They tend to maintain themselves by fairly rigid prescriptions of fixed adult roles into which both men and women are socialized. These expected social roles define the limits of aspiration for each generation. When status is ascribed rather than achieved, individual effort toward excellence is not directed through any form of innovation; rather, the enhancement of status occurs only through the realization of a previously well-defined role position. It is only with social change or when some form of continual dynamic disequilibrium occurs in a society that we begin to think of achievement motivation in its modern sense.

As has been well pointed out in different contexts by Tonnies,[5] Redfield,[6] Riesman,[7] and others, many societies that previously were relatively static are moving today with increasing acceleration from folk-type societies, with their traditional cultures based on a kinship network of ascribed status to societies of the "marketplace." In the latter one can attain status only through some form of self-initiated personal achievement requiring well-directed and integrated motivation toward realizing social standards that are to different degrees defined either by firmly internalized patterns or by contemporary patterns of social approval.

Achievement or accomplishment itself can be a form of personal validation. In this sense, achievement must be considered to be motivated by some psychological patterning that guides behavior in accord with a value system. Such a value system is "sacred," in Durkheim's terminology, even when it embodies the value orientations of a thoroughly secularized culture. This fusion of internalized achievement needs and the necessity for personal validation through economic success is what seemingly occurred in premodern northern Europe, according to the differing interpretations of Max Weber[8] and R. H. Tawney.[9] Such a fusion also occurred in Japan during the Meiji period. During this period of self-conscious, government-directed modernization, the quasi-religious feudal social values of the former samurai were

---

[4] Weber, *Wirtschaft und Gesellschaft* (1925).
[5] Tonnies, *Gemeinschaft und Gesellschaft* (1940).
[6] Redfield, *Peasant Society and Culture* (1956).
[7] Riesman, *The Lonely Crowd* (1950).
[8] Weber, *Wirtschaft und Gesellschaft* (1925).
[9] Tawney, *Religion and the Rise of Capitalism* (1926).

transmuted into an entrepreneurial ideology that directed behavior into life-long patterns of economic activity, contributing to the rapid economic development of Japan.[10]

Without the presence of some widespread, subjective need for personal validation, through economic and other forms of achievement, to guide the behavior of a large group of the members of a culture, there is a question whether one can speak of a society as being "achievement oriented." Cultures differ radically in how they foster modes of personality integration resulting in economic or social innovation, or in how they foster a facility for acculturative borrowing, or in both.

Awareness of the role of cultural differences in modern economic development has increased. These differences, however, cannot be understood without further exploration of underlying psychological mechanisms. Robert LeVine, in his introduction to his recent monograph on achievement-motivation in Nigeria, summarizes this point of view very well:

It has become increasingly clear that a high rate of economic development in a country cannot be guaranteed by the presence of abundant natural resources, capital, and even skilled manpower. Consequently, serious attention has been paid to the suggestion that psychological, and particularly motivational, factors may be importantly involved.

The "psychological position" is that an individual drive to excel is required for the entrepreneurial activity which converts resources, capital, and manpower into production and—eventually—income. Where this drive is strong and widespread in a population, the economy will develop rapidly through the cumulative push of entrepreneurial actions; where the drive is weak or infrequent, economic advance will be slow. Proponents of this psychological position attribute differences in the rate of economic growth, between the "have" and "have-not" nations and between rapidly industrializing nations like Japan and those countries which have lagged behind, to corresponding differences in the incidence of this drive to excel among the national populations concerned. Particular ethnic groups specializing in trade have been singled out as having more of this motive than do their neighbors within some of the underdeveloped countries. Thus a psychological factor—an acquired drive for excellence or need to achieve—is held to be unevenly distributed in the human species and to be at least partly responsible for the major national and other group differences in economic growth which are so conspicuous in the contemporary world.[11]

It is my further contention, however, that achievement motivation is not to be found in the same social and psychological context of values in every culture. It can produce similar results without being

---

[10] Bellah, *Tokugawa Religion* (1957), and Hagen, *On the Theory of Social Change* (1962).

[11] LeVine, *Dreams and Deeds: Achievement Motivation in Nigeria* (1966), p. 78.

identical in nature in every culture. The evidence from Japan con-
tradicts some previously formed generalizations of those who have
attempted comparative research.

COMPARATIVE RESEARCH ON
ACHIEVEMENT MOTIVATION

Crandall [12] has noted that the concept of achievement motivation
as a psychological variable in the educational and occupational activities of adults is not recent and had some status in psychology before
Murray's use of the variable termed "need achievement" in the analysis
of TAT stories and the subsequent application of this concept to cross-
cultural research by McClelland and others. Reviewing its prior use,
Crandall points out that Alfred Adler, the psychoanalyst, and Kurt
Lewin, the social psychologist, made much of achievement motivation
as a central need. Lewin discussed achievement in terms of "levels of
aspiration," and even earlier, Alfred Adler spoke of a need for achievement as a "compensatory motivation" derived from the childhood experience of inferiority in relation to adults. Nevertheless, David Mc-
Clelland must be largely credited with developing over the past fifteen
years a stimulating line of research on achievement motivation in a
variety of cultures.

With G. A. Friedman, McClelland [13] published results of a cross-
cultural study of the relationship of child-rearing practices to achievement motivation. They analyzed the imagery of the folktales of a number of American Indian tribes as it symbolically reflected some form
of achievement need. With John Atkinson and R. A. Clark, Mc-
Clelland [14] published a general description of what they termed the
achievement motive and its association behavior as related to particular
forms of childhood socialization. They proposed, for example, that a
mother of a high achiever teaches her son self-reliance and personal
competition with a standard of excellence. As an adult he will continue
to seek out tasks that will express these now internalized standards. He
will prefer tasks with a moderate amount of risk and a high degree of
personal responsibility. Such an individual likes to pursue energetic
instrumental activity toward goals. He avoids situations in which
the task is either too easy or so difficult as to preclude any chance of
success except through luck. He needs accurate feedback on results so
that he can maintain an awareness of how well he is functioning. Such

---

[12] Crandall, "Achievement" (1963).

[13] McClelland and Friedman, "A Cross-Cultural Study of the Relationship Between Child-Training Practices and Achievement Motivation Appearing in Folktales" (1952).

[14] McClelland, et al., *The Achievement Motive* (1953).

an individual may become depressed with failure, even when he has
had no great control over outcome. When failure is possible as a result
of personal inadequacies, he strives to compensate for or to overcome
the effects of such inadequacies. McClelland [15] noted in a later study
that an entrepreneurial role seems best to suit men who fit this opera-
tional definition of high need achievement.

Winterbottom[16] is credited with developing a fairly tight research
design to help test out the relationship of need achievement and socialization in American culture. Using a series of psychological tests,
she divided a group of boys into high need and low need achievement
types. She then systematically analyzed the child-rearing practices of
their mothers. She found striking confirmation for the general hy-
potheses proposed by McClelland and his associates. She discovered
that mothers of the high need achievement boys continually stressed
the importance of the child's ability to take care of himself and to
make his own decisions at an early age; the mothers of boys classified
as low need achievers did not stress this requirement until a later age
or not at all. It must be noted that in the study the class variable was
held constant. It should also be noted that American fathers were not
considered an important socialization variable in this particular study,
possible differences among the fathers being ignored.

There is some controversy about the effect of the father on need
achievement. Rosen and D'Andrade[17] suggest that an authoritarian
father when he inhibits the eventual development of high need achievement interferes excessively with his son's attempt at mastery. Bradburn[18] suggests that in certain cultures such as that of Turkey, socialization is more fully in the hands of the father, so the father's role
is pervasively more important. Where the father concerns himself
minutely with the son's behavior, as in Turkey (and apparently also
in other Moslem countries such as Algeria and Egypt), variations of
the father's behavior may have no less effect, and perhaps more, than
do variations of the mother's behavior toward her children. Further,
Bradburn,[19] in commenting on Winterbottom's research, notes some
need to qualify findings derived specifically for the white middle-class
American subculture.

Training involved in achievement orientation is not of a unitary

---

[15] McClelland, "Some Consequences of Achievement Motivation" (1955).

[16] Winterbottom, "The Relationship of Need for Achievement to Learning Experiences in Independence and Mastery" (1958).

[17] Rosen and D'Andrade, "The Psycho-Social Origins of Achievement Motivation"
(1959).

[18] Bradburn, "Need Achievement and Father Dominance" (1963).

[19] Bradburn, "The Cultural Context of Personality Theory" (1963).

nature. There are three somewhat interdependent considerations: first, "independence" training per se; second, "mastery" training; and third, "caretaker" training. According to McClelland,[20] only variations in types of mastery and independence training can be shown to correlate cross-culturally with need achievement. D'Andrade,[21] in examining the development of need achievement, stresses that the affective concern conveyed by the mother to the child in her attempts at independence training produces high need achievement. In fact, under certain conditions, independence training can be construed by the child as a form of rejection by the mother if it is not accompanied by a very positively affectful concern over successful acts of independence. It is the nature of this concern itself that induces an internalization of standards of excellence. However, some evidence in Japan, on which I will comment later, goes somewhat contrary to the usual formulations concerning early independence training.

Turning from considerations of theory to those of method, we find that McClelland's influence has been equally strong. In 1953 he made a detailed exposition of his scoring system. Child, Storm, and Veroff [22] further applied McClelland's methods to a total of fifty-two cultures and found to their satisfaction a definite correlation between folktales and particular socialization practices. They made use of ethnographic records concerning child-rearing to seek out correlations between particular practices and the manifest content of the folktales.

Parker[23] used a similar method in analyzing and comparing Eskimo and Ojibwa mythology with respect to achievement motivation. He pointed to the greater amount of individual achievement orientation found in Ojibwa culture, in contrast to that of the Eskimos, who often appear to be more concerned with affiliation than with achievement. Parker's results support Landes' [24] previous conclusions concerning Eskimo personality.

Others have attempted to apply McClelland's methods to an historical analysis of need achievement by turning to written literature. Cortes[25] made a study of shifts in achievement motivation in Spain from the thirteenth century to the eighteenth by analyzing popular

[20] McClelland, *The Achieving Society* (1961).

[21] Rosen and D'Andrade, "The Psycho-Social Origins of Achievement Motivation" (1959).

[22] Child, Storm, and Veroff, "Achievement Themes in Folktales Related to Socialization Practice" (1958).

[23] Parker, "Eskimo Psychopathology in the Context of Eskimo Personality and Culture" (1962).

[24] Landes, "The Abnormal Among the Ojibwa Indians" (1938).

[25] Cortes, "The Achievement Motive in the Spanish Economy Between the Thirteenth and the Eighteenth Centuries" (1960).

Spanish literature. Bradburn and Berlew[26] similarly related the era
of English industrial growth to themes found in the popular literature
of the time. DeCharms and Moeller[27] suggested that observable variations in achievement themes of American children's readers are related
to fluctuations in American economic expansion from 1800 to 1950.

Barry, Child, and Bacon,[28] using materials from relatively simple
cultures, found interrelationships between types of subsistence patterns
and childhood training that caused them to infer that societies dependent for food on hunting and gathering are more interested in training
children toward independence and self-reliance than are societies having a technology that permits them to accumulate and store food.
LeVine[29] takes exception to their somewhat simplistic attempt to
utilize Hull's reinforcement theory as an explanation for this interrelationship. He points out that one cannot compare the very simple
cultures examined by Barry, Child, and Bacon with other cultures
employing a more complex technology. For example, differences between Poland and England with respect to achievement motivation can
hardly be reduced to simple questions of basic subsistence.

Rosen[30] has made an extensive comparison of ethnic variations in
achievement, using samples of Canadians, Italians, Greeks, Jews, Negroes, and white New England Protestants. He concludes that class and
ethnic factors are more important than religious affiliations in explaining observed differences. Rosen[31] also used TAT scores for need
achievement to compare Brazilians and Americans. He infers from his
data that childhood training is the key differential in distinguishing
the achievement behavior of the two cultures. American culture, compared with that of Brazil, more pervasively stresses independence,
autonomy, and self-reliance, and induces the child to compare himself
competitively with idealized standards of excellence.

McClelland's volume *The Achieving Society*[32] reviews a number of
other related studies in more detail. Throughout, he finds a relationship between entrepreneurial behavior and modes of child-rearing
that stress early independence and a sense of personal mastery. As one
of his conclusions, he cites evidence that seems to support Weber's

[26] Bradburn and Berlew, "Need for Achievement and English Industrial Growth"
(1960).
[27] DeCharms and Moeller, "Values Expressed in American Children's Readers,
1800–1950" (1962).
[28] Barry, Child, and Bacon, "Relations of Child Training to Subsistence Economy"
(1959).
[29] LeVine, "Behaviorism in Psychological Anthropology" (1963).
[30] Rosen, "Race, Ethnicity and the Achievement Syndrome" (1959); and Rosen and
D'Andrade, "The Psycho-Social Origins of Achievement Motivation" (1959).
[31] Rosen, "Socialization and Achievement Motivation in Brazil" (1962).
[32] McClelland, *The Achieving Society* (1961).

postulated relationship between Protestantism and capitalist economic activity.

Hagen,[33] borrowing loosely from McClelland and other sources, proposed a general theory explaining differential responses to economic development in a number of cultures on the basis of some form of status deprivation. Status deprivation serves as a stimulus to a particular minority of the population, inducing it to undertake compensatory forms of innovation, some of which relate to the eventual economic development of the entire society.

A particular social segment separated by religious or ethnic distinctions can be affected by a withdrawal of proffered status. Some of such groups may become demoralized and manifest various forms of deviance or social pathology.

Such a group may also be prompted to find alternative means of reestablishing itself. Minority groups can become innovative either positively or negatively to produce some form of social change that eventually brings about change in the total society. Hagen considered the situations in which innovation occurred in the economic sector in such a way as to generate general economic development, and concludes that types of authoritarian or nonauthoritarian personality patterns fostered within innovating minorities were of crucial importance in this process. He draws a great deal on previous studies of need achievement and, unfortunately, somewhat oversimplifies his discussion of the psychological variables involved.

Taken as a whole, Hagen's theory offers a direct challenge to those economists who ignore the significant psychocultural variables in their observations of how economic development is supposed to occur. In the following chapter I criticize some of the specifics of Hagen's theory as applied to the case of Japanese modernization. Nevertheless, Hagen does afford us a very valuable insight into the complex manner in which differences in social status and in socialization experiences bring about tensions and disequilibria resolved only by some form of social change.

THE CULTURAL CONTEXT OF ACHIEVEMENT: THE CASE OF THE JAPANESE-AMERICANS

Japanese Socialization and Need Achievement

In 1947 I was one of a group of social scientists interested in the relocation of the West Coast Japanese-Americans to the Chicago area. There was an obvious positive occupational and social adjustment being made by the American-born Nisei in the face of what had been a

---

[33] Hagen, *On the Theory of Social Change* (1962).

blatant act of ethnic and racial discrimination resulting in their wholesale deportation from California in a time of war hysteria. The younger
generation of Japanese-Americans located in the Chicago area were, in
1947, entering white-collar and professional occupations in large numbers. Just as the Japanese nation had taken on the ways of the West
in a rapid, self-consciously directed industrialization, Japanese immigrants and their children in the United States were giving evidence,
occupationally at least, of breaking through the barrier of color discrimination in the United States.

I contend that neither sociological theories about discrimination nor
economic theories, by themselves, can explain the acculturation of the
Japanese-American in the United States and in such Latin American
countries as Brazil, nor can they explain the economic development
within Japan itself. A complementary psychological theory related to
the socialization of human motivation is also necessary.

The psychological theory of achievement motivation presented by
McClelland and others, however, does not seem to fit Japan well in all
its contentions. In the samples of TAT materials obtained in Chicago
and in various settings in rural and urban Japan we have found a
pervasive preoccupation with achievement and accomplishment, no
matter what group of Japanese was tested, but the achievement imagery
differs from that found in American samples in respect to the context
within which it appears. Throughout, the Japanese materials also show
both very high need affiliation and concern with nurturance and de-
pendance, conflicting with American data, which usually suggest a
negative correspondence between the appearance of need achievement
and need affiliation.

It is obvious that this difference relates to differences in socialization
experiences within the American and Japanese cultures. The generalizations by McClelland, Winterbottom, and others concerning the socialization pattern characteristic for high need achievement differ
greatly from the common experiences of Japanese children. The Japanese child is not trained toward independence or self-reliance as are
those who manifest high need achievement in the United States.[34]

Ezra Vogel [35] and William Caudill [36] have conducted intensive de-

---

[34] Caudill and Weinstein, "Maternal Care and Infant Behavior in Japanese and
American Urban Middle Class Families" (1966); Caudill and Schooler, "Symptom
Patterns Among Japanese Psychiatric Patients" (1966); Doi, "Some Aspects of Japanese Psychiatry" (1955); Doi, "Theory of Narcissism and the Psychic Representation of Self" (1960c, in Japanese); Doi, "Psychopathology of 'Jibun' and 'Amae'"
(1960b, in Japanese); Doi, "Parental Identification of Delinquent Boys" (1960a,
in Japanese).

[35] Vogel, *Japan's New Middle Class* (1963).

[36] Caudill and Weinstein, "Maternal Care and Infant Behavior in Japanese and
American Urban Middle Class Families" (1966).

tailed observations of mother-child relationships in middle-class families in Japan. Vogel's observations of mothers' interaction with school-age children indicate that Japanese children of this age receive relatively little of the American type of independence training. Nevertheless, an intensive concern for educational achievement on the part of the mother is imparted to the child; this is accomplished in a manner quite different from that in the American household. In Japan, the mother and child act almost as one in meeting the demands of the school.

The family, rather than the individual, has tended to be the traditional unit in Japan. Success only for oneself has been considered a sign of excessive, immoral egoism; one learned to aim at high standards of performance as a quasi-religious act of dedication and lost one's selfish feelings in the pursuit of goals benefiting one's family. The family, not only the self, suffered the consequence of any failure. I have discussed in Chapter 5 the subjective sense of need to repay the parents for their self-sacrificing care as a strong moral imperative impelling the individual toward the actualization of achievement. Because of the sense of dedication of individual Japanese and the nature of group cohesiveness and group processes within the Japanese community, it is important for us to understand how the need for social belonging is structured in Japanese economic development, as well as to note the individual need to achieve.

As was discussed in some detail in Chapter 1, motives related to affiliation and nurturance play a continuous role throughout the life cycle of the Japanese. My formulations concerning Japanese need achievement, give much more attention to cultural patterns operative in the structuring of guilt than McClelland's theory does. I am as concerned with the social sense of belonging manifest in the Japanese culture as McClelland is concerned with the sense of self-reliance and individualism manifest in the American. McClelland overgeneralizes Western European and American psychological patterns as the only possible ones expressing need achievement.

Role Dedication and Economic Development

In considering economic development within given particular historical circumstances, McClelland somewhat single-mindedly emphasizes the role of individualistically oriented entrepreneurial behavior.

McClelland's suggestion[37] that Hermes is the most suitable figure in Greek mythology to symbolize the achieving personality is rather curious seen from the vantage point of Japanese concepts of achievement realization in the context of social role dedication. Hermes, in addition

---

[37] McClelland, *The Achieving Society* (1961).

to being a messenger and an athlete, was given to "entrepreneurial" activities aided by his capacity for outrageous lying, stealing, and trickery. This suggests to me an individualistically oriented concept of need achievement, which, if present only by itself in a culture, even in a large number of individuals, would hardly contribute optimally to national economic development. To illustrate, the Chinese who have settled in other sections of Asia have been eminently successful as merchants and as entrepreneurs, but within China itself social and historical circumstances made China an easy prey to the incursions of colonial powers. The fact that the Chinese value system emphasized only the immediate family and deemphasized any wider sense of social integrity or honesty in service to the national entity was a crucial factor in helping to explain both the political collapse and the lack of general economic development in China in the late nineteenth and early twentieth centuries. The rampant corruption in the Chinese government until the Communist takeover made it impossible to resist foreign incursions and to modernize internally. As a second example, in India today one finds good evidence of individualistically structured need achievement in particular subgroups, but of itself this cannot bring about widespread economic development. Ethnic minorities such as the Parsis and the Jains manifest a high degree of individual entrepreneurial activity, and, like the Chinese, overseas Indians in minority enclaves in Africa or Asia show a great deal of economic prowess. Nevertheless, there have been counter forces within Indian culture that have prevented a more rapid rate of economic development on the Indian subcontinent itself.

McClelland's theory is that national economic development is instigated internally from within a population high in the entrepreneurial virtues of self-reliance and initiative. He sees need achievement as ideally embodied in a particular socially mobile, expediential, instrumentally oriented personality type dedicated to the pursuit of selfish gain. McClelland's theory of economic development is the psychological counterpart of Adam Smith's "Wealth of Nations" theory of free enterprise. As such it is as much a one-sided vision of social processes deriving directly from an implicit nineteenth century rationalist ideology, as is the instrumentally oriented Communist interpretation of history built around a progressive political and economic exploitation of subordinate groups by a power elite. Neither variety of rationalist-individualist theory can be applied with cogency to what has occurred in Japan.

Economic development in Japan depended not only on individuals ready to take chances to further their individual aims but also on the cooperative, concerted efforts of many persons imbued with a relatively high sense of mutual trust and social responsibility. These individuals were distributed throughout all ranks of a rigidly stratified society. The desire for individual social mobility of itself is not necessarily conducive to a social climate that results in economic development if there is no fair level of integrity in government bureaucracies and if the legislative and judicial processes are subject to widespread corruption. Japanese society developed very little sense of class alienation during its major phases of modernization. As is discussed in detail in Chapter 8, Japanese entrepreneurial attitudes involve trust and patience on the part of the young entering into lifelong patterns of paternalistic reciprocity. Those undergoing a period of learning through apprenticeship expect future support as well as present dependency. Japanese need achievement is often couched in long-range terms. Earlier loyalty toward superiors by subordinates is eventually rewarded by assistance—financial as well as social—by one's former patron when the subordinate seeks to initiate his own entrepreneurial activities.

Japanese need achievement has also indirectly influenced the way past overall economic development was realized through non-economically oriented social roles in the modernizing Japanese society. From Meiji Japan to the present, individuals have been stimulated to actualize such selfless roles as teacher or civil servant, as well as the more direct economic roles of merchant or entrepreneur.

One cannot overemphasize the need to look at the total cultural configuration and the various alternative roles both economic and non-economic through which achievement motivation may be directed. Dedication to a wide variety of occupational roles on all levels within a national entity is necessary in contributing to economic development.

McClelland ignores the cultural configurations in which need achievement does or does not become relatively manifest. He is, therefore, not really contributing a more complex picture of the psychological dynamics underlying social change. Rather, he is suggesting that there is only one type of internal-combustion achievement engine that is able to motivate the "economic man."

There is no doubt that McClelland's model well suits the American culture, but as it now stands it is less applicable elsewhere. Even from the limited perspective afforded by projective materials in a culture such as that of Japan, one gains the impression that human psychology as it influences history cannot be so facilely reduced to a single paramount motivation.

In examining what can be determined by quantitative approaches to projective test materials somewhat less focused than those used by McClelland, I find a more complex configuration of internalized values motivating individual Japanese. This configuration is common to Japanese artists, scientists, scholars, government officials, and soldiers, as well as to businessmen and entrepreneurs. The elements of the configuration include more than achievement motivation; however, one cannot gainsay its strong central influence.

McClelland in emphasizing a particular type of socialization related to need achievement tends to ignore how such a need can be interpenetrated by various other expressive cultural values. In Chapter 7 I discuss the striking parallels between the internalized quasi-religious ethics of the Japanese, which led many of the early business leaders in the Meiji period to feel a sense of social purpose, and the Protestant sense of self-actualization through hard work and success. Robert Bellah[38] has noted such similarities in his volume on Tokugawa religion. One must also note, however, the following singular difference: in the nineteenth century, in Western Europe, individualism was the reigning ideology; in Japan, in contrast, the individual found his overriding sense of purpose in a dedication to his occupational and vocational role somewhere within the hierarchical Japanese social structure, rather than in salvation in relation to a personal God. The Western ideal of personal self-realization apart from family or social group has, until recently, been entirely foreign to the Japanese system of thought outside the thinking of a small group of alienated intellectuals. The ultimate goals of life were centered on noninstrumentally organized, quasi-religious concepts of family continuity. Legally and morally, individuals in nineteenth-century Japan defined themselves in the context of family roles and their attendant obligations and expectations.

To recapitulate the point made in introducing this chapter: One cannot afford to overlook the expressive elements in any culture in any truly scientific behavioral analysis. This is especially apparent in the case of Japan. As we shall continue to demonstrate, in Japan actualizing oneself through meeting social challenges takes place within an overall context of strong nurturant and affiliative needs. Dedication to social service in one form or another in the performance of a designated role, even on the lower rungs of the status ladder, is a strong Japanese traditional social value. This value is based on the traditional psychological motivation, although in modern times it has come to be redirected toward new social purposes.

The individual's successful dedication brings with it internal satisfaction where the role is well accomplished. Sustained long-range, goal-directed behavior for the samurai class, for example, was directed at one period toward serving successfully as a warrior-administrator. Similar underlying psychological motivations were transferred to successful accomplishment in activities by many former samurai when their social role was abolished at the beginning of the Meiji period. At this period the government turned its attention to consciously directed programs

---

[38] Bellah, *Tokugawa Religion* (1957).

of economic and political modernization and found ready recruits, psychologically primed to undertake the new challenges of the changing culture.

One can understand a great deal of modern Japanese achievement motivation in terms of the continuing need to prolong and to participate cooperatively with others, collaterally, as well as in terms of hierarchically structured mutual needs for nurturance and support that unite individuals. These latter needs not only help cement the bonds of family, but also form pseudo-kinship economic ties in a variety of what are called *oyabun-kobun* relationships.[39] Internalized sanctions make it difficult to conceive of letting down one's family or one's social groups and occupational superiors. In turn, those in authority positions must take paternal care of those for whom they have responsibility. Abegglen[40] has described the way in which this social framework of paternalism has been introduced into many Japanese factories. For some time, paternalism in factory settings increased with modernization, but the trend since the 1960s has been in the other direction (see Chapter 7).

The motives discussed above are as strong determinants of Japanese behavior as is any sense of individual accomplishment. To be fully understood, Japanese achievement drive (as perhaps all achievement drives elsewhere to some degree at least) must be seen as motivated by irrational, unconscious forces as well as by the immediate benefits to be derived from economic success. The sense of validating the self through sustained work activity is now being transmuted into modern goals. This interrelationship of instrumental and expressive motivational factors takes place in the context of socially defined role relationship.

In the West, similarly, the sense of satisfaction in rational, autonomous individualistic behavior is in many respects "expressive" of a value orientation. Instrumental behavior and expressive needs are congruent for many Westerners whose behavior is oriented toward economic accomplishment. It is only when there is some such congruence between the instrumental and underlying expressive needs in goal-directed behavior for a sufficiently large number of people within a culture that one can talk about an "achieving" society. McClelland and his associates have successfully hit upon how particular socialization patterns common within the United States contribute to such an achievement syndrome. We would argue on the basis of the Japanese evidence, however, that other culturally determined syndromes, psychologically different in some respects, may also lead to economic develop-

---

[39] Bennett and Ishino, *Paternalism in the Japanese Economy* (1963).

[40] Abegglen, *The Japanese Factory: Aspects of its Social Organization* (1958).

ment without being as directly "individualistic" or "rational" in nature. In short, the system of classical economics developed in Britain and the United States must be seen, to some degree at least, as "ethno-economics" with an implicit ethnopsychology as a motivational base. Its emphasis on the source of human motivation (like that of Communist theory) is too much dependent on a view of human nature as individualistically motivated and solely instrumental.

McClelland's concept of need achievement has the virtue of taking into account some internally motivated processes antecedent to goal-directed behavior. But, with his emphasis on achievement as something generally going counter to strong need affiliation, for example, McClelland reveals the ethnopsychology from which his generalizations are derived. His hypothesized underlying general patterns of motivation make good sense in a Western setting but do not necessarily hold for others.

In the case of the Japanese-American minority in the United States, discussed in Chapter 9, and the Japanese in Japan, as discussed in Chapter 5, we find expressed in the projective psychological materials obvious effects of the cultural tradition and of a pattern of socialization that leads to considerable concern with achievement, although in quite a different context from that of American society.

There are also psychocultural considerations related to a *failure* to achieve in terms that are positively sanctioned in any culture. Patterns of achievement or failure to achieve are disproportionately distributed among different segments of a complex society. A relatively greater prevalence of "failure" is found in traditionally disparaged minorities in both Japan and the United States. Achievement motivation is also indirectly related cross-culturally to patterns of deviancy, and to such psychocultural concepts as negative self-identity and alienation. These topics are further discussed in Part III.

Chapter VII

Achievement Orientation, Social Self-Identity, and Japanese Economic Growth

The proposition set forth in this chapter is two-fold.[1] First, given traditional Japanese culture—especially its *expressive* values related to the prevalent patterns of psychological organization found among pre-modern Japanese of the late Tokugawa period—it is not surprising that the Japanese developed quickly into the first economic industrial power of Asia. Second, the ethno-economics and political theory developed by the Japanese themselves as an ideology directing their modernization make more sense from the standpoint of Japanese culture and personality variables than the simplistic application of Western classical economics or Marxian theory. An understanding of the psychological characteristics that make Japanese social organization work is necessary to explain the relative success of Japanese industrialization.

A CRITIQUE OF NINETEENTH-CENTURY ECONOMICS FROM A CROSS-CULTURAL PERSPECTIVE

Both Marxian economic theory and classical economic theory, products of nineteenth-century social science, put too heavy an emphasis on man as functioning rationally toward the achievement of instrumental goals. The Marxian dictum that religion is an opiate refers to a vast spectrum of seemingly irrational behavior on the part of un-enlightened or duped masses, who refuse to be motivated to a proper extension of their own interests through revolutionary self-assertion.

In similar fashion, in the vision of theorists of a free economy related to the Protestant ethic of personal salvation, and blended at the end

[1] This chapter previously appeared as "Achievement Orientation, Social Self-Identity and Japanese Economic Growth," *Asian Survey* (1965), Vol. 5, No. 12, pp. 575–589.

of the nineteenth century with social Darwinism, economic success was not only equated with self-justification in religious terms but viewed as evidence of biological superiority in a competitive world wherein only the fit deserve to survive. With this latter philosophy, it is entirely consistent to consider specific races and societies as inferior and sometimes requiring the guidance and supervision of those who have demonstrated their fitness to govern others.

In the latter half of the twentieth century, self-satisfied assumptions of social and intellectual superiority, among theoreticians at least, have given way to new philosophies. The Communist revolutionary ideology is being countered by attempts at some form of evolutionary capitalism that vainly seeks social means of raising economic standards everywhere so that unregulated explosive population growth will not cause irreversible political upheavals. Proponents of both ideologies, however, face considerable frustration when they seek to actualize programs for economic betterment. On the one hand, programs based on the Communist theory that people can be rationally motivated to act out of a totalitarian concept of altruistic social interest, and, on the other, capitalist programs to induce individuals to benefit the general good by acting out of motives of enlightened self-interest are continually meeting with difficulty. Not only are these difficulties apparent in the application of these programs to economic-political satellites, but also they are manifest within the Soviet Union and the United States. Traditional rationalist economic theories, whether Communist or capitalist, based as they are on the premise of economic rationality and the application of political power as a means of implementing planning, tend to ignore determinants of human behavior related to specific cultural traditions and general psychological processes.

Direct concern with the recognition and surmounting of the difficulties experienced in actualizing economic goals has had some effect on recent theory. Modern economists, dealing increasingly with the non-Western world, have come to place greater value on the study of cultural traditions by historians and anthropologists for the understanding of economic development. Some have come to realize that classical economics itself has been a product of Western culture and, as such, is what might be termed "ethno-economics," based on some postulates that do not bear up so well when examined cross-culturally.[2]

THE ROLE OF PSYCHOLOGY IN ECONOMIC THEORY

Theorists have readily conceded the relevance of the disciplines of political science, history, anthropology, and sociology to an understand-

---

[2] Economics is not the only social science affected by ethnocentric cultural assumptions.

ing of economic development; however, there is still a general reluctance to acknowledge psychology as a relevant social science—a neglect that can lead to serious theoretical difficulties. Knowledge of psychological processes adds another dimension to an understanding of the vicissitudes of economic development. As discussed in the last chapter, an understanding of irrational motives as related to expressive behavior serves to correct what might be termed the instrumental bias still found in most of social science.[3] Man, no matter in what culture, in creating a meaning for his existence, orients himself toward nature and his fellow man in terms of values not directly derived from instrumental activities or goals. He derives satisfaction from behavior that is expressive of psychological processes, as well as guided rationally toward the realization of culturally defined ends. The study of psychology reveals why this is so. When we apply psychological principles to any investigation of the learning processes and of the means by which goals are internalized or activated in any particular culture, we gain clues to why people of that culture behave as they do and why it is difficult for them to modify their behavior to conform to some new form of planned change, be it economic or political.

Being socialized within a particular culture may, in many subtle ways, either internally incapacitate or motivate the individual and externally impede or facilitate the achievement of goals set by the politically dominant element of the society. The degree of sustained effort that one puts into adult occupational roles, including the work role, is determined not only by immediate social inducements but also by a complex series of prior experiences.

An illustration is the work of Inkeles, Bauer, and others,[4] who have studied tensions between the Communist party cadres and ordinary citizens in the Soviet Union. These authors point out the continuous tension between the dedicated party members whose psychological structure is congruent with national objectives, on the one hand, and, on the other, the large mass of ordinary Russians who cannot be sufficiently mobilized to carry out the economic programs put forward by the social planners. The type of psychological structure derived from previous cultural patterns operates as a continual source of disharmony and frustration to those seeking to effect new economic and social programs.

---

[3] Parson's description of the dichotomy between instrumental and expressive social role relationships is congenial to the following argument. Parsons, Bales, and Shils, *Working Papers in the Theory of Action* (1953).

[4] Bauer, *The New Man in Soviet Psychology* (1952); Bauer, Inkeles, and Kluchhohn, *How the Soviet System Works* (1956); Inkeles, Haufmann, and Beier, "Modal Personality and Adjustment to the Soviet Socio-Political System" (1958).

It is precisely the neglect of the expressive, persistently irrational, elements in man's social behavior that often confounds economic programs based too heavily on abstract theories of economic and political behavior. Expressive behavior is found institutionalized not only in the religious life of a people or in its art, but also in the very patterns of social and sexual relations in family life to which a group is heavily committed. To understand what motivates members of a particular culture, one must place political or economic motives within their proper social-psychological context. What gives man "meaning" is the ideas and values embedded in the symbols of social life. The economic system of the culture itself must be seen in expressive as well as instrumental terms. Some of the profundity in Max Weber's sociological analysis derives from his recognition of this role of what he terms "meaning" in social processes.[5]

The sacred cow of India confounds Indian economic development. As an expressive symbol, it points up several of the anti-economic values of Hindu culture. The economist would do well to discover that every culture has some form of sacred cow. It is from this vantage point that I would like briefly to examine, in a psychological frame of reference, the achievement orientation of the Japanese as related to their economic growth.

MOTIVATIONAL OR EXPRESSIVE ELEMENTS IN ACHIEVEMENT BEHAVIOR RELATED TO THE JAPANESE FAMILY SYSTEM CONDUCIVE TO ECONOMIC GROWTH

For many economists viewing economic progress in Japan, the Japanese family system may seem to be analogous to the sacred cow of India. It has been seen by some as an impediment to a more rational form of modernization of the Japanese economy. I would like to take a contrary position; I maintain one can demonstrate that, viewed historically, particularized traditional Japanese social values (as they were inculcated within the context of family life) were to no small extent responsible for a prevailing type of personal motivation, expressed both in the implementation of government policy and in social relationships centered around work, that made possible the rapid industrial modernization of Japan. Both in its instrumental and in its expressive aspects, socialization within the Japanese family inculcated a type of self-motivated achievement orientation in a sufficiently numerous segment of the Japanese population to adequately man the opera-

---

[5] Cf. Weber, *The Theory of Social and Economic Organization* (1947), pp. 88 ff.; Gerth and Mills, *From Max Weber: Essay in Sociology* (1946), pp. 350 ff.; Parsons, *The Structure of Social Action* (1949), pp. 666 ff.

tion of the society, which was being consciously guided toward a position of eminence in a world heretofore exclusively dominated by Western states.

The Quality of Responsible Paternalism
and Mutual Trust in Japanese Social Organization

In this adventure in modernization all important segments of Japanese society including those in newly founded economic enterprises were guided and organized by a quasi-religious paternalistic familism that united its members more than it divided them into economic classes, created more harmony than dissension, fostered morale rather than alienation. Japanese familism in its psychological and attitudinal aspects has been a strong integrative force constraining all segments of the society toward cooperation. In contrast, one might compare it to the type of familism reported for southern Italy. Banfield [6] describes what he terms "amoral familism" as operative in the southern Italian family. The family is a fortress held against the outside society, which is perceived with hostility and distrust. Life and social relationships are seen as tragic and defeating—there is a general tone of pessimism, deprivation, and distrust of man and nature. This type of familism is in direct contrast to that in Japan, where the community beyond the family is united by a network of interpenetrating obligations and expectations. The individual Japanese may be concerned with personal inadequacies and the difficulties of his environment, but he does not perceive himself as being defeated by the malevolence of his fellow men. He sustains himself by hard work and ultimately accomplishes some social goal; he remains optimistic through adversity and does not view society with distrust. He may fear to stand out unduly from his fellows, but he disguises such fear by emphasizing cooperation rather than by offense or retreat. Above all, he is guided by a sense of self-dedication.

Many of the political and even the economic leaders of Meiji Japan operated within a framework where such dedication as a consuming expressive need was not rare. They could count on others, now no longer dedicated to feudal loyalties, to advance the totally conceived national interest. In the Meiji period, both the ex-samurai leaders and their followers as well as members of the farming and mercantile classes joined in common enterprises. All of their children were educated toward the realization of common policies in the schools. The Japanese intellectuals—whatever strain they experienced in the course of relating Westernized conceptions of science and economic rationality to their own country and to their personal lives—were not overwhelmed.

---

[6] Banfield, *The Moral Basis of a Backward Community* (1958).

The Japanese values were not inundated, but during the Meiji period at least, they crested this tide of new experiences.

The point is this: the assimilation of aspects of Western culture did not alienate the leadership from the common people. The expressive ties of an intricately interwoven family society did not break. Also, from a psychological perspective, one can observe that the new leaders in significant numbers had learned to dedicate themselves to newly evolving social roles, the manner of their dedication peculiarly derived from the previous Japanese culture. This sense of dedication did not become individualistically conceptualized in Western entrepreneurial terms; self-justification to a great degree in a large number of individuals was permeated with a strong sense of social service. It was not only the warrior who gave his life; the bureaucrat, the educator, even the humble official running the railroad station, all derived "meaning" in Weber's terms[7] from their occupational roles. They did not work merely to earn their livelihood or to aggrandize themselves. Many worked to achieve a sense of self-realization through service to family and nation.

This paternalistic structure of society, in individual psychological terms, was motivated from within. The early experiences of family life were sufficiently rewarding and sufficiently gratifying to give life meaning without any transcending recourse to more universalistic roles and values or to individuated purposes, as occurred under a more universalist Western social philosophy.

In Chapter 17, on Japanese suicide, I discuss the extreme form of dedication to a particularistic social role found within Japanese culture, a dedication that was originally part of the samurai sense of self. With the abolition of the samurai class, self-actualization found new expression in the roles of Meiji government bureaucrat, of teacher, and of entrepreneur. This kind of dedication, stemming from the internalization of social values within the family, peopled the new bureaucracy as well as the economic and political parts of the social system with individuals who had sufficient morale to make these parts work with a fair degree of success. There was a feeling of "we-ness" in the society, a sharing in which class divisions did not interfere with a sense of cooperation and common purpose throughout the society. The former samurai, as an educated class, became devoted to the total national polity. A tremendous resource of human energy was directed into new channels. An important function of the family system and the reorganization of the society in familial terms, often overlooked in an instrumentally oriented economic theory, was that it helped maintain a high morale by its expressive emphasis on harmony instead of

---

[7] Weber (1925).

permitting energies to be dissipated by an undue amount of social dissension or apathy in the face of economic change.

There was a dedication to role in all minor jobs that at times approached the ludicrous but at all costs kept the system working.[8] The paternalism within the system stressed obligations on the part of superiors as well as their subordinates. Employees held occupational security to be dominant over efficiency of operation. What appeared to be inefficient, from an impersonal economic standpoint or on a day-by-day level, sustained concerted group action over the long period. Strikes or other forms of crippling dissension were rare.

For stable industries, Japanese modernization was aided by the fact that employees considered job security more important than wages. When industries became stable, they looked to the "fringe welfare benefits" of the workers and tolerated an uneconomic work force instead of discharging faithful workers. In less stable industries, rural family ties provided an economic and emotional cushion against unemployment. Unemployed family members were readily reabsorbed within a rural village. They did not simply become unattached urban proletariat faced with the total consequences of particular economic reversals, as occurred under European conditions of industrialization.

Some of the major factors often referred to in purely economic explanations of rapid industrialization and economic expansion of Meiji Japan prove on closer scrutiny to be derived from the psychologically satisfying familism permeating Japanese society. The example given above of reabsorption of unemployed urban workers into the village is often used only as an economic explanation. A second factor usually presented only in economic terms is the role of government paternalism. The Meiji government sponsored and subsidized heavy industries that were subsequently taken over completely by private enterprises. This government paternalism prevented inefficient experimentation and possible loss by private entrepreneurs, who could not immediately compete successfully in the international market. Social trust was evident in a readiness to invest savings in new enterprises which depended on trust in the government and its directives. Moreover, an appeal could be made to stoicism and frugality, rather than to hedonism, in encouraging the saving of capital. In these factors and others by which economists themselves explain Japan's rapid industrialization, there are uniquely Japanese cultural-psychological features found in their particularistic, paternalistic familism.

---

[8] Raucat, *The Honorable Picnic* (1955). Under a pseudonym, "Thomas Raucat," a Belgian diplomat, in 1924, wrote a satirical novel which points up in a most compelling fashion the obsessive rigidity found in small officials in carrying out their functions.

Lockwood directs attention to yet another dimension.[9] He does not disagree with the theory that much of the rapid industrialization of Meiji Japan is due to the government's initiative and sponsoring of heavy industry (a policy that took advantage of overpopulated farming villages as sources of cheap labor). Lockwood, however, attributed even more importance to the role played by thousands of frugal, small-scale Japanese entrepreneurs who worked hard and long in their own house-workshops, often with their own family members as sole employees. Here too, as is pointed out in the following chapter, one is referring to an abiding quality in the cultural psychology of the Japanese; the concerted effort was on the part of families, not of individuals alone. The "house," not the person, was being advanced by the small entrepreneur. Again, one had a strong sense of self-motivated achievement—but in the context of affiliative nurturant expressive concerns.

Briefly, the role of the Japanese family as a socializing agent, as a permanent recourse in times of stress, and as a keystone of Japanese social values must be considered in an understanding of both Japanese achievement motivation and the capacity for concerted instrumental group efforts that went into the rapid economic change witnessed in Japan. The point is that there was a sufficient percentage of the Japanese population psychologically ready to make government-directed modernization succeed.[10]

This consideration must not be removed from context, however. What we have to say on this point is not to suggest an entirely new theory of economic development, one that ignores other complex determinants already fully considered by the economic historians. It is simply an attempt to bring motivational determinants into proper focus; such factors are an essential characteristic for any population in the achievement of social change. In the last analysis, internally induced and lasting social change in the economic sphere must be congruent, to some extent, with the psychological motivation of at least a good number of the participants in the economy.

CRITIQUE OF HAGEN'S THEORY OF SOCIAL CHANGE

Although much of what we have to say here runs parallel to the arguments of Everett E. Hagen in his volume *On the Theory of Social Change*,[11] our contentions and propositions are somewhat different. His theory suggests that innovation and creative behavior are due to a tendency for elements of the population to retreat when they be-

---

[9] Lockwood, *The Economic Development of Japan: Growth and Structural Change* (1954).

[10] See discussion in Chapter 9.

[11] Hagen, *On the Theory of Social Change* (1962).

come alienated from traditional values as a result of the loss of expected status within the traditional society. While I agree that some such process seems to have been taking place at the end of the Tokugawa period in Japan, Hagen's arguments do not touch upon some unique features of Japanese psychology. These features are expressed externally in an ideological emphasis and on the development of capacities for sustained application to tasks in the face of present frustrations and temporary defeat as one persists toward ultimately successful future goals. The virtues of endurance and perseverance, the capacity to put off pleasure and to endure suffering, characterize Japanese culture to a degree not paralleled elsewhere.

Nor is Japanese economic development to be explained simply by saying that the Japanese were more willing to accept foreign values than were other Asian societies, since it was part of their tradition to do so. My position is that the political leaders of the Meiji Restoration were able to call forth efforts from the Japanese population by a reinterpretation of the familial structure of the society on the basis of a hierarchical system of loyalties and trust. It made emotional sense and was appealing to the Japanese because it was entirely consonant with learned behavior within the primary family; such behavior could easily be transmuted to the economic political plane in sustained work patterns phrased in social terms. The Japanese sense of accomplishment or achievement could be satisfied ultimately only by being defined as relevant to a sense of self as part of family, or part of something larger than the individualized self. The sense of self, for many Japanese, is realized only through repayment of deeply felt obligations, which, if not fulfilled, give rise to a sense of intolerable guilt. This sense of loyalty to authority and need to repay obligation stems from interaction of the child with its parents before there is any verbalization of an ideology of loyalty beyond the primary family itself. The emotional impact of life within the primary family sets the keystone to life's meaning. The traditional family system must be perceived as having a quasi-religious connotation for the adult Japanese. In his perceptive work *Tokugawa Religion*,[12] Robert Bellah demonstrates from a somewhat different perspective that it was not uncommon in Tokugawa times to find religious affirmation of the virtue of work and the diligent pursuit of one's occupation. Simplicity, frugality, and diligence were inseparably woven into the fabric of one's filial duty to family and society, and thence to the supernatural extension of the family. It should be pointed out, also, that such feelings were an emotionally relevant part of personality integration, whether expressed by the individual secondarily in the Japanese religious system, or pri-

---

[12] Bellah, *Tokugawa Religion* (1957).

marily as part of being a member of a Japanese family seeking family continuity through time. This sense of self-justification through work, as Bellah pointed out, is remarkably similar to what has been called the Protestant ethic in Western culture.

Hagen notes the similarity of the puritanlike ethic in Japan to the ethic of English nonconformism, with its doctrine that service to God lies in a diligent attempt to glorify Him by making the earth fruitful. This doctrine in the English, Hagen points out, was associated with a deep pervasive sense of guilt that is central to puritan psychology. Although he sees the same ethic appearing in Japan, Hagen does not presume that in Japan it is related in a similar fashion to a sense of guilt; rather, he concludes from some of the written literature, that it is related to a sense of inadequacy and shame. This conclusion is unwarranted according to my view, which is that whereas a sense of guilt in the West was often associated with individualized problems related to sexuality, in Japan there was a strong sense of guilt if one strayed from the path of work. Only through repayment of parental efforts could a Japanese find satisfaction in life and freedom from a sense of guilt.

FAMILY STRUCTURE:
SELF IDENTITY IN ACHIEVEMENT ORIENTATION

In contrasting Japanese traditional cultural concepts of self and society with those prevalent in western Europe in the nineteenth century during its industrial revolution, one finds that the Japanese placed little value on individualistic self-realization in either the spiritual or the material realm. The ideal found in the West of self realization apart from family or social group has been entirely alien to the Japanese system of thought (outside that of a small group of intellectuals) until very recently. The religious ideals of Buddhism emphasize loss of self or selfish preoccupations as a means of release from worldly problems. Confucianist ideology, which colored the thought of the governing classes throughout the Tokugawa period as well as that of the subsequent innovators of modernization in the early Meiji period, kept its central focus on the position of the family in the social system. The ultimate goal of life was a noninstrumentally organized, quasi-religious family continuity. Legally and morally an individual defined himself in the context of family roles and their attendant obligations and expectations. The state was defined not only in terms of a class or occupational hierarchy but also as a pyramid of social obligations in which all Japanese were interrelated in a hierarchical structure. It was within the context of this ideal social structure that the Meiji government defined its social and economic goals. Economic theory stressing individualized laissez-faire attitudes would have made little sense in Japan as a mandate for modernization or development. Such individualized economic theory, even though it may have influenced Japanese theoretical economists, could not actually describe the Japanese atmosphere. The self concept under individualism, the economic man as instrumentally oriented, could not form the basis of a viable social or economic theory directly pertinent to the events taking place in Japan.

The Western ideology sprang from a different tradition, the seeking of salvation or self-realization. Personal freedom as a goal of human endeavor and creative individualism were the paramount virtues in western Europe at this time, to be realized especially in a newly emerging United States. The individually internalized Christian conscience was given priority over the laws of the state and even over the traditional organized bureaucracy of the Roman church. The struggle for individual liberty became a source of considerable religious and secular social conflict. It is not coincidental that this Western ideology appeared as a main feature of the economic theory of the nineteenth century. Theories of Adam Smith gave reassurance that the individual was morally justified in seeking to maximize his individual interests, since through the operation of the impersonal market these interests were ultimately consistent with the social good, and could lead to benefit for the total society. The illusion that rational self-interest properly understood did away with any need for a controlling government apparatus made sense emotionally to individuals reared consciously by parents who at the same time trained their children to control their impulses and to feel guilt for unacceptable physical sexual urges, but also trained them to rely on a direct dependent relationship with their deity. No other form of psychological dependency was considered mature. Assured of God's help, the individual could attribute personal failure only to moral flaws or an incomplete conquest of internal evil propensities or lack of proper motivation. One learned not to turn too readily toward one's fellow men for social assistance, since by doing so one demeaned oneself. With God's help, one could become sufficiently self-reliant not only to overcome one's baser urges, but also to find sufficient strength to endure adversity and achieve long-range goals. The weak or incapable could be given alms, but the idea that poverty was a stigma of the intellectually and morally inferior lessened the feeling of oneness of the righteously successful with the underprivileged. In its later development the religious aspects of this ideology were replaced with more secular arguments. One finds such an ideology, however, still of considerable import in American society; thirty years ago, Robert Lynd, in *Knowledge for What?* [13] amply

---

[13] Lynd, *Knowledge for What?* (1939).

demonstrated how such thinking was (as it still remains) an essential aspect of American life.

The point being made here again is that the system of classical economics developed in Britain and in the United States must be seen as ethno-economics. Its emphasis was very much on an instrumental view of human nature and its motivation. On the contrary, the type of economic social system envisioned by the Meiji government officials directing modernization was much more expressively oriented and centered on the family and the nation as an extension of the family itself. To the Japanese, this kind of integration made sense. Also, it created a system under which morale was high and class conflict was minimized. The feelings of mutual expectation between superior and subordinate were strongly operative in motivating those involved in economic pursuits. In addition to the goal of maximizing profit, employers felt a series of obligations to their subordinates. This made some, at least, come to emphasize fringe benefits very early, and led to a reluctance to discharge individuals once they had been brought into the organization. These particular features have been criticized by Western economists as irrational, but one could argue, on the contrary, that they contributed to the high morale that prevented significant conflict in Japanese industrialization, a conflict resulting from alienation of the worker, which occurred with European capitalism.

Western economics is based on a commonly held assumption about the nature of achievement motivation as it relates to occupational self-justification among dominant social elements of the culture producing such motivation. Rational self-interest assumes the rationalization of the economy in accord with impersonal laws; when these laws work ideally they require freedom from interference by government; such interference may be guided by noneconomic considerations and hence prevent the maximization of self-interest. In the twentieth century this system has been considerably modified in an attempt to make it work better. Curiously, many of these modifications are in the direction of a greater consideration for expressive elements in human motivation among workers. In contrast, in the Japanese system, one finds an increased recourse to instrumental concerns, with the gradual dropping out of the family system as the major guiding ideology within Japanese thought. From the 1920s on, Japanese intellectuals became more and more concerned with a Marxian interpretation of the social structure. The emotional climate of Japan, however, has not completely altered. The structure of Japanese feelings about self and class identity and about social authority still makes class warfare of little appeal. The Japanese even more than the American identifies himself as middle class—an old tradition of the Japanese rural farmer which seemed to have been transmitted to the industrial worker. The company president, in the fantasy of many Japanese, has replaced the daimyo, or feudal lord. Individuals are still motivated by feelings of loyalty to the organization, feelings that an individualistically organized middle-class American would see as interfering with his achievement career, which demands a degree of mobility not possible within the Japanese system. The idea of loyalty to a business or factory strikes the ordinary American industrial worker as absurd, to say the least.

It is noteworthy that even today, as demonstrated by the material we have been accumulating, in the expressive fantasy of lower-class urban Japanese, as well as in that of rural folk, the status position often spontaneously depicted as that of an adviser is held not only by the teacher but also by the head of a company or an entrepreneur who takes a paternal position and acts as adviser to his subordinates. This perception of paternalism also affects the individual when he reaches such a status position; he feels he is expected to protect and maintain his subordinates in a way entirely in line with the familistic pseudo-kinship structures that were part of the old society. From the standpoint of some economists, the system in a Japanese factory described by Abegglen[14] looks uneconomical and inefficient; however, it is the force of this very system that helped the Japanese adapt to the modern age. The internalized personality structure, the concept of goals and of interconnected relationships, the pattern of social expectations focused on the familial pattern—these were exactly the emotional and motivational forces within the Japanese system that helped maintain and direct Japanese society successfully in the new direction of industrialization.

SUMMARY

Social scientists concerned with problems of economic development have only recently become cognizant of a need to consider psychological factors as relevant to the study of economic growth and change in particular cultures. Both classical economics and Marxist theory, in their heavy emphasis on man as a rational animal maximizing his political or economic power, tended to overlook or deprecate the influence of the expressive aspects of human behavior. These culturally determined but psychologically structured expressive aspects must facilitate a sense of achievement and accomplishment in the context of economic productivity within the motivational structure of a sufficiently large segment of a particular population, if political policy decisions and social planning, whatever their theoretical validity, are to be adequately implemented.

---

[14] Abegglen, *The Japanese Factory: Aspects of Its Social Organization* (1958).

Socialization experiences in the context of Japanese society result in a strong need for self-realization through work and a sense of accomplishment defined in social terms. These psychological features were common to a sufficient number of Japanese to make possible a successful transmutation of a feudal society into a well-functioning industrialized modern state. Japanese achievement drive must be seen as motivated by irrational unconscious forces as well as by socially defined goals. The system of familial obligation related to Japanese internalization of feelings of potential guilt and the lack of easy expression of hostility or aggression, if given the proper cultural-industrial context, can result in self-dedication to social role and to the maintenance of relatively high morale and harmony in work situations.

The social climate within the family was readily transmitted in particularistic terms to a larger social context.

I do not presume here to formulate alternative theories of economic growth, but simply to supplement existing theories with the insight afforded by an examination of the role of psychological variables in determining the differential rate of economic change among different cultures entering the modern industrial age. Psychological factors contribute both in respect to achievement motivation and in respect to the effectiveness of the social organization in bringing about commonly accepted new goals.

Chapter VIII

The Entrepreneurial Mentality
of Lower-Class Urban Japanese
in Manufacturing Industries

with HIROSHI WAGATSUMA

When the anthropologist concentrates on a simple rural community with at most a thousand or so inhabitants, he can, in a relatively short time, gain an overall view of how basic subsistence is obtained in that community by using resources for the production and distribution of food, shelter, and clothing. The pattern of internal distribution and of external trade may be complex, but the analysis of modes of work and of how property and wealth are distributed does not necessarily demand specialized knowledge of economics, even though it may at times demand an acuteness of observation that goes beneath the deceptive surface of events.

It is far more difficult to describe the interdependent economic functionings that tie together the smaller segments of any urban structure. Such segments are internally and externally integral parts of a vast complex of international and national trade. Yet, to gain any adequate understanding of a local specialized community within a larger national state, it is vital to understand its internal economic functions as they are intertwined with other social relationships. In doing so, the anthropologist or sociologist has a task far different from that of the economist.

In studying Arakawa, a lower-class Japanese ward in Tokyo, Hiroshi Wagatsuma and I were interested in its total ecological organization, not as the subject of an economic treatise, but rather so that we could

present the psychocultural thought patterns of a social segment of a
Japanese city in some form of dynamic interplay with the basic economic structure of the total society. In the course of our study of a city
ward and problems of delinquency,[1] we were interested, first, in how
the thought patterns of the group examined conformed to or deviated
from basic cultural values. Second, we were concerned with how members of family units think and feel about themselves in relation to
their community in respect to basic economic conditions and to other
forms of social organization.

More specifically, we developed considerable interest in the psychocultural aspects of the economy, in how the personality patterns of
people in this ward were reflected in their economic activities. What
we report about the interplay between personality and culture in
Arakawa Ward in Tokyo should be of interest to the economist as
well as to the generalist in social science theory, for there are motivational patterns apparent in Arakawa Ward that shed light on the
history of Japanese economic modernization in a more general frame
of reference.

What we present here is a brief glimpse of the economic structure of
Arakawa Ward, showing how the marginal economic activities of
urban lower-class Japanese are in slow transition and how the goal-
oriented achievement motives energizing this part of the Japanese

---

[1] Portions of this chapter will appear as chapter 2 of *Heritage of Endurance*
(DeVos and Wagatsuma), to be published. The anthropological field research on
which this particular chapter is based was done between 1966 and 1968 principally
by Hiroshi Wagatsuma in Arakawa Ward, Northeast Tokyo. Informal interviews of
a number of Arakawa residents rounded out our knowledge of the community context of the fifty families we were investigating intensively by standardized interviews and projective psychological tests. The more formal aspects of our research
design were directed toward a study of the genesis of delinquent behavior in adolescents living in a lower-class area with a relatively high rate of delinquency. Both
parents and subjects of thirty experimental and twenty controls were interviewed
and tested for an average of six hours apiece. Additionally, we interviewed teachers,
social workers, police, and community volunteers to gain a picture of how members of the community were dealing with delinquency among youth. In the course
of this research on delinquency we found it necessary to think of Arakawa Ward
as a segment of the still continuing urban *shitamachi*, or townspeople culture of
Tokyo. We conducted interviews on informal voluntary organizations and a number
of other topics related to community organization. These fieldwork results are reported in our forthcoming volume. Also included are several chapters on the
economic conditions and occupations of Arakawa residents derived from the statistics available through the ward offices. To trace out in more detail a typical occupation representative of the ward we decided to find out how the pencil-making
industry operated as part of the economic life of Arakawa. Wagatsuma therefore
interviewed a number of pencil-makers ranging from individuals working on subcontracts with one or two machines to "company presidents" with three or four
workers to workers in larger factories. The material in this chapter derives from
these interviews as well as secondary statistical sources.

economy influence and are influenced by the massive shifts in technology and industry now going on in Japan.

TRANSITION FROM PREMODERN TO MODERN INDUSTRIAL LIFE

The economic life in Arakawa Ward typifies that of a significant segment of the Japanese urban lower class. In studying this ward in some detail, we gained insight into one of the enigmas that have puzzled Western economists. Many questions concerning the source of the hidden strength that keeps the Japanese economy viable have defied easy answer. For example, how were the Japanese able to launch a large-scale industrialized war effort against the United States, and to maintain it so long, without the extensive plant facilities any Western industrial nation would have considered essential? Where were the machines? Where were the skilled laborers? How could the tiny workshops forming part of individual homes housed in flimsy wooden structures possibly compete with the large developed factories of the United States in mounting a significant war effort? Obviously they did, but how?

In our investigation of Arakawa Ward we found a still viable economic system in which an individual family owned from one to three machines placed in one room of a small frame-and-paper dwelling, while characteristically the family lived in one or two additional rooms. These home-factories were found in narrow irregular streets periodically cut through by major traffic arteries having more modern stores, sidewalks, and larger concrete buildings. Only here and there in this ward, located to the north of the center of Tokyo, was there a factory of any significant size. According to Lockwood and other economic specialists on Japan, this type of urban factory setting was typical. During the prewar period, such neighborhood areas accounted for nearly 30 percent of all Japanese production, and it was in such areas that the most significant developments of the Japanese economic modernization occurred. For example, Lockwood writes:

The founding of large-scale industry in Japan, because of its political support, its strategic implications, and the striking contrast it offered with traditional Japan, attracted a good deal of attention from the outside world, but it was the expansion of Japan's basic economy—agriculture and small-scale industry built on traditional foundations—which accounted for most of the growth of national productivity and income during [the early Meiji period].[2]

---

[2] Lockwood, *The Economic Development of Japan: Growth and Structural Change* (1954).

Lockwood notes how difficult it was to make comparative statistical measurements of overall growth in the Japanese economy. The workshop industries, or house-factories as we have termed them, most of them employing fewer than five workers, were not actually reported in the statistics prior to 1939 except in a few of the major manufacturing branches.[3] He states:

The myriads of tiny establishments comprising workshop industries . . . continued to account for a major sector of manufacturing activity. Only slowly did they yield to factory competition. In fact, one of the striking aspects of Japanese industrialization has been the strength and staying power of the small industrialist, especially where he has been fitted into a framework of large-scale organization providing him with other marketing arrangements, credit, and cheap electric power. Here it may be recorded that as late as 1930 plants of less than five operatives still furnished 30 percent of the net product of all manufacturing establishments in Japan.[4]

Lockwood reports the estimate that in 1930 more than half of the nearly six million men, women, and children employed in some branch of manufacturing or construction in Japan worked in establishments of fewer than five workers. He writes that there were at least one million tiny shops, each engaging fewer than three persons on the average. In effect, these were nuclear family enterprises.[5] He says:

To discuss the growth of industry without reference to the masses of workshops which crowd the sidestreets of Japanese cities and give employment to many a rural village is to leave out a considerable sector of the industrial economy.[6]

Although gradually declining in relative importance before World War II, the small plants—more than half of which were actually one-man shops—still contributed a quarter or more of the Japanese industrial output during the 1930s'.[7]

Looked at anthropologically, these house-factories developed out of particular Japanese premodern cultural traditions. Carried over into Japanese industrialization were many of the premodern, so-called feudal, social-structural elements. Nevertheless, Japan was transformed into a modern industrial state with relatively little major disruption of the total social fabric. As I have contended in the previous two chapters, in addition to certain social-structural elements that contributed heavily to this successful transformation, one must also consider the psychological dimension of Japanese culture if one is to understand the peculiarities of the way in which achievement motivation was and is structured in the Japanese national character.

---

[3] *Ibid.*, p. 109.   [4] *Ibid.*, p. 110.   [5] *Ibid.*, p. 112.   [6] *Ibid.*
[7] *Ibid.*, p. 203.

An intensive examination of family units in Arakawa Ward has helped us understand why and how the traditional patterns of thinking adapted to city life. For example, we found that farm youths who came from isolated rural areas were treated in ways already familiar to them when they came to find jobs in the city. Ties with the family often remained unbroken, and even when such ties were ruptured, many employers in the city acted with traditional paternalism. It was not unusual in premodern times for second sons of farmers, as well as those of petty merchants and artisans, to be apprenticed to a wealthier artisan or merchant family. The underlying patterns in the vicinity of Tokyo—as far as the social arrangements for in-migration are concerned—remain in many respects much as they were in the past. Urban migration was a feature of Japanese culture during the Tokugawa period, especially from the late eighteenth century onward.

In our sample, some of those whose ambition was to stay in the city and establish an "independent house" were encouraged to do so by their city mentors, and some employers helped to find a wife or husband for the country employee. Within our particular sample of households, we found numerous examples of individuals who eventually established themselves by purchasing machines, and who, with their wives, set up household economic units that were readily incorporated into an already existing organizational network. This assumption of an entrepreneurial role depended heavily on traditional forms of mutual expectations and responsibilities between a master artisan or merchant and a former apprentice.

Many of the studies of urbanization reported in the sociological literature are based on experience within the United States. Urban immigration into the United States from a foreign country, and the attendant impossibility of ready transportation back and forth to the old home, meant for many a complete split with their place of birth. This has not been true in Japan, where the urban dweller, given economic or other difficulties, could always go back to join his rural relatives. In fact, a great many such returns occurred with fluctuations in economic conditions within the city. The case of return to the country meant that the Japanese urban in-migrant did not have to make a complete break with his previous network of relationships. Two features of Japanese urbanization—first, the pattern of occupational paternalism, and second, the capacity to maintain some continuity with the family network—ensured that the change to city life could be accomplished without a great deal of psychological insecurity or anomic disorientation.

The thought patterns of the new factory worker in modernizing Japan did not have to vary greatly from traditional patterns. The relationship of apprentice to master artisan or merchant was defined so that there were expectations of dependency directed toward the employer, who in turn felt a responsibility toward his employees, although this expectation was often breached in practice. Most importantly, a sufficient number of employers took seriously this moral paternalistic directive to meet the expectations of their dependent workers, to some degree at least. It was mutually understood that hiring could involve a long-term commitment of both employer and employee. Traditionally, learning a skill in Japan meant that a young employee or apprentice would work a good many years for food, shelter, and low pay toward the day when he would be recognized as worthy of some sponsorship in a semi-independent role, very often in a subsidiary shop, while still drawing on the continuing sponsorship of his former employer. In more modern times this has taken the form of a loan to enable a former employee to invest capital in his own machinery, be it only one or two simple machines. The faithful apprentice would expect to be rewarded for his past loyalty by benevolent support as he embarked on his own increasingly independent occupational career. He could, therefore, expect some financial support as well as other forms of security and would feel entitled to his employer's encouragement when he felt ready to initiate activities of his own, either as a *shokunin* ("artisan") or a *shonin* ("merchant").

Naishoku, or work within the house by both middle- and lower-class women, is related to patterns traditional in rural farm families. For example, such "side" activities as raising silkworms in a rural house were part of the expected occupation of women in many of the rural areas from which the new city dwellers came to provide labor for the new industries of Japan.

These traditional Japanese economic-occupational models of artisan, merchant, and farmer, therefore, blended readily into the newer machine industries developed for trade. In textiles, for example, although cotton products manufactured by large-scale factory units were one of Japan's early big export industries, the silk industry, which was still important, continued to be essentially small-scale and rural in character. Lockwood notes that before the incursion of nylon and other synthetics "nearly one-third of the households of the country derived some supplementary income from the raising of cocoons." [8]

A large consumer market was at hand in Japan for the cotton textile industry from its beginning. There was a quick development of internal demand as well as export. Labor was available. It was relatively easy to adapt handicraft skills and unskilled low-wage labor to the operation of power machinery for weaving and spinning. We learned that in Arakawa Ward, by 1899, eighty-three cotton mills had

---

[8] *Ibid.*, p. 28.

already been established, run chiefly with low-wage female labor. Girls were recruited on a contract basis from peasant homes in the rural countryside, and were housed and fed in company dormitories. As Lockwood puts it, these dormitories "blended the factory system of the West with the paternalism and strict discipline of Japan." [9]

We contend, on the basis of this evidence, that one of the basic reasons for the ease of Japanese modernization was that urbanization was already a developed feature of Japanese life. Moreover, both the familial network and the traditional paternalistic psychocultural patterns of mutual expectation that existed in all classes from samurai on down, helped the total Japanese society adapt with relative ease to the new industries developing with modernization. We contend further that the Japanese-type familism and paternalism were as adaptable to industrialization as were the more individualistically oriented patterns of socioeconomic relationships found in northern European countries and the United States. It is an ethnocentric fallacy to assume that only Western psychocultural conditions could be readily transmuted into a modern industrial economic social system. Japan offers an example of an alternative system of cultural adaptation to social change. On a more strictly psychological level, also, there are peculiar Japanese modes of achievement motivation that contribute to the energy and drive that have allowed the modern transformation to occur with such success. In Japan, family and pseudo-kinship ties kept a firm hold on most individuals both socially and motivationally as they gradually shifted into newer forms of commercial and industrial economic life.

Bennett and Ishino see two general features which characterize paternalistic economic organizations.[10] First, there is a degree of hierarchy which is not purely a matter of instrumental necessity, but in which there is a cultural or ideological element suggesting that the employer is more than just an employer. As was indicated in previous chapters, there are, on a psychological level, expressive elements to the employer-employee relationship, as well as the direct power and economic elements, that serve as major determinants of behavior.

A second characteristic is an institutionalized concern by the employer for aspects of the personal lives of his employees, a concern that has nothing to do with the actual work performed or the organization for which it is being performed. That is, the employer's responsibility extends beyond the economic sphere itself, even to helping the families of employees. A great deal of Japanese economic and social history is to be understood in terms of such paternalistic

---

[9] *Ibid.*, p. 30.

[10] Bennett and Ishino, *Paternalism in the Japanese Economy* (1963), especially pp. 225 ff.

structures which permeate the entire culture. For example, as Bennett and Ishino point out, the pattern of migration of rural people to the cities and towns has actually reinforced paternalistic practices, since youthful migrants were often the types of people who *needed* the kind of dependent relationships to which they had become accustomed in their families and communities.[11] A number of the employers themselves were at one time migrants from a rural social structure and its involved network of expectations. Our volume on Arakawa[12] will discuss in detail how this worked out in particular families, as well as in particular situations where the individual took on a pseudo-familial relationship to a particular boss.

These paternalistic structures still exist in relationships throughout Japanese society. In the past, they characterized the apprenticeship structures and *dōzoku*, or branch family organizations of the merchants and artisans; the hierarchical loyalty and responsible paternalism often cited as part of the code of the samurai were found to exist even in outlaw organizations and in the entertainment industries that still operate on the peripheries of the regular social organization (see Chapter 11). Such paternalism is also an integral part even of the Japanese outcaste communities (see Chapter 15).

THE ENTREPRENEURIAL MENTALITY OF SMALL-SCALE MANUFACTURERS

It is interesting to note that, according to Lockwood, of the nearly thirty million Japanese gainfully employed in 1930, more than six million reported themselves in the census as "employers." Two-thirds of these were in agriculture and fishing, but there were also about two million in nonagricultural pursuits who so classified themselves. Another three and a half million Japanese, listed as "independents," made a living on their own in one way or another. Thus, Lockwood points out, almost one-third of the working population of Japan, the lower class as well as the middle class, were classified as "entrepreneurs" in some sense, as far as their principal occupation was concerned.[13]

The difference between the use of the term *entrepreneur* in Japan and its use in Europe or the United States should be noted. In its Western usage, the term connotes a degree of independence; "middle-class" well-being is associated with owning and controlling one's own business. The Japanese, however, use the term in a more extensive

---

[11] *Ibid.*, p. 226.

[12] DeVos and Wagatsuma, *Heritage of Endurance* (to be published).

[13] Lockwood, *The Economic Development of Japan: Growth and Structural Change* (1954), pp. 584–585.

sense and include individuals we would consider to be of lower-class status. They are motivationally, in effect, what we call "lower-class capitalists." Such individuals may not have any higher economic status than does a simple factory worker and may possess only the barest of capital resources or skills; nevertheless, according to our evidence, they exhibit attitudes and maintain social self-identities that motivate them to behave in a manner much different from that of the simple, employed factory workers in the United States or Europe. Lockwood points out, for example, that the rickshaw pullers, carrying passengers, and cart pullers (whether gatherers of refuse or movers of material for particular small companies) were classified as "entrepreneurs" and were considered as much entrepreneurs in Japan as were such independent craftsmen as carpenters or fishermen, who had some investment in their special tools and gear.

As we can document in detail, individuals with an entrepreneurial mentality (as our lower-class ward) include men and women at the very bottom of the Japanese social hierarchy. We contend, therefore, that, psychologically at least, Japanese entrepreneurs of the lower-class as well as the middle-class level of social participation share many motivational features that are characteristic of only the middle class in the West.

As some of our materials illustrated, there is room even at the lowest levels of entrepreneurial endeavor for minor types of technical innovation. Japanese of all classes are interested in gadgetry and technology for its own sake and as an instrument of competition. A lower-class Japanese who owns his own machine will try to invent some technological gimmick that will give him an advantage over others doing the same work. When he develops an innovation he guards it as a trade secret which will help to ensure his survival. Covert competition with peers is a curiously pervasive psychological feature among Japanese of all classes. Competition is a heady stimulus among these lower-class entrepreneurs who maintain their optimism despite the strong possibility of failure. The fact, for example, that in one year in Arakawa Ward there were 5,000 bankruptcies did not seem to deter others from continuing their competitive behavior vis-à-vis one another.

Lockwood points out that the "independence" of the small businessman is an illusion. He must secure his raw materials, his credit, and his market from a merchant or large industrialist whose financial resources and knowledge of market conditions far exceed his own. Thus the small fellow, whether industrialist or merchant, in reality is often "reduced virtually to the status of a wage worker squeezed between the price he paid for his credit and supplies and the price he can get for his product." [14]

---

[14] *Ibid.*, p. 211.

Although this is increasingly true, the point still must be made that for psychological reasons the Japanese miniature entrepreneur maintains his illusions with optimism. He feels that if he works sufficiently hard he can somehow beat nearby competition and is sustained by the hope that he himself can escape failure by competing better—by somehow devoting more time, energy, and dedication to his work than does his failing neighbor.

There have been no really successful fraternal organizations or associations of the small industrialists and traders to relieve their continual involvement in a cut-throat competition. Among the pencilmakers we studied in Arakawa Ward, for example, we found that some belonged to informal groups whose families would picnic together, but in no instance did these informal groups include two families doing the same type of work; their occupational functions were complementary to one another, even though every member of a group was involved in some phase of pencil making.[15]

Intense competition persists in most of the small-scale trades. No controls exist to regulate output, prices, wages, or working conditions. This sellers' competition tends to be ruthless wherever many small, lower-class industrialists supply a common market. Individually, the little man can exert no influence on price and must adjust himself as best he can to the overall conditions of demand and supply. In this kind of situation a good producer can enter very easily with a minimum amount of capital and technical experience. There is comparative freedom for the small producer to risk his tiny savings, get loans, engage in labor, and arrange the production process according to what he can see locally. This is all well illustrated in the pencil-making industry, which we have studied in considerable detail. In the study of this industry and others, I find a reaffirmation of the general motivational features discussed in other chapters of this volume related to the social structure and familial origins of Japanese achievement motivation.

There are nevertheless a number of differences among merchants, artisans, and farmers which cannot be discussed here in any detail. Suffice it to say that there are functional differences related to traditions that either facilitate or hamper the operation of the lower-class entrepreneur. To give one example, the shokunin, or artisan, is considered to have—as they put it in Japanese—"a slow mouth" (kuchi ga omoi), which means he has no experience in salesmanship. Therefore he usually finds it expedient to work through a merchant, who

---

[15] A similar tendency is to be noted in such American fraternal organizations as the Lions, Elks, and Rotary; businessmen in direct competition with each other tend to join different groups, and mutual business patronage is a tendency among members of one organization.

acts as an intermediary in the selling process. Those of merchant background do not have difficulty in selling, but they lack some of the sustained discipline learned in growing up within an artisan family that leads to diligence in applying oneself to particular types of mechanical operation. Therefore, it is interesting to note that in Arakawa Ward, and perhaps elsewhere generally, there is even today some division of labor between those of artisan and those of merchant backgrounds in lower-class entrepreneurial activities.

OCCUPATIONS AND INDUSTRY IN ARAKAWA

Arakawa industry is particularly characterized by the small-scale factory. Many of these are typical "house factories" that provide living space for a nuclear family, sometimes, with aged grandparents, other times including a young married couple who have not been able to locate independent housing. Eighty-five percent of the total number of factories listed in Arakawa employ fewer than nine workers. The major products of the small-scale factories are furniture, metal work, ready-made suits and dresses, leather products, toys, and pencils. Arakawa retail and wholesale commerce is also characterized by its small-scale units. Larger stores such as one often finds in the commercial areas of Ueno and Asakusa are rare in Arakawa. Except for a few wholesale dealers, most of the shops and stores found in Arakawa are run by individual proprietors and their families.

In Arakawa one can observe how and why the small-scale factories have played an important and unique role in the development of Japanese industry. They are, in effect, marginal enterprises that suffer most from fluctuations or adjustments in the Japanese economy. They demonstrate the functioning of a free-enterprise system in that relatively inefficient or poorly managed economic units go out of business. They are, in effect, a cushion or shock absorber that allows the Japanese national economy to adjust to minor as well as major changes in demand. Economists who note this type of market function very seldom concern themselves with the psychological price paid by the individuals and families forming this cushion.

For example, there was a slight recession in the Japanese economy in 1965, which affected Arakawa industry and commerce. The recession led to a decrease in demand for furniture and ready-made suits. Though the total output was not too seriously affected, the profit rate was reduced to keep sales going. Similar adverse conditions occurred with leather manufacturing and in the pencil industry. The year 1965 saw a total of 6,141 bankruptcies in Arakawa, a 50 percent increase over 1964. They reflected not only the excessive number of small units that could not maintain themselves in the competitive market, but also the increasing inroads made in the small manufacturing units by the growth in the automation of larger factories.

A bureau of economics in the Arakawa Ward office made a desperate attempt to overcome the short-term effects of recession. The bureau held lectures and short training courses on the improvement of machines and management of small factories and offered guidance on taxation and bookkeeping, and diagnosed the functioning of individual factories, with suggestions on how to bring about improvements. The bureau furnished loans to some small firms and helped to reorganize some cooperative groups, even holding fairs to advertise Arakawa products. It suggested means of maintaining employee morale by commending excellent workers and supplying recreational activities. In spite of programs of this kind the forces of a free enterprise economy dictate that there will be an inevitable number of failures and that this number will fluctuate with conditions in the market.

As an example of how the people of Arakawa provide a cushion for larger units of economic enterprise, we can cite how during this period the department stores dealt with individual families in Arakawa who manufactured shirts. These shirts were not bought outright from those manufacturing them but were placed in the stores for sale. During this period of recession the unsold shirts were returned to the shirt makers so that the store itself suffered no loss in unsold inventory; the smaller factory units of subcontractors absorbed the loss.

Flexibility and Demand Change in Small Industries

These small enterprises must use their own capital to replace outmoded machines. There are numerous examples of change within Arakawa industry. The manufacture of celluloid toys, once produced on a large scale in many Arakawa houses, has almost completely stopped, largely replaced by the manufacture of plastic toys. The toy industry is meeting stiff competition from toys produced in Hong Kong. Similarly, the production of artificial flowers, once a very important source of income for housewives working at home, has all but disappeared, driven out of the market by the cheaper labor in Hong Kong. Machines for the manufacture of ballpoint pens and cheap mechanical pencils are appearing in workshops that formerly worked exclusively on wood pencils. Furniture manufactured in Arakawa used to be made completely of wood, but recently metal-pipe furniture is becoming popular and machines have been adapted to its construction. There is still some demand for traditional products such as the various kinds of hair accessories and a number of tiny articles called *komonotayo* ("small things"); tiny fans and other articles for Japanese dolls are still made in Arakawa by housewives doing *naishoku*.

Stuffed toys are another important product of Arakawa; bears, dogs, lions, and the like are exported in large numbers. In this industry, the Arakawa Gangu Kanushiki Kaishi (the Arakawa Toy Manufacturing Company) directly employs only twenty or thirty persons but subcontracts widely, buying raw materials and having toys made by several smaller factories, which in turn employ housewives working at home for some parts of the manufacturing process. For example, stuffed animals are delivered to homes for housewives to sew on the glass eyes and the ears, and then are carried back to the small factories for further processing.

Ups and Downs in a Pencil-maker Family

Mr. Arai, approximately sixty years old when this was written, and owner of a woodworking factory, exemplifies the vicissitudes of a career in the pencil-making business. He first started in the business of transporting pencils for various processors. He came to know many of the pencil-makers personally and, with some backing from a pencil firm (the Home Run Pencil Company), he set up his own lead-processing factory. After the war, Mr. Arai handed over his lead-processing factory to his second son and established a woodworking, painting, and printing factory in which he began manufacturing pencils of his own brand, Indian Pencil. He notes that immediately after the war was a good time for small business, but gradually, as the larger makers became better equipped and more automated, there was less demand for cheaper pencils, and the competition intensified among the small-scale makers who subcontracted with the larger firms.

According to his daughter, Mr. Arai began to lose out because, although he was a good businessman, he was an amateur (*shirōto*) in pencil-making. By 1956 Mr. Arai stopped making his Indian Pencil and was forced to close down his painting and printing factory, saying, "If you don't print pencils with your own brand name, you need no painting shop." Thus an individual who attempted to become an intermediate pencil-maker was forced to concentrate on the woodworking process. Mr. Arai now does woodwork for some of the leading companies such as Globe-Flag, Ribbon, and Cherry Yacht. These companies usually buy lead from Mr. Arai's son's lead factory and boards from other dealers and have them delivered to Mr. Arai's woodworking factory. Globe and Ribbon pencils are sent back for painting to the painting and printing shops owned by these companies. Cherry Yacht sends its pencils to another painting and printing factory on a subcontracting basis. The packaging of these pencils is done by housewives as *naishoku*. According to his son-in-law, Mr. Tateno, Mr. Arai is not too successful as a woodworker. He has not had as intensive experience with his machines as have other woodworkers who are real artisans (*shokunin*). In spite of his years of working in the pencil-making process, he is still considered by his son-in-law to be an amateur.

Mr. Arai himself recognizes that he is getting old and considers himself semi-retired. He says that as long as he can make enough profit to permit him and his wife to live without discomfort he will be contented. The rest of what he makes he adds to the wages he now pays his employees, expressing the ideal of benevolent paternalism. His employees' daily wages range from 600 yen (less than $2), received by an unskilled woman, to 1,000 to 1,300 yen ($3 to $3.50 a day) received by men.

Mr. Tateno, age thirty-nine, Mr. Arai's son-in-law, works for himself as a special printer. He was born in Gunma Prefecture, the second son of a farmer who had five sons and two daughters. After finishing technical high school, where he enjoyed working with a lathe, he was sent to a kamikaze pilot training center, but the war ended before he was called upon to fulfill any suicidal mission. He returned home for a short period and then came to Tokyo when he was twenty-one. When he arrived in Tokyo he started working for Mr. Arai's company, which was then making Indian Pencils, and was put in charge of sales. He obtained this job through family affiliations; Mr. Arai had been twice married—his second wife was a cousin of Mr. Tateno. Shortly after he married Mr. Arai's daughter, the pencils went out of production and Mr. Tateno received from his father-in-law the painting machines of his former company, whereupon he set himself up as an independent special printer. At present he has three machines in his six-by-nine-foot factory room. On one of these machines he does the special printing of company, bank, or hotel names on pencils and ballpoint pens.

Mr. Tateno has been inventive. He has modified his machine to prevent it from crushing the resilient body of the ballpoint pen, thus permitting his wife, who is less skilled, to work on this machine. He prints "Tombow Pencils" in silver on a small plastic box with another machine he also improved.

Mr. Tateno has liked machines since his youth, and he finds his work interesting. His attitude exemplifies a number of traits observable in lower-class Japanese entrepreneurs, not the least of which is a basic feeling of dedication and enthusiasm for his work, as well as pride in his own inventiveness in improving and adapting machinery.

To modify or produce the parts necessary for improving his machines, Mr. Tateno divided the work between two machine shops,

so that neither of them really understood what was being done to the machine. This was necessary to keep my improvement a secret. Once I made a mistake and had a machine improved by one machine-maker, the maker immediately thought it was a good idea, he stole my idea and started selling the same machine with the improvements and everyone in Arakawa began using the new model.

When asked why he did not have his invention patented, Mr. Tateno said:

It's no use. They can still copy the crucial part of my invention, and by changing other parts of the machine, putting in other metal pieces sideways instead of lengthwise or something, they can claim it is a different machine. The patent does not protect us. The only way is to keep your idea secret.

This concept of secret improvement is part of the folk culture of the house-factory entrepreneurs of Arakawa. It is a way of getting ahead of others in the competitive game.

In addition to competition there are also forms of cooperation. Mr. Tateno has upon occasion made design changes in the machines of his friends. Mr. Arai's son, who is now a lead-maker—and Mr. Tateno's brother-in-law—has asked Tateno to help invent a better machine for extruding the lead and cutting it automatically, and is now working on this.

It is interesting to note that in spite of his inventiveness and his obvious capacity for hard work, Mr. Tateno does not present himself as having any high ambitions.

I don't have any ambition to become great, I never wished to be a *shachō* ["president"].[16] I will be well satisfied as long as I and my family can live a normally comfortable life with an occasional vacation trip. I wish for nothing more. I enjoy my work. I want to keep working with printing machines so that I can finish my job faster than other people can or do the kind of work with my machine that others cannot do with theirs.

He believes that the special printers will not so easily be driven out of their business by the larger pencil-makers since "it is still cheaper for large-scale makers to depend upon us than to have their own machines in a larger factory."

Five years ago, Mr. Tateno invited four of his friends to form a kind of economic friendship group. None of the five is in direct competition with another. The members of this group take their families out together on a recreational trip once a year. As he puts it, this group is strictly *yukō-dantai* (an association for social and friendship purposes), "but certainly we help each other by introducing one another to customers, and so forth." He says that because nobody in the group does

---

[16] It is very interesting to note how the folk hero of today's Japan is the *shachō*. For example, a TAT card used in our research depicting an older man is seen by young people as a *shachō* giving advice to a younger man; older people more frequently see the older man as a father or a teacher. The *shachō* seems to be replacing the teacher as a source of wisdom.

the same kind of work "we can get along well with each other. People with the same type of work would not be good members of the same group—they are too competitive."

Since the house-factory entrepreneurs are in essence competing with one another, they do not form unions to guarantee any basic profit for their labor. They are thoroughly imbued with the competitive spirit of free enterprise.

The House-Factory Processors: Why They Do Not Become Company Entrepreneurs

Many processors and machine owners are ambitious to expand and to develop into a "company." This is rarely successful, but nevertheless the expressed ambition of many individuals who run house-factories is to capitalize more and more machines and to take over more and more phases of the pencil-making process. However, these individuals usually lack organizational ability and, more importantly, have no experience in selling or contact with wholesalers. They have no way to learn how to sell directly to the outside nor do they have the experience to organize or to establish an enterprise that handles several machines.

Unlike those of merchant background who start companies, the woodworkers and painters are basically *shokunin*, or artisans, either because of their background or by virtue of their having had some form of apprenticeship when they arrived in Arakawa from a rural area. (The case of Mr. Tateno well exemplifies this learning sequence.) Working daily for long hours in their small factories, these artisans fail to develop business connections. As was mentioned previously, it is often said of shokunin by the merchants that they are heavy-mouthed; they lack the capacity to sell themselves or their products.

The fact that, statistically, very few can expand their businesses or run them well if they do, does not prevent this hope from being a constant preoccupation and a spur for the artisans of Arakawa. As we can document from our projective psychological tests and interviews, a great deal of internalized achievement motivation is found in Arakawa, as it is in other segments of the Japanese society.

It is perhaps difficult for those familiar with the more impersonal forms taken by capitalism in the West to understand immediately why factory owners would encourage their workers to buy their own machines. Owners or management in a Western context would normally be motivated to keep all phases of production under direct control and would pay wages and give incentives to workers to stay within a firm instead of fostering the greater independence of a worker running his own machine on a subcontracting basis. Implicit in the Japanese system, however, are some basic psychocultural attitudes about the nature of motivation to work, of loyalty, and of obligation that were central to the traditional economic system. There is an ideal of paternalistic benevolence that has helped to keep the organization of small entrepreneurs going, a concept which is carried over from the nature of contractual relationships among both merchants and artisans of premodern Japan. From that background it is somewhat easier to comprehend why a patron would encourage an ambitious worker to become a petty entrepreneur, establishing in effect a "branch" business.

Paternalism still has economic advantages in Arakawa. Risk is spread among the small entrepreneurs; in times of recession a larger company simply cuts back on its subcontracting, and its own machines do not stand idle, nor does it have to pay wages or maintain workers. The system of obligations in paternalistic relationships, which is now dying, thus sometimes serves the large company to whom these small entrepreneurs are obligated. Failure is the responsibility of the individual, so the competition between the small entrepreneurs for high productivity is also to the advantage of the larger company, which can selectively subcontract with those who work the hardest, spurred by their own competitive incentive rather than by receiving a fixed wage.

There are strong economic reasons for the continuation of paternalism in marginal industries. If a particular activity fails for any reason, or if demand for a product is reduced, each machine owner takes a loss, and the contractor takes a smaller loss than he would if he owned all the machines. Also, this system deters formation of antagonistic labor unions and obscures awareness of common problems on a class basis. Relationships remain on an individual basis between subcontractor and patron. The small entrepreneurs are competitive rather than fraternal. Herein is perhaps one explanation for the fact that many lower-class Japanese have little of either the emotions or the self-identities that are part of the class consciousness that, according to Marxian theory, arises out of capitalistic exploitation. There was a time when the Communists were active in Arakawa, but they were not successful, and Arakawa remains conservative. There is, nevertheless, a small but continuing group of Communist supporters, and there are a few ward assemblymen belonging to the Japan Communist party.

The motivational pattern of people who own their own machines gives us further knowledge of Japanese psychological patterns of motivation related to hard work and achievement. The lower-class entrepreneurs are psychologically different from ordinary factory workers; their motivational pattern is different; their work patterns are different; their family life is different; and naturally their ideology is quite different. Arakawa remains basically conservative in its political and economic theories. Throughout Arakawa there are people whose life styles integrate their family life around their ownership of small machines. They process some product as part of a chain of households united, in effect, in a complementary system of subcontracts into an invisible factory in which they spend their lives.

This system is slowly disappearing as the rate of automation of larger factories increases. The disappearance of paternalism is evident in Arakawa and elsewhere, and what we are describing must be considered a transitional phase in Japanese capitalism. We would guess that this is probably the last generation that will operate in this fashion. Today in Arakawa the independent processor is slowly being squeezed out. It may soon be impossible for former employees to set themselves up independently.

According to Mr. Sakurai, one of our best informants, the older pattern of paternalism has almost disappeared from Arakawa. Fewer employers today encourage their workers to become independent by lending them money and promising them jobs. Also, compared to the profits possible for the tiny entrepreneurs, the pay of workers in larger factories is now fairly good and the jobs are more secure. There is less incentive therefore to take on the risks of individual ownership. As the owners of large pencil factories acquire more efficient machines, they become more impersonal toward their workers; fringe welfare benefits are granted as impersonal contractual obligations rather than as paternalistic benefices.

Mr. Tateno is pessimistic about the future of the small-scale pencil-maker.

The price of a cheap pencil remains 5 yen, leaving very little for profit. The larger companies like Tombow and Mitsubishi manufacture "high quality" or "deluxe" pencils that are sold in stores for 20, 30, or even 50 yen apiece. There is much greater possibility for profit margins with such pencils. It is left to the marginal businesses to make 5-yen pencils.

Again, according to Tateno, the pencil-making business does not pay.

If it did, gigantic corporations like Sumitomo, Mitsumi, and others would certainly have invested some capital into this business. There is no possibility of a new small-scale factory being established by an individual today. Such chances no longer exist. After all, factory workers are *shokunin*. They know how to make pencils but they don't know how to sell them.

Mr. Tateno thinks that eventually small-scale pencil-makers will all disappear and pencils will be made exclusively in automated factories. He hopes, however, that special processors like himself will somehow survive.

A few of our informants reported that the large-scale pencil-makers

are now having some difficulty in recruiting workers for their factories.
One notes:

Young people in Arakawa are too familiar with pencil-making factories to be
willing to work there. The companies must therefore depend on recruits from
distant places like Kyūshu and Tōhoku. The companies have to provide them
with dormitories and various recreational facilities. Young people nowadays
would not work for a factory unless they are satisfied with its recreational
facilities.

Mr. Tateno notes that young workers first ask about recreational
facilities and other contractual fringe benefits and then ask about how
many holidays they can get and only then ask about their wages. This
is partly because wages are pretty much standardized these days, but
also because "the young worker's attitudes are very different from
those in the past. It is not easy today to run a factory." Mr. Tateno
notes further that this spring a number of middle-school graduates
came up to Tokyo and were assigned to various companies according
to their choice. Tombow Pencil Company had wanted a sizable number
of new recruits, but only one boy agreed to work in the Tombow
factory.

High-school graduates do not want to work in pencil-making. If the middle-
school graduates are unwilling to work in a pencil factory, the only possible
solution is to automate the manufacturing process. If you have enough capital to invest in an automated factory, you can make better pencils more
easily and less expensively. This is happening now, therefore small-scale pencil-makers will go out of business sooner or later.

Enterprise shifts with the times, and according to Mr. Tateno,
pencil-making companies are now supplementing their income by
using empty areas around their factories as parking lots and charging
daily or monthly rates. Others are constructing apartment houses on
their land. Tateno claims that more than thirty of the intermediate-
scale pencil-makers now also own apartment houses and that pencil-
making activity is being continued in a small space next to the apartment houses or parking lots, which are becoming an increasing source
of new revenue.

Chapter IX

Achievement, Culture, and Personality: The Case of the Japanese-Americans

with WILLIAM CAUDILL

Much of the older literature on achievement in relation to intelligence has focused on the importance of either hereditary or learned individual abilities, as in the relationship between IQ scores and educational or occupational success.[1] In these studies, when there are discrepancies between predictions and observed fact, the discrepancies are attributed to "other factors." For example, Terman and Oden[2] use the added factor of individual personality traits to distinguish between otherwise matched groups—their high achievers being greater in "prudence and foresight," "self-confidence," "will-power and perseverance," and "desire to excel." More recent workers have gone on to emphasize that such traits should be seen not only within the framework of the individual personality structure, but also in relation to cultural values receiving different emphasis in lower and in middle-class levels of American society.[3]

Some attention has also been given to the factor of ethnic background in accounting for differences in achievement. For example,

---

[1] This chapter first appeared as "Achievement, Culture and Personality: The Case of the Japanese Americans" (William Caudill and George DeVos), *American Anthropologist* (1956), Vol. 58, No. 6.

[2] Terman and Oden, *The Gifted Child Grows Up: Twenty-five Years Follow-up of a Superior Group* in *Genetic Studies of Genius* (1947).

[3] Davis, Eells, Havighurst, Herrick, and Tyler, *Intelligence and Cultural Differences* (1951); and Havighurst and Taba, *Adolescent Character and Personality* (1949).

Terman and Oden[4] found that their Jewish subjects, although not differing significantly in mean IQ scores from the total group, had higher grades in college, received a higher income, and were concentrated more heavily in professional occupations. Thus, the indication is for something specific in Jewish culture to account for these differences, but beyond allusion to its probable importance, this factor has received little systematic elaboration.

Early psychological studies comparing Japanese-American children with other social and racial groups in California public schools[5] indicate a cultural factor at work which was not fully recognized or explored at the time. Strong,[6] in summarizing the achievement tests, grades, and Binet IQ scores of Japanese-American pupils in comparison with other groups in California schools, asks:

How shall we explain the fact that the Japanese pupils in Los Angeles have about the same IQ as the average pupil and score about the same on educational tests but obtain strikingly better grades? It may be that they possess to a greater degree than whites those qualities which endear pupils to a teacher; that is, they are more docile, occasion less disciplinary trouble, and give the appearance of being busy and striving to do their best. . . . Another explanation would be that they come from poorer homes than the average and early realize that they must make their own way in the world; in consequence, they are better motivated to do their best.

Strong does not develop the further question of why the Japanese-Americans, out of the numerous low-income ethnic groups in California at the time these studies were done, should show this remarkable striving and intensity of purpose.

Much further study of the cultural variable in achievement is needed; we must understand (1) the achievement goals that are emphasized in the value system of the specific culture from which the subjects are drawn; (2) the processes by which these goals are implemented in the interpersonal behavior of individuals in the family, the peer group, the school, on the job, and in leisure-time activities; and (3) the range and most frequent types of individual personality adjustment to these goals within the context of the specific culture, rather than a consideration of personality traits solely as an inde-

---

[4] Terman and Oden, *The Gifted Child Grows Up.*

[5] Darsie, "The Mental Capacity of American Born Japanese Children" (1926); Clark, "Differences in Accomplishment in Schools of Varying Average Intelligence Quotient" (1927); Fukuda, "Some Data on the Intelligence of Japanese Children" (1930); Bell, "A Study of Effects of Segregation upon Japanese Children in American Schools" (1933); Kubo, *The Revised and Extended Binet-Simon Tests Applied to the Japanese Children* (1934).

[6] Strong, *The Second Generation Japanese Problem* (1934), p. 2.

pendent variable. The methods used in the research reported below
were both quantitative analysis of data on the groups in question, and
intensive clinical analysis of testing, interview, and psychotherapeutic
data on specific individuals.

THE ACHIEVEMENT ORIENTATION OF
JAPANESE-AMERICANS IN CHICAGO

Between 1943 and 1946, approximately 20,000 Japanese-Americans arrived in Chicago from relocation camps set up by the federal government when all persons of Japanese ancestry were evacuated from
the Pacific Coast shortly after the United States entered World War
II. Roughly a third were Issei—first generation immigrants who came
to America during the early part of the century; the other two-thirds
were Nisei—second generation, who are American born children of
the Issei, and U.S. citizens. The cultural and personality adjustment
of this group to life in Chicago was studied for three years (1947–
1950) by an interdisciplinary team from the University of Chicago.[7]
Although the problem of achievement was not a central focus of the
research, the data serve to point up the success of the Japanese-
Americans in this regard and to show the necessity of a thorough
consideration of cultural factors in the further study of achievement.

In terms of the usual sociological or anthropological approach,
there are many reasons why the 342 Japanese-American families represented in the Chicago research, or the Japanese-American group in
general, should experience great difficulty in achievement in the
United States. Japanese culture, social structure, values, and religion
are traditionally thought of as alien to those of the United States.
Moreover, the Issei had a background of rural, peasant, subsistence
farming, and came to the United States intending to settle only temporarily. Most important of all, the Japanese are a racially visible
group to race-conscious Americans.

[7] Details of this project, and a fuller exposition of the data may be found in
Caudill, "Japanese-American Personality and Acculturation" (1952). Briefly, the interdisciplinary team included two anthropologists, William Caudill and Adrian
Corcoran; three sociologists, Setsuko Nishi, Alan Jacobson, and Lee Rainwater; a
clinical psychologist, George DeVos; a psychoanalyst, Dr. Charlotte Babcock; and a
psychiatric social worker, Estelle Gabriel. Collectively, the data gathered consisted
of (a) interview schedules obtained from a random sample, selected from a directory
of Japanese Americans in Chicago, of 342 families representing 1,022 persons; (b)
evaluations by employers of Japanese-American workers in 79 firms; (c) abstracts of
all the cases of Japanese-American clients seen by Chicago social agencies between
1942 and 1948; (d) investigation of the child-rearing practices of 50 Nisei mothers;
(e) the collection and analysis of 100 TAT and 150 Rorschach records; and (f) psychiatric data consisting of diagnostic interviews with 40 Issei and Nisei, brief psychotherapy with 10 Nisei, and psychoanalysis of 3 Nisei.

Yet the data show that by 1947 the Nisei, almost as a group, held white-collar and skilled trade jobs within the general employment market of the city. White employers and fellow employees were enthusiastic in their praise of the Nisei. The median level of education for the Nisei in Chicago was, as it had been on the Pacific Coast, beyond high-school graduation.[8] Almost all who did not go on to college took vocational training in order to become secretaries, laboratory technicians, beauty operators, or skilled workers. It must be noted, however, that the Issei had a surprisingly high level of education for immigrants—a median of 10 years.[9] Educational data about Japanese Americans are summarized in Table IX-1.

The Japanese-Americans first found housing in some of the least desirable sections of Chicago. However, they disliked living in these sections and many families soon moved into predominantly white upper-lower- and lower-middle-class neighborhoods. The Japanese-Americans were accepted in these areas. Neighbors and landlords liked them because they improved the property, paid their rent promptly, and were quiet and courteous. In their clothing and general appearance the Nisei were almost stereotypes of the American middle class. This was particularly true for the women, who invariably appeared well-groomed, in conservative but chic dresses, snow-white blouses, nylons, and high heels. In their attitudes and aspirations the Nisei were oriented toward careers, white-collar work, or small businesses. They were not interested in factory jobs. They saw in unions a block to rapid advancement through individual achievement. In their social life the Nisei tended to stay within their own group. While they interacted freely with their white fellow workers

---

[8] In 1940 the educational level of the Nisei stood at 12.2 median years of school completed, as compared with 10.1 median years for American-born white children in the Pacific Coast states (War Relocation Authority of U.S. Department of Interior, *Wartime Exile*. Washington, D.C.: Government Printing Office, 1946, p. 93).

[9] The high level of education for the Issei in our sample demonstrates a certain selectivity in the Chicago population as compared both with the total previous West Coast population and with Japanese in Japan. The slightly higher average education in the Chicago population is probably in part because Issei who came to Chicago were mainly urban small shopkeepers. The median education level for the total Issei population in the relocation center was eight years (War Relocation Authority of the U.S. Department of Interior, *The Evacuated People: A Quantitative Description*. Washington, D.C.: Government Printing Office, 1946, p. 80). The average level in Japan at the time of major immigration was closer to six years than to the eight-year average of the immigrants. Hence we may assume a certain selectivity in immigration of individuals who on their own, or under family pressure, sought and found educational opportunities greater than the six years required by the laws of Japan. Nevertheless, the values which went into this emphasis on education are the values reported in the literature as generally prevailing in Japan.

TABLE IX-1

Education of Japanese Americans Compared with American Sample
(in percent)

Education level	Issei (277 persons)	Nisei (488 persons)	Chicago Americans (60 persons)
Elementary school			
Uncompleted	7	0	0
Graduated	34	2	12
Secondary school			
Uncompleted	10	8	35
Graduated	32	56	40
College			
Uncompleted	11	21	10
Graduated	6	13	3
Total	100	100	100

Note: Includes all persons from 342 Chicago families who had completed their education as of January 1, 1947. Vocational and trade school training is not included. Right-hand column is a normal control sample.

on the job and in casual social intercourse at lunch, they had not yet achieved close intimate social contact with the white middle class they emulated. Yet they had achieved more in the space of four years in Chicago than other ethnic groups who had long been in the city and who appear far less handicapped by racial and cultural differences.

Since occupation (as well as education) is a major avenue to achievement in America, it is worthwhile to look in a little more detail at the Japanese-American data in this respect. The jobs the Japanese-Americans were first able to obtain in the city were menial, unskilled, and poorly paid. Very shortly they left such jobs for semiskilled factory and service work at which the Issei stayed, while the Nisei, having higher aspirations, moved on rapidly to better employment. By 1947 the Japanese-Americans showed the occupational distribution presented in Table IX-2, where it can be seen that 19 percent of the Issei and 60 percent of the Nisei were in the categories of skilled workers, white-collar workers, small-business owners, or managerial and professional personnel.

There were some interesting job differences between men and women. The Issei men were concentrated in semiskilled factory and service jobs. In the factories they worked on the assembly lines, as machine operators, or at such jobs as carpenters in trailer manufac-

TABLE IX-2

OCCUPATIONS OF JAPANESE-AMERICANS
(in percent)

Occupation category	Issei (197 persons)	Nisei (383 persons)
Unskilled workers and laborers	1	1
Domestic and service workers	24	7
Semiskilled workers	56	32
Skilled workers	2	10
White-collar workers	2	35
Small-business ownership	13	6
Managerial and professional	2	9
Total	100	100

NOTE: Includes all members from 342 Chicago families who were employed as of January 1, 1947.

ture. Their service jobs were as kitchen helpers, cooks, waiters, elevator operators, and janitors. There was also a considerable percentage of Issei men in building ownership and management, but the buildings were deteriorated and were operated as cheap hotels, or rooming and boarding houses. Even more Issei women than Issei men were found in semiskilled factory and service jobs. Forty-three percent of all Issei women in the sample worked in the garment trades.

The occupations of Nisei men were distributed throughout all categories. Their major concentration was in apprentice and skilled trade jobs and in white-collar occupations. In the skilled trades the Nisei men worked as printers, welders, electricians, mechanics, and jewelry and watch repairmen. Some of these Nisei men had achieved jobs as foremen and supervisors, where they had authority over white workers. In the white-collar field the Nisei men worked as clerks, draftsmen, laboratory technicians, commercial artists, and studio photographers. The percentage of Nisei men in managerial and professional positions was of considerable significance. As managers they worked in personnel departments, as laboratory heads, and as editors. As professional men they were doctors, dentists, lawyers, pharmacists, research workers, and teachers.

Nisei women were concentrated in white-collar work, with 49 percent of the sample so employed. Here they were evenly distributed between secretarial-stenographic and clerical duties. There were also Nisei women in the garment trades, but far fewer than Issei women. Other important jobs for Nisei women were as beauty operators, social workers, and registered nurses.

The demonstrated aspirations of the Nisei indicated that small businesses would become increasingly important to them. The Nisei men in the sample owned grocery stores, garages, and cleaning shops, while Nisei women owned such businesses as beauty parlors. All of these served the general public, not just the Japanese-American community.

It must be remembered that the individuals sampled had been in the city for only a few years, and that the Nisei were young—clustering between twenty and thirty years of age—and had not yet reached their occupational peak.

Alan Jacobson and Lee Rainwater[10] investigated employers' evaluations of their Japanese-American employees in seventy-nine firms. These were owned by white businessmen, within the general economic and industrial structure of the city, and drew their employees from the general employment market. Firms owned by Japanese-Americans were excluded, as were such organizations as social agencies, which might be expected to be somewhat liberal in their employment policies. More than two-thirds of the employers were positive in their evaluations of Japanese-Americans as workers; they considered them to be as good as the best employees they had ever had. Approximately one-third of the employers considered Japanese-Americans to be no better and no worse than their average employees. A few employers criticized the Nisei for being too ambitious and wanting to move on to better jobs too quickly. In general, Japanese-Americans were praised for their technical abilities, for their speed and efficiency, and for their honesty, punctuality, willingness to work overtime, general moral standards, and personal appearance. They were also praised for the way they got along with other workers in informal relations. Japanese-Americans had been upgraded in job and salary in forty-six of the seventy-nine firms, and in five others in salary alone. Seventeen Nisei were promoted to jobs that gave them authority over white workers.

Why was this so? How was it possible for the children of an immigrant group to succeed as well as the Nisei did in Chicago in approximating the American middle-class way of life, when the culture of their parents seemed to diverge in so many respects from the American pattern?

Certainly relocation was a factor. No matter how well the Nisei were prepared in attitudes, behavior, and education for living a middle-class life, it seems unlikely that in 1947 they would have been

---

[10] Jacobson and Rainwater, "A Study of the Evaluations of Nisei as Workers by Caucasian Employment Agency Managers and by Employers of Nisei" (1951); "A Study of Employer and Employment Agency Manager Evaluations of Nisei Workers" (1952).

able to do so well on the Pacific Coast because of anti-Oriental prejudice. Also, the Japanese-Americans on the Coast had formed tight, self-contained communities controlled by parental authority and strong social sanctions, from which it was difficult for the Nisei to break free. Furthermore, Chicago had had a Japanese population of only 390 persons, and had no social techniques for dealing with this group. A third factor was the scarcity of labor during the war; the highly trained Nisei were in a relatively favorable position in terms of the employment market.

These reasons may help to explain why the Nisei got their jobs, but they do not satisfactorily explain why they were able to keep them and to please their employers and fellow workers.

A major hypothesis orienting our research was that there seems to be a significant compatibility (but by no means identity) between the value systems found in the culture of Japan and the value systems found in American middle-class culture. This compatibility of values gives rise to a similarity in the psychological adaptive mechanisms most commonly used by individuals in the two societies.

This hypothesis does not assert that the social structure, customs, or religion of the two societies are similar. They are not; indeed the Japanese and the American middle classes differ greatly in these respects. But the hypothesis does point out what is often overlooked, that the Japanese and American middle-class cultures share such values as politeness, respect for authority and parental wishes, duty to community, diligence, cleanliness and neatness, emphasis on personal achievement of long-range goals, and the importance of keeping up appearances. Equally, the hypothesis does not suggest that the basic personality or character structures of Japanese and middle-class Americans characteristically utilize the adaptive mechanisms of great sensitivity to cues coming from the external world as to how they should act, and of suppression of their real feelings, particularly physically aggressive ones.

Given this sort of similarity between the two cultures, when they meet under conditions favorable for acculturation (as in Chicago) Japanese-Americans, acting in terms of their Japanese values and personality, will behave in ways that are favorably evaluated by middle-class Americans. Nevertheless, because the values and adaptive mechanisms are only compatible (and not identical), and because the social structures and personalities of the two groups are different, there are many points of conflict as well as of agreement for the Nisei individual attempting to achieve an American middle-class life. Certain points of conflict are made all the more poignant by the fact that the points of agreement are sufficiently strong to hold out much promise to the individual that he will succeed.

The direct relation of our general hypothesis to Japanese-American achievement involves the problem of variant cultural orientations.[11] When cultural values are considered in current research studies on achievement, it is usually in terms of the dominant cultural values, whereas there may be many subgroups and individuals who do not subscribe to these values and who are, in this sense, variant. As Brim[12] says in an unpublished paper,

> What is necessary is some systematic knowledge of differences between groups in the acceptance of the goals of the larger society, and it is of high importance that research operations be developed which will enable us to appraise the hierarchy of goals perceived as desirable by different *segments* of society, whether these be religious, ethnic, economic, or the like. Once accomplished, future studies could be directed toward relative individual achievement within discrete subcultures, with each of these sharing homogeneous goals.

The Japanese-Americans provide an excellent example for Brim's argument. The fact that they succeed in approximating middle-class American standards in education and occupation does not necessarily mean that they are motivated by middle-class values and goals, nor that their achievement orientation should be thought of in these terms. What is needed is an analysis of the Japanese-American values and psychological adaptive mechanisms underlying those goals that are of crucial importance to Japanese-Americans in their conception of what constitutes achievement.

From the foregoing, it appears that much more than a surface evaluation of behavior is necessary for the understanding of achievement. Japanese-American and white middle-class behavior looks very much the same in many areas of life, but the psychological motivations underlying such behavior may occur within quite different cultural matrices. The following sections of this chapter will present material illustrating this problem, as well as the further problem of individual differences in achievement within the Japanese-American group itself.

CULTURAL VALUES AND PSYCHOLOGICAL MECHANISMS IN THE ACHIEVEMENT ORIENTATION OF JAPANESE-AMERICANS

To further understand the success of the Japanese-Americans in Chicago, we used Thematic Apperception Tests, Rorschachs, and

---

[11] F. Kluckhohn, "Dominant and Variant Cultural Value Orientations" (1953).

[12] Brim, "Ability and Achievement: Summary of Selected Research on Gifted Children," unpublished paper (1952).

psychoanalytic and social-agency case studies. This chapter is limited to the projective material pertaining to those aspects of personality dynamics that seem most relevant to achievement among Japanese-Americans.[13]

TAT material will be discussed first, because it tends to provide data on the more conscious aspects of the personality structure—internalized values, goals, and preferred ways of relating to others and to oneself. The Rorschach provides data concerning more generalized, and perhaps deeper-lying and unconscious attributes of the content and structure of the personality. Thus, the TAT can be useful in indicating the manner in which an individual approaches problems of achievement. The Rorschach can then suggest related, but often hidden, motivations and conflicts in this area.

A random sample of Murray TAT records was gathered from Japanese-Americans and compared with samples from white Americans from several socioeconomic levels.[14] In this chapter the material from TAT pictures 1 and 2 will be presented in detail. The manifest content of these pictures is such that they usually elicit stories concerning achievement. Picture 1 is of a young boy looking at a violin on a table in front of him. Picture 2 is a country scene: in the foreground is a young woman with books in her hand, while in the background a man is working in the fields and an older woman is looking on.

The rank order of positive achievement responses to both pictures goes from the Issei who have the highest proportion, through the Nisei and white middle class, who are roughly equivalent, to the white

---

[13] Details of method, and a general personality analysis of the Japanese-Americans, can be found in Caudill, "Japanese-American Personality and Acculturation" (1952); and DeVos, "Acculturation and Personality Structure: A Rorschach Study of Japanese Americans in Chicago" (1951), and "A Quantitative Approach to Affective Symbolism in Rorschach Responses" (1952). Caudill collected the TAT records, DeVos collected the Rorschach records, while Charlotte Babcock did psychotherapeutic interviews and psychoanalysis with Nisei patients.

[14] The white TAT records that are here compared with those of the Japanese-Americans came from normal people in everyday jobs. The middle-class women's records were drawn at random from a previous study of Warner and Henry, "The Radio Daytime Serial: A Symbolic Analysis" (1948), on lower-middle- and upper-lower-class housewives. From other research projects (carried out in the Committee on Human Development of the University of Chicago) with businessmen, retail department store employees, and factory workers, it was possible to obtain a sample of records from lower-middle- and upper-lower-class men. The terms "middle" and "lower" class are used in the text to avoid awkwardness in discussion. In all cases, what is meant are the more technical designations "lower-middle" and "upper-lower" class. (See Caudill, "Japanese-American Personality" (1952), and Warner, Meeker, and Eells, *Social Class in America* (1949). Sex distinctions are not recorded in Tables IX-3 to IX-5, which are based on samples divided as to sex as follows: Issei, 15 men and 15 women; Nisei and white middle class, 20 men and 20 women; white lower class, 8 men and 12 women.

TABLE IX-3

POSITIVE ACHIEVEMENT RESPONSES TO TAT PICTURES
1 AND 2, BY CULTURAL GROUP

		Positive (in percent)	
Group	Total cases	Picture 1	Picture 2
Issei	30	67	83
Nisei	40	43	55
White middle class	40	38	48
White lower class	20	0	30

lower class, who have the lowest percentage of positive responses.
(Table IX-3.)

In rating the stories told to picture 1, responses were considered to
be positively achievement-oriented when (a) the boy wants to be a
violinist (a long-range goal) and succeeeds by working hard; (b) he is
puzzled about how to solve the task but keeps working at it; (c) his
parents want him to become a violinist and he does so successfully;
and so forth. Stories were considered to be negatively achievement-
oriented when (a) the boy openly rebels against his parents' wishes for
him to play the violin (against a long-range goal) and seeks immediate
pleasure gratification in baseball or in breaking the violin; (b) he com-
plies in a negative mood with his parents' demands and does poorly;
(c) he engages in fantasy about becoming a famous violinist, but gives
no indication of how he will realistically reach this goal; and so forth.

Positive achievement-oriented responses on picture 2 were scored
when (a) the girl wants to leave the farm for a career, does so successfully (with or without the help of her parents), and either returns later
to help her parents, or is of benefit to society elsewhere; (b) the farmers
in the picture are continually striving to do a better job; and so forth.
Negative achievement-oriented stories were those in which (a) the girl
wants to leave, but feels she cannot and so stays and suffers; (b) she is
disgusted with farm life and wants to see the bright lights of the city.

Picture 1 reveals a second point of difference: the boy can be seen as
self-motivated, or he can work on a task because it is assigned to him
by his parents or other adults. The distribution of the four cultural
groups in this respect is shown in Table IX-4.

On picture 1, then, the Issei are high in positive achievement orientation and self-motivation. Taking these characteristics with a content
analysis of the stories, a major value and psychological adaptive mechanism found in the Issei is the determination to strive for success at
all costs. Even if one is tired and puzzled, and the outer world presents

TABLE IX-4

SELF-MOTIVATION AND TASK ASSIGNMENT RESPONSES
ON TAT PICTURE 1, BY CULTURAL GROUP

Group	Total cases	Self-motivated (in percent)	Task assigned (in percent)
Issei	30	93	7
Nisei	40	62	38
White middle class	40	75	25
White lower class	20	35	65

many difficulties in living, one must keep on and never give up. Such a characterization is frequent in the literature on the Japanese,[15] and is often referred to as "the Japanese spirit" or *yamato damashii*. The Issei attempt to live up to this value by hard, realistic work with little use of fantasy or magical thinking, as can be seen in the following story:

(Issei W, age 44, picture 1) What is this? A violin? He has a violin and he's thinking, "How shall I do it?" It looks very difficult and so he rests his face on his hand and worries. He thinks, "I can't play it yet, but if I study hard, someday maybe I'll be a good musician." In the end because he holds steady, he becomes a good player. He'll grow up to be a fine persevering young man.

Like the Issei, the Nisei see the boy as positively achieving and self-motivated, but they also often see him as assigned a task and in conflict with his parents. In the latter case, the adaptive mechanism is one of negativistic compliance and self-defeat. As will be seen later, this method of adapting is in considerable contrast to that used by the white lower class, who tend to be openly hostile and rebellious. Typical Nisei stories:

(Nisei M, age 25, picture 1) Probably gifted along musical lines. . . . Perhaps mature enough to realize it isn't a plaything but something that, well, takes both skill and practice to master. . . . Perhaps he's been playing but still can't get the same tone or master it with such ease as an accomplished musician could. Doesn't seem to be thinking of baseball or anything like that that would be keeping him away. . . . Well, if he had real talent, lived for music and was guided and counseled in the right manner by his parents and teacher, he might have the making of a musician in the real sense, toward classical rather than modern big-name dance orchestras . . . probably strive more for immaterial things to make his life satisfactory in a spiritual sense

[15] Benedict, *The Chrysanthemum and the Sword* (1946); Haring, "Aspects of Personal Character in Japan" (1946); Nitobe, *Lectures on Japan* (1938); *Japan: An Attempt at Interpretation* (1904).

rather than purely monetary, economic. Probably would be a musician in some large municipal symphony orchestra or through his love of music be a teacher in some university. He never would be very rich, but probably won't regret it and through his music he will be living a full rich life. That's about all.

(Nisei W, age 26, picture 1) Is he supposed to be sleeping? Probably practicing. I guess the mother must of—something the mother is forcing on him. He's a little bored and disgusted, but he can't go against his mother's wishes. He's probably just sitting there daydreaming about the things he'd like to do rather than practicing. Something that was forced upon him. He'll probably be just a mediocre player.

The stories from white middle-class subjects, in their emphasis on self-motivation toward long-range goals, are similar to those told by the Nisei. The situation is reversed in stories from lower-class subjects, in which such goals are not valued and the boy is largely seen as assigned a task. When parental pressure is applied in the lower-class subject stories, the reaction is either one of open rebellion and refusal or one of doing only what one has to and then quitting.

An example of a story from a white middle-class subject:

(White M, age 21, picture 1) He is an intellectual looking young man. He probably has had an inspiration from some other violinist. He is intelligent. There seem to be two possibilities. Either he isn't too well prepared, or he wonders why he isn't getting the same results from his violin that greater musicians get. He doesn't seem to register despair of any kind. Probably making an analysis of why he doesn't get the results, although he seems rather young for much in the way of analytical work. He will probably go on with his studies of the violin and do quite well.

Whereas, the following stories from white lower-class subjects:

(White F, age 32, picture 1) Doesn't want to play his violin. Hates his music lessons. His mother wants him to be a musician but he's thinking about breaking the violin.

(White M, age 45, picture 1) It strikes me as if he isn't thinking about the music there. He is thinking about a swimming hole, something like that. He has a violin there but he has his eyes closed and he's thinking about something else, probably what the other kids are doing out on the play- ground. He'll probably grow up to be a fiddler like Jack Benny. Probably grow up to drive a milk wagon [which is the subject's job]. When his mother quits pushing the violin on him, he will break away from it altogether.

In general, it may be said from an analysis of picture 1 that the Issei, Nisei, and white middle-class individuals are self-motivated and achievement-oriented, whereas white lower-class individuals are not. The determination to push ahead no matter what the obstacles, which is evident in the Issei stories, is a part of the Japanese value system and character structure, and this orientation has been passed on to

TABLE IX-5

RESPONSES ON TAT PICTURE 2 INDICATING "ABILITY
TO LEAVE FARM," BY CULTURAL GROUP

Group	Total cases	Leave positively (in percent)	Leave negatively (in percent)	Other responses (in percent)
Issei	30	37	7	56
Nisei	40	35	25	40
White middle class	40	35	28	37
White lower class	20	10	50	40

the Nisei in somewhat attenuated form. In addition, the Nisei give evidence of being in some conflict with the Issei parents, although they cannot openly express this. A further aspect of this conflict can be seen in the stories to picture 2 summarized in Table IX-5.

When the Issei tell stories of the girl leaving the farm to further her ambitions, it is usually in a positive manner. This is because it is a Japanese value that parents should help their children achieve long-range goals since it is (for the Issei) the unquestioned expectation that the children will then return to fulfill their obligations to their parents. For example:

(Issei W, age 52, picture 2) This child is going to school. It's morning and her parents are farmers and they work and she's off to school. Her mother wants her to do well in school. In the end this girl goes to school to improve herself, and she wants to grow up so she can repay her obligation to her parents.

As in response to picture 1, the Issei are primarily concerned with working hard in a difficult environment in their stories to picture 2, and such stories make up the bulk of "other responses" for the Issei in Table IX-5. A typical story is:

(Issei M, age 58, picture 2) Papa and Mama is working hard. One girl is about to go to school, I think. This picture mother work hard. She is working hard at something. This life is pretty hard. That's what these two are thinking—look like girl must see this situation and decide she must study diligently because Papa and Mama are concerned over her. Finally the girl becomes a nice girl, looks nice.

The Nisei, unlike the aging Issei, must find achievement and success within an American white middle-class world. The Japanese values and adaptive mechanisms learned from the Issei help the Nisei in such achievement, but they cannot live up to the expectations of the American world and at the same time fulfill their Japanese obligations to their parents. The Nisei tell stories to picture 2 which indicate this conflict.

(Nisei W, age 22, picture 2) Well, let's see. This older woman over by the tree is watching her son till the soil. The younger girl with the books is this woman's daughter and this boy's sister. She sort of has disdain for this life in a farm community, it's so limiting, so she goes to a nearby school in hopes of emancipating herself from this environment. But in her face you could see that she feels a very real sense of responsibility to her family and almost a guilty feeling for not sharing the life that her family had tried to create for her. And her feelings are always changing. She feels one day that she should stay and be contented with this life, and the next day that she should go on and seek a new life, but she is committed to school, so she guiltily looks back at her family and proceeds to school.

Like the Nisei, the white middle class see the girl in picture 2 as leaving the farm to achieve a career or higher education. Almost no lower-class subjects see the picture in this way. Unlike the Nisei, the white middle class see the girl not so much in conflict with her parents as being neither helped nor hindered by the parents but simply leaving and becoming successful. Often this success is stated in too pat a fashion to be realistic, reflecting the American lower middle-class overvaluation (particularly in the women's stories) of education as morally good in its own right; also, one "gets an education" as a status symbol much as one buys a new car or a house. Education is valued as a status symbol by Japanese-Americans also, but their emphasis is more on the knowledge and learned background it gives one, or as a down-to-earth means to further achievement. A representative middle-class woman's story to picture 2 follows.

(White W, age 37, picture 2) The daughter was brought up on a farm. She is striving for better things. She wants to read books, go to school, see the rest of the world. She is now in the process of going away from the farm, the early things you see on the farm. She will succeed in her book learning and will become a very successful author, authoress.

The lower-class responses to picture 2 are quite distinctive. When a lower-class subject sees the girl leaving the farm, it is not to seek a long-range goal, but instead because she is "disgusted with farm life" and wants to go to the city:

(White W, age 27, picture 2) What kind of a field is that? It must be a wheat field. Girl is coming home from school. She's disgusted with the farm, doesn't like the farm. Like to get away from it all to the big city. Woman standing by the tree is her stepmother. She's very selfish. Father is a nice person. Looks to me like a very disgusted girl.

The TAT material presented above shows some of the similarities and differences in Japanese and American achievement orientations in the area of life concerned with education, occupation, and other long-range goals. It would also be possible to make the same sort of analysis for parental, sexual, general interpersonal, and other aspects of life.[16]

The Rorschach data offer a complementary analysis of Japanese American personality structure. A full treatment of these data and results, only summarized here, can be found in De Vos.[17] The areas of mental striving and ambition drive as usually reflected in the Rorschach Test can be seen by comparing representative samples of fifty Issei and sixty Nisei with sixty American normal controls ranging from lower- to middle-class socioeconomic status.[18]

The perceptual organization of both the Issei and Nisei, when compared with that of the American sample, proves to be much more concerned with a straining to produce some overall response to a Rorschach card (scored as W), with a neglect of both the easily perceived details (scored as D), and the smaller, usual detail responses (scored as Dd). The data are summarized in Table IX-6. The Japanese-American approach in Rorschach terms is approximately 35 percent W, 60 percent D, 5 percent Dd, in contrast to the American normal sample's 20 percent W, 72 percent D, 8 percent Dd. This sort of approach, along with an effort to organize the blot into complex concepts or configurations, indicates a great deal of striving in the intellectual sphere. The results also show a significantly large number of individuals among the Japanese-Americans who exhibit an imbalance between an ability to be freely creative and spontaneous (as measured by movement re-

---

[16] William Caudill, "Japanese-American Personality and Acculturation" (1952); DeVos, "A Comparison of the Personality Differences in Two Generations of Japanese-Americans by Means of the Rorschach Test" (1954).

[17] *Ibid.*

[18] The original study from which the details reported in this paper are derived consisted of Rorschach records from 50 Issei, 60 Nisei, and 50 Kibei (American-born Japanese-Americans who were sent back to Japan for an extended period during childhood). These records were obtained by taking a random sample of Rorschachs from individuals included in the Chicago sample of 1,022 persons. See DeVos, "Acculturation and Personality Structure: A Rorschach Study of Japanese Americans in Chicago" (1951). The American comparison groups used consisted of 60 normal, 30 neurotic, and 30 schizophrenic Americans, obtained from the normative files of Dr. S. J. Beck, with Rabin, Thiesen, Molish, and Thetford, "The Normal Personality as Projected in the Rorschach Test" (1950). Two papers by DeVos, "A Comparison of Personality Differences" (1954), and "A Quantitative Rorschach Assessment of Maladjustment and Rigidity in Acculturating Japanese Americans" (1955), give a detailed statistical analysis of the Rorschach variables. The first consists of a detailed analysis of the American and Japanese-American groups in reference to (1) intellectual functions and ego control, (2) emotional organization, (3) affective symbolism. The second paper considers the quantitative results as they relate to maladjustment, and the nature and types of rigidity prevalent in the records.

TABLE IX-6

COMPARISON OF ISSEI, NISEI, AND AMERICAN NORMAL SAMPLE ON CERTAIN MEASURES OF MENTAL APPROACH

Group	Mean responses total	W (whole)	D (detail)	Dd (race detail) (in percent)	Mean organization score (Beck's Z)
Issei (N = 50)	18.8	35.6	58.8	5.7	24.7
Nisei (N = 60)	26.0	34.8	59.3	6.6	35.9
Am. Norm. (N = 60)	30.9	18.6	73.5	8.7	22.4

Group	W. on color cards, percent of individuals			Ratio of W:M, percent of individuals			Mean number of space responses, percent of individuals			
	0	1–2	3+	High*	Med.†	Low‡	0	1–2	3–4	5
Issei										
Total	26	40	34	30	58	12	56	40	4	0
Male							68	28	4	0
Female							44	52	4	0
Nisei										
Total	16	42	42	25	57	18	42	27	21	10
Male							41	44	11	3
Female							43	10	30	17
Am. Norm.										
Total	47	38	15	12	51	37	30	48	13	8
Male							27	46	17	10
Female							33	51	10	6

SOURCE: Condensed from tables appearing in DeVos, George, "A Comparison of the Personality Differences in Two Generations of Japanese Americans by Means of the Rorschach Test," *Nagoya Journal of Medical Science*, Vol. 17, No. 3 (1954), pp. 153–265. Refer to this publication for complete statements concerning significant tests of differences and other tabular material on which the present summary of achievement aspects of personality is based.
* 3W:1M (W6).   † W < M.   ‡ W = or < M.

sponses on the Rorschach) and their intellectual strivings (as measured by whole responses). This finding suggests that the strong drive to accomplish outstrips, in some persons, the actual capacities available to the individual.

Although there is an overall agreement as to striving among both Issei and Nisei, the personality context in which this striving is manifested is markedly different between the generations. The indications for a somewhat extreme intellectual constriction among the Issei are not as readily found in the Nisei. In both groups, where this constriction appears it sometimes leads to excessive associative blocking (refusal to continue responding to a particular Rorschach card) that suggests a lack of liberation of intellectual abilities, and at other times to intense preoccupation with bodily functions, and a considerably narrowed range of interests or contacts with the outer environment. The associative blocking prevalent in the Issei was frequently accompanied by verbalization of a sense of defeat when the individual could not give an overall response. When in a test of limits the examiner attempted to have the individuals respond to the details, many subjects would not respond, feeling that they had already failed the task. Many would say only, *"Ammari muzukashii"* (It's too difficult). This response of the Issei is similar to their refusal to use fantasy or magical thinking even in the face of defeat, as described in the TAT analysis. The American normal group, on the other hand, shows a greater tendency to caution and momentary blocking in associative functioning, rather than the severe blocking found in the Issei; those in the American normal sample who show some sign of blocking recover and give responses, whereas many of the Issei totally reject the stimulus material.

The data suggest that oppositional trends (as measured by the frequency of white-space responses) are most prevalent in the Nisei women, less common in the Nisei men, and notably lacking in the Issei group. Psychotherapy material from the extended treatment of three of the Nisei women supports this conclusion. A strong theme running through many of the therapy cases was opposition to the mother to the extent of acting out rebellious behavior in various subtle ways. In none of the cases treated, however, was continuing difficulty with authority or supervisory figures expressed through direct opposition, probably because such direct opposition is not allowable in Japanese values. Instead, opposition was more indirectly manifested in the ways that assigned tasks were done. The rebelliousness toward authority was prompted more toward women than men. Some break with the family always appeared, with the girl determined to make her own way, but with considerable turmoil and strong guilt feelings over neglecting the internalized obligation of obedience to family.

The kind of breakdown in ego controls observed in the Japanese-American records often seems to be related to their sense of striving. The tendency to respond to the Rorschach cards in terms of confabulatory wholes found in both Issei and Nisei, the presence of vague abstract responses, the use of poorly conceived anatomy responses in which the parts were ill-defined at best, all serve to confirm the implication of an overstraining to accomplish. This strain to accomplish in spite of severe limitation is particularly present in the Issei. The selectivity of immigration from Japan does not allow the inference that our results would hold true for all Japanese, and controlled studies in Japan should substantiate or modify these findings (see Chapter 2). The American normal group used here, in comparison with whom the Japanese tendency toward striving seems so marked, may reflect a certain environmental selectivity related to their occupational framework. There is a tendency for this group to show a certain sluggishness of intellectual drive in comparison with the usual expectations of Rorschach workers. The American normal group used as a sample in this study is composed of lower- as well as middle-class persons (unskilled and semiskilled, as well as skilled and executive groups), and the greater striving shown in the Nisei results would indicate that the orientation of the Nisei is more of a middle-class sort than is that of the normal sample itself. The Japanese-American Rorschach material has yet to be compared with Rorschach data gathered from a group of subjects with a strictly middle-class background.

In general, the overall results of the research on Japanese-Americans in Chicago seem to bear out the hypothesis that the values and adaptive mechanisms of the Japanese-Americans and lower middle class are highly compatible, whereas the upper lower class diverges from both these groups and presents a different psychological adjustment. Where Japanese-American values differ in emphasis from middle-class values, these differences are not such as to draw unfavorable comment from the middle class. Indeed, the differences would probably be considered praiseworthy by the middle class, if a little extreme, as in the extent of duty to one's parents and the need to be of benefit to society.

The Issei place a high value on the attainment of such long-range goals as higher education, professional success, and the building of a spotless reputation in the community. These goals the Issei have passed on to their children, and the Issei willingly help the Nisei to achieve them because it is the unquestioned expectation of the Issei that their children will in turn fulfill their obligations to their parents. It is this "unquestioned expectation" that is the source of greatest conflict for the Nisei, who feel deeply their obligations to their parents, but who also are striving for integration into American middle-class life.

What appears to have occurred in the case of the Japanese Americans is that the Nisei, while utilizing to a considerable extent a Japanese set of values and adaptive mechanisms, were able in their prewar life on the Pacific Coast to act in ways that drew favorable comment and recognition from their less prejudiced white middle-class peers and made them admirable pupils in the eyes of their middle-class teachers. This situation repeated itself in Chicago, and personnel managers and fellow workers also found the Nisei to be admirable employees. Peers, teachers, employers, and fellow workers of the Nisei have projected their own values onto the neat, well-dressed, and efficient Nisei, in whom they saw mirrored many of their own ideals.

Because of this situation, the Nisei are usually favorably evaluated by the American middle class, not only as individuals but also as a group. Hence in Chicago, where they were removed from the high level of discrimination to be found on the Pacific Coast, the Nisei can be thought of as mobile toward, and attempting to achieve in, the American middle class. They were tremendously helped in this process by the praise of their parents and of the white middle class; conversely, they were thrown into conflict over their inability to participate as fully as they would like in the middle-class way of life and at the same time fulfill their Japanese obligations to their parents.

A simile is useful in pointing up the similarities and differences between Japanese-American and white middle-class achievement orientations: the ultimate destinations of individuals in the two groups tend to be similar; but Japanese-Americans go toward these destinations along straight narrow streets lined with crowds of people who observe their every step, whereas middle-class persons go toward the same destinations along wider streets having more room for maneuvering, and lined only with small groups of people who, while watching them, do not observe their every movement. In psychoanalytic terminology, this means that the Japanese-Americans have an ego structure that is very sensitive and vulnerable to stimuli coming from the outer world, and a superego structure that depends greatly upon external sanctions. This tends to be true of middle-class Americans as well, but not to such a degree. For example, individuals in both groups are interested in acquiring money in amounts sufficient to be translated into the achievement of social class prestige; however, every move of a Japanese-American toward amassing money is carefully watched by the community, and the way he does it and the ultimate use he makes of it in benefiting the community are equal in importance to the financial success itself. This is less true of the American middle class, where an individual can make his money in a great variety of ways and, so long as these are not dishonest, the ways are sanctioned because of the end product—the financial success.

The Japanese-Americans provide us, then, with the case of a group who, despite racial visibility and a culture traditionally thought of as alien, have achieved a remarkable adjustment to middle-class American life because certain compatibilities in the value systems of the immigrant and host cultures operated strongly enough to override the more obvious difficulties.

The foregoing summary should by no means be taken to imply that all Japanese-Americans will meet with success. What is meant is that, because of the compatibility between Japanese and American middle-class cultures, individual Nisei probably have a better chance of succeeding than individuals from other ethnic groups where the underlying cultural patterns are less in harmony with those of the American middle class.

INDIVIDUAL INTEGRATIONS OF THE ACHIEVEMENT VALUE

Through the analysis of individual cases by means of psychological test data and psychoanalytic interviews, it is possible to show how similar values and adaptive mechanisms are variously integrated in the personality structures of individual Nisei. There are, however, certain types of adjustment that are more favored by the culture, and these provide modal points in the total range.[19] The responses of three individuals briefly considered show how essentially the same values and broad ways of adjusting to life are differentially combined so that one individual is more likely to succeed in the achievement of his goals than another.

All three of the following Nisei stress, in their TAT stories, the positive achievement value of determination to get an education and to succeed in a career; likewise, all three see that in order to achieve these goals they must adapt themselves by working hard and forgoing immediate gratifications. This similarity in orientation is set, in the first case, within a relatively flexible personality structure in which energies are partly directed into achievement because of, rather than in spite of, certain apparently unresolved emotional problems. In the second case, the overall picture is one of successful achievement within a pattern of rigid conformity. Many neurotic conflicts are evident in the third case that prevent the satisfactory expression of the need felt by the individual for achievement.[20]

The first example is that of a twenty-nine-year-old married Nisei man with two small children. He has had two years in college, and

[19] The class-stratified comparison sample of sixty white records was obtained from Beck's American normal group, "The Normal Personality as Projected in the Rorschach Test" (1950). Beck's group was gathered from the occupational hierarchy of a large department store and mail-order house. The individuals were classified originally on a seven-status occupational scale. For purposes of simplification, this scale was reduced to the categories of unskilled, semiskilled, and executive. The class range extended from lower to upper-middle, according to the criteria of Warner, et al., *Social Class in America* (1949). The predominance of the individuals in the group were upper-lower to lower-middle. No attempt has been made to date to examine the strata of the sample separately by statistical techniques.

[20] The material for these cases is taken from Caudill, "Japanese-American Personality and Acculturation" (1952), where they are presented, along with others, in a more detailed and within a more systematic theoretical framework.

is now doing well in a responsible white-collar job where he is continually meeting the general public. In his work adjustment he seems to have been able to reconcile in a positive, nonhostile manner whatever problems have arisen. From the TAT and interview data it appears that he has not rebelled against Japanese values nor, on the other hand, has he lost his individuality and self-assertion in overconformity. His is one of the very few Nisei TAT records that indicates a sense of humor, an ability to laugh at oneself occasionally.

This Nisei man is strongly self-motivated toward long-range goals. Like all Nisei who are similarly striving, he has some conflict with his parents, but he is able, overtly, to handle the conflict satisfactorily. For example, the daughter in his story to picture 2 goes ahead and makes her own decisions, then talks it over with her mother, who is at first displeased but later reconciled, and the daughter is able to leave the family without guilt and with feelings of warmth toward her parents. In almost all his stories, this man is able to depict his characters as self-assertive but desirous of talking things out with family members or other older people whose advice they respect. He sees himself as very fond of his parents and wants to visit them as a pleasure rather than as a duty.

Like most Nisei, this man does not like to display his personal emotions. He is much less sensitive about this, however, than are other Nisei.

The adjustment outline above gives evidence of a great many positive qualities—the self-assertion, the flexibility, the seeking for and acceptance of advice without seeming hostility, and the ability to build one's own life while retaining pleasant, respectful ties with one's parents.

The Rorschach picture, however, is somewhat at variance with the impression gained from the attitudes and values presented in the TAT stories. There are signs of what in a clinical record would be considered serious underlying emotional maladjustment (a preoccupation with oral-sadistic fantasies, and indications that authority figures are seen as very threatening). The achievement drive to this individual, however, is so pronounced and so invested with energy that these underlying conflicts do not greatly impair his functioning. On the contrary, ambition becomes an avenue through which some of these conflicts are discharged. As was already indicated, the average Nisei record is characterized by a strong drive toward organizing the Rorschach cards into integrated responses. This individual exemplifies this trend by producing thirteen overall responses, many of them of a rather complex nature (a W percent of 76 compared with the mean of 35 for Nisei generally and 20 for the normal sample). He pushes himself very hard.

This individual does not use ego-constrictive defenses. Although sensitive to social norms, he is not stereotyped. His is an open, rich record with both inner and outer controls of a complex nature utilized in the integration of his personality. However, he does show egocentric tendencies, which are only partially offset by a readiness to respond to others with anxiety and compliance.

He faces evident difficulty in regard to handling underlying hostile impulses. In spite of what seems to be his relaxed attitude toward people on the TAT, the Rorschach suggests that deeply felt relationships toward people are productive of considerable anxiety. He shows an underlying hostility to both male and female figures (he perceives human beings on the cards as distorted into witches or animals engaged in human activity). He is consciously aware of his inner tensions, as indicated by his response to color (the red symbolizinz hell, blast furnaces, and sunsets hidden behind clouds). It is as if he were sitting on a volcano. The skill with which he handles the TAT cards with little indication of these underlying tensions demonstrates the value of combining projective evidence dealing with several levels of consciousness in gaining a total impression of an individual. This individual has been able to integrate himself quite well on a conscious level in terms of what are usually considered mature social attitudes. However, the Rorschach suggests caution about assuming that all is as well at deeper levels of his personality.

There is another and more frequent type of fairly successful Nisei adjustment that involves a much more rigid conformity to parental standards and less conscious flexibility and ease in meeting problems. An example of this second kind of adjustment is a twenty-three-year-old single Nisei man who is completing his medical training in Chicago while his family are in California on a farm. In an interview, this Nisei man frequently referred to the strictness of his parents when he was young, and told how his behavior was always compared unfavorably with that of an older brother, and how most of his social life centered around the Buddhist church, where his father was always on committees and hence able to observe his son's activities. When asked how he had decided to become a physician, he said, "My mother decided for me; she thought it would be a good idea."

In the projective material there is no warmth in this Nisei man's TAT stories about his parents. The adaptive mechanism is to comply completely with the parental demands, to internalize the parents' goals, and to suppress all personal individuality. Only through such a stereotyped conforming adjustment does the subject feel secure.

This Nisei man is able to strive realistically for long-range goals, but the striving is unimaginative and overconventional. His values are the same in many areas of life as the values of the well-adjusted

Nisei discussed earlier, but in his life they appear as philosophical clichés. The subject, however, is not aware that his behavior is over-conventional; he sincerely believes in it and it is his main source of strength. In his story to picture 1 there is competition and then identi-fication with the father; there is also the necessity of being of benefit to society; and there is realistic recognition of the work necessary to attain the father's goal.

In this man the Rorschach analysis is in almost direct agreement with that drawn from the TAT. Whereas the first case demonstrated the utilization of achievement as an outlet for energies of a pathologi-cal as well as a healthy nature, this individual presents a picture of persistence, tenacity, and conformity in the face of severe anxiety that tends to block and immobilize his actions. The severity of his emo-tional blocking is well brought out by examining his time of first response to the Rorschach cards. He averaged over ninety-five seconds before giving a response. On two cards (8 and 9) he took more than four minutes before he was able to give a response. During all the time he was trying, he gave no indication that he considered rejecting the card. He was able to maintain a fairly systematic approach to the cards in spite of these constrictive tendencies. He showed no originality or imagination, but rather a plodding persistence.

The anxiety aroused in this man by affective stimuli is countered on the Rorschach by anatomical-vocational responses indicating how his concentration on work and achievement is used to avoid difficulties with the spontaneous expression of emotions. There are indications on the Rorschach also that in spite of his rigid conscientiousness he has managed to preserve a retreat within himself, so that, although he is not a particularly insightful individual, he is on fairly good terms with his impulse life. He is therefore capable of a certain level of understanding in his relationship with others, although he may be awkward in establishing contact. In general, this is an individual who has to overcome considerable blocking and constriction in working out his drive toward achievement.

It is more difficult for Nisei women who aspire to a professional career to be successfully adjusted than it is for those Nisei women who are housewives or office workers. This can be illustrated by the case of one of the psychoanalytic patients—a twenty-five-year-old, single Nisei woman who is a university-trained professional worker. The TAT material reveals the lack of real satisfaction afforded this subject in her striving for education and a career. The conflict with her par-ents is shown in her story to picture 1.

(Nisei W, age 25, picture 1) This boy doesn't seem to want to play on the violin, way he's looking at the violin. And the expression on his face seems to be that of, what is it? Not rebellion but, uh, well, the feeling that he doesn't want to do it. Doesn't want to play the violin but someone like his mother has made him take lessons and is trying to make him practice. He probably feels quite [long pause] resentful of his mother's forcing him to do it against his will. He'll probably [long pause] refuse to do it at all, or else he'll play it so badly he won't have to take lessons any more.

In this story, the demands made by the mother touch off an emotional conflict for the subject, and at first the defense of being outwardly aggressive is considered—"refuse to do it at all." This defense is abandoned, probably in part because the subject's internalization of Japanese values makes her say "not rebellion but. . . ." The defense finally utilized is one of negativistic compliance, suppression of hostility, and a turning inward of aggression.

The subject's story to picture 3BM shows that her parental conflicts are carried over into her relations with other people, including her employers, so that in her own words she "no longer is able to distinguish between people." The Japanese value that rebellion against one's parents is also a rebellion against the whole structure of society is shown here, along with values of correct speech, close attention to personal appearance, and careful observation of the proprieties.

(Nisei W, age 25, picture 3BM) Well, a young fellow who wanted very much to do something and then was told that he couldn't by his parents and he was very broken hearted about it and he is crying. I don't think he'll say or do anything externally to show how he feels toward his parents but he will carry a deep resentment towards them inside himself and probably show his hostility through devious means such as refusing to carry out an order or refusing to obey his parents when a request has been made. [What happens to him?] He becomes a delinquent and he's referred to juvenile court. He carries resentment and so becomes bad for mother and child and society. He becomes careless in his speech, his attire, his contacts with other people, and transfers this resentment towards his parents to society and no longer is able to distinguish between people.

The lack of adequate satisfaction of this woman's basic dependency needs causes her to have poor and nonrealistic interpersonal relations. She has developed an unconscious defense of using practical and intellectual interests as an approach to people (such as her employers and friends) from whom she actually wants nurturant affection. The people respond practically and intellectually to her, she resists and resents this, and the relationship bogs down. Another major defense for this Nisei woman lies in withdrawal from problems and situations that precipitate emotional conflict. Early in the course of therapy (the fourth hour) she said, "I keep rejecting people. . . . I feel rejected and I reject them. It has something to do with my always having to fight with my mother and my family. I can't fight any more. I just withdraw instead of expressing things—withdraw completely from the situation."

The Rorschach analysis of this case brings out the interference of neurotic inhibition with need for achievement. This subject was in therapy, and was not a case in our representative sample. In comparison with the total sample of Nisei, her Rorschach record shows some interesting similarities and differences. Her most notable difference from the representative sample is her difficulty in producing a whole response. She manages to produce only one whole response out of thirty-four responses. This result suggests a neurotic difficulty in externalizing her desire for achievement. A second discrepancy, from both clinical norms and those of the Nisei group, that reinforces the impression of neurosis is the imbalance in the ratio between human and animal movement responses. Contrary to the usual picture, she has a predominance of animal movement, which, along with certain features of the content, suggests definite immaturity. She also shows the tendency that is characteristic of many Nisei toward a high number of space responses. Analysis suggests that this indication of rebelliousness is on a rather immature level and may be related to the neurotic maintenance of certain impulsive and childish ways of meeting problems in daily life. There are indications in the record, however, that this rebelliousness may remain covert, as her Rorschach manifests considerable underlying passivity and dependence on others. She is more apt to modify her ideas than to assert herself openly, in spite of a critical undercurrent in her personality.

As positive characteristics, she has a strong sense of the popular and the expected, and has an ego with a great deal of strength and resiliency. Also, the overall affective tone of her responses is more positive and optimistic than one would usually expect in an individual seeking therapeutic help. Although there is a certain tendency to force or formalize her emotions, she probably can, with help, respond positively to friendliness in others. An attempt to push herself intellectually beyond her capacity in order to meet internalized social demands may develop into a serious source of conflict.

In general, the picture presented in this Rorschach record is one of neurotic incapacitation, without the personality constriction of the second record, or the more severe underlying disturbance of the first record. Of the three cases, this record shows the most direct interference with achievement itself. In this it is different from the usual Nisei record with regard to the variables considered in relation to achievement.

As a summary of this case, and as an indication of how the analyses

of the projective data (done before therapy had commenced) fit with
the clinical material, it is useful to quote part of a tentative formulation written by Charlotte Babcock after eighty-five hours of analytic
therapy:

The patient's problems center around her extreme dependency and helplessness, which result from her early emotional deprivations, and her defenses
against her hostility, which are totally unacceptable to her family. Much of
her hostility arises because of the failure of her emotional environment to
provide for her any support adequate to meet her infantile impulses and
needs, of which she was ashamed and frightened. Intelligent and capable
of considerable independent thinking, she has been in great conflict because of the discrepancy between her ideals for herself (one should be independent, achieve high status, be successful in the eyes of the public, and
never show any negative attitudes) and her abilities to obtain in a concrete
form any of her ideals. . . .
  She talked a great deal of her job in which she was very interested, but
whenever something was hard for her at work, she would deny the reality
setting of the situation. If a certain service seemed needed, and she thought
her employer would not permit it, she would rebel in her feeling, but fail to
take up the problem with her employer. Instead, she would physically avoid
the employer, and in many other withdrawing and stubbornly denying ways
circumvent the problem.

  These three records demonstrate the complexity on a psychological
level of the structuring of certain similar culturally induced attitudes
toward achievement. Although the overt attitudes and aims of these
three individuals were quite similar, they were embedded in differing
overall personality structures. Such differences in total personality
have a great deal to do with how an individual attempts to actualize
his desires for achievement and the degree to which he succeeds in
achieving his goals.

CONCLUSION

  In the consideration of the achievement orientation of the
Japanese-Americans, we have followed a different path from the more
usual consideration of genetic and learned abilities, and the attribution of discrepancies to "other factors." The way of looking at achievement presented here stresses the need for systematic investigation and
interrelation of (a) overt and underlying culture patterns, (b) individual psychodynamic factors, (c) the structure and emotional atmosphere of crucial small-group interactive settings in the home, on the
job, and at recreation. A knowledge of these three related variables—
the cultural, the personal, and the interpersonal—when coupled with

genetic data, should greatly increase the ability to predict the achievement possibilities of particular individuals in a group. Even in the illustrative material given here, it can be seen that the inclusion of culture as a residual "other factor" is theoretically and methodologically insufficient until it is related to the personal and interpersonal variables. In future research, a thorough analysis of individuals within a cultural context will be necessary for a better understanding of the factors making for achievement.

Part Three:

Deviancy and Alienation

Part Three Introduction

Anomic Conditions in Japanese Society

Cultural definitions of achievement and the normative expectations of any society have negative as well as positive sides. The final series of essays in this volume is concerned with anomic conditions in Japan both traditional and modern. Robert Merton[1] in his discussion of social structure and anomie[2] has given a cogent analysis of the negative aspects of achievement in American society. He discusses the economic and social conditions that influence such negatively sanctioned behavior as suicide and various forms of deviant behavior including crime and delinquency, very often by members of minority groups. Although there is a great deal of cogency in the sociological approach, theoretical criticisms are nevertheless possible from the vantage point of a psychocultural analysis.

The following chapters although heavily influenced by Durkheimian sociology are not uncritical of it as it is applied to an analysis of Japanese social data. I believe I am able to show the insufficiency of a totally sociological perspective by demonstrating the additional value of a psychocultural approach that takes into account the subjective experiences of individuals and their personality determinants.

Seen from a sociological perspective, Durkheim's basic concept of anomie is valid and useful, an excellent orientation to the meaning of deviant social behavior, but it does not refer directly to psychological states. There is often the mistaken notion that this concept refers to individual subjective experiences. As Durkheim sought to use it,

---

[1] Merton, "Social Structure and Anomie" (1949).

[2] According to Talcott Parsons ("Emile Durkheim," 1968), "Anomie may be considered the state of a social system which makes a particular class of members consider exertion for success meaningless, not because they lack the capacity or opportunity to achieve what is wanted, but because they lack a clear definition of what is desirable. It is a 'pathology' . . . of the collective normative system."

251

it refers to the states of relative integration or disintegration of society that induce feelings of alienation or malaise.

In the following chapters, therefore, when I use the term *anomie* it refers to anomic conditions as distinct from experiences of personal alienation. From a psychocultural frame of reference there is no necessarily invariable direct correspondence between the two. As I shall discuss in the context of my criticism of Durkheim's theory of suicide in Chapter 17, the assumption that suicidal behavior is directly determined by social conditions, a view taken by some sociologists, ignores a number of psychodynamic features related to personality theory. Interpersonal problems between two or more individuals are only in the most indirect way related to overall conditions of social cohesion.

All societies at all times are anomic to some degree. That is to say, they are to some extent in disequilibrium and as a result "deviant" behavior is always present. Nevertheless, the amount and intensity of anomie varies with time, and therefore the use of specific indices does indeed shed some indirect light on the processes of social change taking place.

SOCIAL PROBLEMS IN JAPAN: CRIME
AND DELINQUENCY, MINORITY STATUS, AND
PERSONAL ALIENATION

In my collaborative research with Japanese, I have concentrated on three social-problem areas: juvenile delinquency and youth problems in a period of social change, minority status, and personal alienation. In this collection of essays I have included excerpts from these continuing research activities, which I hope eventually to treat fully in individual volumes.

I have included, first, four chapters, three done collaboratively with Keiichi Mizushima, dealing with general issues of crime and delinquency in Japan seen from a cross-cultural perspective. In these chapters and an additional chapter on student politics and violence I have paid particular attention to the subjective sense of alienation as well as anomic social conditions specifically influencing youth in Japan.

Second, I have included two chapters on minority social status and deviancy in Japan. (Hiroshi Wagatsuma and I have already published a fuller treatment of the Japanese outcastes as a persisting socially disparaged minority in *Japan's Invisible Race.*)

Lastly, I report on the ongoing collaborative study by Hiroshi Wagatsuma and myself on the subjective experiences of personal alienation among Japanese intellectuals living in a changing culture. Our psychocultural analyses of Japanese literary figures and my work on Japanese suicide are represented in the material presented in the last two chapters.

Each of these three topics dealing with socially deviant behavior is introduced by some general theoretical issues raised by a comparative psychocultural approach, which differs from that usually taken in straight sociological writings. Again, as in other parts of this volume, the methods used to gather material for analysis are eclectic, ranging from statistics and historical research, on the one hand, to depth interviews and the analysis of literary works, on the other.

Crime and Delinquency: Culture Patterns and Social Change

In Chapters 10 and 11, Keiichi Mizushima and I make a historical examination of attitudes toward what is deviant or criminal and of the nature of the Japanese underworld and its organization. It is quite apparent that the underworld and its mores, as well as what is defined as "crime," reflect the overall changes occurring in Japanese society. Ample evidence is available in Japan to support contentions of Merton and others that patterns of achievement within the American underworld are in effect caricatures of those holding for the society at large. In Chapter 12 I contend that social definitions of adult roles have changed, actually creating "delinquency," a concept that did not exist in premodern Japanese society. In Chapter 13, which deals with juvenile delinquency in postwar Japan, Mizushima and I relate changes in juvenile behavior to conditions of rapid social change in post–World War II Japan.

In Chapter 11 we note the appearance of fairly independent peer-group-oriented, basically lower-class juvenile gangs, whereas in the past Japanese youth were incorporated directly into adult gangs as apprentices. The fictive kinship bond that cemented underworld organizations in the past is no longer as strongly operative. In many organizations a breakdown of the formal system of loyalties and commitments is becoming evident, although the Japanese *oyabun-kobun* type of organization among artisans and merchants described in Chapter 8 still functions in the more traditional gangs. A pattern of occupational self-selection in underworld activity also carries some psychocultural continuities from premodern Japan.

Cross-cultural parallels between the Sicilian "Mafia" and the Japanese "Yakuza" would be interesting to pursue from a psychocultural approach. An interesting parallel to the American social scene is the conservative political ideology of underworld Yakuza groups, which tend to support rightist political causes and conservative social ideals and are therefore sometimes in covert or even overt conflict with leftist elements critical of the social structure. These attitudes are directly opposite to those dominant among Japanese students alienated from and critical of their modernizing society.

In a comparison of the past with the present, the cult of masculinity, the need to demonstrate aggressiveness, is seen to change in content but not in psychological function. The personalities of modern, prevailingly lower-class delinquents seem to show striking similarities to those of outlaws of the past, as reconstructed through documents.

Another interesting continuity in the Japanese criminal element, differing somewhat from the American situation, is the pains taken to limit violence to within the criminal group. In present-day delinquent subgroups the innocent outsider is no longer so well protected from gang activity, a symptom of the peer group age-grading alienation that separates youth from adults in deviant behavior as it does also in normative role behavior of nondelinquent students who express their alienation more directly in political terms.

The postwar social scene has been characterized in Japan by noticeable trends toward increased deviancy, especially in violence, and political confrontation among youth. In Chapter 13 Mizushima and I discuss some of those postwar trends, drawing on Japanese police statistics up till 1965. In Chapter 16 I present vignettes of violence in the Japanese student movement. The rapid culture change taking place in Japan is most manifest in the younger generation. Seen in the context of American social values, the younger Japanese are concerned positively with individual effort and personal liberty. The increase in deviant behavior in the fifties and early sixties and the rebellion manifest against various forms of authority are the negative sides of this search for individual values in young people who are shedding the vestiges of a hierarchical, collective past. The post-war increase in juvenile crime has been until the last few years similar to that reported in other modern nations, with a characteristic trend in the post-World War II statistics toward the geometric increase in crimes of assault and violence. By 1956, according to the statistics of the Ministry of Justice, more than 30 percent of all crimes in Japan were committed by individuals under twenty years of age, and 53 percent of reported rapes and 39 percent of robberies were by legal juveniles. Recidivism showed radical increase, and the age at which deviant behavior was first reported was increasingly early. I shall cite some of my reservations regarding straight sociological-ecological explanations of these phenomena. Certain cultural differences and certain mechanical features of Japanese resident patterns contradict some of the conclusions of previous ecological studies of crime and delinquency made in the United States.

Chapter 16 on the Japanese student movements and its general question of violence in modern Japan is little more than a brief reminder that the role of uncommitted youth in society is a central issue in modern Japan as elsewhere in industrialized states. This topic bears much more elaboration than I have devoted to it. I have included this chapter, prepared originally for an international symposium on violence, just to round out somewhat better the presentation of my perspective on alienation in youth. Increase or decrease in lower-class alienation is most often neatly represented by statistics on delinquent behavior—while in middle-class youth it is represented by eloquent and disturbing vocal political as well as social criticism. It is not that middle-class youth have lost their need for achievement; it is more that they raise questions concerning the total context in which it takes place: what sort of achievement, and for what ultimate social ends?

Minority Status and Deviancy

In the United States many of the negative aspects of "failure" to achieve are related to the problems of ethnic pluralism. Japan, strictly speaking, is not a pluralistic society, but the presence of former outcastes and Korean minorities make possible some comparison with the United States. Modern Japan and the United States share the sustaining social ideology that all social strata and all ethnic subdivisions, where they exist, are imbued with sufficient goal-directed achievement motivation to undergo the sustained periods of vocational training after puberty required to equip the oncoming generation with the specialized skills necessary to maintain a very complex technological society in operation.

It has long been evident to American social scientists that this ideal of effecting the technological competence of the entire society is not being realized. From the vantage point of the psychological anthropologist, one can contend that there are limiting psychological as well as sociological forces operating to prevent the optimal educational and vocational advancement of members of particular subgroups within the American society. In other societies, such as Japan, similar evidence exists of social dislocation and deviancy that inhibit the optimal exploitation of the natural environment and the optimal allocation of human resources, viewed in economic terms. It is apparent to the American social scientist that deviations from optimal expectations are especially prevalent in particular ethnic minorities, who are barred from full participation in the society by barriers of caste or racial discrimination. Achievement behavior, with or without this complication, is nevertheless influenced also by other factors affecting the disproportionate distribution of ethnic minorities among social class levels. It is sometimes erroneously concluded that differences in social and occupational distribution are due simply to different value

orientations within ethnic groups; on the contrary, economically depressed groups often show considerable concern with their marginal
economic and social position and a strong wish to better it.

From a psychological perspective there are complex internalized
concepts of self in relation to society that operate in systems of social
stratification. Differences in the possible intensity with which values
are held must be considered, as well as those differences that are related to various forms of discrimination and lack of opportunity; but
also to be considered is how within any minority group a sense of
social self-identity comes to be internalized. A number of psychological
problems arise from types of personality integration that result from
socialization experiences within particular socially disparaged ethnic
groups.

Both advantaged and disadvantaged ethnic minorities are found
within most pluralistic societies. Some minorities come to play specialized roles of one sort or another; for example, Jews, Parsees, Chinese,
Armenians, and Hindu Indians take on entrepreneurial-commercial
functions in minority enclaves in a number of different societies in
Africa, Asia, and Europe. These groups usually give other evidence of
high need achievement—Jews, Chinese, and Parsees, in particular,
emphasize taking advantage of formal educational opportunities.

There are also widespread examples of degraded and defeated ethnic
or caste minorities. In Pacific settings such as New Zealand and Hawaii and in African societies such as Rhodesia and South Africa, the
white colonists have established cultures in which defeated indigenous
groups, no matter what their relative numbers, became ethnic cultural
minorities, forced to evaluate themselves in a subordinate relation to
a dominant European-derived society. Africans originally brought into
Brazil as slaves may be much worse off economically today in a
Brazilian society relatively free of rigidities of color caste than are
Afro-Americans living within a society that has not as yet freed
itself from racial restrictions. Throughout the former Spanish colonies
of Latin America a cultural separation is strictly maintained between
the indigenous Indians and the descendants of the Spanish conquerors.
In all these societies, looking at the problem from a psychological as
well as a sociological perspective, one can find in the subordinate segments of these nations internalized psychocultural impediments to
achievement as compelling as the external force of the discriminatory
practices of the elite.

The plight of the Maori in what is often considered a relatively
harmonious pluralism in New Zealand is a case in point. Ausubel's
research in New Zealand [3] carefully documents the fact that there are

---

[3] Ausubel, *Maori Youth* (1965), and *The Fern and the Tiki* (1965).

no really significant differences in the stated achievement objectives of Maori youth and those of European-derived New Zealanders (the so-called Pakeha). Controlling for rural-urban sampling differences and using a battery of questionnaire-type instruments, Ausubel found that conscious attitudinal differences by themselves would not account for the fact that, in comparison with the Pakeha youth, Maori do less well in school, drop out earlier, and have four times the rate of adjudicated juvenile delinquency. These differences are due not solely to external forces related to discrimination but to unconscious, internal psychological characteristics influencing the structuring of need achievement as well as the capacity to order behavior toward long-range goals.

The problems of adolescent "delinquency" that come to the attention of the police, in New Zealand as elsewhere, are usually evidence of social alienation and as such are a negative index of aptitudes for, or inclinations toward, actualizing school and vocational achievement. There is evidence of considerable social alienation among Maori youth, their high delinquency rate comparing with that of some American ethnic minorities. Similarly, among young Hawaiians of Polynesian background a disproportionately high number are in trouble with the police, and on the mainland, blacks and Mexican-Americans are generally low in school achievement and high in delinquency. The statistics for the state of California demonstrate a delinquency rate among former peon Mexican-Americans of five times that of the majority, European-derived, white population. The former enslaved blacks have four times the rate of arrests that whites have.

In all these instances, discrimination has operated over several generations—enough to influence family patterns of socialization. The social behavior of the children of Japanese immigrants, discussed in Chapter 9, is in sharp contrast to these findings. These immigrants brought with them no traditional social stigma, but instead a sustaining cultural tradition stressing education and long-range goal-oriented behavior. Their children were socialized within the context of strongly integrative family units and now show both a high level of educational achievement (more than two years of college as an average) and a low delinquency rate (in California approximately one-fiftieth that of the majority of Californians).

In Japan itself one finds the differentiating effect of minority status on those of a former pariah caste reported in Chapters 14 and 15. In spite of the legal guarantee of full citizenship, Japanese outcastes continue to experience various forms of social and economic discrimination, a continual reminder of their supposed biological inferiority as descendants of an infrahuman social caste. The systematic comparative studies of the Burakumin or "Eta" and the general population, using such measures as I.Q. tests or achievement tests, show that Buraku children do relatively poorly, even when they are tested in integrated schools. Also operating in this group are the effects of socialization experience different from that of the majority group. Most of all, however, we find compelling evidence of an internalized negative social self-identity, which must be regarded as having considerable influence on the school and vocational behavior of the Burakumin.

Social Alienation and Suicide

Suicide, in its broadest perspective, also reflects upon the nature of achievement motivation with given societies. The values of the society are reflected, on the one hand, in the actualization of achievement, and, on the other, in the social failures that lead to suicide. It was Durkheim's observation of the consistencies of rhythms in European suicide rates that helped established the value of the statistical method in sociological research. Durkheim established that variability in suicide was related to other indices of social cohesion in society. As a result of these observations he developed his classic theory of suicide as related to forms of maladaptation, reflecting either chronic or acute difficulties in social role cohesion, which he found to differ among specific classes and groupings within society. Sociologists following Durkheim have continually stressed that stable persistent differences among countries in suicide rates reflect chronic persistent differences in the nature of social cohesion in those countries. Periodic increases reflect temporary disruptions of the norms regulating social cohesion.

While criticizing an exclusively sociological approach, nevertheless, I would join with those who maintain that the willful act of self-destruction remains irreducibly social, for the social environment must in some way determine it. This environment must be perceived as depriving or frustrating or in some way devoid of meaning. The question of personal meaning demands an investigation on a psychological as well as sociological level.

In Chapter 17 I examine the social and personal meanings of suicide in Japan. The socialization experiences common to Japanese, already discussed in the context of achievement motivation, are reexamined with reference to how they contribute to suicidal reactions. What I term "role narcissism" occurs dramatically in given cases of Japanese suicide. Peculiarities of Japanese role socialization create an "emotional logic" that makes suicide a feasible alternative in particular impasses occurring in the lives of both youth and adults.

Finally, in Chapter 18, Hiroshi Wagatsuma and I look at Japanese alienation as revealed in life histories and creative literature. In the writings and biographies of three Japanese literary figures we find the complexity of the subjective experience and relate it to the theory of suicide found in Chapter 17. A muted theme running through this material is how actualization of oneself is achieved or not achieved by Japanese in the first half of the twentieth century.

The sense of self in modern Japanese intellectuals is inextricably interwoven with the necessity to resolve what it means to be "Japanese" separate from, but increasingly permeated by, the aggressive, but seductive Western culture that stimulated Japan to enter the modern age.

Chapter X

Criminality and Deviancy
in Premodern Japan

with KEIICHI MIZUSHIMA

Japan had a well-developed legal system elaborated to apply sanctions against behavior considered dangerous or repugnant to the dominant political-social group. The behaviors chiefly subject to sanctions can be divided into those considered politically criminal and those considered socially criminal. We shall not discuss the periodic political problems and the severe sanctions to which the premodern feudal shogunate had recourse. Suffice it to say that many thousands of individuals and families were executed, tortured, imprisoned, exiled, or stripped of property as a means of preserving the Tokugawa dictatorship for 250 years.

The social crimes were related to the violation of person, property, or social mores. Some of the cultural peculiarities related to definitions of crime reflect differences between Japan and the West. For example, definitions of criminality in respect to sexual mores are in some respects notably different. However, the similarities between Japanese and Western cultures are perhaps more striking than such differences. Attitudes toward crimes committed against personal property are relatively similar, and, as we shall discuss in the following chapter on the Japanese underworld, Japan's organized criminal underworld bears comparison with the world of crime in the West; at the same time, there are emphases in its organizational features that reflect the proper Japanese society whose "improper" needs they covertly serve.

260

TRADITIONAL AND MODERN SANCTIONING
RELATED TO CULTURAL DEFINITIONS
OF PROPERTY AND PERSON

Robbery and Theft

For a culture to have concern over theft there must be a well-developed sense of personal property. Japanese culture is little different from Western culture in this respect. Concern with property, hence with theft and stealing, was prevalent in feudal Japan, and piracy and banditry were widespread in pre-Tokugawa times. Throughout the waters of Southeast Asia as far as the coast of Australia, in addition to legitimate traders, there were Japanese pirates dealing in slaves and attacking vulnerable cargo ships. The edicts of the Tokugawa government that protectively sealed off Japan during the period of Spanish expansion in the Philippines seem to have eliminated these activities. In Japan itself bandit gangs were common during the Sengoku period preceding the unification of the country in the latter part of the sixteenth century. In this extremely unsettled period, bands composed of ruffians and former warriors attacked villages for food and loot or set upon unwary travelers. Such bands were all but eliminated from the more settled areas in Tokugawa times, but mountain bands still made unaccompanied travel dangerous in less populated regions.[1]

Individual assaults for robbery were fairly common in the early Tokugawa period.[2] Such offenses were committed by the more violent among the unemployed samurai, or *rōnin,* whose numbers increased in some areas owing to their increasing unemployment following the stabilization under the Tokugawa regime. There was a folk expression that "killing, stealing, and robbery are a way of life for the rōnin." A favorite mode of attack was to station oneself at a crossroad and, with a quick unsheathing of the sword, to slice down on an unwary pedestrian who might have a fat purse on his person.

In the middle of the Tokugawa period, thievery by ordinary folk (as opposed to professional criminals) was greatly increased. Police practices were gradually shifted from tracking down known members of a criminal class to the solving of individual crimes committed by folk within the noncriminal classes.[3] Later in the seventeenth century, stealing accompanied by arson became more widespread and was greatly feared and severely punished. In addition to crimes for gain

---

[1] Mitamura, *The Life of the Samurai* (1956, in Japanese), pp. 63–88.

[2] *Ibid.,* pp. 7–36.

[3] Mitamura, *The World of the Police* (1959, in Japanese), pp. 149–176.

there were crimes for retribution, such are arson, committed by embittered Hinin, or social pariahs.[4]

During the late Tokugawa period, minor forms of theft seem to have been very widespread. One complaining samurai said, "There is no one in my household with the exception of my horse who does not steal from me." [5] It is suggested by Mitamura that, in addition to the very poor and outcaste Hinin, servants who had been discharged by the samurai or feudal lords committed a good number of these crimes. Many of these dissident servants were from among those who disliked the hard life of the farmer and were drawn to the towns. Some who were not employed long or who found the life of a servant too unrewarding, would, instead of returning home, turn to a life of professional thieving. A group might form a band for robbing; a form of intimidation and robbery still prevalent was for one or more members of a group to bump up against some unsuspecting victim and then, blaming him for his rudeness, to start a scuffle during which he was relieved of his valuables.

During the latter part of the Tokugawa period there were numerous professional pickpockets known as *kinchakukiri* (analagous to the medieval English "cutpurse"), a term which defined the common practice of cutting through some of the victim's clothes to get at his purse. The dexterity of some pickpockets inspired many stories of fabulous feats of deception by the *ninjutsu-shi*. These individuals, supposedly thieves or pickpockets originally, seem to have been comparable to modern magicians and could cause objects, or even themselves, to suddenly appear or disappear. Such people were sometimes compelled by the police to apply their skill in prestidigitation to the practical art of police spying.[6]

In the next chapter we discuss the romantic traditions attached to some outlaw figures who, like their Western counterpart Robin Hood, were reputed to rob the rich to care for the poor. Although mostly fictitious, these stories illustrate the attitude of many of the common folk, who were helpless to prevent social inequities or sharp practices by merchants, moneylenders, or rich landowners.

Aggressive Crimes Against Person

The worth of the individual in premodern Japan was relative to his social status and his lineage; crimes of violence were measured according to this relative scale of social worth. Samurai could, with little

[4] DeVos and Wagatsuma, *Japan's Invisible Race: Caste in Culture and Personality* (1966), p. 11.

[5] Mitamura, *Criminals in Edo* (1933, in Japanese).

[6] Usatake, *Research on Gambling and Pickpocketing* (1948, in Japanese), pp. 165–262.

provocation, cut down a commoner, but should the commoner kill an official not only was the culpable individual punished but also those related to him. Family households tended to be the unit of sanctioning as well as of ownership, and there were instances of a family disowning a child who committed illegal acts so that subsequent punishment would not be visited on the family.

Under conditions stipulated in Tokugawa law, revenge could be exacted by members of the family of the injured. If his intent was previously reported to the government, a samurai could seek to kill such a private enemy without further punishment. In the famous case of the forty-seven *rōnin* who avenged their injured lord, they were guilty of legal transgression, since in order to throw their intended victim off guard, they had not officially declared their intention of revenge. Avenging parents or a master was considered an act of filial piety, almost the supreme requirement in the traditional Japanese code of social morality.[7]

Outcastes could sometimes be attacked with impunity. In a famous judicial decision following the murder of an outcaste Eta, a judgment was rendered that the murderer would be punished by death if six other outcastes would come forward to be killed, since the worth of an outcaste was approximately one-seventh that of an ordinary human.

The Personal Rights of Parents Over Children

Parents exercised exclusive rights over the persons of their children, and it was legal for children to be sold into various forms of apprenticeship, including those in which the daughter would be trained to become an entertainer or a prostitute.[8] This practice was widespread throughout the chronically impoverished sections of northeast Japan until very recent times. During the Tokugawa period, it was also a not infrequent practice to kidnap a girl and sell her into prostitution, since the monetary gain was worth the risk of official punishment.

The Buddhist concept that the soul enters the fetus at about the fifth month, the time of quickening, removed abortion from the area of religious sanctions; doctors performing abortions were relatively well patronized, and several means were known to bring about the abortion of an undesired child. Infanticide was widely practiced to insure that the first living child was a boy, and one twin was often permitted to die, since twin births were considered "too animal" and unpropitious. The attending midwife would "guess" the intent of the parents, and without any spoken interchange she would report

---

[7] Shinshi, *The Life of the Samurai* (1963, in Japanese), pp. 259–272.
[8] Mori, *Human Trade* (1959, in Japanese), pp. 1–14.

that the dead infant had been too frail to survive. Technically such acts were punishable, but they were usually carried out in such a way that they were never prosecuted. The Tokugawa government would periodically castigate either the farmers or the samurai for "criminally keeping down the population," more, perhaps, from the standpoint of having its wishes for a larger population in some areas flouted than from any humanitarian considerations. For some time before World War II a larger population was encouraged as part of the effort to increase military strength.

Today, the Japanese continue to practice abortion as well as birth control without any punitive enforcement of laws to limit abortions strictly to those sanctioned by definitions of legal cause.

Cultural Persistences in Present-Day Delinquent Behavior

Today the most frequent types of stealing among juveniles are petty thefts from small stores and thefts of cash or small items from their own homes. Children who steal money from their own family know where the household money is kept and also find it easy to take money from mother's handbag or from father's clothes, which he changes upon arrival at home to put on the more comfortable *yukata,* or kimono. Wealthier upper-middle-class households have a separate storehouse, or *kura,* guarded by elaborate locks, where valuables are kept. There are no locks in Japanese traditional houses, except for the locks on the outer doors, but most Japanese are extremely loath to leave their houses unattended, and when the entire family is absent the house is usually guarded by a *rusuban,* someone left behind for that purpose.

The ordinary Japanese home does not contain much that is worth stealing; the main object of thievery is usually any loose money that might be found in the drawers of the *tansu.* Little vandalism occurs, in spite of the houses' vulnerability and fragility. Windows are rarely broken to effect forced entry, which is usually gained by opening an outer lock with a wire or similar device; when entry is made through a window, it is usually by means of a glass-cutter.

To generalize, in Japan there is very little expression of diffuse aggression in burglary or in stealing, nothing comparable to the vandalism and willful destruction of property found in American cities. Vandalism in schools is also extremely rare, although cases of arson are not uncommon; those wishing to destroy property rather than to damage it will resort to fire, fear of which is traditional in Japan.

Aggression is usually directed not toward property per se but toward specific individuals living in particular houses. Most of the more violent street robberies involve some kind of group behavior and take place in territory familiar to the aggressors. The individual delinquent usually acts more meekly when he is outside his own territory.

There are still well-defined cultural expectations as to when a person can or cannot be aggressive or assertive. Hierarchical considerations of status remain extremely important. Aggressive behavior under the influence of alcohol is more permissible, since the individual is not held fully responsible for his behavior. (This link between aggressiveness and alcohol is particularly apparent among the lower class, whereas the middle-class use of alcohol is directed less toward the release of aggressiveness and more toward the relaxation of social distance.) Traces of traditional attitudes are still to be found in Japanese gangs, which condone aggressive activity between rivals but consider it improper for a gang to attack an innocent outsider. This attitude is part of the spirit of bravado that permeates much of youthful gang activity in which aggression is often directed toward rivals rather than toward outside victims.

There are certain peculiarities in Japan in respect to the use of weapons. Japanese laws governing the carrying of weapons, especially since World War II, are very severe. Guns are fairly difficult to obtain, and those who are proficient in karate must, in essence, register their fists as "dangerous weapons." Guns and pistols have always had a foreign, "non-Japanese" connotation, and an attitude persists that the use of a gun or weapon, even by adult hoodlums in fighting, is almost "unfair." When a gun is used it is always with a great deal of romantic flourish, as a particularly heinous act. Such crimes as armed robbery are extremely rare among adult criminals and almost unheard of on the part of young delinquents. When a weapon is used, it is usually a knife of a length that comes within the limits of the law. Most threats or acts of violence involve the use of fists or a stone or a piece of wood.

Aggressively inclined youths sometimes attempt to learn boxing, and informal boxing clubs very often have indirect connections with underworld gangs. Karate clubs frequently have a rightist political patriotic orientation, although kendo (Japanese swordsmanship), which used to have a "militaristic" political meaning, has lost popularity as a rightist or traditional sport. Judo has wide acceptance as an art increasingly removed from direct aggressive connotation, and it is now considered quite separate from jujitsu. Those interested in defense learn either karate or judo as a part of their aggressive physical armamentarium.

THE SANCTIONING OF SEXUAL BEHAVIOR IN JAPAN

The sanctions applied to sexual behavior in many societies are as stringent as those applied to violence or theft. Regulations governing sexuality can be analyzed psychologically and sociologically as performing a number of functions. For example, in societies emphasizing kinship relationships, some unions are forbidden as incestuous when they would violate the kinship classifications regulating social interaction and lineage. In some societies where the status of woman is very low, having a sexual relationship with another's wife is not too different from violating his sense of property or ownership. In Japan, the first overriding considerations in defining the legal sanctions, if not the moral aspects, of sexual behavior were questions of status, both in respect to the differential status of men and women and of the rigidly stratified classes of society. A second paramount consideration of the Tokugawa government was that sexual liaisons should in no way disturb the rigid sense of order or escape the surveillance of police spies.

In Japan the sexual act never took on the sacred sacramental aura bestowed upon it in the West. Abstinence was never considered a virtue; the Japanese attitude toward the body was generally freer than that in the West, but it was recognized that strong human passions could be disruptive to the social order and had to be kept rigidly under conscious control.

In peasant groups premarital sexual intercourse was frequently practiced, but sexual fidelity and devotion to children was expected and rigidly sanctioned after marriage in all classes of Japanese society. Men, if they could afford it, could have periodic recourse to prostitutes or entertainers, but no system of concubinage was developed in Japan comparable to that of China. In the merchant class it was not uncommon for a man to have a mistress; indeed, in wealthier groups, keeping a mistress was a symbol of social prowess, but the children of a mistress were usually not legally recognized by the father.

From about 1300 onward, monogamy was the rule in Japan. Although men of high status could readily take on additional mistresses, they could be legally married to only one wife. For persons of low as well as of high status the permanence of a marriage was often determined by the appearance of an heir, although a man who loved his wife might resist pressure from his family to divorce and instead resort to some form of adoption. A frequent pattern of adoption for a childless couple was to adopt a baby girl in infancy and then to adopt a young man at majority who had already shown some indications of wishing to marry the adopted daughter.

Once a child was born, divorce was rare, since a child was brought up to be the heir of the family into which the mother married. Remarriage of a wife upon the death of the husband was almost impossible, whereas in the case of a widower remarriage was quite usual.[9]

---

[9] *Yuzankaku Series of the History of Japanese Folk Custom* (1959, in Japanese).

As was mentioned in connection with premarital sexual activities in rural Japan, what was expected and condoned in sexual behavior was regionally variegated. In some regions rapelike activity was condoned, whereas in other areas it was stringently prohibited. Premarital intercourse among rural farmers was generally treated lightly, and in some villages unmarried or divorced women were regarded as the common property of the young men. Adultery with a married woman, however, seems generally to have met with more stringent sanctions.[10]

Although private prostitution periodically was stringently prohibited by the feudal Tokugawa government, among the warriors, merchants, and artisans, there was ready recourse to public prostitutes. After a boy had gone through the *genpuku* ceremony (see Chapter 12), he was expected to visit the prostitution quarters openly. Use of prostitutes was considered light entertainment, to be enjoyed by those who could afford it.[11] The traditional attitude toward the life of prostitutes and the area in which they lived had a certain romantic flavor. Although prostitution was looked upon with disfavor by many, it was also related to the supposedly freer life of the gay-quarters, an area of escape for mind and body from the strictures and rigid sanctions applied to ordinary social life. Themes of romantic love and tragedy were often woven around the women who lived as entertainers or prostitutes. The inhabitants and frequenters of the gay-quarters, instead of meeting with the universal disapproval of their society, were often looked upon as arbiters of taste in the world of art or fashion. Certain aspects of prostitution in Japan retained this romantic flavor until very recently.

According to Takikawa,[12] there was no clear separation between entertainment and prostitution. Prostitution took many forms during the earlier feudal period but it never was so organized as it became under the direction of Hideyoshi, the general who integrated the whole of Japan after the anarchic period of war preceding the seventeenth century. The early Tokugawa government followed his lead in establishing entertainment in houses in particular areas, and it rigidly prohibited any form of private prostitution except in the designated areas. These quasi-public houses of prostitution were owned by particular families, who looked upon their activities as purveyors of prostitution much as did other merchants in the business of selling. This family tradition in the ownership of houses continued until 1956, when such houses were finally put out of business by more stringent legislation. These merchants of prostitution, many of whom became quite wealthy, very often validated themselves socially through patronage of the arts.

---

[10] Nakayama, *History of Japanese Youth* (1930, in Japanese), pp. 151–169.

[11] *Yuzankaku*, pp. 202–208.

[12] Takikawa, *A History of Women Entertainers* (1965, in Japanese).

During the early Tokugawa period the government, as a means of maintaining control over prostitution, gave an official monopoly to owners of houses of prostitution in the Yoshiwara district in northeast Edo. Any form of prostitution outside this area was severely repressed by the police, and pimps operating elsewhere were severely punished; some were even executed. Private prostitutes who were picked up would, after receiving some minor punishment, be turned over to one of the public houses in the Yoshiwara district.

A system of prestige and social stratification developed among the Yoshiwara prostitutes. The most talented and beautiful among them were termed high-status *oiran* and received much the same kind of adulation and attention now accorded to well-known entertainment figures. By the middle of the Tokugawa period, the geisha (literally "artists") tradition developed out of the combined prostitute-entertainer role; ordinary prostitutes who remained in the Yoshiwara district were more and more relegated to the role of hired sexual partner, whereas the entertainer became recognized as an artist who, according to personal choice, could act as a prostitute or become the mistress of a wealthy man or have sexual relationships with various men. The more desirable and popular the entertainer, the more her leeway in such matters. The geisha still remained in semi-bondage to a particular house, but her value as an attraction for customers made it possible for her to make many of her own decisions concerning her sexual life. Individuals of higher status consorted with geisha, whereas those of lesser means were limited to the ordinary prostitutes in the Yoshiwara district. With the departure of the geisha as entertainers of higher status, the artistic tone of the Yoshiwara district deteriorated considerably.

The inmate of the house of prostitution was usually a girl who had been purchased at a fairly early age from a dealer who had paid her parents. In general she had very little personal freedom. She could not leave the house before her "debt" was paid, and since she continually incurred costs for her clothes and other items, this was often not until the expiration of her contract period of fifteen years of service. In some fortunate cases, a man would fall in love with a prostitute or geisha and would have sufficient funds to buy her release from a house. The age-graded order among prostitutes was fairly well regularized, as it was for other specialized occupations in Japan. Girls would be brought to live in the prostitution quarters at about twelve or thirteen years of age, acting first as servants (*kamuro, kaburo*) to the regular prostitutes. During this time they watched and learned. When the madam in charge of the younger girls considered a girl "ready," usually at about age fourteen, she would try to find someone willing to pay a special price for deflowering her. Afterward a girl would become a *mizuage,* assisting the older prostitutes, serving the guests, or sometimes serving directly as a prostitute when desired. At about eighteen, which was considered the peak age of beauty and experience in prostitution, the girls usually became classified in some relative status as an *yūjo.* Girls received classification in degrees of beauty and aptitude.

In addition to the selling of children into prostitution, numerous men among the impoverished population would pay off an incurred debt by *tsukasegi,* or the provision of the wife's sexual services in lieu of money. In spite of government sanctions, private prostitution remained widespread in the Tokugawa period, and there were also numerous illegal houses with male prostitutes for homosexuals.

Attitudes Toward Homosexuality

According to Takikawa,[13] there are records of homosexual behavior in Japan from the earliest period. The poems (*kwaka*) written by monks of the Heian era often referred to such relationships, and there is considerable evidence of homosexuality among monks through the Tokugawa period.[14] Monks would sometimes abuse the young boys sent to the temple for lessons and special training.[15]

Samurai warriors would select a particular youth as a favorite, and like the Homeric Greeks, a samurai would keep a particular lover by his side during battle. The Ashikaga shoguns, who followed the Kamakura period and moved from Kamakura to Kyoto, were considered particularly prone to homosexual tastes. During this time, it appears that the entertainment girls would sometimes dress boyishly to be particularly enticing. The noh drama was developed by a young outcaste male entertainer, a *dengaku* dancer who was brought by the shogun to his court as a sexual favorite. This youth, Zen-ami, who was gifted with great artistic talent, almost singlehandedly developed the noh tradition out of elements of morality plays and entertainments put on by itinerant *dengaku* outcastes.[16]

Takikawa also mentions in some detail the activities of homosexual prostitutes in Edo, many of whom were actors but some of whom were directly employed in private houses of prostitution. Some of these male prostitutes habitually dressed in women's clothes. This is of special interest in regard to the history of the Kabuki drama. Kabuki

---

[13] *Ibid.,* pp. 209–220.

[14] Inagaki (ed.), *Encyclopedia of Edo Life* (1959, in Japanese).

[15] *Yuzankaku.* In addition to the homosexual relationships of monks and apprentices (*chigo*), the homosexual relationships between lords and young boys (*kusho*), older samurai and youth (*wakashū*) are also discussed. See especially Vol. 3, pp. 236–241.

[16] Personal communication with Benito Ortolani.

seems to have developed out of the erotic dancing of women prostitutes, which was extremely popular in early Edo. Dramatic plots were also developed about contemporary incidents as well as about historical figures and events. After this activity moved into theaters, the government banned women from the stage, since they were also involved in prostitution. The men actors who replaced them were subsequently also banned as a result of their sexual behavior, and thereupon dramatists resorted to writing plays for puppets. When living actors were reintroduced after the ban was lifted, some of their gestures imitated those of the puppets with whom they were competing for audience.

There is much less written evidence of overt homosexual activities during the Meiji period, raising the question whether actual homosexual behavior declined or whether it merely disappeared from view. Neither in pre–World War II criminal law nor in the postwar criminal code did Japan prohibit homosexual intercourse. However, overt homosexual soliciting is sometimes classified by the police as "obscene" or as a form of prostitution and therefore subject to arrest.

Homosexual congress, then, has not been illegal per se, and specific homosexual behavior that does not involve prostitution lies outside the province of the police. Compared with the United States there is considerable difference in legal and emotional attitudes toward homosexual behavior within Japanese society. There is very little emotional pressure from the public in Japan for direct punitive action against homosexuals, and therefore they are less likely to become involved in forms of illegal behavior and are not easily subject to blackmail. The Japanese attitude toward homosexuality seems to be that it is an expression of personal preference or evidence of a pathetic incapacity rather than of a criminal or immoral tendency.

Sexual gratification was not considered a matter involving sin or morality, nor was the "naturalness" of any sexual act a matter of concern. The concern of the government in the sanctioning of sexual behavior during the Tokugawa period was based on the idea that uncontrolled sexual behavior of either a heterosexual or homosexual nature might possibly weaken the rigidly guarded status stratification of the society. Social control over prostitution was exercised mainly to keep individuals from undue dissipation of a sort that would distract them from diligence in the pursuit of their occupation as warrior, merchant, or farmer. Private prostitution was less open to the surveillance of police spies than was public prostitution and therefore was considered a potential danger to the government.

The most severe forms of punishment of unsanctioned sexual behavior were reserved for acts that went counter to status considerations. If a person of lower status raped, or even found willing access to, a woman of higher status, the most severe punishment could be inflicted.

Maternal closeness
is a key to Japanese socialization
(see Chapter 1).

The Japanese family has not been "Westernized" despite the vast changes accompanying industrial modernization. For psychological reasons, an arranged marriage is still considered the most proper (see Chapter 5). Abstract social attitudes may accept free marriage, but arranged marriages still prevail (see Chapter 2). Here the go-between plays a principal role in the ceremonial meal between bride and groom in their new home in Niiike village.

Eagerness for success appears early. Attitudes toward education are intense; guilt over failure also can be intense (see Chapter 5).

Hard work is part
of the Japanese "Puritan" ethic
both in traditional agriculture
and in modern industry,
whether in a large plant
or in a small home factory
(see Chapters 2 and 8).

(The photographs on these facing pages were taken in the late 1860s, shortly after the invention of the camera in the West.)

Youthful Satsuma samurai were leading figures in the Meiji Restoration of 1868. They readily took to articles of Western dress (see Chapter 12).

A group of samurai,
aged 16 to 21 years.

Youthful brothers
of Shimazu Tadayoshi,
Daimyo of Satsuma in 1867.

Two members of the Tokugawa family.
Tokugawa Yoshinobu (*above*) in 1866,
an able administrator who worked
with his brush instead of a sword
(see Chapter 7).
Tokugawa Akitake (*left*);
already officially an adult at 15 years of age,
he was sent as a representative of Japan
to the World's Fair in Paris
(see Chapter 12).

Contacts with Western technology and enterprise resulted in the appearance in Japan of entrepreneurs motivated to achieve by becoming industrial "tycoons" (*taikun*) (see Chapters 6, 7 and 8).

Baron Yataro Iwasaki (1835–85), founder of the Mitsubishi Zaibatsu.

Nakamigawa Hikojiro (1854–1901) at the time of his appointment as executive director of the Mitsui Bank in 1893.

Fujiyama Raita (1863–1938), founder of the Fujiyama "Konzern."

Contacts with Western ideas gave form and content to the alienation experienced by modern Japanese intellectuals (see Chapters 17 and 18).

Natsume Sōseki (1867–1916), author of *Kokoro,* at the height of his fame in 1912. He suffered continual internal conflict between traditional and modern attitudes.

Akutagawa Ryūnosuke (1892–1927), author of *Rashōmon.* A withdrawn commentator on the human condition, he ended his tormented life by suicide with a Christian Bible at his bedside.

Dazai Osamu (1909–1948), author of *No Longer Human,* shifted from Western-oriented Communism to fervid support of the Emperor before committing suicide after the Pacific War.

Mishima Yukio (1925–1970), author of
The Temple of the Golden Pavilion,
in 1961. Retreating from
Westernized sophistication,
he ended his life dramatically
in enacting a warrior's suicide.

University students are today the most alienated segment of Japanese society (see Chapter 14).

Armed confrontation between students and police in Tokyo, 1968.

Crucifixion and public exposure of the bodies both before and after death were used as ultimate punishment for an adulterous couple when a woman of high status was involved. Concern with family lineage and blood purity, as well as with the unseemly nature of status reversal, made such an act subject to the most severe repressive means possible.

Continuance of Traditional Attitudes Toward Sex in Present-Day Japan

Semilegal prostitution continued in Japan in modified form until 1956. Each large city had a well-delineated area of houses, usually in proximity to the railroad station. After World War II there was some legislation outlawing public prostitution, but the houses in such districts as Yoshiwara continued to exist semilegally, since the laws were not stringent enough to allow the police to close them down completely. Moreover, in the immediate postwar period, there was a rapid increase in prostitution related to the presence of the American military; prostitution areas were located near every American military facility. A new style of entertainer and prostitute, the "bar" girl, appeared at this time. Bars, cabarets, and dance halls, offering various levels of cost and degrees of sophistication, began to supplant the traditional houses and the geisha tradition. These new establishments varied considerably as to direct availability of the women for prostitution; in many such establishments the role of women has shifted to that of helping the management by leading on the interested customer to run up large checks.

Very little is known about what eventually happens to modern prostitutes or semiprostitute bar girls or how their life patterns compare with the life patterns of those who in the past were placed in traditional houses of prostitution. In 1954 De Vos interviewed some owners of houses of prostitution, who stated that the average length of time spent by a young woman in traditional houses of prostitution in Nagoya at that time was less than a year. It often happened that a young lower-class worker who had no other means of meeting young women in the city would meet a girl as a prostitute and marry her, cutting short her career in prostitution.

In Japanese culture, unless the family makes marriage arrangements, it is very difficult for many young people to come together. This postwar phenomenon among lower-class Japanese, which is totally unknown in the middle class, can be considered a continuation of a traditional pattern in Japan of a young unmarried man buying a woman free from a house of prostitution. Such arrangements had no negative connotations, and similar attitudes toward this practice are probably found among many of today's bar girls.

The "panpan" girl, or modern prostitute, is usually regarded as a "tougher" person than the more traditionally docile girl who served in a house of prostitution as a result of economic need rather than by personal choice. Many Japanese men felt more comfortable with the traditional prostitute than they do with the panpan girl.[17] In many respects, the bar hostess is the modern version of the geisha; she enhances the ego of the customer, but she need not prostitute herself unless she finds the man and the situation agreeable. Other forms of direct prostitution are more furtive. For a time, inns marked with an *onsen,* or hot spring symbol, were disguised brothels, or houses to which to take a sexual partner. More recently massage parlors that offer extra "services," usually of a masturbatory or "heavy petting" variety, have become popular.

Prostitution and sexual activity with prostitutes is generally viewed in present-day Japan as a form of play and as a means of physiological relief. Seduction of an ordinary married woman, however, would be considered a highly immoral act by both parties.[18] Considerations of sexual morality in the present day are still related rather specifically to expected role behavior.

The lower-class youth in Arakawa Ward in Tokyo where Hiroshi Wagatsuma and I have interviewed are little interested in premarital chastity. Both temporary and permanent sexual liaisons can start during middle and high school, but there is a difference in this respect between families with middle-class pretensions, who supervise their daughters more carefully, and frankly lower-class families, who exercise relatively little control over either girls or boys. In some lower-class behavior a distinction is made between the proper woman and the seductively available woman, a differentiation similar to that reported in lower-class American groups. Individuals who participated in group rape and who were interviewed by Mizushima often justified their behavior on the ground that the young woman involved was herself very promiscuous; although they therefore had no compunction about the act, they would abhor the idea of such aggression on an innocent woman.

Higuchi[19] indicates that delinquents, as compared with nondelinquent controls, are likely to have a greater amount of premarital sexual experience of various kinds. Among delinquency-prone junior high school youth in playgrounds and public places "pink play,"

---

[17] The Japanese traditional attitude toward the entertainment world is rather well exemplified in novels of Nagai Kafū. See, for example, *A Strange Tale from the East of the River* (1937), and *Geisha in Rivalry* (1918, both in Japanese).

[18] A small-scale Japanese comparison with the American Kinsey report attests to a much lower rate of adultery among Japanese women as compared with that among American women.

[19] Higuchi, *Criminal Report of Edo* (1962, in Japanese).

momoiroyūgi, has appeared. This "pink play" sometimes takes the form of kissing or heavy petting—playing with one another's genitals —among thirteen- or fourteen-year-olds. Kissing is a fairly new phenomenon in Japan and has only become a part of erotic play generally in the postwar population. Such "pink play" is not considered acceptable among ordinary students, and willingness to indulge in it, especially by the younger girls, is considered a prodromal symptom of sexual delinquency. Some of these cases have been found to develop toward later prostitution. The uniquely new feature of pink play is the age at which it occurs. Another recent phenomenon is the forming of "pink groups" among youth, usually under twenty, for sexual intercourse. These consist of six to eight couples who continually interchange partners.

In lower-class communities such as Arakawa, premarital sexual behavior is not always related to other forms of delinquency. There are many premarital sexual partnerships that eventuate in marriage. A room may be rented for sexual activity by a couple neither of whom considers the liaison permanent, and gradually a marriage situation may develop. Such a pattern seems to be quite prevalent in the lower-class districts but is unheard of in middle-class Japanese communities.

Middle-class Japanese attitudes about sexuality today closely resemble middle-class attitudes in the United States at the turn of the century. Modern middle-class adolescents are awkward with one another, and easy familiarity between high school youth of different sexes is avoided. Adolescent "crushes" are apparent among girls of this age.[20] Dating is becoming increasingly acceptable in Japan. Coffee houses, dance halls, and theaters have become popular places for dating but still have a somewhat illicit flavor. Youth society is in a stage of transition; generally speaking, it is becoming more and more similar to that in Europe and the United States.

TRADITIONAL AND MODERN ATTITUDES
TOWARD ALCOHOL AND DRUGS

The Japanese attitude toward the subjective experiences of alcohol, like that toward sexual experience per se, is generally positive. Drinking is usually thought of in social terms, in the context of conviviality and the momentary shedding of responsibility. It is considered a relaxing leisure-time activity, principally for men although some women in the entertainment world also drink freely. In drinking, individuals are momentarily freed from the necessity to maintain formal barriers of status that operate when they are sober. Behavior

---

[20] Takarazuka dance group composed solely of girls who take both male and female parts, is still very popular among teenage women.

under the influence of alcohol is considered unrelated to one's usual social role; a drunken person cannot readily be held culpable for what he does or says, and under many circumstances the courts tend to treat lightly acts committed by persons when drunk.[21] Attempts to legislate against the use of alcohol have been infrequent. Sakamoto[22] reports that during the early feudal Kamakura period the government passed edicts prohibiting the sale of sake as a means of curbing drunkenness.

It is difficult to identify or define alcoholism in Japan, since tolerance for heavy drinking is very high. In our interview material from Arakawa Ward in Tokyo, numerous individuals are cited whose work and family life have been seriously affected by heavy drinking, but there is a reluctance to label such individuals as alcoholics. Such "problem drinking" is probably not new in Japan; in many of the cases we interviewed, a father or grandfather living in his traditional village was considered by the son or daughter in retrospect to have been an excessive drinker. The parent would be described as having a tendency to be drunk to the point of neglecting his work and receiving the disapproval of other villagers, but there were few such individuals in any particular village. There is little research to indicate that in either premodern or modern Japan the use of alcohol has in any way been connected with antisocial activities.[23]

Although some authors today claim a relationship between the early drinking of alcohol and other forms of delinquent behavior, it is difficult to assess the age of onset and the amount of drinking among delinquent adolescents; in one attempt, Higuchi[24] found that 8 percent of his delinquent sample manifested what might be called tendencies toward excessive drinking.

Narcotics and Stimulant Drugs

There has never been a widespread use of drugs in Japan comparable to the use of opium in China. In regulating trade, the Japanese government from the very beginning of the modern period, for example in the first treaty with Holland in 1857, made specific prohibition of any trade in opium. The use of opium was defined as a

---

[21] Until about 1953 it was possible in some instances for an automobile driver involved in an accident to plead mitigating circumstances if he could demonstrate that he was drunk at the time of the accident. With the increase in automobiles this means of escaping punishment has disappeared.

[22] Sakamoto (ed.), *Encyclopedia of Folklore* (1957, in Japanese), p. 340.

[23] M. Takahashi, *Research on Alcoholic Crime* (1963, in Japanese), reports that after the Meiji Restoration one can trace in the statistics a relationship between the number of injury cases proportionate to the population and the relative use of alcohol in the area.

[24] Higuchi, *Criminal Report of Edo* (1962, in Japanese).

crime in 1907, but it was not until 1930 that any specific law was enacted in Japan to define the use of narcotics and other drugs as a crime. In the postwar confusion after World War II there was some increase in the importing of heroin from Hong Kong, and special laws were passed between 1946 and 1953 enabling the government to control the importation of narcotics into the country more stringently. What illegal drugs there are in Japan now are imported by particular gangs.[25] The government has very carefully prevented the cultivation in Japan of the opium poppy or any other drug plants.

Recent statistics indicate a small increase over the last few years in the number of drug addicts, principally heroin addicts, who are located mostly near the major ports of Yokohama and Kobe. In 1962 there were approximately 2,000 addicts registered by the Ministry of Health and Welfare, 75 percent of whom were addicted to heroin; approximately 1,500 of the total were male and 600 female, and 57 were physicians, the largest number in any demographic category being males between the ages of twenty and thirty-four. According to the official figures, supported by the additional survey done by Shigemori,[26] the number of juvenile addicts is low (a total of 75 males and 27 females officially registered); a case of narcotic addiction in a juvenile detention home is extremely rare.

In contrast to the lack of problems with the use of opium derivatives, there has been increasing concern over the use of stimulant drugs and barbiturates by juveniles. For a short postwar period there was a rapid increase among Japanese youth in the use of a drug called philopon, a stimulant resembling benzedrine, injected intravenously, that could be obtained for about ten yen (three cents) around places of amusement such as pinball-machine parlors. The excessive use of this drug produced psychotic reactions, usually of a delusional paranoid nature. The philopon problem was quickly controlled by the government through rigid prohibition of the manufacture of this drug and the institution of tight supervisory controls by the police. In 1952 there were 2,923 arrests involving philopon; in 1953, 4,010; in 1954, 5,404; in 1955 the arrests dropped to 3,112, in 1956 to 547, and in 1957 to 640. After 1957 the use of the drug practically disappeared as a social problem. Among those arrested, juvenile offenders were 12 percent of the total in 1954, but only 3.2 percent of the total in 1956. More than half of the arrests were for either manufacturing or distributing the drugs. The Japanese government unofficially estimated that there were as many as 440,000 users in

<hr>

[25] Seki, "A Study of the Personality of Heroin Addicts" (1964, in Japanese); Sugawara, *Japan, the Narcotics Paradise* (1962, in Japanese).

[26] Shigemori, *General Study of Narcotics* (1964).

1954, a number that had diminished to about 10,000 by the first half of 1958.

More recently, the sleeping pill has come into vogue among youth as a form of "amusement." The peculiarity of this fad is that it is particularly popular among the very young, and it is not uncommon for fourteen- and fifteen-year-olds to gather for "sleep play." According to a survey made by Katō and Imada[27] among approximately 2,000 police contacts reported, the peak usage of the sleeping pill was found in the fifteen-year-old age group. Pills were obtained by direct purchase in pharmacies or indirectly from friends, and were used mostly by groups. Only 20 percent of the total users were not involved in other forms of delinquency and more than 20 percent of those who used the pills had a record of some fairly serious criminal offense. These pills are often used by groups gathered at a coffee shop or in some secluded place, and the barbiturates are often put in a drink, the object of the game being to see how close one can come to falling asleep without actually doing so, and to enjoy the pre-sleep, pleasant, anxiety-free mental condition. In some situations sadomasochistic cutting or burning or self-burning with cigarettes is practiced as a means of demonstrating daring and to keep oneself awake. In some amusement areas youngsters can be observed walking around unsteadily under the influence of barbiturates, but very recently the government has put stringent restrictions on the sale of sleeping pills, as well as more careful controls over their manufacture.

Generally speaking, there is a sharp distinction in Japan between the use of alcohol and the use of drugs. The use of alcohol to influence ego states is generally considered a social activity rather than one done in isolation, in keeping with the general tone of Japanese culture. Statistically, the misuse of alcohol or drugs cannot be said to be as serious a social problem in Japan as it is in the United States today, but the increase in the use of drugs by younger individuals symbolizes some form of emotional and social dislocation among an increasing number of young people.

TATTOOING AND ITS RELATION
TO SOCIAL DEVIANCY

An interesting recent phenomenon is the fairly high incidence of tattooing among delinquency-prone youth today. Various forms of scarification appear in early Japanese history.[28] There is some evi-

---

[27] Katō and Imada, "The Conditions of Sleeping Pill Misuses Among Juveniles" (1963, in Japanese).

[28] Sakamoto, *Encyclopedia of Folklore* (1957, in Japanese), pp. 33 ff.; and *Yuzankaku Series of the History of Japanese Folk Customs* (1959, in Japanese).

dence that tattooing had a magical meaning in ancient Japan as protection against witchcraft, and there are also indications that some form of tattooing was used in the Nara era as a means of punishment. During the Heian period, records indicate that monks tattooed the figure of Buddha upon their persons. Again, there was frequent use of tattooing in the Kamakura period as a means of punishment, and the Tokugawa government used tattoos to mark criminals. During the late Tokugawa period it became popular to have a large portion of the torso tattooed with rather elaborate designs, many of which had direct sexual connotations. This practice was especially popular among gamblers and other outlaw groups (yakuza), among whom some form of tattoo was a membership badge. The Tokugawa government periodically prohibited tattooing but was unable to curb its popularity. During the Meiji period tattooing continued to be popular among gang members, manual laborers, and the military, especially among naval personnel. In a study of prisons by medical researchers in the late Meiji era,[29] it was found that among 720 male prisoners investigated, 215 had had themselves tattooed. Tattooing is still popular among daylaborers and among individuals who are related to yakuza groups of one kind or another; this will be discussed further in the next chapter.

Japanese tattooing has some unique features. Some clubs of individuals who are tattooed meet at public baths to reveal their designs to one another. The tattooing often covers the body extensively; the arms will be tattooed from the shoulders midway to the elbow, and the legs down almost to the knees, the entire torso being covered with elaborate designs. According to Honjo,[30] tattooing is usually started during adolescence, and is most frequently requested by individuals between the ages of sixteen and eighteen. Honjo also sees a relationship between tattooing and the use of drugs. Tattooing is fairly rare among girls, and a disproportionate number of girls who use drugs, or who are prostitutes, or both, are also tattooed.

Horiye[31] did a study of female juvenile delinquents who were tattooed. The favorite designs were playing cards, dice, hearts, roses and other flowers, maple leaves, cherries, and peaches. Generally the left arm was used. Among the most frequently stated motives for tattooing were "as a playful act," "as a form of amusement," "just because others did it." Very little thought was given to the permanent consequences, or the reaction of others to the tattooing.

Tattooing and other forms of scarification are widespread among the world's cultures. There seems to be some definite satisfaction to be gained from marking the body. Motives stated in many groups are

---

[29] *Yuzankaku.*

[30] Honjo, "Tattoo and Delinquents" (1955, in Japanese).

[31] T. Horiye, "Tattooing Among Juvenile Girl Delinquents" (1958, in Japanese).

related to cosmetic purposes of "beautification." Tattooing seems to reassure and to give form to the individual's concept of himself. The psychological motivations for tattooing bear much more careful examination than they have been given to date. One could speculate that the act of being tattooed is an attempt to validate one's sense of self somehow and that it is particularly frequent among the young because they are still in the process of actualizing themselves and becoming recognized in some fuller status by others. The present-day affinity between delinquent behavior and tattooing suggests that those with a more motoric, body-oriented concern with self-validation may also be prone to engage in behavior that causes them to be considered delinquent. Their emotional and mental makeup is such that they are not apt to validate their masculinity or daring through conventional channels related to goal orientation.

GAMBLING

Some form of gambling is to be found in most cultures. Gambling can become such a preoccupation as to injure the gambler's social capacity to the point of distracting him from adult responsibilities. Gambling debts can lead to crime or to some form of bondage, and professional gamblers can ensnare unwary dupes. Many governments have sought to regulate or to eliminate gambling, but the ordinary citizen continues to woo fortune by magical means and condones games of chance in one form or another.

Gambling has always been very popular in Japan as recreation, as well as a means of improving one's fortune. In the recreation areas or gay-quarters during the Tokugawa period, there were various forms of gambling, most of which were considered illegal by the government and harassed to varying degrees. As is discussed in the following chapter, most gambling operations have traditionally been conducted by criminal gangs called *bakuto,* one form of *yakuza* group.

Japanese gambling is not too dissimilar from the forms of gambling found historically in the West. In the Nara period there was a dice game played on a board, and by the late seventh and eighth centuries there were government prohibitions on record against gambling. In the Kamakura period, a great deal of gambling was found in connection with sports, races, and such activities as dog fights; Iwai[32] discusses the moralistic tone of the government prohibitions of gambling in this period.

In the Tokugawa era new kinds of gambling games using playing cards were introduced; one, *hana karuta,* became popular and was

---

[32] Iwai, *The Structure of Pathological Groups* (1963), p. 34.

spread by professional gamblers' organizations. During the Meiji period and afterward, certain public forms of gambling were legalized.[33] Horse racing, government lotteries, bicycle racing, and a minor type of gambling for commodities on pinball machines all came within legal jurisdiction. However, it remains illegal to gamble with cards or dice or to use money in games of mah-jongg either in private houses or public places. In the statistics quoted in Chapter 11, it is to be noted that in recent years gambling has not been a problem among juveniles—at least the number of arrests of minors for gambling is extremely low; this constitutes a curious discrepancy in an overall comparison between juvenile and adult crime.

---

[33] Sakamoto, *Encyclopedia of Folklore,* pp. 32–574; Kida, *Gambling in Japan* (1966, in Japanese), pp. 10–49; Usatake, *Research on Gambling and Pickpocketing* (1948, in Japanese), pp. 65–90.

Chapter XI

Organization and Social Function
of Japanese Gangs:
Historical Development and Modern Parallels

with KEIICHI MIZUSHIMA

One feature of Japanese culture and social structure least known to the West is the nature of the Japanese underworld.[1] Some Japanese writers have examined the functioning of professional criminal groups within Japanese culture in preindustrial feudal society and in the present time of rapid social change; but the subject has not received the detailed attention it deserves.

In all complex societies, heroic legends about the innovator, the out-law, the rebel, and the deviant are part of the common lore and are available as justification for deviant behavior in the present. The social scientist can better understand the nature of present social functions by reference to generally popular legends which glorify defiance of legitimate authority.

Knowledge of both the actual structure of the underworld and its legends is especially pertinent to an understanding of the foci of power within the total political structure of society. The overt exercise of power is often closely, though covertly, related to officially illegal groups. The American big-city boss at the turn of the twentieth century, as described by Lincoln Steffens, does not appear to be much different in social function from his Japanese counterpart, the so-called

---

[1] This chapter has previously appeared in modified form as "Organization and Social Function of Japanese Gangs" (DeVos and Mizushima), in Dore (ed.), *Aspects of Social Change in Modern Japan* (1967), pp. 289–325.

oyabun.[2] What does differ is the degree and cultural content of the loyalty demanded of the *kobun,* or followers.

Delinquent and criminal gangs within a culture reflect conflicts going on in the society generally, especially in times of change. Deviant individuals may act as innovators helping to influence patterns of change, or as conservative forces attempting to resist change and to maintain older forms of behavior.[3]

Japanese outlaw gangs have acted generally as a conservative force within the society.[4] Like the Mafia in Italy, gang traditions that are still influential today in Japan had their origins within the feudal structure of the preindustrial society. The outlaws drew their cohesiveness and strength from their organization along the quasi-familial lines of loyalty so characteristic of Japanese society generally during that period.

Conservative traditions, both on a legitimate level and an outlaw-racketeering level, are residually operative in present-day industry. Such traditions help maintain marginal operations that would disappear if they were more subject to modern labor-management operations. For example, the coal industry of the southern island, Kyushu, is in large part economically marginal. Smaller mines are kept in operation by labor oyabun who keep groups of workers together on an oyabun-kobun basis. Gangs of oyabun and their henchmen sometimes resort to violence against one another over controlling "territory," and workers can be forced to continue to work on a level of marginal existence as "loyal" kobun. Unionization would put these marginal mines out of business.

Today a new kind of gang, called *gurentai,*[5] is becoming consolidated around activities related to prostitution, which has been stringently outlawed only recently. This new type of organization does not rely, as earlier groups did, on traditions of personal loyalty. However, the older traditions still maintain some force.

---

[2] In American vernacular, "boss," directly translated, "parent part" or "role," in a gang relationship. *Kobun,* or follower, directly translated means "child role." See Ishino, "The Oyabun-Kobun: A Japanese Ritual Kinship Institution" (1953).

[3] Robert Merton has discussed this relationship between alienation, deviancy, and innovation in *Social Theory and Social Structure* (1949); see especially pp. 133–149.

[4] Nevertheless, at the time of social revolution occurring with the restoration of the emperor in 1868, these gangs were found operating on both sides. Some assisted the feudal shogunate, while others backed the clans and other forces that were seeking to overthrow the Tokugawa regime and establish the emperor as head of a modern state. Their purpose was not modernization but indirect political advantage.

[5] According to some, the origin of the word *gurentai* is a combination of a slang word, *gureru,* to turn bad, and *rentai,* a unit of military organization. Also, the prefix *gu* usually suggests stupidity or foolishness.

A new phenomenon was noticeable in the early 1960s, the *chimpira*, or juvenile gangs.[6] These gangs, usually of a shifting, impermanent nature, are only most indirectly related to the professional adult gangs. They draw their models of swagger and bravado chiefly from American cinema. Nevertheless, the *yakuza* tradition still contributes to the masculine "heroics" through which the youth seeks to demonstrate and validate his masculine "tough guy" identity.

THE GANG TRADITION: ROMANCE AND ACTUALITY

Gang Activities during the Tokugawa Era

The feudal period of Japanese history is far enough in the past to be used by present-day Japanese for the construction of legends. It can now be exploited romantically much as the opening of the American West has become a focus for romanticism concerning heroes and villains. There are curious parallels between Japanese society and American society in the formation of legends around outlaw heroes. In the American tradition, the Western hero is a man who lives by his wits, and although given to being a law unto himself, he often fights for the forces of good against corruption and evil in his society. Similarly, certain types of Japanese outlaws known as *Yakuza* have been turned into heroes fighting oppression and misrule on the side of the underdogs. In both countries the type of violence expressed by modern delinquent youth is influenced by this legendary past.

In America, the fast draw and the ability to handle a weapon in all circumstances have crept into the delinquent picture. In Japan, the tradition of violence is focused more on the sword as a weapon and a symbol of masculinity.

The Tokugawa period (1603–1868), the subject of so many modern legends, was radically different in social organization from the open-frontier West. But both eras have contributed the outlaw as a symbol of the individual against society, providing a source of legends quite different from the true facts. The *yakuza* were either gangs involved in shady activities as itinerant merchants (*yashi* or *tekiya*) or gangs whose chief occupation was gambling (*bakuto*).[7] To understand how

---

[6] Etymology of this word is obscure. We suspect it partially derives from a Japanese word for penis.

[7] Today, in common parlance the collective term for both *tekiya* and *bakuto* is *yakuza*, but this is not quite appropriate historically. Originally, according to Tamura, *Yakuza-kō* ("A Study of the Yakuza") (1958), the word *yakuza*, or *ya-ku-sa*, (eight-nine-three) was used among gamblers to denote something "no good" or useless, because eight, nine, and three add up to twenty—a losing number in gambling. Later the word *yakuza* came to be used outside the gambling world by

some of the leaders of these gangs of gamblers or petty racketeers and confidence men were turned into legendary heroes, one must examine in detail certain features of the feudal Japanese society.

The origin of Japanese gangs in the form they were to take during the Tokugawa period can be traced back to the chaotic times before the establishment of the rigid social structure by the Tokugawas after 1600. Before the Tokugawa period there had been many confused years of continuous civil war among feudal lords who controlled the various decentralized government units. When a feudal lord was defeated, his former retinue of samurai sought to support themselves by violence and looting. They often formed roving bands in the best tradition of banditry. This period was well illustrated by a recent popular picture shown in the United States, "Seven Samurai," or "The Magnificent Seven."

The consolidation of political power under the Tokugawa shogunate ended this period of political confusion. To maintain power and to police this centralized government it was necessary to control the gangs of gamblers and street merchants involved in criminal activity. To accomplish this, the government indirectly supported some of the better-established gang leaders and unofficially helped them consolidate their positions.

For example, a bureau called Kanto Torishimari-jo, or Hasshu-Torishimari, was established in 1805 to strengthen the public peace and order in territories directly supervised by the *bakufu* government, and in the landholdings of temples and shrines and of other lords in the Kanto plain. Eight assistants worked for this bureau as *hasshu-mawari,* comparable to traveling marshals; their job was to travel around the Kanto area, conducting a periodic roundup of outlaws.

During this period, samurai police officers often freed prisoners to serve as informants, known as *me-akashi* (originally meaning "eyewitness"). The informants were pardoned after they had contributed

---

the general public to denote people who are useless and good-for-nothing. The word gradually came to designate outlaws generally. At present the word is used collectively to designate *bakuto, tekiya, gurentai,* and other professional and semi-professional outlaws.

The word *tekiya* is relatively new; in the past *yashi* was the more common term. According to one theory, *yashi* derives from *no-bushi (no-bushi—Noshi—Yashi;* the same character is pronounced both *no* and *ya). Nobushi* were bandits, mostly warriors serving defunct feudal lords who had lost their jobs. Bandits were very active in Japan during the Sengoku period of continual warfare (about 1500 to 1575). The origin of the word *tekiya,* according to one theory, was a reversal from *ya-teki* ("arrow" and "mark"). The word "mark" had the same meaning as that used by American confidence artists. Usually *tekiya,* when selling small commodities on the street or at a fair, cheated the customers by using many of the techniques still practiced by confidence men today, including the use of decoys or shills.

sufficient useful information to the police. The traveling marshals depended heavily on these informants. Police also developed informal relationships with some of the recognized leaders of gambling groups. Gamblers were often forced into spying to escape arrest or to protect others of their gang from arrest.

The leaders of gamblers were thus supported indirectly by the government, and their leadership position was consolidated with the indirect approval of the police. The structure that developed in these groups, when they stabilized, resembled the patterns of formal loyalty that served as the code of ethics for the samurai themselves. The head of the gamblers became an oyabun, and his subordinates were his kobun. Quasi-familial ties of loyalty came to bind these individuals together. The followers and leaders were bound—often by a blood oath—in a code of behavior that could not be broken with impunity. The ethics of such groups thus reflected, in some respects, the ethical code of the warrior, although their activities were mostly illegal.

Groups of itinerant merchants who gathered at fairs and ran small portable stalls in the market areas banded together to form organizations of *yashi*. These groups often depended on shoddy goods or trickery to fool the public,[8] and from 1735 to 1740 the Tokugawa government appointed "supervisors" to regulate them and keep them more "honest." The supervisors were allowed *myoji-taito* (that is, they were permitted to have a family name and to wear a sword, the symbol of status below samurai but above the ruled commoners). They were held responsible for supervising street merchants and maintaining order within a certain territory and in turn were given the implicit right to collect money from the merchants. Later, shrines and temples within their holdings followed the example of the government and appointed "supervisors," to function on those ceremonial days when many merchants gathered.[9] These "supervisors" were responsible for allocating lots to each merchant, and for maintaining order; in return they received the difference between the money they collected and the sum charged by the shrine or temple for the use of its land.

---

[8] The cheating activities of *tekiya* descendants of *yashi* are called *hattaribai*. Some examples follow: *gane-neta-bai* consists of selling commodities under a false name, such as selling a cheap fountain pen as a "Parker." *Kisuguro* is pretending to be drunk and making a show of selling things cheaply so that customers are fooled into believing the seller does not know what he is doing. *Montan* is selling shoddy cloth under false pretenses, making a buyer believe he has bought enough good cloth for a kimono when the cloth is really unusably bad quality, or of insufficient amount. *Kaboku* is selling a miniature plant (*bon-sai*) without roots. *Gesoya* is selling old, worn shoes that have been glued and painted to look new under the feeble light of a lantern.

[9] Market days in medieval Japan, as in medieval Europe, were held in accordance with the religious calendar.

Usually elderly, influential yashi who were well respected by their fellow merchants were appointed "supervisors" by the government or a particular temple or shrine, and in this way the otherwise more-or-less informal position of the yashi leaders became more formal and public, especially after they were given special status of semi-samurai. Merchants under the supervision of one leader came to be regarded as a recognized group, identified often with the leader's family name, and the territory within which each group functioned came to be fixed. Later, to increase their income, the leaders of yashi groups began to conduct their own fairs, in addition to the fairs held on ceremonial days. Besides keeping street stalls, the yashi (today called *tekiya*) engaged in running small-scale circuses, show booths, and exhibitions, somewhat like "carnival people." The rise in importance of the yashi organizations in the late Tokugawa period was related to the developing market function of towns and of certain castle cities. The Yashi groups were bound by formal rituals as well as by social and economic ties.

In the early Tokugawa period, the yashi came to worship Shinno, a mythical Chinese god-emperor, who was credited with discovering medicine and who helped the sick and the poor. The reason yashi came to worship Shinno is not quite clear, except that he was a deity of "patent medicine," which to the yashi was an important commodity. Even today, in the house of some traditional oyabun of the tekiya group, we find an altar to Shinno, and ritual exchange of a sake cup and other important ceremonial activities cementing oyabun-kobun relationships still take place in front of the altar. An oyabun would often be called "Shinno," and some tekiya have termed themselves "Shinno Gyosha" (merchants protected by Shinno).

One of the chief functions of both bakuto and yashi was to limit competition in the interests of those who were already "in," and to protect territory or income; for this it was necessary to maintain an aggressive military attitude. Factional conflicts over territory were constant; "hired swords" were sometimes attached to one group or another, but usually the yashi and bakuto did their own fighting.[10] As specialists in "self-protection" and aggression, these groups developed other functions. They sometimes served as private police for outsiders not actually in the underworld who wished to use the threat of violence. Their disciplined organizational loyalty enabled their leader to control their use of force.

As this military function was stabilized and traditionalized, these gangs developed a morale somewhat similar to that of the samurai, and ordinary folk talked about the *yakuza-katagi,* or "yakuza tempera-

---

[10] Ohashi, *Urban Lower Society* (1962, in Japanese).

ment." Their code was a parody of the samurai's Bushido, and their hero ideal was drawn on samurai models. Their preoccupation with violence and controlled aggression could be romanticized as manliness. Violent death, for the yakuza as for the samurai, was seen as a poetic, tragic fate.

Yakuza heroes owe their romanticism in part to the difficulty, under the feudal regime, of expressing social criticism. Stories about yakuza could indirectly criticize injustice without incurring government suppression, and the yakuza, an outlaw living outside the structures of society, was used by the oppressed as a symbol of resistance and of the free spirit. In the towns, the yakuza were identified with the tradition of the *machi yakko*, or "town servants," who protected town commerce from the aggressive acts of *rōnin*, who no longer had feudal political strife to keep them busy.

By the early seventeenth century, the Japanese countryside was settled and peaceful, and the earlier virtues of an age of constant war became obsolete. Bushido degenerated, as luxury and easy living became common, even among the samurai class. In reaction to this tendency, a group of samurai of lower status appeared and tried to restore the older "virtues" of warriorhood. They dressed distinctively to draw attention to themselves, and developed ceremonials pledging group loyalty. They disciplined themselves strictly, trained themselves in swordsmanship, and promised to be always ready to sacrifice themselves. They were, so to speak, reactionary protagonists of lost warrior values, and find a parallel in right-wing groups today. They were called *kan-ei yakko*, kan-ei being the name of the era, and yakko, or servant, designating samurai of lower status.

Samurai who belonged directly to the shogun, called *hatamoto* ("under the banner"), had low incomes, and peace time deprived them of the occasional plunder of war. They were continually in financial difficulties, and they felt out of place. Their ancestors' job had been to fight and be killed in protection of their lord, Tokugawa, and in peaceful times the hatamoto had no real function. Rough young hatamoto (often in their late teens) formed groups called *hatamoto yakko* who roamed the city of Edo looking for excuses to vent violence on innocent commoners or *chonin* (townsmen). The commoners met this menace by supporting the counter activities of machi yakko, who were groups of tough chonin youth. There is some historical evidence to suggest that some feudal lords secretly opposed the Tokugawa shogunate, and gave covert financial aid to the machi yakko and sometimes provided them with teachers of swordsmanship. Later, the Tokugawa government suppressed the conflicts between hatamoto yakko and machi yakko; by the end of the seventeenth century, both groups of yakko had disappeared.

The machi yakko, protectors of citizens and fighters against the ruling class, were heroes of the common people in folk tales and songs, and similar legendary attributes, were inherited by various later groups. Such "protective" heroics came to be attributed to yakuza groups as well as to *hikeshi* (firemen), *meakashi* (police detectives), leaders of labor gangs, and even to sumo (wrestlers).[11]

Occasionally one or another of the oyabun acquired and maintained status within the structure of regular society and was deferred to as a person of power to be consulted and at times placated. Many of these wealthy oyabun were trained not only in swordsmanship but also in literature and the arts, since one means of rising in social status was to cultivate the appearance of the samurai,[12] and some had connections with the more dissolute members of the nobility. The oyabun were expected to demonstrate the "manly" virtues of endurance, to bear cold and heat, hunger, pain, and imprisonment with a show of stoic unconcern. There was emphasis on *noblesse oblige* toward the poor; charity was a means to social mobility, as it is in modern society,[13] and it served to distract attention from the source of income and to help others "forget."

Some bakuto and tekiya had formal charters regulating gang functions. A modern one, quoted by Berrigan,[14] had the following rules:

(1) Do not touch the wife of another member.
(2) Do not do anything other than the regular "business" (that is, gang activities), even under the pressure of poverty.
(3) Do not reveal secrets of the organization to the police when caught.

---

[11] For instance, in the Tokugawa period there were two different groups of firemen in Edo City. The first, who were called *gaen*, were fire-fighters hired by the feudal lords and warrior class to take care of the warriors' residences. The other group, who were called *tobi* ("birds," or Siberian black kites; the word came from *tobiguchi*, fire hook: the bill of a Siberian black kite), were fire fighters for the commoners. Usually they were engaged in construction work, especially building houses, but when a fire broke out, they would act as firemen. The term *tobi-shoku* or *tobi* is still used today to designate construction workers. During the late Tokugawa period there were nearly a hundred groups of *tobi* in Edo City; they had a reputation for being quick-tempered, brave young fellows. *Gaen* and *tobi* were involved in constant brawls. See Ogawa, "Juvenile Delinquency in the Ten Years After the War" (1956, in Japanese). On present-day documents referring to lineage belonging to *tekiya* one finds imprinted a symbol for *tobi*. The reason is not clear, but it suggests some historical connection between groups of *tobi* and *tekiya*.

[12] In a sense, *yakuza* activities were due to the limitations of the "opportunity structure" of a strict feudal society. See Merton, *Social Theory and Social Structure* (1949), or Cloward and Ohlin, *Delinquency and Opportunity* (1960).

[13] See Warner and Lunt, *The Social Life of a Modern Community* (1941).

[14] Berrigan, *The Society of Gangs* (1955, in Japanese).

(4) Keep strict loyalty in the *oyabun-kobun* relationship.
(5) Do not use ordinary language; use the gang's special terminology.[15]

These groups needed to justify their activities to themselves. The tekiya leaders could easily rationalize their taxing of itinerant merchants as part of needed regulation to prevent excessive exploitation and irregularity. The status of the oyabun could be maintained only if the merchants enjoyed a degree of trust, and therefore even honest merchants were benefited by affiliation with the tekiya. This relationship parallels that of certain racketeers with labor unions that they control; exploitation is rationalized both to the bosses and to the membership as necessary for the well-being of the group.

Maeda,[16] a specialist in problems of Japanese criminal sociology, describes a handbook circulated among the tekiya today which contains similar rationalizations. It states that there are two kinds of merchants: the ordinary merchant who owns a shop, and the itinerant merchant who works on the street. The former has sufficient capital to maintain a store and residence, but the latter is without such capital, and resembles a laborer who works hard for his everyday living, his one advantage being independence from others. Without definite residence, itinerant merchants must band together for mutual protection. Behind this façade of democratic cooperation, the actual organized activities of these groups are quite another matter. As we will discuss later, the tekiya today are extremely conservative, usually supporting the most reactionary political groups. In developments within the construction industry, bakuto oyabun have played an important role; many gambling halls have become hiring halls controlled by oyabun, some of whom have become modern contractors, securing exclusive rights in a given territory through threats of violence.

Some Historical Examples of Yakuza Legends

Stories about the yakuza are very popular in Japan and are similar to our own Westerns with "good guys" and "bad guys." Their legendary exploits are found in all forms of storytelling and folklore. For example, musical ballads (*naniwa bushi*), set forth in endless verse the romantic exploits of these men, and in modern Japanese movies yakuza themes are very popular. The story of Shimizu-no-Jirochō, or Jirochō of Shimizu, a representative boss figure among the gamblers at the end of the Tokugawa period, can serve as an illustration. There

---

[15] The development of a special criminal argot is characteristic of Japanese gangs, as it is of the Western underworld—an obvious parallel in the secretive function of argot.

[16] Maeda, *Problems in Criminal Sociology* (1955, in Japanese).

are many romantic stories about this man, and a recent movie concerning him is summarized below.

The first scene is in the home of a local gambling leader, "Dragon," who is playing a game of go with "Black Horse" (Kurokoma-no-Katsuzō), the big gambling boss of three prefectures in the underworld of the time. Black Horse is extremely crafty, ruling his territory by a combination of guile and personal force; he maintains strict order and makes sure that no one contravenes his authority. Dragon is one of his subchiefs, responsible for part of the big boss's territory. Many of Dragon's immediate subordinates are sitting around watching these two leaders at play. Jirochō, a minor gang leader, enters and politely informs Dragon that one of Jirochō's subordinates has been killed by a roving unemployed soldier (rōnin), who is reportedly being protected by Dragon from the revenge of Jirochō's group. Prevention of such justifiable retribution is against the rule of the yakuza code. When Dragon seeks to ignore his complaint, Jirochō becomes extremely angry and is about to draw his sword against Dragon. Immediately all Dragon's subordinates rise to kill Jirochō. Assuming the quiet authority befitting him, Black Horse stops the fight and suggests that an individual duel be fought between the rōnin who has killed Jirochō's follower and another one of Jirochō's subordinates. An agreement is reached, the fight takes place, and the rōnin is killed. However, because the government has a severe prohibition against unauthorized fighting, Jirochō has to flee from the police as the man responsible for the murder. The film indicates that this banishment had been intended by Black Horse to rid himself of Jirochō.

On his flight, Jirochō stops at the home of the father of one of his previous subordinates. This subordinate, now reformed and a hardworking merchant, is in love with a young woman who is also wooed by a government official. The girl and her mother have refused the official's marriage proposal, but he forces the marriage by threatening prosecution of the girl's father for his criminal past. The father decides to kill the official at the marriage ceremony. Dragon, the antagonist of Jirochō, and a friend of the official, is to attend the marriage ceremony. (The collusion between political and underworld figures is depicted here.)

Jirochō, hearing about what is to take place, goes to the ceremony with two of his subordinates. A fight occurs between Jirochō's group and Dragon and his followers, and Dragon is killed. The government official, sensing that Jirochō has become a power, quickly calls off the marriage and makes overtures to Jirochō. Since the official is feared as well as hated by the people, Jirochō gains status through this and becomes a strong figure in the gambling world. The big boss,

Black Horse, seeing in Jirochō a coming competitor for his power, provokes him by holding a gambling game in territory controlled by Jirochō. Black Horse's men are found by Jirochō's followers and they hide in a farmer's house, where Jirochō's followers kill them. In the course of the fighting, Jirochō's men set fire to the house. This makes Jirochō extremely angry because it violates the yakuza code against damaging the property of the common people. He tells his subordinates to pay for the damage with his own money, and the guilty retainers are put under house arrest. (Note the romantic concept of the yakuza's protection of the poor and the use of violence only against enemies.) When they reach the place where they are to stay, they find that one of Black Horse's groups has been swindling one of their friends out of his property. To redeem themselves, Jirochō's followers attack this group and kill a number of Black Horse's men. Black Horse then attempts a frontal assault upon Jirochō and his men, and the story ends with Jirochō's killing Black Horse and becoming the big chief of the yakuza.

A number of attitudes are exemplified in this film: first, the heroic, swaggering quality of the yakuza group; second, the emphasis on the code of "honor," and the anger aroused when it is violated; third, the importance of territorial domains and the fights over territory which resemble the disputes among American gangsters in the prohibition era; fourth, the deference paid by government officials to the outlaw groups shows that they had great status among the people, the outlaw's power often being greater than that of the official government representative. The heroic quality of Jirochō's character is emphasized in the film, but from what we know of history, the reality was considerably different.

The actual Jirochō was born in 1820 and lived to be seventy-four years old.[17] His father, who had a violent temper, was reported to be the skipper of a ferryboat. There is no record of his mother. Jirochō was adopted by a neighborhood storekeeper; he was an unruly child, noted for a variety of delinquent activities. When he was fifteen, he asked his stepfather for permission to go to Edo, and on being refused, he stole money from his stepfather and ran away. On his stepfather's death, his stepmother ran away with another man, and at this point Jirochō came back to his home and started his gambling career. When a man to whom he was heavily in debt asked him to pay up, Jirochō is reported to have killed him by throwing him into a river. This crime was supposedly the factual basis for the flight described in the motion picture, but there were several other periods in his life when he had to flee the police.

---

[17] Tamura, *A Study of the Yakuza* (1958, in Japanese), pp. 190–200.

One recorded account resembles an incident in the picture. Jirochō returned after his first flight and was accused of several murders. "Dragon" (actually, in the film, a composite of a number of Jirochō's real-life rivals) was acting as a friend of a corrupt government official and attempted to assist the government in capturing Jirochō, who instead was able to kill him and who subsequently fled. There is no historical record of Jirochō's fighting against unjust government officials. The real Black Horse was a gambler of the area who was in constant dispute with Jirochō, and according to the official records he was killed, not by Jirochō, as was depicted in the film, but by the police.

Jirochō's help was actively sought by the government, and he played an important role in the civil war which ended the Tokugawa period and reestablished the emperor as supreme authority. Both the revolutionary army and the army of the Tokugawa government attempted to gain the assistance of yakuza groups, since they were well-organized fighting forces. Jirochō was employed by the revolutionary forces, and all his previous crimes and murders were pardoned. In 1868, the year the Meiji government was established, more than 3,000 defeated soldiers of the Tokugawa army fled by boat from Tokyo to Shimizu, where they were killed by the combined forces of Jirochō and the revolutionary military. Many of the corpses were abandoned in the neighboring sea, and Jirochō, who felt this was inhuman, had them buried; the legends concerning Jirochō's humane activities appear to stem from this act. He died of old age in his home, a respected figure in his community.

Another famous yakuza, Chuji Kunisada, met a different end; he was beheaded and his head was put on display for the public to see. His life, too, has been a source of many legends. Chuji lived somewhat earlier than Jirochō, and according to legend he rescued many people from a variety of difficult situations. He is reputed to have been instrumental in starting a better system of rice farming in his area and was said to be responsible for killing government officials who were exploiting the common people.

As far as Chuji's actual career can be traced, there is very little basis for the romantic character ascribed to him. He was the son of a rich farmer and started gambling as a means of earning easy money before he was nineteen years of age. He exploited his wealthy background to attract followers and used his connection with a corrupt government official to further his gambling activities and to establish control over the underworld in his area. Chuji was not satisfied with the location of his activities, which was too far from the national highway where the gambling take was much greater; he sought to expand his territory into that of another gang. According to the yakuza code, warning had to be given before war was declared against another individual, but since Chuji's group was inferior in number, he found it more expedient to attack without notice, and by this means he was able to kill a more powerful figure and to establish his position on the national highway. As a further indication of Chuji's character, it seems that the man he killed had, on a previous occasion, caught him carrying on activities within his territory and had let him go. Chuji had a reputation for violating the yakuza code by thieving and pilfering in addition to gambling, and was hated by other gamblers because such activities brought them into difficulty with the government. To explain why Chuji became a legendary hero in the face of such facts, certain other aspects of his character must be considered.

According to Mitamura,[18] who made an extensive study of the subject, there were certain characteristic patterns in Chuji's behavior. Although he committed crimes of violence and robbery in other areas, he strictly forbade them within his own district. He was known to give money, clothes, and food to the neighboring poor, and he would advise rich young boys who came to his gambling dens to stay out of gambling in order not to ruin their futures. Chuji's domination of his own territory was so complete that he was able to prevent almost all minor burglary and other such crimes, and the common folk were thus thankful to him. Further, in times of stress, Chuji used his own money to help in various emergency situations.

There is a certain aura of mystery about Chuji's personal activities. For example, he is reported to have left his home every evening alone; no one knew where he went. One curious individual once followed him but was later found killed. No one ever discovered the purpose of Chuji's night prowling.

Tamura[19] also studied the life of Chuji, but does not treat him so gently. According to him, most of Chuji's supposed kindnesses can be directly attributed to his foresightedness in expanding his gambling activities by gaining the good will of those about him. The degree to which the legend of humanistic concern is attached to the yakuza is illustrated by a very touching scene in which Chuji, when an uncle of one of his retainers is killed, takes over the care of an infant child with a great show of maternal affection.[20] The truth seems to be that

---

[18] Mitamura, *World of the Police* (1959, in Japanese), pp. 303–313.

[19] Tamura, pp. 143–181.

[20] This incident is the burden of a very popular ballad, sung with great sentimentality at sake parties, "Chuji's Lullaby," or the "Lullaby of Mount Akagi" (Chuji's "territory"):

> Don't you cry—just go to sleep.
> Even though the crow caws in yonder mountain,
> You musn't cry but sleep.
> If you weep he will only caw more.

this particular man was killed on the direct orders of Chuji, who felt that he might betray him to the police.

The yakuza themselves did not see their activities in the heroic light later shed on them by others. Many self-abasing statements are attributed to yakuza, such as "I am a bad man and worthless, just like an insect," but they go on to justify themselves with "I am doing wrong things, but I never hurt ordinary people."

YAKUZA IN MODERN SOCIETY

Recent Activities in the Underworld

The traditional forms of yakuza have continued to exist since the industrialization of Japanese society, although they have somewhat changed their financial activities as well as their morals to adapt to the modern environment. The bakuto could not continue their fairly open activities in the new state. Police control became more severe, and their open brawling and territorial disputes were no longer tolerated. Open gambling was forbidden, and the gambling bosses had to conceal their sources of income by carrying on respected economic, social, or political activities as a façade. In a number of documented instances, the gambling boss gained protection from the police by a direct donation of money to police chiefs, with the result that police were discouraged from observing any gambling activities in their area. Where disruptive violence has occurred, the direct relationship between the police chief and the gambling boss has been used to "solve" the problem. It has sometimes been easier for the gambling boss to hand over one of his subordinates as guilty of subcriminal activity than for the police to find the real culprit.

The tekiya, or former yashi, have shifted with modern times. Extortion from small street stalls or itinerant selling has become less and less lucrative with the development of modern commercial activities. To keep up with the times, tekiya bosses have tended to go into modern industry themselves, some of them actually managing companies, and some tekiya going into large-scale activities have become "legitimate." (In the confused period after World War II, when businesses were conducted on a shoestring, tekiya appeared in their more traditional form for a brief period.) The tekiya today have become semilegitimate, and are in a stronger position than the bakuto, who have not adapted themselves so much to changing times.

The façade of "knightly spirit" appropriate to the feudal period has largely disappeared from yakuza groups. Since World War II, it has been very difficult for these organizations to cloak themselves with any form of social purpose. It must be noted that, previous to this period, these yakuza groups played a considerable political role in the far right. Such ultranationalist parties as the Genyosha, and later the Black Dragon (Kokuryukai), included some yakuza leaders, and in the twenties and thirties these groups were not above using violence or terrorism as a means to political or economic ends. Yakuza acted as mercenary strikebreakers and intimidators, and yakuza leaders, by engaging peripherally in politics as enthusiastic anti-Socialist and anti-Communist militants, could claim some legitimacy for their violent activities. As Japanese politics in the late twenties became more and more militaristic, yakuza groups cooperated with the militarists by going to Manchukuo or China to participate in "land development" programs. This period was a heyday for the yakuza, a return to the good old days of feudalism, but when war broke out, the yakuza were suppressed by the military government, no matter how willing or co-operative they were, and many were brought into the military system or imprisoned.

In the postwar period, yakuza appeared rather openly, sometimes as mediators, sometimes as contractors providing materials for the American military, who were not aware of their background and sources of procurement. The postwar yakuza, however, never recovered the power they had been able to maintain during the prewar period, and the ultra-rightists today are a strongly disparaged group. Certain rightist groups practicing karate[21] have a number of members who also have some affiliation with the yakuza, but it is not possible to generalize and say that there are direct links between the yakuza and the political right.[22] However, the appeals to violence and aggression found in both movements are similar, and therefore may attract the same individuals.

Iwai[23] notes that the old-time yakuza are much concerned with the changing conditions of today. He quotes one of the traditional bosses as saying,

What is happening today has never happened before. The traditional yakuza used to fight among themselves and sometimes steal, but it was only a matter of living in underworld society. If a yakuza caused injury to ordinary people, we used to punish him immediately. It was not permitted by our rules to

---

[21] A skill used to subdue or cripple an enemy using the open hand. The side of the hand, used by experts, can be a lethal weapon.

[22] The relationship between some yakuza bosses (disguised as presidents of construction companies and the like) and politicians was illustrated by an incident which took place a few years ago. At the funeral ceremony of a yakuza leader a large expensive bouquet was openly sent by a noted politician of ultraconservative orientation.

[23] Iwai, *Antisocial Group and Social Tension* (1954, in Japanese); see also Okada et al., *Study on Social Tension* (1954).

hurt the weak; however, today, force is used against weak people indiscriminately, and there is no longer any sense of order in the yakuza world.

Iwai observes the increasing encroachment of the *gurentai,* or modern mobsters, into the traditional areas of the bakuto, who now practice extortion or blackmail as major sources of income. Bakuto who have sought to stick mainly to gambling have often been pushed out by the gurentai. Many bakuto groups have had to form some kind of liaison with the gurentai in order to continue to exist.

As the boss quoted by Iwai observed, the prohibition against injuring ordinary folk is less true for yakuza today. The traditional bakuto felt some responsibility for protecting his own territory from the encroachment of thieves and other criminals, but modern urban districts cannot be as well controlled and such protective functions are no longer much in evidence.

On the one hand, today's criminal boss tends to establish a fairly impersonal relationship with his underlings and feels little responsibility for their well-being. On the other hand, several cases have been reported in which the subordinates of a boss have ganged together and attacked him. The unquestioned authority and control of the boss is losing force, and if he shows any weakness, his underlings tend to take advantage of him. In one minor youthful gang, for example, one of the underlings stole his boss's bicycle and sold it. Such insubordination would have been unheard of in the past.

The gurentai are more modern organizations which, although they imitate some of the characteristics of the traditional tekiya or bakuto, well exemplify modern changes in underworld relationships. These organizations received a great deal of impetus after new laws made traditional forms of prostitution impossible, and the gurentai took over pandering and protection.

As we noted earlier, in Tokugawa times houses of prostitution were operated by families who behaved very much as merchants in any other activity. They considered that they were in "business," and since the government condoned legal prostitution, these families, although classified as *senmin*[24] or outcastes, in the Tokugawa period, received a degree of acceptance in the social world. Some of these wealthier families, like the wealthiest bakuto, made a show of being patrons of culture and the arts and sent their children to expensive schools. Primogeniture was practiced in such families, requiring the eldest son to continue in the father's business.

This attitude existed as late as 1955, as exemplified by a yearly "open

[24] The "base people," as groups variously called in Tokugawa records as Eta or Hinin collectively. See Dore, *Aspects of Social Change in Modern Japan* (1967), p. 340.

house," held by the wealthiest house of prostitution in the city of Nagoya, attended by the author, De Vos. The affair was attended by numerous government officials and executives of large companies important in the commercial life of the city, and by representatives of the press and television. Each of the many rooms of this house of prostitution was done in the characteristic architectural style of one or another period in Japanese or Chinese history. Representative tea-masters of various schools conducted the tea ceremony in a number of the rooms.

The aged father of the proprietor of the establishment had retired to practice the art of Chinese brush-painting. His son, a man in his forties, who was a graduate of the University of Tokyo and a person of considerable accomplishment, lived in the establishment with his wife and several children. He said that he himself did not like the business, but felt an obligation to continue it at least as long as his father lived.

This incident illustrates several points, namely, that the business of prostitution could be carried on at that time with considerable status, and that it was run not by underworld figures but by individuals who had certain pretensions to social acceptance. It must be noted, however, that prostitution was never completely legal, and was tolerated only in certain areas. Even from Tokugawa times, some forms of prostitution had considerable underworld influence. When laws were passed and enforced making all prostitution illegal, the underworld, which had had control over "street girls," became the dominant force in the operation of houses of prostitution as well.

Gurentai gangs have become increasingly powerful in pleasure-resort areas. They protect undercover houses of prostitution both from minor criminals and from the law, and prevent prostitutes from running away. Some are employed by cabarets and bars as bouncers and strong-arm specialists. Like the yakuza, each gurentai group controls a recognized territorial area. In districts where the yakuza are more powerful, the gurentai sometimes function as a suborganization under the jurisdiction of a yakuza boss. In general, the gurentai, which lack the formal patterns of oyabun-kobun relationship, are the newer form of the modern underworld organizations now shaping up in modern Japan. They function in places where businesses are operating on the fringes of the law. They are intermediaries in personal negotiations of competitors who use rival gurentai for protection, with threat and counterthreat, such confrontations are of financial benefit, at least to the gurentai.

The tendency to limit violence to individuals already within the underworld—an attitude derived from gang activities in the past—is apparent within organized gangs even today, though the activities of those outside the gang itself are not controlled. This limitation on violence prevents the stirring up of unnecessary attention from the police. In committing aggressive acts, most gangs therefore attempt to distinguish between the nondelinquent world and other criminal or delinquent groups or individuals. Even the gurentai try to prevent their members from attacking individuals outside their world, and most of their aggressive activities are directed against other gangs or individual delinquents. Casual stealing may also be tabooed.

In our research with the TAT it is noteworthy that in the fantasy stories constructed by delinquents, violence, when depicted, occurs only among members of a delinquent gang. In stories told by American delinquents, no such distinction appears, and instead, aggressive activity is usually directed against some nondelinquent. In Japan there is evidence that a strong tradition in the underworld keeps most aggression directed toward members of outlaw groups; it seldom erupts in attacks on the outside population. There are still special prohibitions, in youthful gangs against the rape of nondelinquent girls, for example; the inference would seem to be that only girls who are demonstrably delinquent are fair game.[25]

Public concern regarding the increase of violence in Japan results not only from the rise in absolute number of assaultive crimes, but also from the fact that the violence seems to be spreading from within the delinquent groups themselves into attacks on the public in general. However, most assaultive crimes occur principally in areas frequented by gangs—pleasure-resort areas, houses of prostitution, cabarets, dance halls, or racetracks. As in the United States, the people from the nondelinquent world who have most contact with these gangs are usually unskilled laborers or other members of the lower class; most white-collar and blue-collar workers have very little contact with any of the criminal elements. Fringe groups, such as street merchants and street musicians, having no well-defined social role, continue to have a great deal of social contact with the criminal element.

Political Activity of Japanese Gangs

Before World War II, many right-wing political parties were directly or indirectly related to yakuza groups, and similar indirect liaisons continued in the postwar period. Today certain gang activities are camouflaged behind a political right-wing ideology; that is, the gangs disguise themselves as minor political parties.

Iwai made a study of seven cases of criminal activities by gangs to see in what way they affected the ordinary populace. These activities

---

[25] Instances are sometimes cited indicating that former outcastes do not limit themselves so readily to these rules.

well illustrate the type of violence and fighting occurring today between gangs.[26] One case cited by Iwai resulted from the arrest of two bakuto groups who were struggling over control of an entertainment district that serviced American soldiers. Another case involved a tekiya group picked up by the police after a struggle with a group of Korean nationals. A third was a conflict between two policemen over their "pay" relationships with a tekiya group. The fourth case involved a somewhat different type of tekiya group, which functioned near a coal mining area. In this case, the police picked up a gang who were acting as strikebreakers and who had gotten into a fight with the labor union. The conflict between the labor union and the gang resulted in the murder of a local policeman and hence came to the specific attention of the authorities. In a fifth case, the publicity given by the *Asahi* newspaper to a particular yakuza group working in the vicinity of an American military base resulted in action by the American military occupation and by the Japanese to stamp out their violence and extortion. The sixth case is an example of the right-wing political activity of yakuza groups; a bakuto group sponsored an attempted assassination of a well-known Communist leader. Case number seven occurred when some younger members of a yakuza group organized strikebreakers in the coal-mine area and tried to kill a union secretary who was considered a Communist. These particular cases illustrate features of gang function that we have previously noted. First is the tendency to support a conservative political ideology and to function against unions and other such organizations, sometimes simply because of the leftist ideology of these organizations, and sometimes because the gangs are paid mercenaries of conservative business interests. (Conservative politicians have on occasion made blatant mention of the support they have received from a tekiya group.) Second is the tendency to direct a great deal of gang violence against other groups like themselves.

A statement in a weekly news magazine, *Shūkan Asahi,* made in 1952 by a right-wing politician, further illustrates the tie with yakuza groups. The particular law referred to was fought very bitterly by liberal elements in the government, since it had to do with the suppression of meetings that could be construed by the police as being in some way "potentially destructive" of the country. The law was very vague and was reminiscent of some of the prewar totalitarian edicts. To quote the politician:

One of the greatest successes of our party was to have enacted a law which is strongly resisted by socialist forces. When the bill came to the Diet, many left-wing students appeared to make a petition. I was warned of this by the

---

[26] Iwai (1954), pp. 104–105.

police beforehand and I was personally asked by the Minister of Justice to try to do something to take care of the situation. I called a tekiya boss, and approximately 100 members of his group got together around the Diet. I am one of the bosses of the tekiya in Tokyo, so that my order was carried out smoothly by every one of our groups in this area. Thus, the students as well as the other left-wing forces were unable to make this petition and to disrupt the discussion of the law, which went on smoothly in the Diet resulting in its enactment. The Minister of Justice as well as some cabinet members gave me many thanks for my assistance.

Another characteristic of the activities of the yakuza groups was their antagonism to the underworld activities of the Chinese and Korean minorities in Japan. After the Japanese defeat, many Korean and Chinese reacted violently against the Japanese authority that had so long exerted severe pressure on them, and some Chinese groups became extremely provocative and openly aggressive in their underworld activities with the weakening of the government under the American occupation. During the occupation, Chinese, Formosan, and Korean groups could use their privileged status as foreigners in smuggling and in black-market operations, and thus had an advantage over their Japanese counterparts. The tekiya felt themselves pushed by the Chinese, and a great deal of tension developed, with Japanese gangs seeking to regain lost power. On one occasion, for example, a member of a tekiya group attacked a Chinese, and so a Chinese group, in retaliation, forced their way into the tekiya headquarters and killed the individual who had committed the assault. A battle broke out, with the tekiya counterattacking the headquarters of the Chinese group with drawn swords. A number of Chinese gathered in the open space by the emperor's palace, almost in battle formation, to launch an attack on the Tokyo tekiya groups generally. A main boss of the tekiya ordered all his organizations to cooperate and armed them with swords and other weapons. Ordinary individuals in the vicinity cleared out to avoid being hurt. The police were unable to cope with the situation, and the American occupational military police were brought in. It was rather ironic that through the action of the tekiya here, against the Chinese underworld, attention was focused on what was becoming a growing problem. This event, as well as others, caused the American military to restrengthen the Japanese police so that they could cope with underworld activities.

Japanese professional criminal gangs have informal relationships with professional groups elsewhere, notably in Hong Kong, the Philippines, Hawaii, and the mainland United States. Although gambling is the chief activity of these groups, smuggling of narcotics, guns, or illegal currency is also quite common. Japanese gangs previously were quite active in narcotics trade with China, but there seems to have been relatively little attempt to push narcotics into Japan itself. Whether this relative lack of narcotics activity in Japan is due to a lack of receptivity on the part of the Japanese to drugs, or whether the Japanese criminal element has some traditional reluctance to push these drugs, cannot be clearly determined.[27]

Japanese Juvenile Gangs

The juvenile gang, as such, was not a characteristic of pre–World War II Japanese society. The recruitment of juveniles into the adult criminal world was always practiced, but the large-scale appearance of highly organized juvenile gangs having indirect relationships with criminal adults is something new to the Japanese scene. Such gangs are in varying degree a symptom of modern industrial urban societies throughout Europe as well as in the United States.

The basis on which some of these juvenile delinquent gangs are related to adult professional groups seems to be an extension of the symbolic oyabun-kobun relationships that still exist in the adult criminal world. An adult subordinate of the criminal boss may develop around himself a small gang of juvenile members toward which he acts as boss. These minor gangs are not formally affiliated with the adult gang in any way, but they assist the activity of their adult sponsor.

Juvenile gangs today are called *chimpira*. Not all chimpira have any direct or indirect connection with adult criminal gangs. Some are groups of aggressively oriented high school students who hang around a pleasure-resort area and engage in minor bullying of one sort or another. When their activities become more definitely delinquent, they usually come in contact with the adult group in whose *nawabari*[28] they function. Sometimes the chimpira will attack a member of a yakuza group without knowing his identity, only to be confronted with the formal organization. In Japan, these juvenile groups seldom find themselves strong enough to cause the type of disruption of the adult organized gangs that has been reported in the United States.[29]

There are two routes through which members of the juvenile gang establish contact with the adult professional group. In one mode of contact a subordinate member of the adult gang meets with the leaders of the juvenile gang and recruits them as loyal but loosely attached

---

[27] In 1960 in all Japan there were approximately 2,000 police cases involving narcotics. Most of these involved stimulant drugs.

[28] Literally, "roped-off area," or jurisdiction.

[29] In this context there is a report that the operation of juvenile gangs in a particular district of New York was so disruptive that members of the organized underworld moved to a new location after unsuccessful attempts to prevent disturbances drawing police attention.

subordinates. This is considered quite an honor by the juveniles so approached, and they then have higher status with rival groups when the affiliation becomes known. A young yakuza who is officially a member of some adult gang (*sakazuki o moratta*) often acts as a leader of a delinquent group, whose members sport a common badge as a symbol of their group membership. Out of such delinquent groups the more promising "tough boys" are later recruited as full-status members of the adult gang organization.

Another mode of recruitment is on an individual basis. When some juvenile gang members become notorious in one way or another in respect to the police or the community, and at the same time handle themselves well, they may be contacted by the adult group and taken in; often this incorporation takes place after some form of conflict. In such situations, members of the juvenile gang who have been disturbing the area sometimes are taken to a room or a quiet street and beaten up by adult yakuza. If the juvenile survives this ordeal in a manly enough fashion and shows himself to be tough and "takes it," the adults may suggest that the youth become a member of their gang. The juvenile, thereupon, is expected to swear loyalty to the adults and become a gang member. This method of recruitment is not unknown to the juvenile gang itself as a means of taking on new membership. Sometimes one gang will defeat another delinquent group and as a consequence form an amalgamation.

Groups considered too young to meet at ordinary pleasure-resort areas, such as dance halls, cabarets, or gambling houses, will seek an occasion for gang activity at some particular shrine festival. "Territorial" fighting much like that described for American gangs is one of the main characteristics of these groups.

Hierarchy is emphasized, starting at a relatively early age within the gangs and throughout the process of recruitment into the adult criminal world, and it is relatively rare today that an individual is recruited into an adult gang without prior apprenticeship, in one form or another, as a juvenile. There are exceptions when an individual of extremely high intelligence and better social background is able to short-cut his way into the professional criminal world, but such individuals are a distinct minority.

Junkichi Abe,[30] much as did Cavan,[31] described four stages of the delinquent's alienation from his own society and attachment to that of the criminal. These stages have geographic as well as psychological distance. The first stage is one in which the delinquent activities occur

---

[30] Abe, "Social Psychology of Delinquency" (1960, in Japanese); see especially pp. 204–225.

[31] Cavan, *Criminology* (1948), pp. 120–125.

in the individual's own family and social setting, either at home, at school, or at work; in this stage, the normal frame of reference is dominant. In the second stage of development of a delinquent identification, the delinquent acts take place outside the home, usually at a place of amusement or in some other questionable area which the delinquent frequents while living at home. In the third stage, the individual has shifted his main activities and relationships outside the home; his major contacts are now in the geographic area of delinquency itself, and characteristically he is with others who are also engaging in delinquent activities. In the fourth and final stage, delinquent identification has become complete and the individual is now an integrated member of a professional delinquent group, in which he finds his major role behavior.

The process of alienation is demonstrated by the author Mizushima, who cites the following case out of his own experience in a juvenile detention home to illustrate a typical development from juvenile gang relationships to adult professional crime.

Kazuro had a very poor school record in primary school and took part in some minor delinquent activities, such as stealing, with his play group, which itself was never defined as specifically delinquent. When he graduated into secondary school at twelve, the group with which he associated gradually became increasingly delinquent in their activities. At first, the group would play truant together, walking around the neighborhood and sometimes stealing iron or steel from a nearby company yard. Since Kazuro was above average in strength, he frequently fought with his friends and readily dominated those boys with whom he came in contact. He was continually disobedient at home, but the family was rather indulgent with him and there were no serious overt conflicts with family members.

By the time he had finished nine years of compulsory education at fifteen, he had developed a reputation in his area as a "tough guy." He seldom committed actual delinquent acts, but by threatening his friends he would extort money from them, which they would then replace by going out themselves and stealing. Older boys who had graduated from the same school heard about him, and one of these youths proposed that he join their delinquent gang. Such a "pickup" by an older group is not accidental, but is done, as in this case, on a somewhat systematic basis. Every year new recruits are looked over much as university graduates are "scouted" by major business companies. Thus, Kazuro became familiar with the amusement area where the gang operated and also became acquainted with other boys who had graduated from school and become leaders of some of the other gangs operating out of the same area. Nevertheless, he continued his contact with the previous group in his old school and sought to introduce others of his friends to his new associates. This affiliation to the previous group was necessary as a source of funds for his amusement in the pleasure resorts, and also because he, in turn, was required to give money to his new associates.

At this stage, Kazuro sometimes left home for considerable periods of time, during which he stayed with his associates. He showed considerable bravado in his new group and took easily to drinking and gambling. He found it not difficult to establish his domination over others among his new associates, and gradually gained in stature in the new group. He was arrested by the police and brought to court several times, but was never put in any institution, because the police could not cite him for any major offense. After some time, he became personally acquainted with a member of an adult gurentai group which had jurisdiction over this particular amusement area, and it was not long before he was invited to join the adult group. His contacts with this group in a minor amusement area permitted him to go to the larger resort area more central in the city.

By this time he had broken completely with his family and lived most of the time with his adult companions in a gurentai group. He gave up the minor job he had held since graduation from school, and the gurentai gave him the job of getting acquainted with managers of pinball establishments and thus finding ways to buy back cigarettes, candy, and cake from the winners who preferred cash. These articles, bought cheaply from the customers, could then be sold at a profit to an ordinary store. This is one type of petty business activity through which minor gurentai obtain funds. When such business did not go well and the group lacked money, they would go out on the street and extort money from passers-by, threatening them with violence.

Kazuro was arrested for extortion and sent to a reformatory. He showed no regret concerning his arrest because his time spent at the reformatory was one indirect means of gaining status in the underworld. Indeed, when he was interviewed at the prison he explained that having now obtained sufficient status within his group he would no longer have to occupy himself with minor activities, but upon his release would have subordinates working for him.

A second illustration of a Japanese juvenile's entrance into the adult world of crime is provided by Berrigan,[32] who describes the life history of a rather well known yakuza boss. Oza was born into the family of a small lower-middle-class manufacturer. The father, who loved the boy's stepmother, a prostitute, to an inordinate degree,

---

[32] Berrigan, *The Society of Gangs* (1955, in Japanese).

ignored his clever son. The stepmother was cruel to Oza and used to beat him, and he, in turn, became a bully at school. At last he ran away from home and became a vagrant, begging from adults in a Tokyo park and sleeping in the park at night. Sometimes he was beaten up by other vagrants or criminals in the area, but finally an older boy picked Oza as his kobun and from that time he was trained, under the supervision of his mentor, as a member of a pickpocket group. Later, he became acquainted through the group with the tekiya operating in his area, and because of his violent, strong, "masculine" personality he rapidly rose within the ranks of this group until he became an oyabun.

These two cases illustrate the gradual mobility that is usual within the hierarchy of the Japanese criminal system, although individuals from a higher-class background sometimes move along more rapidly in the recruitment system.

Berrigan also cites the case of a doctor's son, Tsutomu, who was forced by his father to follow the father's career and go to medical school. Tsutomu hated his studies and looked for some opportunity to quit. One day he went into a restaurant where two young men were fighting. When the fighting became so furious that the tables and chairs of the restaurant were being broken, an old gentleman came in, intervened, and with a mild smile was able to stop the fighting immediately. The old gentleman said something to the young men and left the restaurant, still smiling in a gentle way. The medical student, amazed at this man's personal force and wondering what the source of such control and presence could be, asked the bar girl who he was and she identified him as the famous "boss" of that area. Tsutomu wanted desperately to meet the old man, and although the bar girl said it would be impossible, he was so insistent that he located the old man's residence and followed him around. Tsutomu abandoned the study of medicine, and at last met a subordinate of the old man who was impressed by the seriousness of his attitude and introduced him. The student thus became a member of the yakuza group and was given high status from the first because of his serious attitude and his good social background.

Such cases are very rare; they illustrate, however, many of the Japanese virtues, such as intensity of allegiance and seriousness of purpose. Recruitment into professional gangs out of the middle class is not in itself a rare phenomenon.

The author, De Vos, interviewed Masao, a young man of nineteen in prison, whose induction into the underworld is a good illustration of another type of recruitment, one based on quasi-familial ties. It is clear in the previous case of Tsutomu that part of the appeal of the old man was as a father symbol, and similarly in the case of Masao the need for some familial tie was most evident.

Masao, whose father was killed in the war, was the son of a wealthy upper-middle-class family. His mother became the mistress of a wealthy oil industrialist, and at an early age Masao was sent to live with his grandparents. Eventually his mother married the industrialist, and Masao at the age of nine was brought to live with his new stepfather and mother. The boy was highly rebellious in this relationship and did poorly in school, opposing all efforts of his parents to send him to special schools. In adolescence Masao took up with delinquent groups and spent much of his time in amusement areas. Unusual circumstances brought him into contact with the wife of a yakuza leader, who became maternally attached to him. As a result of this relationship, Masao became a courier for the yakuza group, delivering stolen commodities. He was eventually caught and sent to a training school. His fantasy now is to "go straight" and open a barber shop, a trade he has been learning in the reformatory. However, one may speculate about whether, upon release, Masao will not rejoin his yakuza group and take up his position not only as a kobun of the chief but also as a favorite "son" of the chief's wife.

CONCLUSIONS AND DISCUSSION

An historical perspective on Japanese gangs affords, as does any historical approach to groups of individuals in Japanese society, a view of both continuity and change with modernization. Some supposed changes, however, upon closer scrutiny often turn out to be mere surface phenomena rather than symptoms of basic shifts in group behavior. History teaches that one must exercise great caution in assuming that any form of social behavior is without precedent in the past. Yet, however critical we may be of attempts to define that vaguely felt social ambience we call modernization, we cannot escape an awareness of its presence throughout today's world. In discussing the underworld, as any other feature of Japanese culture today, it is necessary to make as careful an effort as possible to delineate how the past continues into the present so as to assess with some degree of cogency what is "modern" about what we observe.

Alienation and the Adolescent Social World

One basic conceptual change seems to differentiate delinquent and criminal behavior today from that noted in the past. The necessary specialization of industrial urban society in its need for increased specialization in all class segments has been changing the definition of adulthood. Adulthood is now preceded by a less socially responsible, transitional, preparatory period called adolescence. Adolescence has become so universally recognized as a definite period in social maturation that it is difficult for many to conceive of a culture in which it does not exist. A careful study of Western culture as well as of Japanese culture, however, reveals it to be an essentially modern concept.

In the next chapter I discuss more fully how social definitions of adulthood are related to youthful alienation. Adolescence, as a separate, legally defined, "age-graded" period in the technical usage of anthropology is socially visible in deviant as well as in conforming behavior within Japanese society. As a reflection of the modern age it seems apparent that there is a proneness for what is termed personal or social alienation to occur within this adolescent period in forms not as directly visible or as easily defined in the past. Amorphously structured juvenile gangs are a new feature of Japanese society, at least insofar as they are defined as distinct from the adult world.

The gangs of yakko that appeared in a previous unsettled period in Japanese history could possibly be considered as parallel phenomena to youthful gangs today. But their social function and definition by society were quite different. Delinquent gangs today conform neither to the majority society nor to the professionalized world of crime. They are essentially an expression of alienated social behavior without any clear definition of purpose.

Alienation and the Loss of Fictive Kinship

A second major change noted in Japanese gang behavior is a shift from adherence to a system of personal, pseudo-kinship loyalties to a more overtly expediential, less formal, more impersonal structuring of relationships. While ties between outlaws in the past were often expediential, motives had to be cloaked in the garb of personal, family-type relationships, virtuously expressed through the exercise of a system of mutual obligations. The criminal world reflected the value system of the majority society in this respect.

In the modern period the breakdown of this formal system of loyalties is to be found also in the changing structure of the underworld. The old *yakuza katagi* is breaking down. Members of this segment of society are consciously bemoaning the fact that no such ties seem to inhibit or guide the behavior of the newer gangs. Before concluding, however, that this shift in ideology represents an actual shift in behavior within the underworld, considerable caution must be exercised. As we have indicated, some dispassionate studies of the past would show that the influence of outlaw codes or behavior can readily be exaggerated. Nevertheless, the shift from personalized ties, whatever may have been their breach in behavior, to impersonal expediency in the underworld must be considered a symptom of modernization.

The Function of Outlaw Legends in Modern Society

In our discussion of the Japanese outlaws of the past we have briefly noted how they serve as heroes of legends. The function of these legends, however, has shifted somewhat with modernization. Today outlaws are no longer direct symbols of revolt from arbitrary political oppression. The more recent use of these legends in Japan, we would suggest, fulfills the same sort of need that is so apparent in the American concern with the cowboy. Legendary outlaws become symbols of unfettered masculinity and freedom of initiative, even violence, within societies in which such outlets are less directly available for most. The sense of confinement has become more internalized, in a sense more psychological.

Today both Japan and the United States comprise highly complex, commercial-bureaucratic social organizations. They are "service" societies in which one must please one's clients and superiors for self-advancement. Attainment of social status within an acceptable position in the dominant class demands a sustained commitment to a long-range career. The direct expression of aggressive feelings is severely inhibited lest one irreparably damage one's chances in a society with a well-organized memory file that records even inconsequential events throughout one's career. In other words, the romanticized cowboy figure which has become a fantasy outlet for an increasingly conformist American society has a parallel in yakuza legends which serve as a similar expressive outlet in Japan.

Legends of undomesticated, untamed outlaws of the past or of the present, uncaptured by commitment, have a particular appeal to youth during adolescence, since these echo their own desires to remain uninvolved—to escape from what appears to them to be a confining, unrewarding, continuity of adult existence.

Persistence of the Gang Member as a Personality Type

Case histories suggest that certain patterns tend to appear in the family histories, both of famous yakuza of the past and of modern delinquents. Although materials are sketchy and unclear, we can gain from such histories an impression of some selective features in the family which would seem to be conducive to delinquency formation in the present-day society just as in the past. Repeatedly mentioned are experiences such as running away from home at an early age, rejection, or some form of alienation from parents and a social environment during childhood filled with sexual irregularities or preoccupation with sexual activity on the part of parents or other close figures. Such material suggests that whereas the overall social structure may be changing in Japan, underlying personality variables orienting an individual toward deviant behavior are less changed by modernization.

A perusal of personal descriptions of yakuza in the past as well as of delinquents in the present leads one to infer continuity in those personality factors and social attitudes that selectively lead an individual to enter upon a career of crime. In the literature of the Japanese concerning the yakuza, one is repeatedly impressed by descriptions of certain characteristic aggressive personalities found in the criminal world. "Masculinity," as an exploitative aggressiveness, and a concern with either dominance or submission are much emphasized.

There is some continuity in the oyabun-kobun relationship of the Japanese criminal world because it is emotionally satisfying. This formal structure not only is a means of organizing or controlling criminal activity itself, but also allows for types of dominant-subordinate relationships in which personal expression of aggressive masculinity, and at the same time a strong dependent relationship on a dominant figure, are part of the rewards to be gained. Even though these organizations are diminishing, today's juvenile delinquents in Japan seem to want to belong to something which might provide such a relationship. We are finding evidence in our empirical data of such concerns in adolescents.

There seems to be, in delinquent as well as in nondelinquent youth, the need to find a suitable father figure with whom to identify, in an active or a passive sense. By itself, such concern has no specific relation to delinquency. However, once this preoccupation in individual cases becomes intermeshed with pressing, ill-controlled needs for self-gratification at the expense of society, without tolerance for delay, or in a context of violence, the deviant society of the underworld becomes an attractive arena for personal activity.

Political Ideology and the Personality of the Gang Member

Perhaps the most interesting aspect of the organized yakuza gang member's ideological adaptation to recent social change is his ready adoption of conservative nationalist philosophies and his periodic appearance as a force in the political arena. This affinity with right-wing attitudes may well be partially explicable in terms of the personality factors we have just mentioned, namely, his concern with dominance and subordination as well as a propensity of violence. Some types of personality structure cannot well tolerate types of association demanding mutual internalized self-control and self-discipline. One type of delinquent cannot express aggressiveness through intellectual channels; he is more likely to employ physical means. Such a modern institution as a give-and-take political discussion is somewhat alien to his makeup.

Rightist organizations in Japan give an outlet for a more physically aggressive type of expression and allow for certain political-social rationalizations of this aggressive behavior. A need for some form of strong external authority, also a part of the criminal personality in many cases, puts emphasis on the virtues of manliness and bravery in a manner harmonious with a rightist ideology but basically antithetical to a more liberal approach to public affairs. Hypernationalism goes well with the caricature of the romanticized warrior's code that is used in yakuza groups even today. More immature personality types with incomplete control systems feel more at home in situations of officially tighter social control. Attempts at implementing a challenging, emotionally difficult, democratic social atmosphere bring forth uneasiness and a tendency toward the outer expression of physical aggression. The yakuza gang today in Japan in many instances has become a group of bully boys who are found useful to others in situations such as labor-management conflict or in political demonstrations of the extreme right. They have little else to recommend them, in spite of the legends of humanistic activity to which they have supposedly subscribed in the past.

In one sense the personality predispositions of the yakuza "fit" better in the past. They are ill-suited to the modes of egalitarian, nonaggressive behavior now predominant in modern society. Such individuals are now perceived as delinquent rather than "hot-blooded" youth.

In the present age, however, we have seen frightful throwbacks to barbarism with such shifts in the control of power as occurred under the Nazis and the Japanese militarists. These reversions struck the unprepared modern conscience as somehow unreal atavisms until it was too late to control them. The fact that modern society generally condones only less direct forms of aggressive behavior does not change human nature and its proneness toward violence, nor does it put an end to its lust for activities and releases not overtly countenanced by the legal codes reflecting majority consensus. The Japanese underworld, in its recruitment of professional personnel as well as in its providing for the periodic indulgences in unsanctioned activities on the part of otherwise conforming citizens, performs apparently inescapable social functions today as it did in the past.

Modernization and Changes in Institutionalized Social Sanctions

It is not possible to determine objectively the validity of the lament of present-day yakuza about an increasing absence of self-control in youth which would serve to delimit the perpetration of haphazard delinquent acts. The yakuza today tend to see themselves as being able to exercise less control not only over other criminals operating in their own territory but also over the tendencies for their younger members to victimize innocent outsiders. Such acts are seemingly part of a general tendency on the part of uncommitted segments of the modern younger generation toward more "impersonal," less socially inhibited attitudes. Police reports suggest that robbery and rape committed by individuals under age twenty have increased radically in recent years. Youth now comprise a notably larger proportion of offenders brought to the attention of the police. While the concentration of reported criminal acts still is heaviest in entertainment areas, their surrounding vicinities as well are no longer considered safe for the casual visitor.

What one could gather from reports of this nature is that the adult criminal organizations seem to have less direct contact with or control over alienated delinquent youth. These youths, motivated by their own interests, are detached from direct influence of sanctions applied to them either by legitimate society or by the underworld itself.

There is no doubt that the forms of social control are changing in the more stable modern societies. Not only are police agencies encouraged toward increasing impersonal and systematic exercise of justice extended to all levels of society, but other newer welfare agencies are increasingly instituted to "treat" the deviant or criminal offender as well as control him through punitive sanctions. With the lessening of the harshness of punitive sanctions more deviant behavior is readily visible and, perhaps, earlier in the life cycle. Less concealment due to the lessening of repression indicates not a greater degree of potential for deviancy in the society but a greater awareness of these suppressed elements in human nature.

We believe that modernization in Japan, to an extent difficult to assess, is represented not only in some changes in the structure and functions of criminal gangs which we have examined in this chapter, but more generally in the way social sanctions are institutionalized, by what agencies they are exercised, and to what degree they partake of what we may call a modern professionalization and depersonalization of social facilities through special training of agency personnel. Modernization as it affects the expression of deviant behavior, singly or in groups, may result more in a change in the institutionalized social perception of behavior in some instances rather than in gross changes in the total incidence of specific deviant behavior itself. Nevertheless, changes in social perception in turn strongly influence the openness, the group context, and the social circumstances in which behavior can be expressed—so too with gang behavior within modern Japan.

Chapter XII

Adolescence and Delinquency
in Cross-Cultural Perspective

"ADOLESCENCE" AND "DELINQUENCY"—
MODERN AGE-GRADING CONCEPTS

Anthropological material on crime and custom contains no data that can be related directly to the concept of "juvenile delinquency" or simply "delinquency" as the term is now used in criminology. It is not that anthropologists concerned with criminal or deviant behavior in primitive social systems have ignored the subject; it is simply that such a concept has no real relevance in preindustrial social structures. If a delict is committed by an individual considered a minor, and the age of the offender is of no importance to the society, there will be no formal indication of his age. Although there are societies, such as the Zuni, which have institutionalized systems to keep children in line, the age level at which this sanctioning system operates is certainly far below the "adolescent" level in society today. In most societies, until recently, minors have been "children" who if they committed acts that needed serious sanctioning were then regarded as having acted as adults. Individuals in preindustrial societies whose behavior is counter to that expected are treated either as children or as adults. "Adolescence" as a transitional age does not appear in such societies in any form resembling that in modern society, and it certainly does not appear in respect to any concept of criminal behavior.

There is a tendency, however, for modern social-science writers, even those taking a cross-cultural approach, to overlook this cultural-historical fact. For example, although they have assembled a tremendous amount of cogent material concerning the nature of youth societies and deviant behavior in youth, in non-Western as well as Western cultures, Gottlieb, Reeves, and TenHouten in their recent volume, *The Emergence of Youth Societies*,[1] use the term "adolescence" as if it were universally applicable to preindustrial societies. But the evidence they present does not establish that the concept of adolescence, as they use it, is appropriate to describe a preadult stage in most of the cultures they cite. They interpret the initiation ceremonies of primitive societies as moving an individual from an "adolescent" to an adult status, but the evidence of anthropologists, who almost invariably avoid using the term, would suggest that the transition is more often directly from childhood to an adult status with no recognition of an intermediate adolescent period.

The age at which an individual arrives at adult status varies widely among the world cultures and is highly dependent on the technology and social organization of the society considered. Adult status may be acquired abruptly as an end to childhood, or the individual may go through an elaborate series of age-grades—with minutely defined roles and status prerogatives—none of which would properly be designated as "adolescence." In modern societies arrival at the status of adult is governed less by the biological change of puberty than by the social recognition that the individual male or female is ready to assume the occupational responsibilities assigned an adult. Arensberg[2] cites the extreme case of rural Ireland, where property ownership helps define the adult status and where individuals as old as forty-five may be referred to as "boy," symbolizing their lack of right to marry or to assume any of the usual prerogatives of adult social status.

In most preindustrial societies that celebrate any formal ceremonial passage into adulthood this usually occurs not so much with reference to when the individual is able to function adequately in an adult social role, but more directly with reference to his biological puberty and physiological capacity for reproduction. Until recently, the age of adulthood was defined in most simple societies as earlier than it generally is in modern cultures. For example, circumcision rituals, usually held at the time of puberty, admit boys into the order of men in many societies.[3] From this rite are derived the bar mitzvah of the Jews, which takes place after age twelve, and Christian confirmation. In Japan there was the rite of *genpuku* (clothing initiation), the formal recognition of adulthood, which could take place as early as fourteen, to mark the attainment of manhood among samurai, and, later, among farmers, artisans, and merchants as well.

From the perspective of the social anthropologist, delinquency is essentially a modern concept related to the appearance of a self-con-

[1] Gottlieb, Reeves, and TenHouten, *The Emergence of Youth Societies* (1966).

[2] Arensberg, *The Irish Countryman: An Anthropological Study* (1937).

[3] Van Gennep, *The Rites of Passage* (1960).

sciously transitional adolescent period in industrial societies. Modern definitions of "delinquency" reflect ambivalent social attitudes concerning the ambiguous status of youth during adolescence, and have been used only recently to legally separate the concept of juvenile delinquency from that of adult crime. It is necessary, therefore, from an anthropological perspective to examine the function of the adolescent period in the total life cycle of members of an industrial society. The occupational complexities in modern societies have brought about a necessary period that is termed "adolescence"; thus the age at which a person arrives at social maturity has been deferred a significant number of years. Biological deferment of human adulthood has previously occurred in human evolution; the uniquely long cultural-physiological extension of childhood in humans already allows for cultural learning to take place over a longer period than in any other related animal species. This physiological moratorium on reproductive capacities and the associated deferment of hormonal activity allow for greater ingestion of culturally oriented knowledge of the environment with a diminution of egocentric, bodily oriented physiological preoccupations.

In all human societies, including modern industrial ones, the definition of adulthood as the achievement of the biological capacity to reproduce is further superseded by even more strictly cultural definitions as a capacity to assume occupationally productive work and to participate in the decision-making functions of adult society.

In industrial societies the social structure requires that the individual assume a technologically specialized vocation in order to care for a family of procreation, and a complex social organization is also less dependent than a simple one on kinship or lineage considerations. In societies organized on the basis of a lineage or extended kinship, adult responsibilities are less independently focused on a nuclear biological family, reproduction can occur earlier, and fewer independent decisions are required of the individual members. More technologically complex societies emphasize the individual rather than the lineage, and require considerably more experience for independent decision-making than is usually available to postpubescent youth of fourteen or fifteen. Adulthood is deferred by a period of adolescence in the total age-grading system emerging within modern societies.

In general, age-grading systems are attempts at relating various social maturation stages to appropriate culturally determined social statuses. Age-grading systems are seldom determined only by biological considerations, although the maturation of socially useful talents is involved; they recognize more or less formalized or ceremonialized changes of status reflecting changes in prowess or in capacity or in the assumption of responsibility. Within the more complex achievement-oriented societies of the present day, there are implicit, if not explicit,

definitions of roles related to the complex system of acquired statuses
that demarcate the sequence through which all adults must pass.

THE ONSET OF ADULTHOOD IN PREMODERN JAPAN

During the chaotic period preceding the Tokugawa shogunate,
when government control was inconstant and continual conflicts between warring factions kept the martial virtues of the samurai in the
forefront, physical maturity was necessary to becoming a man. The
age of childhood was more protracted, therefore, than it was during
the Tokugawa period, when considerations of family liaisons led to
lowering the age of marriage. During the long feudal era, although
there was no social concept resembling modern adolescence, the elaborate clothing ritual, *genpuku,* marked the ceremonial day of transition
from childhood to adulthood. The performance of the genpuku ceremony designated both readiness for a final commitment to a particular
adult career and the age after which marriage could appropriately
take place, the individual thereafter being accorded full adult status in
all civil respects. Genpuku was modeled after a Tang dynasty Chinese
custom and in some form is thought to date back at least to the seventh-
century Nara period (646–794); historians note the first recorded reference to it at about 714 A.D.

The age of adulthood recognized in Japan varied by period and by
social class. The age at which a genpuku ceremony was given for a
particular individual also varied depending on the judgment of his
readiness to assume full adult status. Usually the ceremony took place
sometime between a youth's twelfth and sixteenth years[4] but occasionally it was delayed until he was almost twenty.

During the premodern Tokugawa period, expected social role behavior in the class-caste system of Japanese society was minutely defined by sumptuary laws. The warrior-administrative class, including
various ranks of nobility, was the governing body of the nation. The
ordinary folk consisted of the merchant, artisan, and farming classes
in that order. Below these classes were the outcaste pariahs, or Senmin,
considered to be two grades of "subhumans," the Hinin and the Eta,
ritually polluted either by occupation, circumstance, or heredity.[5]

For the youthful samurai, marriages were very often put off for from
one to two years after the date of the genpuku ceremony, which was
used in the warrior class to establish a particular *oyabun-kobun* relationship.[6] The ceremony bound a youth entering manhood to a

---

[4] *Encyclopedia of Japanese History* (1959), p. 156.
[5] DeVos and Wagatsuma, *Japan's Invisible Race: Caste in Culture and Personality* (1966).
[6] Bennett and Ishino, *Paternalism in the Japanese Economy* (1963).

prominent high-status warrior, the *eboshi-oya,* who placed his helmet on the head of the youth being initiated to signify that he would accept him as a follower and would see to his fullest development in his newly entered warrior-administrative career.

The genpuku ceremony served to confirm the relative social status among samurai families. For example, if one family was traditionally in servant status to another family, the boy of the first family at the time of genpuku would begin his retainer role at the house of the higher status family.

There was no elaborate ceremony to mark adult status for women, who were always, officially at least, in a dependent, subservient position in respect to men. Women were subject to criminal procedures from the age of fourteen. In the Tokugawa period, among the samurai the marriage ceremony itself was the occasion for recognition of a woman as an adult, and at that time a woman was usually given gifts or possessions belonging to her house which she would find of use in her new career.

In times of strife, the young warrior could become a full participant in battle following the genpuku ritual. As indicated in the previous chapter,[7] groups of young warriors, called *hatamoto yakko,* would periodically terrorize the townspeople, and youths from among the *chonin,* or townspeople, would form counter groups, called *machi-yakko,* sometimes with minor battles as the result.[8] In more peaceful times the young warriors sometimes formed what were called *waka-mono-gumi,* or youth groups, which might be said to represent a transitional status somewhat resembling adolescence, although youths in these groups had full adult status.

In southern Kyushu in the Kagoshima area it was the custom for those youths who passed through the genpuku ceremony at approximately fourteen or fifteen years of age to join a young man's group which was made responsible for the protection of the neighborhood and for police activities, as well as for carrying on cultural and welfare projects. At about the age of twenty-five they would move from such a group into a group of older men; very often marriage would take place at this time, marking the transition to a full level of adulthood.

In the Kagoshima young men's groups there were strict rules and routines to be followed and improper behavior was severely punished. The overall purpose of the young men's groups was physical and spiritual training as well as intellectual study. Casual communication with members of other groups was strictly prohibited, and harmonious and cooperative feelings were encouraged within each group formed by

---

[7] Chapter 11.

[8] Nakayama, *History of Japanese Youth* (1930, in Japanese).

youths of the same genpuku period. Members of these groups were instructed to obey their elders and were not permitted any form of criticism, and the elders in turn were expected to supervise and be responsible for them. This particular Kagoshima pattern somewhat resembles the pattern of preadults in the role of "students" in modern society.[9] By no means, however, was it a prevailing pattern in Japan.

According to Mitamura,[10] in the early Tokugawa period the genpuku ceremony among warriors was held for youths as old as twenty years, but by the middle of the period the usual age had dropped from fifteen to seventeen, and in the late Tokugawa it was lowered again to between thirteen and fifteen. Mitamura suggests that this was because in the early period of political uncertainty it was not considered advisable to ready youths who were still physically immature for full warrior status, whereas during the long periods of peace in the later Tokugawa era the pressure for earlier marriages to insure the family succession increased so that the marriage age was lowered considerably, and, therefore, the genpuku ceremony took place at an earlier age.

During the Muramachi period (1338–1573) the custom of having some sort of genpuku ceremony spread from the samurai to the wealthier segments of other classes as a means of designating entrance into occupational roles. The farming-class families developed their own usage for this ceremony similar to that of the warrior. For most of the Tokugawa period the males of this class were regarded as coming of age between their fifteenth and seventeenth years.[11] After the ceremony, farmers' sons changed their hair styles, and many also changed their given names. Thereafter the young men were expected to work equally in the fields with their parents and to assume special roles during the shrine ceremonies that marked their higher status in the neighborhood; also they now had the right to marry.

The form taken by the ceremony among farmers varied from region to region, in some places being held individually and in others collectively. Sometimes the youths were gathered together and each one was presented with a tool for farm labor or a shirt to wear in the fields as a symbol of his initiation into his adult occupation. Initially, entrance into the young men's group and genpuku had different origins, but by the middle of the Tokugawa period the ceremony of adulthood was necessary to enter into the young men's group.[12]

As we noted above, after genpuku young farmers were eligible to

---

[9] Dainihon Rengō Seinendan (Society of Japanese Youth), *Wakamono Seido no Kenkyū* (Research on Young Men's Organizations) (1936).

[10] Mitamura, *The Life of a Samurai* (1956, in Japanese).

[11] *Ibid.*

[12] Kitajima, *The Edo Era* (1958, in Japanese).

marry,[13] but many of them remained for some time within the young men's group. This group was most active in setting up shrine festivals and other community recreational activities, as they still are in many rural areas of Japan. At such periodic rituals, usually in commemoration of a local tutelary diety, vigorous physical behavior, approaching violence, was manifested to symbolize the prosperity and productivity of the village or township.

The age range of individuals included within particular festival groups was wide; sometimes those remaining in such a group were as old as thirty-five. Nevertheless, a genpuku ceremony always marked the lower age of eligibility. By late Tokugawa, as noted above, genpuku and entrance into a young people's group were generally blended together.[14] Sometimes the youth, accompanied by his father, would ceremonially promise the group to abide by its rules. In addition to their recreational and festival programs these groups supervised training activities and maintained a continuous night watch, which could also mobilize for fire-fighting.

These groups also functioned as policing or sanctioning agents for the community. If a group member or some member of the community committed a minor violation, he might be beaten or prohibited from wearing a particular item of warm clothing on cold days. Such a person, if a group member, might leave the youth group or if he had committed a more serious offense he could be subjected to a form of exclusion called *murahachibu*. This punishment cut off, either temporarily or permanently, the usual interpersonal communication with other villagers and was often extended to include members of the offender's family. The most extreme punishment was banishment, but when *murahachibu* was practiced, a direct order of banishment was often not necessary, the individual or family being constrained to leave because life within the village became unbearable.

For farm women from thirteen to seventeen years of age there was sometimes a minor ceremony related to preparation for marriage. They would join in a sewing circle or in groups concerned with other activities preparatory to marriage. This would mark the girl's accessibility for either casual or more permanent sexual liaisons with unmarried members of the young men's group, depending on the region or village.

Social intercourse between the young men's and young women's groups was fairly free, and sexual liaisons occurred without any of the strictures observed among the samurai. The form of these relationships and the emotional tone taken toward them varied greatly

[13] *Heibonsha Dictionary for World History* (1959).

[14] Kitajima, *op. cit.*

by village and region; extremes were practiced that amounted to the condoning of rape, whereas in other settings, the mutual consent and affection of both parties was expected.

The practice of "night crawling," or *yobai,* was widespread in rural Japan as a means both of condoning and of controlling premarital affairs. After dark a young man would visit a girl's house "in secret" with a towel disguising his features, often merely as a symbol of anonymity to avoid embarrassment in the event that his advances were rejected. Such liaisons often became formal if a child was born. Official marriage consisted of the entering of the bride's name into the young man's family register, and was often withheld until the fertility of the couple was demonstrated. If a liaison remained too long infertile, official marriage would not be recognized even though the girl had already come to live in the man's household.[15]

Among the artisan class, the *shokunin,* the age of the onset of adulthood was related to a system of apprenticeship closely resembling that developed by European guilds during the Middle Ages. When a child reached the age of eleven to thirteen, if he was not apprenticed at home, he went to live as a servant with a master from whom he was expected to learn a particular skill. Before the Tokugawa period this period of training, *nenkibōkō,* was relatively short, but it became more and more protracted as masters were motivated to exact as much cheap labor as possible from their charges. Although the artisan class held a genpuku ceremony, they did not recognize adulthood until the apprentice was considered ready for independence (sometimes not until he was from twenty to twenty-two years old), and the termination of *nenkibōkō* thus became more important in designating adult social status than the official initiation ceremony. For Japanese artisans, the gradual extension of a transitional period functioned as a form of adolescence and was related both to economic motives and to the increasing difficulty in gaining the technical competence required by many of the more refined Japanese crafts. By the end of the Tokugawa period, among the merchants as among the artisans, the period of dependent apprenticeship grew very protracted. During this late feudal period, the head of any prosperous merchant establishment demanded a long strict period of training for those youths who were assigned to him.

We can cite one specific instance as illustrative. In a well-known apprenticeship with numerous employees, the employer selected boys of eleven or twelve from among the "good" families of his own district. Assigned various minor jobs, these youths were kept as *koyo,* or errand boys, for their first five years. When they were sixteen or seventeen,

---

[15] *Ibid.*

an official genpuku ceremony of adulthood marked the end of this period and began the progressive assignment of more responsibility. Even so, they were not considered adults in either occupational or marital status and were retained as apprentice merchants for approximately another eight years. They were then allowed to return home and could establish some affiliate activity or continue to work for the merchant in a higher capacity.

It was not unusual for a dependent relationship to continue so long that marriage and full independence were put off until the man was from thirty-five to forty.[16] This delay in marriage among the merchant class was functionally related to the semipublic role of prostitution in the towns and cities; large numbers of unmarried apprenticed merchants swelled the crowds in the Japanese gay-quarters.

Little data are available on the practices of the hereditary pariahs. In a sense, they never reached the status of "human," much less that of adult. It can be assumed that only a few outcastes who were economically or politically better off than their fellows would seek to emulate the practices of the majority people by observing some formal initiation into adulthood. However, in some special groups of entertainers or artists whose families were originally of outcaste origin, elaborate ceremonial occasions did develop to signal mastery of an art form.

With the acquisition of higher status, special types of apprentice systems were instituted to mark progressions in proficiency. For example, among geisha the end of a *maiko* apprenticeship and entrance into the full role of adult woman entertainer usually took place when the girl was fifteen or sixteen—an occasion that is still marked by an arranged act of deflowering by a wealthy patron, who pays heavily for the privilege. Subsequently, this patron will often support the geisha for a protracted period, during which time he claims exclusive rights as her lover.

In the world of the Japanese theater there are acts of recognition to separate the various stages of proficiency marked by the progressive forms of apprenticeship, resulting for the more talented in final full recognition as a mature actor or performer. No one of these stages can logically be designated as "adolescence." The concept is not useful in attempting to describe the age-grading of proficiency and experience in the art and entertainment world of Japan.

In summary, in Japan it is only among the town-dwelling artisans and merchants that anything like an adolescent moratorium of the modern type appears. It is specifically among the merchants and artisans that the genpuku initiation ceremony gradually lost its original symbolic meaning as marking full adulthood. In these groups it came

---

[16] *Heibonsha Dictionary for World History* (1959).

to be used to define entrance into a more advanced preparatory stage of training, and in this sense some concept of a subadult stage preceding full adulthood came into being among the town-dwellers in Japanese society as a precursor to modern urban concepts of adolescence. The putting off of adulthood in these groups can be related directly to an emphasis on the increased time necessary to acquire technical competence. No such extension of adulthood appeared in rural regions. Adult-type farm work could be started at an early age, and the warrior class had strong motivation for early recognition of adulthood to assure proper marriages and thus maintain the ascribed status of their lineages.

More recently in Japan there can be traced the gradual universalization throughout the society of a preadult adolescent stage comparable to that found in modernizing western societies. Such a general stage was not to be found, however, in the divergent social classes that comprised the traditional Japanese culture.

ADOLESCENCE IN MODERN SOCIETY

In modern society emphasis on *achieved* status rather than on *acquired* status has, as a by-product, placed greater emphasis both on individualistic endeavor and on the necessity for individual decision-making. Where an individualizing value orientation prevails, the extended family as a formal structure becomes increasingly dysfunctional, hampering the realization of individual potential achieved by means of extrafamilial occupational relationships.

An unresolved comparative problem for anthropology is the extent to which a society can become industrialized while remaining firmly committed to an extended lineage system. Japan did for some time succeed in maintaining its traditional lineage family system in spite of modernization, but recent trends indicate that this has been a transitory phenomenon. In the past ten years, at an increasing rate, the nuclear family has become an independent decision-making unit in Japanese urban life. Adult, individual decision-making responsibility increasingly includes job choice and choice of a mate. Even family decisions today are made more in respect to the possibilities of personal and social mobility than in respect to maintaining a quasi-religious sense of continuity of lineage.

Those who would contrast the rapidity of Japanese industrialization with the difficulties encountered in the attempted modernization of other Asian cultures based on lineage are often not aware of the degree to which the Japanese in the past subordinated hereditary considerations to pragmatic considerations of competence in selecting household heads to continue the lineage. The widespread Japanese practice of adopting children or young adults as family heirs permitted a continuity of lineage, even where the blood heir was incompetent or no heir existed. Japanese society actually covertly countenanced a great deal of individual and family social mobility within its rigidly segmented class-caste social structure.

Adolescence in Modern Society as a Crisis Period

Kinship or hereditary lineage and acquired social status have little remaining functional value in an individualistic society. Subjective considerations of social status acquired by birth have given way to concerns over individually achieved status as necessary for personal validation. Indeed, through the extension of compulsory formal education beyond the usual period of puberty, modern societies seek to motivate their members toward technological competence. Some young people lack sufficient motivation, a sense of commitment, or the type of personality organization to accept further training as it is organized within the school—a social institution dedicated to the development of achievement-oriented individuals. Such individuals, whose occupations are no longer predetermined, tend to lack a socially approved social role until they are employed. There are various inherent difficulties in the adolescent transition to adulthood and a social occupational commitment. Various forms of deviant behavior arising in modern societies considered "delinquent" in nature must be examined in this total context.

With the highly specialized division of labor appearing with industrialization, social control is shifting from an elite based on hereditary considerations to a technological elite of so-called "middle-class" persons who are expected to be achievement-oriented as individuals. This new elite increases in power and importance as the variety of technical skills and the complexity of the social organization increases. Political power as well as social leadership gradually pass into the hands of an advantaged class that must perpetuate itself through education rather than direct inheritance. The variety of positions demanding special skills accelerates recruitment into the elite and, concomitantly, social mobility so that the family-oriented institutions found in traditional communities can no longer operate as the organizing focus of the total social pattern. Sociologists have called attention to the decline of the stable face-to-face birth-to-death community as an organizing force in social relationships in modern societies. This decline varies with differences in modern cultures in rapid geographic and social mobility. For example, stable face-to-face communities remain relatively numerous in Japan in comparison with the United States.

As an age-grading period, adolescence occurs directly as a result of the shifts in social role definitions and in the expectations of individual, family, and community that accompany changes toward a more mobile, modern social structure. In any discussion of cross-cultural comparison of delinquency, one should be directly concerned with the general social, political, and other issues of industrialization, as well as with the specific implications for the individual of the loss of family lineage and community sanctions, particularly in regard to role definitions in adolescence.

As the newly dominant professional, commercial, and managerial class comes to command a central position in society, it establishes its own occupational-technological criteria for adulthood as part of an achievement-oriented value system and seeks to universalize these criteria at the expense of those held by the less specialized, less achievement-directed lower classes. The merchant class, already technologically oriented most readily to industrialization, thereby tends to become the dominant class in society.

As the demands and pressures of industrialization increase, and the structure of the society depends more on highly motivated individuals seeking their place in a money economy, the criteria for educational accomplishment become more important than age or physical maturity in defining adult social status. In a growing industrial society, adequate training and experience require a longer and longer preparatory period, and it takes a longer time for the individual to be recognized as an adult, taking full part in decision-making and exercising political power. Most societies relate readiness for marriage with the capacity to assume adult occupational responsibility, and the time before official marriage in industrial societies is therefore also delayed.

In Japan, especially, one notes how sexual tension in youths increases as a result of middle-class insistence that heterosexual interests must not interfere with occupational preparation. In the higher professional segments of the middle class in Japan as elsewhere a double standard has permitted some sexual outlet for males during the preparatory period and avoided premature commitments. An individual who makes a premature permanent marital liaison is considered to have jeopardized his total career pattern, as he does also if he fathers children before his occupational stability is fully assured.

Modern society, which stresses achievement and the necessity for geographic and social mobility, also expects these values to be spread throughout the society. This universalization of values underlies the social definitions of adulthood and goals throughout the various social strata of modern society, and is encouraged by legislation. Political responsibility becomes universalized, at least in theory, and all segments of the society are expected to participate in the political power structure at least officially and formally. The definition of adulthood, therefore, must be the same for the lower segments of society and for the technological elite. However, the lower segments of a national culture, both because of recently acquired attitudes and because of their traditional socialization practices, often do not prepare their members adequately for "adolescent" deferment of an adult role. They are not so readily imbued with the internalized constraints and prohibitions expected by the dominant elite, whether in a communist-oriented state or in a political democracy.[17] Modern societies therefore develop special problems of class background, afflicting and alienating certain of their youth, who sometimes become socially deviant in behavior, hence "delinquent."

A major problem of an advanced technological society, such as the United States, is technological unemployment; with automation, those who perform simple manual work are gradually being replaced by machines. Increasingly, specialized technical competence is a necessity and is required of all individuals. All segments of the society, then, must become motivated to undergo longer preparatory vocational training. The modern high school's "commencement" exercises mark formal entrance into an adult vocational role only for those who do not continue their preparatory careers in college, and the proportion of the American population continuing their education beyond high school is increasing yearly.

Public educational facilities are made available to all, but the preparatory socialization experiences of a large percentage of urban youth do not involve them sufficiently in the educative process. Out of this group come the high school "dropouts," most of whom are poorly equipped for technically specialized roles because they lack psychological or intellectual capacities, or integrative personality mechanisms, or the motivation.

The urban area dropout differs from the rural youth who, in the past, left school to take on a man's job. The urban dropout has no job commitment to absorb his energies or to give him increasing competence or skill, and he is recognized as a potential social problem. Another problem discussed only briefly and tangentially in Chapter 16 of this volume is the alienation of advanced college students who do not necessarily drop out of the educational process in secondary schools but instead become politically as well as socially revolutionary as their education continues. Student unrest affecting Japan as well as elsewhere bespeaks the crises occuring in the formal educational process in industrial societies due to rapid expansion of numbers of students and the impersonal group processing of classroom education without

---

[17] Inkeles, Haufmann, and Beier, "Modal Personality and Adjustment to the Soviet Socio-Political System" (1958); Inkeles and Levinson, "National Character: The Study of Modal Personality and Sociocultural Systems" (1954).

direct apprentice-like interpersonal communication between teacher and student. The students in an advanced mass production educational system are not positively related to the society in which they are supposed to take on "adult" roles only after a long-drawn-out, increasingly impersonal apprenticeship as "student." They turn to each other as a reference group and turn away from their elders in increasing mutual distrust.

In modern societies the sanctioning of individuals passes from the face-to-face community to impersonal social agencies, such as the legal court system and the police, and with this shift there may be alienation of given segments of the society, including the youth, who feel that professionalized social agencies are external forces of oppression rather than positive agents of social control. A complex society develops specialists, technically trained in their professions, who make the laws, judge infractions, and arrest and punish "deviants" not only of lower-class origin, but alienated middle-class youth as well. These specialists are imposed on segments of the population with whom they have no other direct contact. In American cities the local police are becoming alien professionals who have little informal contact with the community they are "protecting." The professional police force is so alienated from the communities it supposedly serves that adequate functioning has become impossible in many places. The very definition of delinquency and of other less manifest forms of alienation in adolescence is related to this shift within modern cultures toward impersonality of authority and the professionalization of such sanctioning agencies as the police. Where ethnic as well as class variables segment the society, a greater proportion of alienated youth interact as part of ethnic sub-cultures. As Wagatsuma and I will indicate in Chapter 14, an antagonistic attitude toward social authority exists within the Korean and outcaste minority communities in Japan, as well as within the black, Puerto Rican, and Mexican communities in the United States. One must examine this phenomenon in a cross-cultural perspective, as well as from the standpoint of social-class theory, to understand how such processes of alienation came to occur within specific social segments.

American theorists who argue that "differential opportunity structure" is a determinant of delinquency regard the discouraging features of urban lower-class life as central in the failure of many modern youths to develop specialized, technological competence. Such single-minded interpretations overlook the complexity of the determinants that precede adolescents' actual knowledge of the social opportunity structure. This lack of motivation to acquire necessary specialization is not limited to capitalist societies; within the Soviet Union, there appears to be a significant number of uninvolved youths, uncommitted to any preparation for an adult occupational role. One must examine the question of why this alienation occurs even without technological unemployment.

I do not propose to develop any major theses concerning the nature of age-grading in modern society, but have attempted simply to examine the relationship of the concept of "adolescence" to that of "juvenile delinquency" in Japan. The concept of "delinquency" seeks to differentiate criminally deviant acts of postpubescent juveniles who are no longer "children" from such acts committed by adults, so that there can be differential treatment of the offenders. This attempt at differential treatment is related to the concepts the society holds as to the vocational educability of individuals and the desirability of their "rehabilitation," as well as the responsibility of society for attempting such education.

Most modern societies have recognized that the "adolescent" period is one of crisis, a time of difficult transition for many of its members. In the past the difficulties associated with adolescence were regarded as principally characteristic of the more educated segments of the society, where the crisis experience was one of involvement and commitment in an ideational or religious context. The lower social and ethnic segments of society, now more universally included in the preparatory role of "student," increasingly express the crisis not in ideational terms, but manifest instead deviant acts that mutely signify the difficulties of the transition required. There is considerable resistance in adults to face directly the extent to which the tensions that occur in adolescence are the result of a deferment of both sexual reproductive activities and *meaningful* vocational interests. These tensions are of course not simply biological. The crisis occurring in adolescence is also symptomatic of occupational-economic tensions and inconsistencies occurring within the total social structure itself. The characteristic modes through which the adolescent seeks to cope with the tensions of this period reflect indirectly the characteristic modes of coping with tensions within the adult society itself. From this viewpoint, the study of adolescence reveals in exaggerated form the nature of social and economic tensions existing in society generally, as well as specifically in different class and ethnic segments of complex societies.

The expression of social tensions such as those that occur in adolescence must be viewed not only in a sociological context but in a psychological context as well. Different class and ethnic segments of the society have different specific socialization experiences and develop different social role expectations, including those deviating from the prevailing legally sanctioned expectations of the total society. The development of a relatively high incidence of deviant or delinquent orientation in some areas of society is due not only to the immediate

social inducement of peer groups, but also to a total subcultural climate of values and expectations, on the one hand, and, on the other
hand, to individual psychological factors and primary family relationships that lead to a selection of particular reference groups out of the
alternatives available. These forces are at work in student movements
as well as in special minority segments such as the ghettoed outcastes
discussed in chapters 14 and 15. Physiological incapacities or peculiarities can indirectly predispose the individual to develop deviant attitudinal patterns. But, more than any of these direct personality factors, it
is the formative experiences within the matrix of the primary family
that serve to develop delinquent attitudes and behavior.

Delinquency is less dependent on personality structure per se
than upon social definitions of self and society derived from unsatisfactory primary family relationships experienced within a particular
social environment.

This topic is too large to deal with in the present volume. The whole
issue of the effect of family interaction on delinquency formation is a
separate study which Wagatsuma and I are publishing subsequently in
our projected volume *The Heritage of Endurance.*

Viewing adolescent "deviant" behavior cross-culturally allows for a
type of analysis that helps one perceive more clearly, and in better
balance, delinquency as a social phenomenon. It is an overt expression
of underlying societal and/or psychological dysfunctions. In this sense,
I have been most specifically interested in changes in delinquency as a
manifestation of changing tensions related to rapid social change in
Japanese culture. The next chapter is a very partial and specific use
of statistical data as one approach to this problem.

Chapter XIII

Delinquency and Social Change
in Modern Japan

with KEIICHI MIZUSHIMA

THE RELATION OF DELINQUENCY
TO SOCIOECONOMIC CONDITIONS

Since World War II, the pace of social change in Japan has stepped up appreciably. The defeat of Japan and the subsequent American occupation provided a revolutionary opportunity for consciously planned change that was almost as fundamental as that occurring after the Meiji restoration of 1868. The basic constitution was changed; economic reforms of great importance were brought about in both agriculture and industry. Other reforms changed laws of land tenure and discontinued primogeniture as the basis for inheritance. There was a general restructuring of the business community with the temporary abolition of cartels. The political-legal system was revised and based more directly on democratic principles, and the court system and legal procedures were radically modified. The role of the school in society was reinterpreted; its primary function, which had been to stimulate loyalty to the nation, is now to develop the individual potential of the students. In the course of all these modifications the law relating to the basic institution of the family was changed to correspond closely to that in advanced Western cultures.

These have produced noteworthy results. Economically, Japan has attained an unprecedented level of prosperity and a degree of political freedom also without precedent. Changes in social attitudes are particularly evident in the younger generation; individual interests previously submerged within a network of family and community obligations are now being asserted more openly as orienting guides for behavior. The younger Japanese are more self-consciously concerned with individual liberty and self-motivated achievement, which in the past had to be couched in terms of fulfilling a family destiny. Ideally, the individual today has become more an end in himself no matter how much the strictures of Japanese occupational or family organizations still circumscribe actual behavior.

In the 1950s and early 1960s there occurred a radical increase in social deviancy and crime among younger Japanese adolescents. The relationship of the changes in social values to the nature and incidence of social deviancy in juveniles cannot be demonstrated, but adolescent behavior generally, whether positive or negative, must be seen as inextricably related to the ferment occurring in a Japanese society seeking new ends both individually and collectively. To draw balanced and meaningful conclusions concerning the nature of delinquent behavior in modern Japan, one must study the entire society, especially its differential appearance in various social classes. Delinquent or deviant behavior cannot be viewed in isolation from other social occurrences, nor can one type of deviancy be singled out and discussed apart from other forms of behavior; for example, in Japan today one must note not only the relative increase of delinquency in lower-class young people, but also, observe, how it relates to the strikingly high rate of suicide for middle-class individuals under twenty-five (see Chapter 17).

New fads, both acceptable and unacceptable, more quickly permeate younger groups who are less committed to previous ways of behaving. In modern cultures these fads may be limited to the period of youth and not carried over into more conservatively oriented adult behavior. In Japanese youth, especially in college students, the assumption of adult commitments brings about a sudden dramatic shift in attitudes and behavior, and an individual may move from a radical political philosophy to a conservative one when his employment changes his reference group from the student world to the business community.

It has been said by Japanese social critics that modern youth are more overtly pleasure-seeking than their predecessors and that many seem little concerned with long-range goals; the concept of hard work as a social virtue is said to be disappearing in Japan. However, the intensity of effort put forth by young people to pass the examinations for the major universities suggests that one cannot so quickly generalize that all Japanese youth are more pleasure-oriented than were those of previous generations.

At any rate, a society as complex as that of Japan is bound to manifest divergent patterns in its various social segments. Emphasis on education and social advancement may continue to characterize the modern urban middle class while an increased rate of deviancy may characterize lower-class segments of modern Japan, just as they do in the United States. To determine whether this is so, we turn to some overall statistical evidence. The following materials do not provide any definitive answers. They comprise our review up to 1966 of the specific reports of a number of Japanese social scientists and when compiled do give some overall picture permitting at least some considered opinions.

POSTWAR TRENDS AS REVEALED
BY STATISTICAL EVIDENCE

Unresolved Problems of Validity
in Regard to Statistical Evidence

The comparative approach would be vastly simplified if we could rely on the accuracy and comparability of statistics presented by various governments and governmental bureaus. No one working directly with statistics in any setting can accept them as a direct reflection of social conditions, but when they are qualified by critical judgment they offer some basis for controlled comparison of past with present trends both within a particular society and between nations.

One may certainly question today the validity of some of the statistics used by Emil Durkheim[1] in his pioneering study of suicide. But only a radical skeptic can question the value of using statistics at least as an approach to defining comparative trends. What is necessary, rather than an abrupt dismissal of the possibility of cross-national comparison, is a series of dispassionate scientific studies of how statistics are compiled in each of various countries, by whom and with what intent. It is our conjecture that the cultural traditions that go into various stages of gathering and presenting statistical data in particular settings can be defined and that knowledge of these traditions will help considerably in weighing evidence in the actual comparison of data. For example, a law enforcement agency budgeted by the United States Congress, such as the Federal Bureau of Investigation, has a positive investment in painting a gloomy view of crime, since, as a self-perpetuating governmental agency dependent on congressional appropriations, it seeks to assure its own development and a larger and larger budget.

There is a generational tendency to see crime on the increase. The general impression of a sharp rise in various forms of crime in the United States is in part the product of increases in urbanization and total population growth, which make the crime rate seem larger than it actually is. The meaning of police statistics as well as of those supplied by federal agencies must be judged in the context of local as well as

---

[1] Durkheim, *Suicide* (1951).

general social conditions. Statistics can be very misleading when approached without judgment.

Research at the University of California on police-arrest patterns of the Oakland, California, Police Department[2] demonstrates that there is a relatively fixed tradition in arrest patterns and learning it is part of the necessary training of new police officers. Too zealous an arrest record, for example, evokes just as strongly negative sanctions of an informal or formal kind on the part of peers toward a new officer as would neglect of duty. Judgment and discretion as to who is to be arrested and under what circumstances are acquired as part of the learning process that orients a new policeman to an ongoing frame of reference within a particular department. More stringent or more lax application of discretionary powers by police can cause a "crime wave" or a reduction of the incidence of crime to appear in the official records, and such variations must be explained. Therefore, radical changes in arrest practices or recorded reports are usually avoided.

Statistical averages, therefore, tend to persist and are resistive to abrupt change. Significant changes signal changes in bureaucratic structure. A decrease in the recorded incidence of crime may bring increased criticism of the agency as not performing its duties or may suggest to economy-minded legislators possible curtailment of the personnel budget for the following years. Changes in the statistics on crime very often simply reflect the institution of new police policy.

In cross-cultural comparisons of statistics on crime, the difficulties are compounded because methods of recording vary greatly. Law-enforcement practices differ radically from country to country. Certain illegal activities are condoned in some countries or overlooked by police, or are so widespread that official police action becomes impractical. In some places police action is so unrewarding or involves such complications that the police are not called in by injured parties; for example, statistics on arrests for theft in Cairo, Egypt, are completely out of line with the amount of minor and major theft that must surely occur in a city of four million people.

The statistics on delinquency for any country, therefore, not only depend on the professional competence of the statisticians assembling the data, but also must be seen as a function of the nature and organization of law enforcement, its stringency, its efficiency, and how discretionary powers are exercised.[3]

---

[2] Personal communication with Scott Briar and Irving Piliavin in School of Social Welfare, University of California.

[3] For example, the tendency to view more gravely a "disrespectful" attitude toward authority by black youths than by white youths in the United States is often cited as swelling the arrests for minor offenses in this minority group.

The Validity of Japanese Statistics

In assessing the comparability of material from Japan with that from the United States, we have the impression that official action in respect to delicts or potential delicts by minors is in some respects more careful and more stringent in Japan than it is in the United States. Youths in Japan are more likely to be officially sanctioned for lesser delicts, or even for "tendencies" toward what might be defined as delinquent behavior, than they are in the United States. Anticipatory attention to younger individuals, termed "predelinquents," is more careful than in the United States and raises the rates obtained in the official statistics.

Japanese statistics, as far as the professional competence of the compiler is concerned, are probably among the best in the world. Modern statistical reporting has received strong interest and support in Japan since its introduction in the early Meiji period. Government statistics were first compiled in 1872, and statistics on every subject are available in various governmental agencies. Police statistics, arrest and court statistics, and penal statistics have received continuous detailed attention from the beginning of the Meiji period. Numerous Japanese research workers in epidemiological studies of one or another aspect of society have made interpretations of how various phenomena may be symptomatically related to the incidence of crime or delinquency. A number of these studies have been concerned at various levels of generality with the major recognizable fluctuations in society that we shall consider in detail. First, the relationship of economic conditions to the incidence of crime and delinquency; second, the effect of war and its disruptions on the delinquency rate; third, rural-urban differences; and fourth, some major effects of social change that followed the war. In the following material we will evaluate the adequacy of the statistics we cite to remind the reader that statistics in themselves must never be taken at face value.

*Comparative Estimate of the Present Overall Incidence
of Delinquency in Japan and the United States*

It is of some importance for this cross-cultural comparison to estimate the present absolute incidence of juvenile delinquency in the United States and Japan. Since it is very difficult to get overall national statistics on juvenile delinquency in the United States, we have tried to compare the incidence of delinquency in selected major cities in the United States and in Japan.

Table XIII-1 compares the age structure of delinquents shown as percentages of the total of the same age group in Japan. Table XIII-2

TABLE XIII-1

PERCENTAGES OF DELINQUENT ARRESTS WITHIN AGE GROUPS 14–19, JAPAN

Age group	1955*	1960	1963†
14–15	0.62	1.14	1.34
16–17	0.88	1.32	1.30
18–19	1.31	1.61	1.65

NOTE: Arrests were for offenses against criminal code excluding traffic offenses.
* Ministry of Justice: *Delinquency in Japan* (1958), p. 1.
† Ministry of Justice: *White Paper* (1965), p. 255.

TABLE XIII-2

ABSOLUTE NUMBER OF DELINQUENT ARRESTS AND PERCENTAGES OF
AGE GROUPS INVOLVED IN THE SIX LARGEST CITIES OF JAPAN

Year	Absolute number	Percentage
1955	21,832	1.21
1960	42,823	1.85
1963	51,227	——*

SOURCE: Ministry of Justice: *Delinquency in Japan* (1958), p. 4.
NOTE: Arrests were for offenses against criminal code excluding traffic offenses.
* Population statistics not clear.

shows the absolute number of delinquents and rate in the six largest
Japanese cities.

Delinquent acts comprising these figures are fairly well defined as
offenses coming to the attention of the family court (excluding traffic
offenses, offenses against special laws, vagrancy, prostitution, and some
minor misdemeanors). In comparing figures with the United States,
we have attempted to isolate similar categories from the available
statistics. Tables XIII-3, -4, and -5 cite rates of incidence of delinquent offenses in various age groups for three major cities of the
United States in 1950. It is generally believed in Japan that delinquency is as serious there as it is in the United States, but it is our
judgment that the relative incidence of delinquency is still considerably lower in Japan than in the United States, insofar as trends in
the urban rates in major cities indicate. However, by 1960 in Japan
the rate per year per total of the same age population was at least
more than half that found in the United States in 1950 and it was
steadily increasing. Therefore, although the rate of delinquency seems
lower than in the United States, Japan's increasing concern with the

TABLE XIII-3

DELINQUENT OFFENSES IN NEW YORK CITY, 1950 (AGES 16–20)

Against persons	907
Sex	841
Against family and child	92
Gambling	1,960
Drug	43
Against property	6,230
Total	10,573

SOURCE for Tables XIII-3, 4, 5: U.S. Bureau of the Census: *U.S. Census of Population, 1950.* Vol. II, part 5 (Calif.), part 13 (Ill.), part 32 (N.Y.). U.S. Government Printing Office, Washington, D.C., 1952.

NOTE: Population of age group 16–20   487,935
Rate (percent)   2.2

TABLE XIII-4

DELINQUENT OFFENSES IN CHICAGO, 1950 (AGES 15–20)

Age	Number/Population	Percentage
15	1,297/39,660	3.27
16	1,305/38,960	3.34
17	964/38,650	2.49
18	874/41,690	2.09
19	875/44,285	1.97
20	772/47,515	1.62
Total	6,087/250,760	2.93

SOURCE: See Table XIII-3.

NOTE: Offenses exclude disorderly conduct, traffic offenses, drunkenness, violations of liquor laws, prostitution, vagrancy, gambling.

TABLE XIII-5

DELINQUENCY IN SAN FRANCISCO, 1950 (AGES 14–17)

Age	Number/Population	Percentage
14	150/6,470	2.3
15	154/6,415	2.4
16	176/6,420	2.7
17	148/7,060	2.1
Total	628/26,315	2.38

SOURCE: See Table XIII-3.

NOTE: Offenses exclude traffic offenses, prostitution, state misdemeanors, malicious mischief, vagrancy, disorderly conduct, violations of liquor laws, city ordinances, and bench warrants, and drunkenness, held for investigation.

delinquent activities of its youth was justified in 1965. As we will discuss below in our detailed comparison of postwar trends in Japan, the
changes noted cannot be attributed solely to changes in police action.

Although one can note changes in arrest policy that undoubtedly
influence the statistics presented, there are three other considerations
involved in comparing prewar and postwar Japanese police activities
related to youth. For example, the increased rates of violence in those
under twenty in the postwar statistics reflect the fact that there were
certain forms of violence that remained unreported in prewar Japan
and therefore did not come to the official attention of the police. First,
informal sanctioning within social groups in instances of rape, for
example, were operative, and would tend to exclude the calling in of
the police since this would disrupt the interaction going on among the
families within the communities concerned. Second, some aggressive
acts on the part of the military were not touched by the police but
were considered the province of military authority. Third, the police
seem to have become more and more sensitive in regard to certain
forms of youthful predelinquent activities. The surveillance of youth
in some areas is more intensive than it was in prewar Japan, and there
are now specialists in the police department trained in the area of
youth surveillance. Taking all these features into account, however,
one must still attribute a large percentage of the increase noted in
the statistics to some change in the actual incidence of more directly
aggressive types of delinquent activity and a proportionate increase
of delicts at lower age levels.

Delinquency as Statistically Related to Economic Conditions

In a work written in 1917, George von Mayer[4] reported that in
Bavaria in 1867 the crime rate increased with the increase in the price
of grain on the stock market. Ogburn,[5] an American sociologist, in
a 1923 study of crime rates between 1870 and 1920 in New York found
a negative correlation between the prosperity of the nation and the
number of criminal arrests. In 1930 Radzinowicz[6] found in Poland
that crime increased with economic depression; similar results were
obtained by Bonger[7] in 1916 in the Netherlands. Exner[8] in 1949 in
another German study found a correlation between the number of
unemployed and the incidence of theft between the years of 1925 and
1936.

---

[4] Von Mayer, "Statistik und Gesellschaftslehre" (1917).
[5] Ogburn, "Factors in the Variation of Crime Among Cities" (1953).
[6] Radzinowicz, "The Influence of Economic Conditions on Crime" (1941).
[7] Bonger, *Criminality and Economic Conditions* (1916).
[8] Exner, *Kriminologie* (1949).

In Japan, Iwasaburo Takano,[9] in a prewar study, found parallel relationships between the increased price of rice and the higher incidence of crime in the period 1884–1895; after this period, however, irregularities in the statistics made any similar analysis rather difficult. In another Japanese study by Seiichiro Ono,[10] in 1947, the price of rice and the average daily wage were found to be almost directly correlated with the crime rate until 1900; after 1900, with the increase in Japanese industrialization, this relationship became progressively less clear. In a study made in 1960 by Takemura[11] of the period from 1956 to 1959, economic prosperity measured by the general wholesale price index is related to decrease of adult crime.

Studies such as those given above, whatever the statistical limitations on which they were based, demonstrate some consistent influences at work relating the incidence of crime to economic conditions. Most of these studies indicate that adult crime increases in time of economic difficulty and decreases in time of prosperity. More recent studies concerned specifically with juvenile delinquency seem to indicate that the relationship is somewhat different in the case of minors. Some studies of juvenile crimes report reversal of the relation that pertains in adult crimes; the incidence of juvenile crime seems to increase with economic prosperity and to decrease with economic depression. In 1944, in Los Angeles, Bogen[12] found that juvenile delinquency, in direct relation to measures of economic prosperity that he used as indices, increased from 1924 steadily and reached a maximum in 1929. From 1929 to 1933 there was an economic decline, and the incidence of delinquency during this period also declined. In general, Bogen found a definite positive relationship between economic prosperity and juvenile delinquency. Results suggesting similar conclusions were obtained by James E. Sterner[13] in 1935 in Detroit; he found that in the period 1921 through 1935 the number of juvenile cases paralleled industrial employment. John Otto Reineman[14] in 1947 studied the relationship of economic conditions to juvenile delinquency from 1923 to 1945; he concluded that delinquency remained at an average level during periods when the economic situation tended toward neither extreme and that rates increased with extreme depression or with extreme prosperity. These findings would somewhat parallel the

---

[9] Takano in Takemura, "Sociological Study of Juvenile Delinquency" (1953, in Japanese).

[10] Ono, *Hompō Hanzaigenshō no Ninshiki* (1951).

[11] Takemura, "Poverty and Crime" (1960).

[12] Bogen, "Juvenile Delinquency and Economic Trends" (1944).

[13] Sterner and Rosemont, *Manual of Juvenile Court Officers of the State of Michigan* (1935).

[14] Reineman, "Juvenile Delinquency in Philadelphia and Economic Trends" (1947).

greater incidence of suicides that Durkheim[15] found during periods of unusual economic activity, both in depression and prosperity, and would seem to indicate that the delinquency rates are somehow related to anomic social conditions.

In 1959 Daniel Glaser[16] found that poor economic conditions, as reflected by the unemployment of adults, have a positive direct relation to adult crimes, whereas in individuals under twenty the situation appears to be reversed—that is, when economic conditions are generally good, the juvenile crime rate appears to be higher.

The findings in Japan are quite similar.[17] The period from 1892 to 1896 was a time of very high prosperity in Japan, one of the major periods of capitalization and development in the economy. Looking at the rate for this period, one finds it higher than at any period until after World War II.

Recent rates for juvenile delinquency increased up to the time Table XIII-6 was published, but they seem to have leveled off. Adult crime reported to the courts apparently leveled off earlier, close to the beginning of what has been a general period of increasing prosperity[18] in spite of minor fluctuations. The relationship of crime to prosperity is not simple; however, many of the authors cited differ from one another on the measures used to define prosperity. Also, certain periods of prosperity and depression differentially affect different class levels in the society. Moreover, one has also to differentiate among the types of crimes considered; for example, in general, crimes against property have a generally negative relationship with measures of prosperity, whereas crimes against persons go up with better economic conditions.

Adult crime rates show a direct relationship between increased availability of employment and decreased criminal activity, but the rate of juvenile crime is affected by factors other than occupational opportunity. One principal factor is the nature of family relationships under conditions of prosperity. It is in this regard that Durkheim's understanding of anomic conditions has its greatest relevancy; unusual prosperity or unusual depression affects not only the individual but also the nature of family relationships. Unusual prosperity may cre-

---

[15] Durkheim, *Suicide* (1951).

[16] Glaser, "Crime, Age and Employment" (1959).

[17] Takemura, "Sociological Study of Juvenile Delinquency" (1953, in Japanese).

[18] The report of Tamanyu, "One of the Preventative Methods of Juvenile Delinquency by Dots-Mapping of the Marginal Areas" (1964), shows that the correlation between the consumer's price index (Fisher's Effective Price, that is, $EP = \dfrac{MV}{T}$ Money times Velocity over amount of Trade) and a delinquency quotient runs consistently high from 1946 to 1962. Both increased rapidly and in almost parallel lines. This article includes a detailed ecological study of Saitama Prefecture.

TABLE XIII-6

COMPARISON OF THE PROPORTIONATE INCREASE IN JAPANESE RATES OF ARREST
TO SPECIFIC JUVENILE AND ADULT POPULATION USING 1941 AS A BASE YEAR
(CORRECTED FOR AGE)

Year	Juvenile	Adult	Year	Juvenile	Adult
1941	100	100	1953	204	118
1942	132	82	1954	191	114
1943	119	100	1955	196	116
1944	140	80	1956	198	112
1945	100	65	1957	221	109
1946	213	118	1958	126	105
1947	198	114	1959	264	103
1948	238	132	1960	291	100
1949	236	138	1961	298	99
1950	264	136	1962	296	93
1951	272	132	1963	302	97
1952	232	128	1964	323	107

SOURCE: Ministry of Justice: *Crime and Its Prevention* (*1960*), p. 417. Ministry of Justice: *White Paper* (1965), p. 247.

ate an attitude of free spending and permit indulgence in various forms of entertainment not possible in more normal times, and this can be quite disruptive to the usual family pattern. Also, in such times there is a dramatization of quick gain and direct access to a hedonistic life, which affects the more volatile youths who are not yet committed to a stable occupation or to family responsibilities. It follows that there would be a greater tendency at times of prosperity for youths who have no regular occupation or fixed status to seek irregular means to obtain money for pleasure. Such a situation is especially apparent in present-day Japan, where most delinquency revolves around entertainment activities which become much more active and exciting in times of free spending. The adolescent is drawn to "where the action is," and the steady day-by-day pattern of hard work leading ultimately to very distant goals becomes a pallid alternative to more immediate pleasure. It may be that this tendency toward hedonism influences lower-class youth more directly than middle-class youth, who perhaps remain more committed to long-range goals.

According to Sutherland,[19] who is concerned with traditions of delinquency within specific neighborhoods, the continuing general effect of marginal economic conditions is related to high delinquency in particular areas, and this factor is more important than the shifts that occur periodically within the overall economic climate. Studies have

[19] Sutherland, *Principles of Criminology* (1947).

been made of particular neighborhoods and occupational areas in Japan, but so far as the authors know, no one has studied the differential effect of economic conditions on delinquency in specifically defined ecological areas to ascertain whether the delinquency rate in these areas is related directly to employment or to rapid rises in living standards.

EFFECTS OF WARTIME AND
ITS AFTERMATH ON DELINQUENCY

The social dislocations resulting from war have been one of the major causes of periodic fluctuation in crime and delinquency rates. War exerts disruptive influences, not only specifically as a result of economic dislocations and the displacement of people, but also more generally from the loosening of social controls in the face of emergency conditions. Such effects are most apparent in communities directly involved in combat, but they are more or less apparent in areas out of reach of actual hostilities.

War can be so completely disruptive that the statistical recording of its effects becomes a parody of actual conditions. Wartime crimes commited by soldiers are usually not represented in official statistics. In wartime police action is not normal, and the recording operations of government bureaus are disrupted. In spite of such obvious limitations it may be useful to cite briefly European and American data on the effects of war, and the Japanese statistics that compare the situations obtaining in Japan during and immediately after the war.

European and American Data on the Effects of War

There are a number of reports on crime and delinquency in Germany after the first and second world wars. The official statistics[20] tend to show a rapid increase in juvenile crime in the immediate postwar period, with the peaks occurring in Germany some time considerably after the actual end of combat. In France, which suffered considerable damage during both world wars, a similar rise in juvenile crime appeared immediately after the cessation of hostilities.[21]

According to Tappan,[22] who summarizes various findings concerning the influence of the war, in the United States during the war there were trends similar to those appearing in European countries, but the postwar period did not show the radical increase in juvenile crime reported in the European countries. The figures on juvenile delinquency

---

[20] Bundes Kriminalamt, *Polizeiliche Kriminalstatistik* (1958).

[21] Ministère de la Justice (France), *Compte Général de l'Administration de la Justice Civile et Commerciale et de la Justice Criminelle* (1952–1955, 1957).

[22] Tappan, *Crime, Justice and Correction* (1959), pp. 183–187.

before and during World War II, in the United States as well as in
other countries, show a considerable rise in delinquency among
younger age-groups, especially among females. The United States
Children's Bureau statistics, as interpreted by Tappan, report that delinquency cases increased 60 percent between the years 1938 and 1944,
with an increase of 54 percent for boys and 88 percent for girls. Tappan also compares these results with those reported by Cyril Burt,[23]
who found that in England male juvenile delinquency increased 60
percent but female delinquency increased only 20 percent. These increases occurred especially in evacuation areas and where air raids
were most intense.

Going back to World War I, there are official statistics that indicate
an increase in juvenile delinquency between 1914 and 1918 of 69
percent in England, 63 percent in Germany, and 52 percent in Austria.
The figures given show a decrease in the number of attacks on persons
and an increase in larcenous types of delinquency.

Both the English and American data during and after World War II
reveal an increase of delinquency in lower age-groups, particularly
those under fourteen. Burt attributed the high incidence of delinquency in England to the break-up of homes, evacuation problems, the
absence of fathers in the services, the necessity to spend time in air-raid
shelters, blackouts, decreased opportunities for maintaining normal
educational and recreational activities, and the increased overall atmosphere of violence. Disruption of life patterns was much less extreme in the United States, but nevertheless, there were disruptions
of home life, increased geographic mobility in the population, and a
lessening of supervision over children with the employment of mothers and the young in wartime industries.

In the United States offenses by juveniles under eighteen rose for
the entire period of World War II in contrast to a general lowering of
the crime index for the country.[24] The most noteworthy decrease in
crime was in age group 21–24, a decrease greater than that of either
the next older or next younger age group, reflecting the proportionate
numbers of each age group drafted into the military services.

Neumeyer[25] has done perhaps the most intensive survey of delinquency in the United States immediately after the war and has made a
thorough systematic attempt to interpret the influences at work. His
report takes into account so far as possible the actual complexities of
the situation. He demonstrates that the statistics were by no means
uniform throughout the United States during this period; the general
postwar trend was toward an increase in delinquency, but some areas
reported decreases.

---

[23] *Ibid.*, p. 184.   [24] *Ibid.*, p. 185.
[25] Neumeyer, *Juvenile Delinquency in Modern Society* (1961).

A special study made in small cities, towns, and rural communities in four states from 130 judicial districts showed that 73 of these reported increases, 49 reported decreases, and 8 showed no change. Another later report demonstrated that the number of delinquency cases handled by 304 courts in various sections of the nation increased 31 percent in one year.

Population shifts make accuracy of reporting difficult. For example, 83 juvenile courts which served areas of 100,000 or more population reported a 16 percent increase in cases handled in the immediate prewar period 1940–1942. Forty-one of these areas, where the population was increasing at this time, reported an increase of 18 percent, whereas the remaining 42 areas, where population was stable or declining, reported only a 9 percent increase. This would indicate that part of the reported percentile increase may be due to a lag in applying the population statistics to the crime rate.

The U.S. National Probation and Parole Association, in an annual report covering 117 judicial districts, showed that the volume of delinquency remained on a high level during the period of war. Immediately after, however, there was a marked decline. Unfortunately, in this report, changes in the volume of delinquency were not sufficiently correlated with the population changes in those areas submitting reports, a number were urban areas that experienced a considerable increase in population during the war. The greatest proportionate increases in juvenile court cases were in areas that had gained extensively in population because of an increase in the number of war industries. Neumeyer, therefore, points out that both the increase in population and the immediate overcrowded situation may have served to contribute to the increased rate.[26]

Neumeyer points out that urban areas usually have higher general crime rates for most offenses than do rural areas and, therefore, the increase in urbanization in the United States leads to an increase in the crime rate.[27] In regard to delinquency, Neumeyer notes that starting with the early years of the war there was an increase in the delinquency rate not only of girls but also of minority groups. The number of cases involving delinquent girls went down abruptly with the end of the war, but the increase in male juvenile cases continued somewhat longer. Following the war, there was a rapid decline in delinquency for at least two years, but since 1948 the statistics again show a sharp upturn for both male and female delinquents. Neumeyer considers that statistics related to the age composition of the delinquent population are less reliable than those pertaining to sex differences in rates of delinquency. The crime reports to which Neumeyer refers

---

[26] *Ibid.*, p. 68.   [27] *Ibid.*, p. 69.

show the predominant age for arrests as fluctuating considerably. During the prewar period 1939–1941, the most arrests were made among nineteen-year-olds. The peak age for arrests dropped to seventeen during 1944 and 1945, and rose to twenty-one in 1946 and then to twenty-three in 1951. These fluctuations are seemingly accounted for in large part by the extent to which youths were enlisted or drafted for military service. Misconduct of military personnel was handled mainly by the military authorities, rather than by the regular law enforcement agencies, hence there is a drop in civilian statistics.[28]

The American uniform crime reports also indicate that considerable fluctuation occurred in types of offenses. Offenses against persons, although always a small proportion of the total, increased relatively during the war period. While offenses against property showed a general sustained tendency to increase, there were also periodic decreases to be noted in the statistics. Immediately postwar, decreases occurred especially in crimes against persons. By 1952, however, increases had occurred in almost all categories of crime, but chiefly in those of aggravated assault, robbery, auto theft, burglary, and larceny.

Delinquency Related to War in Japan

Contrary to the situation reported for the United States, immediately following World War II the Japanese statistics show a rapid increase in delinquency similar to that reported in the German police records. It is hard to distinguish in these overall statistics between causes related specifically to conditions of postwar disruption and those related to general social change or simply to postwar police-arrest policy.

By 1932 the "prewar" period was a militaristic one in Japan; the Japanese nation was generally mobilizing itself for a deeper involvement in its military adventure in China. In the statistics obtained during that period we find a drop in the total number of individuals of all age levels cited for criminal activity. Several reasons have been proposed by Japanese authors to explain this phenomenon. Among the most cogent reasons are the general tension throughout the society related to the mobilization of national effort and the sense of danger to the national entity, a state of crisis daily expressed in newspapers and in other mass media. The military forces had been increased yearly since 1932 and at the same time the government was actively pushing a colonization program in Manchukuo. Those intent on the expression of aggression could find ample outlet in the military; the army was known for its brutality, the lower ranks, especially privates, being easily victimized by rather sadistic noncommissioned officers,

---

[28] *Ibid.,* p. 70.

and the subject non-Japanese populations, in turn, being helpless against the Japanese military. Japanese soldiers capable of aggressive dominance were encouraged and rapidly advanced.

The decrease in crime in Japan leveled off in 1940–1941. With total mobilization another decrease appeared in the criminal statistics for 1942, but by 1943 there was some disillusionment with the war effort, especially in regard to the excesses practiced by the military upon their own people, and during this period the criminal statistics show a slight increase. By 1944–1945 there was considerable disruption in the urban centers. Bombings by the American Air Force dispersed the population into the countryside. Goods and materials of all sorts were in extremely short supply and the threat of famine was not far off. Given the disruption of bureaucratic procedures, it is not surprising that the official statistics of this period show a decrease in recognizable criminal activity. Nowhere in the official statistics for this period or for the early postwar occupation is there any adequate reflection of the magnitude of the black market activities throughout Japan. According to some Japanese analysts such as Takemura,[29] the actual incidence of criminal activity had not decreased in the late war period, but the police organization had been generally disrupted. Japanese statistics during this period bear certain similarities to German statistics for World War I as reported by Exner[30] and Liepmann[31] and for World War II as reported by Bader.[32] The totalitarian aspects of the government under war conditions in Germany and Japan must be considered in an interpretation of the statistics of this period.

Whereas the overall statistics in Japan showed a decrease of crime from 1936 to 1941, juvenile offenses showed a continual slight increase (see Table XIII-7). As in wartime America, a considerable number of young people were left without supervision and some were earning money in factories, a situation that may be related to the appearance of delinquency in this age group.

Immediately after the war, offenses against property increased, reflecting the chaotic economic conditions obtaining, but the long-term postwar increase in crime has been especially in acts involving physical aggression, intimidation and extortion, and sexual violence. Unaccountably, Japanese statistics show a continual postwar decrease in the incidence of arson, for which there has not been a good explanation.[33]

---

[29] Takemura, "Sociological Study of Juvenile Delinquency" (1953, in Japanese).

[30] Exner, *Kriminologie* (1949).

[31] Liepmann, *Krieg und Kriminalität in Deutschland* (1930).

[32] Bader, *Soziologie der Deutschen Nachkriegskriminalität* (1949).

[33] Arson, which threatened vulnerable wooden communities, was considered one of the most reprehensible crimes. The gradual change to more modern structures may lessen the emphasis on the use of arson as a means of covert retribution.

TABLE XIII-7

Number of Juveniles Arrested in Japan: By Year and by Type of Offense

Date	Murder	Robbery	Rape	Arson	Theft	Obscenity	Gambling	Fraud	Embezzlement	Injury
1936	153	311	197	266	29,750	76	1,425	3,297	3,491	..
1937	155	310	172	272	26,783	79	1,307	3,006	3,269	2,631
1938	161	302	211	279	32,503	88	1,355	2,973	3,207	2,596
1939	123	310	217	291	21,409	87	1,639	2,787	2,801	3,073
1940	146	475	230	263	35,999	188	2,072	2,361	2,485	2,901
1941	107	436	255	256	36,954	180	2,188	2,028	2,111	2,997
1942	126	406	328	213	47,267	361	2,121	2,184	4,028	3,106
1943	94	377	335	204	45,113	439	2,941	1,552	1,358	2,998
1944	177	442	294	215	54,852	417	5,765	1,767	1,148	2,968
1945	149	455	218	92	42,818	308	2,637	1,044	603	1,746
1946	249	2,903	258	164	87,825	282	3,271	3,193	1,132	1,874
1947	216	2,851	298	116	77,514	163	4,127	2,999	1,209	3,059
1948	354	3,878	584	173	90,066	272	4,720	4,173	2,020	(3,264)
1949	344 (333)	2,866 (2,832)	1,176 (1,165)	340 (199)	94,214 (78,900)	283 (265)	2,954 (2,902)	4,470 (4,332)	2,475 (2,347)	(13,731)
1950	369 (362)	2,897 (2,824)	1,538 (1,508)	470 (264)	111,526 (85,490)	497 (404)	2,346 (2,246)	6,368 (6,109)	3,148 (2,945)	(18,784)
1951	448 (443)	2,107 (2,133)	1,530 (1,509)	446 (246)	127,122 (97,439)	347 (310)	1,556 (1,527)	4,886 (4,670)	3,142 (2,931)	(15,296)
1952	393 (389)	1,927 (1,899)	1,870 (1,840)	530 (299)	104,344 (78,841)	338 (318)	733 (717)	4,954 (4,752)	3,117 (2,850)	(14,923)
1953	383 (376)	1,582 (1,533)	1,535 (1,497)	410 (225)	88,586 (64,435)	407 (365)	443 (441)	4,875 (4,651)	3,155 (2,955)	(14,105)
1954	411 (404)	1,830 (1,800)	1,977 (1,935)	407 (228)	81,298 (58,198)	459 (389)	371 (355)	(4,090)	(2,602)	(15,495)
1955	345 (342)	2,003 (1,969)	2,121 (2,078)	328 (182)	80,626 (58,458)	495 (420)	322 (301)	(3,151)	(2,218)	(18,107)
1956	(323)	(1,998)	(2,010)	(148)	(57,261)	(475)	(176)	(2,964)	(1,841)	(22,488)
1957	307	2,173	2,823	162	59,877	533	189	(3,077)	(1,889)	(29,615)
1958	359	2,348	4,605	183	56,856	832	151	(2,693)	(1,500)	(37,754)
1959	415	2,550	4,530	189	64,447	947	183	(2,372)	(1,444)	(40,851)
1960	423	2,646	4,232	203	68,779	988	263	(2,198)	(1,311)	(40,364)
1961	440	2,380	4,106	210	77,542	(1,064)	313	(2,112)	(1,151)	(41,726)
1962	336	2,169	3,866	154	83,105	(1,129)	442	(1,661)	(900)	(41,821)

Source:: National Police Bureau Criminal Statistics, 1950 and 1963.
Note: Figures for 1936–1956 include all those under 20 years of age; figures in parentheses represent the 14–20 age group; the figures under 14 years of age are not given for the years 1957–1962; a new method of classification was used for 1949–1962.

The Japanese statistics indicate that although adult criminal activity reached its peak in 1949 and has shown very little rise since, the increase in juvenile crime has been steady. All criminal statistics supplied by the National Police Bureau contain abrupt discrepancies between the years 1948 and 1949, which would indicate that some change in policy, either in arrest practices or in recording, occurred at that time. (By 1972 one notes a declining rate from 1968 on.)

There are some general contrasts between the American postwar statistics on delinquency and those reported for Japan. In the American case, juvenile delinquency seems to have had a temporary decrease immediately after the war. The American statistics seem to show much less effect of wartime dislocation than do the Japanese statistics over the same period. The shift in the United States to a prevailingly urban population has been going on for a long period and preceded World War II. The trend in Japan is increasing in intensity; while the United States shifted from a 14 percent to an 8 percent rural population from 1946 to 1960, Japan shifted from approximately a 45 percent to a 22 percent rural population in the same period. The long-range trends toward increased delinquency with urbanization would thus be recognizable in Japan at a later date than that already noted for the United States. (Now, despite increasing urbanization, delinquency rates are dropping.)

GENERAL POSTWAR TRENDS IN JAPAN

The outstanding feature of juvenile delinquency in Japan today is the apparent increase in the rate of deviant behavior among individuals of an increasingly younger age. The present trends reported in Japanese statistics (see Table XIII-8) cannot be considered solely an artifact of changing police methods or policies of classification. The evidence seems incontrovertible that there are radical increases in juvenile crime, especially that involving extortion, threat, assault, or violence. Most of the increase in all crime is due to the increased rates among juveniles, which exceed those increases to be expected solely on the basis of population growth. In Table XIII-7 arrests for robbery of individuals under twenty years of age jump from lass than 500 in 1945 to 2,900 in 1946 to 3,900 in 1948, and from 1949 on, the rate is more than 2,000 arrests a year. Juvenile arrests for various forms of threat, assault, extortion, and injury (reclassified in 1949) have increased from almost 1,400 in 1949 to almost 42,000 in 1962. Juvenile arrests for rape have increased from 200 to 300 a year through 1947 to almost 600 cases in 1948 to a peak of 4,600 cases in 1958. Arrests for lewd or obscene behavior (a rather vague category) of juveniles have increased from about 300 a year to more than 1,000. Theft has

TABLE XIII-8

JUVENILE ARRESTS FOR OFFENSES AGAINST THE PENAL CODE, JAPAN
1957 AND 1964, COMPARED WITH TOTAL NUMBER OF OFFENDERS

Crime	Number of juvenile offenders		Ratio of juvenile offenders to the total number of offenders (in percent)	
	1957	1964	1957	1964
Rape	2,823	4,181	53	50
Robbery	2,173	1,909	39	48
Theft	59,877	95,219	29	49
Violence, bodily injury, threat, and extortion	29,615	44,778	23	29
Arson	162	150	18	19
"Obscene" behavior	533	1,347	17	23
Murder	307	356	16	14
Embezzlement	1,889	856	10	10
Fraud	3,077	1,636	8	7
Gambling	189	649	2	5
Bribery	0	2	0	0
Abortion	0	0	0	0
Other offenses	13,657	39,359	11	15
Totals	114,302	190,442	21	28

SOURCE: For 1957 figures, Ministry of Justice (Japan), *Juvenile Delinquency in Japan* (1958), p. 12; for 1964, Ministry of Justice (Japan), *White Paper on Crime* (1965), p. 253.

fluctuated with no notable upward trend in arrests since 1945, and gambling at least no longer appears in the statistics as a juvenile problem according to the arrest records; from highs of 5,700 in 1944 and 4,700 in 1948 arrests have dwindled to a low of 151 in 1958 and to approximately 400 in 1962. The radical general increase in the arrest rate for crimes against persons attests to changes in the attitude of juveniles. It also indicates the growing concern of the police and the public over prevalence of aggressive behavior and the tendency of subadults to use the threat of force interpersonally.

In arrests of those under twenty the greatest proportional rise continues to be for acts involving display of aggression or threat. This increase in actual or potential crimes against person is without any radical increase in the use of such weapons as guns or knives; threat often consists of allusion to membership in a gang or in a feared Korean or outcaste minority group. By 1957, 21 percent of all crimes were committed by individuals under twenty years of age, as compared with the base year 1941, and by 1964 the proportion of juvenile

346   DEVIANCY AND ALIENATION

crime had risen to 28 percent. By 1957 arrests of juveniles for theft
represented 29 percent of all such arrests (Table XIII-8), but this
increase was due not so much to an increase in juvenile arrests as to
a decrease in theft arrests in the adult population.

The ratio of juvenile delinquents to the entire juvenile population
is higher in the six largest urban areas than in rural and other areas;
1.5 percent of the juveniles in urban areas were investigated by the
police for offenses against the penal code, as against 0.9 percent in
the rural regions (see Table XIII-9). More than one-third of the

TABLE XIII-9

Juvenile Offenders in the Six Largest Cities in Japan (Tokyo, Osaka,
Nagoya, Kyoto, Kobe, Yokohama) Compared with Those in Other Areas

	Six largest cities			Other areas		
Year	Number of juvenile offenders	Total same-age population	Percent-age	Numbar of juvenile offenders	Totel same-age population	Percent-age
1950	27,150	1,363,436	1.99	101,659	9,021,000	1.13
1955	21,832	1,809,801	1.21	75,124	8,781,000	0.86
1960	42,823		1.79	105,096		
1963	51,227			123,124		

Source: Adapted from Ministry of Justice, *Crime and Prevention* (1960), p. 297.

TABLE XIII-10

The Number of Delicts Committed by Juveniles in the Six Largest
Cities, Compared with Those in All of Japan in 1958

Type of offense	In six largest cities (c. 20 percent of total juvenile population)	Total offenses for all of Japan	Juvenile crime in six largest cities as percentage of total
Extortion	4,112	11,588	35.5
Robbery	809	2,348	34.5
Threat	227	798	28.4
Injury	4,050	15,557	26.0
Theft	14,487	56,856	25.5
Murder	75	359	20.9
Assault	2,033	9,811	20.7
Rape	928	4,605	20.2
Other crime	5,509	22,457	24.5
Totals	32,230	124,379	25.9

Source: Same as for Table XIII-9.

reported cases of robbery and extortion occur in these larger cities, which have 20 percent of the juvenile population. Acts of threat, injury, and theft are also overrepresented in the largest urban centers (See Table XIII-10). The more recent trend, however, may be increased delinquency as population goes down in rural areas.

The largest increase in the arrest rate is of individuals 14–15 years of age. Table XIII-11 shows that the number of arrests yearly for individuals 20–24 years old is essentially the same as it was in 1948; except for a peak postwar increase in 1957, there has been only a slight increase. The number of arrests of 18–19-year-olds was highest in 1948 (61,000) followed by a steady decline to about 44,000 in 1954; since then the number of arrests has gone up to 62,750 in 1961 and is dropping slightly (as of 1963). Arrests of 16- and 17-year-olds (treated separately in the statutes only since 1953) increased yearly until 1960, after which they leveled off at about 50,000 arrests a year, about five-

TABLE XIII-11

NUMBER OF JAPANESE JUVENILE OFFENDERS (POLICE ARRESTS), 1941–1963, BY AGE

Date	14–15	16–17	14–17	18–19	20–24
1941	....		22,731	19,876	....
1942	....		30,256	25,649	....
1943	....		28,116	23,427	36,308
1944	....		36,722	26,678	37,453
1945	....		26,208	22,314	27,300
1946	....		47,479	51,910	92,446
1947	....		45,831	46,720	100,718
1948	....		52,453	61,310	141,582
1949	....		60,405	53,126	135,478
1950	....		73,075	55,734	133,119
1951	....		75,626	58,030	136,752
1952	....		64,776	49,405	130,991
1953	....		54,321	44,283	132,130
1954	20,687	29,780	50,467	43,875	135,229
1955	21,769	28,721	50,490	46,466	143,633
1956	22,316	30,141	52,457	48,301	145,213
1957	26,278	38,254	64,532	49,770	148,207
1958	29,260	44,114	73,374	51,005	146,270
1959	35,897	47,111	83,008	56,610	143,180
1960	35,375	50,550	85,933	61,966	140,455
1961	44,909	51,217	96,126	62,758	141,130
1962	60,615	43,089	103,704	59,237	134,515
1963	65,957	50,000	115,957	38,394	142,617

SOURCE: Adapted from Takemura (1953), p. 172; and National Police Bureau: *Criminal Statistics* (1963), p. 257.

sixths the number for the 18–19-year-olds. The number of police arrests of 14–15-year-olds rose steadily until 1948 and increased rapidly from almost 10,000 a year to approximately 66,000 recorded in 1963, more than for either the 16–17- or 18–19-year-old groups.

We have more detailed figures for Arakawa Ward in Tokyo and we find there that the police contacts for behavior categorized as "suspicious" or "predelinquent" contribute heavily to the relatively high delinquency statistics coming yearly from this ward. If this situation obtains elsewhere, increased police surveillance of questionable activities of very young juveniles contributes significantly to the continuous rise in the delinquency rate. The rate of arrests for individuals 16–20 years of age is decreasing slightly.

GENERAL URBAN-RURAL DIFFERENCES IN CRIME AND DELINQUENCY

A great part of the study of crime and delinquency in the United States has been devoted to the city and its effect on delinquency formation. Much less is known of the nature of antisocial behavior in rural areas. Overall statistics indicate that generally in the American urban environment official police response to certain forms of antisocial adolescent behavior is much more evident than in the rural environment. According to Sutherland the per capita rates in major crimes are related to the size of cities; in the United States in 1940, for example, there were approximately two and one-half times as many robberies per person in the urban areas as in the rural areas. Sutherland notes, however, that this proportional increase is not directly related to community size; the rate of crime was lower in cities of over 250,000 inhabitants compared with that in cities of more than 100,000 but less than 250,000. The United States statistics also appear to show that the proportion of murder and rape in relation to other forms of crime is higher in rural populations of less than 1,000 than in small towns and cities.

More recently Clinard [34] reports continuing evidence that urban county crime rates have been considerably higher than rural county rates within various states. He notes that the robbery rate in urban areas reached almost three times that in rural areas.

Another study pointing to urban-rural differences is Wiers' [35] intensive study of juvenile delinquency in Michigan, based on the composite index of population density, size of largest city, and occupation, which has shown that the rural counties have a lower incidence of

---

[34] Clinard, *Sociology of Deviant Behavior* (1957), pp. 59–70.
[35] Wiers, "The Juvenile Delinquent in Rural Michigan" (1939–40).

juvenile delinquency, the rural county rates for juvenile court hearings being one-half those for urban counties. Caldwell's[36] study of the extent of juvenile delinquency in Wisconsin for the years 1935–1940, based on the percentage of delinquents in the school population, also found that the predominantly urban areas in the state had the highest rates, whereas the essentially rural northern areas of Wisconsin had the lowest rates of delinquency.

In the more recent figures in the United States, the continuing rapid disappearance of forms of relatively isolated rural life is reflected in statistics on crime and delinquency. To quote Bloch and Flynn:[37]

Although urban delinquency still outnumbers rural delinquency at least 3.5 to 1 and will probably continue to do so for an indefinite period, we can conclude that the increase in rural juvenile offenses is significant and that the upward trend may continue at a rate comparable to and even greater than urban rates. Further, in selected rural areas that are beginning to experience the impact of industrialization, the rates appear to be rising precipitously. That this is being borne home in many rural districts can be seen in the mounting public clamor in such regions for the establishment of special facilities in courts where this need was not apparent a scant two decades ago.

It appears, therefore, that it is in the nature of the urban environment to produce more of certain forms of both adult and juvenile criminal behavior.

Japanese social scientists have been impressed with this ecological approach to social problems and have made a number of studies directly comparable to those done in Chicago and other U.S. cities, tracing the relative rates of delinquency and crime for rural and urban populations. With the exception of crimes of passion such as murder and rape, which are higher in rural areas, the general trend in Japanese statistics is directly comparable to American findings that the per capita crime rate for both adults and juveniles increases in almost direct relationship to increases in total population or density of population within each of the prefectures. The general evidence seems to be that juvenile crime has roughly similar patterns to crime generally. In the United States, juvenile crime rates for burglary, robbery, and theft have been especially high in the urban areas, whereas those for murder, manslaughter, and rape have shown less urban-rural difference. In Japan the relative rate of juvenile delinquency in each prefecture is almost identical to the relative rate for adult crimes. Rates for crimes involving some form of extortion, robbery, or threat are especially high in the urbanized prefectures as compared to the more rural ones (see Table XIII-10).

---

[36] Caldwell, "The Extent of Juvenile Delinquency in Wisconsin" (1942).
[37] Bloch and Flynn, *Delinquency* (1956), p. 50.

There are numerous theories as to the factors contributing to a higher delinquency rate in urban areas. It does not seem probable that delinquency can be directly related without qualification to industrial concentration, overcrowded housing, poverty, or the other socioeconomic factors often cited as contributory to delinquency in urban areas. One cannot dismiss the fact that certain neighborhoods and areas may have all these component features without at the same time having a high delinquency rate, whereas others show a high rate but without such economic disadvantages.

According to Clinard [38] the relationship between juvenile gang behavior and adjudicated delinquency applies chiefly to cities. He found that two-thirds of the farm boys arrested for stealing had not been associated with others who stole, and if serious thefts only were considered, 87 percent had had no such previous association.

In rural areas there is less mobility than there is in urban areas. People have had face-to-face relationships over several generations, and neighborhood ties are intimate, or, if not intimate, at least known and clearly defined. Community sanctions have a direct effect upon the individual, and everyday life involves the community more than it does in the city. Not only does the family as a social institution act as a sanctioning agent, but the neighborhood and community also perform this function. The community can operate informally in relation to the individual in a rural area in the United States in a way that seems impossible in the city, and therefore professional legal sanctions are less likely to be invoked for minor offenses.

In Japan some of the characteristics of the traditional feudal society are still apparent in the rural areas, and these traditions serve to reinforce the very tight nonprofessional, informal sanctioning system of the local community. In Japan, rural delinquents tend to go into neighboring cities for their activities, and as their delinquency increases they are less likely to remain in a rural setting and tend to migrate permanently to the city. The modern type of juvenile gang is not found in rural areas and would not be tolerated there. On the other hand, rural regions have a relatively high rate for crimes of passion and violence resulting from impulsive outbursts. According to statistics, rape in the Japanese rural areas is notably on the increase; one may well ask, however, if there has not been a change in the extent to which police officials are notified about such acts. Sexual activities involving forced intercourse in the past were sometimes condoned as the "natural" behavior of young men in certain rural communities, and in certain instances there seemed to be direct acquiescence on the part of the adults of the community to such be-

---

[38] Clinard, "Rural Criminal Offenders" (1944).

havior. At any rate, it was inconceivable to call in the law and make a legal issue of such acts. Even when the rape was not condoned, it was considered so disgraceful an occurrence that it would permanently damage the reputation of a girl who made a public complaint before the law. These rural patterns are changing and there is more recourse to legal sanctions, although many of the more remote areas in Japan are still characterized by what would be considered by modern urban Japanese deviant standards of sexual conduct.

A study by Hiroshi Hasegawa[39] reports a rural group rape among juveniles which seems to have been influenced by a number of deviant cultural factors. Apparently in the culture of this area there was not merely tolerance but a certain acknowledged admiration for violent "phallic" sexual activity on the part of young men. However, such traditional influences were responsible only in part; in addition there was the indirect influence of the behavior of a criminal gang from a nearby city, which seems to have been emulated by the rural youth in question.

The relatively frequent appearance of crimes of violence, either with or without sexual motivation, in the rural areas may also be related to the relative isolation of village life in some regions of Japan. In northeast Japan, for example, villages are virtually isolated during the long winter months by heavy snowfall. People are snowbound in their own homes over long periods, and in this situation any tension that may occur within the family will have little opportunity of finding outlet elsewhere. Very often it is in such a setting that a murder or injury occurs within the immediate family.

Arson also seems to result from pent-up tension within the home. Rural arson is often committed by a young maid or apprentice who has developed a grudge against an employer, and frequently relates to interpersonal conflict involving resentment that cannot be otherwise expressed. Choice of employment is still very often a family rather than a personal decision, and no outlet for mounting personal tensions is permitted the young worker. Feelings of homesickness or resentment over what is perceived as harsh treatment are released in both minor and major recriminatory acts. Recriminatory fire-setting has long been a major fear of Japanese living in vulnerable, closely spaced wooden dwellings. Any form of arson has always been met with severe sanctions.[40]

High delinquency rates in given Japanese prefectures are related to the overall density of the area, the prefectures containing the major cities of Tokyo, Yokohama, Kyoto, Osaka, Kobe, Fukuoka, and Hiro-

---

[39] Hasegawa, "A Study on Group Rape in Juveniles" (1955, in Japanese).
[40] Nakada, "Psychological Study of Arsonists" (1953, in Japanese).

shima having the highest rates. This pattern has remained fairly
stable.

There is as yet no certain evidence that can be interpreted as
demonstrating that the crime rate in Japan for rural and urban areas
is becoming increasingly similar, as suggested by Bloch and Flynn for
the United States. Such a trend has not appeared in Japanese statistics, although the proportion of rural to urban population is changing.
In 1950 the arrest rate for juvenile delinquency per total juvenile population, 14–19 years of age, was 1.99 per 100 in the six largest cities and
0.86 in other areas. When we compare these rates we find no rural-
urban shift between 1950 and 1955. A breakdown according to type
of offenses shows that offenses traditionally higher for the rural area
are continuing their relative increase there, while offenses more characteristic of the urban areas are increasing proportionately even more
in these areas. Total increases noted in increasing delinquency rates,
then, are differentially related to whether the area is rural or urban.
In American rural regions the advent of the automobile and other
modes of transportation as well as modern means of communication
such as television have had an impact that is just beginning to be felt
in rural regions in Japan.

Yuriko Horiye[41] (1954) conducted an intensive study of delinquency
patterns in a particular region of Yamagata Prefecture. In this rural
area many of the delinquents studied were from poor farm families of
low social status. Many of those convicted of delinquent behavior had
moved away from home at a relatively early age, seeking unskilled
daily employment in nearby urban centers, and many had fallen into
some form of delinquent behavior as a result of economic frustration.
The author considers that an important factor in inducing this delinquent behavior is the hostile attitude of the residents of certain of
these poorer farming areas toward government or authority generally.
We shall discuss this issue further in respect to the Korean and outcaste minority populations in Japan in Chapter 14.

The special social attitudes of some rural communities can be
related to the chronically poor economic conditions. In the northeast,
as we have indicated in Chapter 12, selling daughters into prostitution
was a well-established means of relieving economic hardship. Unless
a general community attitude had at least condoned such practices, it
is unlikely that they would have continued. Economic privation in
many areas is considered more degrading than the commercial use of
the body in prostitution.

It has been noted in some Japanese studies of urban-rural differences that small cities and the towns near large cities have very high

---

[41] Y. Horiye, "A Study on Criminal Environment" (1954, in Japanese).

rates of delinquency. It is our impression that the higher delinquency rates in satellite towns have been insufficiently examined in respect to overall mobility patterns in urban migration. Peculiarities in the development of Japanese cities that are different from the patterns of development taking place in American cities have not been sufficiently documented by Japanese sociologists concerned with urban development. To illustrate, Kashikuma et al.[42] report that six medium-sized satellite cities on the periphery of Tokyo have a slightly higher rate of juvenile delinquency (1.22 for the year compared) than has the metropolitan district of Tokyo itself (1.14). These peripheral urbanized areas have a higher proportionate rate of urban-type crimes than have the more rural surrounding areas, which are relatively high for injury and rape and other forms of sexual offenses.

Wagatsuma and De Vos,[43] in an intensive investigation of Arakawa Ward in Tokyo, found evidence for a pattern of geographic mobility that may be fairly general for Japanese cities, and that may shed light on delinquency rates in satellite communities. Very recently, Arakawa, a traditionally lower-class northern peripheral ward of Tokyo, which has been termed the "wastebasket" of Tokyo, has been gradually improving as far as delinquency is concerned. We are gaining evidence of a slow but perceptible differential migration pattern; if families prosper sufficiently, they seek housing in a more central middle-class ward such as Setagaya-ku, whereas if they cannot afford even the minimal low rentals of Arakawa, they move to Adachi Ward or to nearby Saitama Prefecture, a satellite urban area.

This outmigration occurs selectively among the more personally disorganized families. In general, what we see in Tokyo is an urbanizing phenomenon quite unlike that occurring in Chicago or other American cities. Although there is also a very apparent suburban growth pattern, the city of Tokyo is not deteriorating in the central area under the pressure of land values and changed forms of usage. The problems of buying and selling property, the transportation problems and the peculiar residency patterns of petty artisans and merchants continuing from the premodern economy prevent a general retreat to the suburban areas. Rather, there is a steady pressure for improvement of more centrally located areas, while some peripheral areas are selectively less desirable and attract the poorest individuals. The fact that satellite cities show high delinquency rates seems related therefore to economically determined patterns characteristic for Japanese urban residential migration.

In both Japan and the United States, urban and rural differences

---

[42] Kashikuma, "Ecological Study of Juvenile Delinquency in Tokyo" (1958).
[43] DeVos and Wagatsuma, *Heritage of Endurance* (to be published).

have been analyzed almost exclusively in sociological terms. No one
has made a serious attempt to study whether possible differential
socialization experiences and community sanctions may contribute
to these different statistics. One would suppose that there may be
vicissitudes in personality development that are directly or indirectly
related to features of urban society not found in the traditional rural
environment. This needs further explanation. Some serious attempts
should be made to test, on a more general level, the personality variables related to selective patterns of urban migration. In a major
personality survey of rural and urban Japanese conducted in 1953–
1957, we did find systematic differences between the two groups in
personality rigidity and authoritarian and conservative attitudes. However, we did not attempt to trace and test specifically those individuals
who had already left the three villages studied.

DIFFERENTIAL RATES OF DELINQUENCY
WITHIN URBAN AREAS

High Delinquency Areas in the United States

So-called high-delinquency neighborhoods in urban slums have
been much studied since the pioneer work of Shaw and McKay[44] on
the differential distribution of the incidence of delinquency in the
Chicago area. Specific areas of the city of Chicago were carefully sur-
veyed for three periods, 1900–1906, 1917–1923, and 1927–1933. The
distributions of alleged delinquents brought before the juvenile court
of Cook County, of delinquents committed by the court to correctional
schools, and of delinquent boys dealt with by police probation officers
in each of these periods were plotted on a map of Chicago. Three
methods were employed to determine the extent to which the evaluations corresponded with the rate of delinquency in the respective
periods. First, by comparing city zones, the authors found that Chicago
delinquents were principally concentrated in the central areas of the
city. Moreover, the relative concentration of delinquency in certain
areas, especially in the central part of the city, did not change from
1900 to 1933.

The high delinquency area was characterized as an area in transition in which the social relationship of the people was always changing. Shaw and McKay also studied the economic and cultural condition of these areas and pointed out that delinquency is thus largely
related to transitional slum conditions. However, as Shaw stated in a

---

[44] Shaw and McKay, "Are Broken Homes a Causative Factor in Delinquency?"
(1932); *Social Factors in Juvenile Delinquency* (1931); *Juvenile Delinquency and
Urban Areas* (1942).

later chapter, poverty in itself in the sense of purely economic considerations does not show a direct relation to delinquency. The important determinant seemed to be, rather, the poverty area and its group influences in which other conditions of disorganization were to be found.

The recent view of the high delinquency area in terms of subcultural continuity also stems directly from their work. From the standpoint of anthropology, however, their work shows a lack of comprehension of the role of cultural traditions in the data they were examining. They concluded that family and ethnic cohesion were irrelevant to the overriding effects of neighborhood continuities in the peer-group patterns influencing delinquency. They cited the fact that although other ethnic groups, such as the Negroes and Mexicans, living in the high delinquency areas studied, showed signs of family disorganization, the Sicilians living in the same area had strongly knit family configurations, yet all had high rates of delinquency. The generalization by Shaw and McKay was made without regard to other possible influences making for similarity in the groups considered. An important consideration is similarity in previous traditional attitudes toward the police. The traditional general attitudes of Sicilians toward government and police authority are not dissimilar to those of the Mexicans or American Negroes, although all these groups differ in family patterns. The Sicilian ethnic traditions of gang behavior goes counter to "law and order" concepts of middle-class Americans. The ethnic tradition of the Sicilians put a higher value on interpersonal loyalties and commitments than on respect for police or legal authority. The Mafia as a social force operated counter to legal authority. This did not preclude the operation of strong familial ties within Sicilian culture. The Shaw and McKay generalizations deserve some reinterpretation in respect to the role played by cultural traditions among immigrants as an equal force in determining reactions to a high delinquency neighborhood environment. Their generalizations did not operate when Japanese-Americans moved into high delinquency areas in Chicago.

In observing the post–World War II pattern of Japanese immigration of more than 17,000 into the city of Chicago owing to the enforced relocation of Japanese-Americans from the West Coast, author De Vos[45] was particularly interested in whether there would occur some noticeable increase in social problems, including delinquency, among this minority group faced with problems of extreme racial discrimina-

---

[45] DeVos, "A Comparison of the Personality Differences in Two Generations of Japanese-Americans by Means of the Rorschach Test" (1954); and "A Quantitative Rorschach Assessment of Maladjustment and Rigidity in Acculturating Japanese Americans" (1955).

tion. Examination of the records of social agencies and police showed a minimum number of problems in spite of the fact that the Japanese families were constrained to find housing in the ghetto areas open to minority groups in Chicago. Japanese American youth did not succumb to the influence of the high delinquency neighborhoods in which they were living. It is our view that the ethnic family patterns and values of the Japanese made them resistive to the delinquency-producing forces of these neighborhoods in which they were living.

The influence of family patterns on delinquency formation in Japan is discussed in another volume.[46] Suffice it to say here that cultural traditions operate in family units as well as in community reference groups. They are as determinative of the continuity or lack of continuity of delinquent activities in urban neighborhoods with high delinquency rates as are the atmospheric conditions of the neighborhood itself.

Differences in the ecology of high delinquency areas between the United States and Japan became very apparent in some of the published statistics. Kashikuma[47] studied the rate of delinquency in the various districts of Tokyo.[48] The overall rate of juvenile delinquents in the city area of Tokyo is 0.54 percent.[49] When the Tokyo area is divided into small population units consisting of about 10,000 each, several areas have a comparatively high concentration of delinquents, but none of these has the very high rates reported in the American results. A detailed estimate of the juvenile population was made in the highest delinquency areas of Tokyo, and the rate of juvenile delinquents there per total juvenile population was found to be 3.7 percent, approximately three times the concentration of delinquents found in the entire city of Tokyo, which has a 1.4 percent delinquency rate per total juvenile population for the same period. It is highly questionable whether this "high delinquency area" would be so called in the American frame of reference.

There are differences between the Japanese lower-class and the American lower-class value systems and patterns of living.[50] Even in

---

[46] DeVos and Wagatsuma, *Heritage of Endurance* (to be published).

[47] Kashikuma, "Ecological Study of Juvenile Delinquency in Tokyo" (1958).

[48] Time has passed since the study of Kashikuma et al., and delinquency has increased in Japan. After ten years, Kashikuma is trying to replicate the study. Although the results are not yet obtained, it is his personal impression that the place of concentration changed and that the total tendency found in the 1958 study changed by 1966.

[49] The exact total of the juvenile population was not available at that time; therefore, to compare the American results by Shaw and McKay, which use the rate of the delinquent per total juvenile population, we have estimated the juvenile population.

[50] DeVos and Wagatsuma, *Heritage of Endurance* (to be published).

poor areas, family structure is not necessarily unstable; it is often characterized by the maintenance of traditional familial ties. There is less "anomie" in the city in Japan than in the United States. On the whole, the common belief of American sociologists that unsuccessful families move into the central areas of the city with their social maladjustment and disintegrated family life does not seem to apply to Japan.

The Distribution of Delinquency Rates Within Japanese Cities

In spite of the effects of commercial and industrial growth on the development of urban complexes in Japan, there are obvious differences between Japanese and American cities in their patterns of growth differences that have to do with traditions of property transactions, tenacity of residence, and transportation facilities that create a different structuring of the ecological environment within the Japanese and the United States city. Change of residence is difficult in Tokyo for a number of economic reasons inhibiting property transactions. There is also a reluctance to give up property in order to move to a more convenient location. Once a family residence is established, individuals will travel great distances from residence to job rather than move. The housing market is very tight and prices are constantly rising. The prevailing mood is to cling to what one already has or to make improvements on existing housing rather than to exchange houses or move out farther to the peripheries into new housing areas that are more inconvenient to the central city.

Relatively little has been done to relate the type of growth pattern of the American city to the early appearance of the automobile. The possession of private transportation by the middle class is just now being felt in already established European cities and in Japan. The role of public transportation in the development of Japanese cities has made for a residential distribution in Japan resembling the European pattern more than that of the United States. Nevertheless, the nature of public transportation and traditional patterns of leisure and entertainment make for some features in Japanese city life not duplicated elsewhere.

The Ecological Structure of Tokyo

In the city of Tokyo, now with a total population of twelve million within the metropolitan area, there is a large web of transportation facilities—subways, trains, buses, and trolleys—serving the city in all directions and circling it in the center. At several points various modes of transportation come together to form major ganglia in the circulatory system of the city. It is at these points of transfer that one finds the principal areas of delinquency and crime. These transportation hubs are extremely active areas both in selling various forms of merchandise and in providing entertainment for the teeming population of Tokyo. Around each of these principal areas is an amazing number of coffee shops, bars, restaurants, cabarets, nightclubs, and small hotels (used by prostitutes and by individuals carrying on affairs away from home). These areas provide for all the needs, both legitimate and unsanctioned, of the large population of Tokyo.

Although these areas are similar in many respects, certain of them have peculiar characteristics that account for a differential incidence in crime. Many of the juvenile delinquents in these areas are seen wearing characteristic dress; certain modes of haircut and certain types of shirts are used as symbols by this group. In 1960, for example, one could observe a great many terry-cloth short-sleeved shirts and "shintaro" haircuts made popular by books and motion pictures about the *taiyozoku* or "sun tribe." These stories had a rather sadistic "phallic" tone, romanticizing the activity of wealthy youth in the pleasure-resort area of Kamakura. These styles were subsequently replaced by "Teddy boy mod" clothes and Beatle-type haircuts. Attempts at beards are now appearing as well.

It is difficult to describe the crush of crowds and the general atmosphere of a Japanese entertainment area to those unfamiliar with it. One may find bars and coffee shops appealing to every taste and inclination; certain of the Japanese coffee shops feature classical hi-fi music and others offer a steady diet of American-type "rock and roll" and "country" music for the price of a cup of coffee. The decor in some coffee shops beggars description; for example, De Vos recently visited a coffee shop in Tokyo decorated by a large fifteen-by-twenty-five-foot backlighted stained glass reproduction of the painting by David of the coronation of the emperor Napoleon.

The bar-girl, or "hostess," has become a Japanese institution. Girls will keep amiable company with the customer while he is drinking, but there is relatively little pressure in most places to raise the bill by having the girl drink colored water, as is done in other Asian countries catering to G.I.'s. The Japanese bar-girl is mainly for Japanese customers, and any sexual activity on her part is usually on a voluntary or individual basis arranged between herself and the customer, although in some places the "madam" helps out in such arrangements.

Much of the activity of these entertainment areas attests to a wide-scale chronic isolation and anomie existing within the modern Japanese city, where many individuals must seek some paid contact to round out their otherwise isolated social lives. For some married men these areas also form a stopping-over place between work and home. Since the pattern of family life in Japan includes very little visiting or social communication by a man and wife with others, the man often finds his entertainment by himself while the woman remains home. One can readily understand why entertainment areas of this nature provide such a fertile field for delinquent activity in the city.

Under the leadership of Koji Kashikuma and others[51] the Supreme Court of Japan has published a detailed ecological study of juvenile delinquency in the Tokyo area. This large-scale survey reported on all delinquents taken into Tokyo Family Court in 1956, except for those arrested for accidental violations and traffic offenses. Included were all violators of the penal code and of certain special laws concerning the handling of weapons, drug addiction, and prostitution. This survey of Tokyo delinquents was an elaboration of a more modest survey conducted three years before. The second survey included data on 14,325 individuals under twenty years of age. Distribution maps were made of the residence of delinquents as well as of the actual places that delinquent activities occurred. There tended to be little correspondence between these two distributions. The area of residence of delinquents in Tokyo is not concentrated in the central area of the city, but tends to be distributed throughout most of the major population districts. Relatively high residential concentration of delinquents was observed in some areas located between the central and peripheral districts or wards. However, these areas are proportionally much less concentrated than are the "high delinquency areas" in the United States. According to American research reports, delinquents reside in the area where their delinquency occurs. Relatively little differential in the rate of delinquency exists in comparison of the twenty-three wards of Tokyo. However, as in the United States, socially transitional areas had a somewhat higher rate of delinquency than other areas. The distribution of delinquents by residence seems related to the nature of the growth of residency in Tokyo, which has led to a relative lack of differentiation of large areas by class. Although the correspondence is not remarkable, the general economic and cultural level of specific areas seems to have a somewhat low correlation to delinquency. As the city developed, transitional areas were characterized by minor industries and poor residences, and included some amusement centers.

Actually, the areas with the largest concentration of delinquent residents either are peripheral to certain amusement areas, or are located in special areas noted for their private gambling facilities; the gangs operating in the Tokyo area are most active in both of these areas. This pattern is obviously related to transportation facilities; three of the five major areas of residence of delinquents are relatively close to one of the major transportation hubs of Tokyo. Four of the five major poor residence areas are well known for their commerce,

[51] Kashikuma, "Ecological Study of Juvenile Delinquency in Tokyo" (1958).

and contain many small stores and small industries where many young people, both males and females, work away from their families and live in small stores and factories. These boys and girls living outside a family network are considered more apt to become delinquent.

The relationship in the United States between a high rate of delinquency and some of the social factors mentioned by Shaw and McKay[52] does not seem equally operative in Japan. Although in Japan there is some slight correlation between the rate of delinquency of an area and the rate of infant mortality, it does not accord with their findings for the United States. Also, there is no consistent relationship reported in Japan between the rate of delinquency and the amount of public assistance for an area. There was no relationship between the rate of delinquency and the number of families who have radio or television. It seems that in Tokyo, at least, the relationship of economic conditions and health and social conditions to delinquency is less apparent than that reported for the United States.

Recently, Yoshimasu[53] made a comparison of two contrasting areas of Tokyo, the former an "uptown" Yamanote district and the latter a "downtown" Shitamachi district. The subjects of the study were all the juvenile delinquents from these two areas arrested in 1960 and in part of 1961. Sumida Ward, the "downtown" area, showed a notable recent increase in the number of juvenile delinquents, whose homes are distributed over the area, suggesting no particular area of the ward as contributing to the increasing total. The average age of the delinquents is decreasing in respect to incidence of theft and larceny, but there are an increasing number of violent offenses (threat, violence, injury, etc.). Nearly half the delinquents (44.3 percent) were classified either as factory workers or as shop assistants. The educational level was generally low. Many came originally from rural areas outside of Tokyo. In Setagaya-ku, the "uptown" middle-class area, the delinquents' homes tend to be concentrated in a certain area on the distribution chart. No particular pattern of delinquency stands out, except for a fairly high rate of arrests for prostitution. Yoshimasu found that 40 percent of delinquents were classified by occupation as students. Little or no difference among these delinquents was found when they were compared on other features such as differences between the place of residence and the place of acting out or the actual, economic conditions of the household, the rate of infant mortality in the area, and the distribution of radio and television. One will note that subsections of Setagaya Ward are lower-class although the ward as a whole is one of relatively high income people.

---

[52] Shaw and McKay, *Juvenile Delinquency and Urban Areas* (1942).

[53] Yoshimasu, "Regional Study of Juvenile Delinquency in Tokyo" (1961, in Japanese).

Fukutomi and Saito[54] made an ecological survey in Kawasaki City, immediately south of Tokyo, including in their survey all the juveniles appearing in Yokohama Family Court in 1954 and 1959 who either resided in or committed delinquency in Kawasaki City. They analyzed the mobility pattern of these delinquents, sampling the daily movement and the residential mobility of the whole population of the delinquency area and comparing it with other areas. They found that the "acting" circle of a juvenile delinquent is usually within a five-kilometer radius of his residence, and that he is most likely to commit his delinquent acts at a large amusement center within this circle. The delinquent tends to move residence to gain easier access to a delinquency area. Fukutomi and Saito also found that the daily movement of the residents in the higher delinquency areas of Kawasaki is more intense than that of those residing in other areas. However, change of housing for the residents in a high delinquency area is not greater than for those in the other areas. These findings again conform with our generalizations concerning the differential ecological effects of the Japanese city compared with those of the United States.

Some Japanese Interpretations of the Significance of Postwar Trends

A 1958 summary by the Japanese Ministry[55] indicates that there has been a continual increase in recidivism in the postwar period. By 1956 one-third of the cases handled by the family courts were concerned with individuals who had previous delinquent records. There was a definite trend toward an earlier age of recorded commission of the first act of delinquency, which is related to this increase in recidivism rates for the entire juvenile population.

In analyzing such postwar trends, Taro Ogawa[56] attempts to break down the postwar trend into several subperiods. According to Ogawa, using 1941 as a base year (100), the peak year for delinquency was 1951, when the rate had increased to 300. There was a subsequent decline, until in 1954 the rate was down to 228. From 1954 to 1957 the juvenile crime rate increased to 274, a trend that is continuing upward since Ogawa's report was written. Ogawa sought to analyze these changes as they related to variations in the social climate in the postwar period. In the earliest postwar period, from 1945 to 1948, there was large-scale disorganization, and robbery and offenses such as gambling especially were on the increase. From 1948 to 1951, there

---

[54] Fukutomi and Saito, "Delinquency and Life Structure in Urban Community" (1962, in Japanese).

[55] Ministry of Justice, Japan, *Juvenile Delinquency in Japan* (1958).

[56] Ogawa, "Juvenile Delinquency in the Ten Years After the War" (1956, in Japanese).

was an increase in burglary and crimes against property which reached
a maximum in 1951. From 1951 on, the types of crime on the increase
were crimes against persons, especially injury, and forms of sexual
delinquency. Ogawa related these fluctuations in the incidence of
juvenile crime to the patterns of economic recovery in postwar Japan.
Ogawa has attempted to point out that delinquency as a long-range
general trend in Japan is turning from a more socially withdrawn form
to a more aggressive type of acting-out. The trends observable since the
publication of Ogawa's review have continued in the direction he
indicated. Very recently, joy-riding and theft related to automobiles
are increasing proportionally with the number of automobiles appearing on the Japanese streets.

Except for the absence in Japan of the use of weapons, it is the
author Mizushima's first-hand observation in both the United States
and Japan that delinquency in Japan is coming more and more to
resemble that in the United States. It may be said that delinquency
related to economic difficulties is being replaced by delinquency as
an assertion of dominance or power, or as a means of immediate gratification.

When psychiatrists compared their studies of the personality composition of delinquents in the postwar period with diagnoses done in a
previous period, they concluded that fluctuations in the postwar social
conditions are influential in producing delinquency in what in other
circumstances would be essentially normal individuals. Higuchi,[57] in
an early postwar study, examined a group of seventy-three juvenile
vagrants, most of whom were lost or separated from their parents
owing to wartime circumstances. Nearly half of those examined were
found to be of essentially normal personality; however, of the remaining half, nearly one out of three was found to have some major
type of mental defect. In general, they maintained themselves by
begging, shoe-shining, or other types of "street business." They were
becoming habituated to forms of illegal and criminal behavior in the
course of making their livelihood. A number of them had already
developed contacts with professional and criminal gangs.

A second group studied by Higuchi was composed of 313 institutionalized delinquent children, most of them under fourteen years of
age. The rate of mental deficiency in this group was found to be much
lower than that in samples of prewar delinquents. This group did not
differ basically from the juvenile vagrant group Higuchi had previously studied in respect to the proportion of normal and so-called de-
fective individuals. Among the so-called defectives, however, the rate
of what the author considered "genetic personality defects" was lower

---

[57] Higuchi, "Psychiatric Study of Juvenile Delinquency After the War" (1953).

in general, and the rate of what he termed "environmentally induced defects" was higher. Families from which this group was derived were found to be more disorganized than those of prewar institutionalized groups. Higuchi did considerable study of the environmental and personal historical background of the children in his sample.

Higuchi's third empirical study was done with a group of five hundred institutionalized juvenile delinquents of a somewhat older age. Of this group, 73 percent had been institutionalized for theft. Among the older boys there was a higher incidence of adjudicated acts of threat, bodily injury, fraud, and larceny; the younger boys more often were pickpockets or individuals who had simply been picked up for running away from home. Higuchi notes that there seems to be more crime committed in a group context among these institutionalized youngsters than was true for the prewar delinquents he had observed. In his statistics he cites a rate of mental deficiency in this group of 20 percent, as compared with the prewar figure of 31 percent.

Vagrancy among youth from families that had been broken or made destitute by the war was a transient phenomenon that disappeared fairly rapidly with postwar economic gains. However, these studies do indicate that the effects of wartime disorganization coupled with lack of economic opportunities could lead very quickly to criminal associations and criminal activity on the part of otherwise normal youngsters.

We plan to discuss in a future publication some other studies that seek to affirm that social conditions within a society at any time can radically alter the effect of what might be considered the psychological or physical determinants of delinquent behavior. Early family experiences in one situation may not lead to delinquency, whereas, given a change of conditions, the same experiences would be highly conducive to delinquent conduct. Psychiatrists such as Higuchi and Yoshimasu seem to say that postwar social conditions have been more influential in producing delinquency than were the conditions obtaining in prewar Japan.

One cannot, however, neglect to point out that the perception of the investigators themselves has changed. With the general attention now being paid to environmental conditions, even psychiatrists who have had training in a German psychiatric tradition with a relatively strong constitutional orientation have come to respect the influence of environment on socialization experiences. Such a change must be regarded as part of a general change in the professional perception of specialists in the field of delinquency and criminology in Japan. How much increased sensitivity influences the results of comparative studies of the pre- and postwar periods is hard to determine. It may well be that in the prewar period an individual would be more readily diagnosed as having some physical or mental constitutional defect contributing to his delinquency than he would when examined in the present era.

THE INFLUENCE OF MASS MEDIA AS AN INSTRUMENT OF CULTURAL DIFFUSION AND SOCIAL CHANGE

One of the unresolved issues on which there has been considerable controversy is the relationship of delinquency to the postwar increase in exposure to mass media. The publication of books and magazines emphasizing sex and violence, and the distribution of movies in which sex and violence are openly portrayed, have been freed from the rigid censorship applied before the war in Japan. It has been argued that the mass media may be a causal influence in provoking crime and delinquency. Less attention has been paid to how the models presented in the mass media may influence the particular style of delinquent or criminal acts.

In a careful early study done in the United States, Blumer and Hauser[58] reported that among 368 male delinquents studied, 10 percent believed that their delinquent activities could be related to movies they had previously viewed. The authors concluded, however, that only the delinquency-prone and already deviantly predisposed children were actually motivated to delinquent activity by the movies themselves. They suggest that the impression a film makes on a viewer in its capacity to incite action is a function of the total personality integration of the individual at the particular time.

Sutherland [59] cites a report that a movie, *Wild Boys of the Road,* was played in 1933 in Evanston, Illinois, during the Christmas vacation and that within one month fourteen children in this community ran away. Of four of these children subsequently caught by the police, three said they had been strongly influenced by seeing the movie. Similar reports by police are not infrequently recorded in Japan; for example, a group of boys is reported to have seen a gang movie and immediately afterward, caught up in the mood of the film, to have acted out violently.

One of the authors, Mizushima, in his role as clinical psychologist, had occasion to interview intensively four boys who were involved in a group rape. These boys, sixteen and seventeen years of age, had formed a gang which previously had been involved only in very minor infractions, including truancy. One evening the four of them had seen a picture, *Ali Baba and the Forty Thieves,* which had a generally

---

[58] Blumer and Hauser, *The Movies, Delinquency and Crime* (1933).
[59] Sutherland, *Principles of Criminology* (1947).

arousing effect on them. Afterward they walked about the street pro-
claiming in loud voices what tough fellows they were, that like the
hero of the movie they were virile, masculine, and aggressive. They
came across two young girls of a somewhat sexually provocative nature who walked about with them for awhile, and they finally convinced one of them to accompany them to a quieter place. One of the
boys, by now sexually very excited, forced the girl into intercourse,
and the three other boys, although initially somewhat hesitant to join
in, were induced by a feeling of masculine bravado and the wish not
to show weakness or lack of courage to participate in a group rape. One
can say in this instance that the movie was a general instigation to the
boys, who in having formed the gang already showed need to proclaim
their masculinity and give it behavioral evidence. This incident perhaps illustrates the capacity of a movie to act as a specific catalytic
stimulus to trigger already potentially available behavior.

There have been some studies in Japan that indicate that delinquent
boys and girls attend movies more frequently than do nondelinquent
youth. Although such studies do not demonstrate in any way that
specific movies are the direct cause of delinquency, one cannot overlook the fact that in making available the stimulation of various simu-
lated acts of violence they offer a form of social learning to individuals
who have internal motivations and personal propensities for expressing some form of antisocial behavior. Such an individual finds in
movies and in television external sources of identification beyond
those immediately available in his environment through the sub-
stitution of a necessary provocation supplied by the movie or the
television scene.[60]

Kiyoyasu Kamei[61] made a study of the influence of so-called bad
pictures or books on one hundred delinquents. He concluded that
although sexual or violent pictures and books did not seem to have a
direct influence upon the specific delinquent acts of these boys, many
of the delinquents were very familiar with how to obtain such pornographic material, which seemed to exert some sort of indirect influence
on them.

How mass media are related to social change is a much broader issue
than the specific issue of the provision by mass media of models for
incitement to delinquency. It is the general impression of the authors,
for example, that the presence of American servicemen in Japan had
much less effect in changing patterns of behavior than did the showing
of American movies in Japanese movie houses. Only a very small per-

---

[60] Mizushima, *Social Disease* (1956). See also Keiichi Mizushima, "A Study on the
Prognosis of Social Adjustment of Delinquents" (1955, in Japanese).

[61] Kamei, "Delinquency and Bad Pictures or Books in Iwate Prefecture" (1957, in
Japanese).

centage of the total Japanese population had contact with American service personnel in Japan, whereas many Japanese now see weekly movies about American and European social and personal life. These movies graphically present a way of life and behavior that differs from that of traditional Japan. From the standpoint of cultural diffusion, the visual immediacy of movies or television has a much more lasting effect than did the importation of European literature in the late nineteenth and early twentieth centuries, which influenced only those capable of the sustained act of reading.

There is no doubt that movies throughout the world tend to change youthful behavior. Such phenomena as the wearing of black leather jackets has been noted in Japan and in such widely separated places as Chile, France, and Sweden. It is apparent that certain symbols in form of particular clothing styles, for example, can quickly become universalized and can become a manifest means of expressing already present delinquent attitudes.

One must note a selectivity in those who choose particular models of a delinquent nature in contrast to other models available in the way of media used for nondelinquent behavior. With shared sources of communication, such as the movies and television, the content of adolescent behavior is becoming progressively similar throughout the world. Popular figures set the tone and express the content through which the various propensities of youth everywhere find expression. The development of periodic outbreaks of youth in countries such as Germany and Sweden, in the 1960s as well as such activities in American cities, suggests a confluence in the patterns of adolescence in a negative as well as a positive sense in a developing world culture stimulated by interpenetrated mass media. Delinquency-prone individuals are influenced by what they see and may choose to act out violently in patterns suggested to them by movies that offer scenes of violence and sexual activity.

Less obvious, but equally potent as a stimulus for behavior, is the continual viewing of opulence and wealth by youth throughout the world. Movies continually suggest that individuals through a stroke of luck or some unusual prowess, can suddenly obtain a luxurious way of life, and thus offer uncommitted and personally vulnerable adolescents everywhere an inducement to attain goals by illegitimate means no less influential than the more obvious scenes of violence and sex. Nevertheless, one cannot say that the movies increase the number of individuals within the society who have antisocial propensities. Although the content of delinquent behavior can change, it has not been demonstrated that the actual incidence of antisocial behavior in any country is greater now because of the influence of mass media.

Discussion: General Trends of Social Change
as Related to Delinquency in Postwar Japan

Our discussion of the recent increases in certain forms of delinquency in Japan, and our strong impression that delinquent activities in Japan are coming to resemble forms of behavior observed in other modern countries to a much greater degree than previously, may seem to be somewhat at odds with the extremely low delinquency rates obtaining among Japanese-Americans in the United States. The statistical reports of California, the state with the largest mainland Japanese-American population, indicate that, whereas the Mexican-American and Negro minority groups contribute approximately five times their proportionate number of adjudicated delinquents, the rate for the Japanese-Americans remains approximately one-fiftieth that of the majority white population. One can say that until recently, at least, the Japanese-American population in California had no delinquency problem whatever. This raises the question of why and for what reason one finds in Japan at times a considerable fluctuation in delinquency. There is no doubt that there was some selectivity of emigraton to the United States, with 84 percent of the individuals coming from rural districts. Yet when one investigates the population of Tokyo, one finds there also a very large percentage of individuals who, though now living in Tokyo, were born in rural regions. Therefore, rural background by itself is not a significant selective feature.

It may well be that living in an alien culture and sharing particular cultural traditions, as in the case of the Japanese-Americans, somewhat solidified community structures. This, together with a strong tradition of low divorce or separation may explain why both the family structure and the community structure of the Japanese population living in the United States have maintained a remarkable stability in the American setting. Knowledge of the cultural values that the rural Japanese farmers brought with them to the United States is essential in understanding their adjustment to a minority ethnic status within American life. These immigrant farmers had had in Japan a relatively respected social status within their own society, and in their value system they combined respect for and interest in learning and obedience to community sanctions with a family life of an extremely close and intimate sort. Their values made it imperative for the children to exert themselves to their utmost in the school situation in meeting standards set by American middle-class teachers and in other contacts with American social institutions. Culturally sanctioned attitudes toward learning and scholarship plus primary family socialization practices led to an optimal readiness for learning within American educational institutions and tended to inoculate the growing Japanese children against the alienation experiences in American society that confronted many other immigrant groups coming from different traditions.

The fact that in urban Japan today one finds delinquency problems at least equal to those of other industrial European societies demonstrates that resistance to such larger sociological forces has not been any more possible for Japanese society than for other modern nations.

POSTSCRIPT 1973

The above chapter written originally in 1966 manifests some of the problems of writing about a very rapidly changing society. Despite the fact that Mizushima and I attempted to take the longest range historical view possible on post war delinquency rates, recent changes demonstrate a downward trend in delinquency rates we would not have predicted. The question arises as to how any of our above interpretations should be modified to better explain these recent events.

If I were to attempt to modify them in any way it would be only to give more stress to the continuing integrative features of Japanese social life in urban communities, as Wagatsuma and I have done in our forthcoming report on Arakawa ward. I would also emphasize the continuing capacity of the Japanese primary family to "inoculate" children against potentially alienating social conditions.

The concluding of this chapter as previously written sounds now to me to give too heavy a weight to the larger sociological industrial processes at work—rather than to appreciate sufficiently the continually amazing integratives force of Japanese cultural traditions related to community participation, and intimate family life whether they are manifested in Tokyo or in Japanese Americans in the U.S.A. Witnessing the rapidity of physical change one must marvel at the fact that Japan has evidently crested a wave of post war delinquency. And, indeed, Tokyo's present statistics suggest the lowest level of deliquent activity to be found in any capital of an industrial society!

Chapter XIV

Minority Status and Delinquency
in Japan

with HIROSHI WAGATSUMA

MINORITY STATUS AND AUTHORITY

To understand socialization one must understand the way in which social discrimination tends to induce deviancy and lack of respect for constituted authority.[1] The following generalizations suggest themselves regarding these conditions in American society. Not only do minority group members often lack the incentive to internalize conformist attitudes toward the law, but there are also active personal and community inducements to flout the rules of the majority society in some form, either symbolically or by actual behavior. The use of trickery to outwit authorities is among the basic defensive maneuvers of an individual in an exploited role position that excludes him from equal participation in his society. By using such methods, the minority group member salvages some aspects of self-esteem and "gets back" at an authority structure that is perceived as operating to perpetuate his degradation or to hinder his freedom rather than to benefit him in any way. What happens frequently in a minority-group role, therefore, is that the individual tends to become in some way deviant from the standards set by the dominant groups in the society. He may not identify strongly with formal authority, as it is represented in either the school or the legal system. He may not subscribe readily to patterns of marriage stability set by the majority society. He may develop

---

[1] The major content of this chapter previously appeared in DeVos and Wagatsuma, *Japan's Invisible Race: Caste in Culture and Personality* (1966).

linguistic usages, and language patterns that distinguish him from the majority society. He may be less apt to control his aggressive feelings or his sexual urges sufficiently to meet the standards of impulse control maintained by individuals more motivated by conformist needs and who are seeking to keep their social status in the majority society.

Generally, the majority society is less apt to exercise police powers over sexual or aggressive activity of minority group members than it is over such activity of majority group members. In its pejorative perception of a socially degraded group, such behavior is expected, and so long as the injuries suffered are by individuals within the minority group, they are covertly condoned. The majority society is sensitive, however, to assaults on the persons or property of the majority group, and legal sanctions toward minority members are apt to be interpreted as more severe in such situations, deepening a sense of expected injustice on the part of minority group members.[2]

In our cross-cultural research on delinquency and social deviancy in Japan[3] we were interested in determining whether a functional social parallel could be found to the high incidence of delinquency in certain minority groups in the United States. Four groups have minority status in Japan. The Ainu of Hokkaido are a separate aboriginal cultural group many of whom have become assimilated into Japanese society; they are relatively insignificant in number and are found in groups only in Hokkaido, the northern Japanese island. A second minority group, also relatively small, are the Chinese (many from Taiwan)[4] living in Japan; this group is not easily studied, and very little research has been done regarding their adjustment. A third group, more socially visible, are the Koreans; some Koreans are assimilating into Japanese culture to the extent of taking Japanese names, but a larger number keep their ethnic identity. They are recognized as constituting a social problem in Japan. So far we have not had the opportunity to investigate this group to any degree. A fourth, and for us a more interesting group, is one we were able to investigate using social anthropological methods. This group comprises the former outcastes, who were treated like the pariah caste of India until 1871, when they were "liberated" and supposedly accorded full citizenship. Through somewhat unusual circumstances, we were able to gain the trust and cooperation of some members of this group, which permitted us to initiate our study of them.

---

[2] Cf. Merton, "Social Structure and Anomie" (1949).

[3] Comparative research on delinquency and social deviancy was sponsored by a grant (MH-04087) from the National Institutes of Mental Health, Bethesda, Maryland.

[4] Both the Taiwan-Chinese and the Koreans in Japan were legally citizens from the time of the Japanese annexation of Formosa and Korea.

THE PEOPLE OF "SPECIAL" COMMUNITIES—
SOCIAL DISCRIMINATION IN JAPAN

In present-day Japan, there are an estimated one to three million people residing in more than six thousand communities, rural and urban, who are identified as *tokushu-burakumin* (people of special communities).[5] These people are referred to as *mikaihō-burakumin* (people of unliberated communities), which has a leftist connotation, or, paradoxically, as *dōwa-chiku-no-hito* (people of integrated districts). There are pejorative forms, seldom heard now, such as *eta* (filled with dirt) or *yotsu* (four-legged). The neutral descriptive abbreviation, acceptable to all, is *Burakumin*. These Burakumin are the descendants of the "outcastes" or the "untouchables," who are still socially and economically discriminated against as the result of prejudice by members of the majority society. Not racially different in any way from the majority Japanese, they can be identified certainly only by the registry of their place of birth and residence. Nevertheless, many Japanese believe that they are in some way or other visibly identifiable, and that they are mentally inferior, incapable of high moral behavior, aggressive, impulsive, and lacking any notion of sanitation or manners. Very often they are "the last hired and the first fired." Marriage between a Buraku individual and a member of the majority society, if not impossible, is frequently the cause of tragedy and ostracism.

A Brief Historical Background

By the fifteenth century, various groups of people collectively designated as Senmin ("lowly people") had appeared in Japan. Very roughly, they were classified in two large groups: (1) artisans, mainly engaged in leather and bamboo work, or dyeing, or serving as executioners, and (2) itinerant entertainers, prostitutes, and quasi-religious itinerants. The leather workers were engaged in the slaughtering and skinning of animals, the tanning of leather, and the making of leather goods, such as foot gear, saddles, and armor. Because of the Shinto tradition of disdain for whatever was considered "polluting," such as the handling of carcasses, and the proscription in Buddhism against the killing of animals, these leather workers were shunned by ordinary folk. These artisans, who were avoided, but were certainly needed, often lived in settlements on dry river beds (*kawara*) or on tax-free barren lands (*san-jo*), away from the communities of "decent" common people. The second group of Senmin, the itinerant entertainers, were

---

[5] Mahara, "Buraku Society" (1960*a*, in Japanese); see also, Mahara, *Present Situations in Buraku* (1960*b*, in Japanese).

engaged in singing, dancing, acting, performing in puppet shows, or in fortune telling and other magico-religious practices, or prostitution. Both groups of senmin were believed to have special magical power and to be "different," and were the objects of suspicion, fear, condemnation, and avoidance by the general public. The Japanese word *iyashii*, "lowly," derives from *ayashii*, "mysterious and suspicious." The Senmin included beggars, fleeing criminals, and the crippled. They also often cleaned roads and gardens, carried baggage for travelers, escorted and executed criminals, disposed of their corpses, and some of them built gardens and houses.

With the establishment of the Tokugawa government in the early seventeenth century, Japanese society was further organized into a rigidly hierarchical structure. At the top was a warrior-administrator-ruling class (*shi*), with numerous strata of subranks; the ruled consisted of peasants (*no*), artisans (*ko*), and the merchants (*sho*), and beneath this structure of accepted citizens were the "outcaste," or Senmin class, into which all the lowly people of previous times were integrated. Two major groups of outcastes were designated as the Hinin (nonhuman) and the Eta. During the Tokugawa period, the status of an Eta was inescapably hereditary; one was born, lived, and died as an Eta. This was also generally true in fact for Hinin, but in principle a Hinin individual could, by securing a respectable sponsor and paying a certain fee, gain the status of a commoner, a practice called *ashi arai*, or "foot washing." Commoners could be forced into Hinin status as punishment for certain crimes, such as adultery, or for attempting double suicide. They could become Hinin as a means of escaping the death penalty. Because of the slight mobility that was possible between "nonhuman" and "human" status, Hinin was considered to be a higher status than Eta. Eta and Hinin maintained separate endogamous groups. They were made to live in particular parts of the cities and were forced to walk barefooted, use straw to tie their hair, and many of them were required to wear a patch of leather on their clothes signifying their pollution.

Buraku Movements in Modern Japan

In August 1871 a Meiji government edict officially abolished the outcaste status and described the outcaste people as "new citizens" (*shin-heimin*). According to this government document, there were about 280,000 Eta, 23,500 Hinin, and 80,000 miscellaneous outcastes at the time of the emancipation. Legal emancipation did little to alter the discrimination against the so-called shin-heimin.

A political movement, the "integrationist movement" (*yūwa undō*), began against prejudice and injustice and was joined by wealthy paternalistic Buraku leaders and the sympathetic elite of the majority society. The core of the integrationist movement was the Great Japan's Fellow Citizens Integration Society (Dai Nippon Dōhō Yūwa Kai), established in 1903, which worked for "self-betterment" through "self-improvement" (*kaizon*) of shin-heimin, such as the improvement of morals, customs, manners, sanitation, and so forth. However, discrimination continued; for instance, when recruited into the Imperial Army, a new commoner (shin-heimin) was usually assigned to the transportation corps or maintenance corps responsible for making and repairing shoes and other leather goods. When assigned to the infantry, such a soldier had no hope of moving up, even to a rank of noncommissioned officer.

Following a series of "rice riots" by impoverished peasants at the time of the inflation after World War I, a militant liberation movement was organized; in March 1922 the National Suiheisha (Levellers' Association) was inaugurated, and it adopted as its flag "a crown of thorns the color of blood against a black background of darkness." An early objective of the Suiheisha was "an eye for an eye" counterattack against discrimination, resulting in frequent bloodshed. From 1924 to 1930 the movement suffered from internal conflicts among anarchists, Communists, and nonrevolutionists, but in 1930 it took a clearly leftist orientation and established close ties with laborers' and farmers' unions. The fight against discrimination was incorporated, both in theory and strategy, into the broader context of the class struggle and the fight for the proletarian revolution, and for nearly ten years the Communists' red flag and the flag of the crown of thorns often flew side by side. As the militarists gained power and Japan moved into war, such movements, together with other leftist activities, were either rendered "harmless," forced underground, or broken by the action of special police. At its last national meeting before final dissolution in August 1940, the Suiheisha vowed loyalty to the emperor.

After World War II, in February 1946, the National Committee on Buraku Liberation was formed. The committee, which "inherited the revolutionary tradition of the Suiheisha," later changed its name to the Buraku Liberation League; known as the Kaihō Dōmei, it continues its active attempts to end discrimination toward Buraku people.

Burakumin Response to Discrimination

Many Burakumin find outlets for their simmering discontent through leftist political organizations. Such political movements seek to change social attitudes by creating a new pattern of political-legal sanctions within the society. Through political involvement, the individual may participate in politically deviant behavior instead of resorting to forms of individual extralegal deviancy. Far-left political movements, although at times questionable from the standpoint of unrealistic assessment of possible influence and in some cases characterized by the overly emotional approaches taken by the reformer involved, are socially integrative at least insofar as they seek means of effecting change without denying self-identity or resorting to deviant mechanisms of expressing hostility toward authority through extralegal or unsanctioned behavior. The individual who takes political action is mobilizing his energy toward a cause rather than falling back in resignation or apathy, as do a great majority of the Burakumin.

Black and Mexican-American minority groups in the United States have backgrounds and traditions similar to those of the Burakumin. It is to be expected, therefore, that the Burakumin, like their American counterparts, will exhibit higher-than-average indices of various forms of socially deviant behavior. And the evidence from Japan supports such an expectation.

We find, first, among the Burakumin, a high incidence of apathy and inaccessibility to programs for education, public health, and sanitation initiated by government authority. We find also some deviousness and dependent opportunism in respect to welfare programs sponsored by the majority culture. And we also observe that the incidence of antisocial attitudes expressed as behavior defined as delinquent or criminal in nature is higher than that in the majority culture.

Burakumin and Education

One striking parallel between the situation of black people in the United States and that of the Burakumin is that both American and Japanese culture strongly induce and stimulate occupational and educational achievement in their value systems. Yet, although a minority member is well aware that he should apply himself to his own training and education, he also knows he will be faced with a highly problematical situation when he applies for a job in the profession or skill for which he has trained himself. He has to be willing to persist through a number of situations of self-deflation and rejection. American and Japanese culture both offer career incentives, at the same time producing a potential negative shock should a goal actually be sought. For instance, Mahara[6] reports the employment statistics for 166 non-Buraku children and 83 Buraku children who were graduated in March 1959 from a junior high school in Kyoto. Those who were hired by small-scale enterprises employing fewer than ten workers numbered 29.8 percent of the Buraku and 13.1 percent of the non-Buraku children; 15.1 percent of non-Buraku children obtained work in large-scale industries employing more than one thousand workers, whereas

---

[6] Mahara, "Buraku Children and Their Guidance" (1961, in Japanese).

only 1.5 percent of Buraku children did so. Working conditions in large-scale industries are generally much better than those in small-scale enterprises. The average first salary was 5,196 yen for non-Buraku children and 4,808 yen for Buraku children. Ishida[7] reports that at another junior high school near Kyoto, almost 100 percent of the non-Buraku graduates found jobs in April following their March graduation, or in May at the latest, whereas only 39 percent of Buraku graduates could find jobs in April and May and the rest had to wait longer. Many Buraku children are actually unqualified for jobs, but it is also true that many employers are unwilling to hire Buraku children, even when they are well qualified. Table XIV-1, based on Mahara's results in the report mentioned above, illustrates this tendency.

TABLE XIV-1

PERCENTAGES OF BURAKU AND NON-BURAKU JUNIOR HIGH SCHOOL GRADUATES
AT VARIOUS ACHIEVEMENT LEVELS HIRED BY LARGE-SCALE INDUSTRIES

Results of Objective Achievement Tests of graduates	Percentage hired	
	Buraku	Non-Buraku
Poor (10–29 points)	19	25
Average (30–49 points)	36	41
High (50–69 points)	50	53

There is a consistent pattern in which children of Buraku background are hired less often than non-Buraku children having the same achievement ratings. However, the higher the achievement results the less discrimination seems to operate as a factor in the selection by prospective employers.

The following story, told by a woman doctor[8] who worked among Burakumin for more than ten years, also well illustrates the adverse effect of collective or family anticipations on the aspirations of individual youth. It also illustrates a characteristic ambivalence: the desire for occupational success opposed to the fear of alienation and the social isolation that may result for the Burakumin from such success.

Mr. Y's second son was graduated from a special high school for commercial and industrial training in Nara and found a good job with a large company in Tokyo. The boy had been captain of his high school baseball team and was a promising and happy young man.

---

[7] S. Ishida, "Guidance and Problems of an Entire Class Entering High School" (1961, in Japanese).

[8] Kobayashi, *Woman Doctor in a Buraku* (1962, in Japanese).

When he left for his job in Tokyo, he was full of buoyant expectation. Everyone in his family and in the community was enthusiastic about his prospects.

When he returned home for his first vacation visits, he exhibited his usual optimism and good spirits. However, some time later he complained about living alone in Tokyo and indicated that he was homesick. His parents began to press him to quit his job and return home.

Eventually, he told his employer that he intended to quit, apparently giving homesickness as his reason. But there were obviously other reasons, because he did not accept his employer's offer to transfer him to a branch office in Nara so that he could live at home and commute to work. It appears that there was some basic ambivalence about occupational success leading to alienation and to disturbances in integrity and self-identity.

The parents' reactions were revealing, although they refused to advance specific reasons for their son's action. His mother said, "We feel relieved." The father said, "It is better that a boy of the Buraku comes back to his own community and learns how to make *zori;* this is a Buraku industry." The father also told the story of a well-known and successful outcaste in Kyoto. This individual, a brilliant student in college, became a Ph.D. and a professor. Because he was so eminent, no girl in the Buraku was "good enough" to marry him. Neither could he marry a woman from the majority society. He remained a bachelor and died of tuberculosis at an early age. The father said that, although the professor was a great man, he was not happy. And the father applied the lesson of this story to his own son. If the son were, as seemed very probable, to be successful in Tokyo and if he happened to fall in love with a girl from the majority society, he would also be seriously unhappy. The greater the success for the Burakumin the greater the potential for unhappiness.

In the face of discrimination, the easiest solution is not to try or to discredit the goal. A protective self-identity with a submerged group eliminates the necessity for trying. Although a number of individuals from minority groups have the strength of purpose and the ego capacities to survive in spite of discrimination, a good number react with general apathy and lack of involvement in the educational process.

Buraku school children are less successful compared with the majority group children. Their truancy rate is often high, as it is in California among the black and Mexican-American minority groups. The situation in Japan also probably parallels the response to education by certain but not all minority group children in the United States.

In Izumo (Shimane Prefecture), on the Japan Sea in southwestern Japan, there is a long tradition of belief in fox possession. The potentiality for being possessed by a fox descends along the family line, and such families, *kitsune-mochi* (those who have a fox), are labeled as "black" in contrast with other, "white," families. In many communities in this area, people are classified either as "black" or "white," and marriage across the black-white line is tabooed because it is believed that if a member of a white family marries a member of a black family all the other members of the white family become "black." In this area, Burakumin are treated even more stringently as outcastes than elsewhere, ranking below the "black" families. Nomura[9] compared the "intelligence" of students in three junior high schools where children of "white" families, "black" families, and Burakumin matriculated. He used two different kinds of "intelligence" tests, the nature of which are unfortunately unclear from his report. On both tests and in all three schools the results were uniform: "White" children averaged significantly higher than children from "black" families, and Buraku children, although not markedly lower than the "blacks," averaged lowest.

TABLE XIV-2

COMPARISON OF INTELLIGENCE TEST SCORES OF BURAKU CHILDREN WITH THOSE OF CHILDREN FROM "WHITE" AND "BLACK" FAMILIES

	School A		School B		School C	
	Test A	Test B	Test A	Test B	Test A	Test B
"White" children	50	53	46	49	49	49
"Black" children	45	50	44	46	46	47
Buraku children	45	50	41	45	43	45

NOTE: The nature of the test used and the meaning of the numerical scores are not explained by Nomura, the author of the table.

According to Tojo,[10] the results of a Tanaka-Binet Group I.Q. Test administered to 351 fifth- and sixth-grade children, including 77 Buraku children, at a school in Takatsuki City near Osaka shows that the I.Q. scores of the Buraku children are markedly lower than those of the non-Buraku children (see Table XIV-3).

Recently reported test results from a school in Fukuchiyama City show the same differences between Buraku and non-Buraku children.[11]

The Buraku children in Fukuchiyama City are doing less well than their non-Buraku classmates at both primary and junior high school.

---

[9] Nomura, "Psychology of Fox Possession" (1956, in Japanese).

[10] Tojo, *Debate on Assimilation Education* (1960a, in Japanese), pp. 11–12.

[11] Nishimoto, *Buraku Problems and Assimilation Education* (1960, in Japanese), p. 71.

TABLE XIV-3

COMPARISON OF THE TANAKA-BINET I.Q. TEST SCORE PERCENTAGES OF BURAKU
CHILDREN WITH THOSE OF MAJORITY GROUP CHILDREN IN A CITY NEAR OSAKA

I.Q.	Non-Buraku children (274)	Buraku children (77)
Above 125	23.3	2.6
124–109	31.8	19.5
108–93	23.3	22.1
92–77	11.7	18.2
Below 76	9.9	37.6

TABLE XIV-4

COMPARISON OF TANAKA-BINET TEST SCORES OF PRIMARY SCHOOL
CHILDREN IN FUKUCHIYAMA CITY

	I.Q. average
Buraku boys (10)	89
Buraku girls (9)	87
Non-Buraku boys (10)	105
Non-Buraku girls (12)	103

TABLE XIV-5

COMPARISON OF GRADE-POINT AVERAGES IN PRIMARY AND
JUNIOR HIGH SCHOOL IN FUKUCHIYAMA CITY

Primary School	
Buraku boys (12)	2.29
Buraku girls (10)	2.59
Non-Buraku boys (10)	3.29
Non-Buraku girls (15)	3.16
Junior High School	
Buraku students (8)	2.2
Non-Buraku students (11)	3.3

Mahara,[12] in his aforementioned report, compared the scores on
standard achievement tests devised by the Ministry of Education of
247 subjects, 83 of them Buraku children, at a junior high school in
Kyoto. The average in four subjects consistently showed higher functioning by the non-Buraku youth than by Buraku students.

---

[12] Mahara, "Buraku Society" (1960a, in Japanese).

TABLE XIV-6

COMPARISON OF STANDARD ACHIEVEMENT TEST SCORES IN FOUR SUBJECTS
IN A KYOTO JUNIOR HIGH SCHOOL

	Non-Buraku children	Buraku children
Japanese	55.5	46.5
Humanities	61.8	46.6
Mathematics	49.9	36.4
Science	51.1	41.0

Numerous studies in the United States similarly attest to the substandard functioning of minority group children from culturally underprivileged ethnic backgrounds. Racists would argue that this reflects innate differences in ability; we would argue that in both Japan and the United States the results reflect early damage to social self-identity and self-respect vis-à-vis cultural expectations.

Burakumin Attitudes Toward Health and Welfare Authorities

Members of a minority group, having experienced a long tradition of discrimination, develop certain characteristic ways of handling their relationships with dominant elements of the society. They not only develop a defensive hostility in respect to the dominant groups, but they are also likely to develop ways of expressing ambivalent attitudes of dependency toward the economically dominant majority group members. The minority member's dependence on the majority group is given an expediential flavor by his finding means of being devious in how he "takes"; deviousness is a balm to the ego and allows the individual to maintain his self-respect by feeling less than completely helpless. Individuals from the majority group are sometimes angry to discover "relief cheating"; it confirms their prejudice concerning the worthlessness of the individuals who are being "helped" through the efforts of the more humane elements within their community. There is considerable division of opinion in American society today concerning the effects of the relief policy. Analogous to the situation in the United States, the Burakumin have developed the attitude that they are "due" economic assistance from the majority society, tending to see this as a right that goes with their minority status. Dr. Kobayashi, the woman doctor mentioned previously,[13] tells of an incident illustrating the "expediential-dependent" attitudes of the Burakumin toward welfare programs.

Mr. T., a tailor who is very poor, lives in the Buraku; he is not a

[13] Kobayashi, *Woman Doctor.*

Buraku person, but his wife is from the community. She was working in a bar in a nearby city when Mr. T. met her. Mr. T. did not know that his wife was of Buraku background, but he was not concerned when he learned about it. However, his wife remained very much concerned; she was always talking about it and felt inferior to other people. Mr. T. did not like his wife's attitude about this, so he went to the library of the town and started reading books on the history of the Burakumin. He wanted to educate his wife and to free her from her own prejudice, but he was not very successful. He felt he could not persuade her to believe that he was not prejudiced against the Burakumin people, and as a last resort he decided to move into his wife's community, where he is now living.

The doctor asked Mr. T. to comment on life within the community. Mr. T. said he feels that the people of this community behave in such a way as to cause social discrimination on the part of the general society. Within this community he, as an outsider, is not accepted and meets with discrimination. About six months ago he wanted to take care of a man living in the next apartment who had wandered into the community from the outside. This man had no job and no money, so Mr. T. took him to a local branch of the city office that takes care of the jobless to register him as eligible for relief. The public employees there told Mr. T. that the number of people who could receive governmental unemployment relief money was limited and that they could not help Mr. T.'s friend at that time. Mr. T. was told that they would have to wait for a while, so they waited, but nothing happened. Then Mr. T. learned that immediately after they were refused people of the Burakumin community were accepted and registered in the office. He also found that people with considerable income were receiving relief money; some of these relief recipients even owned electric washing machines, telephones, and television sets. Mr. T. got very angry and went to the public employment security office and criticized them very severely. He was very angry that the man from the outside society could not receive relief, while the people with Buraku background could register and receive money even when they had enough money to own a television set or telephone. Through Mr. T.'s efforts, his friend was accepted and registered for relief money; minor officials at the office had been forced to admit that they were doing something technically wrong, but they still did not reject the Buraku people, merely accepting his friend on the rolls. Mr. T. says that in this community receiving unemployment relief is considered a kind of job, and in order to get this "job" the people use all kinds of political pressure tactics on the ward office. If an individual has influential relatives and many other relatives living in the community to give him strong support, he will be successful in getting relief funds. Mr. T. himself rejected strongly the clannishness of the Buraku people and their exclusive attitude directed toward members of the majority society.

As another example of the expediential "take what you can get" attitude of the Buraku toward the outside society, Dr. Kobayashi writes that many families in her community, although relatively poor, use electricity generously for cooking, warming up rooms, and so forth. They pay only the basic fee for electricity and have their own devices for using electricity without having it register on the meter. The people of almost every house do this, and they do not think they are doing anything wrong in cheating the company.

Dr. Kobayashi was the only doctor living in this relatively poor community and she was well accepted and well liked by the people, but she had a hard time getting her patients to pay her fees. She received a salary from the hospital that owned her little clinic and she wanted only enough money to maintain the clinic and to pay for drugs and other supplies. She had to collect fees to defray these minimum expenses, but her patients were reluctant to pay even a little, although they had the money to pay. The social apathy of the community was such that they could not "give" even to a cause of direct benefit to them.

Burakumin seem prone to more illness and endemic disease than residents of other communities, apparently not because of a lack of effort on the part of public health officials, but rather because of the community's resistance to governmental officials, whatever their purpose.

According to Dr. Kobayashi, trachoma was very common among the Burakumin. In 1953 at the junior high school in which most of the children were Burakumin, 64 percent of the total 400 students were suffering from trachoma. The district commission on education was alerted, and the next year the percentage dropped to 30 percent. Nevertheless, the health programs initiated were met with a certain amount of apathy and resistance.

Inoue,[14] a well-known historian and active protagonist of Buraku liberation movements, also points out the frequency of "dependent-expediential" attitudes in older members of the Buraku:

In their campaigns aimed at the prefectural or central governments demanding further administrative measures for Buraku improvement, some of the older members of organized movements express the feeling that they have the "right" to demand things in compensation for a long period of discrimination, since they have not retaliated in any way against the majority society. People frequently fall into the mood that they have a special right to ask

[14] Inoue, "Lessons We Receive from the History of Liberation Movements" (1961, in Japanese).

for governmental help for improvement because they are Burakumin . . . but this is wrong.

In leveling this criticism of the Burakumin, Inoue pays little attention to the fact that this demanding attitude is a consequence of a long experience of social discrimination through a number of generations. Such underlying antagonism to legitimate authority is particularly disturbing to majority Japanese, since there is little tradition other than conformity to authority within the regular culture.

RELATIVE INDICES OF DELINQUENCY AND CRIME

There is strong evidence in the United States associating delinquency with the social dislocations of mobility and migration and with ethnic minority status. In California, for example, Mexican-American youth are committed to correctional institutions approximately five times more often and Negro youth approximately four and a half times more often, per capita, than are whites of European background.[15]

Long-term absenteeism, truancy, and dropping out of school are all serious problems among Buraku children. Tojo reports, for instance, that in Kobayashi Buraku in Nara Prefecture, for the four-year period between 1950 and 1953, after the establishment of a new junior high school under the revised educational system, a total of 740 students matriculated to finish the obligatory three-year period. Of these, 171 students, or 23 percent, did not finish school. Of the total 740 students in attendance, there were 237 non-Buraku children, only 9 of whom did not receive certificates of graduation; that is, only a little more than 3 percent of the non-Buraku students became dropouts, whereas 162 of the 503 Buraku children, or more than 30 percent, failed to graduate.

Sustained periods of absence from class are also common for Buraku children. At the same school in Nara Prefecture, in 1953, 78 of the total 445 students were absent from school for extended periods. Research revealed that when students were old enough to help their parents at work they were increasingly absent from school.[16]

---

[15] It must be noted that some other minority groups have escaped a negative self-identity through the effects of strong, cohesive, well-integrated communities that do not bring them into conflict with the majority society. In California the Japanese-American and the Chinese-American minority groups have the lowest delinquency rate of any distinguishable group (see California Department of Corrections Statistics).

[16] Tojo, "Postwar Education for Assimilation" (1960c, in Japanese); see also, Tojo, *Assimilation Education* (1960b, in Japanese), pp. 49–98.

TABLE XIV-7

BEGINNING OF SUSTAINED PERIODS OF ABSENCE BY STUDENTS OF A
JUNIOR HIGH SCHOOL IN NARA PREFECTURE

Time absence started	Number of students
Fourth grade (and before)	17
Fifth grade	7
Sixth grade	14
Seventh grade	24
Eighth grade	8
Ninth grade	8
Total	78

TABLE XIV-8

REASONS GIVEN FOR SCHOOL ABSENCE BY STUDENTS IN A JUNIOR HIGH
IN NARA PREFECTURE

	Non-Buraku students (148 total)	Buraku students (297 total)
Poverty	1	32
Work for family	0	11
Lack of parental understanding	0	9
Laziness	0	24
Physical disability	1	0
Total number absent	2	76

As shown in Table XIV-8, research also revealed that most long periods of absenteeism from school are explained by the students themselves as resulting from the poverty of Buraku families and the felt necessity for the children to work for their parents. Other students explain absence as due to "laziness" and to lack of parental understanding.

According to the investigation carried out by the Welfare Department of the Kochi Prefectural Government in Shikoku Island, long-term absenteeism from school is much more prevalent among Buraku children than among non-Buraku children.[17]

Research in Nara Prefecture shows the same general prevalence of long-term absenteeism among Buraku children throughout the schools of the prefecture, as shown in Table XIV-10.[18]

[17] Tojo, *Debate on Assimilation Education* (1960a, in Japanese), p. 15.

[18] Matsuda, Masutani, and Eiichi, *Buraku Problems and Christianity* (1963, in Japanese).

TABLE XIV-9

SCHOOL ABSENTEEISM, SHOKOKU ISLAND
(in percent)

	Non-Buraku children absent from school	Buraku children absent from school
Primary school	0.49	6.26
Junior high school	1.38	32.9

TABLE XIV-10

COMPARISON OF ABSENTEE RATES OF SCHOOLS WITH
AND WITHOUT BURAKU CHILDREN

	Number of schools	Number of children enrolled	Number of children absent	Percentage of children absent
Primary schools with Buraku children	63	34,254	419	1.2
without Buraku children	254	59,516	480	0.81
Junior high schools with Buraku children	49	24,811	1,556	6.2
without Buraku children	76	20,381	520	2.06

As shown in Table XIV-11, the delinquency rate (as well as the rate of households on relief) is higher in school districts with a heavy concentration of Buraku children than is the average rate for the entire Kyoto City.

To learn the delinquency rate among Buraku children, we went through case files of a family court situated in one of the major Japanese cities with a population of more than one million. When the case of a delinquent boy is first brought to the family court, his permanent address, home address, date of birth, the nature of his delinquent act(s), and the kind of treatment received are all recorded on a card which is kept on file; if the same boy is brought back to the court for later acts of delinquency, these are added to his records.

These cards, therefore, provide a general impression as to how delinquency is distributed in different residential sections of the population.

TABLE XIV-11

COMPARISON OF DELINQUENCY RATES AMONG SCHOOL DISTRICTS
WITH BURAKU POPULATIONS (in percent)

District	Delinquency rate	Relief rate
Rakushi (Takagamine)	23.06	95.2
Tanaka	23.02	70.0
Sanjō	19.51	63.4
Shigō	14.30	50.1
Sujin (Uchihama)	35.54	24.7
Kisshoin	17.70	40.5
Uzumasa (Saiin)	11.32	33.7
Mibu	22.45	24.7
Takeda	28.03	70.0
Average	21.51	74.8
Entire Kyoto average	9.48	37.1

SOURCES: Kyoto-fu Seishonen Mondai Kyogi Kai and Kyoto Daigaku Kyoiku Shakai-gaku-bu (Kyoto Prefecture Conference on Youth Problems and University of Kyoto, Dept. of Educational Sociology); *Shonen Hiko no Shakaigaku-teki Chosa Hokoku: Kyoto-shi ni okeru Hiko no Shakai Bunka-teki Haikei no Bunseki* (Reprint of the Sociological Study of Juvenile Delinquency: Analysis of Socio-cultural Background of Delinquency in Kyoto), 1960, p. 11.

NOTE: Although the districts shown above include varying numbers of non-Buraku children, some of whom certainly must be contributing to the rate of delinquency, we can still assume that Buraku children's delinquency rate is higher. Delinquency rate is calculated by dividing the number of delinquent children, age 12–20, by the total number of children of the same age group registered in the district; delinquents/total school children. The rate of relief is figured as the number of households on relief/1,000 households.

We examined a sample period covering more than 13,000 cards. After excluding all cases of traffic violation, we examined every tenth card. The resulting 1,044 cards included boys whose residence was unknown or outside the jurisdiction of the court from which we derived our sample, and these cases were also excluded. We finally obtained a sample of 633 boys aged fourteen to nineteen. Those who were found to reside in districts known as "special" Buraku areas were identified as "Buraku boys," and those living outside known Buraku districts (passing or not passing) were identified as "non-Buraku boys." This classification by residence in known Buraku would therefore include a relatively small number of nonoutcaste children. Conversely, a number, probably larger, of children of outcaste families who were attempting to "pass" were no doubt misclassified in the "non-Buraku" sample. There was no way to avoid such misclassifications since a boy's outcaste identity cannot legally be investigated or documented in official records. The 633 boys also included some Chinese and Koreans and a small number of other foreigners. We obtained estimates of the total population of Burakumin from the city's welfare department. The population of Koreans and other foreigners was obtained from the June 1963 statistics of foreigners' registration.

The general population total in June 1963 was estimated from the census of October 1960. The number of boys in each category was divided by the total estimated population for each group, producing a rough rate of delinquents per 10,000 individuals.

As shown in Table XIV-12, youths of Korean background show the highest delinquency rate—more than six times that of the majority area. Those identified as Buraku boys showed a rate of more than three times that of the non-Buraku areas.

In Table XIV-13, the boys of each group were classified into first offenders and recidivists. This breakdown reveals that recidivism is highest among those living in Buraku areas and is also higher among the Koreans than among those living in majority areas.

TABLE XIV-12

ESTIMATED RATE OF DELINQUENCY IN MINORITY GROUP YOUTH IN KOBE
(in percent)

	Number of cases	Total population	Rate (per 10,000)
Those residing in majority areas	493	1,098,546	4.49
Those residing in ghettoed areas	71	47,023	15.10
Korean registrants	63	22,365	28.17
Other non-Japanese	6	10,468	5.73

TABLE XIV-13

RELATIVE RECIDIVISM RATES FOR MINORITY AND
MAJORITY GROUP JAPANESE IN KOBE
(in percent)

	First offenders	Recidivists	Total
Those residing in majority areas	350 (71.0)	143 (29.0)	493
Those residing in ghettoed areas	42 (59.1)	29 (40.9)	71
Korean registrants	42 (66.6)	21 (33.4)	63
Other non-Japanese	4	2	6

The delinquent acts of the boys were classified into different categories, as shown on Table XIV-14. One characteristic of delinquent acts by those residing in Buraku areas is the very high rate of threat, intimidation, and extortion. However, this probably needs some explanation. In a number of these cases of threat and extortion, the delinquent boy involved is much younger than the individuals threatened. It is not unusual to find that a boy fifteen years old has threatened a group of two or three older boys without the use of any weapon, sometimes simply by stating that he is from a feared Buraku community. By so doing he evokes fear in the minds of the outside children and can obtain either money or goods from them on the basis of simple intimidation.

TABLE XIV-14

TYPE OF OFFENSES IN ARRESTS OF MINORITY AND
MAJORITY GROUP MEMBERS IN KOBE
(in percent)

	Buraku residents	Majority area residents	Korean registrants	Other non-Japanese	Entire city
Theft	41.4	55.5	44.8	41.7	52.6
Intimidation, extortion	42.9	22.8	26.1	16.7	25.3
Gambling, narcotics, prostitution, obscenity	0.7	2.2	1.9	16.7	0.0
Incendiarism, rape, robbery, murder	3.6	2.8	3.9	0.0	3.0
Fraud	0.7	1.4	1.3	8.2	1.4
Criminal inclination	9.3	8.8	8.4	0.0	8.7
Other	1.4	6.5	13.6	16.7	6.8
Total	100.0	100.0	100.0	100.0	100.0

Community control seems to operate to deflect delinquent activities outside the Buraku community. It is widely agreed by our informants that violence, acts of stealing, or other forms of antisocial behavior rarely take place within the outcaste community itself, although the children will be verbally aggressive toward one another. If physical aggression seems to be in the offing, an adult will quickly step in and attempt reconciliation.

The Buraku people do not support outside authority when a child is accused of delinquent behavior but stand behind and support him instead of the authorities. What is important, seemingly, is that the children obey their parents rather than that they show any allegiance to the outside. In court, the fact that children are obedient to their parents is cited as a mitigating factor when the parents talk to court officials.

In Japan when children are on probation they are put under the supervision of a so-called *hogo-shi* (supervisor) within their own community.[19] The delinquent children under the supervision of the *hogo-shi* within the Buraku community do not indulge in any delinquent activities within their own community, and the *hogo-shi* does very little in the way of supervision. He does not seem to be active in preventing individual adolescents from leaving the community and committing delinquent acts elsewhere. The recidivism rate is disproportionately high for Buraku children under probation.

The community is not at all supportive of court decisions to place a child in a correctional institution. When such a decision is made a large number of adults will sometimes gather at the court building and form an organized hostile protest against the action to be taken. They may appeal to the court to cancel the judgment and instead put the child on probation, so that he does not have to leave the community.

A general attitude of hostility is directed toward the buildings that house the prefectural offices, police, and court, which represent for the Buraku people the legal authority of the majority society. In the prefectural office birth records and registry of Japanese families and individuals are kept, and for the Burakumin these offices represent the place where officials keep records of their identity and background.

The police station and the police system come in for considerable criticism. There is an implicitly understood procedure among police that when a policeman wants to get married the social and family background of the young woman is scrutinized very carefully and reported to a supervisor, whose permission is required before any further

---

[19] In the Japanese court system, under Japanese juvenile law, there are two forms of probation, one in the custody of Family Court probation officers, and the other in the custody of officers of the probation bureau of the Ministry of Justice. The first is called *shiken-kansatsu*, and the second is called *hogo-kansatsu*. Usually when the prognosis for the delinquent is favorable, he is put under the probation of the Family Court. When the delinquent is placed under probation to the Ministry of Justice, he is put under the supervision and guidance of some volunteer in the community, whose qualifications are carefully examined by the probation bureau. Those who pass scrutiny are appointed as supervisors of children; they are the so-called *hogo-shi*, many of whom are school teachers, although one also finds small entrepreneurs among them. Usually the number of delinquent cases per probation officer is too large for him to handle personally, and he is therefore heavily dependent on these lay volunteers. Very often a volunteer's motivation for having a boy under his supervision is that he will work at the factory or store of his supervisor.

action is taken. One informant cited a story, which he claimed was not unusual, of a young policeman who fell in love with a girl of Buraku background and whose application for permission to marry was turned down by his supervisor for the stated reason that the girl had an unfavorable background and could not, therefore, become the wife of a policeman. When police are brought up in conversation with Burakumin, such incidents readily come to the minds of informants, suggesting the ready hostility toward police authority.

A criminal career can be one method of "passing" for members of the Buraku community. If a Buraku youth is successful in becoming a member of a criminal gang or yakuza group, his outcaste background is discretely forgotten.

Professional criminals do not scrutinize the past of individuals too carefully, and the Buraku youth may feel more readily accepted than he would in facing the discrimination that occurs in other occupations. In the same way, Buraku women find in prostitution an easy way to "pass" and to remove themselves from the Buraku community.

CONCLUSIONS AND DISCUSSION

Evidence from Japan suggests direct functional parallels between deviant trends in traditionally disparaged minority groups in the United States and Japan. An aggravated delinquency rate is but one symptom of a total situation influencing the internalization of social values. One must note, however, that this internalization pattern in minority groups is influenced not only by the external pressures of discrimination but also by the nature of the response to minority status in terms of the sanctioning methods available to families and to the minority community generally.

Not all minority communities react to discrimination by producing socially deviant members or individuals who flout socially expected behavior. For this to occur, the tradition of discrimination must exist for sufficient time to affect the socialization process of the young. Some minority groups that are acculturating to a new society, but not all, undergo disruptive changes. The Puerto Rican immigrants to New York, for example, cannot sustain their previous community or family relationships in their new setting. The Chinese in the United States, however, formed communities with strong sanctions that prevented any visible individual deviancy from the accepted standards of the majority that would bring members into conflict with the police. Some minority groups meeting a new situation of social discrimination maintain active defenses against legal authority based on previous traditions. The Mexican-American community and family groups, in socializing the young, develop in them attitudes of resistance to legal authority, which is perceived traditionally as an outside force meaning no good to the individual. The Japanese, in contrast, in facing the discriminatory attitudes met as immigrants to the United States, socialized their young toward conformity to legal authority. Through the pursuit of strong Japanese values of education and achievement, the Japanese community, in contrast to other racially discriminated communities, has maintained itself with a significantly low delinquency rate.

Members of minority groups based directly on a disparaged caste position in the society must respond by some form of self-evaluation, which in itself tends to incapacitate the individual from the ready assumption of social expectations. The parallel situation we have documented in this chapter attests to how a tradition of social disparagement continues even after there is some alleviation of overt discriminatory attitudes and practices themselves.

This is another example of the psychological lag found in a changing society, namely, that the effects of a particular social condition continue after the structural elements producing the condition have changed. This continuance occurs because an internalization pattern has been induced in individuals and this cannot readily be changed since internalized psychological mechanisms are involved. This internalization pattern results very often from the sanctioning practices of the primary family. In fact, the primary family itself may have been seriously influenced by aspects of minority status, as in the case of the American Negro, so that a serious disruption from the culturally prevalent family pattern has occurred. In discussing the Japanese Burakumin we have not fully presented the evidence we have gathered concerning their freer sexual practices and more fragile family relationships in contrast to those obtaining among the majority Japanese, but in this area also, we can cite a direct parallel to the family situation of the black American on the basis of the testimony of some of our Japanese informants.

Chapter XV

Socialization, Self-Perception and Burakumin Status

with HIROSHI WAGATSUMA

SOCIAL SELF-IDENTITY AND MINORITY GROUP SOCIALIZATION: SOME ORDERING CONCEPTS

In this chapter we explore the effects of Burakumin minority status on some aspects of personality development.[1] We have found it useful to relate our data to five ordering concepts, which permit us to demonstrate how growing up in a Burakumin community affects the socialization of the Burakumin child and, in creating a subcultural distance, helps to separate him from the majority society. These concepts are "differential socialization experiences," "differential role expectancies," "social self-identity," "selectivity of reference group," and "selective permeability." This chapter expands these concepts with respect to the inner experiences of growing up as an outcaste and problems of self-discovery, self-hatred, and ruptures in affective ties.

Differential Socialization Experiences

Differences in experiences during the socialization process lead to what are "modal personality variations" between groups and subgroups.[2]

---

[1] This chapter previously appeared in DeVos and Wagatsuma, *Japan's Invisible Race: Caste in Culture and Personality* (1966).

[2] Kardiner, *The Individual and His Society: The Psychodynamics of Primitive Social Organization* (1939). For reasons well delineated by Linton we prefer the term "modal personality" to "basic personality" without, however, rejecting most of Kardiner's formulations.

Kardiner and Ovesey have thoroughly discussed a concept of basic personality in reference to non-Western societies and to the Negro in American society.[3] Under the general concept of differential socialization, one can discuss how the nature of cultural values, concepts of adult roles within the family, and child-rearing practices influence the development of modal personalities in distinct class, caste, or ethnic groups. As the word *modal* implies, this concept emphasizes that culture patterns selectively influence the prevalence of certain forms of ego defense mechanisms or control mechanisms and patterns of interpersonal interaction in one group as compared to another. Certain forms of childhood experiences in particular cultural settings predispose the adult to rely upon particular modes of coping with his experiences. It is easy for members of any particular group to come to negative conclusions concerning another group on grounds that they respond "unnaturally" or "immorally."

The concept of differential socialization and possible resultant modalities in personality traits is pertinent to understanding why individuals of any one group or social segment feel some degree of strangeness or cultural distance in relating to those of another. Although a wide range of variation in personality mechanisms is found even in the most isolated societies, nevertheless certain modalities in behavior in coping with situations of acute stress, for example, strike the astute observer of any specific group.

Differential Role Expectancies

Social roles are perhaps best understood as modalities of expected behavior reinforced by formal or informal sanctions and expectancies. At every grading stage within a culture, starting with infancy, behavior is oriented by a series of formal and informal sanctions toward specified role expectancies. These expectancies are fairly uniform within simple societies, but in more complex societies there may be highly dissimilar attitudes and expectancies distinguishing particular social or subcultural segments. For example, parents of different classes or caste segments may differ widely as to the degree of impulse control or responsibility that they expect of a grade-school boy or an adolescent.[4] What is expected of a mature adult or an aged grand-

---

[3] Kardiner and Ovesey, *The Mark of Oppression* (1962).

[4] (a) The Japanese, from his earliest years, is expected to depend more heavily on the *family* social roles, which are well defined traditionally in *family* terms, and is less encouraged to individuate or define social roles in *individual* terms.

(b) In American society, concerned with individual achievement, what is termed by psychologists "independence training" starts very early. Different class segments can be differentially affected. It is in this respect, also, that Alison Davis (Davis and Havighurst, *Father of the Man,* 1947) found striking differences between the social-

parent may also differ, depending on the status position of the family within a culture. These expectancies either become internalized as part of the self or are selectively resisted, depending upon the relative permeability of the individual to the attitudes of various reference groups and upon the degree of his motivation toward conformity or deviancy.

In a complex society, conflicts can occur when there are inducements toward social mobility within a class hierarchy. The individual may be exposed to a series of alternative expectations of role behavior. Given social role expectancies are presented to the individual from the earliest periods of infancy. This concept of social role expectancies is therefore intimately related to the nature of the differential socialization experiences.[5] A mother's perception of an infant's capabilities is in a very real sense the earliest appearance of a social role expectation. The concept of "role expectancies" more often has been used in discussing adult social roles than in discussing attitudes toward the young infant, but there is no reason to limit this concept to the adult. In a sense, attitudes taken toward toilet training, masturbating, and the like are closely related to what is expected not only from the child but also from the future adult.

Social Self-Identity

A third ordering concept, "social self-identity," or ego-identity, is discussed thoroughly and illustrated in the writings of Erik Erikson.[6] Erikson uses this concept as a bridge between the psychoanalytic and the sociological framework. He points out that the period between adolescence and young adulthood in modern society is of major importance because definitive decisions on future life roles have to be made at this period. As one moves from simple, rigid societies, with few alternatives in adult roles, to more complex, segmented societies, this concept becomes increasingly important. It must be seen in the

---

ization practices of middle-class and lower-class Negroes, for example. The parental concern for mobility and for helping the child to get ahead in the world often results in very severe toilet-training practices toward the middle-class Negro infant, more severe, in fact, than that practiced by the white middle-class counterpart.

(c) There is some indication that socialization practices are changing in our culture. The recent work by Miller and Swanson, *The Changing American Parent* (1958), would suggest that some of the striking differences between classes in socialization practices have tended to disappear, with the American lower-class taking on more of the middle-class attitudes in some respects and with an increasing general permissiveness in the middle class, tending conversely toward methods of socialization formerly more prevalent in the lower class.

[5] Cf. Whiting and Child, *Child Training and Personality: A Cross-Cultural Study* (1953).

[6] Erikson, *Childhood and Society* (1950), and "Identity and the Life Cycle: Selected Papers" (1959).

context of a psychodynamic theory of internalization or "super-ego" formation, as well as in the light of theories of social determinants derived from social structure. For the individual oriented toward cultural or social determinants, the concept of social self-identity implies the attempt to assume an integrated consistency toward a series of roles in various social relationships. For Erikson, in his analysis and use of this concept, these roles are integrated within an encompassing idiosyncratic self-concept that, contrary to some sociological theory, is not simply the sum of specific roles. That is, the self, or the social self-identity is not the sum of various roles, but a unique integration of roles which encompasses also certain elements of self-perception that, properly speaking, cannot be said to be related to roles at all. This concept has particular pertinence to problems of self-acceptance and self-hatred related to minority status.

Selectivity of Reference Group

Our fourth ordering concept, that of a "reference group," is taken from social psychology. It is perhaps best discussed and illustrated by Muzafer Sherif [7] and, in another context, by T. Shibutani.[8] This concept is particularly useful in understanding some of the stresses, conflicts, and frictions experienced by the Burakumin both intrapsychically and interpersonally. The individual's standards, attitudes, and status aspirations stem from and are related to certain groups, which we shall call the individual's reference groups. Many of these reference groups are groups of which the individual is an actual member—they are then "membership groups." This is not always so, however; the individual may be a member of one group but, through direct or even indirect contact with the attitudes and aspirations of another, he may do his best to relate himself, his standards, his aspirations, to that group. Individuals in the middle class may try to relate their standards and aspirations to leisure class values, and an individual may live with a group to which he does not relate himself. With these situations in mind, it is useful to have two different concepts—membership groups and reference groups—although usually one's reference groups and membership groups are the same. The discrepancy between the two—that is, when an individual lives in one group but aspires to belong to or relates himself to another—causes a number of conflicts and frictions. Shibutani[9] suggests a further refining of the reference-group concept to emphasize salient characteristics of mass societies, in which individuals frequently internalize discordant values from different groups.

---

[7] Sherif, *An Outline of Social Psychology* (1948).

[8] Shibutani, *Society and Personality* (1961).

[9] *Ibid.*

Shibutani believes that this concept gives insight into situations in which the individual is confronted with the necessity of acting on the basis of alternate definitions, that is, in which he must make a choice between two or more organized perspectives. The key problem in understanding a reference group, then, or in learning how it influences the individual, is that of ascertaining whose confirming responses are the strongest in creating a consistent point of view. Defined and used in this way, the concept of reference group may not only point to audiences otherwise unsuspected by the observer, but also focus attention on the more subtle nuances of identification and loyalty.

In using the concept, however, social psychologists sometimes neglect to emphasize the deeper and more rigidified internalizations in how they relate to reference groups. One can look at super-ego formation as an early manifestation of the internalization of the reference groups represented by primary family and religious ideology. We use the concept this way in our discussion below of social solidarity and of the appearance of in-group, or we-group, identifications, and out-group, or they-group, hostilities, both of which receive negative projections from the individual. We are also relating this concept to, but at the same time maintaining some distinction from, the psychoanalytic interpretation of super-ego. The emphasis in the more sociologically oriented theories using this concept is on the actual groups to which an individual refers rather than on the operation of internalized processes.

The concept suggests to us, however, that in addition to what has been inflexibly internalized as early super-ego, the individual is continually ordering his behavior in terms of a primary reference group and that his behavior is in a sense being continually judged either by himself or by others in accordance with the norms and standards of this group. (At critical stages of development the individual shifts from one reference group to another; for example, in many societies there is a shift somewhere in childhood from parental figures within the family to the peer group. Numerous conflicts can occur when these reference groups have conflicting expectancies and sanctions.)

In relating super-ego internalization to reference group, one must start by saying that the socialization has its psychological origin within the family and that the first reference group is the primary family or parental image, psychologically speaking. This image is internalized and becomes part of the ego structure and part of the moral and super-ego structure of the individual. As the individual becomes more aware of the outside world, the force of the immediate dependent relationship on the parent is shifted, and peers become a very important source not only of social activity but of self-identity. They therefore begin to influence the standards and norms of the individual and his behavior. According to the relative rigidity of prior internalization, the individual will be more or less inclined to take cues from his most immediate, important primary group relationships. Internalized standards of behavior learned in the family, set up in a formal sense in many societies by the religious orientation of the family, will determine how permeable the person is to the values of his peer groups, and will help him select among alternatives in the peer groups available to him. In one sense, for certain individuals the most important "reference group" remains that of their God; an individual who truly believes in an organized dogma may be relating to the sanctions of his deity more than to his immediate human contacts.

It is obvious from looking at the multiplicity of potential reference groups that there are possibilities for all sorts of conflicts between the role expectations of one group and of another, especially in hierarchical societies that have become increasingly mobile with social change. Our examination of the Burakumin will show particularly poignant examples of individuals caught between social directives and a confusion as to what group they are to relate. Individuation is never a complete process, and a good deal of behavior if not personality must be understood in terms of the group with which an individual feels he is most closely associated.

Selective Permeability

Finally, we are ordering our interpretation of data according to a concept of relative or "selective" permeability. This concept puts some emphasis on the mechanisms within the ego concerned with selective cognitive perception and interpreting the outer social reality. With this concept we are attempting to relate certain structural components of personality to the concept of reference group. The concept is basically borrowed from biology; it is an analogy to the phenomenon of the relative permeability of various living cell membranes. A living, permeable membrane of the cell is selective in what it allows to enter the cell. In an analogous sense, the ego is a membrane that selectively allows certain experiences to penetrate and become an integral part of the total self. This concept is especially important in understanding the psychological barriers creating persistent cultural distance between contiguous but different cultural or subcultural groups. It is important in implementing the concept of reference groups, for in a sense the most important reference group is the one whose influence can penetrate the most readily into the individual without protective resistence. Relative selectivity of penetration depends upon the relative congruence with previous experiences. Usually in a well functioning culturally conditioned ego structure, hostile or contradictory ideas will not be allowed to enter. So too with attitudes in opposition to those of the primary reference group. This concept of permeability is related to what has been said about the need for consistency within the self structure. Inconsistent or discordant elements that are potentially disruptive are protectively kept out so that they do not upset the viable homeostasis of the living structure.

There is a prevalent misconception that cultural modes of living themselves are so different as to cause lack of understanding among individuals. We could argue that it is not the differences in behavior that cause misunderstanding, but the need to use even slight differences symbolically to preserve barriers between individuals and groups. Barrier-preserving operations are particularly noticeable where sensitive distinctions can be used to signify particular caste or class membership. Differences are emphasized as a barrier to the assimilation process, or they are used defensively to enable the individual to maintain his integrity when he meets with lack of acceptance in the assimilation process.

DIFFERENTIAL SOCIALIZATION
WITHIN THE BURAKU COMMUNITY

The Burakumin are considered to be more impulsive and volatile than the majority group in their behavior patterns, and sometimes this is related to widespread opinion of them as hostile and aggressive in their relationship to individuals from the outside society. We have discussed elsewhere the relationship of hostile behavior to in-group solidarity; here we would like to further suggest that there is some evidence that in socialization practices the Burakumin actually tend to be less restrained in the expression of aggression toward their children than are parents of the majority group. According to some of our informants, many parents, especially fathers, in the outcaste community do not hesitate to resort to physical punishment in handling children. Children do often fight with one another, but within the outcaste community fighting is discouraged when it becomes too serious. However, Burakumin children are not scolded with any severity when they get into a fight with children outside the community, and sometimes are even encouraged to do so. We suggest that a considerable amount of hostility and aggression is implanted in outcaste children by the nature of the parental control of aggression. The amount of aggression experienced by the child in his socialization may affect the evaluation by the outside community of the Burakumin child, as well as of the adult Burakumin. Hostility, hate, aggression developed within the family or peer group are readily displaced outward toward people of the outside community, who are judged to merit them because of their prejudice and discrimination. It is not implausible to explain the father's physical aggression toward his own children in part as a displacement of hostility induced by elements of his relationship to the outside community. The material, although extremely limited, definitely suggests that there may be a greater display of aggressiveness in the interpersonal relationships of the Burakumin child than is common in the outside Japanese society. One must quickly add that there is no valid quantification of these differences, nor do we have any way of comparing the Japanese lower class generally with the Buraku members.

The Burakumin child is most probably more overtly exposed to and made aware of adult sexuality than is general for the total Japanese society. There is less hiding of sexual relationships, and Burakumin children seem to have less of a latency period in some respects than is true for children coming from more restrained Japanese households. In general, although our sources of information are secondary, less stringent impulse control of both sexuality and aggression would seem to be demanded of the Burakumin child in his social roles. His perception of the adult relationships in his group also shows him that adults act impulsively and can vent their feelings when they are under the influence of strong emotions.

One reliable informant without Buraku background, who spent his childhood in the district near the outcaste community and had many friends among Buraku children at school, stated that Buraku children are precocious and "know more about sexual matters than ordinary children." He thinks two factors contribute to this precocious knowledge of sex. It is his impression that, although their houses are no smaller than many non-Buraku houses, Buraku children have more opportunities to witness parental coitus. These opportunities may be the result of fewer restrictions and less concealment practiced by adults in intercourse. Also, Buraku adults are more apt to talk openly about sex. Children have more opportunities to learn about sexual behavior both visually and verbally, and the mechanism of repression is less operable in such an open atmosphere.

An informant from within the Buraku told us that he does not have any memory of having been punished by his parents for his sexual curiosity and sexual play when he was a child. He told us that he used to engage in sexual play with both boys and girls. He recalled that once, when he was in the first or second grade, boys and girls from his neighborhood came to his house and they went together into a room upstairs and examined each other's genitals, shouting their comments rather freely and loudly. He remembers that in the living room downstairs, there was always either his father or his mother, and he believes that these adults must have known or at least had some vague notion of what was going on upstairs. No one paid them heed or told them to stop what they were doing. The same informant also commented on the fact that in the Buraku community, the houses are rather small and there is little privacy, especially in summer. In Kyoto it gets very hot, and people leave their windows open all night, making it easy to observe what is going on inside their houses. The informant recalls from childhood several experiences of witnessing adults in neighboring houses in the act of intercourse. In this way, Buraku children are exposed to sexual matters from a relatively early age.

DIFFERENTIAL ROLE EXPECTANCIES IN RELATION TO BEHAVIOR RELATED TO SEX, PROPERTY, AND AGGRESSION

In certain Buraku communities, at least among the lower strata of the community, there is considerable casualness about marriage ties and sexual fidelity, and temporary liaisons are reported to be common. For example, a husband may go to a distant place to work and be gone for a year or two. Most probably the husband will find another partner in the place where he lives and works, and it is not unlikely that his wife will take another man if the opportunity offers. In the majority society, such a situation would provide people with a good subject for gossip or criticism, but in the Buraku it is taken more as a matter of course. There it is considered necessary for a woman to have someone to rely upon for income and for the training of children, as well as for her own pleasure, which is an acknowledged part of the relationship of the sexes. Such "freer" behavior is not necessarily highly evaluated by the Burakumin themselves, but they take a rather matter-of-fact attitude toward it. One informant, who is now living in an outcaste community, told us that a husband's sleeping with a woman other than his wife is not considered seriously wrong but is taken for granted or accepted, especially if the man is a good hard worker and earns money to support his family.

Traditionally this kind of attitude toward a husband's sexual infidelity has been found also in the majority society. However, there is a noteworthy difference in social role expectation between the Buraku and the outside majority. According to informants, more lenient attitudes about premarital sex and infidelity also apply to Buraku women, in contrast to the double standard operative in the majority society, in which men could traditionally enjoy sexual freedom but women were under very severe requirements of loyalty and chastity. In the Buraku the general expectation toward unmarried girls does not include premarital innocence. If a girl becomes pregnant, the general attitude, although disapproving, is protective. The baby is usually registered as its mother's younger brother or younger sister, or a marriage is quickly arranged between the unmarried mother and her lover, or occasionally with another man, in which case the baby is registered as the child of the newlywed couple.

Relative freedom in sexual experience by Buraku women does not seem to carry over into equality of status between man and wife. The Buraku wife is expected to fulfill a subordinate role in relation to a dominant household head. One of our Buraku informants illustrated the social attitudes in this regard by the following occurrence. In one of the outcaste communities of Kyoto a husband took as his mistress a young woman who was suspected of having been a prostitute. His wife found out and got very angry. Husband and wife had a vigorous quarrel, and the husband ordered his unruly wife to leave the house. This wife had a somewhat unusual character and was quite strong willed. She set out a wooden box in the street in front of her house and, standing on the box, waited until the curious neighbors began to gather about. She then started telling the crowd the long history of how she had been harshly treated by her husband, how her husband had been disloyal and unfair to her, although she in her stead had always been loyal, obedient, and subservient as a wife. The crowd increased, with many individuals sitting around her on the box listening to her story, expressing amusement. They seemingly enjoyed this incident, but no one expressed any sympathy with the wronged wife. The crowd's attitude seemed to be that after all this woman was rather crazy, because it was to be taken for granted that a man might be interested in a woman or women other than his own wife, and it was the general contention that in such cases the wife should not make an undue fuss about it. A wife was supposed to endure and accept whatever happened to her. This woman, in acting in this unusual way, went completely against the general understanding, and any negatives that were expressed were not toward the husband, but toward this rebellious, disobedient woman. After this incident, the wife was driven from the house by her husband, and his young mistress came into the house as his wife. This incident reflects both the casual attitudes about sexuality as well as the traditional or feudal concepts of the position of women and men. Women among the Burakumin, as in the traditional society, were required to be subservient, docile, and non-aggressive, at least as far as their husbands were concerned. A husband beating an unruly wife was not considered uncommon.

We have already noted that Buraku men are allowed, if not expected, to be impulsive and quick-tempered and physically aggressive. When they lose their tempers, they often direct their physical aggression toward their wives and their children. Physical aggression from husband to wife, or from parents, especially to children, is frequent.

Girls are not spared physical punishment; both boys and girls may be beaten by their fathers. Mothers usually do not resort to physical punishment or aggression toward their children as often as do fathers. However, when they are compared with mothers of the majority society, especially those of the middle class, they seem to take to physical aggression much more rapidly. Physical aggression between women is within the experience of our informants.

Among the Buraku the upper-class families express aggression in ways which seem to be closed to those of the majority middle-class society, which acts as a more compelling reference group for them. General Buraku identification, however, makes even the middle-class families of the Buraku feel somewhat uncertain about their ability to control their passions.

SELF-IDENTITY AS A BURAKUMIN

Perhaps the most poignant material we have gathered concerning the social self-identity of the Burakumin has to do with early experiences by children in discovering themselves and their families to be members of a disparaged group. The examples we cite speak for themselves and need no special interpretation.

There are some differences between the roles of the Burakumin today and those of black Americans. Horace Cayton,[10] Richard Wright,[11] and others have shown that in his relation to majority whites, the Negro has to handle within himself a complex patterning of hate and fear. He well knows the stringent sanctions that have been used against members of his race by the majority society in maintaining its dominance. He is also aware that he is feared and that whites have a perception of him as capable of acting out impulses that they themselves feel, although they prefer to project them as being in the Negro and not in themselves. In the self-identity of the black, there is the fact that he must be afraid of the white and at the same time the knowledge that he is seen as a potential sexual and aggressive threat to him. In the case of the Burakumin, there seems to be less acting out of aggressive sanctions by the majority Japanese against members of the outcaste group, who are seen, rather, as potentially frightening, capable of violence and aggression toward members of the majority society. This was not always the case in the past, when Burakumin could be subjected to violence by samurai, or even by commoners, with impunity. Today, however, the majority attitude both in the distribution of relief funds and in other matters is non-

[10] Cayton, "The Psychology of the Negro Under Discrimination" (1955).
[11] Wright, *Black Boy* (1945).

violent and mollifying, and aggressive sanctions are not used to maintain dominance. It is the Burakumin, if he is at all permeable to the role expectations defined by the majority group toward him, who has to cope with a self-concept that includes a potential display of unacceptable aggression toward the majority group individual. Majority Japanese are expected to maintain dominance not by sporadic aggression but by attitudes of innate superiority. It is the Burakumin who is constrained to conceptualize himself as potentially violent as well as basically inferior.

The following incident reported by a university student with Buraku background illustrates the experience of self-discovery related to negative identity. It illustrates the problem of having to internalize an image of oneself as a feared object, to deal with fear both of others and of oneself, and shows how a small child tries to cope within himself with the definition of himself as a fearful object.

One early morning, when our informant was four or five years old, he wandered out of his community to a neighboring hill in search of butterflies. When he turned around to return by the little path winding along the hill, he encountered two children approximately his age. They stood for a while looking at him, and suddenly they screamed and started running away. This particular hill separated the Buraku community from a residential district of ordinary folk. These two little children probably had been told by their parents not to go beyond the hill, into the district where the frightful, untouchable people lived. The two little children must have become extremely frightened when they suddenly realized they had met a boy from the prohibited area. When they started to run, the little children cried out the word, "yotsu," meaning "four," a harsh tabooed word designating the outcaste group.[12] The student does not remember quite how he felt when these two little children cried out the word, a word he had already come to know was a dreadful one and not to be used. He remembers only that a shudder went through his body, and he felt a mixture of fear, sorrow, and anger. He started running after the two children and, catching up with them, he hit them, choked them, and shouted meaningless words at them in an excited voice. The children did not try to defend themselves but remained passive, pale with fear. Later, our informant again visited the little hill, and upon his return he met a boy coming along from the direction of his own community. Without exactly comprehending what he was doing, he started crying out "yotsu" and began running away from the boy. Somehow, he was attempting to understand the overwhelming sense of fear he had witnessed in the other two children. At first, when our

---

[12] *Yotsu* implies a four-footed animal—used in reference to the outcastes.

informant was relating this experience, he could not recall what he had cried out; even in recounting the story, the emotional impact of the word came back to him with extreme force.

Another informant, from a family that had successfully passed, relates a number of episodes from his childhood, illustrating the feelings of secrecy and shame relating to self-discovery. They also convey a sense of discovery about the meaning of outcaste parental roles compared with those of the larger society.

At about the time that this informant was ready to go to grade school, his father decided to move out of the Buraku community. The first step in this process was to open a small shoe store in a neutral neighborhood. In addition to selling new shoes, his father continued his previous occupation of repairing shoes and sandals. Since our informant now lived a considerable distance away from the community, he went to grade school with children of the outside society, and at school he was not known as an outcaste by the other school children. In other words, he was passing, although in his immediate neighborhood his father's occupation made it evident that the informants' family was of Buraku background. When he was in the second or third grade, our informant recalls that he drew for his art teacher a picture of his father at work. He was afraid of his strict father, but at the same time he loved him and felt proud of him, and he drew his picture out of innocent pride. After completing the drawing and showing it at school, he brought it back triumphantly to his home to show to his parents, expecting praise. He had been complimented by his teacher, who said that the picture was well done. However, when he showed the picture to his parents they suddenly paled and became upset. His parents then told him never again to draw a picture of his family at work, or any pictures of their shoe store. He was not told why, but from the reaction and the tone of his parents' voices, he could sense that he had done something seriously wrong and that there was something about his father's job that other people should not know. He felt then that there was something secret about his family that should be hidden from the eyes of ordinary people. In other words, at this point he suddenly came to look upon himself not simply as another ordinary child in school. This was his painful initiation into the understanding that he was marked as a Buraku person.

The same informant relates another incident, which took place when he was in the fifth grade at school. When he delivered a pair of shoes to a customer's house, the man brought out a bamboo stick at one end of which he had tied money. He then stretched out the stick and proferred the money to the child, in this way avoiding the child's coming close to him or approaching the house. Later our in-

formant found that this was not an unusual way of giving money to
the untouchable Burakumin: some Kyoto residents made a point of
indicating that members of the Buraku were too "dirty" to be allowed
to receive money directly from the hand of an ordinary citizen. As he
now recalls the incident, the informant as a child did not respond with
anger to this behavior, but instead felt very lonely and helpless. He
felt that he would like to be accepted more warmly as an ordinary
child. It was not until after his family moved out of the Buraku
community itself that the small boy was progressively exposed to the
harsher aspects of people's attitudes toward Burakumin. Among the
Burakumin, as among groups subject to discrimination in our own
society, internalized disparagement is turned toward members of one's
own group in times of stress. Our informant recalls the following
incidents that well illustrate this phenomenon. Not far from his
family's store was another small shoe store. From their occupation,
it was evident to the neighborhood that the owner of this store and
his family were also Buraku people. The wife of the owner of this
little shoe store for some reason chose our informant as a target for
her aggression. Every time she encountered him, she would cry out
repeatedly in a loud voice, "Eta, eta!" or "Yotsu, yotsu!" The informant felt sad and angry, and when he told his mother of this
woman's behavior she became incensed and told him to tell her immediately the next time it occurred. The next time the woman shouted
at him he quickly ran home and told his mother, who dropped what
she was doing and ran out of the house into the street. She ran to
the woman, grabbed her by the hair, and pulled her down on the
street, hitting her and shouting wildly. This behavior took place in
the middle of the street, with many curious passers-by, and the boy
felt like hiding in fright and shame. He had never seen his mother
act this way before, and he was particularly frightened by the violent
behavior of his mother, whom he had usually seen as a calm, gentle
woman, submissive to her husband. He can still recall the wild expression of his mother's face at this time, and he still remembers with
a shudder the unspeakable fear and threat he felt looking at his wild
mother hitting another woman on the street. He recalls vaguely, in
this context, that earlier, in the community from which he and his
family had moved, he had seen other such wild scenes, expressions of
physical aggression between women. He thinks now that he had attempted in his own mind to separate his mother from any connection
with what he perceived to be the wild and rude women of the community from which he came. This incident destroyed the image that
he sought to maintain of his mother as a gentle, calm, and refined
person.

This story reveals that this young man had psychologically sought to separate himself from the Buraku community at a fairly early age. His ego identity was no longer with the Buraku but with the outside society. Nevertheless, the impulsive, passionate behavior of his mother destroyed a previous defensive idealization and caused him to feel consciously that he could not completely escape his past.

The journal *Buraku*[13] reported a tragic case of self-discovery and its aftermath: Etsuko took her life at eighteen years of age, using an agricultural chemical obtained at school. A local newspaper reported that her suicide was due to a nervous breakdown resulting from excessive adolescent sentimentality, and the national newspapers, the *Mainichi* and *Asahi*, each reported a different cause. The *Mainichi* reported that the girl killed herself because she had been suspected of theft, and *Asahi* attributed her suicide to discrimination at her school. The complete story was complex. One of Etsuko's friends at school, also a Buraku girl, was quoted as saying, "Etsuko was the only Buraku girl in her class; therefore, it was she who was suspected when there were a number of thefts in her classroom. I am certain she did not do it, but she became very upset when she was suspected. Shortly before, a thoughtless inquiry had been made at the school to identify the Buraku students in every class. I am not saying that this inquiry made Etsuko kill herself, but it certainly was one of the causes. It was thoughtless of our school to make such an inquiry; instead of giving warmth or help to Etsuko who needed it, the school actually increased discrimination by carrying out such a strange inquiry."

Etsuko's father was of the Buraku, but in attempting to pass, he had moved out of the Buraku community a long time before, and had had very little subsequent contact with his former community. The family was relatively well off, and the parents did not want to inform their children about their Buraku background. Etsuko and her three sisters grew up without any knowledge about their outcaste background. Further, according to Etsuko's friend, Etsuko had even exhibited some prejudice against Buraku people. However, in some manner or other, shortly before her death, she had come to learn about her own identity, and at school there were some students who became suspicious about her hidden background. Then came the inquiry by the school held supposedly for the purpose of finding "Buraku problems" in the school. Etsuko must have developed a complicated, ambivalent feeling toward her own identity as a Buraku person. The inquiry at the school, which made all the students aware of Etsuko's

---

[13] Buraku Henshūbu (editorial staff of *Buraku*), "Discrimination at Hirooka Junior High School" (1957, in Japanese).

being a Buraku individual, must have been a severe shock, and this was followed by the suspicion of being a thief, which is sufficient explanation for the tragic suicide that followed.

THE BURAKUMIN'S NEGATIVE SELF-IMAGE

A very difficult aspect of minority status is the continual need to cope with the negative self-image that is automatically internalized as one becomes socialized within the context of a disparaging majority society. A self-image is not always conscious; sometimes, under a situational stress, one comes face to face with attitudes toward oneself that have been consciously repressed, as we shall illustrate below.

Passive, Intrapunitive and Conservative Elements in Conscious Self-Images

Some revealing materials have been gathered by Japanese social scientists concerning the Burakumin's conscious self-concepts. Koyama[14] cites four types of tension consciously experienced on the part of Burakumin in their relationships with majority society. They are aware of their extreme poverty and often resolve their tension in this regard by supporting leftist policies. Koyama suggests that many Burakumin have a strong sense of personal inferiority that leads to resignation or passive resentment; in critical situations, these resentments come to the surface and there is resort to impulsive aggressive behavior. The third tension, one found more in the educated, is a sense of injustice, which leads to a continual sense of indignation against the majority society; Koyama sees relatively few such Burakumin able to overcome this personal indignity to the degree that their anger is sublimated into more constructive channels, and they function below their optimal capacities, debilitated by unresolved feelings. The fourth tension, experienced by the more educated Burakumin, is a state of continual anxiety over passing.

Koyama relates these feelings to answers on a questionnaire he used in research within Osaka City. He asked, "What do you think is the best way to abolish social discrimination against Burakumin?" He classified the answers in seven categories. Of ninety-seven persons approached, 18.5 percent gave what Koyama terms "ignorant" responses, or "I don't know" answers; 11.3 percent gave what he terms "no solution" answers, or "I know something must be done, but I don't know what to do"; and 6.2 percent gave what is called by Koyama "avoidance" answers, such as "I do not want to think about it; I want to be left alone." These three groups, consisting of more than one-third of

---

[14] Koyama, "The Nature of Social Tension in Outcaste Communities" (1953, in Japanese).

the individuals approached reveal a general attitude of passive resignation, helplessness, and avoidance toward the problem of discrimination.
The fourth group, 29.9 percent, gave what Koyama terms "self-reflective" answers, which reflect, though not completely, passive helplessness and a great deal of intrapunitive thinking, such as "We should
behave better; we should give up our slovenly behavior and keep our
houses and clothes clean; we should seek more education; we should
cooperate with one another; we should move out of this dirty area;
we should change our occupations to more decent and respectable
ones," and so on. In contrast with these passively oriented attitudes,
the fifth group, 15.5 percent, gave what Koyama terms "extrapunitive"
responses, which put all the blame on the majority society: "We should
destroy discrimination; we should make them learn that we are all
equally Japanese; those who have prejudice should be legally punished," and so forth. The sixth group, 10.3 percent, also militant, is
termed "passionate" by Koyama, because in their attempt to answer
the interviewer they were too much overwhelmed by their own emotions of anger and resentment toward the outside society to verbalize
their opinion adequately. The last group, 8.2 percent, is considered by
Koyama the most objective or realistic; their answers pointed out the
necessity of both enlightenment of the outside society and actual improvement in the Burakumin's life situation.

Men tended to be either intrapunitive or extrapunitive in their
attitudes, whereas women tended to "don't know" or avoidance answers. Most self-reflective and objective-realistic answers were given by
people between thirty and fifty-five years of age. People older than fifty-
five tended to be extrapunitive, and those younger than thirty tended
to fall into the "passionate" group.

John Cornell [15] cites some interesting results of research carried out
by Yamamoto on the Burakumin's image of himself and his image
of the outside society. According to these findings, the Buraku people
think they are more filial, more respectful to ancestors, more stringent
in the observation of arranged marriages, and more deferential toward
persons of higher status when compared to the Ippan ("ordinary") outsiders. They also think that they are harder working, more cooperative,
and more egocentric than the outside people. Outside people, they
think, are better reared, better educated, more hygienic, better dressed,
and with higher and better sexual morals and better speech habits. It
is apparent that Burakumin balance their traditionalist attitudes as
a counterpoise to a self-disparaging image. They regard themselves as
more conservative and as subscribing more strongly to traditional
values such as arranged marriage and the expression of deference

---

[15] Cornell, "Matsunagi—a Japanese Mountain Community" (1956).

toward persons of higher status. According to our own informants, Burakumin seem to take a certain pride in being more traditional than others; older and intellectual members of the Buraku community like to refer to the general deterioration of ethical standards among postwar youth, and they like to point out the importance of the traditional, conservative Japanese values of conduct. In this respect the Burakumin in general inferentially put less emphasis on individualism and innovation and more emphasis on the maintenance of traditionally sanctioned social-role behavior. These community attitudes foster a conservative traditionalist self-image and serve as a preventive against anomic or deviant tendencies becoming unduly disruptive in stabilized outcaste communities.

Unconscious and Suppressed Negative Self-images

We have illustrated already the difficulty experienced by a passing Burakumin in freeing himself from his own concept of himself as an outcaste person. Here are some examples of the presence of negative self-images on less conscious levels of awareness. Our informant, who still lives with members of his own outcaste community in Kyoto, is passing as a city official in the municipal government of Osaka. Every day he commutes to the bureau where he works, and in the one-hour train trip he changes his identity. At his bureau, he is treated as an ordinary person, both by his supervisors and by those whom he supervises; at home, he remains an outcaste. He is looked up to by the members of his community as a success and serves as a symbol of achievement for the outcaste people because although he has become a fairly high city official in Osaka he has not deserted his own people.

When we asked this informant whether he thinks the Buraku people are visibly discernible, his answer was affirmative. He said, "Yes, the Buraku persons are usually identifiable," and he hastened to add that at least for other Buraku persons they are identifiable. He said that when he sees or meets somebody with a Buraku background who is successfully passing, he can rather easily tell that person's hidden background. We asked him to specify how Buraku people are identifiable, at least for other Buraku people; he could not give us any precise explanation, but he still felt he could always do it. After thinking for quite a while, he finally gave us this explanation: Living conditions within the outcaste community are terrible—torn-down houses, unsanitary conditions, distasteful occupations, dirty food, bad language, violence, fighting, laziness—everything that is bad and distasteful is found in outcaste districts. He believes that these conditions produce "something vicious, something dirty, something unnamable, but something that can be felt, like a strong odor. This something horrible permeates the people who are born and reared and live in this area. It is something like a bad body odor. Even when an individual leaves the community, wherever he may go this something horrible is discernible and always accompanies him." He said that this "something" may be the impression that one gives to another as an end result of his way of speech and mannerisms of facial expression and gesture, and all those personal expressions usually not perceived very consciously. He said that he believes that a Buraku person gives an impression that differs from what one receives from a non-Buraku person. Here, inadvertently in a way, a man of considerable learning who is successfully passing, told us that he himself has an image of his people as somehow unclean. We could not assess how much of this negative feeling he directs consciously toward himself.

The following story was told us by a young unmarried informant who is now successfully passing as a teacher. Although he could not provide us with the information on the traditional occupation of his own family, he knew that his family, through many generations, had enjoyed upper-class status within an outcaste community, and his family certainly had been very wealthy. However, the financial condition of his family suddenly deteriorated because his grandfather, who was considered a very handsome man, spent his money on women, gambling, and drinking. It is interesting to note that this grandfather was an adopted son (*yoshi*).[16] By the time this informant's mother came to his house as the young bride of his father, his grandfather was reduced to working as a repairer of *geta*. Every day he walked from house to house repairing the footgear of the outside society. Although his mother came from a family whose traditional social status and prestige were lower than the declining prestige of his own family, her family had accumulated more wealth. Needless to say, given the conservative definitions Burakumin have of "proper" behavior, the marriage of his father and mother followed the traditional arrangement form. Owing to the poverty caused by the profligacy of the grandfather, his father had to start working while still a small boy. He quit grade school and started working as an assistant to the grandfather; he worked very hard and soon took the place of the lazy grandfather, who disliked any form of work. Working as a repairman of geta, the father nevertheless found time to read books, and later managed to go to night school. He was well known in the community as a good son, a virtuous, hard-working young man, and he managed to pay back the debts the grandfather had incurred. When the informant's mother married the informant's father, he was working,

---

[16] The *yoshi* is adopted as heir and takes his wife's family name. He "inherits" the house, becoming the head of his adopted father's lineage.

as his grandfather had, as a repairman of geta, covering long distances in the outside community. With hard work and frugality, his father eventually saved up sufficient money to rent part of a flower shop as a little store for repairing shoes and wooden clogs. In prestige as well as income, it was a step upward, because there is a big status difference between a person without a store of his own and one who owns his own repair shop, however small it may be. Then an opportunity arose to purchase the flower shop, a five-room house with what was considered an ample living area. The father borrowed money and bought the shop and all the family members moved in. Gradually the father expanded the store, and in addition to his repair work he started selling new shoes and clogs. The informant remembers very well how hard his father worked from very early morning until late at night, and also how very strict he was in saving money. The business thrived, and the father did not change his occupation, so it could be said that although the informant's father had become successful in his upward mobility, he did not attempt to hide his background. Passing had to wait until the next generation, that of the informant himself. The father's business expanded, so that almost twenty years after leaving the Buraku community, the father now owns one of the biggest shoe stores in his city. He has many non-Buraku employees working in his establishment.

The father was very much interested in his children's education; he was stern to the point of harshness, and the informant was made to study hard. Although the father was extremely frugal, he was generous as far as the expense for his children's education was concerned. He managed to send his two sons to good private schools, and they both were graduated from the university. Being obedient to the father, the informant and his elder brother studied hard and always remained at the top of their classes.

When he was a child, the informant went through painful experiences; he was discriminated against, laughed at, and pointed out as a yotsu. When the boy mentioned the harsh treatment or cold and hateful attitudes of others, his father never failed to tell him that the only way to be freed from such painful experiences was to achieve, to get ahead, to pass as a successful member of the majority society. So the informant told us that in his mind achievement and passing were identical words: "Unless you are successful in your achievement, you cannot be successful in your passing." The informant told us that his father's attitude toward passing was rather contradictory. When the informant as a young boy told his father about mistreatment by the outside people, his father, especially when he was in a bad or irritated mood, told him not to run away but to fight—to go back to the other children and beat them up. The informant also recalled his father telling him to say to other children, "What's wrong with being four-footed?" The father was telling his son two contradictory things, to hide his identity and be a successful passer, and to strike back as an outcaste rather than hide his background.

This confusion in parental directives explains, at least in part, why this informant remains basically ambivalent toward his own successful passing. He was a successful student at the university and was also successful in passing examinations toward his eventual goal of becoming a teacher. After going to a univerity near his own community, he transferred to an institution in Tokyo, where he faced keen classroom competition with a more highly select group of students and where he also found his new life in the big city away from friends and family a little difficult. He began to feel himself inferior to the others in his class, and one day when he could not respond well to questions given him by his instructor, he became depressed. On his way to his boarding house on a train he noticed that one lady was looking at his face, and he suddenly became panicky. He felt that everybody on the train was gazing at him, and it seemed to him that his face started to become distorted in a strange way. He felt that he was becoming ugly and that everybody on the train was noticing the distortion taking place. Remaining mute in his panic, he inwardly prayed and pleaded for the people on the train not to look at him, saying to himself that he was a harmless person. He felt a strong surge of anger at the people who were gazing at him, but at the same time, he felt himself becoming weak; he wished he could ask for the favor of not being stared at any more. In his panic, he was perspiring all over, and his body and his hands were trembling. He got off the train as quickly as possible and had to take a long rest in the station. Afterward, this painful delusion of being stared at would come back occasionally. To avoid it, every time he got onto a train he would stand facing away from the other passengers close to the doorway, looking outside, or, if this procedure was not possible, he would hide his face with a magazine.

When he began relating his experiences to the interviewer, forgotten incidents would come back to him, and he experienced considerable cathartic relief. He remembers that in second grade he was depressed when he was told by his teacher that he was second rather than at the top of his class, and he urinated in his pants. Another long-forgotten memory was of a fearful experience he had when he was a high school student. One day he went to see a movie in which the victims of a vampire themselves became vampires, their faces gradually changing into the ugly, fearsome vampire visage. This change of face was shown close up on the movie screen, and he was horrified. He told us that he usually liked to see horror movies and had never been frightened by them, but this time he was so horrified he could no longer stay in the theater and he ran out. That night he had a long nightmare, and for about a month he could not free himself from the horror and panic produced by this particular movie. He had completely forgotten this incident until it suddenly came back when he told us the story of his fear of his face suddenly starting to change.

The interpretation of his fear of facial change is clear in the light of the other material we have presented. The ugly face symbolized for him his self-image as an outcaste person, an image similar to that held by the passing public official mentioned before. The man who passes may maintain the common prejudices of the majority society toward his own people, seeing them as dirty, ugly, and full of vice and violence. In passing, he consciously thinks that since he is no longer an outcaste he himself is free of these characteristics, but unconsciously he has internalized them as part of a disavowed self-image. When success of achievement becomes threatened, security about successful passing also tends to become shaky, and anxiety over failure is experienced in a symbolic way. In our informant this anxiety was expressed in the fear that his face would reveal his ugly identity. He was so horrified by the movie of the vampire because it suggested that one's hidden or ugly impulses might disclose themselves. Unconsciously he must have identified with the fearsome, hideous creature, that is, the vampire, who preyed on ordinary good folk. When he witnessed the scene of the vampire's face changing, he must have felt that the same thing could happen to him, that his outcaste face might suddenly appear, revealing his hatred of others.

Another experience suggests a further reason for our informant's sense of a Jekyll-and-Hyde potentiality within himself; he had witnessed in individuals a radical change of behavior within the Buraku and outside it. His family lived outside his community when he was going to grade school, but his grandfather was living in the house that had long been owned by his family in the outcaste community, and as a child he visited his grandfather and other relatives still living in the Buraku. He remembers that his parents, especially his mother, showed a drastic change in speech and manner and way of dressing when they visited the outcaste community. When she was in her house outside the community, his mother was careful in dress, speech, and manner, and today in her late fifties or early sixties, she behaves traditionally, identifying with ordinary middle-class persons with whom she associates. She was proficient in adopting the behavioral patterns of middle-class non-Buraku ladies and was genuinely spontaneous in her behavior, but she reverted to the "ruder" forms of speech and behavior whenever she visited the Buraku. The informant told us that the change was so extreme that sometimes as a young boy he wondered if his mother were a single integrated person. He felt as if he had two different mothers, one within the outcaste community and another outside.

There was once the belief that the Burakumin bore upon their persons an inherited physical stigma—a bluish birthmark (*asa*), under each arm. The following poem written by a Buraku poet, Maruoka Tadao, depicts a tormenting aspect of his negative self-image, a sense of being branded with an inescapable stigma—or worse—carrying deeply within himself a never-to-be-removed sense of his own marred nature.

Let Come the Day to Say "Once It Was So"

I heard whispering
Like the flow of wind from mouth to mouth
That under each armpit I am marked,
The size of an open hand.
Was it inherited from an ancient time?
My parents, so too I've heard
Were also bruised by nature's brand.

Yet of them no memory affords
Sight or feel of such a spot.

But in childhood I learned,
Through cruel heavy winks, how instinctively to hide.
What was it I so naïvely wrapped with rags,
And hidden, dragged, through dark months and years?

In these concealing rags, I had hid my heart,
When refound, it was sorely bruised
Shrivelled red from stigma I sought to lose.

Without some fresh exposure, my songs would end in lies;
Such bruises tightly bound but increase the inner plight.

Who marked my sides? For what unknown cause?
Why such a brand upon my very self and soul?

Even today, my ebbing thoughts,
So pale and cold, transparent as glass,
Hold me awake.

THE TRAGIC FATE OF LOVE CROSSING THE CASTE BARRIER

The following are reported examples of the effect of social pressure on the lives of those who transgress caste in marriage; they illustrate how intervention occurs. A number of reported suicides among known Burakumin are traceable to ruptures in love relationships

brought on by social discovery or disapproval of an intercaste relationship. There is no way at present to substantiate speculation about the
actual suicide rate among Japanese Burakumin compared with that
among the general population. The official statistics do not separate
groups on this basis nor do they record suicide motivated by outcaste
status.[17]

Often the rupture in a love affair occurs with the discovery of the
background of one of the principals.

Matsumoto Kinue, of Fukuchiyama City in Kyoto Prefecture, was a factory
worker. One day she met Chihara Akira, a member of the Japanese self-
defense corps, and signs of mutual love were soon exchanged. After initiating
sexual relations, they decided to marry. At that time, the young soldier did
not know that Kinue was a girl of Buraku origins. On making inquiry about
the family background of his fiancée, as is often the custom in Japan, Akira
discovered her Buraku past. He was shocked and his love quickly cooled. On
a cold January evening, he told her in a voice full of blame, "Why didn't
you tell me you are a Buraku woman? I walked with you arm in arm, I am
too ashamed to see my friends." Akira did not show any concern for Kinue's
hurt feeling, nor would he take any responsibility for their having had
sexual relations. Kinue, not knowing how to face the cruel reality of such
a harsh rejection, killed herself three days later by throwing herself in front
of an oncoming locomotive. It was January 19, 1954.[18]

Men as well as women have recourse to suicide:

A Buraku youth fell in love with the daughter of his employer. They lived
together for forty days, until the girl's parents found out and separated them.
The possibility of marriage was not considered because of the boy's Buraku
background. Shortly after the separation, the boy killed himself.[19]

The intervention of the majority-group family is the usual cause
of rupture. The act of suicide sometimes takes the form of a self-
sacrificial removal of the self as a source of problem for the other
person.

A Buraku girl twenty-three years of age died of poison. She left a message for
her mother that the only possible way she saw to make her fiancé and others
happy was to kill herself. The girl and her lover had wished to marry, but
he worked for a company headed by his uncle, who threatened to fire him if
he persisted with his plan to marry a Buraku woman. The boy's relatives also
directly insulted the girl, by pointing out to her how presumptuous it was
of her to even think of marrying a non-Buraku boy. The boy reaffirmed his

---

[17] Burakumin probably share the general motivational patterns of Japanese generally in respect to suicide, which are discussed in Chapter 17.

[18] From Mahara, "Social Situations in Buraku" (1960, in Japanese).

[19] From *Buraku*, July 1951, p. 26 (in Japanese).

love for the girl and said that he still wanted to marry her, but knowing her fiancé was in serious trouble, the girl decided to kill herself.[20]

The suicide often sees his or her act as a moral protest, beneficial in possibly alleviating future problems for others.

Knowing that he could not marry the non-Buraku girl he loved, a Buraku youth tried to kill himself with poison, leaving behind a note addressed to the *Mainichi* in Osaka. He wrote, "I sincerely hope that discrimination practiced against three million Burakumin will be abolished by power of the press.

"By the time this letter reaches your newspaper office, I shall be dead. I fell in love with a girl, and after six months of dating, I decided to marry her. But by that time, I had been found out to be a Burakumin, and our marriage was strongly opposed by the parents and relatives of the girl I love. Her mother said that she would not allow her daughter to marry a man with dirty blood. She even threw a handful of salt toward me." [21]

The note was mailed to the newspaper, and a newspaperman was dispatched to the boardinghouse where the youth had swallowed poison. He was found to be still alive and was quickly carried to a nearby hospital, where his life was saved. He had been working for a department store in Kyoto City, and had fallen in love with a fellow employee with non-Buraku background.

The boy also left a will, addressed to his mother and brother, in which he wrote, "I do not want to live longer with the cursed brand of the Burakumin upon myself. I cannot love, because I am a Burakumin. I kill myself in my protest against those who are wrong."

The suicide in intercaste love affairs is not always that of the helpless offended party, but may be in the form of a protest suicide by a thwarted parent.

In November 1957, in Hiroshima, Mr. Tanaka, a fisherman, drowned himself in a well; he was opposed to his second son's marriage to a girl with a Buraku background. In July, Mr. Tanaka's son met a nurse in the hospital, with whom he eventually fell in love; they decided to marry the following November. Shortly before the date of their planned marriage, in the course of checking the girl's family background, Mr. Tanaka discovered that the nurse had come from a Buraku. Mr. Tanaka and his wife asked their son to cancel his plan of marriage, and they also urged the girl to withdraw. Disappointed and depressed, the girl, who had seemingly not known about her own background, tried to kill herself at the hospital by swallowing poison

---

[20] From Buraku Henshūbu, "Demanding the Life and Rights Guaranteed by the Constitution," *Buraku*, June 1961, p. 19 (in Japanese).

[21] Throwing a handful of salt toward a person is a magical practice believed to purify the one who has done something polluting, like attending a funeral. When it is done to a Buraku person, it is probably not to purify him, but simply to indicate that he is polluted. And it may also have the meaning of purifying the air, which was "contaminated" by the presence of a Buraku person. (From *Buraku*, April 1962, p. 71, in Japanese.)

but was unsuccessful. A little later the boy and girl tried to commit a double
suicide in the girl's home town, but they were discovered in time by a
patrolling police car and saved. The Hiroshima branch of the Burako Kaihō
Dōmei, learning about this near tragedy, attempted to persuade Mr. and Mrs.
Tanaka to allow their son to marry the girl. Mr. Tanaka, still stubborn but
finding no way out, finally himself committed suicide, leaving a note saying,
"Please solve the problem in such a way that everybody can become happy."
The Social Welfare Department of Prefectural Government and City Office
decided to conduct a full investigation of the case to prevent the future
occurrence of such a tragedy.[22]

Outsiders who become aware of an intercaste relationship are prone
to interfere. Moreover, it is hard for a love affair that lacks the approval of family to survive the vicissitudes of quarrel and discord
when they occur.

In 1954, a girl twenty-four years old from a Buraku in Nagano Prefecture was
working at a small restaurant in Shinjuku, Tokyo. She met a student of
Senshu University in Tokyo who was also from Nagano-Ken, though not from
a Buraku. He lived in a boardinghouse nearby and regularly had his meals at
this restaurant. The girl and the student, exchanging conversation every
day, gradually became close and eventually found themselves deeply in love.
In November 1954 the student heard that the girl was from a Buraku from
the owner of the restaurant, who had noticed the relationship. Although the
girl admitted this was true, the student said it was no problem for him, and
in February 1955 the couple started living together in a nearby apartment.
The girl asked the student to marry her, but he said that they would have to
wait until he was graduated, since he did not receive enough money from
home for both their support and his schooling. The girl then borrowed money
from her own relatives and began to support the student. By March 1955,
the girl was eight months pregnant and the student told her to get an
abortion. She borrowed money from her sister, and underwent the operation
at National Hospital in Nagano Prefecture. While in the hospital, she began to wonder whether she was being deceived by the student, and she
wrote him a letter, saying that she would not return to Tokyo. Upon receiving the letter, the student sent her the transportation expenses and
begged her to come back to him. The girl returned to Tokyo, where she again
worked at the restaurant to help the student through school. The student
was finally graduated from the university, but had difficulty in finding a job,
and his older brother came to Tokyo and took him back home, leaving the
girl. Soon her lover returned to her and they lived together once again. In
February 1956, when the girl gave birth to a boy, the youth asked his mother
to come up to Tokyo to see her grandchild. Upon her arrival the proprietress
of the apartment house where they lived told the mother that her son was
living with a woman of Buraku background. The youth's mother was shocked
and went home crying. A few days later, the boy received a letter from his
elder brother telling him that if he continued to associate with the Buraku

---

[22] Yamamoto, *Basic Problems of Assimilation Education* (1963), in Japanese.

woman, he would be disowned and would no longer be treated as a member of his family.

The man and woman decided to stick it out together. They appealed for help to the Buraku Kaihō Dōmei in Nagano Prefecture, and the secretary of the Dōmei visited the man's parents in Nagano Prefecture. The man's father gave the secretary four reasons why he was opposed to the marriage. First, his son had no income. Second, his son was too young to marry. Third, his son and the woman could not make any adequate preparation for their own marriage. Fourth, all the man's relatives were opposed to such a marriage. The man's mother said that as long as she was alive, she would never allow her son to marry the Buraku woman. The parents also made it clear that they would not be willing to support the baby born to this woman.

After this visit the man's brother wrote him asking him to tell the secretary of the Dōmei, who would call on him, that because of character incompatibility he and the girl could not consider marriage. The youth was then visited by the secretary of the Dōmei and the woman's brother, and he told them that although he loved his child and the woman, he thought that love itself was not enough for the marriage. He said he had been scolded severely by his parents and relatives and felt unable to marry against the will of his family. He added that he was afraid of being cut off from his relatives and of losing all his friends by marrying the Buraku woman.

Soon after this the lovers had a quarrel and he struck her. That night, she fled to her younger brother's, and later moved to her sister's in Nagano Prefecture. The girl was completely desperate, and expressed her wish to kill herself. The secretary of Kaihō Dōmei, Nagano branch, and the girl's father both came up to Tokyo and talked again with her lover and his brother. Their conversation lasted for four hours, but the man's brother never changed his mind, making it clear that the man would not marry the woman, that the baby should be taken care of by its mother, and that no money would be paid either to the woman or to her baby. The Nagano branch of the Dōmei decided to sue the man and his brother for their failure to fulfill their responsibilities to the woman and her baby, and for the violence the man had inflicted on the woman. The Dōmei also demanded that the man legally recognize the child as his own, and assume financial responsibility for its upbringing.[23]

No report on the final outcome of this case was published.

Sometimes the rupture of an intercaste love relation occurs after a number of years of marriage. The following episode also illustrates a recurring theme in many reports—that somehow the implications of Buraku membership are repressed or denied to consciousness.

A Buraku woman named Niwa Mariko sent the following letter to the journal *Buraku*, describing her experiences.

I was born in a Buraku, as a youngest daughter. Although my family was relatively well off in the Buraku, I had to work hard as soon as I finished

[23] From Buraku Henshūbu, "Discrimination at Hirooka Junior High School" (1957, in Japanese), pp. 46-49.

junior high school. Although I was small, I was healthy and worked as hard as any boy. I found a job at Nishijin, a woven-goods company in Kyoto, and there I met my husband. We fell in love, and after talking it over with my brothers and sisters, I married him. This was five years ago. We loved each other very deeply and I had never been happier. A few years after our marriage, my husband was promoted to the position of supervisor of the factory. I was happy.

Last year, I went to the factory to see my husband, and there I happened to meet a former acquaintance who knew I was a Buraku girl. My old acquaintance showed in an exaggerated manner her surprise that my husband was a factory supervisor. I felt disgusted at the expression on her face but I did not realize fully that the woman thought it was simply too much for a Buraku girl like me to be married to a factory supervisor. About ten days later, my husband came home sullen and morose. After finishing dinner without speaking to me he said he was not feeling well, and left the house. I could not imagine why he was angry. He came home late that night. I asked him if I had done something wrong. He asked if I knew why we had not received many visitors of late, saying that I should know the reason. I said I could think of nothing.

From that night on my husband became a changed person; he began abusing me, and often even inflicted some form of physical abuse upon me. But still I could not guess why he had so suddenly changed and become so mean to me. I kept asking what was wrong; and he said, finally, that I was from a Buraku, and that it was all wrong. It may sound too naïve, but until that time I had not fully realized what it meant to be a Burakumin. I had never been told very clearly that I was a Buraku woman and was therefore the subject of discrimination. I later discovered that my old acquaintance had told everyone at the factory that I was from a Buraku. My husband kept mistreating me, almost cruelly, when he was in a bad mood. He also started saying that I had deceived him. I said that I had had no intention to deceive him; but my husband, and also his brother, accused me of deception. They said they did not want to see me any more. I had to leave my husband's home to stay at that of my elder sister. I thought I would stay away from my husband for a while, never thinking of divorce. But by that time, my previous intense love toward him had changed into hatred.

There was a branch office of the Kaihō Dōmei in the village where my sister lived. My sister's husband was a member of the Dōmei. They suggested that I ask for help from the Kaihō Dōmei, but I did not want to disclose my problem to those outside my family. Meanwhile, I received a letter from my husband's brother telling me to sign a divorce paper so that my husband could marry someone else. I wrote back a letter that I would not consent to the divorce unless I was fully persuaded it was best for me. I went to my husband's house with my sister to pick up my belongings. There I found my bedding thrown into the garden like some object of filth. While married, I had made bedding for us of the finest quality, but only the poorest set was given back to me. My sister and I also found two suitcases in the garden, filled with the things I had used before my marriage. I could not meet with my husband; he was out. I had been thrown out of the house, like filth. I trembled with anger and returned to my sister's home, angry, sad, and exhausted.

My husband and his brother still insisted that I sign the divorce document. I hated them and had no intention to remain his wife, and yet I did not like to consent to a divorce, because the stated reasons for divorce were my weak health, my inability to have a child, and character incompatability. These were all untrue. I did not believe that my husband had had any feelings of discontent before his discovery of my identity.

I had an opportunity to meet the man who was secretary of the Kaihō Dōmei. He told me that discrimination against Burakumin would never end unless Burakumin themselves fought back. He said I should overcome my own depression and fight for all the Burakumin, who were sufferers from discrimination. One of my sisters, married to a non-Buraku man, wanted to keep our background hidden from her husband. If I stood up to fight, my sister's marriage would probably be threatened. I talked with the secretary of the Dōmei several times and, although I am ashamed of my indecisive attitude, I still cannot make up my mind. I know that eventually I will have to get over this conflict in myself and stand up and fight.[24]

Not all intercaste love relationships end in rupture or divorce, but for such a relationship to survive demands much more of the partners than is required for those sanctioned by family or social group. Members of the Japanese culture, with a strong sense of family belonging, are particularly vulnerable to family disapproval.

---

[24] From *Buraku,* August 1955, pp. 30–35.

Chapter XVI

Violence and Change:
The Alienated Japanese Student

After World War II, the Japanese constitution was redrawn under American tutelage to renounce violence and warfare as an instrument of policy in foreign affairs.[1] In the following discussion of the nature and concept of violence now surfacing in Japan in student movements, I am concerned with the concept of violence as an instrument of internal political change. I shall briefly consider both the ideology and the practice of violence in Japanese political and intellectual history, giving principal attention to the political ideology behind the present-day student movements.

Internal violence or advocacy of violence has been present, to some degree, in Japan in the past hundred years. There have been rebellions and riots, although none serious enough to bring about major disruption of Japanese society. A more important form of violence in the late twenties and early thirties in Japan was the assassination of political figures, assassinations that helped the military considerably in their assumption of power in the pre–World War II Japanese government.

After the restoration of the emperor, a brief unsuccessful civil revolt by certain clans was put down by the newly formed national army, and from this time on there was no question concerning political legitimacy of government by force. In the 1880s there were some minor revolts of conservative groups against modernization programs instituted by the government; these revolts were usually put down after brief skirmishes with police. There were several rice riots in Japan

---

[1] This chapter will appear in a volume of the papers of the International Association for Cultural Freedom Conference on Violence, to be edited by Crouch and Martin and to be published at the London School of Economics and Political Science.

immediately after World War I, a time of economic dislocation. All in all, however, compared with other countries over the same time span, threats of political dislocation in Japan have remained fairly minimal. Similarly, Japanese economic modernization has been characterized by a singular lack of major crises in the form of strikes or shutdowns in any part of the economy.

The Japanese consider themselves a homogeneous nation without major minority factions. Generally speaking, the Japanese have not suffered visibly from serious tensions among ethnic minorities or from regional cleavages or religious disputes. The minority-group situation, however, can be oversimplified, since there are indeed ethnic and caste minorities in Japan that have been a periodic source of minor if not major tension. The former outcastes or Burakumin discussed in the two previous chapters comprise only about 2 percent of the population (approximately two million individuals), and therefore their problems do not reach the proportions represented by Welsh or Scottish separatism in Britain, or the regional tensions between the central government of France and the inhabitants of Brittany, or the extreme tensions existing between the Flemings and Walloons in Belgium. Nevertheless, there is a history of ideas within the outcaste movement that parallels the ideological preoccupation of alienated intellectuals from the 1920s on in Japan. Politically committed outcastes today are generally associated with the communist and socialist movements in Japan, and in some instances they have been the backbone of serious protests erupting in southwestern Japanese cities. These protests are little known outside Japan and the Japanese themselves generally choose to ignore what they consider minor social problems.

The remaining Korean minority in Japan is relatively small. Before World War II, Korea was a source of serious unrest in the Japanese empire, and today the tensions between the North and the South Korean governments are reflected in the division found among Koreans in Japan. However, the problems presented by the Korean minority in Japan do not represent anything comparable to the social problems posed by Mexican-Americans in the United States, for example. In sum, in looking at the history of alienation and social criticism and the philosophies of violence and nonviolence in Japan, one must recognize that the students and professional intellectuals of Japan were operating in a social system of relative ethnic homogeneity, of relatively little peasant or labor unrest, and of relatively little religious or internal ethnic tension as compared with the situation in European states, where there are established traditions of internal and external conflict. The geographic location of the Japanese is analogous to that of the British in Europe, so also are the traditions of governmental stability and legitimacy of power which have been contravened rela-

tively seldom by historical events such as foreign invasions or wars on
the soil of the homeland.

THE PRECURSORS TO JAPANESE MILITARISM
THE TAISHO ERA OF PARLIAMENTARY DEMOCRACY,

Japanese industry and trade were expanding at an unprecedented
rate up to the outbreak of the first world war. With her Western competitors diverted for four years to war economies, Japan enjoyed an
almost complete monopoly of trade in southern and eastern Asia. The
military requirements of Russia and the worldwide demands for merchant shipping were reflected in a spectacular expansion of Japanese
heavy industry. Japanese military leaders saw political opportunities on
the continent of Asia, just as bankers and industrialists saw economic
opportunities. With all the attention drawn to the European holo-
caust, Japan could extend her control over China quietly and inex-
pensively, without arousing serious opposition.

In the middle twenties, China had a new nationalist government
that was attempting unification under a single administration. Ambitious and chauvinistic, the Japanese did not like this turn of events.
A modernized and efficiently governed China would not merely put
an end to Japanese political influence, but might eventually lead to
China's regaining control of the rich and populous Manchurian provinces. Thus China might well come to rival Japan as a leading nation
in Eastern Asia.

A more aggressive foreign policy came into being in Japan when
political leadership changed in April 1927. A moderate cabinet under
Wakatsuki was replaced by a new ministry headed by General Tanaka,
leading advocate of a "strong" policy toward China. There is a con-
troversial document of this time that purports to predict the way in
which the Japanese would attempt to take over China. The so-called
Tanaka document is reputed to be fraudulent, but the realities of
history came very close to meeting the predictions of this supposedly
spurious document.

Japanese interference did not prevent the unification of China. In
Japan itself the Tanaka cabinet's policies were repudiated and it was
forced to resign in 1929 in favor of a more moderate ministry once
again. This return to moderation, however, was short-lived. The policy
of nationalist China became a matter of increasing concern, and by
midsummer of 1931 it was apparent that Sino-Japanese relations in
Manchuria had approached the breaking point. The more fanatical
young officers in the Japanese army took advantage of a flagrantly
trumped-up incident at Mukden and, forcing their older superiors to
go along in the name of patriotism, they deliberately eliminated all

vestiges of Chinese authority and brought Manchuria completely under Japanese control. The League of Nations was impotent, and although the assembly of the League formally condemned Japan's action, the only effect was that Japan was the first great power to withdraw from the League. The militarists in Japan informed the rest of the world that Japan and Japan alone would assume responsibility for keeping what was described as the peace in East Asia.

The internal tensions and conflicts in the intellectual history of the 1920s and early 1930s in Japan give evidence of a great deal of opposition to Japan's external expansion. Japanese intellectuals, like those in Europe, failed to give sufficient support to the parliamentary form of government that was attempting to maintain itself. The ideology in Japan had become polarized toward the far left and the far right.

Someone unfamiliar with Japan, ignorant of the fact that the Japanese, statistically at least, are the most literate nation in the world and that all major Western authors are translated very quickly after their publication, might ask where the Japanese intellectuals got their inspiration. Already by the 1880s and 1890s, only twenty-five years after the restoration, there was a heavy flow of intellectual and ideological literature, as well as material on business, government, and economics. Almost immediately after the Russian Revolution, Marxism became the single most dominant influence among Japanese intellectuals. By 1920 the Japanese were as familiar with the intellectual currents of Europe as were the citizens of any Western nation. Arishima Tatsuo, for example, a Japanese novelist of the early twenties, was strongly influenced by a personal meeting with Kropotkin. Arishima and his group had previously been influenced by Tolstoi, and before committing suicide, in a Tolstoian gesture Arishima turned over his lands to the tenants working on them. By the late 1920s Japanese literary movements were almost exclusively dominated by Marxists, who considered literature an arm of political propaganda. It was difficult for the other leading literary figures of the time to resist the continual critical harassment of their works, which were held up as examples of bourgeois decay. The purpose of literature, according to the Marxists, was to affirm the class struggle and the nobility of the oppressed; a familiar type of novel dealt with the inner agony of the individual as an example of the sickness of the society. The politically uninvolved novelist was put down as decadent and ineffectual.

The Japanese youth of the 1920s were influenced by the Russian Revolution as much as were the youth of any country in Europe. Their Western reading often was not profound and was sometimes distorted in interpretation, but it was part of their total picture of themselves vis-à-vis the Western world. It was part, also, of their total picture of the nature of their own government. They were intensely aware that the older Japanese intellectual was ineffectual and that Japan was soon to embark upon a military course. As a matter of fact, fear of the youth-led anarchistic and communist movements in Japan helped directly to sway public opinion to support police activities against so-called foreign ideologies, especially after the militarists took over.

For all the theoretical talk of the Japanese anarchists, it was not they but the younger army officers, most of them sons of farmers and less educated than the youth of the cities, who in their fervent "national socialist attitudes" most seriously threatened parliamentary authority and eventually forced others in power to comply with their fanaticism. The assassinations in the late 1920s of several liberal political figures by fanatics of both the left and the right undermined the courage of the moderates in the government and helped the militarists in their take-over of the state and their stifling of all opposition to Japan's military domination of Asia.

The present situation in Japan bears similarity in some respects at least, with public opinion allowing police activities against youth in the universities on a scale unprecedented in Japan, even during the military period of the thirties. Students are losing the sympathy of the public. The airport assassination in Israel and the "red army" shoot-out in the mountain resort of Karuizawa in 1972, followed by the discovery of the bodies of comrades killed because they were "too soft," has swelled a wave of public revulsion against immoderate idealism. Unlike the previous period, the police today are using restraint in arrests. They have not lost their "cool." Nevertheless, political radicals continue to hold control of many student bodies, and hazing, including beatings, is used covertly to keep individuals in line. Liberal and radical faculty tend to remain silent or excuse such activities as due to the "intensity" of youth. They are ineffectual in protecting the less "intense" students from harassment. The major portion of the student body withdraws individually from such activities, forming no countermovement.

THE CONTEMPORARY POSTWAR INTELLECTUAL CLIMATE: THE CRISIS IN THE JAPANESE UNIVERSITY

Marxism today is the major ideology of the Japanese student. In a recent poll 63 percent declared Marxism to be of major interest to them. Less than 10 percent of Japanese students have any interest in religion. It must be noted, however, that the Marxism of the 1960s is far different from the Marxism of the 1920s and 1930s, when Marxism was illegal in Japan; today the Communist party is legal, but criticized from within.

Today's student is critical of all ideology and eclectic, whereas those in the late twenties and thirties were dedicated in ideology, self-sacrificial, and guilt-ridden about their bourgeois origins. Although these traits are still present, a far larger percentage of students now are sympathetic to Marxism thought without a sense of total commitment.

Peer group influence is great. It has been noted [2] that peer groups are most important and university professors relatively unimportant as sources of political education. Some young people, however, attribute their interest in Marxism to their high school teachers, a group that in general has radical affiliations in today's Japan.

"Positive" and "negative" reasons for Marxist interest are about equally divided. Among the positive reasons are humanistic feelings (25 percent), sympathy for suffering (10 percent), and the quest for truth (5 percent). Among the negative reasons are anti-establishment sentiment (23 percent), and revolt against the older generaiton (13 percent). A single student only lists a sense of guilt for being privileged, another a sense of responsibility, and so on.

In an ironic way the present university crisis in Japan summarizes Japan's present concepts about violence. The students are toying with means bordering on violence to keep Japan nonviolent in its external foreign relations.[3] Student strikes in the Japanese universities preceded the free speech movement in Berkeley in 1964. In 1961 there were already 6 Japanese universities having some major student dispute, and there were 10 in 1962, 9 in 1963, 13 in 1964. Perhaps influenced by the Berkeley activities, more than 50 universities were in some kind of major conflict in 1965. By 1968 the high point was reached with the temporary closing down of 110 schools of higher education, more than 10 percent of the nation's total of 845 colleges, including the two-year colleges. Moreover, those closed down tended to be the major centers of learning rather than minor schools. As of January 1969, there were still 65 universities, including many of the major ones, closed down, or working under serious threat of being closed.

The large number of institutions of higher education in Japan reflects the fact that Japan is about halfway between Europe and the United States in the creation of a mass educational system at the higher levels. Now approximately 40 percent of all Americans of college age attend a college or university. Approximately 20 percent of Japanese of the same age attend an institution of higher learning. The percentage for Japan is more than twice that in either Britain or France, each with somewhat under 10 percent, and it is approximately three times the

---

[2] Research report by K. Tsurumi, "The Japanese Student Movement: Group Portraits" (1969).

[3] Much of the following material is contained in more detail in two issues of the *Japan Quarterly*: Vol. 16, No. 1 (January–March 1969), and No. 2 (April–June 1969), in which there are a great number of summary materials on the present strikes in the universities.

percentage in Germany, which has now reached about 7 percent. Many of the specific problems relating to attempts to change the university as an institution better fulfilling the needs of a modern state are thus perhaps more evident in Japan than they are in any European setting. Japan is ahead of Europe in the training of its youth, just as it is drawing ahead of Europe in its per capita commercial and industrial production.

The issues around which closings and disruptions occur are highly varied. We list below ten of the concrete issues raised.

(1) A number of institutions are concerned with rising tuition fees.

(2) A number of student groups are concerned with the democratization of the administration of the mass university and with greater student participation in every aspect of the university life.

(3) Various problems have arisen involving the operation and management of student dormitories and meeting halls.

(4) Demands are being made for facilities within the university itself. (Japanese universities are physically antiquated, with primitive facilities and buildings below the standard provided in other sectors of the society. Although Japan is pouring a tremendous amount of money into new commercial and industrial buildings, the physical plants of the universities tend to be totally neglected.)

(5) A related issue is the need for the decentralization and relocation of university buildings out of the center of the city. (Many Japanese universities, for example, are crowded into the city of Tokyo, where land values make it totally impossible to extend facilities, and yet students and faculty are unwilling to support a move out of the city, where land values would allow for a new plan to be established.)

(6) A number of disputes concern dissatisfaction with university presidents or members of academic governing boards.

(7) Specifically for the University of Tokyo, the whole university exploded over the initial issue of changing the internship system of medical students.

(8) There are demands for the revocation of disciplinary measures taken against students; these are similar to some of the demands made in American universities in recent years.

(9) Discrimination is charged in examinations for the selection of teaching personnel.

(10) There are allegations of graft or corruption in the use of funds by faculties or administration of the university.

These upheavals involve the private as well as the public universities in Japan; major institutions such as Waseda, Meiji, Chuo, and Hosei were plagued with waves of strikes, reactions by authorities, and new student protest strikes, and ultimately police intervention. Much of the student activity in the university is directed and guided by student organizations, perhaps the best known of which is the official Zenga-kuren, or All Student Association.

Students for some time have been able to mobilize considerable public opinion outside of their own membership on American-Japanese treaty relations and, more particularly, on the Vietnam war. Japanese generally fear possible involvement in the war through the presence of American military forces in Japan. This concern with the Vietnam war can be illustrated by two incidents. In the fall of 1967 at Tokyo International Airport 2,500 students massed to demonstrate their opposition to Prime Minister Sato's departure to South Vietnam; a clash with riot police resulted in the death of one student and hundreds of injuries to both students and policemen. The second incident occurred in the same year on November 12, when Prime Minister Sato's departure to the United States triggered a similar police battle, resulting in a total of 266 injuries on both sides.

Inspired by these two incidents there was an efflorescence of student activities. Two demonstrations by students gained popular support, but most of the others were generally disapproved. When the nuclear-powered American battleship *Enterprise* docked at Sasebo in Kyūshū in January 1968, public opinion was generally negative. A powerful campaign followed, opposing the establishment of an American Army field hospital at Ogi in Tokyo's northern district. From a psychological standpoint these two incidents gained a great deal of popular support for the students because of the Japanese concern with radioactive contamination and a fear of disease that might be said sometimes to border on hypochondriasis. Permeating all Japanese society is an intense fear of the effects of radiation dating from the Japanese experience with the atomic bomb, victims of which are still treated as pariahs who might contaminate others. Several incidents with radioactive fish have frightened the general public, and the idea of a nuclear submarine or nuclear aircraft carrier brings with it the fear of possible radioactive contamination. In the case of the field hospital, the American policy was totally lacking in sensibility to the Japanese feelings about illness as mentioned above. The hospitals were to treat victims of malarial disease and other jungle illnesses, and the Japanese were frightened by the idea of infestation of tropical diseases brought into Japan by American G.I.'s.

These two student protests, therefore, were among the most popular; some student activities that followed met with less popular approval. Violent student protests were directed against the construction of the new Tokyo International Airport in Chiba Prefecture, and again clashes with the riot police made headline news. Perhaps the most dramatic recent incident receiving attention outside Japan occurred in 1968, when students demonstrated at Shinjuku railroad station against Japanese railroad trains loaded with oil for the American Armed Forces. These newer activities rivaled the 1960 mobilization of thousands of Japanese students against the Japanese–United States Security Treaty, which resulted in the cancellation of Eisenhower's planned visit.

In 1968 Tokyo University, the most prestigious university in Japan, was closed down. After months of futile negotiation there was a dramatic take-over of the buildings by riot police. The event looked like the seige of a medieval castle, except that a helicopter with water guns and tear gas was included. Whatever the origins of the disputes at the various campuses during 1968, there is now a general concurrence on the part of both faculty and students that the whole system must somehow be changed.

In the reorganization of the university many see the basic issue as the movement of the university from elitist education to mass education. The Japanese faculty and students blame their plight on following a nineteenth-century German-inspired organization of the educational system, and the conservatives, conversely, blame the American-inspired postwar decentralization of the educational system. The prewar doctrine of higher education is supposed to have been inspired by Karl Wilhelm von Humboldt; prewar education is described as following the "Humboldt doctrine"—that the university is an ivory tower existing for the sole purpose of educating the social elite. After the war, the American concept of education was introduced in Japan and has now been in existence for close to twenty-five years. The number of four-year Japanese universities has been increased from 48 to 377, and there are now 1,500,000 university students each year in Japan. In prewar Japan only 16 percent of the youth went beyond the compulsory six-year primary education into secondary schools. The postwar mass enrollment of students at universities founded on the concept of an elitist education caused serious disruption; the faculty structure based on a European model could not meet this vast increase in students.

The elitist model of the university was based on the idea of mentorship or, in effect, apprenticeship relationship between the university professor, his staff, and his students. Japanese students now complain that they can go four years through a university without exchanging a single word with a faculty member. They are tremendously impatient with lectures delivered by microphone in overcrowded classrooms. Rejection of the earlier model of the university leads to the feeling that the idea of tuition, which is part of the elitist concept, is outmoded. Students in Japan, like those in the United States, are concerned also with questions of the relevancy of curriculum; they see that the previous elitist education did not question the fixed nature of the material to be conveyed. Present-day Japanese students, like their counterparts in Europe and the United States, are intensely interested in social conditions; they become both politically and socially revolutionary and extremely impatient with lectures that package patterns of the past.

Fukashiro,[4] writing in the *Japan Quarterly* on student thought and feeling, suggests two other interpretations:

Students have come to consider themselves as taking the initiative in the society's resistance to the intensification of human alienation in all spheres of life brought about by technical innovation and the increasing control in business management of small cliques with very little perspective on modern life as a whole. Some students feel that they are the only force left to raise a fundamental challenge to the existing social order. Students are well aware that there is very little general social unrest in Japan today; there is increasing prosperity, and the supporters of the left-wing political parties and labor unions are becoming more conservative, increasingly content with a gradual, moderate approach to social reform. In Japan today there is a widespread concept that one can pursue one's own personal happiness, and this concept—an American ideal—is very disturbing to younger students in radical politics. The question might be asked whether students in radical politics, in whatever country, share certain psychodynamic similarities. Idealism is very often part of an ascetic puritanical defense against heterosexual relationships. There is a misconception that student radicals are sexually uninhibited and that those students who are for greater sexual freedom are also the leaders of the radical political movement. There has not been sufficient empirical study, but my hypothesis would be that students who are for sexual freedom may support student radical movements but are not usually the leaders of these movements. I believe that, quite the contrary, the leadership tends to be puritanical in its outlook.

Settling for a feeling of personal satisfaction is seen by some students as a "cop-out" in Japan, as it is in the United States. Fukashiro presents some material concerning a student activist who was killed in the police-student battle at Hanada Airport in October 1967; let me quote from this as illustrative.[5]

Yamazaki Hiroaki was born in November 1948 in the southern Japanese prefecture of Kochi. He entered a public high school in Osaka in 1964. While in high school he took part in the struggle against the Japanese-South Korean talks for normalization of relations and against the Vietnam war; he was also

---

[4] Fukashiro, "Student Thought and Feeling" (1969).

[5] *Ibid.*, p. 151.

active in creating an antiwar organization of high school students. On entering the department of literature at Kyoto University in 1967, he joined the
Marxist Student Alliance and participated both in demonstrations to oppose the government's attempt to expand the American military base located
in Tokyo's western outskirts and in an antiwar rally at Hiroshima. On October 8 of the same year, he was killed at the height of the student-police battle
near Hanada Airport when Prime Minister Sato was leaving on a trip to
Southeast Asian countries, including South Vietnam. After his funeral, a
notebook was found in a drawer of his desk. Yamazaki writes,

> . . . in order for man to free his spirit from all encumbrances he must
> have the capacity to analyze his own spirit and that capacity is called
> self-consciousness, but there exists one thing which, clouding over self-
> consciousness, restrains our spirit and that restraint is called material.
>
> I know very well that I have little courage. I am essentially an op-
> portunist. Even my courageous support of one side remains susceptible to
> attack from the other. In short, I am not qualified to live; I am a weak
> human.
>
> I came into existence eighteen years and ten months ago. What have I
> done to live during this period? I can feel no sense of responsibility, either
> for the present or for the future. I constantly find myself doubtful if not
> indifferent and I borrow other words to defend myself. What on earth am
> I? In my opinion, it is man's fate that to live is to sin; that man becomes
> more guilty by choosing to live. Our life has meaning only insofar as it
> functions to purify sin.

After his death his briefcase was found to contain the following:
Marx, *Philosophical and Economic Manuscripts*; Trotsky, *History of
the Russian Revolution*; Lenin, *What Is to Be Done*; Uno Kozo,
Marxist Political Economy: A Study into Basic Theory, and *A Theory
on Economic Policy*; Asahi Shimbun, "Okinawa-United States Strategy," an article: Kierkegaard, *The Diary of a Seducer*; J. N. Shklar,
After Utopia: The Decline of Political Fate; and two textbooks, one
for French and one for German.

What one sees in this brief look at a dead student is an intense
idealism and a sense of sinfulness. These traits are not unusual in
Western students of the same age, nor is it unusual for one moving
into adulthood from adolescence in modern society to attempt political
dedication.

In an *Asahi* public opinion survey a large number of students were
asked what books most influenced them. (I am quoting from a report
on the results of this that was published in the April–June 1969 issue
of the *Japan Quarterly*.) Of the twenty books that students stated had
the most influence on them, it is interesting to note that heading the
list at the four universities in which this survey was made (two in
Tokyo, one in Kyoto, and one in Kyūshū in southern Japan) were a
number of Western books.

(1) *Crime and Punishment,* by F. Dostoevski

(2) *Kōkōro, by N. Sōseki* (a leading Meiji intellectual)

(3) *The Brothers Karamazov,* by F. Dostoevski

(4) *The Stranger,* by A. Camus

(5) *Jean Cristophe,* by R. Rolland

(6) *The Good Earth,* by P. Buck

(7) *War and Peace,* by L. Tolstoi

(8) *Hakkai,* by T. Shimazaki (an interesting Japanese book which is the story of a member of the former outcaste group of Japan who had to make his way in Japanese society. He finally stops "passing," and in a very dramatic episode reveals his outcaste status.)

(9) *Yujo,* by S. Mushakōji

(10) *Unterm Rad,* by H. Hesse (a romantic German novel featuring a youthful suicide by an idealistic student. The emotional tone is very similar to that of Japanese youthful idealism.)

(11) *Ningenshikaku* (No Longer Human) by O. Dazai (The context of this book perhaps graphically represents what I was describing about Yamazaki, the dead student. The author, Dazai, epitomizes a convoluted feeling of personal worthlessness. He, himself, was a member of communist youth movements before the war: he became a conservative after the war, and ended his rather desolate life in a suicide pact with a woman. (See Chapter 18.) This book by Dazai has extremely wide currency.)

(12) *Les Thibaults,* by R. Martin du Gard (the story of the Thibault family)

(13) *Jirō Monogatari,* by K. Shimomura (a Japanese historical novel)

(14) *Miyamoto Mushashi,* by A. Yoshikawa (another Japanese historical novel about the ideal samurai, an interesting book from the standpoint of youthful idealism. Many conceive of the samurai as a swashbuckling warrior, but Miyamoto represents, rather, the tradition of intense self-discipline and dedication and a Japanese version of idealism. The ideal samurai does not have heterosexual contact with women, because women are seen as pure beings; he is dedicated to his craft; he is always ready but does not use his sword; he is capable of single-minded, intense dedication. In descriptions of Zen Buddhism one sees this in the concept of ideal swordsmanship. This attitude is still influential in young Japanese.)

(15) *Saredo Waraga Hibi,* by S. Shibata

(16) *Thus Spoke Zarathustra,* by F. Nietzsche

(17) *Yukigumi* (Snow Country), by Y. Kawabata

(18) *Escape from Freedom,* by E. Fromm

(19) *Le Rouge et le Noir,* by Stendhal

(20) *The Bible,* and *La Porte Étroite,* by A. Gide, and *Gone With the Wind,* by M. Mitchell

This list should give one some insight into the present nature of the Japanese intellectual climate and the mind of the youth in Japan. Of the first ten most popular volumes, three are by Tolstoi and Dostoevski, and another two by the contrasting figures of Camus and Romain Rolland; these are rounded off by *The Good Earth* and only three Japanese volumes. Incidentally, the theme of *Kōkōro,* the second-place volume after *Crime and Punishment,* which is vastly appealing to Japanese youth, deals with the suicide of an individual who felt himself to be an alienated, guilty man.

In the previous chapters I have contended that the sense of guilt is very deep in the Japanese character and that Westerners have been deceived by a superficial knowledge of the great concern of Japanese with their relative presence in the world, which makes their culture seem to outsiders a shame-oriented one. The Japanese operate individually out of an intense sense of guilt related to achievement. They need to dedicate themselves somehow to social purpose, and in the modern world social purpose is no longer seen in terms of immediate dedication to family objectives, as it was seen in the past. The modern intellectual in Japan is searching for an other than familial definition of his relationship to the world. Japanese intellectuals as a whole are wondering where to go and to what to dedicate themselves. They strenuously reject the idea that the objectives of present-day society are simply material well-being. Yet Japanese society, like every present-day society, is oriented toward an increase of material comforts and material well-being. The youth of Japan find this very difficult to accept and are looking elsewhere for social purpose. Japanese youth see the university as an institution perpetuating the status quo; they want something else, but they don't know what. They can focus clearly on foreign relations, but they are far less certain about domestic issues in a climate of increasing prosperity. They certainly enlist no public approval for changing the economy. They are in concert with the public only on issues of pollution and inflation.

In opinion surveys on student unrest, one finds general public support for the idea that there is something wrong with the university, but the public as a whole is extremely antagonistic to the students' choice of methods. The public's attitude as to the purpose of the university bears out the students' contention about materialism, for most of the adults polled see the objective of the university as training the young in vocational competence. The overall impression of the Japanese people is that their concern is extremely pragmatic, as these specific figures illustrate: of those polled, 54 percent want to send their children to a university; another 16 percent say this choice will depend on their ability. Only 17 percent see university education as unnecessary to their children or to the children of others. The purpose of the university is seen by 46 percent as practical education; another 27 percent see its purpose as cultural enrichment or character building in some form, and 18 percent see the role of the university as basically related to scholarly research in specialized subjects.

With respect to the government of the university, the public is not opposed to student participation, for example, in the election of a university president. Forty-six percent said that students should be permitted to participate, whereas 36 percent regarded such participation as unnecessary.

When asked who was responsible for the trouble in the universities, 53 percent of those polled held both the students and the universities responsible; 16 percent held students responsible, and 17 percent, the administration. Opinion is split here almost half and half between the views that responsibility is the university's and that it is the students'.

In the answers to questions as to the cause of university trouble a number of alternative possibilities were given relating either to the university system itself or to students' dissatisfaction or behavior. Of those polled, the cause was seen by 22 percent as inherent in the fact that the system itself is outdated and old-fashioned, by 27 percent as poor administration of the universities, by 28 percent as too many students and inadequate education, and by the largest number of those polled (43 percent) as students' dissatisfaction with the present government. Worldwide student dissatisfaction with modern society was given by 28 percent as the cause of trouble in the university. The view that a small group of students was causing agitation was held by 28 percent. The belief that the student movement is a worldwide phenomenon was held by 12 percent, and another 12 percent felt that many students behave rationally, considering the circumstances.

It should be noted that the public was not against a mass bargaining session with students or against direct negotiation with university officials. Protest meetings were regarded by 75 percent of those polled as good, but 81 percent felt that striking or nonattendance was a bad way of handling things. Picket lines that prevent students from going to class were seen as bad by 92 percent of those polled, and occupation of classrooms and offices was similarly viewed by 92 percent. In regard to police action on the campuses, 55 percent felt such use of police should be avoided as far as possible, whereas 21 percent view the university as having no special privileges with respect to the use of police; 14 percent say that under the principle of university autonomy, police should not be called.

Recently the Japanese government abolished university sanctuary, and new laws permit police action on campuses and provide that the salaries of professors be abrogated during a period in which the university does not function. The responsibility for the continuing functioning of the university is put on the faculty and administration, and it is up to them to call in the police when they need their assistance. Evidently these laws are working; since this threat to faculty salaries, university administrators have been prompt to call the police in cases of disturbance.

The opinion survey showed that 52 percent of the Japanese public believe that using the police is an ineffective way to resolve troubles in the university; only 14 percent see them as effective. The Japanese public, in this respect, seems to be far ahead of the American public.

In response to questions about student leaders of the current student movement, one finds a generally negative attitude; 30 percent see them as arrogant, and another 29 percent see them as shallow and manipulated by others. Twelve percent, however, see them positively as having a youthful sincerity, and another 12 percent see them as to be admired for putting beliefs into action.

One finds the general public opposed to student participation in political activities. Eleven percent say a certain amount of violence is unavoidable, whereas 38 percent say the students should not take violent action or arm themselves with wooden staves. Another 25 percent say they should not participate in actual political movements, 17 percent say the main task of students is to study and therefore they should have nothing to do with political or social movements.

FACTIONS IN STUDENT POLITICS

The student movement in Japan has a basic core organized around the Zengakuren, the national federation of student self-government associations. Within this large body, which is leftist controlled, a great deal of factionalism has developed over the years. Originally, the Zengakuren was not supposed to have any political affiliation, but it was not long before the organization was taken over by students with very strong leftist orientation. The main factions splitting the student movement today are the Communist party faction, called the JCP, which is regarded as conservative and revisionist, and the ultra-left, which, although at times it goes beyond the Maoist position, is basically pro-Maoist in orientation. It is the latter group, the "anti-JCP" factions of the Zengakuren who have been involved in most of the organizational activities, such as the protests at the Sasebo Naval Base and at Shinjuku Station. The split has become so severe that some of the recent violent student activity is between these factions rather than between the police and the students.

The Zengakuren was organized in September 1948 around the slogan calling for peace and democracy. Since that time, its history has been marked by continual splits and reunions. During the first ten years of its life, the Zengakuren was closely affiliated with the Japan Communist party and may be said to have been controlled by party officials, who imposed rigid discipline, based on party policy, on their youthful adherents. Then came problems within the Japan Communist party itself, especially ideological difficulties related to de-Stalinization, and to the divisions occurring in the communist world.

The Hungarian uprising became a central issue and created a severe split in the Japanese party which no longer could simply unify opposition to warlike imperialists. By 1960 the "antimainstream" Zengakuren faction, which remained loyal to the Communist party, formed its own organization and got back into the Zengakuren, becoming the JCP faction of so-called conservatives. At the present time, there are three further splits in the Zengakuren, the Chūkaku faction, focused on nuclear power, the Hantai, the anti-imperialist faction, and the Kakumaru, the revolutionary Marxist faction.

The ideology of the Communist faction adheres to the primary revolutionary view that the working class and students, as floating intellectuals, should remain obedient to the rules governing the revolution. The JCP program envisions the attainment of full independence for Japan, free of American domination, and its aim is social revolution by means of a united front. The JCP avoid violent clashes with riot police and obey the letter of the official regulations laid down in respect to demonstrations and rallies; they are seldom arrested by police. Their tactics evidence purely political calculation and lessen their popularity with students, who see this behavior as expediential and lacking in sincerity. Students tend to see them as bureaucratic because of the rigid party control over their activities, and a great deal of student sympathy, therefore, goes to the more radical left, which is not burdened by these strictures.

In contrast, the anti-JCP factions in the Zengakuren are willing to clash violently with the police deliberately and to barricade campus buildings and the like, although they make it a rule to issue advance warnings. They have become an almost military organization, arming themselves with staves and going into battle formation with crash helmets of a distinguishing color. They are impressive to the general student body for their uncompromising idealism, particularly in crisis situations on the campus. The communist faction now works through channels in order to gain control over the system, whereas the anti-JCP rejects all activity that would make them tame accomplices of the present system. Very much like the American Students for a Democratic Society, this faction lacks a specific program of any kind.

It is estimated that at the present time two-thirds of the total of one and a half million university students belong to some form of student self-government association. The faction of the Zengakuren that controls a university or a department also controls the revenue from membership fees, and this operates as a kind of "closed shop" in which students have no alternative but to join the faction in control of a particular department of a particular university. At the beginning of every school term the students not only pay their fees for tuition, but they are almost required, by sanctioning of the student body itself, also to pay assessments to the particular organization that has control. Thus a politically organized sanctioning body is in control, and the students, whether they are politically interested or not, are coerced by group atmosphere to join in the activities. Only the most active radicals participate in all activities voluntarily, but there are numerous occasions when there is a compelling force for demonstration exerted upon the students. Of the 830 self-governing associations for Japanese students, 520 belong to one or the other of the four groups of Zengakuren. It is estimated that the pro-JCP faction controls about 65 to 70 percent, and the Zengakuren from 30 to 35 percent of these student self-governing units. Accordingly, as many as 35,000 students can be simultaneously ordered into action by the pro-JCP faction, and about 25,000 to 30,000 by the rival faction.

A final word on the violence and concepts of violence of the more radical faction. Japanese students, like those at the height of the crises in France, set fire to cars and ripped up paving stones to throw at the police lines. (The city of Tokyo went to considerable expense to remove all the loose paving stones from sidewalks in the critical areas of Tokyo and to replace them with asphalt as a means of cutting down this activity.) On the campuses themselves, students make barricades and blockade buildings, using desks and ripping out material to use as part of the barricade. A particularly vicious form of proto-violence engaged in by students is the brainwashing of faculty members; a number of suicides by faculty and the hospitalization of older faculty members for heart attacks and other somatic problems have been brought on by the emotional violence to which they have been subjected by their own students. Radical students openly avow that so long as state power remains a political form of violence the only means by which workers and students can resist is by counterviolence. They maintain additionally that they recognize no institutions of the existing society, including the laws of the capitalist system. Other students argue that violence is justified as a means of demonstrating the reactionary power of the state by causing it to react upon its citizens; that is, they believe in provocative violence as a means of exposing to the world the inadequacies of the government and of such institutions as the university. A large body of students maintain that, although they do not approve of violence, the use of violence in self-defense is necessary to meet the violence of the riot police against them. The general attitudes about violence held by the anticommunist radicals in the student body do not win them much sympathy on the outside. The mass actions with staves have tended to repel the public more and more and the result, as of 1970, has been sympathy with governmental measures strengthening the powers of the riot police.

Chapter XVII

Role Narcissism and the Etiology of Japanese Suicide

THE NECESSITY OF A MULTIDIMENSIONAL THEORY OF SUICIDE

Violence or injury to, or even murder of, another originates in readily understandable human emotions shared by all men whatever the culture. But a desire to annihilate the self, to seek to terminate one's own existence, to suicide, is much less open to easy conscious experience and much more disquieting. It is, for most, threatening to contemplate, hence difficult to explain. Even when an individual lives to relate the state of his mind during an attempt to end his own life he seems to find great difficulty in recapturing in words the emotions and the thought content that could help make his suicidal motivation understandable to others.

It is most difficult, but hopefully not impossible, to enter into the state of mind of an individual to understand his motivation to suicide. However, to understand fully, not only must one look at conscious subjective motives to suicide, but one must also look for the dilemma or crisis leading to suicide as originating in processes not conscious to the suicidal individual. In this chapter I will attempt, therefore, to explain suicide in Japan by integrating theoretically the explanations of the sources of motives to suicide afforded both by psychoanalytic psychology and by the sociological theory originated by Emil Durkheim.[1] These theories both have valid observations to make. I have found them to be complementary rather than in conflict one with the other in understanding forces giving rise to suicidal motivation within an individual. A multidimensional psychocultural approach to suicide, as to any other form of motivated human behavior, benefits

---

[1] Durkheim, *Suicide* (1951). See also Halbwachs, *Les Causes du Suicide* (1930).

438

by recognizing an essential duality of determinants. These determinants pertain both to external pressures originating in the structure of society and to internal pressures originating in the personality structure. Both sets of determinants are aspects of cultural behavior.

Limitations of the Psychodynamic Approach

With the advent of psychoanalysis as a theoretical explanatory system, new understandings of human behavior have become possible. Humans everywhere are found to be motivated by an indescribably complex mélange of unconscious and conscious fears, desires, and hatreds. A dynamic approach to human personality development has placed emphasis on the vicissitudes occurring in the socialization of man's emotional life, making possible more adequate comprehension of all forms of psychopathology, including the psychology of suicide.[2] Nevertheless, the interpretation by psychoanalysis that aggression turned in on the self is a fundamental element in suicide, although valid, is insufficient to give a full understanding. Without discounting that aggression expressed autoplastically on one's own body plays some role in every suicide, one still must look for other essential elements. The strictly psychological approach concerns itself with subjective or unconscious motivational factors and pays relatively little attention to the cultural patterning that is evidenced by the respective relative frequency of suicide and by the peculiarities of the conditions under which it occurs. While effective in giving satisfactory explanations in given instances, it remains insufficient as a general social theory.[3]

Suicide, like other forms of motivated behavior, must also be examined for its "social" forms. There are determinants related to overall cultural traditions, to social context, to factors of age and sex that must be explored. Explanations must be found for the regularities and continuities in the incidence of suicide differing from society to society, since statistically determined rates of suicide, where they are available, have held constant over a long period of time for given nations and cultural entities. The social scientists must investigate the likelihood that continually operative social factors may account for this regularity.

---

[2] Freud, "Mourning and Melancholia," *Collected Papers* (1924); Menninger, *Man Against Himself* (1938); Gregory Zilboorg, "Differential Diagnostic Types of Suicide" (1936a), and "Consideration in Suicide with Particular Reference to That of the Young" (1937).

[3] Menninger, *Man Against Himself*; Zilboorg, "Differential Diagnostic Types of Suicide"; Garma, "Sadism and Masochism in Human Conduct" (1944); O'Connor, "Some Notes on Suicide" (1948); Palmer, "Factors in Suicidal Attempts, a Review of 25 Consecutive Cases" (1941).

Limitations of the Sociological Dimension

A strictly sociological approach limits itself to ordering suicidal behavior around concepts of social status and social cohesion, which are sometimes only mechanically related to the subjective emotional logic of the suicidal act.[4] For the most part, sociological theoreticians following Durkheim have concentrated on a properly cogent analysis of suicide related either to acute disturbances in social status or to chronic loss of cohesiveness of the social fabric itself. When a sociological theory of suicide is applied to a particular culture, however, a single-minded appeal to the differences in either social status or social cohesion to explain variables such as differentials in the rates of suicide in men and women is no more explanatory in itself than a simplistic use of psychological theory to produce the generalization that all suicide is a form of introjected hostility. Such generalizations explain nothing in respect to why a particular incidence of provocation leads to suicide in a particular cultural setting. For example, Ballestros[5] explanation of the male-female ratio in Mexican suicide as being due simply to differential social status of men and women actually explains very little. In general, such sociologically oriented analysis is too directly and mechanically seeking to find cause for all forms of suicidal behavior in contemporaneous social situations that, considered by themselves, do not explain actual suicidal motivation. In a theory productive of both particular explanations and generalizations about suicidal behavior, concepts such as social cohesiveness must be more broadly related to past developmental experiences as well as to present social provocations; that is to say, the concept must be related somehow to the childhood socialization process common to a culture. I suggest that an adequate theoretical analysis must include some explanation of how the primary narcissism of early childhood in a particular culture is successfully or unsuccessfully transmuted to a socially functional or dysfunctional cathexis of outer objects in the course of childhood socialization.

For some individuals within a given culture, earlier acute psychological experiences of object loss may in a culturally patterned way be related to the experiential content through which later inner experiences of alienation and of lack of belonging are given expression in behavior. Given particular later crises in social circumstances,

---

[4] See my further criticism of the sociological approach applied cross-culturally in DeVos, "Suicide in Cross-Cultural Perspective" (1968). Excellent examples of the use of sociological framework in regard to both its virtues and its limitations are found in Henry and Short, *Suicide and Homicide* (1954), and Bohannon (ed.), *African Homicide and Suicide* (1960).

[5] Ballestros, "Suicide in Adolescence" (1953), p. 281.

particular members of this culture may therefore be peculiarly suicide prone. A psychocultural approach lends depth of understanding by attending in particular detail both to psychological patterns and to social content as they are operative in given acts of suicide in a given culture.

Rationale for a Psychocultural Approach

To be fully understood the same suicidal act must be examined in relation to (1) the relative incidence of suicide within a given society, (2) the situational provocations inherent in the social structure, (3) the psychocultural "emotional logic" of suicide within the culture considered. There are three necessary levels, therefore, of data gathering and analysis: the sociological, the experiential, and the psychological. On a sociological level, one determines how a particular act of suicide is statistically related to other similar acts, which relates to the force of given social processes which are not necessarily in the direct awareness of participants. On the second, experiential level one seeks out the "emic" socially aware, motivational categories of suicide defined from within by members of the culture. One seeks to learn what members of the culture themselves say explicitly about the social motivations and explanations for suicide. The third, more "etic" psychological view attempts to make explicit the implicit underlying unconscious emotional logic of the act, which again may not be in the direct awareness of the members of the culture. From this latter perspective the suicidal act must be analyzed, as it is partially at least derived from particular types of socialization experiences that are widespread in the culture. One finds in the theoretical literature on the subject supposed conflict between basically sociological and basically psychological theories of suicide related to one or another level of analysis. The major intent of this chapter on suicide in Japanese culture is to come to some theoretical resolution of the seemingly antithetical positions about suicide by employing as well as is possible what is afforded by all three levels when examined in the context of Japanese culture and personality.

In the course of analyzing Japanese data on suicide I have found it helpful to evaluate critically but constructively the shortcomings of the sociological approach to suicide applied cross-culturally. As a consequence, I have developed a fourfold psychocultural classification that includes the psychoanalytic approach to motivation and at the same time extends Durkheim's sociological classification of types of suicide. My analysis of Japanese suicide suggests how peculiarities in the statistics of Japanese suicide and in the personal crises leading to suicide relate to cultural peculiarities in the development of "object cathexis" in childhood socialization. Cultural peculiarities in Japanese socialization can be related to the resolution or lack of resolution of particular socially determined crises in social roles occurring throughout the life cycle.

The social phenomenon of suicide in Japan raises certain questions in terms of psychodynamic and sociological factors that I contend are operative cross-culturally. In Japan as elsewhere there are social, cultural, economic, and political pressures that affect consecutive generations similarly in inducing a fairly constant number of individuals to resolve these external pressures through suicide. There are also acute social, economic, and political convulsions occurring periodically within Japanese society that make life impossible for some of its individuals. When we search deeper, it is also possible to find prevalent cultural considerations generally affecting the internalized personality mechanisms in Japanese that cause them to manifest suicidal behavior in a culturally patterned way. Following a more general theoretical discussion of suicide in the first part of this chapter is my attempt to explain the peculiarities of Japanese suicide in a context of *both* culturally determined social and personality dynamics by using Japanese data which I have been collecting since 1953.

There are ample data available in Japanese on the subject of suicide. Carefully detailed research by Japanese scholars provides demographic data on age, sex, regional variations, and methods employed in Japanese suicide. There is also considerable material available on cases of suicide recorded in detail both in special reports and in newspaper accounts of suicides that fully discuss supposed motivational factors. There are also numerous presentations of suicidal motivation within Japanese drama and literature. From such sources, as well as from my own projective test materials, I present first, a summary of statistical peculiarities. Next, I list my formulation of six culturally recognized motivational categories of suicide, regardless of their possible relative statistical incidence within the population. Finally, I examine these Japanese data in the light of the general psychocultural theory of suicide posited in the first half of this chapter and the discussion of Japanese socialization already presented in previous chapters of this volume.

A number of subjects related to ego psychology cannot be adequately covered in what follows. In attempting to comprehend the subject at hand, therefore, I must simply allude to topics that of themselves need far more detailed, adequate exposition than I will be able to give within the brief compass of the present chapter. I hope at some future time, for instance, to do a more complete and systematic cross-cultural analysis of the social maturation of the human sense of belonging.

A FOURFOLD CATEGORIZATION OF SUICIDE
RELATED TO THE PERSONAL-SOCIAL POLARITIES
OF SUICIDAL MOTIVATION AND
DISTURBANCES IN OBJECT CATHEXIS

In seeking to understand data on Japanese suicide one finds that the interplay of psychological and of social determinants is highly complex in given instances. Nevertheless, I have found it possible to analyze particular cases by developing an integrated general theory of suicide that intersects sociological concepts of social cohesion or alienation with psychoanalytic concepts of object cathexis and differential forms of narcissistic regression. The accompanying chart (Figure 1) represents briefly in outline form the typology created by this intersection. What follows here is an elaboration of this framework which allows for a psychocultural analysis of any given act of suicide.

Suicide according to Durkheim occurs with greater frequency in situations of acute or chronic disturbance of social cohesion. Different states of social cohesion eventuate in different forms of suicide. First, he cites a polarity in the strength of normative structuring in society that stimulates what he termed *altruistic* behavior, on the one hand, or *egoistic* behavior on the other. Second, he originally paired off social situations that stimulate acute *anomic* reactions as polar to those social conditions that engender *fatalism*. This latter concept proved unsatisfactory to Durkheim; he never developed it in his exposition of forms of suicide. His followers have limited their sociological analysis therefore to three alternative modes of suicide: anomic, egoistic, and altruistic.

From a psychocultural perspective rather than a strictly sociological one, I find it possible, as I have already briefly suggested above, to postulate a different form of a fourth category of suicide to be paired against *anomic* suicide—namely, that of *egocentric* suicide. To fully explicate these four psychocultural categories, one must return to psychodynamic determinants and examine how they are in interaction with societal ones. Sociological analysis cannot of itself explain all forms of suicidal motivation.

There are, indeed, considerable differences in the nature of the subjective experience of social belonging or cohesion in each of the four forms of suicide, but social determinants cannot be found to be as directly operative in what I term egocentric suicides or in egoistic suicides as they are in altruistic or in anomic suicidal reactions. In fact, psychocultural *developmental vicissitudes,* rather than *societal vicissitudes,* are much more directly involved in all forms of suicide

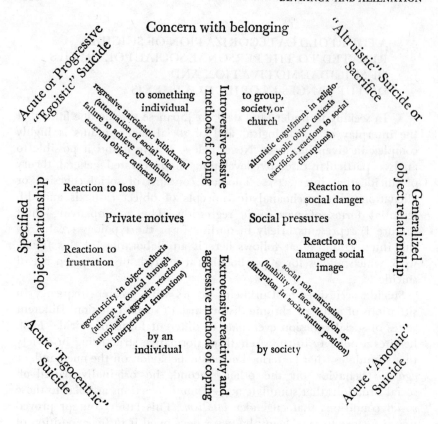

FIGURE 1
*Four Types of Suicide Differentiated
According to the Nature of Object Cathexis
and Personal-Social Polarities of Suicidal Motivation*

than is allowed for in Durkheim's theory. From my psychocultural frame of reference, four forms of suicide are differentiated from one another both by differences in social cohesion and by differences in the psychosocial or psychocultural developmental *level* of object cathexis reached and in the *content* of object cathexis sought.

The Interrelationship Between Affiliative "Object Cathexis" and "Social Cohesion"

All suicide involves what can be termed some form of immature fixation or regressive withdrawal of object cathexis. "Object cathexis" as defined in psychoanalytic theory is the investment of meaning by an individual in the "objects" of his social and natural environment. The objects "cathected," or invested with meaning, can include not only other persons but also inanimate objects or ideas, as well as all or part of one's own body. In the course of psychosexual development an individual is "socialized" out of a state of primary narcissism so as to invest meaning in objects and persons that have social as well as personal value. This process is never complete, and investment in the self is always in dynamic tension with both instrumental and expressive investment in objects outside the self.

To understand how the psychological development of object cathexis is related to the subjective experience of social cohesion, we have to understand how the sense of self is developed in society. The first development of a sense of belonging occurs in the earliest relationship with the mother. This sense of primary belonging is transmuted by socialization into other symbolic representations in every culture. Socialization of social belonging takes place in the context of an available religious cognitive system of beliefs which relates the individual experientially to his environment as a member of a particular culture.

Hence, as a symbolic animal living in culture, man in his psychosexual development comes to cathect not only persons or material objects, but also symbols and ideas. As he becomes socialized, man creates within himself a world of symbolic meaning. Symbolic meanings can become more important to him than the individuals with whom he relates or the material objects that he uses in his environment. Any *idea* of man's social creation, whether it be that of "god" or "society" or "individual" or "self," when examined in its final analysis is a symbol that can nevertheless be experienced subjectively as an overriding reality filled with life's meaning for the individual who cathects it.

Man in culture comes to dedicate himself to some form or system of symbolic representations, whether embodied in a religion or an ideology of society or a philosophy of life. For some, a system of beliefs is as necessary as breathing. Sebastian De Grazia pointed out in his perceptive book, *The Political Community*,[6] that the political system or religious system under which a person lives is for him a psychological security system that prevents the possibility of an individual's re-experiencing the overwhelming primary anxiety.

Every society shapes the elementary instrumental and expressive interpersonal concerns I have discussed in detail in Chapter 1 into some more or less cohesive and consistent system of social relationships. Ideological or religious ideals orient expectations that, however, may not be realizable in actual interpersonal relationships. Sometimes, therefore, religious illusions fulfill expressive satisfactions lacking in the contacts afforded within the existing social network, due to personality limitations both in the person seeking satisfaction as well as those from whom it is sought. Affiliative needs for closeness and "contact" or, more primitively, for fusion are central. Dependent needs, avoidance of a sense of deprivation as well as reassurances of approbation and appreciation countering a sense of worthlessness are also central. (See Table I-5.)

Man's social beliefs are for man his "meaning." This is a way of re-stating Durkheim's perception of society as a "reality" prior to the individual. Should the individual somehow become personally alienated or suffer the consequences of anomic conditions in his society, he can become bereft of meaning and suffer an extreme form of malaise that demands resolution. Bereft of meaning, the individual loses his reason for existence, and life may become so burdensome that he seeks to annihilate himself.

In a final act of desperation he may again turn to some alternative illusory system of fixed beliefs and find in it a reaffirmation of his meaning. William James in his *Varieties of Religious Experience*[7] documents, in case after case, conversion experiences where the individual on the brink of suicide or ultimate despair finds religious meaning and the capacity to continue life; James defined this experience as being "twice born." Many religious thinkers and writers have attempted to communicate this experience of a quest for man's ultimate meaning. Sartre's study in novel form, *La Nausee*,[8] is a fine literary expression of the feeling of intense personal alienation. Man can rescue himself from a quest for necessary meaning only by adapting some symbolic system of belonging satisfying the sense of incompleteness within the self. A conversion experience or a sudden dedication to a cause is for many an alternative to suicide. Jacques Maritain, the French philosopher, in describing his own conversion autobiographically, indicated that for him embracing the Catholic religion was the only way out; he could not otherwise continue to live.

---

[6] De Grazia, *The Political Community* (1948).

[7] James, *Varieties of Religious Experience* (1902).

[8] Sartre, *La Nausee* (1962).

For many, to live is to find expression for a need to relate, to belong, to be sustained. Should this need prove to be unattainable or somehow lack satisfaction, an individual becomes subject to a profound state of despair. Many avoid such despair by means of some sense of relationship created through religious belief and practice, which, seen psychologically, is a dedication to a sustaining set of symbols through which the individual can somehow avoid his essential feeling of separateness. Religion for some provides a means to bridge the gap between himself and others, or, if you will, creates for the believer the illusion of satisfaction to be obtained beyond that of his immediate interpersonal relationships. One *belongs* to a church or other group and thereupon shares with others a sustaining belief in belonging and receiving. For some, although they may remain solitary in the real world, there is possible a special relationship to a deity. In Christianity, God's grace heals the feeling of separation and aloneness; in Buddhistic teaching, the separate ego and the self are acknowledged to be but illusions, but one's true essence partakes of the essential continuity with all life. The gnawing pain of isolation and separation is symbolically healed by such beliefs.

Altruistic and Egoistic Suicide: Belonging and Loss

Egoistic and altruistic suicide, although at opposite poles of a personal-social dimension, both suggest vicissitudes at the earliest level of psychosexual development, a basic disturbance of the most primitive early sense of social "belonging." Such suicides are therefore often symptomatic of a reversion to a very primitive level of narcissism, in which the very boundaries of the self become ill-defined.

According to Durkheim, altruistic suicide is a supreme act of responsibility and of belonging, an example of individual behavior being subordinate to the needs of a cohesive society. Some well-known traditional forms of Japanese suicide, as I shall discuss further, well exemplify this notion of Durkheim, since such suicide includes acts of self-destruction in which the individual's purpose or meaning is defined so strongly in terms larger than himself that he readily sacrifices his life in the name of his social role.

In Japan the suicidal act in the samurai tradition could be conceived as helping a man obtain a closer union with a purpose or force larger than himself.[9] Japanese have been socialized traditionally to find the deepest psychological security in belonging to a family or to a political entity rather than in dedication to a supreme deity. A struggle between adherence to a religious power and loyalty to a

---

[9] Something greater than self as a source of meaning may be a system, like society, or one's family, but it might also be an individual person, representative, more or less, of the system. Emperor Meiji was such a person for General Nogi.

temporal force never appears in Japanese history as it does in the West. There is no parallel in Japan to the emperor Henry IV's kneeling in the snow as an act of penance for his opposition to spiritual power. One could say that the religious security as well as social belonging of the samurai was realized in his adherence to his responsible role as a loyal subject.

Durkheim's concept of altruistic suicide depends upon the subordination of one's self to an outside power, and such suicide, therefore, is in many respects *sacrificial* in nature (see Fig. 1); one feels engulfed in something that is the real essence of life. Looked at from a psychological standpoint, losing of self in a sacrificial act manifests a primitive form of belonging or object cathexis. What bears further exploration, psychodynamically, is under what conditions and in what way such a loss of self may be related to unresolved primary narcissism. The psychological necessity to lose oneself in a cause or a religious commitment in order to survive a diffuse feeling of inner insufficiency is so intimately related to social idealism and to highly esteemed social values that it is difficult to examine it dispassionately. Such social dedication is sacred to some cultures, groups, or individuals; in others it strikes no responsive chord and seems to be a form of madness.[10]

What appears to be altruistic suicide may more likely occur in those whose actual relationships in day-to-day life are somehow insufficient. When examined psychodynamically, as I attempt to do later on, many cases of altruistic suicide may be found to spring from primitive motives rather than from a well-developed and differentiated sense of adherence to mature human values. In my point of view there is often less underlying psychological difference than is presumed between what is termed altruistic suicide as defined by Durkheim and its supposed opposite, egoistic suicide. The insecure or unsatisfactory sense of belonging so directly apparent in egoistic suicide is often present but hidden or cloaked in what on the surface appears to be "altruistic" behavior. The feeling of inner insufficiency, worthlessness, and lack of satisfaction with what life has to offer is the core concern not only in egoistic suicide, but in many supposedly altruistic suicides as well.

Egoistic suicides include those that result when an individual ceases to pretend, to himself or others, to share in group meanings or incentives. For some so alienated, life gradually becomes empty and bereft of sustaining purpose, and the act of suicide can represent the last shedding of the vestiges of one's ties. Egoistic suicide is committed by individuals who have retreated too far from the meanings given them by their society without establishing for themselves a sustaining

---

[10] The perception of British and Japanese role dedication to the outside American in the screenplay *The Bridge on the River Kwai* is a striking example.

individualistic sense of their own purpose. This sort of suicide is well articulated in Japan in the writings of Japanese literary figures, as documented in detail in the following chapter.

Because of the extreme self-preoccupation of the individuals concerned, egoistic suicide can be viewed as an attempt to find meaning in terms of narcissistic preoccupation. Some suicidal individuals try to dedicate themselves to aesthetic refinement as a way of life, but this fails to sustain them, and suicide becomes a way out. For others no religious conversion can solve the continual erosive enfeeblement of all forms of tenuously held object cathexis. Continually compelled to penetrate the veils of illusion that others live by, some become more and more disenchanted with the possibilities of human existence. One can assume from a psychoanalytic standpoint that for such individuals nothing has taken the place of the original primary love object; disturbances and frustrations in this original relationship make it hypothetically impossible for the individual to develop a satisfactory affiliative cathexis of outside objects with enough force to sustain him and give him hope.

A prevalent form of egoistic suicide is that of aged individuals— either those who have suffered the loss of a mate of long standing or those coping with the increasing infirmity or pain of failing health. For such individuals there seems to be insufficient remaining external object cathexis to sustain interest in life. The loss of a vital interest in life can lead to death without recourse to suicide. We do not yet understand the role of a will to live in recovery from illness or in other related phenomena. In the aged, the loss of a marital companion or the final completion of some task is sometimes closely followed by a form of devitalization that results in death. This withdrawal of positive cathexis from body functions to the point of producing death is not "aggressive" and therefore is usually not seen as related to suicide. Nevertheless, the loss of a will to live, whatever its origin, is an essential element in egoistic suicide.

The difficulty in finding a sufficient motive for many suicides resides in the intimate and personal nature of what makes life worth living for any individual, which often is a very private, verbally noncommunicable feeling. It is difficult for an outsider to ascertain what sudden sense of permanent irreplaceable loss another may have sustained that would lead him to suicide. For some suicidal individuals the major libidinal cathexis may have been narcissistically focused on a part of the body or the mind that has ceased to function satisfactorily.[11]

---

[11] One psychologist described to me the circumstances surrounding the suicide of a former prison inmate he had been treating. The inmate compulsively committed rape several times before being apprehended. While in prison he was given psychoanalytically oriented psychotherapy. After receiving a parole, he again raped

The most loved part of one individual may be his intellectual capacity; in another it may be his sexual organ and potency or physical capacity.

To recapitulate, egoistic and altruistic suicide are both related to disturbances in primary narcissism harking back to disturbance of the earliest formation of ego boundaries distinguishing self from nonself. (See Fig. 1.) Such suicides reflect disturbances in the capacity to relate to outside objects of love either because of an incapacity to invest the energy necessary for fulfillment or satisfaction, or because of an incapacity to feel such satisfaction without a total engulfment in which the separateness of the self is lost completely—in the latter context, sense of self is encompassed by an entity larger than itself. Prompting such incapacity is the narcissistic state in which the sense of individuality is felt as a torment; the sense of one's self may be that of a worthless being, incapable of giving or receiving love. This sense of self separation can be lost only by gaining an overwhelming, limitless sense of belonging. These extremes in disturbed social belonging are polar images of each other, and one finds what is termed egoistic torment over loss of meaning being transmuted into attempts at an "altruistic" loss of self. Conversion experiences and some cases of mystical ecstatic transport are subjectively experienced as resolutions transcending previous, abject states of total isolation and aloneness. The individual who becomes an "altruistic" martyr for a cause may have as great a narcissistic incapacity to set limits on what can be expected from human object relations as does the egoistic suicide who despairs of gaining sufficient satisfaction from human contact. In both cases the sense of belonging remains primitively incapable of limitation.

Durkheim, within his sociologistic framework, could recognize the cohesive social belief system that engulfs its members, but he could not recognize the psychodynamic motivational system that causes in

---

a young woman and was returned to prison. He re-entered treatment during the course of which he again came up for parole. At the time of release he had confided to his therapist that he found himself psychically incapable of an erection. Shortly after, he committed suicide. One can infer from the therapy material that this individual was deeply cathected to his penis as an object. Somehow it had become as dead, leading the individual to resolve his state of extreme malaise by suicide.

Another incident of suicide occurring in psychoanalysis suggests how in actual cases it is extremely difficult to judge the degree of actual frustration as related to the degree of unconscionable despair over ever being libidinally gratified on the level at which a need is felt. As reported to me, in the second year of analysis a patient regressed to an extremely primitive oral level of relationship. More and more depressed, he confided to his female therapist a feeling of despair that since she was unmarried and never had children, she could never possibly nurse anyone. A few days later he killed himself.

certain, not all, members of a society a sense of deep need for belonging related to an incapacity to resolve narcissistic needs within the limits of available interpersonal relationships.

Anomic and Egocentric Suicide: Interpersonal and Status Frustration

Durkheim's exploration of the conditions under which anomic suicide occurred progressed into one of his major contributions to sociological theory. It set him to explore the way in which social disturbances may induce a differential incidence of suicide. Sudden disruptions of life patterns by economic, social, or political upheaval can throw individuals into psychological states that call for radical reorientation of previously accepted life goals and meanings. Should psychological inflexibilities make this impossible, the individual may escape the necessity to redefine himself through suicide.

Suicides comprising my fourth, newly posed category, *egocentric* suicide, are only very indirectly influenced by such external fluctuations in social cohesion. The situational stimuli to many suicides in Japan as elsewhere occur in intimate, one-to-one personal relationships. Such personal motivational factors in suicide are relatively neglected by sociologists in their preoccupation with general societal determinants. Particular acute interpersonal crises, marital rifts, and the like cannot be directly related to ongoing overall societal vicissitudes influencing states of social cohesion or anomie. Nor is the proneness to suicide of individuals in such crises explained simply by the presence of a cultural pattern making suicide permissible. One has to examine more fully why a particular culture has a tradition that encourages the suicidal type of autoplastic aggression in interpersonal involvements. Such social behavior is a result, not of direct social pressure, but most probably of some cultural tradition in childhood socialization.

Compared with egoistic and altruistic suicides, the social-personal polarities of anomic and egocentric suicide both are related somewhat more to a sense of acute frustration of interpersonal gratification experienced at a somewhat later "egocentric" level of ego development. At this level, the child is still narcissistically oriented. He is conceptually focused on the self, but the self as gratified by or responded to by others who have their own motivations and thus may thwart wishes or deliberately withhold gratification. An acute sense of frustration of gratification of the self (or later on, the self defined in terms of social role) is reacted to by an inner sense of rage. The individual may be incapable of expressing rage outwardly toward the source of frustration on whom he is also deeply dependent (and in this sense highly "cathected"). Aggression is turned inward or deflected, as is sometimes noted in temper tantrums in young children, which usually deflect aggression from its object. Such tantrums are often minor dramas making a histrionic display of an impasse of frustration to frighten or somehow move the frustrator to desired nurturant action by a "show" of rage; they occur in some adults as well as in children who do not dare attack directly the object of their frustration because they have become heavily dependent on a particular person for a sense of satisfaction.

In egocentric suicide, dependent object cathexis is usually focused on a specific person, whereas in anomic suicide object cathexis has become more generalized and diffused. Suicide is a response to a sudden frustration of a continual need for social recognition and response resulting from a narcissistic preoccupation with the self in respect to status and role. Resultant hostility is manifestly deflected into self-destruction in both anomic and egocentric suicides. In anomic self-destruction, hostility is aroused by the sense of an impending social denial of status. In egocentric crises, hostility results from the feeling that essential acknowledgment is being withheld by some specific "other" who is uniquely capable of gratifying a strongly felt need.

In anomic suicide the individual cannot face a perceived threat of loss of social status, even when the threatened degradation is not due to one's own mistake. Shame and chagrin are so extreme that the individual cannot contemplate life henceforth, and rather than face the necessity of continuing life in an altered or degraded social role, he chooses to end it all. In some instances a society may condone this alternative covertly or overtly; for example, the degraded European officer who has sullied his honor is left by his peers to use a pistol on himself, and in so doing, he recaptures some lost status.

Many Japanese who are prone to acute anomic suicide manifest, for reasons to be discussed shortly, what I term "social role narcissism." They tend to become over-involved with their social role, which has become cathected by them as the ultimate meaning for life. Such individuals are particularly vulnerable to social disturbances or personal mistakes or inadvertencies that may bring about a change in role definition. Whereas the acute anomic suicide is more concerned with injury to one's generalized need for social appreciation, the egocentric suicide is more concerned with receiving nurturant gratification from a specific individual to whom he feels so hopelessly bound in a dependent relationship that he cannot shift to another source of gratification. The person held responsible for the chief source of satisfaction is perceived as deliberately or inadvertently withholding. Characteristically, the suicidal person is in a status dependent or emotionally dependent position that prevents direct aggressive action, control, or manipulation. The evocation of pity or guilt in the other by means of self-inflicted injury is perceived as the only available mode of counterattack or recrimination. Hence, the person either demonstrates symbolically the possibility of suicide, or actualizes it as a final "autoplastic" attack. Such a suicide in a curious way can also be an act of vengeance.

In this form of relationship the dependent person is incapable of getting beyond his own egocentric perception of the other person as an extension of his narcissistic needs. Since the other person is an extension of his own ego he has the sense of wishing to control him to conform to these needs. (Control from a seemingly dependent position is the heart of the concept of "amae," discussed in Chapter 1 on Japanese role relationships.) When this desired control is frustrated, the individual feels a helpless destructive rage, which is autoplastically turned back on his own body in a coercive gesture and with the aim of inflicting retributive destructiveness on the other, who is supposed to feel hurt since the other is still unconsciously perceived as part of the self. This underlies the emotional logic behind many family suicides, of both child and parent, bound together irrevocably in nurturant-control relationships.

The egocentric suicide can be readily differentiated from the egoistic suicide by the greater motivational emphasis in egocentric suicide on a sense of frustration and concomitant aggression in respect to the object cathected rather than on an egoistic withdrawal governed by a sense of loss and despair. (See Fig. 1 and Table I-5.) The individual who commits suicide out of a sense of frustration is apt to be seeking retribution. Such an act of suicide, as was suggested above, is an attempt to control another—the primitive egocentric magical logic of the act involves some sense of hurting another through injuring the self. It can sometimes attempt the manipulation of another's sense of guilt. Such a suicide resembles a gesture of what is termed "sympathetic" magic in anthropology. It is this type of suicide, in its complex primitive psychological ramifications, that has been best explored in the psychoanalytic literature, but relatively neglected by sociologists.

In summary, an evaluation of object cathexis as it is socialized within a culture is a necessary complement to an understanding of the sociological determinants expounded by Durkheim in his theory of suicide. Social theory to be relevant to human understanding is of necessity dualistic; adequate analysis of behavior requires a grasp of personality structure as well as of social structure. This is particularly evident in the analysis of suicide cross-culturally.

First: there are gradations of determinants in suicide between the extremes of internal personality pressures and social situational determinants. Some acts of suicide are determined chiefly by social forces operative either directly or indirectly in society on individuals in given social positions. Other acts, however, are best understood by reference to peculiarities of personality disturbance resulting from interpersonal crises or tensions that cannot be analyzed or satisfactorily understood simply in a social structural scheme. In understanding suicide in culture it is important to know how and at what period there is a culturally prevalent crisis in psychosexual maturation. It is also important in a psychocultural sense to understand how, within particular cultures, early disturbances are related to later experiences that give them content through which they can be socially expressed both to the self and to others.

To illustrate: An early disturbance in primary relationship can lead to an intense sense of incapacity to relate to others with satisfaction. In Japan, in a particular social group, this disturbance can be expressed in the social role of an intellectual who transmutes his personal problems into verbal expression of the social malaise existing in segments of his society. Another individual, who has experienced a different degree of satisfaction of the primary need for mothering, will subjectively experience the same relative malfunctioning of his society quite differently and will express it through alternative culturally available content.

Durkheim's sociological analysis, by itself, does not allow adequate complementary use of psychodynamic and sociodynamic understanding of the suicidal act to achieve a more complete social theory of human behavior, whatever the culture in which it occurs.

Second, in terms of personality theory, one must distinguish between a concern with adhesion and belonging and a reactive frustration as predominant motivational components in suicide. This distinction helps clarify Durkheim's three categories and makes possible the inclusion and relation of a fourth basic form of suicidal motivation.

Third, all actual suicides are impure mixtures of these conceptually *ideal* types. To diagnose a particular suicide is to attempt to discern the most compelling social and personal pressures operating on an individual with a given type of personality structure. It is helpful to consider how suicidal action results, on the one hand, from peculiar combinations of social and deeply internal experience, and, on the other, from a profound sense of loss as contrasted with a profound sense of frustration. Suicide must also be understood with necessary attention to relative maturation in psychosexual development. Cultures differ in their mode and manner of socialization, and socialization is related to the facilitation or blocking of the human capacity to mature in the individuation of the self and *also* to mature in a sense of social belonging. The usefulness of this general psychocultural typology of suicide will be now demonstrated in my attempt to understand suicide in Japan.

DISTINGUISHING FEATURES OF JAPANESE SUICIDE STATISTICS

Several features distinguish suicide in Japan from suicide in Western Europe and America. First, although the suicide rate in Japan has been in some periods one of the highest reported in the world, some countries report rates consistently as high if not higher than those of Japan—namely, Hungary, Denmark, Austria, and Switzerland. It is not, then, the total rate as such that distinguishes suicide in Japan from suicide in other nations. Rather, cultural factors are operative in the age and sex of the persons committing suicide and the locality in which suicides occur.

The most recent statistics on suicide[12] reported in the demographic yearbook of the United Nations, published in 1968, show that Japan, with a rate of 14 suicides per 100,000 inhabitants, is twelfth among the countries listed; in 1964 Japan was tenth (Table XVII-1). In the past, Japan has had a rate close to the top of those reporting, and at peak the Japanese post–World War II suicide rate in 1954 was only slightly lower than that reported for West Berlin.

TABLE XVII-1

SUICIDE AND SELF-INFLICTED INJURY BY SEX, PER 100,000 POPULATION, 1964

	Male	Female	Total
West Berlin	56.3	30.9	41.7
Hungary	40.9	17.1	28.6
Austria	33.2	13.7	22.8
Denmark	26.8	15.3	21.0
Czechoslovakia	29.6	12.2	20.7
West Germany	27.0	13.9	20.1
Finland	30.9	9.5	19.8
Sweden	28.7	10.9	19.8
Switzerland	24.3	10.0	17.0
Japan	17.5	12.9	15.1

SOURCE: Extracted from *World Health Statistics Annual 1964.*

---

[12] The author gratefully acknowledges the assistance of Mr. Hiro Kurashina in the preparation of materials on recent statistical trends in Japanese suicide and in the preparation of bibliographic references. His chief sources were *Demographic Yearbook 1968*; *Japan Statistical Yearbook 1968*; Okazaki, *Jisatsu-ron* (1969); Segi, Kurihara, and Tsukahara, *Mortality for Selected Causes in 30 Countries (1950–61), Age-Adjusted Death Rates and Age-Specific Death Rates* (1966); *World Health Statistics Annual 1964* (1967); *World Health Statistics Annual 1967* (1969).

What has been happening in postwar Japan first to raise and more recently to lower the suicide rate? (See Table XVII-2.) Are these rate changes best accounted for in terms of some Durkheimian sociological explanation stressing recent shifts in economic conditions, or in terms of irreversible changes in Japanese culture with modernization, or perhaps in terms of the deep-set changes in Japanese cultural psychology accompanying modernization?

TABLE XVII-2

RECENT TRENDS IN JAPANESE SUICIDE
(RATE PER 100,000), 1950–1967

	1950–51	1954–55	1960–61	1964	1967
Total	21.6	26.3	21.1	15.1	14.1
Male	26.7	32.5	24.6	17.5	16.1
Female	16.4	19.0	17.6	12.9	12.1

1954–55 (Male)		1960–61 (Male)		1964 (Male)	
1. W. Berlin	32.6	1. W. Berlin	39.9	1. W. Berlin	56.3
2. Japan	32.5	2. Hungary	33.1	2. Hungary	40.9
3. Finland	32.3	3. Finland	33.0	3. Austria	33.2
4. Switzerland	28.7	4. Austria	27.5	4. Finland	30.9
5. Austria	28.1	5. Japan	24.6	5. Czech.	29.6
6. Denmark	28.0	6. Switzerland	23.6	6. Sweden	28.7
7. Hungary	25.1	7. W. Germany	22.3	7. W. Germany	27.0
8. W. Germany	23.3	8. Denmark	21.7	8. Denmark	26.8
9. Sweden	21.4	9. Sweden	21.0	9. Switzerland	24.3
10. France	20.7	10. France	20.1	10. France	22.4
				11. Belgium	20.1
				12. Australia	19.1
				13. Japan	17.5

1954–55 (Female)		1960–61 (Female)		1964 (Female)	
1. Japan	19.0	1. W. Berlin	22.7	1. W. Berlin	30.9
2. W. Berlin	19.0	2. Japan	17.6	2. Hungary	17.1
3. Denmark	12.8	3. Hungary	12.9	3. Denmark	15.3
4. Austria	11.9	4. Austria	11.2	4. W. Germany	13.9
5. Hungary	10.7	5. Denmark	10.5	5. Austria	13.7
6. Switzerland	10.1	6. W. Germany	10.3	6. Japan	12.9
7. Finland	7.5	7. Switzerland	9.2	7. Czech.	12.2
8. Sweden	6.8	8. Finland	8.2	8. Sweden	10.9
9. England and		9. Sweden	7.0	9. Switzerland	10.0
Wales	6.0	10. England and		10. Australia	9.9
10. France	5.7	Wales	6.6		

SOURCES: *Mortality for Selected Causes in 30 Countries (1950–1961): Age Adjusted Death Rates and Age-Specific Death Rates.* Dept. of Public Health, Tohoku University, School of Medicine, Sendai, Tokyo: Kosei Tokei Kyokai, 1966; *World Health Statistics Annual 1964;* and *1967.*

Age-specific Death Rates in 1967

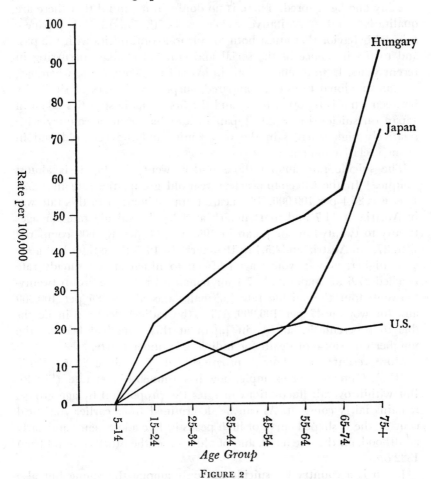

FIGURE 2

*The U-Shaped Curve of Japanese Suicide Rates Compared with **Those in the** United States and Hungary*

SOURCE: *World Health Statistics Annual 1967,* **Vol. I.**

In my opinion no single one of these explanations is sufficient, nor can any one be ignored. There is no doubt in my mind that there are qualitative and quantitative emphases in the nature of Japanese suicidal behavior that attest both to cultural continuities with the past and to the influence of the social and cultural changes occurring in recent years. Despite fluctuations in overall rates one finds, when age, sex, and regional rates are compared, surprising degrees of similarity between what is reported today and the first reliable statistics taken in Japan on suicide in 1882.[13] Japan is, and has been, a country with relatively high suicides in the very young and the very old and in women relative to men.

The suicide rate among those under twenty in Japan is almost unique.[14] In the fifteen-to-nineteen-year-old group, the rate in 1952–1954 was 26.1 per 100,000. The nearest approximation to this rate was in Austria at 11.7 and in Denmark at 8.3. The suicide rate for ages twenty to twenty-four in Japan in 1952 was 60 per 100,000 compared with 27.4 in Austria and 25.4 in Denmark. In 1955 these rates had gone even higher, and in youth aged fifteen to nineteen the suicide rate reached 37.6 for males and 27.4 for females. In the age group twenty-to-twenty-four the suicide rate for males was almost 85 per 100,000 and for women 47 per 100,000. With the radical decrease in deaths due to tuberculosis, suicide in Japan at this time had become the number one cause of death for individuals under thirty.

More recent rates show a progressive decline since 1955 (Table XVII-3). Hungary, for example, now has a much higher rate (Fig. 2). But within overall fluctuations in rates the proportion by age groups remains fairly constant. As can be determined from earlier statistical courses, the U-shaped curve of high peaks in late adolescence and early adulthood, on the one hand, and of old age, on the other is found from 1882 on.

Japan is a country for suicide not only among the young but also among the aged. Although the numbers become much smaller and the other sources of death are much more numerous in old age, for those over sixty the rate per 100,000 increases greatly in Japan, much more

---

[13] In Japanese: "Statistics on Suicide in Japan," *Annual Report on Mental Health* (1958), pp. 74–84; *Japanese Empire Statistical Year Book* (1882), pp. 445–451; *Japanese Empire Statistical Year Book, Statistics Bureau of the Prime Minister's Office* (1950); Jirō Takahashi, "History of Suicide in Japan" (1910).

[14] Kanbe and Ishii, "Japanese Youth's View of Life and of Suicide" (in Japanese), University Studies on Suicide, unpublished; Iga, "Cultural Factors in Suicide of Japanese Youth with Focus on Personality" (1961); Iga and Ohara, "Suicides of Japanese Youths and Family Structures," unpublished; Tanaka, "Statistics on Suicide of Youth" (1907, in Japanese); Osaka Crime Prevention Council, "The Actual Conditions of Youthful Suicide" (1960, in Japanese); Sudō, "High School Students' Views of Suicide" (1959, in Japanese).

TABLE XVII-3

RECENT DECREASING RATES OF SUICIDE IN YOUTH UNDER
TWENTY-FOUR YEARS OF AGE IN JAPAN

	1954–55	1960–61	1967 (WHO Annual)
Male 0–24	20.6	14.5	13.6 (15–24 age group)
Female 0–24	12.7	12.0	11.7 (15–24 age group)

SOURCES: Same as for Table XVII-2.

so than do rates reported in most other countries. For example, in the
United States the suicide rate reaches about 43 per 100,000 between
the ages of sixty and sixty-nine for men, and about 10 per 100,000
for women. In comparison, in Japan the rate is 61 for men and 35 for
women. Even more astounding rates are reported for ages seventy to
seventy-nine in Japan, where the rate goes up to 95 per 100,000 for
men and 60 per 100,000 for women.

For many years Japan had the highest rate of suicide for women in
any country reporting.[15] Only since 1960 has the Japanese women's
overall rate dropped to second, behind West Berlin in 1960, and then
dropped to sixth by 1964. Nevertheless, the ratio of women's suicides
to men's remains higher for Japan than for any other reporting
country. One finds a continuing proportion of approximately two
women's suicides for every three men's in Japan compared with a ratio
of one to two in Denmark, the country with the highest female ratio
in Europe. This woman-to-man ratio is in sharp contrast to that found
in the United States, where there has been a consistant fluctuation
around three and one-half to four suicides of men for every recorded
suicide by a woman.[16]

Suicide in Japan was characterized particularly by suicides among
very youthful females prior to World War II. In the earlier statistics
of 1952–1954 showing the rate of suicides among females aged fifteen
to nineteen, women suicides still outnumbered those of men. This
is no longer so. The suicide rate among women has been dropping
somewhat faster among very young women than among young men
under nineteen. Nevertheless, the overall proportionate rate of suicide
in young women under twenty-four remains very high in Japan as
compared with other countries.

In the past fifteen years the rate of suicide for males under twenty-
four years of age has also been dropping rapidly in Japan so that after
1960 there is little differentiation between suicide rate changes of

[15] Takarabe, "Sexual Differences in Suicide in Japan" (1923).

[16] Statistical Abstract of the United States (1955); and "Why Do People Kill Themselves?" *Statistical Bulletin* (1955).

males and females under twenty-four years of age. (See Table XVII-3.) The Japanese statistics in respect to sex ratios at any age remain unlike any other statistics reported through the World Health Organization.

Notably, the suicide pattern in Japan is not, or has not been, an urban phenomenon.[17] Until the last statistics taken, there were a number of rural provinces that had distinguished themselves through time for maintaining an extremely high suicide rate. Moreover, a number of the suicides reported in urban areas, especially in a cultural center such as Kyoto, are actually individuals from rural communities, who come in to an urban center specifically to commit suicide at some given locality especially noted for the act.

Okazaki,[18] Katō,[19] and other Japanese specialists[20] have well documented the distribution of types and incidence of suicide for various regions and population groupings in Japan. It will not be to the point here to repeat this material; the burden of this presentation is more speculative. One must nevertheless ultimately attempt to explain why certain areas in Japan have traditionally lent themselves to a higher rate than others, just as one attempts to explain total differences between countries.

Methods of Suicide

Hanging is the chief method of suicide reported in Japan, going back as far as records are available. More recently, suicide by the use of sleeping pills has been the most popular method with those under twenty-nine years of age, comprising more than 40 percent of suicides in that age group. Hanging, among individuals over sixty, was used by more than 70 percent of the male and close to 60 percent of the female suicides. Drowning, also a traditional method, especially among women, is still a characteristic method of suicide taken by older women (see Fig. 3).

Throwing oneself in front of moving objects is a method frequently used by youths, forming close to 10 percent of the suicide of those under twenty-nine. Use of poisons accounts for about 25 percent of the suicides of those under twenty-nine and an equal number of those between thirty and fifty-nine; this method is less frequently used by

---

[17] Maeda, "Suicide in Urban and Rural Areas" (1957, in Japanese).

[18] In Japanese: Okazaki, *Social-Statistical Study of Suicide* (1960*a*); "Relationship Between Suicide and Homicide" (1958); "Empirical Study of Suicide" (1958–1959); "Suicide Problems of Youth" (1960*b*).

[19] In Japanese: Katō, "Suicide" (1958); "Way to Suicide" (1947).

[20] In Japanese: Nakano, "Suicide in Japan" (1957); Uesugi, "Empirical Study of Suicide" (1902); Watanabe, "Suicide of the Japanese" (1957); Yakata, "Interruption of Life" (1957); Sonohara, *Psychology of Suicide* (1954); Satō, "A Statistical Observation of Suicide" (1957).

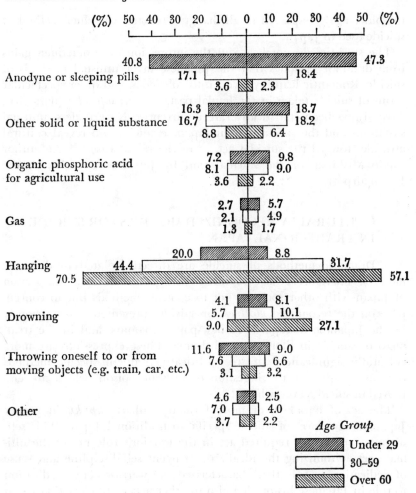

SOURCE: *Nihon-jin no Jisatsu*, by Usui Jisho and Kosaka Masaaki. Tokyo: Sobun-sha, 1966, P. 27.

the older age groups. All in all, hanging remains the chief method of suicide used in Japan.

The statistics do not bear out the impression one sometimes gains from dramatic episodes that the Japanese favor unusual methods of suicide. Romantic leaps by lovers into volcanoes, and other spectacular forms of suicide taken in the feudal past, such as *seppuku* (hara-kiri), have always been statistically rare occurrences. Nevertheless, unusual situations and the spectacular in Japanese suicides do reveal cultural attitudes toward the suicidal act, as in the recent cases of the author Yukio Mishima, or the suicidal raid by Japanese terrorists in the Israeli airport.

CULTURALLY RECOGNIZED MOTIVES FOR SUICIDE IN TRADITIONAL JAPAN

Dramatic methods of suicide are directly related to dramatic motives. Therefore I have found it more profitable in a comparison of Japan with other societies not to contrast methods but to concentrate on the recognized *motives* for suicides presented self-consciously by the Japanese in reports, in newspaper accounts, and in the treatment of suicide in literature and drama. These expressions are more culturally significant than are statistically frequent specific methods such as hanging or the ingestion of pills or poison, which are employed in suicides everywhere.

The act of hara-kiri, or more formally called *seppuku* in proper Japanese, is a form of suicide specific to traditional Japan. This self-disemboweling as a required act in the warrior's role marks the ultimate act epitomizing the idealized, stringent self-discipline and sense of dedication to role that characterized the warrior class. Dedication to role in Japanese history led also to other acts of bravery that could be termed suicidal, since they led to certain death, and they well exemplify Durkheim's concept of "altruistic" suicide, the sacrificial giving up of one's life in dedication to a cause. Warrior ideals of altruistic suicide made their last appearance toward the latter part of World War II in the military's use of kamikaze pilots. As was true for seppuku in the feudal period, the individual involved had little choice between performing such a suicidal act honorably or being ignominiously killed or totally disgraced if he faltered in carrying out his prescribed duty.[21]

Other traditional forms of suicide in Japan are less familiar to the West. There was, for example, the concept of *junshi,* the suicidal act of a faithful retainer who followed his lord in death; this type of

---

[21] Nakahara, *Suicide by Disembowelment* (1960, in Japanese).

suicide romanticized the selflessness of the faithful servant and indicated the ultimate identification of the retainer with the social role of the master. When the emperor Meiji died, less than sixty years ago, General Nogi, a hero of the modern Japanese army, found that his life of dedication to the emperor lost its meaning, and he and his wife chose shortly afterward to end their own lives. Their act of *junshi* was acknowledged with respect by many Japanese but also with incredulity by more modern thinkers in the culture, although even those considering this behavior "old-fashioned" were constrained to feel respect.

There are also other traditional suicides in Japan with special names. One of these is *kangen seppuku*, or "advice suicide," a notable example already cited (see Chapter 5) of which was the suicide of the general sent by Emperor Hirohito to Manchuria to obtain the surrender of the Manchurian forces at the end of World War II. The general was rebuffed by the younger more patriotic officers in charge of the overseas army, who refused to surrender, and he thereupon had his pilot take off from the airstrip and crash the craft in front of the entire body of assembled troops. The commanding officers, responding to this *kangen* or "advice" on the part of a man so altruistically dedicated to the emperor could do nothing but obey and surrender to the Allied forces. Another traditional type of suicide is *shikarare jisatsu*, suicide following upon a scolding or because an individual's honor is impugned or because he is somehow socially compromised and therefore degraded before others.

Also to be noted were several forms of sacrificial suicide (*gisei jisatsu*) of heroic spouses or family members. A favorite theme was that of an ailing wife who, presuming herself to be a burden interfering with her husband's life purpose, removes herself by suicide so as to insure his continued dedication to the success of his endeavor. Proud women of the samurai class were expected to commit suicide by cutting their throats with a small knife should their honor or the honor of their house be threatened by any act of theirs.

Suicide in premodern Japanese literature or drama most often occurred in impossible love situations which were due either to discrepancies of status between the lovers or to the fact that the woman committed an act of adultery. Such suicides combined "egocentric" and anomic features. So-called "double suicides" or "love suicides" (*shinju* —"true heart" suicides) were a favorite theme of tragic dramas.

The general point to be made about the influence of the past on the present is that these various categories of traditional suicide were seen generally as positive acts of dedication or commitment related to a deep sense of responsibility or a sense of protest against an impossible social situation rather than as cowardly escapes or acts of mad or dis-

464 DEVIANCY AND ALIENATION

traught individuals. The theme of suicide in Japanese legend, literature, and drama was given a positive and romantic flavor, an aura that
to some extent holds in the modern age.

The recent suicide of Mishima, of considerable complexity psychologically as seen in its social context, was perhaps a last attempt
to use a traditional form of suicide to elicit a social reaction as well
as to resolve internal subjective needs. The reaction to this suicide
has been mixed in Japan—younger Japanese as a whole tend to reject
it as mad, disquieting, or even pathetic, while some older Japanese
intellectuals have sought to give some social meaning to the act.

Suicide Patterns in Modern Japan

Modern suicides are not as likely to be categorized as were those
of the past. However, there are still a few terms used to describe
special suicidal motives. The Japanese, for example, still discuss the
occasional occurrence of a *shinju,* or double suicide, involving a man
and a woman.[22] One rather unusual suicide of this kind occurred
when a family of noble background attempted to prevent their
daughter from marrying a chauffeur. The young people threatened
suicide, and even though the family relented they went through with
their suicide. The family had made such a point of compromising the
chauffeur that they felt their marital life would be impossible. In the
newspapers there is an occasional report of an "economic" suicide, in
which a head of a family kills his wife and children as well as himself
when he finds himself in desperate financial straits.[23]

The following small sample of Japanese accounts, reported in newspapers or described in novels, express motivations for suicide that
seem strange to Americans.

(1) A safety engineer committed suicide after a mining accident had
killed several miners. He was in no way guilty of any oversight in the
accident since the company records amply demonstrated that he had
given repeated warnings, which went unheeded, of the unsafe conditions in the mine.

(2) A nurse in a hospital made a mistake that caused complications
in a patient and she committed suicide.

(3) In a novel by Osamu Dasai the heroine almost sets fire to her

---

[22] The so-called love suicides, however, when they are examined closely, exhibit
somewhat curious features. In a number of instances they do not actually involve
partners who have had a long, sustained relationship. When they are unsuccessful,
or aborted through circumstances, the partners invariably seem to break off their
previous relationship. In some of these cases, the act appears rather to be of an unconscious symbolic nature and one can infer that the partner clearly represents the
mother.

[23] Burg, "A Psychocultural Analysis and Theoretical Integration of the Dynamics
of Japanese Parent-Child Suicide" (1961).

house accidently and reflects that if a fire had spread to the surrounding village she would have had to commit suicide to apologize for herself and her family.

(4) A Japanese author attempts to find a woman who is willing to commit suicide with him. He is preoccupied for several years with suicide, but cannot find the "courage" to end the misery of life.

(5) A mother, mortified by her son's continued stealing in spite of psychiatric treatment at a clinic, takes him to the seaside and threatens to kill him and commit suicide; the son quits stealing.

(6) In making up a story to a Thematic Apperception Test card, a young farm girl sees a young woman committing suicide so that she can come back to haunt her irascible, demanding mother-in-law.

(7) In another answer to a Thematic Apperception Test card, an inmate of a reformatory sees a mother choking a profligate son and then committing suicide, since she has been a failure as a mother.

These and many other examples that I have gathered were used to determine whether I could abstract from them some culturally peculiar recurring themes. What follows is the result of my attempt at classification.

PSYCHOCULTURAL MOTIVES FOR SUICIDE IN JAPAN

The expressed motives and situations under which suicide occurs among Japanese are quite complex; one therefore cannot reduce such complexity to a simple sorting out of single motives. I have found, however, that one or more of six characteristic culturally recognizable themes are represented in many if not most Japanese suicides.

There are in Japan, as elsewhere, examples of the three general types of suicide described by Durkheim. Durkheim's classification does not, however, include the majority of suicides to be found in Japan. It was as a result of my attempt to understand Japanese suicide as well as suicide generally that I found it necessary to add as well the fourth general type discussed in the foregoing section. "Egocentric" suicides appear to be by far the most common type of suicide to be found in Japan. As I have indicated, this latter type involves psychodynamic mechanisms of introjected aggression related to the frustration of receptive gratification from someone upon whom one is dependent. Such suicides are found cross-culturally and are discussed in detail in the psychoanalytic literature.

These four general types of suicides take on special cultural nuances in Japan and involve in one form or another six thematic emphases that I find most characteristic of Japanese suicide behavior. During the following discussion the reader is encouraged to consult again Table I-5 outlining instrumental and expressive behavioral interaction.

I view suicidal behavior as social behavior, related to cultural pattern-
ings of one or more of the ten social interaction concerns in terms of
which I have been analyzing Japanese behavior throughout this volume.

1. Self Sacrifice and Dedication

There are special culturally stressed themes of sacrificial suicide
in Japan related to Durkheim's concept of altruistic suicide. The idea
of killing one's self as a means of helping one's group or one's loved
ones to reach a desired goal is a favored romantic theme in Japanese
culture, which is positively related to the cultural emphasis on role
dedication developed as part of the warrior code of the samurai. In
its ideal extreme the social self is given over completely to the social
cause, and one is supposed to become a willing martyr to the purposes
of the collectivity. There has been, as part of a romanticized warrior
tradition, advocacy of sacrificial death in Japan, especially among
youth. A young samurai was often poetically compared to a cherry
blossom that dies soon after it reveals its beauty.

The kamikaze pilots in World War II were, in one sense at least,
altruistic suicides. The terrorists who out of ideological conviction
shot up the Israeli airport in May 1972 are in their own logical system
continuing a tradition of personal dedication—no longer to Japan
itself, but as martyrs to the cause of international revolution. I shall
discuss, further on, the possible narcissistic pathology and the self-
destructiveness which can be cloaked in such avowed acts of social
dedication.

SUICIDE AS INSTRUMENTAL BEHAVIOR.—In the frame of reference used
in Chapter 1 to examine Japanese role behavior, altruistic suicide can
be seen culturally as an instrumental act. It can exhibit to various
degrees combinations of *achievement, maintenance of status, responsibility, control,* or *group cooperation* in the realization of a goal. The
warrior, for example, *achieves* his purpose in life by death in service.
This sacrificial dedication to social cause is expected not only of the
male as the ideal worrior but also of the woman as the ideal wife and
mother. It is the woman's role as a bride to dedicate herself selflessly
to the cause of her new family and to her children, even to the degree
of exhausting her life's substance on their behalf, should it be necessary to die to preserve and enhance the *ie,* or house of her husband.
Suicide in this context can be an edifying example of *responsible*
dedication, as in the *junshi* of General Nogi; or it can be an act of
both responsibility and *control,* through reproach to rebellious underlings, as is represented in the suicide of the emperor's emissary to the
Manchurian army. Analogously, a mother in Japan can and does

threaten suicide as a means of *controlling* rebellious or delinquent children.

The traditional cultural logic of *seppuku* as punishment for a warrior is the belief that an honorable suicide responsibly preserves the *status* of the *ie* or "house" of the offender, which is thus freed of the consequences of the behavior of one of its members. By submitting positively to the demands for ritual suicide, the offender affirms both the legitimate control or authority of his superiors and his own responsibility. He "cleanses" out his past deviation from the required code of honor and loyalty. If he did not do so, not only would he be put to death ignominiously but his family would also be punished by loss of status and property, if not killed.

A mother's threat of suicide may be seen positively as an act of extreme dedication to her role of guiding her children to a proper future; it can also be viewed as a threatened "advice" suicide, but in a negative sense it can signify her irresponsibility and failure to maintain herself properly in her role as mother. In this latter sense it is a form of anomic suicide.

EXPRESSIVE ASPECTS OF SUPPOSEDLY INSTRUMENTAL ACTS OF SUICIDE. From the standpoint of expressive behavior what might be considered instrumentally directed altruistic suicides also have expressive features found dominant in anomic or egocentric suicides. There is sometimes an egocentric sense of acute frustration and resultant rage as well as a sense of frustrated need of social *appreciation* in certain forms of what would be regarded sociologically as "altruistic" suicide.

A deep sense of frustrated rage felt expressively can be directed outwardly "altruistically" for what is socially defined "instrumentally" as a just cause. Frenzied social dedication can become an excuse in Japanese for expressing pent-up rage in suicidal or nonsuicidal form involving even brutality. Such was the evident case in the Japanese army in the hierarchical authority relationships within the lower echelons of the army in the behavior on the part of superiors to subordinates. Also such was the case in the war crimes committed against subjected or occupied peoples who could not seem to understand the divinely inspired instrumental purposes of Japanese. All were to harmoniously submit to Japanese hegemony. To resist was to bring out enraged self-righteousness against those resistive to what was conceived of as the superior Japanese will.

Enraging situations of frustrated purpose also occurred on the battlefield. These were to be symbolically if not actually overcome by a collective aggressive banzai charge at the object of frustration in which the sense of personal continuity would be lost in the collective expression of *yamato damashii* ("the Japanese spirit"). To the outside observer such behavior often resulting in needless death appeared quite often to be more expressively motivated than instrumental in purpose or result. The banzai charge seen in the context of suicidal motivation was often an expressive act of rage against a force unwilling to capitulate to one's own egocentric sense of purpose.

Some fanatical behavior is related also to egoistic alienation. The alienated Japanese student who becomes a member of a terrorist group gives himself over to a cause which permits him to kill without guilt less extreme members of his own group as well as to murder others as a supposedly instrumental act of dedication to the cause of humanity. What is often evident when one gets beneath surface ideology in these individuals is a very deep sense of personal worthlessness. The student martyr briefly described in Chapter 16 is an instance in point. The introspective writings of Dazai about his communist activities described in the following chapter is another. The supposedly instrumentally goal-oriented act of dedication turns out to be an unsuccessful attempt to hide from oneself an egoistic incapacity to feel deeply in a loving way toward other human beings. There is an inner self-destructive logic compelling these individuals eventually to seek out situations which result in their destruction whether by their own hands or those of others. This sense of worthlessness is inseparably related to an affiliative incapacity to feel love or a sense of closeness to others. There is both self-hate and a deep despair both about not being loved and about finding in oneself no capacity to reach out affiliatively.

Attempts at a collective dedication by such individuals are acute and feverish in intensity but ultimately without staying power. Rather than finding an enduring sense of social purpose, the individual hastens to some climactic act fearing the pressing self-knowledge that he lacks the libidinal force to maintain a long-term purpose. The supposed "altruistic" suicide is very often a pathetic fraud. He may be acting out of very personal expressive motives while hiding this fact both from himself and others in an instrumental cloak of social purpose.

2. Responsibility and the Rupture of Social Role

Durkheim's conception of "anomic" suicide appears in dramatic forms in Japan. There are numerous situations in which the harmonious adjustment to a given social role is irrevocably disrupted by external circumstances. Such was the case of the mining engineer mentioned above. Not technically responsible, he nevertheless felt an irreparable damage to his status and reputation. To the Westerner there seems to be in Japanese suicide, both past and present, an undue involvement and sensitivity to potentials for damage to one's self-esteem as it is housed in a designated social role. This over-valenced type of object cathexis I have termed "role narcissism." One finds in Japan descriptions of suicidal reactions of chagrin or mortification when the professional or social self is considered irrevocably compromised, whether by one's own mistakes or by situations in which designated responsibility forces one to take blame for a course of events over which one has actually had no control. (Seen positively, such suicides can be viewed as altruistic; seen negatively, as anomic.) "Role narcissism," as an intense identification of one's total self with one's professional or social role, leads in a socially positive way to careers involving long-range endurance of hardships and to lives of seemingly selfless dedication and loyalty of both men and women. In the negative sense, such rigid dedication leads to an inability to regroup one's psychic forces should the role to which one has given such priority of meaning in life be compromised in some way.

On the surface at least, some Japanese suicides related to a rupture of status seem to be acts resulting from overrigid interpretation of responsibility. Examined more closely, however, some of these supposed acts of responsibility prove to be the result of an apparent unwillingness to face circumstances that would force one to live with the consequences of irresponsibility. Such suicidal acts are characterized by the inability to live with a permanent alteration in one's social self-image as seen by others—the chief ingredient of anomic suicide as defined by Durkheim.

3. Suicides of Social Attenuation

A third major characteristic theme in Japanese suicide is what might be considered classic forms of acts that Durkheim termed *egoistic* suicide. Such suicides follow upon a situation of ruptured affiliation and/or social attenuation, usually in marginal individuals such as authors or artists. In Japan there have been a number of dramatic instances of such suicides among well-known celebrities. Several of the most prominent modern authors of Japan have written about suicide as a theme. Of those who have actually committed suicide, Arishima, Akutagawa, Dazai—and most recently Mishima and Kawabata—are numbered among the first ten Japanese authors of Japan's modern century. Each was at the height of his literary career at the time he committed suicide, establishing a very disturbing continuing tradition among literary figures in Japan. One can note in each instance an intense self-preoccupation and other signs of alienation from ordinary affiliative feelings of social belonging.[24]

---

[24] The detailed individual circumstances in these suicides differ and cannot be discussed cogently in the context of this general discussion of suicide in Japan. See the detailed discussion of the lives of Akutagawa and Dazai in the next chapter.

To be human is to have a sense of "meaning." Those who are intensely self-conscious, as are intellectuals, and those who practice the explorative expression of inner thoughts, become very aware of problems in respect to their sense of meaning. Such individuals come to examine critically the system of beliefs their society provides them through the usual modes of cultural transmission. It is particularly true of man living in so-called modern complex cultures that he must, as part of his own maturational process, examine alternatives and select from among them orienting beliefs concerning the meaning of personal and social life.

Intensely introspective individuals do not accept the same levels of belief or of belonging that satisfy the uncritical; they are explorers into the far reaches of the human psyche and as such they often become far removed from the acceptable or the prosaic. They dare give ideosyncratic meaning to life, and some suffer the deep vertigo of profound alienation from others and the loss of all sustaining beliefs. In the Western tradition such profound alienation is sometimes resolved by a dramatic religious conversion in which the tormented individual goes through the subjective experience of reestablishing a sense of relatedness through his relation to a deity, or resolution may be found through dedication to a cause in which the self is lost or engulfed in a new sense of purpose.

In Japan the "religious" conversion has often taken the form of a patriotic loss of self in the name of the Japanese state. During the militarist period, under the forced pressure of the military, there were genuine acts of ideological conversion, some followed by suicide by well-known radicals who had been socially condemned and jailed. In recanting their previous liberal or radical beliefs, they affirmed a rededicated belief in the emperor and in the divinely ordained beneficent imperial destiny of Japan.[25] These men gave up their individuated opposition to the Japanese military state, succumbing to an inundating act of belonging that drowned out their own socially disquieting questionings of the politically prescribed meanings of being "Japanese."

Seen from this perspective, Mishima's recent suicide is a curious egocentric perverse anachronism. Long a critic of Japanese society and Western-oriented in his thinking, Mishima ended his life at age forty-five in a showy bluster of patriotic nationalism ineffectually haranguing uninterested young soldiers of Japan's "self-defense force," who were totally lacking the vulnerability of being controlled by a potentiality for guilt that had characterized the indoctrinated patriotism of the previous generation of soldiers.

---

[25] See H. Tsurumi, *Social Change and the Individual: Japan Before and After Defeat in World War II* (1970).

Seen from yet another perspective or level of analysis, the complexity of motives involved in Mishima's suicide includes also an attempt to resolve his deep chronic sense of personal alienation, which was complicated by homosexuality.[26] By a "manly" affirmation he attempts to dramatize for himself as well as others a traditional supposedly "altruistic" social ritual of "self" destruction. Mishima's suicide is a curiously Japanese form of religious conversion experience resulting from, and in a sense resolving, an inner life of personal "egoistic" alienation, as discussed above. In Western culture the typical experience of conversion is to a belief in God; in Japan, conversion is more typically to belief in and affirmation of the Japanese collectivity. The ultimate loyalty of a Christian is to God; for a Japanese it was to his given role of loyal service to family and social authority in society. The ultimate sense of nurturance expressed in the Japanese concept *on* could extend beyond the family to the Japanese society in the person of its emperor. As I shall discuss further, the need to express gratitude and to resolve resentment cause a Japanese to create for himself a myth or illusion of maternal nurturance which may not always work. The proneness to suicide is related to an inability to create a satisfactory illusion of belonging which is in origin related to a sense of receiving emotional nurturance.

4. The Failure of Purpose Related to a Loss of Physical or Intellectual Vigor

A fourth culturally specific theme related to egoistic suicides generally is associated with the suicides in Japan of aged celebrities or of individuals suffering from illness that causes them continual physical discomfort. The most famous recent example is the Nobel Prize laureate, Kawabata. There seems to be a fairly ready willingness, especially among the aging and including those who are still

---

[26] One must also draw attention to the fact that all the elements of Mishima's suicide are contained in his earlier recounting of sadistic-homosexual masturbatory fantasies in his thinly veiled autobiographical account of his own adolescence, *Confessions of a Mask,* written in the early 1950s. He describes how he identified himself with the Christian martyr St. Sebastian shot through with arrows. After a vigorous course of weight lifting and other forms of body building he actually had his seminude picture taken as St. Sebastian. He describes in the same early volume a fantasy of seeing a young tough who excites him sexually cut open so that his rich red blood stains his white bellyband. He also sexualizes imaginings of the death of soldiers and of decapitations and even reveals a sexually exciting daydream of a cannibalistic orgy in which he cuts open the belly of a handsome youth. Mishima manages to actualize a combination of his earlier sadomasochistic fantasies by an elaborate plan worked out over several years which must have been at least partially conscious. The final drama is enacted under the guise of an act of final "belonging" to his cultural heritage and, as Haruko Tsurumi describes it, the "socialization for death" of the traditional samurai.

considered socially successful and well respected, to resolve difficulties with health or with decreasing prowess by some resigned, simple unaggressive act of suicide. This type of suicide seems to be generally condoned by the Japanese and there is very little negative sanctioning directed toward the memory of those committing such acts. All such acts of suicide can, in part at least, again be related to Durkheim's concept of *egoistic* suicide as it is psychodynamically related to the prevalence of what is usually termed "body narcissism" in Japanese society. The physical body and its failing capacities becomes the principal focus for feelings of love and hate. Life's "meaning" becomes narrowed by the loss through death of others close to the individual, or more narcissistically, even by a sensed loss of capacity in those who received their chief gratification or a sense of personal meaning through some form in intellectual or physical prowess. In such individuals a progressive sense of failing powers becomes an egoistic crisis that the sense of self cannot surmount.

Deaths from a "devitalization" that withdraws the individual from a proper attention to bodily needs are sometimes reported for persons who have recently lost their spouses. These themes of suicide and death among the aged or those failing in physical or intellectual strength are not unique to Japan. However, statistically at least, Japan reports one of the highest rates for suicide in those above sixty years of age. Moreover, despite occasional examples such as Hemingway, one does not in the West find aging entertainers or artists whose talents continue to be recognized committing suicide with the relative frequency found in Japan.

5. Suicide as an Attack on the Vulnerability of Another's Guilt

The fifth theme running through Japanese suicide is an implicit sensitive awareness of the instrumental controlling effects of one's suicide on others, either positively or negatively. The suicidal act is often seen self-consciously as some form of expressive retribution as well as the ultimate attempt to compel action on the part of others. This form of suicide is totally absent from Durkheim's analysis. I have termed such suicides "egocentric" suicides. Implicit in such suicidal behavior among Japanese is the notion that one's own suffering can cause guilt in others and therefore can induce action. The recent suicide of Mishima is, in some of its motivational complexity, also a caricature of this type of suicidal logic; Mishima in effect purported to commit suicide to castigate the Japanese "self-defense forces" for their lack of patriotism, and his suicide was vaguely intended to bring about a military coup by inducing in others a sense of rededication to Japan. The degree to which this generation of Japanese youth has moved away from being influenced by such exemplary acts of "dedication" was most apparent; the attitude held by many about this behavior was an embarrassed sense of the ridiculous. Mishima was an anachronism; respect could no longer be elicited for this mode of compelling action.

Obviously, there is a shift going on in Japanese society. The fact that Mishima could nevertheless still attempt to compel behavior by suicide attests to the vestiges of a Japanese cultural-emotional logic that still exists today albeit in a considerably more attenuated form than in the past.

6. Suicide as a Collaborative Act

A final somewhat culturally unique thematic emphasis in Japanese suicide is evident in the numerous instances in which the individual is not psychologically separated from a very close identification either with family or with a primary social group. There is in the Japanese some propensity to commit suicide cooperatively in agreement with others, often in a curious blend of altruistic as well as anomic or egoistic motives. The group suicide, whether of family or of lovers, or even of a terrorist group, is often an actual murder, agreed to by the victims, who, sharing the intention of the initiator, are killed as part of a collective action.

Such suicides are found with some frequency when families are under economic duress and the head of the family, after discussion with his wife, decides to kill off his family and himself rather than face an unacceptable depreciating or degrading form of poverty. As such these suicides are also a refusal either to face one's sense of incapacity, or to face the lack of concern of an unappreciative, unrewarding world.

In the case of family suicide no thought is given that the children are separate entities apart from their parents—the family is a stronger emotional unit than the individual selves who comprise it.

To the eyes of romantics in Japan another form of a joint suicide, *shinju,* or joint heterosexual suicides, are acts of mutual dedication to one another by a pair of lovers in a socially impossible situation. When examined very closely, however, some of these supposedly "love" suicides are simply acts of two individuals who come together and share a like-minded sense of despair about life. They support each other, creating a temporary bond enabling them to muster the courage to actualize their resolve. In fact they may not be at all deeply emotionally involved with each other, but may have a kind of interdependency and unwillingness to undertake a journey alone. The psychocultural logic of joint suicide demands mutual acquiescence and differs from those situations in which a distraught spouse or lover murders his mate out of anger and frustration and then takes his own life. The best-known example of a somewhat promiscuous need to commit suicide with someone is that of the famous author Osamu Dazai (see Chapter 18). In his youth he experienced two unsuccessful joint suicides with different women, and finally, after the war, his masochistic destiny was successfully consummated on the initiative of a third, more determined and resourceful partner.

Individual cases of *shinju,* or double suicide, differ from one another widely as to circumstances and possible psychodynamic peculiarities. What they share is the peculiarly Japanese logic that makes a joint suicide a way to accomplish suicide through mutual resolve. Ultimately, this logic is related to the lack of total separation of self (*jibun*) from a primary primitive psychological adhesion to others. As has already been amply discussed, a desire to lose one's sense of potential total separateness from others characterizes Japanese culture in other behavior than suicide.

In sum the four elementary forms of suicide—the altruistic, anomic, egoistic, and egocentric—despite wide differences in incidence, are universals to be found in all cultures in one form or another. There are, however, peculiarly "Japanese" intensifications of these forms around specific cultural content.

The next question to ask is whether one can relate the six Japanese suicide themes—(1) sacrificial suicide, (2) suicide to avoid threatened status loss, (3) suicides of social attenuation, (4) suicide because of impaired capacity, (5) suicide as a means of controlling others, (6) collaborative suicide—to given psychocultural patterns in Japanese socialization in order to help explain the characteristic Japanese types of failure in satisfactory object cathexis that lead to suicidal behavior. Can we find patterns in Japanese socialization relating to psychosexual development that help explain the appearance of altruistic dedication, intense role-narcissism, lack of ego differentiation or individuation, egoistic withdrawal resulting from the narcissistic inability to maintain satisfactory object relationships, and, above all, the feeling that others are somehow vulnerable to one's own suffering and death? What are the cultural experiences that increase the incidence of the several suicidal themes within the various age and social segments of the Japanese population?

JAPANESE SOCIALIZATION EXPERIENCES
AND VULNERABILITY TO SUICIDE

Intense Closeness to the Mother and
the Development of Role Narcissism

In the beginning chapters of this volume I have already discussed the extreme closeness between mother and child which is a culturally prevalent traditional pattern in Japan. To recapitulate in this context: The intensity of care given to children is in itself a pattern of woman's role dedication that is reinforced socially; it is essential to the mother's sense of self-validation. Ideally, a Japanese mother can be as "selfless" as a dedicated nun in her absorption in her child's life. This pattern is of course seldom ideally realized despite the shared cultural reinforced producing need to believe in and feel gratification toward an all-giving mother. As Wagatsuma and I illustrate in the following chapter, a profound sense of alienation in particular individuals seems to have some causal relationship to not having had such close maternal experience.

The cultural availability of given social roles such as a literary career encouraging introspection, self-analysis, and self-absorption, as well as the cultural availability of suicide as an act with historical precedent in given occupations makes for some selective choice for alienation-prone individuals to become intellectuals in Japan. One must note, however, that the relative popularity of the tormented writings of a Dazai or the quiet sense of introspective aloneness of Akutagawa or Kawabata are, to some extent, due to the general responsiveness and sensitivity of a large Japanese audience to these potentials within themselves. The Japanese, both positively in their collective behavior and negatively in a proneness to sense social isolation and aloneness, have a particularly acute sense of social belonging related to a very conscious collective fantasy about an uninterrupted lifelong tie to mother and family. Some have had an experiential reality that prevents them from easily sharing such a fantasy of continuity of relationship with a mother. Others create for themselves an illusion of maternal and social closeness whether it actually exists or not.

Chapter 1 has also drawn attention to how bodily pleasures and sensations are cultivated from infancy in Japanese culture. Maternal libidinization of the body receives secondary cultural reinforcement in various ways.[27] The Japanese bath, for example, is one form of direct expressive pleasure and sensory gratification that is elaborated beyond what is customary in the West. The child comes to regard his body as an object of gratification, a source of accepted pleasure that continues throughout life. However, the body loved narcissistically is also a potential source of displeasure, should one's aggressive impulses threaten closeness with others.

Maternal closeness, both physically and psychologically, usually con-

---

[27] Caudill and Doi, "Interrelations of Psychiatry, Culture and Emotion in Japan" (1963); Caudill and Weinstein, "Maternal Care and Infant Behavior in Japan and America" (1969).

tinues for many after infancy into childhood and even into adulthood. There is a continuing and intense relationship around the child's progress through his period of formal education. Teachers often cannot differentiate between a mother's contribution to homework and what is original to the child.[28] Many school children develop very little sense of learning for themselves or of individuation of themselves in a learning process distinct from their interaction with their mothers.

A caricature of the lack of ego-differentiation of mother from child is humorously illustrated in the book *The Honorable Picnic*, by Thomas Raucat.[29] This satirical novel is most perceptive of the various forms of narcissistic preoccupation with roles by the Japanese. The intense narcissism of the Japanese mother finds its outlet in the continual attention given to her child; this is beautifully and humorously presented in the chapter called "The Hat of Tarō-san." Such continual symbiosis must produce peculiarities in the development of ego boundaries. Paul Schilder[30] suggests how the individual ego is not necessarily coextensive with the limits of the physical body. In Japan there is cultural reinforcement of a type of maternal dedication to the child in which the male child seems in some sense at least to become an extension of the mother's masculine principle, to be indulged and directed by subtle controls toward future male social role realization. The focus of libidinal gratification for such a dedicated mother often seems to shift from her own female physical body to that of her male child.

In inculcating social role attitudes in children, Japanese mothers continually reinforce a child's growing concern with the future need to accomplish and to justify to himself and to others his social worth in a covertly competitively organized outer world. The female child, conversely, learns to assume a wholehearted dedication to assisting a husband in his tasks as well as to bringing up children adequate to the challenge of their future roles.

In addition to the intense bond with the mother, there remains in Japan strong continuity of the tradition emphasizing the closeness of the family unit. Until the most recent postwar democratization of Japan and the acceptance of individual goals as morally proper, the highest morality within Japanese society was in an identification of

---

[28] Vogel and Vogel, "Family Security, Personal Immaturity and Emotional Health in a Japanese Sample" (1961); Vogel, "Entrance Examinations and Emotional Disturbances in Japan's 'New Middle Class'" (1962).

[29] This book, written under a pseudonym by a Belgian diplomatic attaché over thirty years ago, still describes a psychological condition found prevalent in today's Japan.

[30] Schilder, *The Image and Appearance of the Human Body*, 1935.

oneself as a family member rather than as a person with individual desires and goals. Even given the present-day conscious desire to find oneself as an entity, many Japanese experience a continuing inner incapacity to realize *jibun,* or a real sense of themselves as something apart from social role expectations.

I contend that the disturbance of a culturally expected intensity of early relationships, sometimes experienced as an intense ambivalence concerning early closeness, may produce a later inability to transfer to others a sense of intimacy at a genital level, and instead may give rise to a strong regressive tendency that prevents an external full free object cathexis. Libido is not readily transferred from its primary object or narcissistic substitutes; the individual may remain, in one form or another, an object to himself. He may continue to be intensely aware of his body experiences, both positive and negative. He may be prone to develop hypochondriacal concerns, the body becoming an object of hate as well as love.

In other individuals, at a somewhat higher level of psychosexual maturation, a narcissistic preoccupation may be transmuted to the mother's expectation of the self in its social role. The occupational or social expectancies of the individual become excessively cathected, substituting for the satisfaction of interpersonal intimacy. Within such individuals there is a continual judgment of success or failure of the self in living up to an internalized ego ideal, which remains an introject of the mother's image of what her child might become. It is not surprising, therefore, that the adult Japanese who conforms well to expectations can make of his or her social-sex role the ultimate moral meaning of life.

This failure either to achieve a capacity for a mature, satisfactorily affiliative form of object cathexis, or to realize *jibun,* an individuated sense of self on the part of many Japanese is a seeming contradiction. One finds, for example, that in spite of a cultural readiness for introspective probings and preoccupations Japanese are at the same time peculiarly resistive to psychoanalytically oriented forms of psychotherapy. To the more individualistically oriented Westerner the immediate explanation occurs that the Japanese cannot for some reason face underlying ambivalent feelings toward parents that go counter to a deeply inculcated sense of "filial piety." While this is descriptively true, if we leave the explanation at this point, we still do not attempt a fully dynamic explanation why Japanese cannot readily criticize a parent or face the fact that a mother or father were not as ideally nurturant or giving as would be required to motivate a sense of grateful repayment, or *on-gaeshi.*

One cannot separate the resistance to psychoanalysis from the fact that it is very difficult for Japanese to transcend the ultimate sense of belonging which is culturally constrained to remain lodged, whether satisfying or not, within the bosom of the primary family. Western culture, whether directly within the Christian system of beliefs, or past Christian constraints toward individualism, forces many to leave go of such primary family ties, to develop beyond them; in short, to critize the past including one's parents in reaching out toward a changing future. Phychological security, as well as is possible, is to be found in present-oriented or idealized future-oriented religious relationships or in present social groupings superseding the family. Psychoanalysis is part of this Western tradition. Ideally it seeks to free the individual from the subjective ties to his dependent past by objectifying what actually occurred. Sometimes it helps create at least a new form of dependency, but one based on one's ability to openly criticize the unsatisfactory nature of the past highly charged, expressive relationships which occurred in childhood within the family.

Japanese forms of psychotherapy either disguised as so-called new religions, or more directly identified in movements such as Morita therapy or Naikan therapy[31] work effectively on another principle. They seek not only to reduce a sense of alienation by reinforcing group belonging, but also to reduce resentment resulting from a frustrated need for nurturances or as a response to excessive control exercised on someone who remains in a socially subordinate role within the family. In Naikan therapy, for example, a delinquent youth learns to be able to sense a feeling of specific gratitude as a means of overcoming the generalized resentment he turns toward society. In some obvious cases it works by helping the individual create a retrospective illusion about the giving nature of his mother or stepmother or the implicitly understanding nature of his father, even though the actual experience when viewed by an objective observer must have been that of a depriving and rejecting parent. This form of therapy probably works in instances wherein the individual has experienced sufficient gratification to allow him to be induced through social authority and cultural stereotypes toward some affirmative belief. In the West a similarly deprived or resentfully antagonistic individual may "find his way to Jesus" and thereby experience symbolically through a belief in the living presence of Jesus some release from the impasse created by a chronic, distressful sense of deprivation or aloneness. Some individuals have a strong pent-up need to feel and gratitude for dependent gratification either directed toward an all-sacrificing savior or the illusion of an all-sacrificing parent. A potential for guilt, as Takie Lebra

---

[31] Ishida, "Naikan Analysis" (1968, in Japanese); Yoshimoto, *Forty Years of Naikan* (1965, in Japanese).

cogently points out,[32] is for a Japanese a problem of having to satisfy reciprocal repayment for favors bestowed.

Internalization of Aggression

The explanation of why the Japanese develop a strong sense of social role and why they are thus prone to suicide in response to social disruptions or feelings of personal alienation does not of itself account for a motive force. To help explain the vulnerability of the Japanese to autoplastic aggressive forms of suicide, it is necessary to examine in more detail how both sexual and aggressive drives are socialized within the primary family. In Chapters 4 and 5 I have described results of an analysis of Thematic Apperception Test stories obtained in various Japanese settings. This material reveals certain masochistic propensities in the internalization of aggression in Japanese culture, especially in women, and shows how the transmutation of guilt into achievement results from a child's experience of the mother in her self-sacrificing, dedicated role. Emphasis on assuring future success as a result of ending present privation predisposes individuals to what Freud first termed "moral masochism." As Reik[33] discusses at length, an unconscious postulate underlying cases of moral masochism is that present suffering will be repaid in future triumph; he who endures, triumphs in the end. The supreme virtue of endurance pervading Japanese culture is perhaps best exemplified in the Japanese strong sense of long-range goals.[34]

The traditional Japanese mother's strongest weapon in disciplining her child is the very self-sacrifice with which she dedicates herself to her offspring. She tends to "suffer" her children rather than to forbid them or inhibit their behavior by resorting to physical punishment or verbal chastisement. The child learns the vulnerability of the loved one and is frightened by his own capacity to injure.[35] Bad behavior can inflict irreversible injuries upon the very person whom one so badly needs; one can make another ill. The mother who exhausts herself on behalf of her child is a source of potential guilt that a Japanese child so brought up cannot escape.

The converse is also learned. A Japanese child learns: "I can control by my own suffering someone bound to me. My illness or death can

[32] Lebra, "The Social Mechanism of Guilt and Shame: The Japanese Case" (1971); and "Reciprocity and the Asymmetric Principle: An Analytical Reappraisal of the Japanese Concept of *On*" (1969).

[33] Reik, *Masochism in Modern Man* (1941).

[34] A favorite Japanese definition of suffering or endurance is "Naranu kannin suruga kannin" (Real forbearance is to forbear something unbearable).

[35] A similar pattern is reported by Hendin in Denmark, in "Suicide in Denmark" (1960).

cause unhappiness, an unending guilt in another." In the traditional culture, the woman's role was doubly masochistic; for both husband and child she must learn to endure, to give, to relinquish, and if necessary, to die. A man in the traditional culture could vent aggression in morally accepted channels—a warrior, for example, had outlets in his role—but a man was never free to direct his aggression toward a constituted authority; he learned from his mother to turn potentially aggressive feelings toward authority back on the self. All authority represented for him an idealized, distant father, whom the mother had taught him to respect at all costs, whereas, he could, at the risk of intense guilt, become periodically aggressive toward a potentially vulnerable mother.

An additional aspect of this pattern of internalized aggression and masochism is a split in the direction of sexual expression. The wife tended to become desexualized and to take on a nurturant role similar to the mother's; she remained a source of bodily comfort and affectional attachment. The husband's aggressive sexuality could be freely expressed toward entertainers, if no deeper dependent attachments arose to complicate obligation to family.

The intensive affective relationship of mother and son in traditional Japanese culture influenced the way in which infantile sexuality was transmuted into adult relationships. Emphasis on family lineage reinforced a tendency to deemphasize the conjugal relationship in favor of a mother-child concern with succession and continuity; the mother's role was focused ideally on the upbringing of a diligent son who would continue the family. Whereas in American society achievement goals are part of an individualistic pattern leading to the setting up of a new primary family unit, achievement goals within Japanese society were expressed in the context of a mother-child relationship unbroken throughout the life span of the mother. For the male child, the mother became a symbol of lifelong dedication and sacrifice, the father, an image of unapproachable authority. In traditional Confucian ethic a woman's ego was actually encouraged to broaden itself to include her male child, and the mother was allowed to maintain her primacy in the son's affection throughout her life, with a resulting disharmony when wife and mother both sought to play the same role for the husband.

Sacrifice and masochism are an unconscious form of control for many women. Covertly, women often perceive men as weak and needing a wife or mother to prop them up and keep them going. A woman desexualizes herself, giving up her directly sexual goals and replacing them with the subtler goals of maintaining a long-range unbroken control over son or husband as a masculine aspect of herself. The image of the terrible mother-in-law in the Japanese family is explicable in terms of the ideal of the self-sacrificing woman; the delicate submissive bride is a larval stage of the mother-in-law capable of terrible rage should her control of her son be threatened.

The general psychocultural considerations discussed above should help explain the social motivational content of the four generic forms of suicides in Japan that are not readily found in Western settings. The tendency to role narcissism and to dedicated altruistic suicide found in past Japanese society were extensions of a masochistic dedication of self to role, which is not inexplicable given the model presented to the child by the self-sacrificing mother.

It should also be added that in the socialization experience in Japan, projection of failure onto outside objects is severely discouraged. In internalizing aggression, the individual focuses on his body as a source of failure and thus is not readily able to project failure onto outside circumstances or persons. If the body fails in carrying out a prescribed role or fails as a result of the aging process, it is apt to become the target of aggression.

The types of attenuation found in Japanese egoistic suicides can be explained in terms of maternal deprivation, which in given instances results in continued primary narcissism and an incapacity to develop relationships that can meet the unbounded sense of need. Individuals suffer such early deprivation elsewhere as well as in Japan, but in the context of Japanese socialization experiences encountered at later stages of psychosexual development, the individual responds to his difficulty with affective bonds in a characteristically "Japanese" way. The individual attempts to resolve his basic sense of injured capacity for social belonging within culturally available forms. In the West a sense of personal isolation can be assuaged by Christian conversion, an outlet not so readily available in Japan as is a suicidal gesture that symbolizes a loss of self in a spasmodic act of dedication. Hence, in a curious way, Japanese religious conversion experiences can lead to suicide rather than to life.

In the autobiographical writings of each of the authors preoccupied with suicide who are examined in the next chapter, as well as in those of Mishima, there are accounts of very early feelings of deprivation and alienation because of separation from the mother. These separations were variously due to the mother's illness, to her insanity, to adoption because the infant was unwanted by the mother, to the obedient mother's release of the infant into the care of a dominant, cold, narcissistic grandmother. In each of the authors studied, maternal deprivation sets the tone of later experiences. It should be noted that the availability of adoption as a cultural form offers frequent occasion for the experience of maternal deprivation, as we shall illustrate in the next chapter.

Crises in Social Cohesion within Japanese Society

Given these explanations of peculiarities in Japanese suicide related to qualitative cultural differences, is it possible also to explain the statistical peculiarities of age, sex, and regional distribution of suicide within Japan? One can do so partially at least, using the insights of a Durkheimian approach, by calling attention to the effect of social and culturally determined disruptions and crises in the life cycle as they affect individuals with the given psychological propensities just described.

One can perhaps account for a higher suicide rate in certain rural sections of Japan by the stronger maintenance of traditional cultural values in these areas,[36] although empirical research would be necessary to establish whether there is an actual correspondence. Suicide rates are the highest in relatively well-to-do farming districts, where there is a strong sense of social status and heavy emphasis on expected role behavior.

The problems of individuation are particularly poignant for Japanese youth. In the Japanese social system the acceptance of adult responsibilities is an extreme crisis point in the life cycle. Many young women still feel a strong conflict between their own personal inclinations and the social directive to be submissive to a family choice of a marriage partner. Young men and women both feel pressured to subordinate individual considerations to family decisions. Young adults face inner turmoil of shifting from a subordinate role within the family, and the men especially must commit themselves wholeheartedly to prescribed goals through active accomplishment whether or not they find willingness within themselves. In their need for occupational commitment, young men must compress their more expansive views of society, to which they have been stimulated in adolescence, into the much more narrow confines of a minor bureaucratic position or an insignificant role in a large company. If theirs is a rural family, they must continue the laborious, exacting farm life, in spite of stimulation to other pursuits; the alternative is to be forcefully ejected from the family, toward which they still feel very strong dependent ties, in order to make a new career for themselves.

These crises in youth are found in all modern societies to some degree, but it is the particular personality propensities of the Japanese and the romantic tradition of suicide that makes Japanese youth par-

---

[36] Some evidence already available would support this contenton in a large interdisciplinary survey study at the Nagoya National University Neuropsychiatric Department by Tsuneo Muramatsu and associates. They found traditional social attitudes most strongly held by what they termed the old urban middle class and farmers in a fairly prosperous farming community.

ticularly vulnerable to resolving their dilemmas by suicide. In spite of wanting to be independent and capable of making new meaningful heterosexual liaisons, for individual youth there seems to be great difficulty in finding oneself as an individual and in achieving satisfactory intimacy with another. In the suicide notes of some youth one finds an overt fantasy of reunion with the mother that runs counter to an avowed disbelief in an afterlife. Some regressive fantasy obviously plays a part in a number of suicides at this age.

After the crisis of youth is past the suicide rate is lower, which is explicable in part perhaps by the paternalistic and protective network of obligation in Japanese society once an occupational commitment has been made. Even though the individual's competence may prove quite doubtful, he continues to be taken care of by the company or organization to which he remains docilely loyal. The middle-aged Japanese remains a fixture until retirement; he does not face the common American crisis of being eased out of a job, a situation well dramatized by Arthur Miller in *Death of a Salesman*.

Marital continuity is the rule in Japan, not the exception. In spite of very liberal divorce laws, in Japan today one finds a phenomenally low divorce rate by American standards. An individual to whom marriage brings little intimacy or companionship, nevertheless finds some protection in the formal structure of the marriage and its relevance to family patterns. A husband expects his wife to continue to fulfill her role while he fulfills his occupational duties. He can find self-validation in the faithful performance of his social role, and by this preoccupation can avoid questions of unrealized intimacy. The American culture, in contrast, delays confrontation with possible failure in intimacy, a confrontation that may occur after the age of forty, with the diminution of physical prowess and decreased possibility of upward job mobility.

Japanese culture permits the individual in the middle years to remain within a continuous network of obligations and commitments, which may be experienced as a burden but which also help prevent social alienation. The suicides committed by individuals in this age group are of the type we identify as stemming from role narcissism and are dramatically associated with trauma inflicted through the individual's social role. In the United States, suicides of the anomic type appeared with spectacular frequency during the depression years following the market crash in 1929.[37] At that time, men accustomed to a high level of income and a privileged social status suddenly found themselves financially wiped out. Too old to start over, to redefine themselves in some less elevated terms, many responded by leaping

---

[37] Hurlburt, "Prosperity and Depression on the Suicide Rate" (1932).

from high windows. Less readily perceived as anomic suicides are the Japanese man who kills his family and himself, refusing to live in abject poverty, or the mother who feels herself a failure in her effort to produce a socially worthwhile offspring and therefore commits suicide, or the nurse who commits suicide over what others regard as a trivial lapse. For the individual involved, however, the disruption of social role is as final and the inability to face a future redefinition by society is as great an issue as these are for the individual who finds himself financially destitute and unable to continue.

Compared cross-culturally, the Japanese seem unduly preoccupied with standards of excellence. The Japanese internalize such standards; they worry about how they appear to others; and, sometimes less obviously, they worry about how they appear to themselves. This preoccupation with standards makes the Japanese particularly vulnerable to social vicissitudes; many Japanese so internalize standards of social expectation in respect to their social roles that they become highly vulnerable to any rupture. Thus the Japanese show a unique subtlety or degree of sensitivity to what others might consider a minor assault on social presence. Status concerns are much more pronounced in middle-class than in lower-class individuals. To some degree this phenomenon is worldwide; overall statistics show differences in class background related to suicide. In countries with chronically abject poverty there is usually a relatively low rate of suicide. What Durkheim calls acute anomic suicide requires the internalization of some sense of potential social degradation.

In old age, as we have indicated, the social role no longer functions to maintain obligations. There is an attenuation of actual relationships; a marriage mate may die; the aging process focuses the individual on bodily preoccupations, and hypochondriasis often occurs; finding himself isolated and ignored, an individual who at a previous age found no occasion to express his vulnerability to suicide may in his final years succumb to the act.

SUMMARY

In brief compass we have attempted to integrate a psychoanalytic approach to suicide with the insight afforded by Durkheim's theory of the social causality of suicide. To integrate the two theories it was necessary to modify the classification system forwarded by Durkheim to include not only his three types, altruistic, egoistic, and anomic, but also a fourth category, which includes a considerable number of suicides in most countries, that of egocentric suicide. In applying the theory to the types of suicide and the distribution of suicide within the Japanese population, I have developed the contention that the Japanese are particularly prone to suicides that involve what I term role narcissism and are particularly vulnerable to socially induced crises. The cultural crisis in individuation is particularly difficult for Japanese youth as a chronic issue. A cultural proneness to maintain a great deal of narcissistic libido tied to the body contributes to a high suicide rate in the aged. A culturally prevalent socialization pattern makes Japanese particularly prone to the logic of inflicting one's suffering or death on others as an autoplastic form of control or aggression. Modern Japanese also manifest forms of alienation that are more apt to result in suicide than in the forms of religious conversion that are alternative to suicide for Christians in the West.

Suicide in Japan, as elsewhere, is as much a failure of love as it is a form of aggression. It is also as much a product of continuities in cultural psychology as it is a product of present-day fluctuations in socioeconomic conditions. It is as necessary to examine the individual psychological motivations of Japanese as it is to examine collective statistics. Suicide is a subject to be understood ultimately in an interdisciplinary psychocultural framework as well as in cross-cultural perspective.

Chapter XVIII

Alienation and the Author:
A Triptych on Social Conformity
and Deviancy in Japanese Intellectuals

with HIROSHI WAGATSUMA

INTRODUCTION: ANOMIC CONDITIONS
AND PERSONAL ALIENATION

Awareness and experience of alienation in modern societies, although common to all age and class segments, is most evident in adolescents. As was suggested in some of the preceding chapters in this section, alienation today in Japanese youth manifests itself much as it does in other urban industrial countries. The increased possibility of personal occupational choice and the quickening tempo of social mobility and social change awaken in many young people the necessity of defining themselves more actively by a self-conscious commitment to an adult social role. Probably more so than at any time in the past, youth must make active choices in respect to career and marriage.[1]

The sense of role diffuseness in adolescents starts with a prior sense of alienation from the primary family and from any strongly adhered-to

---

[1] Erik Erikson discusses the difficulties of achieving adult self-identity in modern society without succumbing to a diffuseness of purpose or an incomplete sense of life goals. Well-conversant with the full spectrum of recent theory, he sets his discussion within both a sociological frame of reference and that afforded by classical psychoanalysis. In Erikson's view it is implicit that social role identity, or its absence, derives from the prior intimate developmental relationships the adolescent has had with his family and from the degree to which his family is functioning in a face-to-face community. Erikson, *Identity, Youth and Crisis* (1968).

face-to-face community relationships. In a mobile, modern urban society, one can quickly lose any sense of community, and if the nature of the relationship as infant and child within the primary family itself has been deficient or even corrosive for the individual, he may find himself completely marginal and alienated. He may come to lack within himself any deeply internalized, unquestioned directives giving purpose and orientation to his life.

It takes more time to grow up in a modern industrial society, with its demand for specialized skills, than it did in earlier societies, since recognition as an adult always comes with some degree of occupational and civic readiness. The universalization and democratization of education create a moratorium after puberty—youth are students of something, or they are marking time. They differentiate themselves from the world of official adulthood with cultural content of their own. They gain status and self-validation from each other if not from the alien adult establishment who run things.

However, our concern here is not with the acutely alienated individual but with the chronically alienated intellectual who in a sense is also an observer. Is it simply his continuing social role as an observer, a moralist, a critic of his society, that creates in him a perduring sense of separation from his culture? We believe not. We believe such a role in itself has psychological determinants which suit those who choose it. The individual seeks such a role. Not all authors become or remain alienated; nevertheless, the sense of alienation lends to the work of some few a depth of poignant feeling; alienation coupled with disciplined talent makes for a sense of greatness that is honored by the society. Three Japanese novelists considered great in this sense are our subjects here.

Alienation, seen psychologically or psychodynamically, is not specific to modern society. It has always existed. There has always been the deviant in society who, either because of infant and childhood experiences or through alienation from a fixed social role later in society, has found himself in a marginal position, motivated by impulses, desires, and goals that run counter to those condoned by society generally. The general lack of fixed role for an articulate minority finding themselves in special roles and at particular points of transition has made the problem more manifest and more socially visible than in the past.

In our pursuit of the study of alienation in modern Japanese culture, we have therefore examined in considerable detail the total life experiences of certain individuals who, by their very role in society, have articulated the inner states of human beings who find themselves marginal, or who experience an inability or lack of motivation to maintain themselves in conformity within society.

In three Japanese creative writers, Natsume Sōseki, Akutagawa Ryūnosuke, and Dazai Osamu, we find ample evidence of their inner experiences of isolation and alienation, not only at the transitional stage of adolescence but throughout their lives from early childhood on. Their own writings and personal documents concerning them well illustrate in dramatic form experiences more or less common to the less articulate Japanese of their times. The form and content of the attempts made by these three men to resolve their feelings in many respects represent patterns of the lives and careers of the Japanese intellectuals of the late Meiji (1868–1912), Taisho (1912–1926), and Showa (1926–   ) periods, respectively. As individuals, these three men varied widely in the means taken to overcome the gnawing sense of incomplete identity and of their own apartness. The resolutions attempted at various times in their life careers included political involvement, immersion in familial obligations and preoccupations, a search for intimacy in marriage and heterosexual relationships, esthetic dedication, religious release, neurotic-psychosomatic sufferings, and self-destruction.

Self-Conscious Alienation and Author's Social Role

As we discussed in the previous chapter, Durkheim in his classic work on suicide distinguishes with great psychological insight a form of suicide that he terms egoistic. Durkheim's description of the psychological state preceding this form of suicide can be matched with statements of inner experiences found in the writings of all three of the Japanese authors we are considering. The following quotations from Durkheim's *Suicide* describe a form of alienation experience common to many intellectuals.

It has been sometimes said that because of his psychological constitution, man cannot live without attachment to some object which transcends and survives him and that the reason for this necessity is a need we must have not to perish entirely. Life is said to be intolerable unless some reason for existing is involved, some purpose justifying life's trials. The individual alone is not a sufficient end for his own activity; he is too little. He is not only hemmed in spatially, he is also strictly limited temporarily. When, therefore, we have no other object than ourselves, we cannot avoid the thought that our efforts will finally end in nothingness, since we ourselves disappear. But annihilation terrifies us; under these conditions, one would lose the courage to live—that is to act and struggle, since nothing will remain of our exertions. The state of egoism, in other words, is supposed to be contradictory to human nature and consequently too uncertain to have chances of permanence. If, in other words, it has often been said man is double—that is, because social man superimposes himself upon physical man, social man necessarily presupposes a society which he expresses and serves. If this dissolves, if we no longer feel it in the existence about us and above us, whatever is social in us is deprived of all objective foundation. All that remains is an artificial combination of illusory images, a phantasmagoria vanishing at the least reflection. That is, nothing which can be a goal for our action. . . .

One form of suicide certainly known to antiquity has widely developed in our day. Lamartine's Raphael offers us its ideal type. Its characteristic is a condition of melancholic languor which relaxes all the springs of action. Business, public affairs, useful work, even domestic duties inspire the person only with indifference and aversion. He is unwilling to emerge from himself. On the other hand, what is lost in activity is made up for in thought and inner life. In revulsion from its surroundings, consciousness becomes self-preoccupied, takes itself as its proper and unique study and undertakes as its main task self-observation and self-analysis. But by this extreme concentration, it merely deepens the chasm separating it from the rest of the universe. The moment the individual becomes so enamored of himself, he inevitably detaches himself increasingly from everything external and emphasizes the isolation in which he lives to the point of worship. Self-absorption is not a good method of attaching oneself to others. All movement is in a sense altruistic in that it is centrifugal and disperses existence beyond its own limitations. Reflection, on the other hand, has about it something personal and egoistic, for it is only possible as a person becomes detached from the outside world and retreats from it into himself. And reflection is a more intense and a more complete retreat. Action without mixing with people is impossible. To think, on the contrary, we must cease to have connection with them in order to consider them objectively, the more so in order to think about oneself. So the man whose whole activity is diverted to inner meditation becomes insensible to his surroundings. If he loves, it is not to give himself, to blend in fecund union with another being, but to meditate on his love. His passions are mere appearances, being sterile. They are dissipated in futile imaginings, producing nothing external to themselves. . . .

The same characteristics appear, reappear in the ultimate social act, suicide, which follows logically from this moral condition. There is nothing violent or hasty about its unfolding. The sufferer selects his own time and meditates on his plan well in advance; he is not even repelled by slow means. A calm melancholy, sometimes not unpleasant, marks his last moments. He analyzes himself to the last. . . .

It is clear how these various peculiarities are related to egoistic suicide. They are almost certainly its consequence in individual expression. This loathness to act, the melancholy detachment, spring from the over-individuation by which we have defined this type of suicide. The individual isolates himself because the ties uniting him with others are slackened or broken, because society is not sufficiently integrated at the point where he is in contact with it. These gaps between one and another individual consciousness, estranging them from one another, are authentic results of the weakening of the social fabric, and finally, the intellectual and meditative nature of suicides of this sort is readily explained, if you recall that an egoistic suicide is necessarily accompanied by a high development of knowledge and reflective intelligence. Indeed, it is clear that in a society where consciousness is normally compelled to extend its field of action, it is also much more in danger of transgressing the normal limits which shelter it from self-destruction. The mind that questions everything, unless strong enough to bear the weight of its ignorance, risks questioning itself and being engulfed in doubt.[2]

It is the role of the dramatist or the author to express those aspects of human experience occurring within his culture that go beyond the mundane, that reach toward deeper human values, even those values possibly not accepted in his present milieu. The creative author or dramatist often functions as a moralist and may criticize society for its failure to fulfill its more lasting and deeper values. He seeks to edify, through dramatic or narrative presentation, the tragic state of man. In an Aristotelian sense, his writing is often cathartic of emotion and elevates and redirects the purpose of his audience. The novelist in contemporary society may not express the morals of the majority or seek to strengthen adherence to the established modes of behavior or political structure of his group; insofar as he has clearer than normal vision, however, he may direct attention beyond the acceptable to a higher goal. When the author or dramatist speaks in these terms, he presents himself in the role of the artist as an innovator and indicator of direction for the values for his society. Today, however, the novelist or playwright is very often expressing the lack of purpose or the quandary of direction experienced by modern man. What he presents about inner experiences may not be readily discernible as moral or moralistic in tone. However, it is interesting to note the moral tone underlying dramas dealing with alienation, such as those of Fellini and Antonioni in recent Italian cinema. One can see in these pictures, which deal with aspects of life that are not condoned within the traditional Christian morality, a search for some moral definition, as well as for some experience of satisfying human intimacy.

If we turn from these examples in the West to the Japanese authors and examine what they have to say about morality or the individual's difficulties with society from the standpoint of his own motivation, we notice a trend similar to that in the West over the past eighty years toward defining the essential problem more and more as one occurring within the individual, rather than simply as a state of tension between the individual and his society. It is this trend that we will illustrate by an examination of our three representative Japanese authors.

In testing the limits of experience, the artist is prone to indulge in

---

[2] Durkheim, *Suicide* (1951), p. 74 ff.

personal impulses and to become tolerant toward behavioral expressions of motivations that are not condoned within the mundane conformity of the culture. He is likely, therefore, to express through his personal experiences the dramatic incidents that he seeks to portray in a novel or play. By the role he takes, which of course is to a certain extent already selected by the nature of his previous personality, the artist is apt to be alienated from his society. He cannot go back and become a conformist without a tremendous sense of personal loss in his expressive life. Functioning with creativity, itself an occupational choice, therefore takes the individual beyond the usual limits of the acceptable culture, and by so doing, it also threatens him with a type of alienation. He seeks to resolve this state within which he finds himself by sustaining himself with new values or by assuming a sense of autonomy in a confrontation not faced by those who simply conform with what is prescribed for them. Sometimes the author or artist, in espousing or criticizing his society, is actually creating a situation for the indulgence and self-expression of uncondoned activities within himself so that the artist even in his personal life in a sense dramatizes for his society the heights and depths of the human problems.

The tragic drama and the novel have changed in the course of modernization in Japan. The theme of the classic dramas of the past presented for the most part the conflict within the individual as occurring between his sense of duty within a rigid class system and his human feelings. This theme, known as conflict between *giri* and *ninjo*, was repeated over and over again in the plays presented on the puppet stage and later by the live Kabuki actors. During the Tokugawa period, the tragic drama depicted the problems resulting from the demands of society upon the individual. In a sense, society was criticized for not allowing legitimate human feelings to be experienced without disastrous consequence. The sharing of personal love and intimacy between man and woman was often cast as a tragic experience that could not be actualized because of differences of class or other circumstances. Chikamatsu Monzaemon, the great dramatist of the eighteenth century who wrote for the puppet stage, voiced these themes with poignant reality for his audience.

In the three authors discussed in this chapter, we find from the Meiji period to the present time a gradual shift in the location of the sense of tension in human experience. Each of the three considered in our illustrative triptych fails to solve the problem of relating himself to society and to others in a continuing experience of satisfying intimacy. The first of these authors, Sōseki, one of the most prominent writers of the Meiji period, sought to understand modern individuation in terms borrowed from the West. In his work he portrays the individual seeking autonomy. His fictional characters almost invariably fail tragically through some inner insufficiency or incapacity.

NATSUME SŌSEKI (1867–1916)— INTEGRITY AND THE ARTIST

Family Identity

In reading Sōseki's work *Within Glass Doors*,[3] one gains the strong impression of consciousness of pride in his family background. The Natsume family had held the position of *nanushi* (ward director) in Edo (Tokyo)[4] since 1702 and enjoyed its influential status as well as wealth. Pictures of great-grandparents and grandparents dignified the ancestral house. Although as a child Sōseki enjoyed a great deal of luxury and privilege, it was under peculiarly Japanese circumstances; he was adopted out to menials beholden to his socially important father.

Born on January 5, 1867, Sōseki, or originally Kinnosuke, was unwanted. His mother had already given birth to four sons and one daughter. Forty-one years old at his birth, she is said to have felt "ashamed" to have given birth again at this unseemly age. Almost immediately after his arrival, Sōseki was given for caretaking to a small merchant and his wife, who was the elder sister of a maid working for the Natsume family. At age three, Sōseki was brought home for a brief period, only to be formally adopted out to a man named Shiobara and his wife.

Shiobara once had worked for Sōseki's father as a houseboy. He proved to be a promising young man, and Sōseki's father decided to act as his guardian, as was often the case in paternalist traditional culture. Sōseki's father had selected a former servant for Shiobara to marry, bought for him the position of *nanushi* of another district, and helped to establish him as a man of considerable social status. For these reasons, the Shiobaras had a sense of personal loyalty and obligation to their patron and were eager to adopt the Natsume's unwelcome child.

Shiobara, at the time Sōseki was about five years old, was appointed ward director of Asakusa. His foster parents lavished an inordinate

---

[3] *Garasu dō no Naka* in Natsume Sōseki, *Collected Works* (20 vols. 1928–29), 358–440. English translation, *Within Glass Doors*, 1928.

[4] The *nanushi* in Edo was an administrative officer in the Tokugawa feudal regime who, under the rule of *machi bugyo* [magistrate of the city], was directly responsible for carrying out governmental orders, taxation, and welfare and security measures within a particular section of the city to which he was assigned.

amount of love and indulgence on their only child. One may judge
that Sōseki retained from his early experiences some sense of maternal deprivation on the one hand, but on the other a strong sense
of being a very "special" person. In *Grass Along the Road*,[5] his most
nearly autobiographical novel, the author writes that his foster parents (called "Shimada" in the novel), who were considered miserly, but
never failed to buy the best clothes and most luxurious toys for their
foster child. At the same time his foster parents, out of a sense of insecurity, would constantly ask him, seeking reassurance, whose child he
was. In *Grass Along the Road*, the author writes:

However, deep in their minds there was always a kind of anxiety about him.
On cold winter nights, sitting face-to-face with an oblong brazier between
them, they would often ask Kenzō, "Who is your father?" Kenzō would turn
to Shimada and point to him. "Then, your mother?" Kenzō would turn to
O-Tsune and point to her. Satisfied, they would nevertheless not stop, but
would ask the same question in a different form. "Well, then, who are your
real father and mother?" Unwillingly, Kenzō had to repeat the same answer,
which for some reason unknown to him continually pleased them. They
would look at each other and laugh. . . . At some periods such an episode
took place almost everyday. Especially O-Tsune was persistent. . . . "Who's
child are you actually? Tell me the truth." He felt agonized. He felt angry.
He wanted to remain silent, rather than giving the answer she wanted.
"Whom do you like the best? Your father? Your mother?" Kenzō disliked
answering just to please her. He stood in front of her, mute. O-Tsune thought
he was too small to answer her question. However, her interpretation was
too superficial. In his mind he detested and hated his foster mother's attitude.
His foster parents did their best to monopolize Kenzō, their foster son. Actually, there was no doubt in him that he was their exclusive possession. Accordingly, the more they took care of him the more, in effect, they deprived
him of freedom. There was already restraint on his body. And the more
dreadful restraint on his mind started casting a shadow of dissatisfaction in
his yet innocent heart. . . . Their attempt to force their kindness into his
mind from outside caused in him an opposite effect. Kenzō felt bothered.
"Why do they have to take care of me?" . . . The couple loved Kenzō for
sure. However, in their love there was a strange expectation of a reward.
Like a man keeping a beautiful mistress and through the power of his
wealth lavishing on her the things she wants, they felt they had to show
kindness to win his heart, rather than simply expressing their genuine love.

One also gains an impression that his foster mother developed in him
a sense of successful primacy in whatever rivalry he felt toward his
foster father. This attitude developed within him a sense of personal
destiny and, inferentially, a sense of potential guilt for having an
advantage in a love rivalry. One can illustrate a number of rivalry

---

[5] *Michikusa* (1915), in *Collected Works* V, 265–380.

situations in his works in which a hero takes a woman already loved or legally possessed by another.[6] As their only child, Sōseki may have experienced the developing motivation for achievement that such a situation induced. He had ample psychological basis for feeling he was a family protégé.

It may not be unreasonable to suggest that Sōseki later came to feel a certain guilt when given special consideration by society. He resisted to an almost paranoid degree any attempt to bestow upon him special honors as a writer or a scholar. In the strong sense of personal autonomy and self-righteousness he sought to maintain, he contemptuously refused official plaudits, which he felt were made without true assessment and understanding of his worth as an individual. He sought to free himself from entangling commitments and avoided any sense within himself that his work as an artist could be tinged with prostituting to the market place.[7]

We might also assume that a feeling of self-importance, developed in early childhood, helped him later when he had to go through what seems to have been a terrible experience of isolation and psychological dislocation at the home of his real parents. When Sōseki was eight years old, Shiobara, his foster father, came to have an intimate relationship with a widow, and quarrels arose between him and his wife. Their marital conflict was not suitable for the education of a small boy. A decision was made that Sōseki was to return to his real parents. Shiobara and his wife were divorced and he married the widow. His wife was also married later to the owner of a liquor store. Sōseki's real father wanted to cancel the adoption but it was discovered that Shiobara, taking advantage of his position of ward director, had registered Sōseki as his real son. The legal complications were not straightened

---

[6] For instance, at the end of *Thereupon* (*Sorekara*, 1909, in *Collected Works* VI, 3–274), the protagonist Daisuke determines to marry Michiyo, in spite of the fact that he has already abetted her marriage to his best friend. In *Gate* (*Mon*, 1910, in *Collected Works* VI, 275–484), Sosuke, whose wife, O-Yone, was once betrothed to his best friend, has to live in continual anxiety and guilt. In *Heart* (*Kokoro*, 1914, in *Collected Works* IX, 3–265), the hero, Sensei, decides to marry a girl whom he loves but who is also loved by his close friend. He causes his friend to commit suicide from despair, and after suffering from a strong sense of guilt on account of his friend's death, he eventually commits suicide himself.

[7] For instance, in June 1909 a literary magazine *Sun* (in Japanese) took a poll in which Sōseki was selected as "best writer." However, he refused the prize, saying that artists should not be ranked in order "like Sumo wrestlers." In 1919 the Ministry of Education decided to confer on Sōseki the degree of Bungaku Hakushi (Doctor of Letters), but Sōseki refused acceptance. In his letter to Fukuhara, the chief of the Bureau of Educational Affairs, Ministry of Education, he wrote, "I have been living as an ordinary individual named Natsume and wish to continue to live as an ordinary individual so named. Accordingly, I do not want to receive any 'Doctor's' degree."

out until 1888, when Sōseki was twenty-two years old, whereupon he was legally returned to the Natsume family.

When he was returned to his real parents' home, as the result of marital conflict between his foster parents, he was still not a welcome child. Quoting again from *Grass Along the Road*:

For his real father Kenzō was no more than a nuisance. The father appeared to be wondering why such a good-for-nothing had to return to his house. His father did not treat him as his son. Such a drastic change of attitude finally dried up all the love Kenzō had toward his father. When Kenzō was living with his foster parents, his real father always showed him a smiling face. Now, Kenzō had become a burden and his father suddenly became sharp and blunt. Comparing these two different attitudes, Kenzō was surprised and then felt disgusted.

As he had many children, Kenzō's father never gave any thought to the possibility of being taken care of by Kenzō in his old age. Having no such expectation, his father did not want to spend money for his child, upon whom he did not expect to depend. The father had accepted Kenzō because Kenzō was his own son, but he did it unwillingly and wanted to do nothing more than to feed him. The father would say, "I will feed the boy as I think I should. However, I cannot afford to do more than that. Shimada should pay the other expenses." Shimada, for his part, had his own selfish view of the situation, and saw his prospects optimistically. "Well, if I leave the boy to his own father, the father will not mistreat him any way. When the boy becomes old enough to work, I will take him away from his father." Kenzō could find no place by the sea nor could he reside in the mountains. Rejected by both, he wandered helplessly in between. . . .

From the standpoint of both his real father and foster father, Kenzō was not a human being but rather a "thing." The only difference was that his real father treated him as trash while his foster father considered him as something of future use.

These early experiences of rejection and hypocrisy on the part of adults may account at least partly for Sōseki's continual deep sense of alienation, his depressed moods, and recurrently pessimistic thoughts. They might also help to account for his almost rigid and indignant moral righteousness and hatred of hypocrisy. But one cannot give final answers to how the human personality draws sufficient strength out of the atmosphere to surmount it and gain some sense of escape through achievement.

Detachment—Attempts at Esthetic Resolution

We find Sōseki referring to pessimistic thoughts and depressed moods at a relatively early age. For instance, on August 9, 1890, when he was twenty-three, Sōseki wrote to his best friend, Masaoka Shiki, a noted poet,

These days I have been feeling thoroughly disgusted with society and life in general. I have tried many times to think and feel differently but to no avail. I still feel disgust. And yet I have no courage to commit suicide; this may mean that I am still human, perhaps. . . .

In another letter to Masaoka Shiki, November 11, 1891, he wrote:

Last year I was a pessimist. This year again I am a pessimist. In my opinion, in order to survive this society, one must be either tolerant enough to accept it or talented enough to be accepted by it. As you know, I have neither sufficient tolerance nor talent. . . .

Two years before his death, Sōseki wrote to one of his disciples:

I consider consciousness as the totality of life, but I do not believe this same consciousness to be the totality of myself. I shall exist after death. I even think that I can return to my real self after my death. At present I do not want to commit suicide. Most probably I shall live as long as possible. As long as I live, I think I shall continue to disclose my weaknesses as an ordinary human being. It is my life. I dislike the pain of it but at the same time I would abhor the extreme pain which would accompany any forced shift from life to death. I therefore do not want to commit suicide. . . .

From childhood on he was fond of nature. For Sōseki's unhappy mind, it offered an escape. Through the classic Chinese literature that he loved and studied so ardently in his youth, he found some consolation of mind, escaping human annoyance in esthetic appreciation of nature. Sōseki manifested a much earlier talent than that for which he became known. Long before his late thirties, which marked his debut as a novelist, he had written a number of poems in Chinese as well as briefer haiku in the Japanese style. These activities were for him an esthetic escape from human problems. However, in his artistic identity Sōseki, even as a successful novelist, failed in his search for a resolution to his personal sense of isolation.

In Sōseki's relatively early work, *Grass for a Pillow* written in 1906,[8] at the age of thirty-nine, he depicts an artist attempting to retreat from the painfulness of human involvements and attachments or maintaining a detached esthetic view of life. The artist retreats to nature and has contact with others only as an observer. This occupational resolution within an artistic role is finally deemed by Sōseki an impossibility. Even while taking a trip into the mountains, making his pillow of grass as a wanderer, he finds he cannot remain uninvolved. Artistic detachment offers no defense against the arousal of vulnerable personal feelings that he cannot help but extend toward others. While Sōseki found great sustenance in his identification with the purpose of creative art, he clearly felt it was not enough for solving personal

[8] *Kusamakura*, in *Collected Works* III, 5–165.

problems. In his later writings, especially starting with *Thereupon*,[9] Sōseki sought to face more squarely the problems of human interaction and their resolution through some moral means.

A quotation from his letter (October 26, 1906) to Suzuki Miekichi, his disciple and a novelist, seems to describe how he felt about life at this time:

. . . from childhood until adolescence I used to think that the world of man was basically good. I used to think that I would come to enjoy delicious meals, refined clothes. I used to think that I could live an esthetic life, married to a beautiful wife, possessing a beautiful home. . . . I used to think that I would try to accomplish such aspirations even if they proved difficult. . . . However, the world turned out to be opposite to my anticipations. That is what life is, after all. Therefore, in this world, however it may be and however unpleasant events, we must simply jump in if we want ever to accomplish anything. . . . To live purely, that is, to live poetically, must be a part of human life, indeed, but must be a very small part of significant life. Therefore, we should not live like the protagonist of *Kusamakura*.

The artistic role for Sōseki was a moral one and continued to be so. In his notes of 1916, the year of his death, one finds, "Only when it is ethical, it is artistic. What is truly artistic is always ethical." For him morality might even bring an individual to oppose society. In an essay of 1906 he wrote: "Sometimes I may be in opposition to the stated morality of society. I may want to indicate what true morality is. I may also write about the values, the positive values of those who break the ordinary morality of the society. I should like to follow my own conscience. . . ."

Sōseki saw the artist as a teacher. In this role, he bore great responsibility. Should he advocate some mistaken view of life, Sōseki thought, he must consider himself severely blameworthy.

One should not forget, however, that Sōseki continued seeking consolation from esthetics until the end of his life. He continued to write a considerable number of Chinese poems, haiku, and even poems in English. He also spent time with calligraphy and watercolors. In a temporary respite from the moral struggle found in his books, Sōseki wrote in 1914 to a friend, "I am less and less capable of finding people in society whom I like. And more and more beautiful to me seem the sky, the earth, grass and trees. Especially beautiful is the recent sunlight of early spring. More and more my living depends on such beauty."

The Struggle for Personal Autonomy

All through his life, Sōseki kept seeking for personal independence from society and the maintenance of self-righteousness. As we

---

[9] *Sorekara* (1909), in *Collected Works* VI.

mentioned earlier, one may presume that somewhere very early in his life, as a foster son of the Shiobaras, Sōseki developed a strong sense of personal integrity as a psychological defense. Part of this defensive armor was his emphasis on conscious self-control and righteousness. Sōseki's sense of personal autonomy was partially sustained by a strong background in the ethical, quasi-religious philosophy of Confucianism he absorbed from his early interest in Chinese classics. The terms and concepts through which he sought to express his sense of righteousness and personal integrity were derived from Confucian literature. In this sense, Sōseki exemplifies many of the Meiji intellectual leaders of his day.

His feeling of isolation was founded on a strong sense of being "different" from others. At the university, he kept to himself and had little association with other students. He would often describe himself as *henbutsu* (a queer one, or strange one). Nevertheless, he continually reaffirmed his right to be different. His pen name, Sōseki, which he used first in 1889 in a collection of essays and original poems in the Chinese manner (*mokusetsuroku*) suggests his delight in his own stubbornness. "Sōseki" consists of two Chinese characters, "to wash" and "stone." They are taken from the Chinese classical phrase *sōseki chinryu*,[10] a term used to describe a bad loser or a person stubbornly unwilling to admit defeat.

The defensive nature of Sōseki's sense of autonomy can be well reconstructed from his satirical novel *I Am a Cat*,[11] published in 1906. The cat is essentially an ironical observer of human foibles. Toward the end of the book, the cat himself is tempted to experience what the humans do when they indulge themselves. He becomes intoxicated, starts acting carelessly, and accidentally drops from a height into a barrel of water. In his resultant helpless struggle, the cat seeks religious consolation and resignation, and dies reciting the Buddhist incantation *Namu Amida Butsu*. Sōseki here, if we can interpret him, suggests the danger of "letting go" and of self-indulgence. To lose control is to fall into self-destructive activity, and worse yet to end up in an act of demeaning dependency—to give up the active struggle and to seek consolation in the deity.

Sōseki avowed that there was more to be feared from one's inner

---

[10] This phrase derives from an old Chinese story. A Chinese man, wishing to retire to a contemplative life in nature, sought to convey his intention to his friend. He used a phrase mistakenly as he talked to his friend about it. He had thought to state his wish "to use a stone for a pillow and a running river to cleanse his mouth daily." Inadvertently he reversed the word order, suggesting the use of "stones for washing and a river as a pillow." When his mistake was pointed out, he denied he was mistaken and stated that he indeed wanted to use small stones to polish his teeth, and the river as a pillow to bathe his ears.

[11] *Wagahai wa Neko de aru*, in *Collected Works* I, 3–466.

feelings, if one does not maintain righteousness and integrity, than one suffers in the social isolation resulting from maintaining one's inner standards against social pressure. In an essay written in 1895 for the magazine of the alumni association of Ehime Junior High School, Sōseki writes:

When you are scolded by your teacher, you should not think that you have lost value or have been depreciated. When you are praised by your teacher you should not be proud, thinking that your value has been raised. A crane is a crane, whether it's flying or sleeping. A pig is a pig, whether it's barking or squeaking. What varies according to the praise and censure of others is a man's market price and not his real value. He who aims at raising his market price, rather than his real value, is called *saishi* ("a smart man"). He who aims at raising his real value is called *kunshi* ("a virtuous man"). Among *saishi* there are many who are socially successful. *Kunshi* do not mind being socially unrecognized.

From his notes in 1905,

It is a disgrace for a *kunshi* to be loved by a *shojin* (a man without virtue). It is disgrace for a *kunshi* to be respected by *shojin*. It is disgrace for *kunshi* to be able to associate easily with *shojin*. It is the duty of *kunshi* to feel contempt for *shojin*.

From *Wintry Blast,* a novel written in 1907:[12]

People glorify the rich. People glorify academic degrees. People do not know how to respect a man's righteous character itself, directly, regardless of position, knowledge, talents or ability. If a society loses one person of good character, it is a loss of one bright light for all. One righteous man is of more value for society than hundreds of noble background, wealth, or scholarly degree. Such a man cannot be replaced.

From notes in 1906:

If the entire world does not accept me, I would depart from the world. Such departure would be better than the shame of bending myself to be accepted. I shall not worry about my lack of friends, family, parents, or sibs. I would only worry about my being mean, cheap and wicked.

In his letter to his friend, Takahama Kyōshi, a noted poet, in 1906:

I think it is my duty to myself, to Heaven and to my parents to do things in my own way. As Heaven and parents gave birth to such a man as I am, I can only interpret it that they wanted me to be just as I am. I cannot be less or more than what I am.

At times he doubted his ability to maintain himself against society. In the same letter he says,

---

[12] *Nowaki* (1908).

I used to think in the past that nothing could be more miserable than to be a righteous man and to be punished on a false charge. I no longer feel that way. I wish I could be such a man. I wish I could fight with the entire world and be crucified, looking down upon people from the cross, disdaining them in my mind. Of course, I am too much of a coward to be able to accept the idea of crucifixion, but I would not mind being hanged perhaps.

To present a balanced picture of Sōseki, one cannot overlook what has been characterized by some biographers as a strong tendency to project into situations a sense that others were seeking to spy on him and catch him in some demeaning act. Sōseki's wife writes:

It was three or four days after his [Sōseki's] returning home from London. Our eldest daughter, Fudeko, was sitting at the other side of a hibachi. For some unknown reason, there was a coin on the flat rim of the brazier. Fudeko did not seem to have brought the coin there. She was not playing with it. Noticing the coin, he said that his daughter had done something obnoxious, and suddenly hit her. I did not understand what it was all about. Fudeko cried. I asked him to explain, and he told me: while in London, he was taking a walk one day and a beggar sorrowfully asked him for money. He gave him a coin. Returning to his boardinghouse, he saw a coin on the window of the toilet. He had previously thought that his landlady always shadowed him and spied on him. Now he was convinced that he had been correct in guessing that he had been watched by his landlady. He thought that she had seen him giving a coin to the beggar and had put the coin on the window to let him know that he was being watched. He felt very angry with her. As he saw the coin on the rim of the brazier he thought that his daughter had tried to make a fool out of him, by doing the same thing, and therefore he became very angry at her. It is a strange story.

He had also been known to accuse others of spying on him or speaking ill of him. At home he would give way to destructive rages, during which he acted irrationally and even smashed objects when he thought that someone was slighting him in some manner. These feelings were often directed toward his wife. They were labeled by his friends as "neurasthenia" (*shinkei suijaku*). These symptomatic occurrences must be considered the obverse side of his continual insistence on personal integrity. Some quotations from his wife's *Reminiscence of Sōseki*:[13]

[In the same year after his return from London] in June and July his head (*atama*) became gradually worse. At midnight, getting angry at some unknown cause, he would become enraged and throw things about. He would become angry when the child cried. He would become furious for no apparent reason and work off his temper on those around him. . . . Dr. Amako told me that he had examined Sōseki. I asked his opinion and he said it was not a simple neurasthenia. He was wondering if it were not some kind of psychosis, but he was not quite sure.

---

[13] Natsume, *Sōseki no Omoide* (1929).

Either having a feeling that somebody was after him or being scared by something, he was excited in a strange way and seemed unable to sleep at night. He would suddenly get out of bed, open the door, and jump out into the garden in the night. Or at midnight he would start banging on things and upsetting and throwing things about, making awful noises. After he left for school next morning I would enter his study to see the mess—his lamp shattered, ashes from the brazier thrown all over the floor, the top of the kettle thrown aside.

One night at about 2:00 A.M. he called me to his study and told me to bring him a meal. I could not wake up our maid but had to manage to gather things to eat and bring them to him. Next morning, I found that he had not eaten the meal at all.

Sōseki himself described his rages in *Grass Along the Road*:[14]

Kenzō's mind was crinkled and crumpled like a scrap of paper. Sometimes he felt in such pain that he had to find some occasion to give outlet to the electric current of his irritation. He kicked off the porch for no reason a vase of flowers which his children had asked their mother to buy. When this brownish vase was smashed as he had anticipated, he felt somewhat satisfied; however, when he saw flower and stem miserably crushed, he was overwhelmed by some helpless feeling. He was made to feel yet sadder by the realization that the beautiful consolation and pleasure of his innocent children had been ruthlessly destroyed by their own father. While he felt regret, he did not dare to confess his misdeed in front of his children. "It's *not* my fault. Who is it that makes me behave like a crazy man? It's this person's fault, whoever it is." There was always such an excuse in the bottom of his mind.

Sōseki's second son, Natsume Shinroku, in his reminiscence of his father, also describes a childhood experience in which as a boy less than seven years old he was suddenly made the target of his father's rage, and was beaten and kicked in public. He also wrote that the children were anxious and afraid of their father when he was "neurasthenic."

Sōseki's National Identity

Having received a governmental order "to study in England for two years," Sōseki left Japan in September 1900 and remained in London until December 1902. Through this personal experience, Sōseki was forced to confront within himself, as do many Japanese intellectuals, the implications of Western contact and its influence on his own culture. Sōseki had eagerly acquired the ideas and poetic expressions available to him from Western sources. He had, like others, thought he was ready for some meaningful interchange and communion firsthand with Westerners. As occurs to many Japanese in-

---

[14] *Michikusa* (1915), in *Collected Works* V.

tellectuals who travel abroad, however, he was confronted with the rude shock of how incomplete was his knowledge of the language and culture of the West. In addition, Sōseki suffered continually from insufficient funds. At times he bought sandwiches and ate them walking aimlessly in the park, or had biscuits and water for lunch. With the money he somehow saved he bought as many books as possible. For Sōseki, with his Japanese view of man-woman relationships the more informal Western patterns of heterosexual relationships were upsetting. In his diary, May 22, 1901, he wrote: "In the evening, I went with Mr. Ikeda to Commons. Here and there sat a couple on a bench or on the grass. Some of them were embracing and even kissing each other. Strange country."

While in London, Sōseki reacted in a typically Japanese fashion to the lack of attention paid him as a visiting scholar. He was a person of no consequence as far as London was concerned. No one paid any attention to his presence in intellectual circles, a not infrequent experience of the visiting foreign intellectual constrained by limited language capacities. A sense of personal alienation can reach critical proportions for many Japanese who, in like circumstances, have little social contact beyond that afforded by the landlady of their boarding-house.

Describing his two years' experience in London, Sōseki wrote in the introductory chapter of his *Study of Literature* in 1907:[15]

The two years of my life in London were my most unpleasant years. I was living a miserable life among British gentlemen like a shaggy dog among wolves. I hear that the population of London is five million. I could almost say that my situation was nothing but an attempt to survive as a drop of water among five million drops of oil. A drop of ink falls on a white shirt just washed; its owner must be very displeased. I feel very sorry, you British gentlemen, for walking around Westminster like a beggar, a drop of ink; and for inhaling over a period of two years thousands of cubic feet of air in this big city so artificially covered with a dirty fog. You British gentlemen, I did not visit your country of my own accord. I was sent by my government. If I had acted according to my personal desires, I would never have stepped onto the soil of England during my entire life.[16]

---

[15] *Bungaku-ron*, in *Collected Works* XI, 17–434.

[16] If we try to analyze the muted, unconscious rage at personal rejection in this statement, we must note that the reaction is somewhat different from that of a Westerner in a similar situation. The Japanese intellectual tends to feel rejected when he seeks out some appreciation or nurturance but meets with indifference. The mechanism involved in this state is a type of psychological projection peculiarly Japanese. What is consciously focused upon is the fact that the individual's own presence is embarrassing or somehow discomforting to the others, so that he projects into others a feeling of discomfort at his having inflicted himself upon them. "Inflicting one's self" is actually one form of unconscious hostility. Such hostility

In Japan, patterns of hospitality developed from a continual necessity to placate feudal dignitaries and superior persons in the political hierarchy who traveled through one's territory. In order to gain good will, it was necessary to put on a big show and make offerings of gifts, seducing the traveler with hospitality, also thereby establishing a mutual obligation. Respected Japanese scholars—consciously or not—carried this tradition with them in their expectation of some reception by foreigners abroad. At least someone of lower status than themselves in the country being visited should provide some form of reception. For Sōseki no such hospitality was forthcoming from anyone; instead the visitor felt complete and sublime indifference. He was impressed with the degree to which he was a "nobody" to foreigners. In Sōseki's description of himself as an ink blot on the white shirt of British society, he felt that at least he should have made a mark, if only a small stain. The painful truth was probably that he was completely invisible to the British intelligentsia, or if visible at all, it was as a curiosity, an Oriental, someone vaguely from the East, Chinese or Japanese. To Japanese, the distinction of themselves from Chinese is important, but to the foreigner, at least at this time in the British nation, the distinction was thoroughly insignificant. Such painful experiences throw a visiting Japanese forcibly back on an imperative need to reconsider his national identity. Sōseki was no exception. In his diary, January 25, 1901, he wrote: "The Europeans are surprised at the development of Japan. The reason for their surprise is obvious. People are surprised when someone whom they feel contemptuous toward suddenly talks or acts in a brash way. Most of the Europeans are not surprised nor interested. I do not know how many years it will take Japan to be able to make the Europeans respect her."

There is no doubt, however, that Sōseki's two years in London aroused in him a continuous subsequent ambivalence toward his own people. In London he wrote on April 9, 1901:

I want to go back to Japan. I visualize Japan and feel miserable. I am annoyed by the lack of virtues, of physical strength and aesthetic appreciation

---

takes on a pathetic quality if we understand that the feelings were in response to experiences of indifference, coldness, and lack of kindness. Actual feelings are reversed in saying, "I'm sorry to have bothered you." When a person says, "I'm sorry to have bothered you," in some circumstances in English it may well be taken as a hostile remark. The Japanese are not necessarily consciously aware of such hostility to the same degree. The problem here is to analyze this very Japanese way of projecting discomfort into others rather than the more usual Western pattern of projecting hostility into an indifferent person. The Japanese consciously experience a feeling of being bothersome to another by existing. One possible explanation psychodynamically is that it is the father who is early perceived as the ungiving person, that this is the way a small child may feel at times when he cannot manipulate the father to change his behavior.

of Japanese gentlemen. I feel annoyed by their being proud of something worthless, their superficiality, emptiness, and vanity—their being content with the present situation of Japan and leading the nation into corruption.

However, as an intellectual leader of the Meiji period, Sōseki, after all, thought as a nationalist. We might safely say that on one level Sōseki could identify himself with the growing status of Japan in the world. For instance, in the introduction to *Study of Literature*,[17] following the statement quoted above about his unhappy experience in London, he writes:

The three and a half years spent after my return to Japan were also exceedingly unpleasant years in my life. However, I am a Japanese citizen. I find no reason for quitting Japan because life is unpleasant. Having the honor and right of being a Japanese citizen, I want to live among fifty million Japanese fellow citizens and to maintain at least one-fifty-millionth of honor and righteousness.

Small wonder that Sōseki was delighted at the victory of Japan over Russia. At the end of the Russo-Japanese war, in his article "Trends in Post-War Literature," [18] August 1905, he writes:

Now we can have self-confidence. Admiral Nelson was a great man but Admiral Togo is even greater. People have been feeling that Japan was inferior to Europe in everything, and that Japan had to imitate Europe, that we should respect and devote ourselves to the cult of Europe. Now we have our self-confidence. Japan is Japan. Japan has her own history. The Japanese have their own characteristics. We should not devote ourselves simply to imitation of the West. Europe is not the only model. We can be a model too.

Sōseki's Religious Quest

Sōseki suggests through certain of his characters a profound inner sense of guilt. In a trilogy,[19] *Sanshiro*, 1908, *Thereupon*, 1909, and *Gate*, 1910, the protagonist, although the name is changed, is used to explore the consequences of insisting on the individual's right to pursue and win the woman he loves, even should it cause sorrow to others. Sōseki's answer to this exploration of individualism is a depressing one. A similar theme in the later work *Heart*,[20] 1914, culminates in the suicidal act of the character Sensei over unavoidable resulting guilt.

One may speculate whether Sōseki is not symbolically representing,

[17] *Bungaku-ron*, in *Collected Works* XI.
[18] "Sengo Bunkai no Susei," in *Collected Works* I.
[19] *Sanshiro*, in *Collected Works* V, 3–304; *Sorekara*, in *Collected Works* VI, 3–274; *Mon, ibid.*, 275–484.
[20] *Kokoro*, in *Collected Works* IX.

at least in the minds of his audience, the potential guilt that would
result from a commitment to any love that would cause an individual
to flout the moral directives of the traditional culture in which marriage was regarded as an obligation to family rather than as the solution to individual needs. In *Gate,* the third work of the trilogy, the
protagonist eventually takes away and marries the wife of his best
friend, but is unable to escape the dark, oppressive shadow of his own
conscience. Sōseki, using an actual experience of his own with Zen,
several years previous, makes the protagonist seek unsuccessfully a
religious solution to his problem. The protagonist knocks at a gate
that will not open; as Kafka later presented this problem, there was no
resolution for his continuing sense of being on trial. Some quotations
from *Gate* will serve as illustrations:

I have come to ask someone to open the door. The guardian of the gate remained within and never showed his face.

He heard the voice state, "Knocking will not do. Open for yourself and
come in." He racked his brain for a way, but could not find within himself
the means to muster sufficient power to open the door. . . .

. . . it seems that he was born to a fate of standing outside. . . .

He was not the one who could pass through the gate, nor was he one who
did not have the need to pass through. In short, he was an unfortunate who
had to stand beneath the gate waiting for the night to come. . . .

Walking in the dark night, he wished to free himself from his own helplessly
weak, restless, anxious, cowardly, niggardly, unstable mind. The pressure in
his chest forced him to look for some practical method of rescue and somehow find a way to disencumber himself from the oppression of his guilt and
error.

As he walked along, he repeated in his mouth the word, "religion." As he
sounded and repeated the word, it seemed to dissolve. For him, religion was
a vain word. Using it was like catching vapor with one's hand.

When Sōseki was still at the university, it was rather fashionable
among intellectuals, politicians, and army officers to practice Zen.
Sōseki had some friends who had been seriously interested in Zen
and through them Sōseki himself became involved. When he was
twenty-eight years old he made a trip to Matsushima, and passed in
front of a famous Zen temple, the residence of a renowned monk.
Sōseki thought of meeting him but for some reason he did not carry
out his wish. In December of the same year (1894) Sōseki, carrying a
letter of introduction from a friend, visited another well-known Zen
monk, Sōen, at the Enkakuji-temple in Kamakura. However, as described in *Gate,* Sōseki's actual experience of pounding at the door of
religion had brought forth no answer.

As is true for many dedicated Japanese intellectuals and for intellectuals elsewhere, the seductive appeal of finding comfort in a sense of spiritual belonging finds no easy reconciliation with rational integrity. For Sōseki, this suspension of his intellect or submission to any proscription against critical inquiry into dogma or belief was too great a price to pay for the consolation of religious nurturance and the seeking of a reunion of man's painfully isolated ego with a mystical sustaining life force. "As I believe in myself, I do not believe in God. Nothing is more valuable than myself in the entire universe. Those who do not consider themselves of value are slaves. Those who leave themselves and go to God are slaves to God." [21]

Seeking Intimacy and Personal Communion as an Answer to Alienation

Sōseki expresses in various places, somewhat arrogantly, a sense of disdain toward people generally as being weak and dependent— qualities he could not admit in himself. Eventually, never admitting such weaknesses of his own for long on any conscious level, he was nevertheless betrayed by his own body. In 1910 he developed a severe ulcer, which caused him recurrent difficulty and ultimately claimed his life in 1916, when he was forty-nine. Consciously, through self-control, he avoided the self-destruction that he sensed would occur with any loss of personal integrity. The ironic tragedy of his life is his inability to master a strongly felt continuing sense of deprivation, which he finally experienced in full agony on a visceral level. In his later novels, written after the first development of his ulcer, one can relate chronologically the more severe attacks to periods during which he was actively engaged in writing novels dissecting the essential coldness and lack of giving that is found in human relationships. In the earlier of these works the burden of blame and the experience of hostility was more directed toward his female characters, but gradually the emphasis shifts toward a sense of mutual incapacity.

However, the resolution in some of these novels was that the hero, the man, saw the necessity to develop self-reliance and an ability to maintain himself in isolation. In writing Reminiscences[22] shortly after he had sufficiently recovered from his first ulcerative attack, he was preoccupied with the necessity to face death and to understand it. Secondly, almost in a surprised vein, he conveyed his experience of the warmth certain of his acquaintances and friends expressed toward him in their concern about his illness. He stated:

---

[21] *Notes* (1906), in *Collected Works* I.
[22] *Omoidasu-koto-nado* (1910), in *Collected Works* XIII.

Having spit blood, I was like a defeated wrestler. Without speaking of my complete lack of courage to fight for my life, I did not even have the consciousness that unless I fought I would die. Lying on my back, managing to breathe weakly, I saw fearsome society in the distance. My illness surrounded my bed like a folding screen and made my cold heart warm.

Previously, even my maid did not show up unless I clapped my hands. I could get nothing done unless I asked people. Things did not go smoothly, however impatient I might have been. However, with my illness, things suddenly changed completely. I was lying down in bed. I did nothing but lie prone. And yet a doctor came. My wife came. Even two nurses came. Everybody came before I had to mobilize my will. Things happened of themselves. "Don't worry but take good care of yourself," a telegraph came from Manchuria the day after I first spit blood. Unexpectedly friends and acquaintances came to my bedside. . . .

. . . lying in bed, looking at the ceiling, I am caused to think that somehow most people in this world have a stronger sense of kindness than I have. In this world that I felt to be most discomforting, I suddenly feel a warm breeze.

After such experience of people's positive attitudes toward him, Sōseki seemed changed in his overt behavior also. In *Reminiscence of Sōseki*,[23] his wife writes: "After this illness, he lost his previous nervous and irritated quality. He became gentle and warm. I thought some drastic change had taken place in his mind."

Contrary to that of many artists, Sōseki's marital career is singularly devoid of any suggestion of extramarital affairs or involvements to any degree with women other than his wife. As indicated before, Sōseki dreaded loss of self-control or behavior that would be visible to others as reprehensible in any way. This may have been instrumental in his lack of involvement with other women—although the relationship with his wife was, throughout, one of battle to see who would give in. Many of the descriptions in his books show the protagonist maintaining a façade of cold aloofness, which was frustrating to both members of the marriage. There are suggestions that he himself recognized the vulnerability of his position and the fact that underlying this aloofness and ungiving attitude toward the wife was a tremendous unresolved need for dependence on her and vulnerability in regard to it.

We may quote from the novel *Grass Along the Road*[24] certain passages illustrating these attitudes; in one part of the novel, Kenzō (the hero), had come down with flu and stayed in bed for several days with a high fever, almost unconscious.

When he came back to himself, he looked at the ceiling as if nothing had happened to him. Then he saw his wife sitting beside his pillow. He suddenly

---

[23] Natsume, *Sōseki no Omoide* (1929).

[24] *Michikusa* (1915), in *Collected Works* V.

recalled that he had been taken care of by her. However, he did not say anything and turned his face away from her. Therefore, his own feelings about the matter never reached his wife's awareness.

He describes clearly his own version of the battle of the sexes:

She is a *shibutoi* ("stubborn") woman. Such words were printed deep in Kenzō's mind, as if they were the sum total of all her characteristics. He had to forget all other things. An idea that she was *shibutoi* became the focus of attention. He threw upon these words the light of hate as strong as possible, keeping the rest of the place in darkness. His wife accepted such hate as silently as would a snake or fish. Accordingly, in the eyes of others, his wife always appeared to be noble in demeanor, while he had to be considered as crazed and an individual given to violent expressions of outrage. The light in his wife's eyes occasionally said to him, "If you treat me so coldly, I'll develop a hysterical fit." For some reason, Kenzō was very much afraid of this message, at the same time hating it with tremendous intensity. Attempting silently to pray for calmness, he showed overtly an attitude of unconcern over his wife's behavior. His wife knew quite well that somewhere in this overtly unyielding attitude was a spot of weakness. "I don't care. I am going to die in delivery anyway," she said to herself in a low voice, knowing full well that her whispers to herself were reaching his ears. He wished in retaliation that he could shout, "Go ahead and die!"

In this passage, we see the feeling of mutual withholding, with foreknowledge that the other was expecting something that was not to be forthcoming. Also in this passage we see that he may have had wishes to get rid of his wife, that he could not express them overtly owing to his deeper knowledge that he really needed her and could not give up seeking from her what he never seemed to find to his satisfaction.

From the very beginning, his wife had basically refused to play the traditional role. For instance, lonely in London, Sōseki wanted to receive more letters from home. However, his wife was not a good correspondent. In his letter to his wife, February 20, 1902, he wrote:

It has been more than a half a year already since I left Japan. I am getting a little tired of my life here and wish to go home. You have written me only twice and I have no way of knowing how things are going with you. I hope everything is well. I suppose I shall receive at least a telegram if you or our child dies. Therefore, I decided not to worry as long as I do not receive any news. However, I feel terribly lonely.

She was given at the first of their marriage to hysterical attacks, even to the point of developing what is described in nineteenth-century literature as a *hysterical arc*, where the body becomes arched and rigid. She refused to provide in any easy fashion the sort of nurturant care he somehow expected, and even after the development of his ulcer, she went to great pains at times to talk to him about matters that were obviously disturbing to him so that he would ask her not to bring up such subjects. There was a continual testing out of the limits, of trying to force the other to give. There is some indication that in the beginning of the marriage Sōseki was more willing to extend himself and that with the wife's hysterical rejection of the role of wife and with the continued obstinacy she was covertly and overtly expressing she wore him down so he eventually went into a long-term battle against her.

Nevertheless, Sōseki realized within himself the kind of coldness that was involved in his contribution to the problem. He says in one other part of *Grass Along the Road*:

Kenzō thought it was her coldness, which she should not have as a wife. His wife, in turn, cast the same blame on him in her own mind. According to her logic, the more he spent his time in his study, the less communication they had, except on matters of formal importance. As the natural outcome of such circumstances, she left Kenzō alone in his study and spent her time with her children. The children themselves rarely entered the study. When they did, they were perceived quickly by Kenzō as doing something mischievous and were scolded. Although he scolded his children quickly in this manner, he also felt a kind of loneliness because they did not approach him.

The essential ambivalence toward his wife in which there is both compassion and continual feelings of hostility is illustrated in Kenzō's description of the pregnant wife. Seeing the pregnant wife lying on the tatami taking a nap, he muses:

She used to stay up until late at night. When he nagged her, she would say that she was wakeful and could not sleep. She stayed up as late as she wished, continually sewing. Of necessity, then, she would have to take naps during the day. He hated this attitude in her. At the same time, he was afraid of her *hysteria*. He was caught by an anxiety that his interpretation of her behavior might be wrong.

He stood there for a while and watched her sleeping face. Her profile lying against her elbow was pale. Standing silently, he could not even call her name. Casting his glance again upon her pale forehead, he saw her sunken cheeks. One of his relatives, upon a recent visit, had been surprised to see his wife's thin face and said to her, "How thin you've become!" Kenzō somehow felt as if he had been the only reason for his wife's pale, thin appearance.

She remained immobile. Pressed against the tatami with her large abdomen, she looked as if she would not mind being beaten or kicked. She had been reticent to speak and came to keep silence more and more, simply watching her husband with a calm stare. He in turn became irritated by her silence.

His wife's hysterical fits were the source of great anxiety for him. Nevertheless, there came to be what might be described as a cloud of benevolence floating above his anxious thoughts. Rather than simply anxiety, he came also to feel pity for his wife. Succumbing to this view of her as a weak, pitiful being, he somehow tried to flatter and please her. At times she appeared pleased at this.

One night, he suddenly woke up and saw his wife, who was looking at the ceiling with her eyes wide open. In her hand was a razor he had brought back from Europe. She had not pulled out the blade, which was folded into the ebony sheath, but was grasping the black handle. Thus, the cold light of the blade did not strike his eyes. But he was frightened just the same. He raised his body and suddenly tore the razor out of her hand. "Don't be a fool!" He threw the razor, which hit the glass pane in the *shoji* ("sliding door"), broke through, and fell down in the corridor beyond. His wife did not utter a word, but remained absentminded like a dreaming person. . . . "Has she really an emotional reason to try to kill herself? Is she just fooling with the knife in a distracted way, losing her presence of mind under the spell of her illness? Does she simply want to shock him, only because she wishes somehow to defeat him? Why on earth does she want to shock him? Does she want to change her husband into a calm and kind man? Or is she driven by a foolish wish to conquer?" In bed, Kenzō thought of five or six different interpretations. Occasionally he turned his wakeful eyes toward his wife to discover what she might be doing. She did not move and he was not at all sure if she were asleep or awake. She looked almost as if she were pretending to be dead. Lying in bed, Kenzō returned to his attempt to solve this problem of the knife. The solution of the problem was much more important for him than giving lectures at school, in terms of its influence upon his actual life. His basic attitude toward his wife could be determined in accord with the solution. In the past, a more simple time for him than now, he simple-mindedly believed that his wife's strange behavior was due to her illness. At that time, during each fit he knelt in front of her with the sincerity of a man who confessed himself in front of God. He believed that his was the kindest and noblest treatment a husband ever could give to his wife. "Even now, if I could find the cause of her behavior. . . ." Such a benevolent feeling filled his mind, but unfortunately, the cause did not seem to be so simple as it used to be. He had to continue thinking. Being tired from attacking an insoluble problem, he fell asleep. When he woke up he had to go give his lectures. He never had a chance to talk with his wife about the previous night. His wife looked as if she had forgotten it all.

In the relationship between the two of them, it seemed that they could tolerate only a certain amount of giving. This is often the situation in Japan, with the excuse of illness—that is, somehow both had to be ill in order to receive what they were attempting to get from one another. He describes also how, after a serious fight and a great deal of acrimony, suddenly they seemed to be united by mutual sexual attraction, and their conflict would end in an embrace. His reaction to this was to feel somehow debased by his own weaker human nature and by being overcome by his physical impulses to succumb and give way from a position that he was seeking to maintain against his wife.

The reason Sōseki's heroes fail tragically in autonomy is that they fail in relationships. They don't fail in themselves or in their attitudes or statements about freeing themselves from the pressures of society, of parents, and of heaven; but failure occurs in relationships, in being able to express in communion with others the feeling that one contains within oneself. Sōseki had a feeling that he was compassionate, that he understood human nature. Yet, what he depicts in the interpersonal heterosexual relationships of his heroes is a failure at intimacy—in relating to another person, especially in marriage. His sense of alienation, therefore, was not so much based on feeling within himself a lack of capacity as on the lack of ability to relate this capacity meaningfully and satisfactorily in his heterosexual relationship with his own wife. He stated in his *Notes,* 1906:[25] "Progress in everything, in knowledge, science, and all kinds of things, tends to make distance in parent-child relationships, teacher-disciple relationships; it tends to split husband and wife and makes friendship based less on mutual liking."

Another quote from *Thereupon:*[26] "The present society is after all an aggregate of isolated individuals. Nature binds the earth together, but when houses are built on it, it becomes discontinuous. People in houses are also unrelated. Civilization makes us all alone." In a lecture entitled "My Individualism," given in 1914, he said: "Stated more easily, 'individualism' is an *ism,* which, without clannishness, simply judges right from wrong. It teaches no party loyalty, nor does it by forming a clique or group move the adherent blindly toward power and wealth. It comprises a loneliness unknown to many. Not forming a group with others, I must go my own way alone." In *Heart,*[27] he says: "We are born in the present time, filled with liberty, independence, and self. But as the price we have to pay for it, we must feel loneliness."

AKUTAGAWA RYŪNOSUKE (1892–1927)— ESTHETICISM AND SUICIDE

An examination of the alienation experience and its resolution in the case of Akutagawa Ryūnosuke is in some respects less complex and less focused than that of Sōseki. Furthermore, we have less actual knowledge of his personal life, since Akutagawa was in many ways less self-revealing in writings than either Sōseki or Dazai. What he does reveal indicates a focus of concern within himself on his attempt to give life meaning through being an esthete. Failing to solve his personal problems, he committed suicide when he was thirty-five years old.

---

[25] In *Collected Works* I.
[26] *Sorekara,* in *Collected Works* VI.
[27] *Kokoro,* in *Collected Works* IX.

Akutagawa as a Japanese

Akutagawa represents one form of political and social escapism prevailing among intellectuals in the late Taisho period. Akutagawa, unlike Sōseki, never had any direct confrontation with Western culture through travel. He was enamored of Western literature at a distance. French, German, and Russian authors, especially Baudelaire and the "fin de siècle" poets strongly influenced his thinking about esthetics. Akutagawa did not find any necessity to define himself as a Japanese in any self-conscious way. He accepted without self-questioning the Shitamachi urban culture of Tokyo, which had developed a generation later than Sōseki's. While there was a considerable continuity with the past, the spirit of Taisho youth of his day contained little of the exuberant sense of national growth so prevalent in the Meiji period.

Taisho, on the surface, was a period of political liberalism, although portents of the future militarist coup were felt by the discerning. In intellectual circles an earlier interest in Christian socialism had been replaced by a variety of ideological positions based more directly on Marxian philosophy. Many of Akutagawa's intellectual contemporaries felt deeply stirred by the possibilities of the Russian revolution and believed that it was the duty of any author to espouse in his work the cause of social and economic justice.

Akutagawa did not feel sufficiently impelled by any such political spirit to become involved in political movements. In keeping with his general personality, he isolated himself from such activities and sought refuge in esthetics as represented by the traditional themes of a now esoteric age. Although influenced by Western writings, he used as content for his work ancient stories and documents—for instance those of the *Konjaku Monogatari* (New and Old Stories), a thirty-one-volume series of ancient Indian, Chinese, and Japanese folk stories and legends, compiled in the twelfth or thirteenth century. Stung by the accusations of some of his peers concerning his escapism, he tried at one point to write more modern stories, but concluded he did not feel they were as satisfying to him as his previous tales drawn from older, more remote themes.

Politically, he did not become involved. Socially, he remained a traditionalist, giving firm adherence to the multiple formal obligations of his prescribed role within the Japanese family system.

Family Relationships and Personal Alienation

It seems probable that at the time of his birth (1892) or shortly thereafter, the author's mother suffered what now would be termed a postpartum psychosis, from which she never recovered. In his late work of reminiscence about his departed parents and a sister, *Necrology*, written in 1926,[28] he describes how his mother appeared to him.

My mother was insane. I never felt close to her as a mother. She was always sitting alone in her home with a particular hairdo called *kushi-maki*, smoking a long thin pipe. Her face was small as was her body. For some reason, I still recall her gray face, without the color of life. I have no memory of receiving any care from my mother. One time my foster mother and I took the trouble of going to the second floor to greet her. I remember how she suddenly hit me on the head with her long pipe. However, generally my mother was a very quiet psychotic. When my elder sister and I pressed her to draw for us she would sketch on a small piece of paper. She was not limited to ink drawings. Using my sister's water colors, she would draw us pictures of colorfully dressed women and children on outings or sketches of blossoming flowers. However, the people in the pictures always had the face of foxes.[29]

The quotation above is almost all the author has to say about his mother in his writings.

His biographers record that at eleven months he was adopted by Akutagawa Michiaki, his mother's elder brother. From childhood Akutagawa had continued contact with his actual parents as well as with those who adopted him. In *Necrology*[30] he writes that his real father was successfully engaged in a dairy business. When he visited him, his father used to serve him rare fruit such as bananas or pineapple, and ice cream, all of which were indeed unusual at this time in Japan.

My father used to give me rare treats and thereby tried to seduce me back from my foster parents. I still remember one night when my father, giving me some ice cream, tried to persuade me to run away from home to join him. Unfortunately for him, such temptations were never successful because I loved my foster parents, especially my aunt.[31]

In the same work he also talks about his actual father's quick temper.

My father was quick tempered and he had frequent fights with people. When I was in the ninth grade, I did *sumo* with him, I threw him down by a favorite technique called *soto-gari*. My father stood up quickly and dashed to me saying, "Let's try again." I threw him again very easily. A third time he challenged me, saying, "Let's try again." His face was convulsed with rage.

---

[28] *Tenkibō* (1926), in Akutagawa Ryūnosuke, *Collected Works* (10 vols., 1934–35) V, 177–188.

[29] It is to be noted that fox possession was a traditional explanation for insanity in Japan. Akutagawa's mother may have been attempting to communicate something about herself by drawing all her humans with the heads of foxes.

[30] *Tenkibō*, in *Collected Works* V.

[31] By "aunt" the author probably meant here a spinster sister of his mother who lived with her brother all her life and had a close relationship with the author.

My aunt, who was my mother's youngest sister and became my father's second wife, was observing us wrestling, and signaled to me with her eyes. As I wrestled with my father this time, I purposely fell down on my back. If I had not let myself be bested, my father must surely have challenged me again and again.

In spite of this passage describing his wrestling activities, Akutagawa saw himself from earliest childhood as delicate and sickly. He was deeply conscious of physical frailty. His constant proneness to physical ailments must be considered of some importance to an understanding of his frequently expressed, somewhat envious feeling about animal vitality.

Also, in understanding the nameless fears leading to his final suicidal act, one may not overlook what he considered to be the hereditary taint of psychosis, which he thought he might have received through his psychotic mother. He expressed his dislike of being the child of his parents, as well as his concern with tainted heredity. In a collection of his essays, *Words of a Dwarf*,[32] he writes:

The first act of the human tragedy starts when an individual becomes the child of certain parents. Heredity, environment, and chance—after all, it is these three factors that control our fate. If one wants to rejoice over these in his own good fortune he may do so, but he should not presume that others are all so inclined.

The author remained a dutiful son to his foster parents, and in the later part of his life he was their chief financial support. During childhood he was closest to an unmarried aunt who was responsible for his rearing, and who spent more time with him than his official foster mother. In spite of his readiness to assume family responsibilities, there is little to indicate any personal warmth toward either of his foster parents.

Toward his maiden aunt his feelings seemed characterized by a strong ambivalence. In his autobiographical work entitled *Life of a Fool*,[33] written in 1927, he writes, "He felt the strongest love toward his aunt. She had remained unmarried all her life, and when he was twenty years old she was already nearly sixty." And yet he wrote to his friend, Satō Haruo, a poet and a novelist, cryptically, without explanation, concerning his aunt. "She was the person who made my life the most unhappy. Nevertheless, it was she only to whom I owed my existence."

Although remaining formally filial toward his foster parents, the author felt a deep isolation. He wrote to his friend in 1913, "I think I am all alone in the world. I think that even the bond afforded by

[32] *Shūju no Kotoba* (1927), in *Collected Works* VI, 57–154.
[33] *Aru Aho no Isshō*, in *Collected Works* V, 549–586.

relatives may turn out to be unexpectedly weak when there are conflicts of interest. After all, it may be that we live in order to be disappointed."

Describing his early contacts and acquaintances in high school he continually stresses his isolation from others. In one of his late works, *The Young Life of Daidōji Shinsuke*,[34] he describes an attitude of careful selectivity. His strong association of love and hatred is also well expressed:

In making friends Shinsuke could not avoid considering relative talents and capacities. Even if he were not concerned by some youth's lack of gentlemanly qualities, should he be without intellectual acquisitiveness, he would treat him as a passer-by. His requirements did not include tenderness of feeling or youthful affection. He had actual dread of having a so-called intimate friendship. Instead, he required his acquaintances to have brains— he loved a sturdy intellect more than handsome manners. At the same time he could hate the possessor of intellectual prowess with much more intensity than he could muster toward someone simply well endowed with virtue. In reality, his friendship was always a passion that, at least to some degree, involved hatred impregnated with love.

Already in his youth, Akutagawa showed the feelings of self-repulsion, withdrawal, and a sense of lacking the inner strength necessary to relate himself freely to others. When he was in his early twenties, he wrote to his friends:

My environment is ugly. I am ugly. It is very painful to live. If this whole thing is god's creation, god's creation is a big joke. I hate it.

It is very unpleasant to reflect on oneself and find emptiness. I feel so disgusted that I want to cover my eyes. There is nothing I can do about it. Unless you discover if the barrel is empty or not, you cannot possibly fill it with wine.

People talk about self-assertion. They say they assert themselves so easily. I may not be too withdrawn but I like to watch myself first, before trying any self-assertion.

When I see people who keep asserting their ugly selves, I feel both hate and disgust, as well as feeling overwhelmed.

Describing his sense of alienation from people (from *The Young Life of Daidōji Shinsuke*): "The people walking along the street were strangers to him. In order to understand such people, in order to know their love, their hate, their vanity, the only thing he could do was to read books. Books, especially novels and dramas produced in Europe at the turn of the century."

In 1915, when he was twenty-three, Akutagawa experienced his first

---

[34] *Daidōji Shinsuke no Hanshō* (1925), in *Collected Works* V, 1–26.

love toward a woman. Their marriage, however, was never consummated owing to the disapproval, for some unstated reason, of his foster parents. There are few instances in his writings of any vivid expression of feeling toward women including the wife with whom he was later married by arrangement. These are a few somewhat vague passages showing a man reaching out toward his wife, coupled, however, with indications of a basic lack of ability to communicate. In *Life of a Fool*,[35] one finds:

On the day following their wedding, he told his wife to be more careful about spending money. It was not his own complaint, but a matter about which his foster-mother had told him to caution his wife. His wife apologized to him and his foster mother in front of a potted jonquil, which she had bought for him.

Night was coming again. The stormy sea kept splashing in the dusk. Under such a sky he married his wife for the second time. It was their happiness and at the same time their suffering. Their three children were looking at the lightning flashing over the distant sea. His wife, carrying one child, seemed trying hard not to cry. "You see the boat over there?" "Yes, I do." "A boat whose mast is broken in half. . . ."

In the figurative phrase "married his wife for the second time" the author implies that the protagonist achieves a closer relationship to his wife and children on some rare occasion when they were away from outside family.

Otherwise, his wife remains a dim figure, considerably younger than Akutagawa by about eight years. One gets no impression as to whether she offered him any genuine companionship or not.

There is evidence that Akutagawa carried on several sexual affairs with other women. Only one of these relationships appeared to have any strong emotional influence on him; it caused him to write what might be considered love poetry manifesting a sense of involvement. In *Life of a Fool* we find the author describing his relationship with this particular woman in fragmentary passages:

Dusk was coming to the park. He sensed in himself a slight fever, as he walked across the park. He stopped on the sidewalk and decided to wait for her to come. After about five minutes she walked up to him, looking tired. Looking at his face, she said, "I am tired," and smiled. Shoulder to shoulder, they walked across the dusk-shrouded park. It was for them the first time. He felt that he would give up anything in order to be with her. After they mounted the conveyance, she watched his face and asked him, "Will you not have any regrets?" He answered decisively, "No, I shan't." Holding his hand, she said, "Although I will never have any. . . ." Her face at this moment looked as if it were in moonlight.

---

[35] *Shūju no Kotoba,* in **Collected Works VI.**

"Do I love this woman?" he asked himself. The answer came back unexpectedly, even though he was accustomed to self-observation. "Yes, I still love her."

The country road smelled of cow's dung in the sunshine. Wiping away sweat from his face, he walked up a hill. The ripened wheat from both sides of the road sent forth its fragrance. "Kill him, kill him. . . ." He found himself repeating these words in his mouth. Kill whom? It was obvious to him. He was recalling a hound of a man with short hair.

Escape into Esthetics

To give some meaning to what he considered the pain of living, Akutagawa had turned early to esthetic creativity. He made his debut into the literary world with his short story *Nose,* to which Natsume Sōseki[36] gave an accolade of supportive praise. He was twenty-four years old and was still a matriculating student at the University of Tokyo. After this auspicious event, his career as a writer was progressively more and more successful.

As we mentioned earlier, Akutagawa's attitude as a writer was basically esthetic without the ethical considerations central to Sōseki. Selecting themes from sources distant in time and place, self-consciously practicing different styles appropriate to each story, the author wove beautiful, though often somewhat too artificial, brocaded works of literature.

Looking back on the time when he wrote his first short stories, the author himself admitted his essentially escapist orientation as a writer. In *About Me at That Time,*[37] 1919, he says:

The short stories I wrote at the time were "Hana" and "Rashomon." I had been deeply concerned with the problem of love for the preceding half year and feeling depressed whenever alone. Therefore, I had wished to write stories as joyful as possible, keeping away from my own reality as much as

---

[36] *Hana* (1917). Akutagawa recognized himself to be beholden to Natsume Sōseki as a disciple. He met Sōseki first in December 1915 through a friend. In his essay of reminiscences, *Ano Koro no Jibun no Koto* (About Me at That Time), written in 1919 (*Collected Works* II, 253–284), Akutagawa writes an impression of Sōseki: "When I visited him for the first time, I was completely tense and nervous. I have not yet completely recovered from such *seishin koka-sho* [words coined by the author, literally meaning "mental rigidification," describing his state of nervous tension]. I visited him a few times and felt afraid that I would be hypnotized. I had a strange feeling that when I published my work if Mr. Natsume were to say it was not good I might believe that it was worthless, even though in actuality it was excellent. It might be called the magnetism of his personality."

At Sōseki's death, Akutagawa wrote to a friend, in December 1916, "I have never experienced such sadness in my life. He was the person who first recognized the worth of what I wrote. It was he who constantly encouraged and guided me. I feel everything has become desolate now."

[37] *Ibid.*

possible. I took materials from *Konjaku Monogatari* and refabricated these stories.

It is noteworthy that even in the writings that he tried to make "as joyful as possible," we very often find coming through the author's basic pessimism and distrust about human nature. For instance, in *Rashomon*,[38] a jobless young man who had been working for nobility in Kyoto, which had been rendered desolate by wars and plague, finds himself at the Rashōmon, a main gate of Kyoto city in the fourteenth century. He is penniless and hungry, not knowing where to go or what to do to survive. In the shadows of the Rashōmon, the young man finds an old frightful apparition of a woman pulling hair from the bodies of those who died there from hunger and epidemic. The young man righteously accuses the old woman of "inhumanity." The old woman says that she wants to remain alive and for that purpose is now collecting the hair from the dead and selling it to a wig-maker. It is the only possible way for her to earn any money. She sneers at the young man's softheartedness and sentimentalism. After listening to her taunts, he suddenly stands up, grabs her, strips her of her clothes and money. He leaves the half-naked old woman sobbing, telling her that he too wants to remain alive. The author's concept of the basic selfishness of humans and their capacity for coldness is clearly reflected in this story. The short story *Within the Grove*[39] also expresses the author's basic negative themes that human beings are untrustworthy, that they want only to justify themselves, and that listening to each person's version of reality leaves one in doubt about the nature of truth.

And yet, it seems that writing such stories did provide the author, at least for a while, with the means of escape into his own world of esthetic standards. In *Life of a Fool*,[40] the author describes his wish for escape through esthetics as treacherously similar to the legend of Daedelus and Icarus:

For him, twenty-nine years of age, life was no longer right at all. However, authors such as Voltaire provided him with artificial wings. Spreading these artificial appendages, he easily flew up into the air. At the same time, under the bright light of intelligence and reason, all the joys and sorrows of human life started fading far below his eyes. Casting ironic smiles upon the miserable dwellings below he soared through the sky directly up toward the sun without hindrance, as if he had forgotten about the ancient Greek whose artificial

---

[38] Not the story depicted in the recent film *Rashomon*, which is mainly taken from another short tale by Akutagawa entitled *Within the Grove, Yabu no Naka* (1922), in *Collected Works* III, 559–578 (English translation by Kojima in *Roshōmon and Other Stories*, 1952).

[39] *Ibid.*

[40] *Aru Aho no Isshō*, in *Collected Works* V.

wings were melted from him by the sun's heat, plunging him to his death in the ocean below.

He was walking along the paved street in the rain. It was raining hard. Suddenly he saw in front of him a broken high voltage wire shooting off purple sparks. He felt a strange excitement in himself. Still walking in the rain he turned around and looked back at the wire, which was still shooting off the fierce sparks. He examined his own life. There was nothing which he especially wished to obtain. He had no desire for any of the things he found around him. However, he still wanted to get hold of this purple spark, this fierce flower of fire in the air, even if he had to trade for it his own life.

There was nothing in his actual life equivalent to the sparks he wanted to hold in his own hands. Nor could he for long fabricate a vital energy through his writings. He was not too different after all from Icarus. His own artificial wings of estheticism failed to carry him to safety. His esthetic transports were not made with wings truly vitalized with blood from within his own being. He could not sustain himself. Like Sōseki's, his body betrayed some symptoms of a debilitating insufficiency.

His health became especially bad after a trip to China in 1921. He started suffering seriously from piles and what was termed "neurasthenia" by others—mostly insomnia, but also periodically severe stomach cramps, diarrhea, and palpitations of the heart.

Meanwhile, from 1920 on, the leftist movement became more and more active in Japan, and these political and ideological tendencies among intellectuals were generally reflected in the literary world. Many literary critics and writers joined leftist organizations, and they gave to Akutagawa the label of "bourgeois writer." He could not remain indifferent to these taunts, but felt inordinantly uncomfortable. In July 1923, a well-known author, Arishima Takeo, committed double suicide with a woman who was a reporter for a popular magazine. Akutagawa seems to have been much shocked by this incident. By 1924 he had attempted to change his attitude toward "escapist literature." He tried to express his feelings toward the people around him. He tried hard to describe human beings rather than creating in his work an artificial beauty of mood and scene. However, he was not very successful in this endeavor. Some critics pointed out that the author's approach to human problems seemed "too cold" and "too intellectual." For example, Sato Haruo,[41] a novelist, commenting on one of Akutagawa's works at this time, stated:

The protagonist of the story looks upon life as would a person from Mars. His head is excessively and abnormally developed and his hands and legs are as thin as needles. Mr. Akutagawa is wearing armor which would become someone from the red planet. The other day a friend advised Mr. Akutagawa

---

[41] In Fukuda, *Akutagawa Ryūnosuke Kenkyu* (1957), p. 103.

to take off his armor. However, he refused. As long as the armor, rather than his own spontaneous self, guarantees him better freedom, he may very well have good reason to remain attached to its use. Although this is simply my guess, it is possible that Mr. Akutagawa considers life as a battle field for defending pride. There is no reason why a man should not entertain such a view of life, but it is certainly not the kind of view of life I have.

It was often pointed out that Akutagawa was not directly facing himself, but was avoiding any direct perception of himself on the basis of his experience of life as painful suffering. Akutagawa was, in the opinion of many people, a sensitive man, and therefore vulnerable to criticism. He realized that in attempting to meet his critics' complaints, he was not being very successful in changing the content, style, or viewpoint of his works. He used to confide to close friends that he was well aware that he was not making any progress in his work as an artist, and to admit that he was suffering because of this. His health kept declining and in his depressed moods he often spoke of death.

Also, certain incidents involving his family disturbed him greatly. For instance, in December of 1924 an uncle toward whom he seemed to have felt some attachment came down with tuberculosis. A marriage arrangement for which he had been responsible was broken and he had to take care of the divorce proceedings. In 1925 he was mistakenly accused of monopolizing the royalties on a joint book he had edited, which actually had not sold well enough to produce any royalty. In February 1925, Akutagawa wrote to a childhood acquaintance: "I am suffering from a bad stomach, indigestion, neurasthenia. I am living with everything sick. I do not think living in this world is pleasant. But on the other hand I think departing from this world is not pleasant either."

Fear of Insanity and Suicide

As we mentioned, there are numerous indications that Akutagawa entertained deep fears of hereditary insanity. His famous novel *Kappa*,[42] which shortly preceded his death, was presented as the writings of a man considered insane and imprisoned in a mental hospital. In addition, there are passages in other works written at this time that are directly suggestive of his fears for his sanity.

There is also considerable evidence that in the last two years of his life he had developed some of the precursory hallucinatory symptoms of schizophrenic withdrawal. He reported in his diary as well as in his last writings that he was subject to visual distortions, such as the impression that walls leaned oppressively toward him, and other distortions in perspective that would not leave him in spite of his attempts

---

[42] (1927), in *Collected Works* V, 269–356. English translation, *Kappa*, 1947.

to make them go away. One of his last works, *Mirage*[43] describes illusions experienced by the author, who was continually taking large doses of sleeping pills during this period. On June 11, 1926, he wrote to a friend, a well-known poet who had had psychiatric training: "Recently when I was about to wake up, various friends of mine whose faces were disproportionately large and whose bodies were as small as beans, wearing armor, ran toward the bridge of my nose, between my eyes from various directions, mostly laughing. I was very frightened."

In his personal diary he wrote:

Among some pine trees I discovered a white house in the Western style. The house looked distorted. I thought it was because of my eyes. However, although I looked at the house many times, I still could not do away with this visual distortion. I felt very frightened.

I was taking a walk along a path among pine trees where no one else could see. In front of me a white dog was walking, wagging his tail. I saw the dog's testicles, and the pinkish color made me feel cold. When it came to the corner for the turn of the path, the dog suddenly turned toward me, and I was sure that he smiled.

In October 1926, preceding his suicide, he wrote to his friend:

Something is really wrong with my brain. For ten or fifteen minutes in the morning after I wake up I can remain all right. However, afterwards any trifling matter, such as a maid's failure to do some work, throws me into a depression. When I think of the number of stories I have to write for the January issues of the magazines, I suddenly feel unable to bear up. When I go to Tokyo I would like to receive some psychiatric diagnosis, but somehow I don't have the opportunity.

In November, he wrote his friend, the poet-psychiatrist:

My stomach is a little better, but my nerves are as bad as usual. The other evening I suddenly saw my mother who had been dead. I was so surprised that I had to hold onto another person's arm who was walking with me. When I see a sign such as *No Trespassing,* I feel that it has been put there especially to block my way in life.

He felt that this sign had special personal symbolic meanings for him —a kind of experience not uncommon in early schizophrenia.

After his death, his wife remarked, "Even when he was sleeping in the middle of a room, he would suddenly feel that the four walls were about to collapse on him. Once when I went out on an errand, I returned to find him violently trembling with fright."

In addition, reality treated him harshly. In early 1927 his brother-in-law's house was burned down. The brother-in-law had been heavily in

---

[43] *Shinkirō* (1927).

debt and had recently taken out an insurance policy, and for these reasons he was suspected of having set fire to his own house. Soon after this, the brother-in-law committed suicide, and Akutagawa had to take care of both the debt and the bereaved. Then his close friend, the novelist Uno Koji, became insane, which was frightening news to Akutagawa. In his last works, published after his death, we gain the direct impression that he was subject to more and more hallucinatory experiences.

The following are quotations from *Gears*,[44] published after the author's death.

In this threatening world, I live pale and helpless, chewing the cud of my own secret suffering. In the back of my right eye, *haguruma* ("gears") are constantly rotating. They gradually increase their numbers until they block a good half of my perceptual field.

Trees along a path in a park and their blackish branches and leaves. Every tree has a back and a front like a human being. These trees almost frightened me. I recalled the hell described by Dante, in which souls were transformed into trees. I decided to walk along the other side of the street where there were no trees.

The sky which had been clear most of the day became clouded over. I suddenly felt that somebody was entertaining some hostility toward me and I decided to hide myself in a cafe.

On a sandy hill a pole for a swing, with the swing missing, was standing alone. When I looked at the pole, I suddenly thought of a guillotine. Actually there were a few crows perched on the pole. They all looked at me but did not fly away. In addition, the crow in the middle raised its big beak toward the sky and uttered a cry four times.

Somebody or something was being aimed at me and I became more and more anxious as I walked along. Then, semi-transparent *haguruma* started blocking off my eyesight. As they increased in number, they rotated faster. I felt my heart beating faster. I wanted to stop short on the road, but I could not, as if I were being pushed by somebody.

For two years before his actual death, Akutagawa Ryūnosuke thought seriously of suicide, spending much thought on the method and place. Quoting from *Notes to an Old Friend*,[45] supposedly written immediately before his death:

. . . for the past two years, I have been thinking about nothing but death . . . pressed by such an impulse to die, any sympathy felt toward my family would mean nothing. This might cause you to use the word "inhuman" to

[44] *Haguruma* (1927), in *Collected Works* V, 471–528.
[45] *Aru-Kyū-yu e Okuru Shūki*, in *Collected Works* V, 587–594.

describe my feelings. If you want to use the word, I must admit that in this one sense I am very "inhuman." . . .

The first thing I thought of was how I would be able to die without suffering too much. Committing suicide by hanging oneself is certainly the best way for such a purpose. However, when I visualized myself dead from hanging, I felt an esthetic disgust. As for death by drowning, it was out of the question, as I swim too well. Even if I were able to drown myself, the suffering involved would be greater than that in hanging. The idea of throwing myself in front of a dashing locomotive also was disgusting from an esthetic standpoint. Any attempt to kill myself by using a revolver or a knife would involve a strong possibility of failure because my hand would tremble. Jumping from the top of a building also appears terrifying. For these reasons, I decided to kill myself by taking drugs. Death by drugs may be more painful than hanging; however, dying by taking drugs not only does not suggest any esthetic disgust, but also promises less danger of recovery.

. . . then what I thought of next was the place for my suicide. After my death my family would have to depend on the property I would leave behind. I thought of the possibility that my family would find it difficult to sell the house if I were to kill myself in it. I felt envious of a bourgeois who can afford to own an extra house or villa in which he can commit suicide.

In contemplating his own death it seemed to the author somehow apt that it should occur as a double suicide with a woman, which is not uncommon in Japan. He selected a woman whose choice he felt would be somewhat ironic; he told his close friend, Koyama Ryūichi, that "since she was a woman with very small breasts, no one would think that our joint suicide had any direct sexual meaning." In *Life of a Fool*,[46] published after his death, the author writes about the woman:

She had a shining face. It was like the morning sun throwing its light on thin ice. He had a positive feeling toward her. However, it was not love. He had never touched her body even with his fingers. "I have heard that you want to die. Is that right?" "Yes. Well, no. Rather than wishing to die, I am tired of being alive." After holding such conversation, they promised each other to die together. "Platonic suicide, isn't it?" "Yes, double platonic suicide."

However, the woman selected refused to die with him. In his "Notes to an Old Friend," he writes about the woman. Even here we find his last attempt, though it is at the time of his death, to be as compliant as possible to the behavior required by his society. In this respect, he makes a significant contrast with Dazai Osamu, who ended his life in chaos. Akutagawa writes:

. . . even after I had decided on the method of suicide, I still felt a certain attachment to life. Accordingly, I needed some springboard for my jump

---

[46] *Aru Aho no Isshō*, in *Collected Works* V.

into death . . . needless to say, it is a woman who can work as a springboard. She was the only woman whom I knew who had showed herself willing to die with me. However, it became impossible for us. Meanwhile, I came to have confidence in my being able to die without the use of a springboard. This was not due to the fact that I could not find anybody with whom I could die. Rather, I gradually became sentimental, and I came to wish to spare my wife from miserable feelings as much as possible, even if, after all, I was going to leave her behind. Also it would be easier for me to kill myself alone than to try to commit double suicide.

At dawn on July 24, 1927, Akutagawa Ryūnosuke took a heavy dose of sleeping pills and ended his life. He died all alone. By his pillow was a Christian Bible.

DAZAI OSAMU (1909–1948)— HYPOCRISY, SINCERITY, AND REBELLION

Of the three authors being considered, Dazai shows the most obvious personal disorganization. The perversely self-destructive course taken in his life is most revealingly documented in his writings and those of his biographers. Neither Sōseki nor Akutagawa indulged in the histrionic self-display that Dazai continually enacted both in life and on the printed page. We can readily obtain a fairly revealing picture of many of the psychological problems in Dazai's personality. But one can also be easily misled and distracted by the obvious.

Alienation from Family and Early Attitudes

Dazai, whose real name was Tsushima Shūji, was born in 1909 into one of the biggest and oldest landowning families in Aomori Prefecture. When Dazai was born his father was thirty-nine years old, and his mother, who was thirty-seven, had already given birth to five boys (two of whom died in infancy) and four girls. Also living in the house were his sixty-nine-year-old great-grandmother, his fifty-three-year-old grandmother, and his mother's younger sister and her four daughters. Including male and female servants, the Tsushima family comprised a household of more than thirty people.

Dazai, who was considered very weak as an infant and young child, had little direct, warm contact with either parent. His mother was an invalid, and he was reared for most of his childhood by servants and a maternal aunt. Several times in his early childhood he was sent to live with others. In a short essay on his childhood he wrote that from an early period he felt alienated from the other members of his family. He recalled one day looking for documents to prove that he was not the real child of his parents. When he could find no such documents among the family's records, he turned to servants and asked them if he actually belonged to his parents. The servants, who had been

working for the Tsushima household when he was born, were amused
and they told him in detail where and how he was born: "It was evening. You were born in that little room—in a mosquito net. It was a
very easy birth. You were a baby with a rather big nose."

In *Reminiscence*,[47] Dazai writes that servants had had a corrupting
effect on him. He was taught to masturbate by male servants working
in his house:

I could not entertain a close feeling toward my mother. . . . I was placed
under the care of a wet nurse. I grew up in the arms of my wet nurse. Until
I was in the second or third grade, I had not known my own mother. . . .
Two of our male servants took the trouble of teaching "it" to me. . . . One
night, my mother who was sleeping beside me noticed that my blanket was
moving. She asked me what I had been doing. I was very much embarrassed
and answered her that I had been giving myself a massage because I felt
pain in my waist. Mother said I should give myself a real massage rather than
stroking. Mother's voice was sleepy.

One of the women servants, however, a maid named Také who was
his constant companion during his sixth and seventh years, exerted a
positive influence. He writes in *Reminiscence*:

When I was six or seven years old, a maid named Také taught me how to
read, and Také and I read various books. Také was enthusiastic about educating me. I was weak and prone to illness; I read many books lying in bed.
When I had read all the books around, Také used to borrow books for children from the village school. She encouraged me to read all these books. As
I learned to read books silently, I did not become tired, however much I
read. Také also taught me about ethics. She often took me to a nearby
Buddhist temple. There she showed me the picture scroll of hell and heaven.
An arsonist was made to carry a burning basket on his back. A person who
kept a mistress in addition to his wife was suffering from being squeezed by
a blue snake with two heads. In a pond of blood, on a mountain of pins, in
a bottomless hole filled with white smoke, thin pale people were crying with
their small mouths open. When I was told that if I lied I would be sent to
this hell and have my tongue pulled out by a devil, I was so scared that I
started crying.

It is perhaps in part as a legacy from Také that throughout his
school career Dazai was usually at the top of his class, although he
was continually absent because of illness. From an early age, he suffered
from sleeplessness and an unwillingness to go to bed at night, and
this also may have been a gift, a more dubious one, from Také.

He was extremely conscious of his father's social position as the big
landowner in his province and a member of the House of Peers in
Parliament. Throughout his writings Dazai expresses ambivalence

---

[47] *Omoide* (1933), in Dazai Osamu, *Collected Works* (12 vols., 1955–56) I, 2–60.

toward his domineering, paternalistic father, who is viewed as lacking
any perception of his son or his feelings. In *Reminiscence,* Dazai writes:

My father was a very busy man, and rarely at home. Even when at home he
did not play with his children. I was very much afraid of my father. When I
was a child, I wanted very much to have his fountain pen, but I could not
tell him my wish. After thinking over and over, I pretended one night to be
asleep in bed and repeated "fountain pen, fountain pen," as if I were speaking
in my sleep. I hoped that my voice would reach my father who was talking
with his guests in the next room. However, my attempt was not successful.
I believe my wish never reached either his ear or his mind. Once I was playing
with my younger brother in a granary which was filled with rice bags. My
father suddenly appeared at the entrance and told us in a harsh voice to get
out of the place. With the sunlight at his back, my father's figure loomed
large and dark. I feel displeased even now whenever I recall the fear and
terror I experienced looking at my father's big, dark figure.

In his later work, *No Longer Human,*[48] one of the two works of his
translated into English, Dazai describes a scene in which a boy's
father, who spent most of every month in Tokyo, asks his children
before leaving what they want him to buy in Tokyo. He writes down
in his notebook what each child wants. The father asks the young boy
what he wants, suggesting a toy mask. Being directly approached by
his otherwise distant and always fearsome father, the boy cannot answer immediately but mumbles. Not understanding what the boy
says, his father looks piqued and asks if all he wants, as usual, is
books. He cannot answer. His eldest brother helps him out by telling
the father that he would like books as usual. The father looks disappointed and closes his notebook without writing. The boy feels he has
made a serious mistake in offending his father, and is afraid that his
father will retaliate in some terrible fashion. He wants to do something
about his mistake and that night, trembling in bed, he seeks a solution.
Finally, he creeps out of the bed into his father's study. Taking his
father's notebook out of the drawer, he finds the page on which the
father has written down the children's requests, and writes down "toy
mask" in his own childish script. The father goes to Tokyo and comes
back home. Later, the boy overhears his father telling his mother that
when he opened his notebook at the store in Tokyo he found "toy
mask" written on the page in his youngest son's handwriting. The
father observes: "When I asked him if he wanted a toy mask, he didn't
answer. Later he must have decided he wanted it and so mischievously
thought of writing in my notebook. He is a strange child."

Dazai describes a home atmosphere in which women are dominant.
He grew up among the women of his house, forming no friendships

---

[48] *Ningen Shikkaku* (1948), in *Collected Works* IX, 363–470. English translation,
No Longer Human, 1958.

with other boys or men, and in his bearing and outlook as well as in his personal habits there were signs of strong feminine identification. Some of his most successful works were written from the standpoint of a female ego-protagonist. In *An Almanac of Suffering*,[49] written in 1946, in recounting his family lineage he maintains, inaccurately, that each of his male progenitors was adopted into the house of the mother. "In my lineage, the women were always stronger and more vital than their husbands. All—my great-grandmother, my grandmother, and my mother—lived longer than their husbands."

Dazai no doubt hated his father and by extension the authority structure of society. However, his more deeply seated difficulties with human communication were to be found in a masochistic need to be manipulated by women. His own destruction was finally accomplished by a woman capable of the task.

According to *Reminiscence*,[50] he had started to think about becoming an author by 1925, when he was in the ninth grade. Already, at sixteen, he had joined a group of classmates in an attempt to publish a literary magazine. The magazine actually lasted a year and four months, all through his last year of middle school. He edited and wrote short stories and essays and his precocious literary talent was well known at school. Describing retrospectively his feelings at this age, he recalls that he felt a need to express his sense of loneliness and alienation. (Dazai throughout his life had a sense of his playing roles and was completely unsure of his sincerity and of the spontaneous emotions of either others or himself.) His preoccupation with sincerity was covering an even deeper sense of hopeless incapacity to reach out and receive.

Walking on the bridge, I recalled many things and dreamed of many others, but at the end I wondered with a sigh if I would ever become a prominent person. Around this time of my life I became impatient concerning my future. I could not feel satisfaction in anything, and I always felt involved in some sort of vain struggle. As I had already been wearing ten or twenty different masks, I could not discover how sad I really was. Finally, I found a sad and lonely outlet for myself. This was creation, writing. I felt that in this field of writing there were many people who were like me, watching their own unknown sadness and loneliness. I secretly wished to become a writer.

When he was sixteen years old, Dazai wrote a short drama *Vanity*[51] in which he already displayed a basically nihilistic attitude toward

---

[49] *Nuno no Nenkan*, in *Collected Works* VIII, 201–212.

[50] *Omoide*, in *Collected Works* I.

[51] Osamu Dazai's *Kyosei* appeared in *Seiza* (A Constellation), Vol. 1, March, 1925. This was the literary magazine Dazai published with his five classmates. It did not last long, and Dazai, in the same year, published another magazine, *Shinkirō* (A Mirage) with his younger brother and nine friends, which lasted for three years.

life—an attitude that was to permeate most of his later works. In this
drama a middle-aged man is living with his second wife and two sons.
The eldest, Teiichi, the son of the first wife, has been blind from his
birth, at which time his mother died. His father, finding that a cure
for his blindness is possible, takes him to a doctor for an operation,
and at twenty-one his sight is restored. After the operation Teiichi declares:

I opened my eyes in the hospital. First I saw my father. Can such a person
be my father? He looked ugly and shabby, even more so than the doctor. At
this first moment I was deeply disappointed in my father's appearance. But
still I was curious. Through this curiosity I timidly followed my father and
came to the front of the room. A pale and dirty-looking man stood before me
in the mirror. When I realized that this man was I, I thought I would faint
from astonishment. At this very moment, through a slightly open door, I
caught a glimpse of a woman, whose face was dark and more disgusting than
any of the other faces. When I sensed that this woman was my mother I could
no longer remain there. I went to the entrance hall and started crying. Why I
cried I don't know. I think you people know better than I do. I wish I could
become blind again.

The events we shall presently relate—Dazai's unstable personal life,
debts incurred but never paid, a scandalous series of unsuccessful attempts at suicide, his affair and subsequent marriage with a country
geisha, his illegal activities in the Communist movement—all served
in Dazai's mind to stain the honor of his house and lineage, a peculiarly
Japanese form of intense perverse misery. In *An Almanac of Suffering*,[52] he sees his disgraceful behavior as unique in his family: "In our
lineage there is nothing complicated, nothing dark. One never heard
any conflict over property. In short, no one ever acted disgracefully.
Ours was one of the most elegant families in the Tsugaru area. I was
the only one in our lineage whose behavior was whispered about and
made a butt of gossip." Dazai's behavior is similar in many respects
to the disreputable extravagances of certain scions of distinguished
European families in the nineteenth century, who seem by their behavior to be destroying themselves as well as their family name. This
destructiveness is not haphazard, but bears testimony to unconscious
motivational patterns. The profligate or prodigal son, by his personal
extravagances, finds a means of destroying those about him. The extremes of his behavior represent a sort of joyless flagellation that
strikes also at those who dare to come too close or who cannot escape
involvement with him. Such behavior in Japanese society is often a

---

[52] *Nuno no Nenkan,* in *Collected Works* VIII.

perverse reversal of the strong concern with achievement induced by socialization within Japanese culture.[53]

Guilt, Rebellion, and Social Criticism

By the time Dazai became a student in high school, communism had gained a strong influence over many Japanese intellectuals. By this time, the trends toward idealism and intellectualism of the late 1920s in Japan had changed to a more direct and active proletarian movement. A large number of aspiring young authors were very much concerned with developing what they termed a proletarian literature. These authors were enthusiastic participants in the intellectual ferment caused by the Russian revolution and the first serious attempt to establish a national state governed by Marxist political doctrines. Such young men also were extremely dissatisfied with the subtle censorship and other forms of social control exercised by the supposedly liberal authorities.

By the late 1920s, Marxist theory had become very appealing to the younger generation, who had developed a distrust of traditional Confucian ethics as well as a lack of interest in the Japanese family system which still formed the core of official "morals" training in the schools. Marxist theory provided rebellious and alienated youth with a strong viewpoint, which allowed them to identify with a new source of power and strength. First, its black-and-white judgments on all social phenomena and its ready solutions to social problems held strong appeal. Second, the actual economic conditions in Japan at this time, in contrast to the picture painted by the government, moved idealistic intellectual youth to a sense of disgust with the hypocrisy of liberal political parties. There was already appearing a widespread feeling of anxiety concerning the future, in spite of the appearance of continuing prosperity. The third, and perhaps most important, factor making Marxist theory popular was the development of an ethical void in Japan's transition into a modern influential state. After the Meiji Restoration, many leaders found a continuity with the past in adherence to Confucian ethics, and for others the social and ethical aspects of Christianity had great appeal. However, by the late 1920s, Christianity had lost its relevancy to social reform. Marxist theory increasingly took over as a code of ethics suggesting goals for political action.

Dazai was swept up in the Communist movement of the time; his own rebellious propensities found expression in the attempts of the Communist groups to flout governmental authority. In March 1928,

---

[53] Life careers such as that of Dazai are periodically noted in Japanese society. For a detailed discussion of the psychological mechanisms involved, see Chapter 5.

at twenty years of age, Dazai published a novel, *A Boundless Abyss*.[54]
The novel exaggerated the dark and sinister nature of his landowning
family: an innocent young maid, beloved of a young man and forced
to become his father's mistress, victimized by the father's profligacy,
eventually becomes insane and dies. Here the author was expressing
his strong negative feelings toward his father, and at the same time, in
line with Communist ideology, was identifying his father's behavior
as a form of social exploitation.

In May of the same year a large number of Communists were arrested in what became known in Japan as the "May 15 incident." At
this time Dazai was a party member and was writing another novel,
which was published in August as *They and Their Darling Mother*.[55]
In this novel he wrote about a poor sculptor and his younger brother
who were totally without hope for future success. They were living
with their ignorant and stubborn but very sweet and gentle mother.
In this novel, with the rich father absent, Dazai describes in a very
touching style the tender emotions binding a mother and her sons.
This novel was without the hatred and animosity he almost invariably
vented upon paternal figures. Throughout his writings one finds no
suggestion of any hostile attitude directly toward a maternal figure,
but toward women generally his attitudes are most complex. He
continually betrays an underlying hatred interwoven with masochistic
passivity.

In October 1928, Dazai published another novel, *This Couple*,[56] in
which the hero, a young author, in one episode is accused by factory
workers of being a worthless bourgeois intellectual. He marries a
good-natured but ignorant geisha and lives out a hopeless and miserable existence in Tokyo. His wife, who lacks much emotional depth,
fails to resist adultery with an acquaintance, and causes the hero
suffering. Written while Dazai was still a youth in high school, this
work foreshadows events in his later life, an augury similar to that in
F. Scott Fitzgerald's *Tender Is the Night*.[57] Authors sometimes predict
their own future experiences with others because they manifest in
their writings evidence of the general human capacity to cause experience by manipulating others to take on the required roles. Not infrequently one can induce others, sought out because they possess the
proper propensities, to act out one's deeper masochistic fantasies of

---

[54] *Mugen Naraku*, in *Collected Works* XII, 120–168.

[55] *Karera to Sono Itoshiki Haha* (1928), in *Collected Works* XII, 182–196.

[56] *Kono Fūfu*, in *Collected Works* XII, 197–219.

[57] The psychiatrist-hero unconsciously sets up the situation where his wife as part
of her recovery from mental illness commits adultery with a more virile, less intellectual type of man.

betrayal and thereby offer the sexual stimulation of being vicariously both the betrayer and the betrayed. Dazai managed well to seek out those who would whet his appetite for stimulation of his sense of inadequacy and worthlessness.

Dazai dramatized his continually operative self-disgust at this period as an unworthiness to be part of the Communist movement. He felt that his landowner background disqualified him from being accepted as a genuine revolutionary. Early in 1929 Dazai made his first suicidal gesture. In *An Almanac of Suffering*,[58] he recalls:

The dictatorship of the proletariat. There is certainly something new to it. It is not compromise. It is despotism. It defeats the opponent without giving quarter. All the rich are bad. All aristocrats are bad. Only the penniless commoners are all right. I agreed with the idea of armed riots. Revolution without the guillotine is meaningless. However, [as a youth] I was not of the common people. My role was to be put on the guillotine. I was a high school student of nineteen and in my class I was the only one who wore luxurious and conspicuous clothes. I thought there was no way out but to kill myself, and I took a large number of sleeping pills but did not die. [Afterward] a friend of mine told me that I did not have to die; I was his comrade. He said he thought I was a promising young man and introduced me to many of his friends. The role given me was to provide them financial support. After transferring to the University of Tokyo, I continued to give them support and was required to pay their room and board.

In April of that year, Dazai entered the University of Tokyo in the department of French literature. By late summer, he published another unfinished work entitled *A Student Group*,[59] in which he describes in great detail a student strike at a high school as the result of the school principal's having stolen public money. Written with a great deal of vigor and sense of action, the work throughout is stylistically unusual for him. It describes the students' first feeling of inadequacy and helplessness at mobilizing themselves and how some students shrink back, not fully accepting the implications of the Leftist movement. These feelings are resolved in the context of the work, and the sense of inadequacy and the questioning attitude are overcome in terms of positive action. At the time this was written, we suspect that Dazai was already facing a dilemma in his attitudes toward his role in the Leftist movement. That he was finding it difficult to reconcile becoming an author with his Communist activities is evident in this quotation from *A Student Group*:

Artistic activity is a brilliant way of escaping class conflict. Art, especially literature, never produces revolutionaries. It produces only romantic attitudes,

[58] *Nuno no Nenkan* (1946), in *Collected Works* VIII.
[59] *Gakusei Gun* (1930), in *Collected Works* XII, 277–348.

and therefore the type of inadequate revolutionary who is bound to fail. Literature can produce sympathizers, and of course it is necessary to gain such sympathizers. However, there is a surer, more steadfast, less expensive way than literature to gain sympathizers; namely, the use of personal propaganda, appropriate agitation at group meetings, and so forth. We intellectuals never learn from what is called Proletarian Literature. The attempt has been made hundreds of times—never resulting in success—to have proletarian novels written by the proletarians themselves. What an irony! The intellectuals can write proletarian novels to be read only by other intellectuals. It is a shame, but it is a fact. If we want to have real proletarian novels we must educate the proletariat. All our work starts from this need. A writer once said: "The revolutionary function of writers of proletarian novels is not to write hundreds of novels filled with the smell of intellectuals, but only to give us the money they earn by writing."

Ultimately, Dazai could not identify himself successfully with illegal Communist activities. Perhaps he felt too critical of those he met in the movement, measuring them by his Procrustean standards. The Communists he met were not ideal models. In Dazai's eyes their sexual morality was loose. Sometimes it was obvious that a leader exercised irrational dominance over his followers. Dazai may have felt alienated in spite of his desire to belong. For all the chaos in his personal life, Dazai was an abused innocent; he could never accept without judgment the actual conduct of himself or others. In his own case, both his personal worthlessness and his wealthy landowning background disqualified him as a Communist, and he felt a sense of deep despair. To him, joining the Communists in their activities meant active rebellion, open fight against his father, elder brother, and any authority. By such rebellion he alienated himself from his primary ties, but he was not free of guilt toward the authority with whom he fought. This guilt deepened his own profound sense of worthlessness and corruption.

During this period of his political involvement and distressing ambivalence toward it, he also first became sexually involved in a serious way with a woman. In this area also he managed to demonstrate his own worthlessness to himself in dramatic episodes. In autumn of 1930 a geisha named Hatsuyo, whom Dazai had known from his high-school days, came to Tokyo to live with him. Dazai's elder brother, exercising his expected family authority over his younger brother, saw to it that she returned home, with the promise that he would consent to marriage at a later date. Her failure to write Dazai after her return further stimulated his masochistic, Dostoevskian helplessness in his relationship with women.

It might not be inappropriate in this context to suggest at least briefly the nature of Dazai's very complex relationships to women from a psychodynamic standpoint. In part at least they involved continual attempts to induce women to act out his fantasy conception of them originating in his own mind. He used women as personifications of his Jungian "anima" or latent female self and found sensuous pleasure in living vicariously through observing their behavior. In his personal relationships with them he ingeniously induced them to act "upon" him, fleshing out his passive fantasies. It is difficult to gain an accurate picture of the women with whom he associated from Dazai's own writings, since those whom he describes are patently so much creatures of his own imagination. Such vicarious living in alter egos is found to some degree in many actors as well as authors, who sometimes find themselves merely an uninteresting residue of the external roles they take or the fictitious characters they create. Some authors create women with qualities of nurturance and care; for others the *femme fatale* is an obsessive source of excitement. The dramatic interpretation Dazai gave to actual events in his life had a particularly masochistic quality, in which female acquaintances continually cause him injury and pain. On the other hand, the second wife he later married according to traditional Japanese practice of an "arranged" marriage is depicted almost as a caricature of the ideal self-sacrificing Japanese woman, a woman one feels Dazai never sought to know as a real person.

In November 1930, at Enoshima, Dazai attempted a double suicide with a bar girl acquaintance in which the girl was drowned, but Dazai somehow survived. He ruminates about his motives in a work entitled *Flowers of a Jester*.[60] At the time of this suicide attempt he was working continuously day and night for a Communist organization, although he felt not only disqualified by background but also inept in performance. He succumbed to what he called "a double despair." He was most aware that his attempt at joint suicide with a casual acquaintance who simply took a liking to him was an act of retaliation toward Hatsuyo, his mistress, for her seeming indifference after being sent home by his brother, but he suggests other motives as well. It appears that in one sense Dazai wishes to recapture a position of being cared for by evoking sympathy in this extreme manner. The act has an expiatory quality, as well as being a symbol of retaliatory hostility. So, too, in much of his debauched behavior can be heard a muted cry for care. As was true in his childhood association with servants, however, those who attend to him seem to do so by means of acts of sensuality that corrupt a passive but excited victim. After the suicide attempt, he wrote:

A woman acquaintance working in a back street bar in Ginza liked me. Everyone, no matter who, has at least one experience of being liked. *But it is his time of defilement.* I invited this woman to go with me into the sea at Kama-

---

[60] *Doke no Hana* (1935), in *Collected Works* I, 241–293.

kura. [In my revolutionary behavior as a Communist] I felt myself a failure in my attack against God. I did not want to be called a coward. Therefore, I accepted work that was impossible for me to carry out physically. Hatsuyo was a woman who could think only of her own happiness. You [addressing Hatsuyo] are not the only woman in the world for me. You have incurred my reprisal because you never tried to understand my suffering. It serves you right.

The fact that I had been alienated from all my relatives made me lonely. The most direct reason for my attempt to kill myself was that I had realized that my elder brother, my mother, and my aunt all had become contemptuous of me and incensed over my affair with Hatsuyo. The waitress died and I lived. A dark spot in my life. I was put in jail. After an investigation and examination, my indictment was suspended. It was the end of 1930. My brothers were kind and gentle to their younger brother, who even failed at dying.

What actually occurred between Dazai and his family after the suicide attempt is not clear. Seemingly he persuaded them to reconsider their attitude toward him and to treat him more kindly. After each later suicide attempt Dazai notes that others felt sympathetic to him.

In February 1931 Hatsuyo returned to Tokyo and Dazai again lived with her, this time with his elder brother's permission and financial help. He rarely visited his classes at the University and kept himself immersed in Communist activities. To disguise his political involvement, he changed his residence several times and used assumed names. He learned that during her separation from him Hatsuyo had slept with another man and he somehow symbolically related this discovery to his leaving the Leftist movement in disgust. In *Eight Scenes of Tokyo,*[61] 1941, he declares:

[After the hints of a friend] I had become unable to trust H. [Hatsuyo] any more. That night I finally made her confess. All that I had heard from the student turned out to be true; indeed it was worse than I had heard. I felt there would be no end to it if I kept asking her questions. I stopped midway. In regard to a matter of this nature, I had no right to blame anyone. I suddenly realized that until that day I had loved H. and had been proud of her, as of a jade in my palm. It seemed to me that I had been living only for her sake. I had believed that [although she was already a geisha] I had "saved" a pure woman. I had been a simple-minded hero and believed what she told me, telling her story proudly to my friends and saying that she was a woman of strong character who had somehow been able to protect her innocence as a young geisha until she came to me. What a fool I was! I found no words to describe myself. I had not known what women were. H. had deceived me, but I could not hate her when she made her confession. I even thought she looked lovely, and wanted to console her. I was simply disappointed. I felt self-disgust. I wished to destroy my own life with a big club. In short, I felt helpless, hope-

---

[61] *Tokyo Hakkei,* in *Collected Works* IV, 49–74.

less, resentful, and disgusted. Thereupon I delivered myself to a police station and confessed my political activities.

When he leaves the prosecutor's investigation, he returns to the room where Hatsuyo is staying: "I hastened to the place where H. was staying. Miserable reunion. Smiling like slaves, we shook hands weakly. We started living together again. My elder brothers at home were amazed and disgusted by my foolishness, but still they were kind enough to keep sending me money."

A Worthless Life

After breaking away from Communist activities in 1932, he started writing a work called *Reminiscences*[62] "as a testament to be left behind." He viewed himself as of no use to anyone. In *Eight Scenes of Tokyo*, he writes: "Even H., the girl to whom I thought myself of some use, turned out to be smeared with someone else's dirt. I had no hope. I had nothing to which to dedicate my life. I thought I was a complete fool and made up my mind to die as a human ruin. I wanted to play as faithfully as possible the role that was given to me, a sad and servile role of being beaten by everyone." His feeling of unworthiness is well represented by another quotation, from *False Spring*,[63] written in 1936. He castigates himself as a traitor to his Communist comrades:

I do not want the factory workers and farmers to lessen or soften the hatred and revulsion they direct toward me. I do not want them to make an exception of me. I love their simple-minded courage and respect above all their simple-minded attitudes. For this reason, I cannot talk about having a view of the world in which I believe. I should not now be allowed to talk about the dawn of the revolution with my own rotten mouth. I am a traitor, therefore I should behave and act as a traitor. I should say to those dirty factory workers and poor ignorant peasants that I feel contempt for them, want to laugh at them, and that I am really waiting only for the day that I am stabbed to death by them.

His life became more dissolute. Whatever money he got by loans he spent on liquor, and he pawned clothes taken from Hatsuyo's closet.

In March 1935 he took an entrance examination for the Miyako Press and failed. The time for completing his work at the university approached, but Dazai had not attended any of his courses and could not be graduated. He went to Kamakura and made another suicide attempt, this time by hanging, and again he failed. Coming home, he found to his surprise that he was treated kindly by everyone. In *Eight Scenes of Tokyo* he writes:

---

[62] *Omoide,* in *Collected Works* I.
[63] *Kyoko no Haru,* in *Collected Works* I, 313–380.

It [the new attempt at suicide] happened five years after I tried to drown myself [at Enoshima] with a woman. As I swim too well, I decided it was difficult for me to die in the sea and, hearing it was a surer way, I tried to hang myself. Again I was a clumsy failure. My breath returned. My neck seemed to be too thick and strong for the effort. With my neck swollen and red, I returned to my home at Amanuma. I had failed to settle my own fate. When I returned, in a weakened state, there was waiting for me a strange world I had never known. At the entrance hall, H. stroked my back gently. Others expressed their relief and consoled me. I was surprised at the gentleness of life. My eldest brother had come from our home town. He scolded me and heaped blame upon me, but I felt my love and attachment for him strongly. Almost for the first time in my life, I was relishing a strange feeling.

Shortly thereafter, Dazai was hospitalized for an appendectomy, and subsequent to this operation he became addicted to a morphine derivative. Thereafter he forced a doctor living in his neighborhood to write certificates allowing him to buy a continuous supply of drugs from the pharmacy. In *Eight Scenes of Tokyo,* he says: "I realized that I had already become a wretched addict. I needed a considerable amount of money daily but my eldest brother refused to give me money for buying more drugs. In the fall of that year I occasionally appeared in Tokyo, a dirty, half-insane man."

In August of 1935 Dazai was nominated as a candidate for the annual Akutagawa literary award and was rated second to the winner. The following year in October, after a year of continuous debauchery in which he borrowed from anyone who would lend, his friends finally had him hospitalized to effect his withdrawal from narcotics. He felt betrayed when he found himself in a mental hospital. In a work Dazai gave the English title *Human Lost* (1936)[64] he depicts his feelings about this experience in an almost incoherent protest. The fact that he interpreted his experience as having a punitive meaning is very clear from his writing. It is filled with angry cries of self-pity: "Shall I say it is whipping a dead body? Or shall I call it squeezing a maimed bird to death?"

His hospitalization, surprisingly, was successful. Freed from physiological addiction, he never again returned to drugs, although he quickly went back to his inordinate use of alcohol. He managed to drink up the royalties of his published works as quickly as they were forthcoming and got even further into debt than previously.

Early in 1937, Dazai's cousin confessed to him that he had had sexual intercourse with Hatsuyo while Dazai was in the hospital. Although the cousin expressed his wish to marry Hatsuyo, he quickly lost interest and, evading further ties, disappeared. In March Dazai took Hatsuyo to a resort where they resolved to commit suicide with sleeping pills.

---

[64] *Human Lost* (in Japanese), in *Collected Works* II, 93–118.

Neither died, and upon their recovery they returned to Tokyo where they separated permanently.

Dazai lived alone for a short period. In *Eight Scenes of Tokyo,* he describes his self-hatred in loving, meticulous detail:

I stayed in my apartment alone, learning to drink *shochu* [low-grade Japanese brandy]. I lost my teeth one by one, my face becoming drawn, ugly, and mean. I am an ignorant and arrogant villain, an idiot, a sensualist of the lowest kind, the meanest kind of a swindler who pretends to be a genius, who wastes his money in a riotous life running about unable to pay his debts, threatening parents by fake suicide, mistreating a faithful wife as if she were a dog or a cat and finally driving her out. There are many other kinds of legends about me which are told by people with contempt, disgust, and anger. I was completely buried by society, treated like a living corpse.

Dazai Attempts Matrimony and the Bourgeois Life

In 1938, when he was thirty years old, Dazai made a decision to become a successful novelist. According to his own explanation in *Eight Scenes of Tokyo,* the sudden change was due to a series of unhappy incidents at home: first, his eldest brother was prosecuted for an election law violation; shortly thereafter his elder sister, his nephew, and a cousin died in short sequence.

Successive unhappy incidents which had taken place at home helped me gradually to raise the upper half of my reclining body. I had felt embarrassed with the large size of my house in my home town. The handicap of being the son of a wealthy family had vexed me sorely. An unpleasant fearful feeling of being unduly favored had made me, since my childhood, servile and pessimistic. I had the belief that the son of a wealthy family should fall into a rather large hell appropriate to the son of such a family. However, I suddenly noticed one night that I was no longer the son of a wealthy family. I was a lonely, humble man without even proper clothes to wear. Within the year I was to receive no more money from home. Even the home in which I was born and reared was now at the nadir of misfortune. I no longer enjoyed privileges which used to cause me to shrink in shame. Rather I had nothing but deficits. Ah, the awareness of it! One thing more I should mention; while lying in my room, having lost even the spirit to die, in some inexplicable way my body rapidly became more robust. Further, my age, the war, my shaken perspectives on history, my distaste for my own indolence, my humility toward literature, God's existence, etc.—all might be mentioned as factors. Yet to explain the change that overcomes the man is for some reason unconvincing. The explanations offered above, even when closely argued and pursued with logic and precision, smack somehow of untruth. Man does not always choose to alter his course by conscious decisions. Most often, without knowing how and when it occurred, he suddenly finds himself traversing a different field.

In January 1939, at thirty-one, Dazai married his second wife, Michiko Ishiwara, through an arrangement made by Ibuse, a well-known novelist, who acted as his mentor. Dazai quickly took on the role of a conformist Japanese bourgeois family man, attempting to solve his personal alienation by living what he deemed to be a "normal" life. His artistic work during the period from his marriage to the end of World War II was most restrained and controlled, and focused on the development of his esthetic style. Throughout this period he frequently expressed a fear that he would not be able to maintain himself as a stable, normal family man.

He remained politically aware, conscious of the rabid militarism dominating Japan, and he never in any way gave the least support to Japan's military efforts. Some of his work during this period was censored by the militarists because it was too "peaceful." Such suppression only spurred him on. It seemed to make him externalize his anger even more toward the military government and to confirm him in his decision to write.

Although he was behaviorally more restrained, in his mind he still did not feel completely successful in leading the life of a common citizen. His sense of belonging to his society seemed generally lacking. In the work *The Sea Gull*,[65] 1940, he wrote:

I have been dead for a long, long time, but people do not notice. Only my soul is alive. I am not a human being now; I am a strange animal called an artist. I am planning to keep this dead body going until it becomes sixty years old to show what an artist actually is. If you want to investigate the secrets of sentences which are written by this corpse, it's useless. If you want to try to imitate such sentences written by a ghost, you'll never be able to do it.

In another work, *A Thief of Spring*, 1940,[66] he writes:

I feel fed up. If this is reality, I don't like it. I can't quite love it. There is nothing romantic about this life. Nobody but me is "psychopathic," and then here I am, too, trying hard to train myself to be a petit bourgeois leading a humble life. I hate it! I don't mind being isolated. Once again I would like to annihilate myself by jumping into that romantic hell of ambition and dedication. Why can't I? Why shouldn't I? "No, you mustn't," I now say to myself, "sad as it is, I must not."

In other works written in 1940 we note also a tone of self-hatred directed at this uneventful, mediocre life. However, after 1941 this tone becomes less strident. Somehow he has made a compromise with the life demanded of him by society. In *Justice and Smile*[67] in 1942 he argues:

---

[65] *Kamome*, in *Collected Works* III, 84–99.
[66] *Haru no Tozoku*, in *Collected Works* III, 110–145.
[67] *Seigi to Bisho*, in *Collected Works* V, 33–190.

Well—from the very start humans are without ideals as such. Even granting some exist, they are appropriate to the daily grind only. Give somebody an ideal somewhat removed from everyday life—ah, that's the road leading to crucifixion—it is a path only for a Child of God. I don't rise above the herd of common folk. I am only concerned with food. These days I have become one of the breadwinners. I have become a bird crawling on the ground. Somewhere, somehow, angel's wings were lost. Flailing about this way, nothing really takes off. This is what's real. You can't kid yourself.

In *A Student Beggar*,[68] he states:

Don't you believe in the "necessity" of order? Ever since the olden days, institutions, custom, and the law have always been attacked and despised by those with the least bit of intelligence. In fact, it makes you feel good when you can make or poke fun at them. However, you should know how irresponsible and dangerous such play is. It is because you don't take any responsibility, isn't it? However meaningless the law, institutions, and customs may look to you, where there are none no knowledge or liberty could be conceivable. To laugh about them is like riding on a big boat and speaking ill of it. Should you jump into the sea, you can do no more than die.

At such times, it is almost as if Dazai were talking to himself through the voice and attitude of his older brother and father about society. He seems in such passages to be attempting to internalize some concept of authority.

It should be remembered that when Dazai was leading this "proper" life, Japan was at war under the direction of its militaristic regime. During this period, open profligacy was impossible. Also it seems that his rebellious energy found sufficient outlet in writing as a nonconformist artist. Unlike many authors of that time, Dazai never wrote work supporting the war or militaristic ideas.

Postwar Disorganization

Not long after Japan's defeat in the war, Dazai lost his insecure grip on a bourgeois life. The military state had been something to oppose; with its external coercion taken away, his inner economy was disrupted. Shortly after the war's end, however, Dazai had his last brief respite from pessimism. He wrote a novel, called *Pandora's Box*,[69] in the form of a letter filled with hope written in a sanatorium by a young man who had recovered from a sense of impending death and deep pessimism. "Both my surroundings and myself have taken on a new brightness. Not too quickly nor too slowly, but with ordinary, steady step I shall proceed walking straight ahead without further

---

[68] *Kojiki Gakusei* (1940), in *Collected Works* III, 281–330.
[69] *Pandora no Hako* (1945), in *Collected Works* VIII, 3–134.

word. Where does such a road lead? I had better ask a vine. The vine would answer, 'I don't know, but it seems that the sun shines its light on me as I extend myself.' " Such vital optimism was rare for Dazai, and even at this time it did not represent a constant attitude. According to a letter written to his mentor Ibuse during the same period he was writing the novel, he repeatedly felt attacked by strange, empty feelings. He brought the novel to an earlier conclusion than he had originally intended. Japan's defeat did not long sustain in Dazai any strong hope for peace.

His spasms of optimism were fairly short lived, and in retrospect he perversely seeks to wipe them out by stressing the negative side of his ambivalent states. In *An Almanac of Suffering*,[70] for instance, written only a short three months after *Pandora's Box*, he states: "Japan had declared unconditional surrender. I felt ashamed. I felt so ashamed that I could not even speak the words. It is not that Japan was defeated; Japan was destroyed, ruined, and exterminated. People who spoke ill of the Emperor abruptly increased, and in such a situation, I suddenly realized how deeply I had loved him." Such statements reveal the loss of moral tonicity formerly maintained by a justified rebellion against militarist authority. Dazai's ability to externalize aggressions toward an opposing force acted for him as a brace. Suddenly the traditional, irrational, authoritarian structure of Japanese society had collapsed completely, and with it somehow an opposing force from which he had gained support. He states in a short work called *Fifteen Years*[71] written in 1946:

The essential nature of liberal thinking is the spirit of rebellion. You may even call it the thought of destruction. It is not the kind of thought that grows after suppression and restriction are taken away, but is essentially a thought that is born as a reaction to suppression or restriction. A dove can fly only when it meets the resistance of air. A liberal thought without its enemy to fight and oppose is like a dove trying to fly in a vacuum tube. It can never rise. The content of liberal thought varies according to the times. In present-day Japan it is no longer liberal to abuse and revile the militarists. It is simply opportunistic. A truly courageous liberal today should cry out, "Hurray for the Emperor!" Until yesterday this cry was old-fashioned and fraudulent. Today it is the newest thought of liberalism.

Without rebellion, regardless of the cause, Dazai could not give a positive, aggressive meaning to his life. Japan's defeat took from him his final means of fighting out some meaning to existence, a means of releasing externally an ever inner-turning hate.

---

[70] *Nuno no Nenkan,* in *Collected Works* VIII.
[71] *Jugo Nen,* in *Collected Works* VIII, 213–236.

In another short work, entitled *The Dead Leaves of Spring*,[72] 1946, one finds again an inner personal state of death rather than life:

For long winter days and nights, buried under heavy snow and enduring its oppressive weight, what have they been waiting for? It makes me shudder. The melting snow has disclosed the filthy appearance of these leaves. Although spring has come, it does not revive them. They only become more rotten. Spring means nothing to these dead, exhausted leaves. For nothing have they endured so long underneath the pressing weight of the snow. Though it is now melted, nothing happens. It is all nonsense. For more than ten years, I have been enduring, suffering, living like a worm. It may be that even before I knew it my existence had already lost its meaning.

In his later writings, he became increasingly critical and sneering toward Japanese postwar democracy. He castigated the new so-called democratic culture and what he liked to call the "insincere liberals." He also increased the tempo of his criticism of the "mediocrity" of the peaceful family life of an ordinary citizen. Soon, his personal life was again in a chaotic state. His complete income was devoted to the pursuit of self-destructive profligacy.

Earlier, in 1942, Dazai had had a brief encounter with Shizuko Ohta, the woman who was later to become the heroine of his most famous novel, *The Setting Sun*.[73] In 1947, after the collapse of his attempt at normal life, they again came together for an intensive week of sexual intimacy during which they conceived a daughter. Shortly after this, he was completely taken over by another woman, Tomie Yamazaki. Although to all appearances Dazai hated and despised her, he was somehow reduced to a state of total passivity and dependence on her, and it was she who eventually contrived to have him commit a successful double suicide with her.

It is the final irony of Dazai's life and a curious outcome of his long preoccupation with suicide that a careful examination of the police reports of his widely accepted double suicide reveals that he was actually murdered. According to accounts at the time, Dazai and Tomie Yamazaki took poison together and threw themselves into the water, but a later critic, who carefully examined the coroner's records and the documents in the files, discovered that Dazai actually was reported as having been strangled and only his mistress took poison, as a means of killing herself after strangling him.[74] It is conjectured that the immediate provocation of her act was Dazai's serious proposal of a separation. There had been several days of quarrels over the fact that

---

[72] *Haru no Kare-ha*, in *Collected Works* VIII, 373–414.

[73] *Sha Yo* (1956), in *Collected Works* IX, 97–242. English translation, 1956.

[74] Saegusa, *Dazai Osamu and His Life* (1958, in Japanese).

52

Tomie wanted Dazai to divorce his wife and marry her; she wanted a complete monopoly over him. The situation, as reconstructed, seems to be that after he had taken a very heavy dose of sleeping pills—as he invariably did to get to sleep—Yamazaki took him, in a semi-conscious state, for a walk to the river bank, and strangled him there, tying his body to hers with a sash. Then, taking potassium cyanide, she managed to drag Dazai with her into the water.

Dazai and the Bible

Our study of these three authors would not be complete without an examination of the fact that in each case of alienation illustrated here there was some attempt to find in religion a means of reestablishing the feeling of belonging. We noted briefly that Sōseki in Gate[75] depicts his failure to find some answer through Zen. Was it a final curious irony that Akutagawa provided his suicidal chamber with a bedside Bible? In Dazai's case the religious theme is stronger; it has been pointed out by some Japanese literary critics that the Bible and Christianity had a strong influence on his thought.

Okuno,[76] a perceptive critic of Dazai's work, points out that the influence of the Bible is clear during the period when Dazai was attempting to maintain normal family life. Okuno states that Dazai looked for God, or became concerned with God, out of his profound and corrosive sense of guilt, and he interprets Dazai's concern with the Bible in terms of love. In his opinion Dazai was basically so narcissistic as to be incapable of loving another. Considering love of others as a duty, Dazai attempted to love without success.

Dazai's ideal was a world in which people could believe in each other, but he found his real world one of utter hypocrisy and continual deceit; he never transcended a feeling of constant distrust. His fate was based on early experiences of maternal deprivation, which colored his life with a continual sense of alienation from others. We find in Dazai's collection of essays, Thus I Heard,[77] 1948: "I could almost say that nearly all my suffering is related to this most difficult task, posed by that man called Jesus—'Love thy neighbor as thyself.'"

In Dazai's mind the Christian God was a punitive god. His image of God was closely associated with his earliest images of a stern father or oldest brother, ready to punish a corrupt, deceitful, and rebellious child, were he to be found out for what he was. In No Longer Human,[78] 1948, Dazai states: "I was afraid of God, too. I could not believe in God's love. I believed only in his punishment. Belief—I feel

[75] Mon, in Sōseki, Collected Works VI, 275–484.
[76] Okuno, Study of Dazai Osamu (1956, in Japanese).
[77] Mozegabun (1948).
[78] Ningen Shikkaku, in Collected Works IX.

that belief consists of facing the seat of judgment, with bowed head, waiting for God's whip. I can readily believe in hell, but I could never believe in the existence of heaven."

It should not be forgotten that Dazai had a strong Japanese sense of duty, although it was so frequently violated by his profligacy. The word *gi* or *gimu* (duty) often appears in his writing, sometimes as the central theme of a story. In 1940, he wrote an essay entitled *Duty*.[79]

It is awfully difficult to carry out one's duty. Nevertheless, one should. Why am I alive? Why do I write stories? The only answer I can make is that it is a duty. I do not think I am living for the sake of pleasure. In love, there is, after all, nothing more than the carrying out of duty. I am living now for the sake of duty. Duty supports my life. As far as my instincts are concerned, I do not mind dying. I think basically it does not make too much difference whether I am dead or alive or ill. However, duty prevents me from dying. Duty tells me to try. Duty demands that I repeatedly, ceaselessly, try. Out of a sense of duty I stand up again and fight. I cannot quit. I am that simple minded.

In his short story *Father*,[80] written in April 1947, among excruciating detailed descriptions of his neglect of family and the suffering he caused his wife and children we find numerous references to the word "duty." For him duty is not the act of writing itself but to use his writing to demonstrate to himself his utter worthlessness as a human being. It becomes a deep perversion of a sense of revelatory sincerity, a self-flagellation, which he could not even believe in as he practiced it. He wrote:

I "amuse" myself out of a sense of duty. I dissipate with hellish suffering. I place a wager on life itself by my dissolute behavior. [To himself] Duty? Don't talk nonsense. You are not even qualified to live. Certainly, this may sound like a feeble self-justification made by a thief. However, the white silk in the deep recesses of my breast is covered with tiny words. I cannot read them clearly. It is as if ten ants have crept out of a sea of black ink and walked around, making little dry sounds scattering some fine-detailed inked prints. In this manner the faint ticklish characters—if I could read them all I would be able to explain to people more clearly the meaning of the duty I am talking about. However, it is very complicated and difficult.

In the same story Dazai illustrates his perverse sense of duty by a disturbing description of a little episode, seemingly taken from his actual relationship with his wife and children.

Around the tenth of January, it was a windy day. My wife asked, "Would you mind staying home, just for today?" "Why?" "There may be a distribution of rationed rice." "Do I have to go for it?" "No." I knew my wife had been

---

[79] *Gimu*, in *Collected Works* X.
[80] *Chichi*, in *Collected Works* IX, 57–69.

down with a cold for the past few days and had been coughing rather badly. I knew it to be merciless to force a half-ill person to carry rationed rice on her back. However, I felt it exceedingly burdensome to stand in a line of waiting people myself. "Are you all right?" I said to my wife. "I will go and get the rice," she said, "but taking the children along is too much for me. Therefore, please stay at home and look after the children. Carrying the rice itself is already hard enough." I saw tears shining in her eyes. She was pregnant with a child in her belly. Carrying one on her back, leading yet another by the hand, herself ill with a cold, and carrying home nearly a half bushel of rice in her arms would be a real tribulation. I understood that even without seeing tears in her eyes. "Sure, I'll be here. I'll stay home," I said. Half an hour passed. "Excuse me," a woman's voice said at the entrance. I went to see. There was a servant girl from a snack bar near Mitaka station. "Miss Maeda is at our place," she said. "Is that so?" I had already laid my hand on my overcoat which hung on the wall near the way out of the room. Unable to think quickly of any lie, I said nothing to my wife in the next room, and put on the coat. Rifling through my desk and not finding much money, I stuffed into the pocket of my coat three checks just sent that morning from publishers. I left. The eldest girl was standing outside. It was she who expressed the awkwardness of the situation in her countenance. "Miss Maeda? Alone?" I purposely ignored my daughter in questioning the servant girl. "Yes. She would like to see you, even briefly." "I see." Miss Maeda was a woman past forty. For a long time she had reportedly worked for a newspaper in Yurakucho. But I had no idea of what she was doing now. I had met her about two weeks before toward the end of the past year. She had come to eat at this snack bar. With two younger friends, I was there completely drunk. I happened to start a conversation, asked her to take a seat with us, and shook hands—that was the extent of my acquaintance with her. "Let us have fun. Let's really have a ball!" When I spoke to her, she said in an unusually relaxed voice, "Only those who cannot enjoy themselves make such an issue of it. You must ordinarily work like a miser." I was startled. "OK. If you say so, when we meet again I'll show you how thorough I am at it." While saying it, inwardly I thought how detestable an aunty she was. Although strange for me to say it, I thought such a person must really be a very unhealthy type. I hate to find amusement without agony. Work well and play well. I approve of play coupled with hard work. Those given only to play irritate me more than anybody else. What a damned fool, I thought. But it was I that was also the fool. I did not like to be defeated. Although she talks big she is basically a square. I felt that next time I would give her a jolt and peel her affectation from her. "Any time you feel like seeing me, come here and send the maid after me," I told her, shaking hands. Although I was dead drunk, I did not forget it. If I write the above only, it sounds as if I was a high-minded innocent. But it was probably only the low, dirty, sensuous end product of my drunken stupor. It might have been nothing more than a grotesque tableau, so to speak, for those who smell the same and find each other. So I hurried out to this unhealthy devil.

He goes to the snack bar and meets this woman again. She is a thin, tall woman, wearing glasses. She looked slightly better when he met

her for the first time, because he was drunk. Now he feels disgusted.
He starts pouring sake into himself and talking to the waitresses. The
woman remains reticent and does not join him in drinking. He challenges her, offering to get drunk together. She says she does not drink
in the daytime.

"It does not make any difference whether it is daytime or night. You are a
'champion' of pleasure, aren't you?" I said. "Drinking is not playing," she
delivered the brazen answer. I felt even more disheartened. "What do you
want, then? A kiss?" A lascivious old bitch! You don't know that only to join
you for pleasure, I have gone so far as to play the role of a father deserting
his children. "I'm going home," the woman picked up her purse on the table.
"Pardon me. I did not call you for that purpose." She looked as if she were
going to cry. She made her face into an ugly grimace. It was so ugly that I
felt pity. "I am sorry. Let's go outside together." She nodded weakly, stood up
and wiped her nose. I said, "I am a savage. I don't know anything about
amusement. If you don't like drinking, I am at a loss as to what to suggest."
Why couldn't I simply leave her? Going outside, the woman became suddenly
cheerful, "I felt ashamed. Although I have known that restaurant for quite
a while, when I told the proprietress today to ask you to come, she gave me
a strangely disapproving look. Disgusting, isn't it? I am no longer even a
woman or anything. What about you, are you a man?" She was becoming
more and more offensive. And yet I could not tell her good-bye. "Let us amuse
ourselves. Don't you have some excellent idea about playing?" I said just the
opposite of what I had in mind, kicking a stone with my toe. "Would you
come to my apartment? I had that originally in mind today. There are some
interesting friends there." I felt depressed. I was simply not willing. "Is there
any wonderful 'fun' waiting for us in your apartment?" She laughed and said,
"There will be nothing. I'm surprised a writer would be such a realist!"
"Well," I started talking and suddenly shut my mouth. There she was, my
wife. My wife, sick with cold, wearing a white mask over her face, carrying
our younger son on her back, standing in line, in a cold wind, I saw her. I
saw my wife. She pretended not to have noticed me, but our eldest daughter
beside her discovered me. Our daughter, imitating her mother, also wore a
small mask. She was about to start running toward her father, who was drunk
in the daytime and was walking with a strange-looking woman. I felt as if I
would almost suffocate. But her mother covered the girl's face with the sleeve
of her overcoat, as if nothing had happened.

He then describes how he gets drunk at the woman's apartment, feeling
nauseated by the pretentiousness of the women companions of his
hostess. He repeatedly says to himself that this is his hell, but yet he
does not give a thought to returning home.

"Duty. What is duty? I cannot explain it but Abraham tried to
kill his only child and Sogoro[81] had to desert his children and I must

---

[81] Sakura Sogoro is a legendary figure, appearing in dramas, stories, and folksongs
in the Tokugawa period. In a dramatic version of the legend, Sogoro, a farmer,
decides to report directly to the shogunate about the sufferings of his fellow villagers

perversely put myself in hell—all for the sake of duty. Duty. Duty. Duty resembles the sad weakness of a man who cannot bear himself."

Political rebellion had led him nowhere; nor did his attempt to be a family man; nor was he sustained by his brief postwar discovery of patriotic love for the emperor. In some sense, at least, this was an incomplete and unsatisfactory "conversion experience," similar to that later avowed by Mishima in attaining a destiny of suicide, as was discussed in the previous chapter. Dazai could not maintain such a pretense of affirmation or belonging even for a short period. Finally, he could not wrest from his capacity as a creative writer any sense of meaning sufficient to sustain him.

In an essay *Faint Smile*,[82] 1948, shortly before his death, Dazai wrote:

What is life? Life is to endure miserable loneliness.
What is art? Art is the color of violet, the flower violet, meaningless.
Yes, art is a meaningless thing.
What is an artist? A pig's nose. . . .

CONCLUSIONS

The three authors we considered, while exemplifying some very characteristic modes of coping with a sense of personal alienation in modern Japanese society, by no means exhaust all possible modes. If we had selected other authors we probably would have had to change our emphasis. We do feel confident, however, that we have covered those modes of adaptation to alienation that are of major importance to intellectuals. Whatever individual Japanese authors had been chosen, we would have found it possible to illustrate from his works cultural changes occurring with Japanese modernization that shift the emphasis of the origin of human tragedy from tragedy occasioned by outer social circumstances to tragedy as an internal human state.

In the later Meiji, Natsume Sōseki was able to represent in his characters tragic tensions related to the newer ideas of individualism. His thoughts and feelings nevertheless still were pervaded with background leitmotifs derived from traditional Confucian ethical values. There is an underlying fear in Sōseki that people, freed from these values, would become egocentric, untrustworthy, cold, and even cruel —and, most importantly, somehow incapable of structuring relationships with others. Failing to find some alternative solution in Zen,

---

under the ruthless rule of a feudal lord. Appealing directly to the shogunate was punishable by death during the Tokugawa regime. In the drama, Sogoro, knowing that he will not return alive after his appeal, takes leave of his home and crying children and sets out on his mission of self-sacrifice.

[82] Dazai, *Faint Smile* (1948, in Japanese), Tokyo: Kodansha.

Sōseki was forced to turn back on himself in disappointment. In the moral ethical code he sought to develop for himself, personal autonomy was more important than political or social reform. This inner-directed attitude,[83] while freeing him from the outer pressure of his society, by no means afforded him any inner sense of personal resolution. Intellectually, he triumphed; emotionally, he achieved nothing better than a stalemate in his relation to his wife. His failure was dramatized in the physiological expression of a sense of rage over personal deprivation that he found impossible to overcome.

Akutagawa Ryūnosuke started with the premise that individuals are nasty, untrustworthy, selfish beings, *as individuals,* irrespective of their membership in a social order. Instead of attempting to cope with an incapacity for true and satisfactory human intimacy or stressing his feelings that only destruction would result from closeness, as did Dazai Osamu, Akutagawa decided from the beginning, so to speak, not to make an issue of his isolation. He tried to escape into estheticism. For a while he succeeded and became genuinely productive as an artist. However, his life was increasingly colored by pessimism, bitterness, and withdrawal. A tenuous balance achieved with wife and family offered very little safeguard to his increasing preoccupation with self-destruction. The specter of his own potential madness hastened his hand.

Osamu Dazai, from the very beginning of consciousness in childhood, continually experienced a deep sense of alienation. He saw all human relationships as façades lacking any honest emotional depth. Truth for him seems to exist in a continual perverse revelation of personal insufficiency and unworthiness. At the same time, he sought means of throwing himself on others, with the expectation of nurturance. In his perverse denial, Dazai ended by directly rejecting family life, or any other possible form of personal intimacy. Dazai's negative message was that human survival is contingent upon the continual practice of hypocrisy. He played at the experience of love, never certain that it actually existed within human beings. During his youth he played at the political resolution of social problems, continually sullying in retrospect any momentary conviction or belief he might have held. The ultimate irony of his life was that he could not actually practice the self-destruction that was for him to be a release. He died not in a true act of individual initiative in suicide, but as a passive masochistic victim, a role he long had played in his fantasy.

The tradition of tragic suicide is not new in Japan. In Tokugawa

---

[83] Throughout our analysis we have found Riesman's formulation concerning the nature of alienation in American society a provocative theoretical framework within which to view Japanese modernization. His trichotomy of "tradition-directed," "inner-directed," and "other-directed" orientations are applicable to Japan.

Japan, for example, the tragic suicide of his day that Chikamatsu Monzaemon dramatized for the puppet stage was in one sense an active defiance of society and its stifling of potential genuine intimacy between individuals. Chikamatsu never examines whether individuals resolved to suicide, if given sudden release from societal pressure, would in fact have found within themselves the real capacity for sustained relationship.

The three authors we considered, however, each gave a different meaning to this act as it relates to human alienation. For Natsume Sōseki the individual may attain his goal and force through to a desired relationship, only to find himself a victim of his own conscience. For Akutagawa Ryūnosuke death is faced from a truly isolated position —a position of real attenuation from all society. The quest for intimacy long since forsaken leaves only the self-imposed standards of artistic refinement and the experience and expression of beauty as a vehicle of human communication. Dazai Osamu mocks the meaning of the suicidal act. For him it takes the form of a histrionic kōan[84] of sincerity, which he himself cannot solve. He is uncertain as to his own sincerity concerning suicide as he is uncertain and doubtful of the sincerity of any form of human communication. There are no standards left for Dazai, no way to judge experience from a firm, unchanging base. Dazai as a modern rebel loses orientation completely without the authoritarian society that once gave opposition purpose. The only positive form of external aggression he had found in his life was in the capacity to express anger toward authoritarian injustice.

Many modern authors, in Japan as elsewhere, in one way or another express what might be called the wounded righteous innocence of the child versus the world. They cannot accept the meaning given to life by the majority who give up the true vision of the child for the hypocritical defensive blindness of the ordinary adult. From what is in essence a position of innocence, they lament the corruption and compromise of adult society. Creative authors in this sense very often remain as critical as a noncommitted adolescent in viewing the world about them. They reject the compromise and conformity in personal relationships that take on the guise of forced social amenities as a means of getting along. Dazai most self-consciously portrays this defensive aspect of social relationships. He portrays hypocrisy from the standpoint of the protagonist himself, whereas in Akutagawa's work the most vivid criticism of society is expressed in his portrayal of the world of the "Kappa." This satire on human nature is still seen from the standpoint of a detached, noncommitted observer. Dazai, in No

---

[84] A kōan is an unresolvable Zen riddle to test the mettle of acolytes—in the hopes of shocking them toward enlightenment.

Longer Human,[85] presents the observer himself as a participant in or protagonist of the hypocrisy practiced between humans.

For the unduly sensitive human, contact implies pain. For Dazai the pain of contact is turned into a sensualized self-flagellation, or, even more cleverly, into a perverse form of *amae*,[86] an expression used in Japanese psychology to describe the passive-manipulative ability to induce in others an active desire to love and care for one. Dazai succeeded in having a woman fulfill the deepest of his passive desires by administering to him the act of destruction through which he sought to lose himself in some form of ultimate belonging.

The early works of Sōseki reveal an attempt to stand aside, to find in the esthetic experience a position of withdrawal from the painful necessity of association. Sōseki cannot maintain this position of esthetic withdrawal; later he shifts to a concern over how to armor the self through autonomy without seeking protective distance.

Akutagawa finds withdrawal the only means open to him. He crosses through the looking glass into the legends and historical, esoteric happenings of former eras and strange situations. By so doing he seeks successful escape from the present. In his own personal life, he does not escape. In a very poignant short story, *Mandarin Orange*,[87] he portrays in very economical fashion his repulsion at vulgarity, at the ugliness of humans; but he is touched, nevertheless, by the capacity of one such vulgar person he observes on a train to maintain a feeling of love and relatedness to others. And in the bleakness of his own experience he is pervaded by a momentary feeling of joy at what it must mean to be able to relate. The story is poignant because one feels the intense isolation of the rider on the train who fills the time with careful observation of others. He touches the reader because everyone at one time or other has experienced this sense of detachment, of riding on a train as an observer. However, when this becomes the mainline of experience for a man, we can say that he is truly alienated.

Man needs to be more than a stranger on a train.

---

[85] *Ningen Shikkaku*, in *Collected Works* IX.

[86] Doi, "Japanese Psychology, Dependence, Need, and Mental Health," in Caudill and Lin, *Mental Health Research in Asia and the Pacific* (1969); and Doi, " 'Amae': A Key Concept for Understanding Japanese Personality Structure" (1962).

[87] *Mikan* (1919), in Akutagawa, *Collected Works* II, 345–352.

Appendix A

Summary Description of Psychological Tests

THE PROBLEM SITUATION TEST

The Problem Situation Test employed in our research is based upon the "Insight Test," [1] a clinical diagnostic personality test originated by Helen D. Sargent. A problematic situation is described to the subject, who is asked to state what he believes an individual would do to resolve the situation, why, and how the individual involved would feel under the circumstances. In adapting the Insight Test for use with Japanese subjects, we were equally interested in the sociological and the psychological values of each item, and therefore freely adapted items to Japanese situations. Only a few of Sargent's items survived unchanged through the revisions which followed the pretesting of college students.

The revised test administered in Niiike consisted of two alternate forms, A and B, for each of 16 items (for which there were also M and W variants for male and female subjects). This use of alternate forms allowed for some changes in wording in items related to similar problems permitting some differences in emphasis. Due to the inappropriate nature of some of the items for younger subjects, only subjects over eighteen years of age were tested. The test was administered to a total of twenty-nine men and thirty-one women in Niiike.

The principal purpose of the Problem Situation Test items used in Niiike was to elicit attitudes toward various forms of interpersonal relationships. We focused on attitudes related to the Japanese family system, and to a lesser degree, relation of family to community. For purposes of analysis we grouped our items into six general categories:

    I. Parent-child relationships
    II. Marriage and parental obligations

---

[1] Sargent, *The Insight Test: A Verbal Projective Test for Personality Study* (1953).

III. Possible marriage choice and attitudes toward arranged marriages
IV. Marital discord and family tensions
V. Reputation and personal sensitivity
VI. Duty, obligation, and responsibility

I. Parent-Child Relationships (7 items)

Item 16. A man has been very much loved by both parents; however, on one occasion his father tells him of his dissatisfaction with his mother. (This item sought to elicit the perception of what role a child might take in relation to parental disharmony.)

Item 21. A young man gets into trouble. If he tells his parents, they can help him but they will be much disappointed and will strongly disapprove of what he has done. (Japanese values have stressed the role of a child as a representative of his family. His disgrace brings disgrace on his parents. This item sought to elicit the degree to which such considerations are of spontaneous concern.)

Item 7. A man is caught in petty theft. His employer offers to let him keep his job if his parents will vouch for him; otherwise he will be forced to look for another job without references. (This item sought to elicit similar concerns as item 21 with the additional factor of employment as a consideration.)

Item 3. A man acquired religious and political opinions away from home which are in direct conflict with his parents' ideas. He is home for a visit, and religious and political subjects are raised for discussion. (This item sought to elicit how differences of opinion are handled in child-parent situations.)

Item 5. A man's parents have always looked forward to having their son take over their business and have educated him for it. The son becomes interested in another vocation. (Occupational succession is put in opposition to individual interests and ambitions.)

Item 10. A young man of poor family wants to go to a senior school after finishing his lower courses and discusses the matter with his parents. He is told by his parents that for the sake of everyone he should not speak more of such a selfish plan. (Poverty and obligation for supporting the home and parents is put in opposition to educational advancement.)

Item 1. A man working (or studying) away from home receives a letter from his mother after the death of his father asking him to move back home. (Living separately and following an individual career is put in opposition to house succession and to care of a mother.)

II. Marriage and Parental Obligations (5 items)

Item 12. A man's parents were habitually indebted to an individual for help. One day this individual asks the parents to accept his daughter as a bride for their son. The man's parents are very happy about the request. (A marriage as a fulfillment of obligation (*giri*) demands that a child sacrifice his future as a repayment for obligation.)

Item 17. A man wants to get married to a girl he loves but he cannot support both his mother and a wife. (This item tests for the priority given a love relationship or care for parents.)

Item 20. A woman's husband dies early. After his death she receives a proposal of marriage from a man to whom she was previously very close. When she talks it over with her parents-in-law, they say, "Don't leave our house; we are planning to leave all our family property to you and your children." (This item concerns itself with the possible marriage of a widow as opposed to the obligation to her new family through marriage.)

Item 14. A man is loved by a girl who is "below" him in wealth and social position. Reciprocating the love, he too wants to get married. When he talks to his parents about it he finds them opposed to the idea. (Love and free choice are put in opposition to questions of social position and parental disapproval.)

Item 19. A man is engaged to be married with a girl whom he loves. However, when he introduces the girl to his parents, one of them raises strong objections. (Love is put into opposition to strong, direct parental disapproval.)

III. Attitudes Toward Men-Women Relationships and Marriage Possibilities (2 items)

Item 13. A man is strongly attracted to a girl who is "above" him in wealth and social position. He hears indirectly that she is interested in him. (The item sought to test the relative weight given love and other considerations such as class position.)

Item 9. A man discovers that a girl to whom he is engaged has a very bad reputation. (This item sought to test sensitivity to criticism about social behavior and manners.)

IV. Marital Discord and Family Tensions (4 items)

Item 25. A man heard that his wife goes out often with another man. (This item, indirectly suggesting unfaithfulness in a woman, sought to test Japanese attitudes in this regard.)

Item 8. A man gets married to a beautiful woman who comes from an honorable family and is much envied by his neighbors. One day he comes to know that his wife loves another man. (This item more directly suggests that the marriage partner loves another. It sought to test the nature of reactions to this type of situation.)

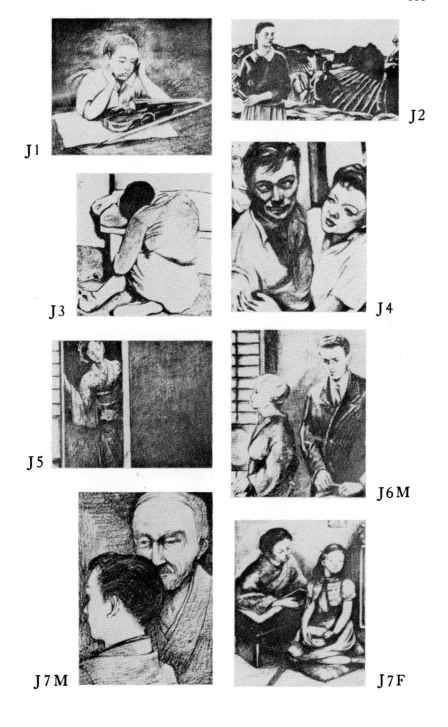

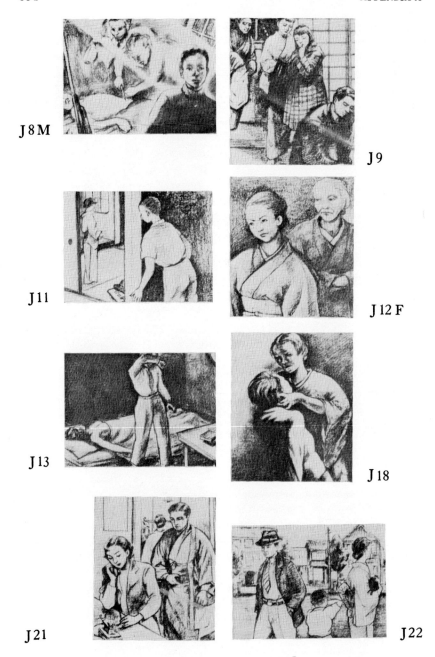

J 8 M

J 9

J 11

J 12 F

J 13

J 18

J 21

J 22

Item 6. A man's wife did not get along with her mother-in-law very well. They had conflicts over all sorts of matters. (6a) As a result his wife one day tells him that she would like a divorce. (6b) As a result her husband one day finally suggests divorce. (This item directly approached the most notable source of family tension in Japan. It was worded to elicit the possible types of reaction to a suggestion of divorce on the part of both the husband and wife.)

Item 26. A woman works as hard as possible every day doing her housework. Nevertheless, one day she overhears her mother-in-law complaining to the neighbors that her son's wife is not a good worker. (This item sought to test the reactions of a wife to an unreasonable mother-in-law.)

V. Reputation and Personal Sensitivity (3 items)

Item 4. A man came from an honorable family much respected by the neighbors, but one of his family does such a dishonorable thing that he is not able to show his face in public. (This item tests family responsibility for the conduct of an individual member.)

Item 11. A man gets the impression that others are discussing him. (Form b—discussing his family). He thinks that the conversation has stopped or the subject changed when he entered the room. (This item attempts to test sensitivity to gossip concerning oneself and family and how it is handled.)

Item 2. A man working in a company is insulted one day by the son of the president in the presence of other employees. (This item poses conflict between economic considerations and personal insult.)

VI. Duty, Obligation, and Responsibility (7 items)

Item 18. A man's superior resigns. Soon after, the man and one of his fellow workers are recommended for the vacated post. He is asked how he feels about this recommendation by his boss. The fellow worker also recommended is an older man who has been working for the firm a longer time. (This item sought to elicit attitudes toward job seniority as opposed to personal ambition. Traditionally, individuals are supposed to exercise reserve about being self-forwarding.)

Item 24. A man is asked by his boss to leave town to carry out important business. At the same time he receives an urgent letter from someone to whom he has been much indebted asking for his immediate help. (This item poses conflict between duty to job (gimu) and obligation to others (giri).)

Item 28. A man's family is in needy circumstances. One day at the town assembly it is decided to collect contributions from all to carry out a group project. (This item poses a conflict between economic duress and duty to support the community endeavors.)

Item 27. A person is told by a teacher to correct certain habits and manners of his child. (This item was devised to gain some insight on the status of the teacher as related to parental feelings about social behavior of a child.)

Item 22. A man who was formerly a tenant farmer was treated badly by his landowner. He now hears that the former owner is very badly off due to the effect of the law reorganizing landownership. (This item was devised to test for the survival of attitudes of obligation toward landowners.)

Item 15a. A man has been feeling quite ill but the doctor tells him not to worry since he is not seriously sick and it will do him no harm to go on leading a normal life. (This item attempted to elicit possible hypochondriacal feelings as well as the relative strength of trust in a doctor's knowledge and authority.)

Item 15b. A man is not well and he is told by the doctor to rest for some time, but if he follows the doctor's advice it will seriously interfere with his life's work. (Conflict is posed between endangering one's health and the necessity to continue work obligations.)

THEMATIC APPERCEPTION TEST

Our large-scale use of the Japanese Thematic Apperception Test had two purposes: (1) the analysis of personality and social values indicated by other material, and (2) the standardization for psychodiagnostic purposes of a TAT suitable for use in Japan. The Thematic Apperception Test consists of pictures of persons in ambiguous situations, designed to elicit in response various stories, which are then analyzed for content and tone. A set of such pictures was first developed by Morgan and Murray at Harvard in about 1935. The idea has since been put to a variety of uses, and the content of the test has often been modified for various types of research. We attempted, in adapting the test for use in Japan, to change as little as possible the cards of the third Harvard edition, which has proven particularly helpful both in clinical and in research work.

The Nagoya edition, or Marui-DeVos Japanese Standard TAT, includes thirty-five cards, not all of which are used with equal frequency in research since only a limited number may be administered at any one time to an individual. The set includes five of the original Murray cards without modifications, fourteen cards from the original series with minor changes of face or background, and sixteen new cards on themes potentially valuable for the eliciting of personality variables or pertinent value attitudes.

Modified Cards

*JM1	Boy with violin
*J2	Farm scene
*J3F	Girl with bowed head at door
*J4	Excited man and woman
*J5	Woman peering into room
*J6M	Mother—adult son
*J6F	Woman surprised by a man
*J7M	Older man—younger man
*J7F	Young girl read to by mother
*J8M	Young boy—operation scene
J8F	Girl dreaming, sitting on chair
J10	Embracing pair
*J13	Seminude reclining woman—distraught male
*J18	Woman with hands on throat of other figure

Murray Set unchanged

*M3M	Young figure slumped against couch
14	Figure peering out at sky
15	Blank card
17	Man climbing
20	Figure under lamppost at night

New Cards

*J1	Boy looking at book
*J9	Family scene
*J11	Boy eavesdropping on woman
J12M	Young man entering room of old man
*J12F	Older woman—younger woman
J15	Buddhist temple and graves
J19	Japanese landscape
*J21	Woman at telephone
*J22	Child crying between two figures —man and woman facing in opposite directions
J23	Very disturbed scene of possible violence
J24	Man at back door
J25	Nude male figure
J26	Geisha
J27	Teenagers in front of coffee shop
J28	Nursing mother and child
J29	Old woman walking in a poor neighborhood
J30	Poor old man in an impoverished setting

* Used in Niiike

Eleven of the nineteen cards employed in Niiike were presented to all subjects. From among them, the cards judged to be most successful in eliciting rich stories were administered to as many as forty persons, but it was planned to present all cards to twenty-five or more subjects. Eighty persons over twelve years of age participated in the test; they were grouped in age as follows:

	Men	Women
12–17	5	10
18–24	6	6
25–34	7	5
35–49	8	13
50–64	6	6
65 plus	4	4
Total	36	44

Most of the pictures that were directly referred to in this volume are reproduced on pages 553 and 554.

THE RORSCHACH TEST

The Rorschach Ink Blot Test has been used in a number of previous personality and culture research projects and has had widespread use in clinical diagnostic practice in both psychiatry and psychology. It consists of ten standardized ink blots which are relatively free of cultural structuring. The basic assumption of the test revolves around the fact that in responding to the test, individuals tend to express in microcosm the way in which they perceive and experience the world about them. The basic determinants of responses—form, color, shading, depth, movement, the distribution of responses to various locations, the nature of the content of the responses and other combinations—are subjected to quantitative evaluations which are interpretable according to certain standard assumptions concerning their relationship to personality parameters. The interested reader is referred to any of several standard texts for further elucidation. For use of the test with Japanese subjects including Niiike, cf. several of the above cited references.

In Niiike the test was administered to the eighty same subjects given the TAT—thirty-six men and forty-four women.

Appendix B

Some Brief Summaries of Death, Illness, Injury, Accidental Death Stories by Niiike Villagers

1. Situational description of death and illness (no expression of feelings)

   J6M, man, age group 50–64.
   A mother is sending off her son who is going to visit a sick person.
   J6M, woman, age group 18–24.
   Village people help a family whose head had died.
   J9, woman, age group 12–17.
   A son came to see his sick father but the father died.
   J11, woman, age group 12–17.
   A child is watching his sick mother walking slowly about.
   J13, woman, age group over 65.
   A wife is sick and not better, her husband is studying.
   J18, man, age group 12–17.
   A mother sees her son who died in Sagami lake. She brings his body back to school and holds funeral.

2. Care and nurturance related to death, illness, and injury

   J4, woman, age group over 65.
   A husband gets excited about his sickness, and his wife soothes him.
   J9, man, age group 35–49.
   A younger sister is trying to console the elder brother, who is sorrowful because of his lover's death.
   J18, woman, age group 12–17.
   A mother examines her daughter's teeth. She will take her daughter to the dentist.

3. Grief, worry, and anxieties concerning death and illness

   J1, woman, age group 35–49.

A boy is studying English, but he is not looking at the book, because he is distressed by his father's death.

3M, woman, age group 25–34.

A woman is worrying about illness of her lover or sibling at a hospital.

3M, woman, age group 25–34.

A girl is sad or worried over her mother or father's illness. She becomes careful over her own health when she becomes a bride.

J13, man, age group 50–64.

A husband is weeping at his wife's death. A young husband will not be married any more and lives in loneliness to pray for the soul of the dead.

J13, man, age group over 65.

A sister or a wife is going to die and a man is weeping very much, since he loves her.

J18, woman, age group 18–24.

A mother has been suffering from T.B. She is sad now, as her child died. She will live on in loneliness.

4. Achievement and hard work related to death and illness

   3M, woman, age group 18–24.

   A girl is crying, as her mother died. She struggles hard and succeeds for her mother.

   J13, woman, age group 12–17.

   A son is weeping very much at the death of his mother, who loved him very much. He is consoled by his father and neighbors. He will become a good man in the future.

5. Reform and expiatory achievement related to death and illness

   3M, woman, age group 50–64.

   A girl is sad over her father's illness or suicide; the father dies and she becomes a serious person, changing her attitudes.

   J7M, woman, age group 12–17.

   A father died and his son walks out as his mother told him repeatedly to become like his father. The mother lives in loneliness. When she finds him again she dies. He becomes a hard-working man.

   J9, woman, age group 35–49.

   The elder brother is going to Tokyo, in order to work. He leaves his sick mother at home ignoring his sisters' opposition. His mother dies, and he becomes hard-working and successful.

   J13, man, age group 50–64.

   A son was surprised at the death of his mother, who has been sick. He will change his attitude and will work hard.

   J18, man, age group 18–24.

   A mother strangles to death a woman who tempted her innocent son. The mother becomes insane and dies. Son begs mother's forgiveness and becomes hard-working.

6. Masochistic themes of self-sacrifice, overwork, and suicide

3F, man, age group 12–17.

A girl is crying over illness or death of her parent. She is sad and thinking of suicide.

3M, man, age group 35–49.

A girl is working too hard at sewing. She is poor and her body becomes weak and cannot keep up. The future is bleak.

J6M, man, age group 18–24.

A son had died from an accident, and his mother is so distressed that she will die, following him.

JM7M, man, age group 12–17.

A father died in an accident. His son loved him so much that he committed suicide. They are ghosts.

J13, woman, age group 12–17.

A husband finds his wife dead (suicide). In her diary she wrote she was going to kill herself, as she was sorry for him being so burdened with her sickness. He weeps, and he will live in loneliness to remember his wife.

7. Poverty and financial concern related to death and illness

J9, man, age group 18–24.

A rich man is economically broken by the father's death, and the whole family is crying.

Bibliography

Abe, Junkichi
1960 "Hikō no Shakai Shinrigaku" (Social Psychology of Delinquency), in Togawa Yukio, et al. (eds.), *Sheikaku no Ijō to Shidō* (Abnormality of Character and Guidance), Vol. 4 of Seikaku Shinrigaku Kōza, Tokyo: Kaneko Shobo, pp. 179–227.

Abegglen, J. G.
1958 *The Japanese Factory: Aspects of Its Social Organization*, Glencoe, Ill.: Free Press.

Akutagawa, Ryūnosuke
1917 *Hana* (Nose), Tokyo: Orandashobo.
1927 *Shinkirō* (Mirage), Tokyo: Chuō Koronsha.
1934–1935 *Collected Works*, 10 vols. Tokyo: Iwanami Shoten.
1938 "Mikan" (Mandarin Orange), English translation by T. Yuasa, "The Mandarin Oranges," in *Contemporary Japan*, Vol. 6.
1947 *Kappa*, English translation by S. Shiojiri, Osaka: A. Kitaya.
1952 *Roshōmon and Other Stories*, English translation by T. Kojima, Tokyo and Rutland, Vermont: Charles Tuttle.

Arensberg, Conrad
1937 *The Irish Countryman: An Anthropological Study*, New York: Macmillan.

Ariga, Kizaemon
1940 *Nōson Shakai no Kenkyū* (Study of Social Organization in Japanese Farming Villages), Tokyo: Kawado.
1948 *Nihon Kon-in shi-ron* (Study of History of Marriage in Japan), Tokyo: Nikkō Shoin.

Ariga, Kizaemon
1955 "Contemporary Japanese Family in Transition," *Transaction of the Third World Congress of Sociology*, Vol. 4, pp. 215–221.

Ariga, Kizaemon; Nakano, T.; and Morioka, K.
1954 "The Japanese Family," *Transactions of the Second World Congress of Sociology*, Vol. 1, pp. 83–89.

Asayama, Shin-ichi
1958 *Nijuseiki no Sekkusu* (Sex in the Twentieth Century), Tokyo: Chuo Koron-Sha.

Ausubel, David P.
1965a *The Fern and the Tiki*, New York: Holt, Rinehart and Winston.

1965*b* *Maori Youth,* New York: Holt, Rinehart and Winston.
Babcock, Charlotte G., and Caudill, William
    1958   "Personal and Cultural Factors in Treating a Nisei Man," in Georgene Seward (ed.), *Clinical Studies in Culture Conflict,* New York: Ronald Press, pp. 409–448.
Baber, Ray E.
    1958   *Youth Looks at Marriage and the Family: A Study of Changing Japanese Attitudes,* Tokyo: International Christian University Press.
Bader, K.
    1949   *Soziologie der Deutschen Nachkriegskriminalität,* Tübingen: J. C. B. Mohr.
Ballestros, Usano A.
    1951   "Suicide in Adolescence," *Proceedings of the International Congress of Mental Health,* pp. 281–289.
Banfield, Edward
    1958   *The Moral Basis of a Backward Community,* Glencoe, Ill.: Free Press.
Barnett, Homer G.
    1959   "Peace and Progress in New Guinea," *American Anthropology,* Vol. 61, pp. 1013–1019.
Barry, Herbert H.; Child, Irwin L.; and Bacon, Margaret K.
    1959   "Relations of Child Training to Subsistence Economy," *American Anthropologist,* Vol. 61, pp. 51–63.
Bauer, R.
    1952   *The New Man in Soviet Psychology,* Cambridge: Harvard University Press.
Bauer, R.; Inkeles, A.; and Kluckhohn, C.
    1956   *How the Soviet System Works,* Cambridge: Harvard University Press.
Beardsley, Richard K.
    1951   "The Household in the Status System of Japanese Villages," Center for Japanese Studies, University of Michigan, *Occasional Papers,* No. 1.
Beardsley, Richard K.; Hall, John W.; and Ward, R. E.
    1959   *Village Japan,* Chicago: University of Chicago Press.
Beck, Samuel J.; Rabin, Albert I.; Thiesen, Warren G.; Molish, Herman; and Thetford, William N.
    1950   "The Normal Personality as Projected in the Rorschach Test," *Journal of Psychology,* Vol. 30, pp. 241–298.
Befu, Harumi, and Norbeck, Edward
    1958   "Japanese Usages of Terms of Relationships," *Southwestern Journal of Anthropology,* Vol. 14, No. 1, pp. 66–86.
Bell, Reginald
    1933   "A Study of Effects of Segregation upon Japanese Children in American Schools," Ph.D. dissertation, Stanford University Library.
Bellah, Robert
    1957   *Tokugawa Religion,* Glencoe, Ill.: Free Press.
Benedict, Ruth
    1946   *The Chrysanthemum and the Sword: Patterns of Japanese Culture,* Boston: Houghton Mifflin.
Bennett, John W., and Ishino, Iwao
    1963   *Paternalism in the Japanese Economy,* Minneapolis: University of Minnesota Press.

Berrigan, Durrel
  1955   *Yakuza no Sekai* (The Society of Gangs), Tokyo: 20-Seiki-Sha.
Bloch, H. A., and Flynn, F. T.
  1956   *Delinquency*, New York: Random House.
Blood, Robert O., Jr.
  1967   *Love Marriage and Arranged Marriage*, New York: Free Press.
Blumer, H., and Hauser, P. M.
  1933   *The Movies, Delinquency and Crime*, New York: Macmillan.
Bogen, D.
  1944   "Juvenile Delinquency and Economic Trends," *American Sociological Review*, Vol. 9, pp. 178–184.
Bohannan, Paul (ed.)
  1960   *African Homicide and Suicide*, Princeton: Princeton University Press.
Bonger, W. A.
  1916   *Criminality and Economic Conditions*, Boston: Little Brown.
Bradburn, Norman M.
  1963a "The Cultural Context of Personality Theory," in Joseph M. Wepman and Ralph W. Heine (eds.), *Concepts of Personality*, Chicago: Aldine, pp. 333–360.
  1963b "Need Achievement and Father Dominance," *Journal of Abnormal and Social Psychology*, Vol. 67, No. 5, pp. 464–468.
Bradburn, Norman M., and Berlew, D. E.
  1960   "Need for Achievement and English Industrial Growth," *Economic Development and Culture Change*, Vol. 10, pp. 8–20.
Brim, Orville G.
  1952   "Ability and Achievement: Summary of Selected Research on Gifted Children," unpublished paper.
Brown, Keith
  1966   " 'Dōzoku' and the Ideology of Descent in Rural Japan," *American Anthropologist*, Vol. 68.
Bunderskriminalamt, *Polizeiliche Kriminalstatistik*, German Government
  1958   Statistics.
Buraku Henshūbu (Editorial Staff of *Buraku*)
  1955   *Buraku*, August 1955, pp. 30–35.
  1957   "Hirooka Chūgaku ni Okeru Sabetsu" (Discrimination at Hirooka Junior High School), *Buraku*, Vol. 7, pp. 4–15.
  1961   "Kempō Dōri no Seikatsu to Kenri O" (Demanding the Life and Rights Guaranteed by the Constitution), *Buraku*, Vol. 10, pp. 16–23.
  1962   *Buraku*, April 1962.
Burg, Moses
  1961   "A Psychocultural Analysis and Theoretical Integration of the Dynamics of Japanese Parent-Child Suicide," *Tōyō Daigaku Shakaigakubu Kiyō* (Department of Sociology) *Bulletin No. 2*, University of Tokyo.
Caldwell, M.
  1942   "The Extent of Juvenile Delinquency in Wisconsin," *Journal of Criminal Law and Criminology*, Vol. 32, pp. 148–156.
Caudill, William
  1952   "Japanese-American Personality and Acculturation," *Genetic Psychology Monographs*, Vol. 45, pp. 3–102.

1962   "Patterns of Emotion in Modern Japan," in R. J. Smith and R. K.
        Beardsley (eds.), *Japanese Culture*, Chicago: Aldine, pp. 115–131.
1963   "Sibling Rank and Style of Life Among Japanese Psychiatric Pa-
        tients," *Proceedings from the Joint Meeting of the Japanese Society
        of Psychiatry and Neurology and the American Psychiatric Associa-
        tion,* Tokyo, Japan.
Caudill, William, and De Vos, George
1956   "Achievement, Culture and Personality: The Case of the Japanese
        Americans," *American Anthropologist,* Vol. 58, No. 6, pp. 1102–
        1126.
Caudill, William, and Doi, L. Takeo
1963   "Interrelations of Psychiatry, Culture and Emotion in Japan," re-
        printed with permission by the U.S. Department of Health, Educa-
        tion and Welfare from *Man's Image in Medicine and Anthropology,*
        Iago Galdston (ed.), New York: International Universities Press.
Caudill, William, and Lin, Tsung-yi
1969   *Mental Health Research in Asia and the Pacific,* Honolulu, Hawaii:
        East-West Center Press.
Caudill, William, and Plath, David
1969   "Who Sleeps by Whom? Parent-Child Involvement in Urban Japa-
        nese Families," *Psychiatry,* November 1969.
Caudill, William, and Schooler, Carmi
1966   "Symptom Patterns Among Japanese Psychiatric Patients," paper
        used at the East-West Center Conference, Honolulu, March 28–April
        1.
Caudill, William, and Weinstein, Helen
1966   "Maternal Care and Infant Behavior in Japanese and American
        Urban Middle Class Families," in Rēne König and Reuben Hill
        (eds.), *Yearbook of the International Sociological Association,* Switzer-
        land: Broz, entire issue.
1969   "Maternal Care and Infant Behavior in Japan and America," *Psy-
        chiatry,* Vol. 32, pp. 12–43.
Cavan, R. S.
1948   *Criminology,* New York: Thomas Y. Crowell.
Cayton, H. R.
1955   "The Psychology of the Negro Under Discrimination," in Arnold M.
        Rose (ed.), *Mental Health and Mental Disorder: A Sociological
        Approach,* New York: Norton, pp. 377–392.
Child, I. L.; Storm, T.; and Veroff, J.
1958   "Achievement Themes in Folktales Related to Socialization Prac-
        tice," in J. W. Atkinson (ed.), *Motives in Fantasy, Action, and
        Society,* Princeton: Van Nostrand, pp. 479–492.
Clark, Willis W.
1927   "Differences in Accomplishment in Schools of Varying Average In-
        telligence Quotient," *Los Angeles Educational Research Bulletin,*
        Vol. 6, No. 4, pp. 13–16.
Clinard, M. B.
1944   "Rural Criminal Offenders," *American Journal of Sociology,* Vol.
        50, No. 1, pp. 38–45.
1957   *Sociology of Deviant Behavior,* New York: Rinehart.
Cloward, R. A., and Ohlin, L. E.
1960   *Delinquency and Opportunity,* Glencoe, Ill.: Free Press.

Cornell, John
    1956   "Matsunagi—a Japanese Mountain Community," Center for Japanese Studies, University of Michigan, *Occasional Papers*, No. 5.
    1964   "Dōzoku: An Example of Evolution and Transition in Japanese Village Society," *Comparative Studies in Society and History*, Vol. 6.

Cortes, J. B.
    1960   "The Achievement Motive in the Spanish Economy Between the Thirteenth and the Eighteenth Centuries," *Economic Development and Culture Change*, Vol. 9, pp. 144–163.

Crandall, V. J.
    1963   "Achievement," in H. Stevenson, J. Kagen, and C. Spiker (eds.), *Sixty-Second Yearbook of the National Society for the Study of Education*, Chicago: University of Chicago Press.

Dainihon Rengō Seinendan (Society of Japanese Youth)
    1936   *Wakamono Seido no Kenkyū* (Research on Young Men's Organizations), Tokyo: Dainihon Rengō Seinendan, pp. 49–63.

Darsie, M. L.
    1926   "The Mental Capacity of American Born Japanese Children," *Comparative Psychology Monograph*, Vol. 3, No. 15.

Davis, A.; Eells, K.; Havighurst, R.; Herrick, V. E.; and Tyler, R.
    1951   *Intelligence and Cultural Differences*, Chicago: University of Chicago Press.

Davis, Alison, and Havighurst, Robert J.
    1947   *Father of the Man*, Boston: Houghton Mifflin.

Dazai, Osamu
    1948   *Mozegabun* (Thus I Heard), Tokyo: Shinchō-sha.
    1955–1956   *Collected Works*, 12 vols., Tokyo: Chikuma Shōbō.
    1956   *Sha Yō* (Setting Sun), English translation by D. Keene, *The Setting Sun*, New York: New Directions.
    1958   *Ningen Shikkaku* (No Longer Human), English translation by D. Keene, *No Longer Human*, New York: New Directions.

DeCharms, R., and Moeller, G. H.
    1962   "Values Expressed in American Children's Readers, 1800–1950," *Journal of Abnormal and Social Psychology*, Vol. 64, pp. 136–142.

de Grazia, Sebastian
    1948   *The Political Community: A Study of Anomie*, Chicago: University of Chicago Press.

De Vos, George
    1951   "Acculturation and Personality Structure: A Rorschach Study of Japanese Americans in Chicago," Ph.D. dissertation, University of Chicago.
    1952   "A Quantitative Approach to Affective Symbolism in Rorschach Responses," *Journal of Projective Techniques*, Vol. 16, No. 2, pp. 133–150.
    1954   "A Comparison of the Personality Differences in Two Generations of Japanese-Americans by Means of the Rorschach Test," *Nagoya Journal of Medical Science*, Vol. 17, No. 3, pp. 153–265. Reprinted as SSRI Reprint No. 14, University of Hawaii, 1966.
    1955   "A Quantitative Rorschach Assessment of Maladjustment and Rigidity in Acculturating Japanese Americans," *Genetic Psychology Monographs*, Vol. 52, pp. 51–87.

1960 "The Relation of Guilt Toward Parents to Achievement and Arranged Marriage Among the Japanese," Psychiatry, Vol. 23, No. 3, pp. 287–301.

1964 "Role Narcissism and the Etiology of Japanese Suicide," paper read at First International Congress of Social Psychiatry, London (August).

1965a "Achievement Orientation, Social Self-Identity and Japanese Economic Growth," Asian Survey, Vol. 5, No. 12, pp. 575–589.

1965b "Social Values and Personal Attitudes in Primary Human Relationships in Niiike," Occasional Papers, University of Michigan Center for Japanese Studies.

1968 "Suicide in Cross-Cultural Perspective," in H. Resnick (ed.), Suicidal Behaviors, Boston: Little, Brown, pp. 105–134.

De Vos, George, and Mizushima, Keiichi
1967 "Organization and Social Function of Japanese Gangs," in R. P. Dore (ed.), Aspects of Social Change in Modern Japan, Princeton: Princeton University Press, pp. 289–325.

De Vos, George, and Wagatsuma, Hiroshi
1959 "Psycho-Cultural Significance of Concern over Death and Illness Among Rural Japanese," International Journal of Social Psychiatry, Vol. 5, No. 1, pp. 6–19.

1961 "Value Attitudes Toward Role Behavior of Women in Two Japanese Villages," American Anthropologist, Vol. 63, No. 6, pp. 1204–1230.

1966 Japan's Invisible Race: Caste in Culture and Personality, Berkeley and Los Angeles: University of California Press.
Heritage of Endurance (forthcoming).

Doi, L. Takeo
1955 "Some Aspects of Japanese Psychiatry," American Journal of Psychiatry, Vol. 3, pp. 691–695.

1960a "Hikōshōnen no Oyakokankei ni kansuru Kenkyū" (Parental Identification of Delinquent Boys), Report of the Science Police Institute, Vol. 1, No. 1.

1960b " 'Jibun' to 'Amae' no Seishinbyōri," (Psychopathology of "Jibun" and "Amae"), Journal of Psychiatry and Neurology, Vol. 62, pp. 149–162.

1960c "Naruchishizumu no Riron to Jiko no Hyōshō" (Theory of Narcissism and the Psychic Representation of Self), Japanese Journal of Psychoanalysis, Vol. 7, pp. 7–9.

1962 " 'Amae': A Key Concept for Understanding Japanese Personality Structure," in R. J. Smith and R. K. Beardsley (eds.), Japanese Culture, Chicago: Aldine, pp. 132–139.

Donoghue, John D.
1957 "An Eta Community in Japan: The Social Persistence of Outcaste Groups," American Anthropologist, Vol. 59, pp. 1000–1017.

Dore, R. P. (ed.)
1967 Aspects of Social Change in Modern Japan, Princeton: Princeton University Press.

Durkheim, Emile
1947 The Elementary Forms of the Religious Life, (translated by J. W. Swain), Glencoe, Ill.: Free Press.

1951 Suicide (translated by J. A. Spaulding and G. Simpson), Glencoe, Ill.: Free Press.

Ema, Tsutomu
  1925 *Nihon Fuzoku Zenshi* (Complete History of Japanese Customs), Vol.
         1, Kyoto: Yamamoto Bunkadō.
Encyclopedia of Japanese History
  1959 Tokyo: Kayade Shobo Shinsha.
Erikson, Erik H.
  1950 *Childhood and Society,* New York: Norton.
  1956 "The Problem of Ego Identity," *Journal of American Psychoanalytic
         Association,* Vol. 4, pp. 56–121.
  1959 "Identity and the Life Cycle: Selected Papers," *Psychological Issues,*
         Vol. 1, No. 1, pp. 1–171.
  1968 *Identity, Youth and Crisis,* New York: Norton.
Exner, R.
  1949 *Kriminologie,* Berlin: Sprenger-Gerlad.
Farberow, Norman L., and Schneidman, Edwin S.
  1958 "A Nisei Woman Attacks by Suicide," in Georgene Seward (ed.),
         Clinical Studies in Culture Conflict, New York: Ronald Press, pp.
         335–358.
Freud, Sigmund
  1924 "Mourning and Melancholia," *Collected Papers,* Vol. 4, London:
         Hogarth Press.
  1955 "The Economic Problem of Masochism," *Collected Papers,* Vol. 2,
         New York: Basic Books.
Fukashiro, Junrō
  1969 "Student Thought and Feeling," *Japan Quarterly,* Vol. 16, No. 2
         (April–June), pp. 148–153.
Fukuda, T.
  1930 "Some Data on the Intelligence of Japanese Children," *American
         Journal of Psychology,* Vol. 24, pp. 599–610.
  1957 *Akutagawa Ryūnosuke Kenkyū,* Tokyo: Shinchō-sha.
Fukutake, T.
  1949 *Nihon Nōson no Shakai-teki Seikaku* (Social Character of Japanese
         Farming Villages), Tokyo: University of Tokyo Press.
  1954 *Nihon Nōson Shakai no Kozō Bunseki* (Analysis of Social Structure
         of Japanese Farming Villages), Tokyo: University of Tokyo Press.
Fukutomi, I., and Saito, Y.
  1962 "Hiko to Toshi no Seikatsu-kozō ni Kansuru Ichikōsatsu" (Delin-
         quency and Life Structure in Urban Community), *Chiken Kiyo*
         (periodical), Vol. 2, pp. 38–52.
Garma, A.
  1944 "Sadism and Masochism in Human Conduct," *Journal of Clinical
         Psychopathology and Psychotherapy,* Vol. 6, Part 2, pp. 355–390.
Gerth, H. H., and Mills, C. Wright (translators)
  1946 *From Max Weber: Essays in Sociology,* New York: Oxford University
         Press. Also Galaxy Books, 1958.
Glaser, Daniel
  1959 "Crime, Age and Employment," *American Sociological Review,* Vol.
         24, No. 5, pp. 679–686.
Gorer, Geoffrey
  1943 "Themes in Japanese Culture," *Transactions of the New York Acad-
         emy of Science,* Series F, pp. 106–124.
Gottlieb, David; Reeves, John; and Tenhouten, Warren D.
  1966 *The Emergence of Youth Societies,* New York: Free Press.

Green, Arnold
1946 "The Middle Class Male Child and Neurosis," *American Sociological Review,* Vol. 11, pp. 31–41.
Grier, William H., and Cobbs, Price M.
1968 *Black Rage,* New York: Basic Books.
Hagen, Everett E.
1962 *On the Theory of Social Change,* Homewood, Ill.: Dorsey Press.
Halbwachs, Maurice
1930 *Les Causes du Suicide,* Paris: Librarie Felix Alcan.
Hallowell, A. Irving
1941 "The Social Function of Anxiety in a Primitive Society," *American Sociological Review,* Vol. 6, pp. 869–881.
1953 "Aggression in Saulteaux Society," in Clyde Kluckhohn, H. Murray, and D. Schneider (eds.), *Personality in Nature, Society, and Culture,* New York: Knopf, pp. 260–275.
Haring, Douglas G.
1946 "Aspects of Personal Character in Japan," *Far Eastern Quarterly,* Vol. 6, pp. 12–22.
Hasegawa, Hiroshi
1955 "Seishonen ni Okeru Shudan-gokan ni Kansuru Kenkyu" (A Study on Group Rape in Juveniles), *Tohoku Correctional Bulletin,* No. 1, complete issue.
Havighurst, R. J., and Taba, H.
1949 *Adolescent Character and Personality,* New York: Wiley.
Hearn, Lafcadio
1904 *Japan: An Attempt at Interpretation,* New York: Macmillan.
Heibonsha Dictionary for World History
1959 Vol. 2, Tokyo: Heibonsha.
Hendin, Herbert
1960 "Suicide in Denmark," *Psychiatric Quarterly,* Vol. 34, pp. 443–460.
Henry, Andrew F., and Short, James F., Jr.
1954 *Suicide and Homicide, Some Economic, Sociological and Psychological Aspects of Aggression,* Glencoe, Ill.: Free Press.
Higuchi, H.
1962 *Edo no Hankachō* (Criminal Report of Edo), Tokyo: Timbutsu-orai-shi.
Higuchi, K.
1953 "Sengo ni Okeru Hikōshonen no Seishin-igakuteki Kenkyū" (Psychiatric Study of Juvenile Delinquency After the War), *Judicial Report,* Vol. 41, No. 1, entire issue.
Honjo, E.
1955 "Bunshin to Hikōshonen" (Tattoo and Delinquents), *Family Court Report,* Vol. 33, pp. 43–184.
Horiye, T.
1958 "Joshi Hikōshōnen no Irezumi ni Tsuite" (Tattooing Among Juvenile Girl Delinquents), *Japanese Journal of Correctional Medicine,* Vol. 7, No. 4, pp. 76–84.
Horiye, Yuriko
1954 "Han-in-sei Kankyō ni Tsuite no Kenkyū" (A Study on Criminal Environment), *Family Court Report,* Vol. 35, pp. 233–270.
Hulse, F. S.
1947 "Status and Functions as Factors in the Structure of Organizations

Among the Japanese," *American Anthropologist*, Vol. 49, pp. 154–156.

Hurlburt, W. C.
 1932 "Prosperity and Depression on the Suicide Rate," *American Journal of Sociology*, Vol. 37, pp. 714–719.

Iga, Mamoru
 1961 "Cultural Factors and Suicide of Japanese Youth with a Focus on Personality," *Sociology and Social Research*, Vol. 46, pp. 75–90.

Iga, Mamoru, and Ohara, Kenshiro
 "Suicides of Japanese Youths and Family Structures," unpublished.

Inagaki, F. (ed.)
 1959 *Edo Seikatsu Jiten* (Encyclopedia of Edo Life), Tokyo: Seiabo, 1959.

Inkeles, Alex; Haufman, E.; and Beier, H.
 1958 "Modal Personality and Adjustment to the Soviet Socio-Political System," Human Relations, Vol. 11, No. 3, pp. 3–22. Also in *Studying Personality Cross-Culturally*, Bert Kaplan (ed.), Evanston, Ill.: Row, Peterson, 1961.

Inkeles, Alex, and Levinson, Daniel J.
 1954 "National Character: The Study of Modal Personality and Socio-cultural Systems," in Gardner Lindzey (ed.), *Handbook of Social Psychology*, Cambridge, Mass.: Addison-Wesley, pp. 977–1020.

Inoue, Kiyoshi
 1961 "Kaihō Undō no Rekishi ni Manabu" (Lessons We Receive from the History of Liberation Movements), *Buraku*, No. 9, pp. 4–17.

Ishida, R.
 1968 "Naikan Bunseki Ryōhō" (Naikan Analysis), *Seishin Igaku*, Vol. 10, pp. 478–484.

Ishida, Shinichi
 1961 "Shinro Shidō to Kōkō Zenraigaku Mondai" (Guidance and Problems of an Entire Class Entering High School), *Buraku*, No. 9, pp. 51–55.

Ishino, Iwao
 1953 "The Oyabun-Kobun: A Japanese Ritual Kinship Institution," *American Anthropologist*, Vol. 55, pp. 695–707.

Iwai, Hiroaki
 1954 "Hanshakai Shūdan to Shakaiteki Kinchō," (Antisocial Group and Social Tension) in Nihon Jimbun Kagakkai (ed.), *Shakaiteki Kinchō no Kenkyū*, pp. 81–122.
 1964 *Byōri Shūdan no Kōzō* (The Structure of Pathological Groups), Tokyo: Seishin Book Co.

Izumi, S., and Gamo, M.
 1952 "Nihon Shakai no Chiiki-sei" (Regional Differences in Japanese Society), in *Nihon Chiri Shin Taikei*, Vol. 11, pp. 37–76.

Jacobson, Alan, and Rainwater, Lee
 1951 "A Study of the Evaluations of Nisei as Workers by Caucasian Employment Agency Managers and by Employers of Nisei," Master's thesis, Department of Sociology, University of Chicago.
 1952 "A Study of Employer and Employment Agency Manager Evaluations of Nisei Workers," *Social Forces*.

James, William
 1935 *The Varieties of Religious Experience*, New York: Random House, Modern Library.

Japan Statistical Yearbook 1968
  1968   Bureau of Statistics, Office of the Prime Minister, Japan.
Kamei, Kiyogasu
  1957   "Iwate-ken Hikōshōnen to Furyō Bunkasai" (Delinquency and Bad Pictures or Books in Iwate Prefecture," *Tohoku Correctional Bulletin,* Vol. 2, pp. 241–255.
Kanbe, Tadao, and Ishii, Kanichirō
         "Wagakuni Seishōnen no Jinseikan to Jisatsukan" (Japanese Youth's View of Life and of Suicide), Kyoto University Studies on Suicide, unpublished.
Kaplan, Bert (ed.)
  1961   *Studying Personality Cross-Culturally,* Evanston, Ill.: Row, Peterson.
Kardiner, Abram
  1939   *The Individual and His Society, The Psychodynamics of Primitive Social Organization,* New York: Columbia University Press.
Kardiner, Abram, and Ovesey, L.
  1962   *The Mark of Oppression,* Cleveland and New York: World, Meridian Books.
Kashikuma, Koji, et al.
  1958   "Ecological Study of Juvenile Delinquency in Tokyo," *Family Court Report,* Vol. 58, entire issue.
Katō, Masaaki
  1947   "Jisatsu ni itaru Michi" (Way to Suicide), *Tōkei* (Statistics), Vol. 8, No. 9, September.
  1958   "Jisatsu" (Suicide), *Seishin Eisei Shiryō* (Annual Report of Mental Health), Japan: National Institute of Mental Health, Ministry of Welfare, No. 6.
Katō, Masaaki, and Imada, Y.
  1963   "Suimin-yaku Ranyōshōnen no Jittai" (The Conditions of Sleeping Pill Misuses Among Juveniles), *Annual Report on Mental Health,* pp. 10–30.
Kawashima, T.
  1948   *Wagakuni Shakai no Kazoku-teki Kōsei* (Familial Structure of Japanese Society), Tokyo: Nippon Hyronsha.
Kida, J.
  1966   *Nihon no Gamburu* (Gambling in Japan), Tokyo: Togensha.
Kiefer, Christie
  1968   "Social Change and Personality in a White Collar Danchi," University of California, Berkeley, Department of Anthropology, doctoral dissertation. Presented at the colloquium of the Center for Japanese and Korean Studies, November 15, 1967.
Kitajima, M.
  1958   *Edo Jidai* (The Edo Era), Tokyo: Iwanami Book Co.
Kitano, Seiichi
  1962   " 'Dōzoku' and 'Ie' in Japan: The Meaning of Family Genealogical Relationships," in R. J. Smith and R. K. Beardsley (eds.), *Japanese Culture: Its Development and Characteristics,* Chicago: Aldine, pp. 42–46.
Kluckhohn, Clyde
  1944   *Navaho Witchcraft,* Boston: Beacon Press.
Kluckhohn, Florence
  1953   "Dominant and Variant Cultural Value Orientations," in Hugh

Cabot and Joseph A. Kahl, *Human Relations: Concepts and Cases in Concrete Social Science,* Cambridge: Harvard University Press, Vol. 1, pp. 88–89.

Kobayashi, Ayako
    1962   *Buraku no Joi* (A Woman Doctor in a Buraku), Tokyo: Iwanami.

Koyama, T.
    1953   "Buraku ni Okeru Shakai Kinchō no Seikaku" (The Nature of Social Tension in Outcaste Communities), in Nihon Jinbun Kagakkai (ed.), *Shakaiteki Kinchō no Kenkyū* (Studies on Social Tensions), Tokyo: Yuhikaku, pp. 395–410.

Kubo, Y.
    1934   *The Revised and Extended Binet-Simon Tests Applied to the Japanese Children,* Pedagogical Seminary, Vol. 29, pp. 187–194.

Landes, Ruth
    1938   "The Abnormal Among the Ojibwa Indians," *Journal of Abnormal and Social Psychology,* Vol. 33, pp. 14–33.

Lanham, Betty B.
    1956   "Aspects of Child Care in Japan: Preliminary Report," in D. G. Harding (ed.), *Personal Character and Cultural Milieu,* Syracuse: Syracuse University Press, pp. 565–583.

Lebra, Takie
    1969   "Reciprocity and the Asymmetric Principle: An Analytical Reappraisal of the Japanese Concept of *On,*" *Psychologia,* pp. 129–138.
    1971   "The Social Mechanism of Guilt and Shame: The Japanese Case," *Anthropological Quarterly,* Vol. 44, No. 4 (October 1971), pp. 241–255.

LeVine, Robert A.
    1963   "Behaviorism in Psychological Anthropology," in Joseph M. Wepman and Ralph W. Heine (eds.), *Concepts of Personality,* Chicago: Aldine, pp. 361–384.

LeVine, Robert A., et al.
    1966   *Dreams and Deeds: Achievement Motivation in Nigeria,* Chicago: University of Chicago Press.

Liepmann, M.
    1930   *Krieg und Kriminalität in Deutschland,* Stuttgart: Deutsche Verlags-Anstalt.

Linebarger, Paul M. A.; Chu, Djang; and Burks, Ardath W.
    1954   *Far Eastern Government and Politics: China and Japan,* New York: Van Nostrand.

Llewelyn, Karle N., and Hoebel, A. Adamson
    1941   *The Cheyenne Way,* Norman: University of Oklahoma Press.

Lockwood, William W.
    1954   *The Economic Development of Japan: Growth and Structural Change,* Princeton: Princeton University Press.

Lynd, Robert
    1939   *Knowledge for What?* Princeton: Princeton University Press.

McClelland, David C.
    1955   "Some Consequences of Achievement Motivation," in M. R. Jones (ed.), *Nebraska Symposium on Motivation,* Lincoln: University of Nebraska Press.
    1961   *The Achieving Society,* Princeton: Van Nostrand.

McClelland, David C., and Friedman, G. A.
    1952   "A Cross-Cultural Study of the Relationship Between Child-Training

Practices and Achievement Motivation Appearing in Folktales," in G. E. Swanson, et al. (eds), *Readings in Social Psychology,* New York: Holt, Rinehart and Winston, pp. 243–249.

McClelland, David C., et al.
1953 *The Achievement Motive,* New York: Appleton-Century-Crofts.
1958 *Talent and Society, New Perspectives in the Identification of Talent,* Princeton: Van Nostrand.

MacNeish, J.: De Vos, G.; and Carterette, T.
1960 "Variations in Personality and Ego-Identification Within a Slavey Indian Kin-Community," *Contributions to Anthropology,* National Museum of Canada Bulletin, No. 190, Part II.

Maeda, Shinjirō
1955 *Hanzai Shakaigaku no Shomondai* (Problems in Criminal Sociology), Tokyo: Yūshindo.
1957 "Toshi to Nōson ni okeru Jisatsu" (Suicide in Urban and Rural Areas), in *Hanzai no Toshika* (Urbanization of Crimes), Tokyo: Yuhikako, pp. 209–221.

Mahara, Tetsuo
1960a "Buraku no Shakai" (Buraku Society), in Buraku Mondai Kenkyūjo.
1960b *Buraku no Genjō* (Present Situations in Buraku), Tokyo and Kyoto: San-itsu Shobo, pp. 131–180.
1961 "Buraku no Kodomo to Shinro Shidō" (Buraku Children and Their Guidance), *Buraku,* Vol. 9, pp. 55–59.

Masuda, Kokichi
1960 *Tekkin Apato-gai no Seikatsu o Saguru* (Exploration of Life in Concrete Apartment Houses), Nishinomiya Educational Commission.

Matsuda, Keiichi; Masutani, Hisashi; Eiichi, Kudō; et al.
1963 *Buraku Mondai to Kirisuto Kyō* (Buraku Problems and Christianity), Tokyo: Nihon Kirisuto Kyōdan Senkyō Kenkyūjo (United Church of Christ of Japan Research Institute for Missionary Work), pp. 84–85.

Menninger, K. A.
1938 *Man Against Himself,* New York: Harcourt Brace.

Merton, Robert
1949 "Social Structure and Anomie," *Social Theory and Social Structure,* Glencoe, Ill.: Free Press, pp. 125–149.

Miller, Daniel R., and Swanson, Guy E.
1958 *The Changing American Parent,* New York: Wiley.

Ministère de la Justice (France)
1952– *Compte General de l'Administration de la Justice Civile et Com-*
1955– *merciale et de la Justice Criminelle.*
1957

Ministry of Justice
1958 *Juvenile Delinquency in Japan.*

Mishima, Yukio
1970 *Confessions of a Mask,* Tokyo: Tuttle.

Mitamura, E.
1933 *Edo no Hanzai Nin* (Criminals in Edo), Tokyo: Waseda University Press.
1956 *Buke no Seikatsu* (The Life of the Samurai), Tokyo: Seikeibo Book Co.
1959 *Torimono no Sekai* (The World of the Police), Tokyo: Seiabo.

Mizushima, Keiichi
1955 "Hikōshōnen no Shakaiteki Yogo ni Kansuru Kenkyū: (A Study on

the Prognosis of Social Adjustment of Delinquents), *Japanese Journal of Educational Psychology*, Vol. 2, No. 4, pp. 45–54.

1956   *Shakai Byō* (Social Disease), Tokyo: Hakua Shobo, pp. 111–112.

Mori, K.

1959   *Jinshin Baibai* (Human Trade), Tokyo: Shibundo.

Murakami, Eiji

1959   "A Normative Study of Japanese Rorschach Responses," in *Rorschach Kenkyū: Rorschachian Japanica*, Vol. 2, pp. 39–85.

1962   "Special Characteristics of Japanese Personality Based on Rorschach Test Results," in Muramatsu, Tsuneo (ed.), *Nihonjin-Bunka to Pasonariti no Jisshōteki Kenkyū* (The Japanese: An Empirical Study in Culture and Personality), Tokyo and Nagoya: Reimei Shobō.

Muramatsu, Tsuneo (ed.)

1962   *Nihonjin-Bunka to Pasonariti no Jisshō-teki Kenkyū* (The Japanese: An Empirical Study in Culture and Personality), Tokyo and Nagoya: Reimei Shobō.

Nagai, Kafū

1918   *Ude Kurabe* (Geisha in Rivalry), Tokyo: Shinbashido.

1937   *Bokuto Kidan* (A Strange Tale from the East of the River), Tokyo: Iwanami Shoten.

Nagai, Michio

1953   "Dōzoku: A Preliminary Study of the Japanese 'Extended Family' Group and Its Social and Economic Functions (based on the research of K. Ariga)," *Ohio State University Research Foundation, Interim Technical Report*, Columbus, No. 7.

Nagai, M., and Bennett, J. W.

1953   "A Summary and Analysis of the Familial Structure of Japanese Society by Takeyoski Kawashima," *Southwestern Journal of Anthropology*, Vol. 9, pp. 239–250.

Nakada, Osamu

1953   "Hokahannin no Hanzai-Shinrigakuteki Kenyu" (Psychological Study of Arsonists), *Family Court Monthly*, Vol. 6, pp. 51–92.

Nakahara, Hiromichi

1960   *Seppuku* (Suicide by Disembowelment), Tokyo: Kuboshoten.

Nakane, Chie

1970   *Japanese Society*, Suffolk, Great Britain: Chaucer Press.

Nakano, Tetsuo

1957   "Wagakuni ni Okeru Jisatsu" (Suicide in Japan), *Shakai Kairyō* (Social Reform), Vol. 2, No. 3 (February), pp. 4–10.

Nakayama, T.

1930   *Nihon Wakamono-shi* (History of Japanese Youth), Tokyo: Hakubunsha.

Natsume, K.

1929   *Sōseki no Omoide* (Reminiscence of Sōseki), Tokyo: Iwanami Shoten.

Natsume, Sōseki

1908   *Nowaki* (Wintry Blast), Tokyo: Shunyōdō.

1928–   *Collected Works*, 20 vols., Tokyo: Sōseki Zenshu Kankō-kai.
1929

1928   "Sengo Bunkai no Sūsei" (Trends in Post-War Literature), *Collected Works*, Vol. I.

1928   *Within My Glass Doors*, English translation by Matsuhara, I., Tokyo: Shinseido.

Neumeyer, M. H.
1961 *Juvenile Delinquency in Modern Society,* New York: Van Nostrand.
"Nihon Jisatsu no Tōkei" (Statistics on Suicide in Japan)
1958 *Seishin Eisei Shiryō* (Annual Report on Mental Health), Japan: National Institute of Mental Health, Ministry of Welfare, No. 6, pp. 74–84.
Nihon Teikoku Tōkei Nenkan (Japanese Empire Statistical Year Book)
1882 Vol. 1, Meiji 15, pp. 445–451.
1890 Vol. 9, Meiji 23, p. 564.
Nihon Tōkei Nenkan (Japanese Statistical Year Book)
1950 *Sōrifu Tōkei Kyoku* (Statistics Bureau of the Prime Minister's Office), Showa 25.
Nishimoto, Sosuke
1960 *Buraku Mondai to Dōwa Kyōiku* (Buraku Problems and Assimilation Education), Tokyo: Sobunsha, pp. 136ff.
Nitobe, Inazō
1938 *Lectures on Japan,* Chicago: University of Chicago Press.
Nomura, Nobukiyo
1956 "Tsukimono no shinri" (Psychology of Fox Possession), in Oguchi, I. (ed.), *Shūkyō to Shinkō no Shinrigaku* (Psychological Studies of Religion and Beliefs), Tokyo: Kawada, pp. 247–257.
Norbeck, Edward
1954 *Takashima: A Japanese Fishing Community,* Salt Lake City: University of Utah Press.
Norbeck, Edward, and De Vos, George
1961 "Japan," in Francis L. K. Hsu (ed.), *Psychological Anthropology,* Homewood, Ill.: Dorsey Press, pp. 18–47.
Norbeck, Edward, and Norbeck, Margaret
1956 "Child Training in a Japanese Fishing Community," in D. G. Haring (ed.), *Personal Character and Cultural Milieu,* Syracuse: Syracuse University Press, pp. 651–673.
Norbeck, Edward; Price-Williams, Douglass; and McCord, William M. (eds.)
1968 *The Study of Personality: An Interdisciplinary Appraisal,* New York: Holt, Rinehart and Winston.
O'Connor, W. A.
1948 "Some Notes on Suicide," *British Journal of Medical Psychology,* Vol. 21, pp. 221–228.
Okada, et al.
1954 *Study on Social Tension,* Tokyo: Yūhikaku.
Ogawa, Taro
1956 "Sengo 10-nen no Shōnen Hanzai" (Juvenile Delinquency in the Ten Years After the War), *Keisei,* Vol. 67, No. 11, pp. 8–16.
Ogburn, W. T.
1953 "Factors in the Variation of Crime Among Cities," in Takemura, Hisashi, "Shōnen Hanzai no Shakaigakuteki Kenkyū" (Sociological Study of Juvenile Delinquency), *Judicial Report,* Vol. 1, No. 4, Tokyo: Judicial Research and Training Institute, pp. 212–233.
Ogyu, Chikasato
1957 "Nihon Bunka no Chiiki-sei to Sono Kōzō-teki Rikai" (Local Distribution of Selected Culture Elements in Japan and the Structural Relationships of Their Lineage), *Minozokugaku Kenkyū,* Vol. 21, pp. 199–206.

Ohashi, Kaoru
  1962   *Toshi No Kasō Shakai* (Urban Lower Society), Tokyo: Seishin Shobo.
Okada, Yuzuru
  1952   "Kinship Organization in Japan," *Journal of Educational Sociology*,
         Vol. 26, pp. 27–31.
Okazaki, Ayanori
  1958   "Jisatsu to Tasatsu to no Kanrensei" (Relationship Between Suicide
         and Homicide), *Jinkō Mondai Kenkyujo Nenpō* (Annual Report,
         Institute of Population Problems), Tokyo: Institute of Population
         Problems, Ministry of Welfare, No. 3.
  1958–1959   "Jisatsu no Jisshōteki Kenkyū" (Empirical Study of Suicide),
         Jinkō Mondai Kenkyū (Journal of Population Problems), Tokyo:
         Institute of Population Problems, Ministry of Welfare, Nos. 74–77
         (December 1958–March 1959).
  1960a   *Jisatsu no Shakai-tōkei-teki Kenkyū* (Social-Statistical Study of Sui-
         cide), Tokyo: Nihon Hyōron Shinsha.
  1960b   "Seishōnen no Jisatsu Mondai" (Suicide Problems of Youth), *Sei-
         shōnen Mondai* (Youth Problems), Vol. 6, No. 6 (June).
  1969   *Jisatsu-ron,* Tokyo: Kokin Shoin.
Okuno, Takeo
  1956   *Dazai Osamu Ron* (Study of Dazai Osamu), Kindai Seikatsu Sha,
         Tokyo.
Omachi, Tokuzo
  1937   "Nihon Kekkon Fūzoku Shi" (History of Japanese Marriage Cus-
         toms), in *Kazoku Seido Zenshū* (The Collected Works on Family
         System), Series 1, Part 1, Tokyo: Kawade, pp. 89–130.
Ono, Seiichirō
  1951   *Hompō Hanzaigenshō no Ninshiki* (Recognition of Crime in Japan),
         Tokyo: Keimu Kyōkai.
Ōsaka Crime Prevention Council
  1960   "Shōnen no Jisatsu no Jittai" (The Actual Conditions of Youthful
         Suicide), *Hikō Hakusho* (Delinquency White Paper), Ōsaka-fu Kei-
         satsu Honbu Bōhan-ka, Ōsaka Bōhan Rengō Kyōgikai (Ōsaka Prefec-
         ture Police Center, Crime Prevention Section).
Palmer, D. M.
  1941   "Factors in Suicidal Attempts, A Review of 25 Consecutive Cases,"
         Journal of Nervous and Mental Diseases, Vol. 93, pp. 421–442.
Parker, S.
  1962   "Eskimo Psychopathology in the Context of Eskimo Personality and
         Culture," *American Anthropology*, Vol. 64, pp. 76–96.
Parsons, Talcott
  1949   *The Structure of Social Action*, Glencoe, Ill.: Free Press, pp. 666ff.
  1951   *The Social System*, Glencoe, Ill.: Free Press.
  1968   "Emile Durkheim," *The International Encyclopedia of Social Sci-
         ences,* New York: Macmillan, Vol. 4, p. 316.
Parsons, Talcott; Bales, J.; and Shils, Edward A.
  1953   *Working Papers in the Theory of Action,* Glencoe, Ill.: Free Press.
Parsons, Talcott, and Bales, Robert
  1955   *Family Socialization and Interaction Process,* Glencoe, Ill.: Free
         Press.

Piers, G., and Singer, M. B.
   1953   *Shame and Guilt: A Psychoanalytic and Cultural Study*, Springfield, Ill.: Thomas Publication Co.
Radzinowicz, L.
   1941   "The Influence of Economic Conditions on Crime," *Sociological Review*, Vol. 33, pp. 1–36.
Raucat, Thomas
   1955   *The Honorable Picnic*, New York: Viking Press.
Redfield, Robert
   1956   *Peasant Society and Culture*, Chicago: University of Chicago Press.
Reik, Theodore
   1941   *Masochism in Modern Man*, translated by M. H. Beigel and G. M. Kurth, New York: Grove Press.
Reinemann, John Otto
   1947   "Juvenile Delinquency in Philadelphia and Economic Trends," *Templeton University L. Q.*, Vol. 20, No. 4, pp. 576–583.
Riesman, David
   1950   *The Lonely Crowd*, New Haven: Yale University Press.
Rosen, Bernard C.
   1959   "Race, Ethnicity and the Achievement Syndrome," *American Sociological Review*, Vol. 24, pp. 47–60.
   1962   "Socialization and Achievement Motivation in Brazil," *American Sociological Review*, Vol. 27, No. 5, pp. 612–626.
Rosen, Bernard C., and D'Andrade, Roy G.
   1959   "The Psycho-Social Origins of Achievement Motivation," *Sociometry*, Vol. 22, pp. 185–218.
Saegusa, Yasutaka
   1958   *Dazai Osamu to Sono Shōgai* (Dazai Osamu and His Life), Gendaisha, Tokyo.
Sakamoto, T. (ed.)
   1957   *Fūzoku Jiten* (Encyclopedia of Folklore), Tokyo: Tokyodo.
Sargent, Helen D.
   1953   *The Insight Test: A Verbal Projective Test for Personality Study* (The Menninger Clinic Monograph Series, No. 10), New York: Grune & Stratton.
Sartre, Jean-Paul
   1962   *La Nausee*, Paris: Gallimard (c. 1938).
Satō, Yasuko
   1957   "Jisatsu no Tōkei-teki Kansatsu" (A Statistical Observation of Suicide), *Jinkō Mondai Kenkyujō Nenpō* (Annual Report, Institute of Population Problems), Tokyo: Institute of Population Problems, Ministry of Welfare, No. 2, pp. 41–44.
Schilder, Paul
   1935   *The Image and Appearance of the Human Body*, London: Kegan Paul, Trench, Trubner.
Segi, M.; Kurihara, M.; and Tsukahara, Y.
   1966   *Mortality for Selected Causes in 30 Countries (1950–61), Age-Adjusted Death Rates and Age-Specific Death Rates*, Department of Public Health, Tohoku University School of Medicine, Sendai, Tokyo: Kosei Tokei Kyokai.

Seki, H.
  1964   "Heroin Shihekisha no Jinkaku Kenkyū" (A Study of the Personality
         of Heroin Addicts), *Japanese Journal of Correctional Medicine*, Vol.
         13, No. 4, pp. 12–30.
Seward, Georgene (ed.)
  1958   *Clinical Studies in Culture Conflict*, New York: Ronald Press.
Seward, Georgene, and Williamson, Robert
  1970   *Sex Roles in Changing Society*, New York: Random House.
Shaw, C. N., and McKay, H. D.
  1931   *Social Factors in Juvenile Delinquency*, Washington, D.C.: National
         Commission on Law Observance and Enforcement, Vol. 2, No. 13, pp.
         401ff.
  1932   "Are Broken Homes a Causative Factor in Delinquency?" *Social
         Forces*, Vol. 10, pp. 514–524.
  1942   *Juvenile Delinquency and Urban Areas*, Chicago: University of
         Chicago Press.
Sherif, Muzafer
  1948   *An Outline of Social Psychology*, New York: Harper Brothers.
Shibutani, Tamotsu
  1961   *Society and Personality*, Englewood Cliffs, N.J.: Prentice-Hall.
Shigemori, Yukio, et al.
  1964   *General Study of Narcotics*, Tokyo: Hokan Koyo.
Shinozaki, Nobuo
  1953   *Nihonjin no Sei Seikatsu*, Tokyo: Bungei Shuppan-Sha.
Shinshi, K.
  1963   *Bushi no Seikatsu* (The Life of the Samurai), Tokyo: Yūzankaku.
Smith, R.
  1956   "Kurusu—A Japanese Agricultural Community," Center for Japanese
         Studies, University of Michigan, *Occasional Papers*, No. 5.
Smith, Robert J., and Beardsley, Richard K. (eds.)
  1962   *Japanese Culture: Its Development and Characteristics*, Chicago:
         Aldine.
Smith, Thomas C.
  1960   "Landlords' Sons in the Business Elite," in *Economic Development
         and Culture Change*, Vol. 9, No. 1, Part 2 (October).
  1966   *The Agrarian Origins of Modern Japan*, New York: Atheneum.
Sonohara, Tarō
  1954   *Jisatsu no Shinri* (Psychology of Suicide), Tokyo: Sōgensha.
Statistical Abstract of the United States
  1955   U.S. Bureau of Census, U.S. Department of Commerce, Washington,
         D.C.: United States Government Printing Office.
Statistical Bulletin
  1954   "Why Do People Kill Themselves?" Metropolitan Life Insurance
         Company, Vol. 26, p. 910.
Steiner, Kurt
  1950   "Postwar Changes in the Japanese Civil Codes," *Washington Law
         Review*, Vol. 25, pp. 286–312.
Sterner, James E., and Rosemont, H. N.
  1935   *Manual of Juvenile Court Officers of the State of Michigan*, Ann
         Arbor: Michigan W.P.A. Recreational Division.
Stoetzel, Jean
  1955   *Without the Chrysanthemum and the Sword: A Study of the Attitudes*

of Youth in Post-War Japan, UNESCO, New York: Columbia University Press.

Strong, E. K.
1934 The Second Generation Japanese Problem, Stanford: Stanford University Press.

Sudō, Shun'ichi
1959 "Kōkōsei no Jisatsukan ni Tsuite" (High School Students' Views of Suicide), Fukushima Daigaku Kyōiku Kenkyū Johō (Report of the Institute of Education, Fukushima University), No. 22 (March), whole issue.

Sugawara, T.
1962 Mayaku-Tengoku Nippon (Japan, the Narcotics Paradise), Tokyo: Soshisha.

Sutherland, E. H.
1943 "Crime," in William Ogburn (ed.), American Society in Wartime, p. 188.
1947 Principles of Criminology, New York: Lippincott.

Takahashi, Jirō
1910 "Honpō Jisatsu no Raireki" (History of Suicide in Japan), Tōkei Shūshi (Journal of Statistics), No. 351 (May), pp. 10–30.

Takahashi, M.
1963 Shusei-sei Hanzai no Kenkyū (Research on Alcoholic Crime), Tokyo: Maeno Shobo.

Takano, Iwasaburo
1953 In "Shōnen Hanzai no Shakaigakuteki Kenkyū" (Sociological Study of Juvenile Delinquency), by Hisashi Takemura, Judicial Report Vol. 6, No. 4, Tokyo: Judicial Research and Training Institution, pp. 212–233.

Takarabe, Seiji
1923 "Honpō Jisatsu no Danjo Betsu" (Sexual Differences in Suicide in Japan), Keizai Ronsō (Journal of Economics), Vol. 16, No. 5 (May).

Takemura, Hisashi
1953 "Shōnen Hanzai no Shakaigakuteki Kenkyū" (Sociological Study of Juvenile Delinquency), Judicial Report, Vol. 6, No. 4, entire issue.
1960 "Hinkon to Hanzai" (Poverty and Crime), Family Court Monthly, Vol. 12, No. 9, pp. 1–68.

Takikawa, S.
1965 Yūjo no Rekishi (A History of Women Entertainers), Tokyo: Shibundo.

Tamanyu, M.
1964 "One of the Preventative Methods of Juvenile Delinquency by Mapping of the Marginal Areas," Japanese Journal of Correctional Medicine, Vol. 13, No. 4, pp. 4–11.

Tamura, Eitarō
1958 Yakuza-Kō (A Study of the Yakuza), Tokyo: Yūzankaku.

Tanaka, Tarō
1907 "Shōnen-jisatsu no Tōkei" (Statistics on Suicide of Youth), Tōkei Shūshi (Journal of Statistics), No. 315, pp. 15–35.

Tappan, Paul W.
1959 Crime, Justice and Correction, New York: McGraw-Hill.

Tawney, R. H.
1926 Religion and the Rise of Capitalism, Frome and London: Pelican Books.

Terman, L. M., and Oden, M. H.
  1947 *The Gifted Child Grows Up: Twenty-five Years' Follow-up of a Superior Group* (Vol. 4 in Genetic Studies of Genius), Stanford: Stanford University Press.
Tojo, Takashi
  1960a *Dōwa Kyōiku Ron* (Debate on Assimilation Education), Tokyo: Shin Hyōron Sha.
  1960b *Dōwa Kyōiku* (Assimilation Education), Tokyo and Kyoto: Sanitsu Shobō.
  1960c "Sengo no Dōwa Kyōiku" (Postwar Education for Assimilation), in *Buraku Mondai Kenkyūjo* (Bulletin of the Research Institute for Buraku Problems), Kyoto.
Tonnies, F.
  1940 *Gemeinschaft und Gesellschaft*, New York: American Book Company.
Tsurumi, Haruko
  1970 *Social Change and the Individual: Japan Before and After Defeat in World War II*, Princeton: Princeton University Press.
Tsurumi, Kazuko
  1969 "The Japanese Student Movement: Group Portraits," *Japan Quarterly*, Vol. 16, No. 1 (January), pp. 25–44.
Uesugi, Shinkichi
  1902 "Jisatsu no Jisshō-teki Kenkyū" (Empirical Study of Suicide), *Kokka-gakkai-zasshi* (Journal of Association of State Science), Vol. 16, No. 190 (December).
United Nations
  1968 *Demographic Yearbook 1968*.
Usatake, T.
  1948 *Tobaku to Suri no Kenkyū* (Research on Gambling and Pickpocketing), Tokyo: Jitsugyo-no-Nihon-sha Co.
Van Gennep, Arnold
  1960 *The Rites of Passage*, Chicago: University of Chicago Press.
Vogel, Ezra
  1962 "Entrance Examinations and Emotional Disturbance," in R. J. Smith and R. K. Beardsley (eds.), *Japanese Culture: Its Development and Characteristics*, Chicago: Aldine, pp. 140–152.
  1963 *Japan's New Middle Class*, Berkeley and Los Angeles: University of California Press.
Vogel, Ezra, and Vogel, Suzanne H.
  1961 "Family Security, Personal Immaturity, and Emotional Health in a Japanese Sample," *Marriage and Family Living*, Vol. 23, pp. 161–166.
von Mayer, George
  1917 "Statistik und Gesellschaftslehre," *Moralstatistik*, Vol. 3, Munich, pp. 10–30.
Wagatsuma, Hiroshi, and De Vos, George
  1962 "Attitudes Toward Arranged Marriage in Rural Japan," *Human Organization*, Vol. 21, No. 3 (Fall).
Wagatsuma, Sakae
  1950 "Democratization of the Family Relations in Japan," *Washington Law Review*, Vol. 25, pp. 405–426.
War Relocation Authority of U.S. Department of Interior
  1946 *The Evacuated People: A Quantitative Description*, Washington, D.C.: Government Printing Office, p. 80.

1946 *Wartime Exile,* Washington, D.C.: Government Printing Office, p. 93.
Warner, W. L., and Henry, W. E.
1948 "The Radio Day-time Serial: A Symbolic Analysis," *Genetic Psychological Monograph,* Vol. 37, No. 3, p. 71.
Warner, W. L., and Lunt, Paul S.
1941 *The Social Life of a Modern Community,* New Haven: Yale University Press.
Warner, W. L.; Meeker, M.; and Eells, K.
1949 *Social Class in America,* Chicago: Science Research Associates.
Watanabe, Jō
1957 "Nihonjin no Jisatsu" (Suicide of the Japanese), *Seimei Hoken Kyōkai Kaihō* (Bulletin of the Life Insurance Association), Vol. 38, No. 2, entire issue.
Weber, Max
1925 *Wirtschaft und Gesellschaft,* Vol. 2, Tubingen: J. C. B. Mohr.
1947 *The Theory of Social and Economic Organization,* translated by A. M. Henderson and Talcott Parsons, Glencoe: Free Press.
Whiting, Beatrice
1950 "Paiute Sorcery," *Viking Fund Publications in Anthropology,* No. 15, New York: Viking Fund.
Whiting, John W. M., and Child, Irvin L.
1953 *Child Training and Personality: A Cross-Cultural Study,* New Haven and London: Yale University Press.
Wiers, P.
1939–
1940 "The Juvenile Delinquent in Rural Michigan," *Journal of Criminal Law and Criminology,* Vol. 30, pp. 211–222.
Winterbottom, Marian R.
1958 "The Relation of Need for Achievement to Learning Experiences in Independence and Mastery," in J. W. Atkinson (ed.), *Motives in Fantasy, Society and Action,* Princeton: Van Nostrand, pp. 453–478.
World Health Statistics Annual 1964
1967 World Health Organization, Geneva, Vol. 1.
World Health Statistics Annual 1967
1969 World Health Organization, Geneva, Vol. 1.
Wright, Richard
1945 *Black Boy,* New York: Harper Brothers.
Yakata, Minoru
1957 "Seizon Chūzetsu" (Interruption of Life), *Tōikei* (Statistics), Vol. 8, No. 9, pp. 10–30.
Yamamoto, Masao
1963 *Dōwa Kyōiku no Kihon Mondai* (Basic Problems of Assimilation Education), Tokyo: Dōwa Mondai Kenkyūjo (Research Institute for Dowa Problems).
Yamata, Kikou
1956 *Three Geishas,* New York: John Day Co.
Yoshimasu, M.
1961 "Shōnen Hiko no Chikuteki Haaku" (Regional Study of Juvenile Delinquency in Tokyo), *Chōken Kiyō* (periodical), Vol. 1, pp. 25–38.
Yoshimoto, I.
1965 *Naikan Yonjunen* (Forty Years of Naikan), Tokyo: Shunjusha.

Yuzankaku Koza Nihon Minzokushi (Yuzankaku Series of the History of Japanese Folk Custom)
   1959   Vols. 1–3, Tokyo: Yūzankaku.
Zilboorg, Gregory
   1936a "Suicide Among Civilized and Primitive Races," *American Journal of Psychiatry*, Vol. 29, pp. 1349–1369.
   1936b "Differential Diagnostic Types of Suicide," *Archives of Neurology and Psychology*, Vol. 35, pp. 270–291.
   1937   "Consideration in Suicide with Particular Reference to That of the Young," *American Journal of Orthopsychiatry*, Vol. 17, pp. 15ff.

Index

Abe, Junkichi, 301

Abegglen, J. G., 185

Abortion, in premodern Japan, 263–264

Accidents, fear of, 103

Acculturation: of Japanese in U.S., 109; of Japanese-Americans in Chicago, 227, 238–239

Achievement, related to guilt, 144–153

Achievement motivation: comparative research on, 175–179; cultural variables and, 220–222; economic growth and, 190–194; within the family system, 23–25, 196–199; and introjection of guilt, 138, 148; in Niiike Village, 67–72; vs. obedience to parents, 92–94; perverse reversal of, 528–529; self-realization and, 196–199; related to self-sacrifice and concern for death, 140; see also Need achievement

Achievement motivation, of Japanese-Americans in Chicago: compared with white Americans, 227, 230–233, 239; individual integration of, 240–247; orientation of, 222–228; psycho-cultural factors in, 228–240

Achieving Society, The (McClelland), 178

Adler, Alfred, 175

Adolescence: and the age-grading concept, 311–314; apprenticeship and, 26–32; genpuku ceremony and, 314–

317, 319–320; and juvenile delinquency, 320–326; in premodern Japan, 314–320; and social alienation, 305–306, 486–487

Adopted son (yōshi), 14

Adoption, 266

Adult status: transition to in premodern Japan, 314–320; criteria for in modern Japan, 322–323

Adultery, 57–58, 271; in Niiike Village, 82, 86–87; see also Sexual behavior, extramarital

Affiliation, intimate: and function of nurturance in dependency, 46–52; and sexual intimacy, 54–56

Age-grading: as a concept, 311–314; and shifts in social role definitions, 321–322

Aged, the: dependency of, 51–52; and enjoyment of old age, 74; suicide and, 458–459, 460, 471–472

Aggression: alcoholism and, 265; and concern for illness or death, 131–132; internalization of, 479–481; women as capable of, 121–127

Ainu (of Hokkaido), 370

Akutagawa, Ryūnosuke (1892–1927), 469, 475, 488; esthetics and, 517–520, 547, 548, 549; family relationships and alienation, 512–517; fear of suicide, 523–524; insanity and, 520–524; as a Japanese, 512; suicide of, 511, 523–524; works of: *About*

157–158, 399–400; premarital, 54–
56, 117–121, 399–400; sanctions of
in premodern Japan, 265–271;
sleeping patterns and, 54; status
and, 270–271; and traditional attitudes in modern Japan, 271–273;
within marriage, 52–54; *see also*
Adultery; Homosexuality; Prostitution

Sexual roles, 38–39

Sexuality: lack of in wife-mother image, 480; leading to a love marriage, 156, 161; *see also* Body

Shame: defined by Freud, 145; as a
basic behavioral motive, 168; as
opposed to guilt, 30, 146–147; related to competence, 30

Shiawase (sense of belonging), 41

Shibutani, Tamotsu, 394–395

Shinju (joint heterosexual suicide),
473–474

Shinno, worshipped by *yashi*, 285

Shintoism, 162; and social discrimination, 371

Shokunin, see Artisan class

Shūji, Tsushima, *see* Dazai, Osamu

Shūkan Asahi (news magazine), 298

Silk industry, 206

Sin, concept of, 162

Slavey Indians, aggression in, 137–
138

Sleeping pills, 276

"Slow mouth," defined, 210

Smith, Adam, 182, 197

Smith, Thomas, 168

Social change: crime and, 253–255;
and critique of Hagen's theory,
194–196; and delinquency, 367–
368; influence of mass media on,
364–366; instrumental and expressive behavior in, 170–175

Social Darwinism, 188

Social organization, and Japanese
paternalism, 191–194

Social problems, in Japan, 252–259

Social role dedication, *see* Role narcissism

Social science, importance of psycho-

logical expressive behavior and,
189–190

Social self-identity, 391; defined, 393–
394; of the Burakumin, 401–406

Socialization: competence and, 30–31;
dependency and, 46–52; need
achievement and, 179–181; *see also*
Child-rearing practices; Family
system; Parent-child relationship

Sorcery, and aggression, 131–133

Sōseki, Natsume, *see* Natsume, Sōseki

Statistics, 329–330

Status: achieved vs. acquired, 320;
competition for, 37; and marital
obligation, 76

Stigma, 413

Strong, E. K., 221

Students: attitude toward education,
429–430; books which influence,
430–432; political factions among,
434–437; preparatory role of, 324,
325

Success, and egoism in Japan, 181

Sunao, see Obedient behavior

Super-ego internalization, and reference group, 395

Suicidal motives, traditional, 462–
464; psychocultural base of, 465–
474

Suicide: admonition and, 151; altruistic, 467–468; altruistic and egoistic, compared, 447–451; anomic
and egocentric, 451–455; by a Buraku girl, 405–406; by mothers, 137;
by wife, 101–102; by youth, 482–
483; conscience and, 99–100; egocentric, 453, 465, 472–473; egoistic,
469, 488–490; formal (*seppuko*),
94–95, 467; four categories of, 443–
444; intercaste love affairs and,
414–416; joint, 473–474; 523–524;
and loss of physical or intellectual
vigor, 471–472; methods of, 460–
462; patterns of in modern Japan,
464–465; and punishment of others, 150; responsibility and, 33;
role narcissism and, 468–469; in